C0-DWL-632

The Microeconomic Foundations
of Macroeconomics

OTHER INTERNATIONAL ECONOMIC ASSOCIATION PUBLICATIONS

MONOPOLY AND COMPETITION AND THEIR REGULATION
THE BUSINESS CYCLE IN THE POST-WAR WORLD
THE THEORY OF WAGE DETERMINATION
THE ECONOMICS OF INTERNATIONAL MIGRATION
STABILITY AND PROGRESS IN THE WORLD ECONOMY
THE ECONOMIC CONSEQUENCES OF THE SIZE OF NATIONS
ECONOMIC DEVELOPMENT FOR LATIN AMERICA
THE THEORY OF CAPITAL
INFLATION
THE ECONOMICS OF TAKE-OFF INTO SUSTAINED GROWTH
INTERNATIONAL TRADE THEORY IN A DEVELOPING WORLD
ECONOMIC DEVELOPMENT WITH SPECIAL REFERENCE TO EAST ASIA
ECONOMIC DEVELOPMENT FOR AFRICA SOUTH OF THE SAHARA
THE THEORY OF INTEREST RATES
THE ECONOMICS OF EDUCATION
PROBLEMS IN ECONOMIC DEVELOPMENT
THE ECONOMIC PROBLEMS OF HOUSING
PRICE FORMATION IN VARIOUS ECONOMIES
THE DISTRIBUTION OF NATIONAL INCOME
ECONOMIC DEVELOPMENT FOR EASTERN EUROPE
RISK AND UNCERTAINTY
ECONOMIC PROBLEMS OF AGRICULTURE IN INDUSTRIAL SOCIETIES
INTERNATIONAL ECONOMIC RELATIONS
BACKWARD AREAS IN ADVANCED COUNTRIES
PUBLIC ECONOMICS
ECONOMIC DEVELOPMENT IN SOUTH ASIA
NORTH AMERICAN AND WESTERN EUROPEAN ECONOMIC POLICIES
PLANNING AND MARKET RELATIONS
THE GAP BETWEEN RICH AND POOR NATIONS
LATIN AMERICA IN THE INTERNATIONAL ECONOMY
MODELS OF ECONOMIC GROWTH
SCIENCE AND TECHNOLOGY IN ECONOMIC GROWTH
ALLOCATION UNDER UNCERTAINTY
TRANSPORT AND THE URBAN ENVIRONMENT
THE ECONOMICS OF HEALTH AND MEDICAL CARE
THE MANAGEMENT OF WATER QUALITY AND THE ENVIRONMENT
AGRICULTURE POLICY IN DEVELOPING COUNTRIES
THE ECONOMIC DEVELOPMENT OF BANGLADESH
ECONOMIC FACTORS IN POPULATION GROWTH
CLASSICS IN THE THEORY OF PUBLIC FINANCE
METHODS OF LONG-TERM PLANNING AND FORECASTING
ECONOMIC INTEGRATION
THE ECONOMICS OF PUBLIC SERVICES
INFLATION THEORY AND ANTI-INFLATION POLICY
THE ORGANIZATION AND RETRIEVAL OF ECONOMIC KNOWLEDGE

The Microeconomic Foundations of Macroeconomics

Proceedings of a Conference held by the
International Economic Association
at S'Agaro, Spain

EDITED BY

G. C. HARCOURT

Westview Press
Boulder, Colorado

© The International Economic Association 1977

All rights reserved. No part of this publication may
be reproduced or transmitted in any form or by any means
without permission in writing from the publishers.

Published 1977 in London, England by
The Macmillan Press Ltd.

Published 1977 in the United States of America by
Westview Press, Inc.
1898 Flatiron Court
Boulder, Colorado 80301
Frederick A. Praeger, Publisher & Editorial Director

Printed in Great Britain

Library of Congress Cataloging in Publication Data
Main entry under title:

The Microeconomic foundations of macroeconomics.

(International Economic Association series) Conference
held Apr. 1975.
Includes index.
1. Economics—Congresses. 2. Microeconomics—
Congresses. 3. Macroeconomics—Congresses.
I. Harcourt, Geoffrey Colin. II. International Economic
Association. III. Series: International Economic
Association. International Economic Association Series.
HB21.M48   1977   330   77-2659
ISBN 0-89158-730-6

HB
21
M48
1975

Contents

Acknowledgements

The International Economic Association wishes to express, as always, its gratitude to the two great organisations which have supported its work and made possible the holding of such conferences as the present one which brings together, for vigorous argument, the experts in various fields of economics, UNESCO and the Ford Foundation.

The conference here recorded was largely made possible by the energies of a Local Committee promoted and organised by the Servicío de Estudios en Barcelona del Banco Uriquijo, with the support and collaboration of the corresponding research departments of the Banco Atlantico, the Banca Catalana, the Banca Mas Sarda, the Banco Occidental and of the Communidad Turística de la Costa Brava.

It was their generosity and active practical assistance which made it possible to hold the conference in the very beautiful and comfortable setting of the Hotel Gavina at S'Agaro. As so often is the case, the arguments of the conference room were continued even more vigorously on the terraces.

The planning of the conference owed very much to Sir John Hicks individually, and to the programme committee listed below. The more than usually full and important record of the discussions has been the work of Susan Howson, helped by Don Moggridge.

Programme Committee

Geoffrey Harcourt   (Chairman)
Sir John Hicks
Takashi Negishi
Luigi Spaventa
Erich Streissler
James Tobin

Rapporteurs

Susan Howson
Don Moggridge

List of Participants

Professor A. Asimakopulos, McGill University, Montreal, Canada
Professor James L. Cochrane, Department of Economics, University of South Carolina, U.S.A.
Professor Paul Davidson, Rutgers — The State University, New Brunswick, New Jersey, U.S.A.
Professor Luc Fauvel, Secretary General, International Economic Association, Paris, France
Professor Dr. Bruno S. Frey, University of Konstanz, Germany, and University of Basel, Switzerland
Professor Pierangelo Garegnani, University of Rome
Dr. C. A. E. Goodhart, Bank of England, London, U.K.
Dr. Jean Michel Grandmont, CEPREMAP, Paris, France
Professor H. A. John Green, University of Kent, Canterbury, England
Professor G. C. Harcourt, University of Adelaide, South Australia
Professor Pierre-Yves Henin, University of Paris I and University of Orleans, France
Dr. L. Hernandez-Albert, Barcelona University, Spain
Professor Sir John Hicks, University of Oxford, U.K.
Lady Hicks, Linacre College, Oxford, U.K.
Dr. Susan Howson, Wolfson College, Cambridge, U.K., (now Scarborough College, University of Toronto, Canada)
Professor Lucio Izzo, Istituto di Economia, Facolta di Scienze Statistiche, Demografiche e Attuaziali, University of Rome
Professor José Jane-Sola, University of Barcelona, Spain
Professor Tjalling C. Koopmans, Department of Economics, Cowles Foundation, Yale University, New Haven, Connecticut, U.S.A.
Professor Axel Leijonhufvud, University of California, Los Angeles, U.S.A.
Mr Edmond Malinvaud, I.N.S.E.E., Paris, France
Professor Alvin Marty, City University of New York, U.S.A.
Professor D. E. Moggridge, Scarborough College, University of Toronto, Canada
Professor Takashi Negishi, London School of Economics and Political Science, and University of Tokyo
Professor Edward J. Nell, Graduate Faculty, New School for Social Research, New York, U.S.A.
Dr. Domenico Mario Nuti, Faculty of Economics and Politics, Cambridge, U.K.

Professor Michael Parkin, University of Western Ontario, London, Canada

Professor Sir Austin Robinson, University of Cambridge, U.K.

Professor Julio Segura, University of Madrid, Spain

Professor Martin Shubik, Yale University, New Haven, Connecticut, U.S.A.

Professor Luigi Spaventa, Istituto di Economia, Facolta di Scienze Statistiche, Rome

Professor Joseph E. Stiglitz, Stanford University, California, U.S.A. (now All Souls College, Oxford, U.K.)

Professor Erich W. Streissler, University of Vienna, Austria

Dr. Richard James Sweeney, Office of Policy Research, United States Treasury Department Washington, D.C., U.S.A.

Mr. Yves Younès, Maître de Recherches C.N.R.S. – C.E.P.R.E.M.A.P., Paris, France

Introduction

G. C. Harcourt
UNIVERSITY OF ADELAIDE

Of necessity this introduction must be personal and uneven, for the subject of the conference, 'no less than the whole of a major (perhaps the major) part of economics, considered . . . from a particular angle' (Hicks, 1973a, p. 1), brought together several traditions and approaches, in not all of which could I claim any expertise.[1] Furthermore, while I hope to escape classification in one Hahn category, that of 'economists [unable to] grow bitter gracefully', I am less hopeful of escaping another, that of economists 'with a theoretical bent [who] . . . cannot now understand what the best minds in their subject are saying' (Hahn, 1973b, p. 322).

The basic architect and the guiding light of the conference was Sir John Hicks. He wrote the first working paper, Hicks (1973a), which was distributed to the original participants. Its outline served to structure the choice of the subjects of the papers and the participants at the conference, though due to last-minute changes in contributors and contributions and near zero-hour withdrawals, the emphasis in fact departed considerably from the original scheme. In my view, the people we most missed, both in discussion and, in some cases, as originally paper-givers, were Tobin (an organising committee member and paper-giver), Bliss (at one stage, a paper-giver), Jorgenson, Phelps and Hahn — quite unpluggable gaps. We were fortunate, however, to have copies of an early draft of Hahn's paper (now printed as Chapter 1, see pp. 25–40 below)[2] before us at the conference and, in some other instances, there were people at the conference who were able most adequately to present the views of notable absentees. The views that suffered most from underrepresentation were those associated with the search literature and the microeconomic foundations of employment and inflation theory, as represented in the famous 1970 Phelps, *et al.*, volume, and of course, those of the American Keynesians, because of the unavoidable absence of Tobin. Hicks also put the closing stamp on the conference with the opening contribution to the final discussion session, see pp. 373–5 below. The final discussion session itself contains the participants' assessments of strengths and weak-

---

[1] I am most grateful to Charles Goodhart, Frank Hahn, John Hicks, Sue Howson, Peter Kenyon, Jan Kregel and Paul Madden for their comments on a draft of this Introduction. Obviously I alone am responsible for the use made of them and, especially, for the contents of the Introduction.

[2] See below, p. 4, n1 and p. 25, n* for the history of this paper.

nesses, achievements and failures, divisions and unfinished business.[1]

At least one of Hicks's original criteria was met: our 'primary concern' *was* with the theoretical, though we had practical men present who made sure that we received many wise asides on measurement and application, testing and falsification, relevance for policy, and so on. Malinvaud, in particular, not only contributed notably to the theoretical discussions but also gave us a wealth of examples from his practical experience in French planning and in applied work, which bore on the operational content of the concepts and models discussed.

Hicks thought that the capital/income family of concepts would be central to the discussions, with their principal characteristics of inter-temporality – 'the certain past and the uncertain future'. We were to devise a means of reconciliation between them, 'the construction of concepts that will stand transmission from past to future, or future to past'; means which, moreover, were not only 'acceptable at the micro-level, but were also capable of being translated into macro-terms'. 'Capital' and 'profits', he thought, could dominate as the central concepts. In retrospect, this proved to be right, though perhaps not quite in the manner that Hicks envisaged originally. Two papers dealt directly with these themes – Koopmans's concept of an invariant capital stock (see below, pp. 144–71) in the context of optimum growth theory, and Asimakopulos's Kaleckian theory of investment (see below, pp. 328–42, in which profits and investment, their measurement and interrelationships figure prominently. Green's paper on aggregation (see below, pp. 179–94) also bore at least tangentially on these issues.

Thirdly, Hicks argued that 'a large part of what we [would be] called on to discuss [would] not be concerned with concepts as such but with the relations between them. . . . How far can these *relations*, on a macro-level, be regarded as projections of accepted (or acceptable) principles in microeconomics?' Again, though his leading examples of the consumption function and the stock adjustment principle were not themselves that prominent, there was very considerable presentation and discussion of relationships, of microeconomic behaviour of individuals and/or firms, the collective outcome of which implied phenomena that are familiar in Keynesian macroeconomics – involuntary unemployment (Grandmont and Laroque, pp. 41–61; Malinvaud and Younès, pp. 62–85), the implications of the introduction of money for the workings of the economy (Hahn, pp. 25–40; Goodhart, pp. 205–27), and so on.

Finally, Hicks argued that as a result of our discussion of relations, we would very quickly become involved in the major unsettled questions which

---

[1] All participants contributed amicably *and* notably to the conference. I am sure, though, that they would not object to my singling out three participants for special mention (in addition to those mentioned in the text): Martin Shubik, for the best allround performance plus imprinting indelibly on us all the phrase, 'in my considered opinion'; Joe Stiglitz, the fastest gun in the west, a rapporteur's nightmare; and Mario Nuti, whose contributions to the discussions positively sparkled.

have come down from Keynes. Hicks himself singled out the questions of equilibrium and the question of money, a divination which proved absolutely right. Several papers (Grandmont and Laroque, Malinvaud and Younès, Leijonhufvud, Streissler) and much of the discussion centred on these concepts and questions. As a postscript, Hicks thought that the areas he had cited had a better claim than other candidates which suggested themselves — the concepts and relations of the international sector and the implications of the public sector. In my view he was right. But, as will be seen from the discussions and the final discussion session, not all contributors agreed. In particular, those who were closest to public policy, for example Spaventa, strongly criticised the relative neglect of the international sector, both in the discussions of inflation and in the theory of the firm. In her contribution to the final discussion session, Lady Hicks (pp. 395–6) appeared also not completely to accept the original judgement.

I

What then are the main strands and traditions that met together at the conference? Before we go into detail, it may be useful immediately to identify two schools of thought. The first asks: Is it possible (say) to obtain Keynesian results by making the 'usual' neoclassical assumptions (Keynes, of course, called them classical) of individuals maximising in the context of competitive markets, or is it necessary to bring in *ad hoc* assumptions such as downward price rigidities, liquidity traps, and so on? Some members of this school are concerned to make the point that '*ad-hocery*' may be dispensed with. The second school, in which we may include, at least sometimes, Keynes himself, argues that the world should be modelled 'as it is' — '[t]he Keynesian method is to describe a set of relationships (intended to correspond to what are believed to be the relevant features of the economic system)' (Robinson, 1975a, p. 92) — and the results obtained may speak for themselves.

We turn now to specifics. There was, first of all, the Continental Walrasian tradition and its modern offshoots, or *Neo-Walrasian Revolution* as Clower (1975, p. 3) recently has christened it. It constitutes that 'long-overdue redirection of economic analysis along lines suggested . . . by Leon Walras . . . a broader and ultimately more influential series of doctrinal developments' within which the Keynesian revolution was but 'an episode' (and Marshall was — seemingly — finally made redundant).[1] They were represented at the conference, first, by Hicks himself, drawing on *Value and Capital* (1939) but now going well beyond and indeed apart from it through *Capital and Growth* (1965), *A Theory of Economic History* (1969) and *Capital and Time* (1973b) to a non-neoclassical approach: see Hicks (1975b). We also had representatives of the modern general equilibrium theory and mathematical economics that is

---

[1] While many may regard this description as the literal truth — it certainly is the theme of Harry Johnson's recent writings — Clower himself writes with subtle irony and, of course, the post-Keynesians and the Marxists would reject it outright.

associated especially with Arrow and Hahn, Debreu and the French school of
Malinvaud and his younger associates – Grandmont, Laroque and Younès.
They take as their base the modern developments of classical general equilibrium theory but they seek to modify them so as to include money and
related phenomena and to derive Keynesian-type results, involuntary unemployment for example. There were three papers in this stream; first, the
paper by Hahn (pp. 25–40); second, the background paper by Grandmont
and Laroque (pp. 41–61); and, third, the opening paper of the conference
by Malinvaud and Younès (pp. 62–85). We were fortunate in having the
illuminating child (prodigy's) guide to money, Keynesian economics and
general equilibrium by Hahn.[1] In the paper he outlined the questions which
the mathematical economists are asking in these areas. He sketched in the
difficulties of modelling rigorously the characteristics of money, the conditions
which produce involuntary unemployment, the problems associated with interrelated decisions being taken under conditions of uncertainty in a complex
series of sequences, and the problems of defining equilibrium (see also Hahn,
1973a) which earlier economists dealt with in a more literary, discursive and
less exact manner. (We were fortunate, too, to have at the conference Hahn's
early collaborator, Negishi, to guide us through these difficult areas with
careful, concisely stated guidelines.)

Though the questions are proving difficult nuts to crack, for some of the
reasons we shall consider in a moment, we nevertheless may take *some* comfort from Stanley Fischer's recent evaluation (Fischer, 1975, p. 159), of
what so far has been and is likely to be achieved in one of these areas, the
new micro foundations of money:

> It will . . . provide more convincing and carefully worked out explanations
> for the use of a medium of exchange than we now have, but . . . [the]
> explanations will not be fundamentally different from the traditional
> verbal explanations, and . . . will not have any major consequences for the
> way in which macromodels are built.

The (so-called) Neo-Walrasian Revolution took at least two roads.[2] One
was through Hicks's *Value and Capital* (1939), which was thought to contain
a general framework in which could be embraced virtually all of economic
theory. This included not only the traditional neoclassical problems of resource allocation and of the general co-ordination of the activities of isolated
economic agents through the price mechanism which Walras set himself, but

[1] Subsequently to the conference, Hahn completely rewrote the paper and also retitled
it as 'Keynesian Economics and General Equilibrium Theory: Reflections on Some
Current Debates! I refer at this point in the Introduction to the earlier version. It was
written as a series of illuminating questions and answers. The paper which is printed in
the volume is equally illuminating but much more grown-up stuff.
[2] This interpretation of the past and the present is based on Clower's excellent
'Reflections on the Keynesian Perplex' (1975). It should be seen as an account, not
necessarily of how it *actually* happened, but rather of how an important and influential
group of economists *think* it happened and of what they believe to be happening now.

also the more immediate and urgent problems of the levels of output and employment for the economy as a whole and of why a competitive capitalist economy with monetary institutions might be sluggish in seeking, or even ever able to find its way to a full-employment equilibrium level of output. These were, of course, the questions to which Keynes was addressing himself at the time that the analysis of *Value and Capital* initially was being worked out by Hicks:[1] hence the manner of Hicks's review of the *General Theory* (Hicks, 1936), which was not a success (with the book's author) and the close following 'Mr Keynes and the "Classics" ' (Hicks, 1937), which was. (The latter drew on the framework that Hicks was working out for *Value and Capital*.) We thus have the paradox, says Clower, setting the Keynesian revolution in the wider context of the Neo-Walrasian Revolution, that virtually all subsequent theoretical contributions to so-called Keynesian economics used Hicks's conceptual framework, so that 'what is now called "Keynesian Economics" owes as much or more to the author of *Value and Capital* and "Mr Keynes and the Classics" as to the author of the *General Theory* . . .' (p. 7).

These developments contained a fatal flaw as far as the questions to which Keynes addressed himself were concerned (and, indeed, the questions which the post-Keynesians subsequently have taken up, especially in the areas of growth and capital theory, including their critique of neoclassical work in these areas). There is, of course, no suggestion that Keynes himself *ever* thought he was working in a Walrasian framework or that he was considering the questions on which Walras concentrated. Clower (1975) says:

> Keynes must rather have intended to offer the world an analytically manageable aggregative version of the kind of *general process analysis* that Marshall himself might have formulated had he ever felt the need explicitly to model the working of the economic system as a whole [p. 4].

This view is amply confirmed by Keynes and also by Joan Robinson's recollections of Keynes's aims. In her review, Robinson (1969, p. 582) of Leijonhufvud (1968), for example, she writes:

> we [the 'British Keynesians'] started from the concept of the Marshallian short-period situation, in which fixed plant, business organisation and the training of labour are all given, and can be more or less fully utilised

[1] It is not possible, though, to accept Clower's statement (pp. 3–4) that Keynes *had* a 'deeply felt conviction that modern capitalist economies tend to adjust *slowly and imperfectly* towards a state in which all productive resources are fully employed' and that the *General Theory* was 'an attempt to construct a theoretical model that would serve to rationalize [his] conviction'. (Tobin, 1975, seems also broadly to agree with Clower's assessment.) The whole purpose of Keynes's book, as both Keynes himself and, now most recently, Kregel (1976) testify explicitly, was to establish the principle of effective demand, the theory of employment and output as a whole, with which was established the distinct possibility of an under-employment equilibrium (in the sense of a sustainable state of rest rather than a consistent set of desired positions for *all* participants).

according to the level of effective demand. A short-period supply curve
relating the level of *money* prices to the level of activity (at given money-
wage rates) led straight from Marshall to the *General Theory*.

The strand of general equilibrium theory which became the core of *Value and
Capital* and which now is associated principally with the work of Arrow and
Debreu,[1] the most authoritative statement of which is Arrow and Hahn
(1971), is not concerned with actual description at all and certainly not with
general process analysis. It is, rather, concerned with the purely logical task
of establishing the 'notional existence and stability' of competitive equilibria
in models with 'no disequilibrium trading' or 'explicit treatment of money'.
Yet the *formal* mathematical structure of this strand and the 'Keynesian'
variety are the same. It is the reaction to this discovery, one made virtually
at the close of the Neo-Walrasian Revolution and which brought about a
realisation that we may well need to start again from scratch as far as the
analysis of Keynesian puzzles are concerned, which draws up the curtain on
the first three papers of the volume: Hahn, Grandmont and Laroque, and
Malinvaud and Younès. (The last paper was presented at the opening session
of the conference.) That is to say, economists are painfully rediscovering the
implications of the important truth that time *is* a device to stop everything
happening at once and that this precludes modelling time as if it were space
(see Bliss, 1974).

   As is now well known, the fatal flaw in general equilibrium theory *for the
present purposes* relates to the fiction of the auctioneer (in his role of dis-
seminating freely information) and so to the absence of 'time', together with
the related concept of uncertainty about an unknowable future, from general
equilibrium models. The assumption of the auctioneer ensures that all prices
actually set — or set up, for, as Clower (p. 9) insists, we are never sure
whether the trades actually do take place — are market-clearing prices. These
postulates rule out the treatment of disequilibrium sequences and monetary
exchanges, whether or not an actual equilibrium ultimately will be attained
following a disturbance. Since the essence of pricing, production and investment decisions in capitalist economies is that they relate to time sequences,
and are based, of necessity, on expectations, an essential characteristic of
time has not been captured in general equilibrium models. Moreover, in
Clower's judgement, general equilibrium theory is

> closed to extensions . . . in those directions that would permit explicit
> formal analysis of Keynesian short-run adjustment processes . . . precisely
> the kind of processes about which economists must be able to speak . . .
> if their science is to be anything more than a body of idle speculation . . . a
> breeding ground for charlatans and quacks [p. 12] .

Joan Robinson, of course, has been stressing essentially the same lesson for
over twenty years — perhaps her most definitive statement is in *History versus*

---

[1] Clower adds Samuelson, Hurwicz, McKenzie, Scarf, Hahn and Negishi.

Equilibrium (1974). The corollary is that as traders with imperfect knowledge try to co-ordinate economic activities over time *within* given markets, there is no guarantee at all, as there is with the overall co-ordination of markets under conditions of certainty in the Walrasian scenario, that co-ordination *as between* markets, overall activity, will be done well. It is no one's specific business to see that it is.[1] This view is shared by Davidson (see his many contributions to the discussions and his opening discussion of Leijonhufvud's paper, pp. 313–7 below) and by Asimakopulos, who in his Kaleckian-cum-Robinsonian paper (pp. 328–42 below) carefully sets out a model that simply encompasses the central idea of an ongoing macro process under conditions of uncertainty in which expectations about the future influence current happenings. Hicks also would probably agree with the main outline but he would deny the overriding importance of there needing to be money in the system in order that unemployment may arise during a process. (In this he is joined by Hahn, see p. 39 below.) One of the results of *Capital and Time* is to show that unemployment of resources may well occur in a system where the structural relationships of production get out of phase with the composition of aggregate demand during an adjustment process, without there being any explicit inclusion of monetary factors (Hicks, 1973b, p. 55). Moreover, as Hicks points out in the opening discussion (p. 88) of Malinvaud's and Younès's paper, it is to credit (or, rather, to its absence) rather than to money as such that we must look in order to obtain Keynesian results in their model.[2] (The latter, of course, is far removed in conception and in form from the models of Hicks, 1973b.)

The direction in which Clower (and Leijonhufvud — see Clower and Leijonhufvud, 1975) wish to see the analysis move is through the introduction of a class of traders whose function is to hold stocks of goods. This allows the implications of incomplete knowledge by other traders of the actual demand curves facing them and/or the nature of the perceived shifts in them — permanent or only temporary — which affect their pricing, production and employing behaviour to be absorbed, to some extent anyway. Malinvaud and Younès, however, seek to tackle the same problems by introducing a broader concept of equilibrium which encompasses price setting that is characteristic of buyers' and sellers' markets as well as including the classical general equilibrium concept as a *special case*. This reflects the view that it is only prices that economic agents (and observing economists) need to take into account — the quantities can look after themselves. The original reaction of Clower and Leijonhufvud was to go to the other extreme and let all adjustments pertain to quantities. They are now moving towards a richer framework in which both can be considered; i.e., they are back, as they say themselves

---

[1] Clower, for one, sees this contrast as the essential difference between the Marshallian and the Walrasian view of the world.
[2] Henin takes up this theme, expanding the context to include the present inflation, in his contribution to the final discussion session (see pp. 375–6 below).

(p. 188), to Mill and soon may reach the point from which Kahn (1931) and Keynes started.

Malinvaud and Younès, however, see the usefulness of their new equilibrium concept (what they call strong non-co-operative equilibrium — see p. 71 below) as applying to a model of a monetary economy *with price rigidities*, a case which they regard as of major importance for a proper understanding of macroeconomics. As we have seen, in the view of both Hicks and now Clower and Leijonhufvud, as well as the original 'British Keynesians' and Kalecki, the existence of unemployment in the sense of Keynes has nothing fundamentally to do with rigid prices. Finally, Tobin continues to be, on the whole, an unrepentant exponent of *LM* and *IS* analysis and, in *his* hands, it *is* a fruitful approach. He uses it to create dynamic processes by identifying the factors and specifying the processes which shift these relationships from moment to moment. (As we shall see — pp. 11–13 below — his method of approach, though not necessarily the specific relationships involved, is closely related to that used by Keynes in the *General Theory* and after.) Tobin continues his usual approach of examining the income accounts and balance sheets of rational individuals and their reactions to external events and the individual and aggregate feedback of these reactions to macroeconomic aggregates. Hicks also mentions unfinished business and unsolved puzzles associated with these aggregates and their relation to the concept of equilibrium in macroeconomics in his contribution to the final discussion session (see pp. 373– 75 below).

II

The next tradition that concerns us is a first cousin of the developments just discussed. It is represented by Koopmans's paper on micro-production relations in optimum growth theory (see pp. 144–71 below). It embodies careful (natural) scientific statements of economic models as exemplified by Koopmans's *Three Essays . . .* (1957) and Malinvaud's classic *Econometrica* paper (1953). It is associated with both the developments of activity analysis and, latterly, dynamic programming in the context of allocation problems over time. Though the actual problem tackled — the concept of an invariant capital stock[1] — was peripheral to the central objective of the conference (which was more to provide the microeconomic foundations for the macroeconomics of actual economies), the methodology itself was very valuable. It showed us the great difficulties associated with the modelling of complex interrelationships between consumption goods, capital goods and production processes over time. The value of mathematical economics was highlighted in making clear the limitations and the limits of the analysis, a view which Shubik stressed in his introductory discussion of Koopmans's paper (pp. 172–

---

[1] An invariant capital stock is one which, if put in the place of the initial capital stock, will not change its structure at the end of each period as a result of optimisation of the production path for capital and consumption goods over an infinite horizon (p. 150).

73 below).[1] Koopmans is an optimist; he believes that the assumption of certainty, so that the models in his paper relate either to planned economies with full knowledge or to perfectly functioning competitive markets under the same conditions, will serve to illuminate (in the sense of serving as the starting point for a study of) the workings of actual economies when the assumption is dropped. Not everyone at the conference shared this view; witness, for example, Goodhart's comments (p. 209, n. 4) on the analysis of transaction costs in economies in which there is certainty.

Though set in the context of optimum growth theory, the analysis and results of Koopmans's paper overlapped into the capital theory controversies of the last two decades; in particular, into those aspects that come under the heading of reswitching and capital-reversing. A feature of the paper is the presentation of a result whereby there is an unexpected (in the sense of counter-intuitive) relationship between the invariant capital stock and the discount factor. This relationship is the counterpart in optimum growth theory of capital-reversing in capital theory. After the conference Koopmans wrote an Addendum in which it is shown that the equilibrium associated with this result is an unstable one and is surrounded by two other equilibria which exhibit normal – i.e., intuitively plausible – relationships between the capital stocks and the discount factor. The moral to be drawn was that this result, like the reswitching and capital-reversing ones, was not very important, a view which Malinvaud endorsed, see p. 174 below. In any event the result easily could be absorbed into the body of orthodox economic analysis, as were Giffen goods and factor reversals. Similarly, Stiglitz (1973a, 1973b) has shown that in the context of dynamic process models, reswitching and capital-reversing are most remote theoretical possibilities. Frey (pp. 175–6) gives an excellent account of the seven steps by which awkward results may be absorbed into orthodoxy. Others, including Koopmans, draw comfort from the title of Joan Robinson's summing up of the debate – 'The Unimportance of Reswitching' (Robinson, 1975b).

To do so, though, is to miss the central point of the critique of orthodox theory as contained at least in Joan Robinson's writings. (As we shall see, Garegnani's stance is a different one.) Her critique relates to comparisons and processes (graphically, differences as opposed to changes) as the appropriate methodology, a point of view in which she now is joined by Clower (1975), Shubik (1975), Hicks (1975b), and Hahn (1973a, 1973b). All now agree that classical general equilibrium theory and its modern offshoots (except, possibly, those of a very recent and different vintage) are unable to tackle Keynesian problems and, as a corollary, the analysis of growth processes including those involving technical advances. It is this point of view which explains Joan Robinson's cryptic comment to Gallaway and Shukla (1974, p. 348, n*):

[1] Koopmans's paper illustrates well Rothschild's recent evaluation: 'The simplicity with which a surprising theorem can be stated is often a good index of the difficulty of establishing it . . . also an illustration of the payoff to be gleaned from an investment in advanced mathematical techniques' (M. Rothschild, 1973, p. 1299, n. 20).

'Do not bother. Neoclassical theory is no better off even when there is no reswitching.'

Garegnani does not agree, as his contribution to the final discussion session (see pp. 381–2 below) and his comment on Samuelson's paper at the Buffalo conference on capital theory and macroeconomics (1976) make abundantly clear. He is loath to drop comparisons of long-run positions, in his view the major method since political economy was a separate discipline of analysing sustained as opposed to immediate or surface forces, in order to make way for the analysis of dynamic processes based on a sequence of short-run equilibria which provide no firm or definite results. (He has in mind the influence of expectations about which so many different assumptions may be made: see Garegnani, 1973.) *His* objection to neoclassical analysis is the attempt by the neoclassicals – he has Walras and Wicksell in mind – to develop a theory of distribution based on supply and demand concepts. He further believes that attempts to escape from these puzzles merely force us to adopt an inappropriate methodology which Garegnani associates with Hicks's *Value and Capital* and the developments that follow from it.

Garegnani believes in permanent sustainable forces and argues that the demand and supply of 'capital' and labour do not fit into this category because results can be derived, using these concepts, which do not square with actual experience: this, to him, is the significance of the reswitching and capital-reversing results:

> Thus, after following in the footsteps of traditional theory and attempting an analysis of distribution in terms of "demand" and "supply", we are forced to the conclusion that a change, however small, in the "supply" or "demand" conditions of labour or capital (saving) may result in drastic changes of r and w . . . would even force us to admit that r may fall to zero or rise to its maximum . . . without bringing to equality the quantities supplied and demanded of the two factors. . . . [N]o such instability [has] ever [been] observed. . . . [I]n order to explain distribution, [we] must rely on forces other than "supply" and "demand" [Garegnani, 1970a, p. 426].

Garegnani therefore would reject Koopmans's and Malinvaud's judgements – 'in the debate between the two Cambridges, Cambridge UK had been right on this point [no necessary one-one relationship between the interest rate and capital-intensity] . . . . [T]he consequences were [not] very profound' (Malinvaud, p. 174 below). The reasons lie partly in the background of Arrow-Debreu general equilibrium analysis which Koopmans and Malinvaud share, while Garegnani explicitly does not want to move in these contexts. He wishes to deal

> exclusively with long-period equilibria . . . in order to focus . . . on one central deficiency [of the demand and supply theory of distribution and show that] the process of transition [may not lead to a] new long-run equilibrium, or to a plausible one because the fall of r might be accompanied

by a *decrease* . . . in the proportion of "capital" to labour in the economy'
[Garegnani, 1970b, p. 439] .

I suspect that Koopmans's paper will reinforce Garegnani's scepticism about
the *neoclassical* concepts but will leave unaffected others who see in the
general equilibrium approach a framework of analysis through which to
obtain rigorous results, some of which may run counter to intuition but *all*
of which have the same logical standing *ex post.* The position of the post-
Keynesians and the Marxists will be considered in more detail when we
discuss Asimakopulos's paper and the Kaleckian-Keynesian-Robinsonian
tradition that it represents (see pp. 328–53 below). As we shall see, it involves
an amalgamation of the need for process analysis within a framework which
puts more emphasis on aggregates and social relationships, less (or sometimes
none) on the logical implications of individual optimising economic agents.
Garegnani perhaps would have *some* sympathy with the modern search for
existence and stability *outside* the classical general equilibrium framework,
(see, for example, Grandmont and Laroque, pp. 41–61 below; M. Rothschild
1973),[1] though not with the concepts and relationships, while the
Robinsonians would have no truck with either.

We may note in passing that Laidler and Parkin refer to these issues and
dilemmas in the early passages of their mammoth survey of inflation (Laidler
and Parkin, 1975, pp. 744–6). They discuss the traditional quantity theory
of money and its modern offshoots and modifications. Analytically, the
traditional theory was a comparison of two equilibrium states, before and
after an actual change, usually in the quantity of money, and the resulting
transition stage. They ask: what if the transition does *not* contain a converging process and what is the relevance of this for an analysis of inflation,
especially one in which the classical dichotomy between a real theory of
allocation and distribution and a monetary theory of prices can no longer
be maintained? Much of their paper is concerned with the detailed answers
to this question.

One subject that received attention at the conference and which is relevant
and illuminating in the present context, in that it suggests a middle ground
towards which movements from very diverse starting points nevertheless
might converge, was a consideration of Keynes's own essential methodology.
This has recently been examined with much insight by Kregel (1976). The
main point may be put as follows: Keynes considered his central contribution
to be the theory of supply and demand and therefore level of output and
employment (and prices) *as a whole*; i.e., the principle of effective demand.
The role of expectations and uncertainty, though important facts of life which
had to be dealt with, were not his central concern; i.e., Keynes's principal
contribution may not be interpreted as that of putting expectations and un-

[1] He would also sympathise with Rothschild's conclusion that 'models of disequilibrium
behaviour do not make sense and cannot serve as reliable guides to further theorising or to
policy unless they meet certain standards of consistency and coherence' (p. 1286), though
I doubt if he would approve of its particular application.

certainty into economics, in the sense of 'an emphasis on the possible difference between *ex-ante* decisions and *ex-post* results or on the recognition that, in an uncertain world, expectations may be disappointed' (Kregel, p. 209). In order to make the analysis manageable, Keynes used three different models of varying degrees of complexity. The first took as given the state of long-term or general expectations, not because they do not change in fact but because he wanted to see the implications for output as a whole when it is *assumed* that they do not change. It is also assumed that *short-term* expectations are always realised, so that not only are the aggregate demand and supply functions given, but also the point of effective demand at their intersection is established immediately without any groping for the equilibrium point as a result of an initial disappointment of short-term expectations. This model is used to make the central point that equilibrium need not be a full-employment one; it is the model of static equilibrium of Keynes's 1937 lecture notes (Keynes, 1973, pp. 179–83, especially p. 181); it underlies his expository 1937 *Quarterly Journal of Economics* article (reprinted in Vol. XIV of the *Collected Writings*, Keynes, 1973, pp. 109–23).[1]

The second model allows for the disappointment of short-term expectations but does not allow this to feedback into long-term expectations, so that they are still regarded as independent and constant (for analytical not necessarily realistic reasons). The system may therefore grope over time for the equilibrium point without causing the point itself to move. This is the model of stationary equilibrium which, in Kregel's view, underlies the first eighteen chapters of the *General Theory* (p. 215). The final complexity *is* to allow a feedback so that in effect movements along the aggregate demand and/or supply schedules as a result of 'groping' for equilibrium in the short run following the disappointment of short-run expectations may affect long-term expectations and cause the aggregate demand and supply schedules themselves to move as well. This is the model of shifting equilibrium (p. 215–17). Thus in Keynes's methodology, '[i]t is not the assumptions made about the economy under analysis that are different [first there is certainty, now let in uncertainty], but the assumptions made about expectations in an economy in which these play an integral part [p. 211]'.[2]

Kregel points out that while Keynes applied these methods to the short-run levels of output and employment, and to prices, the methods themselves are

[1] Tobin (1975, pp. 195–6) is not willing to call this an equilibrium, because if net investment is occurring the stock of capital goods must be changing and so the position attained is not sustainable over time, for these (and other stock) changes 'alter investment, saving and other behaviour'. In Tobin's view, Keynes's tools of equilibrium analysis and comparative statics, though natural for him to use, were 'not the best . . . for his purpose'. For Tobin, '[t]he real issue is not the existence of a long-run static *equilibrium* with unemployment, but the possibility of protracted unemployment which the natural adjustments of a market economy remedy very slowly if at all'.

[2] Tobin's *LM-IS* models (see, for example, Tobin and Buiter, 1974), may be interpreted as an application of this third approach, though obviously the specific relationships of the respective writers do not overlap completely, see p. 8 above.

quite general and have been used by the post-Keynesians for their 'generalisation of the *General Theory*' to the long period. It also explains their initial pre-occupation with Golden Age or steady-state analysis, getting it right before attempting the much harder tasks of studying an economy in actual motion over time. In Kregel's view this methodology differs not only from that of the 'Keynesian' version of Keynes, but also from that of the 'new' interpretation of Keynes of Clower, Leijonhufvud, Grossman, Barro and others. It may perhaps serve as a possible meeting ground, on the one hand, for Garegnani's stress on comparisons of equilibrium positions and, on the other, some other writers' stress on the short period and the processes involved both therein and as between one short period and another.

One final point which Kregel makes is that Keynes took as one of the givens for *his* problem, the existing state or degree of competition – in Keynes's view, it was not (importantly) relevant for his exposition of effective demand. This contrasts with the modern work that we reported above of Grandmont and Laroque, and Hahn, and also with Kalecki's independent version of the *General Theory*, as Kregel and Joan Robinson (1969, p. 582) point out.[1]

III

Green's paper[2] (pp. 179–94 below) provides a summary bridge between theory and practice in that it presents the most recent findings on the aggregation problems associated with the principal variables of macro-economics. His paper is a sequel to his well-known work on aggregation of a decade or so ago (Green, 1964). One gets the impression that not *that* much progress has been made since then, an impression that is confirmed in Bliss's new book (Bliss, 1975). In the chapter on the aggregation of miscellaneous objects Bliss writes: 'There is only one condition. If it is satisfied by any group of inputs, . . . they may be aggregated and treated as if they were one input; if it is not satisfied . . . aggregation is impossible' (p. 144). He concludes that in general aggregation *is* impossible –

[t] he conditions that must be imposed . . . are so strong that we may safely dismiss them from serious consideration as actualities. . . . [A] theory which is genuinely dependent upon the possibility of general . . . aggregation is confined to instances so special that it would be hard to find parallels elsewhere in economic theory for such a constrained theory [p. 162].

Bliss is referring here to capital aggregation. He adds immediately that the conditions for general capital aggregation are identical to the conditions for

[1] See also pp. 15–17 below.
[2] I wrote the first draft of this section just after the shocking news of John Green's death on 4 January 1976 reached me. John was a much-respected and extremely popular participant at the conference and the economics profession could ill afford to lose such a wise and humane member. We are proud to have his paper in our volume.

the aggregation of labour, or of output, so that, in his view, 'the widespread belief that there is a notable, particular and distinct problem posed by capital aggregation is at best an ill-formulated idea, and at worst is based simply on ignorance' (p. 162).

While the point of view which Bliss exposits is correct formally, it ignores a telling argument by Steedman (1975, p. i) in the context of neoclassical attempts to explain the distribution of income in terms of supply and demand concepts rather than in the context of the formal properties of aggregation. Steedman argues that in long-run equilibrium 'capital' has to be aggregated in terms of value because a uniform rate of profits must be paid on it (so raising the well-known circularity that the prices used themselves contain the rate of profits as an element). Aggregation of labour may be sidestepped altogether because there does not have to be a uniform rate of wages unless labour is homogeneous. It must be stressed that Bliss is considering general aggregation, not the more specialised and tractable problem of aggregation over, say, capital goods when already some order has been placed on the economy by supposing that some form of equilibrium structure of the stock of capital goods has been attained already.

Many of the variables that Green considers had their modern origin in the work of Keynes and especially in the *General Theory*. Indeed, Keynes's spirit was rarely absent from the conference discussions and deliberations, to their detriment in some respects, a point that was made by several people in the discussions and final discussion session. Koopmans, for example, objected to argument from authority rather than by analysis that sometimes seemed to prevail. Others pointed out that it was not altogether fair to the authors themselves or especially profitable for us to take dead authors' arguments out of *their* social and historical contexts and apply them to ours. Nevertheless, the central problems in virtually all the papers *were* Keynesian in origin and often in their slant. As we have seen, the 'new' interpretation of Keynes as pioneered by Clower (1965) and reaching perhaps its finest hour in Leijonhufvud's monumental *On Keynesian Economics and the Economics of Keynes* (1968) was well represented, though Leijonhufvud's paper for the conference was concerned with the social consequences of inflation. In the latter area the master's spirit is more of a guide as to what he really meant than are his words, which are few (but certainly not non-existent, as Paul Davidson continually reminded us). Moreover, in relating Keynes's work to the central topic of the conference, both Leijonhufvud and Davidson drew on Keynes's essentially Marshallian (as opposed to Walrasian) background to value theory. For this Leijonhufvud had in mind his recent Marshall lectures, Leijonhufvud (1975), while Davidson painstakingly constructed what he believed to be Keynes's microeconomics in terms of the differing characteristics of spot and forward markets, the interrelationships between them, and the differences in the details of their operation, depending upon whether they related to consumption goods, investment goods, money or other financial assets.

The modern theoretical work on aggregation, as exemplified by Green's

paper and Bliss's chapters, is following out exactly Sraffa's views on the
nature of theory — that 'theoretical measures [require] absolute precision.
Any imperfections . . . were not merely upsetting, [they] knocked down the
whole theoretical basis' (Sraffa, 1961, p. 305). Keynes, too, advocated this
philosophy when he discussed 'the choice of the units of quantity appropriate
to the problems of the economic system as a whole' (Keynes, 1936, p. 37) to
be used in theoretical work of a causal nature, 'whether or not our knowledge
of the actual values of the relevant quantities is complete or exact' (p. 40).
He dismissed propositions about vague concepts such as net output and the
general level of prices as 'not without meaning and not without interest, but
unsuitable as material for the differential calculus' (p. 40) — 'unsatisfactory
for the purpose of a causal analysis, which ought to be exact' (p. 39). Yet the
very paucity of usable results which this approach appears to bring led to a
consensus amongst at least the more applied of the participants that, having
discovered the limitations of rigour, some compromise with vagueness was
necessary in order to proceed with applied work involving the use of aggregates. Streissler, for example, reminded us that each question involved its own
aggregation problem (see pp. 201–2 below). Hicks asked us to keep at the
forefront of our minds the question: When do we *seriously* lose information
by aggregation? (see p. 202 below). Green himself urged the need for approximation theorems (p. 203 below) and Malinvaud stressed that the direct justification of macroeconomic theories (including vague aggregates) could only be
empirical (see p. 204 below). This judgement was a comfort, for it came from
the author of one of the most admired rigorous papers in the literature.

IV

Up to this point the traditions examined are primarily neoclassical, especially
in their microeconomic aspects. The break with them and the switch to a
rival one, namely to that of the classical political economists and especially to
that of Marx, came with Asimakopulos's paper (see pp. 328–42 below). This
paper is basically Kaleckian (and Robinsonian) in spirit, though not completely
in detail. It relates to an endogenous theory of investment and is built on
microeconomic foundations — Kalecki's theory of the (manufacturing) firm.
It also takes account of the Marxian structure of Kalecki's thought, whereby
the basic units of analysis are groups or classes rather than individuals. The
vital social relationships between them are made explicit. The classification
into classes depends in part on the differing characteristics of groups' spending
and saving behaviour and in part on their other roles in the community as
workers, rentiers, organising businessmen and/or managers and whether or not
they own or at least control the use of the means of production as opposed to
having only their labour services to sell. This is allied with Kalecki's theory of
non-competitive markets in the manufacturing sector[1] and his device of
dividing time into sequential short periods. (This device was also, of course,

---

[1] Asimakopulos (pp. 341–2) mentions that in a fuller analysis the competitive structures
of the raw materials sector and financial factors external to the firm would be included.

that of Keynes and the post-Keynesians as well as the Swedes and Hicks.)[1]
It does away with the neoclassical short-period, long-period distinction —
instead the long run is seen as growing out of a succession of short periods, its
characteristics unfolding as the happenings of one short period flow into the
next short period, so creating the initial conditions and helping to form
expectations and influence plans. 'In fact, the long-run trend is but a slowly
changing component of a chain of short-period situations; it has no independent entity' (Kalecki, 1968, p. 263).

As to the use of firms in non-competitive markets as basic micro units,
Kalecki's approach, which supplied 'a missing link in Keynes's theory of
prices' (Robinson, 1969, p. 582), has recently been adopted by Grandmont
and Laroque (see pp. 41–61 below), who argue for a Keynesian model with
monopolistic competition in order to obtain Keynesian results. Hahn, also,
argues that some facet of monopolistic competition may have to be modelled
(see pp. 34–5 below).

The paper further draws on both the Marxian and the Keynesian traditions
whereby investment decisions are guided by the expectations of businessmen
concerning future profitability rather than by the returns to saving by thrifty
households. It stresses, moreover, the two-sided relationship between profits
and investment: that profits are both the reason for *and* a large part of the
ability to invest, in that retained profits are a major determinant, overall and
individually, of the means *to* invest. This post-Keynesian approach is in a
tradition which goes back to Ricardo, as Adrian Wood (1975, p. 11) recently
has reminded us. It is by-passed in the neoclassical approach, at least at the
level of the individual firm, and also in some neoclassical growth models in
which there is no separate investment function, so that saving *is* investment:
see Swan (1956). '[I]n neoclassical theory the availability of finance is not a
problem for the firm [because the] firm is willing and able to finance by
borrowing any investment project that it would be prepared to finance out of
retained profits' (Wood, 1975, p. 4).

That Asimakopulos's approach represents another, not always acceptable,
tradition may be seen from the vigour of the discussions that followed the
paper. Koopmans (p. 350 below) put the point that the model was designed
for empirical testing and wanted to know if this had been done and, if so,
what were the results? As I recall it, the implication was that a theory that
had been around for as long as Kalecki's should have been tested by now and,
if found wanting, discarded. Parkin (p. 351 below) was very sceptical of
the mark-up hypothesis (which is incorporated in Kalecki's and Asimakopulos's

---

[1] Hicks used the device of the 'week' in *Value and Capital* (1939) in order to obtain
market-clearing prices in the short period and in order to discuss the stability problems
associated with differing expectations about prices. Production and investment decisions
were, of course, discussed as well. In *Capital and Time* (1973b), the week analysis is
retained but is now related predominantly to the nature of production processes and to
the gestation and operating periods of investment plans, to their fulfilment or modifications over time, a viewpoint that is very similar to the Kalekian-Robinsonian one.

work). He argued that it had not stood up well to empirical tests, citing pp. 767–78 of Laidler and Parkin (1975).

Laidler and Parkin singled out the work of Godley and Nordhaus (1972) for especially critical comment, arguing that their tests of the normal cost (price) hypothesis which were interpreted by them as not being inconsistent with the hypothesis in fact refuted it.[1] At the conference, Parkin cited United Kingdom and North American work which suggested that 'demand pressures systematically entered into the determination of the mark-up' (p. 351 below). Evidence of variations in the mark-up was taken by Parkin as confirmation of his view that the competitive forces of supply and demand are the dominant factors at work in the explanation of inflation (as in other economic spheres) – the philosophy which·underlies the microeconomic foundations of the monetarist school's work on inflation and other economic problems.

Godley and Nordhaus (1972, p. 869) state quite emphatically that 'because the normal price hypothesis does not explain prices perfectly, there is clearly room for alternative tests and explanations'. Asimakopulos's work, both here and elsewhere (1975), Eichner's work (1973, 1974, 1975, 1976), my own with Peter Kenyon (1976) and Wood's new book (1975) provide alternative approaches which are linked to the investment decision of the firm, including its financial policy, and which are not inconsistent with observed variations in mark-ups over both actual *and* normal costs.

Unfortunately we did not have, as counterweights at the conference, access to either Feiwel's massive volume (1975) on Kalecki's intellectual capital or Arrow's assessment of Kalecki's achievements[2]

> a most original thinker in diverse branches of economics [who grasped] the essential point of Keynesian theory before it ever appeared [and] pioneered remarkable extensions in the political sphere. His integrated approach to monopoly and income distribution and his stress on the risk elements in capital have still never been thoroughly integrated into modern thought.

Hopefully, Asimakopulos's paper goes some way towards doing just that.

V

The five remaining papers[3] – those by Goodhart (see pp. 205–27), Hall (pp. 354–64), Leijonhufvud (pp. 265–312), Segura (pp. 240–53) and Streissler.

[1] I am indebted to Peter Kenyon for helpful discussions of the Laidler-Parkin criticisms of Godley-Nordhaus.

[2] We were, of course, fortunate in having at the conference Mario Nuti, Kalecki's former pupil and editor of a volume of his collected works; see Nuti's comments, p. 343 below. As we remarked on p. 2, n. 1 above, his sparkling contributions to the discussions were a feature of the conference.

[3] They do not appear in this order in the volume, the order of which follows that of the conference programme in order to dovetail in with the cumulative nature of the discussions as each day drew on its predecessors.

(pp. 96–132) – criss-cross the traditions that we have discussed above. Good-hart's paper is a characteristically independent and lucid survey of recent work on the definition and role of money and of the nature of the connection between money's existence and the extent of disequilibrium in a model of an economy in an uncertain environment.[1] In Goodhart's view (p. 208) money (defined as a specialised means of payment) is only needed when exchange takes place under conditions of uncertainty; otherwise a generalised claim on future goods would suffice. Money in turn serves to reduce the effects of uncertainty *and* the inefficiency of barter. Goodhart's paper (and Hahn's) overlap into the search literature, the consideration of the implications of the costs of obtaining information which in the work of Phelps, *et al.* (1970) become the clues to the existence of money, unemployment and inflation: see Laidler and Parkin (1975) and Leijonhufvud's paper in this volume (pp. 265–312 below). Hall's paper is also associated with this literature, on the rather different tack, though, of seeking the optimum level of unemployment for the firm and ultimately the economy.

Segura's paper is partly a discussion of modern theories of the firm, partly a critique of neoclassical (and other) theories of the firm when used as the microeconomic foundations for the study of technical innovations in growth processes. Like many before him, dissatisfaction with some aspects of the orthodox theories in this context sends the writer back to the Schumpeterian 'vision' of innovating and imitative entrepreneurs reacting to gales of creative destruction. But, again like those before him, this suggestive starting point often becomes little more than just that when an attempt is made seriously to model the ideas involved. After all, it *is* very hard to pass the ingenious and exacting test that Shubik set us at the conference: 'If [you cannot] play [the] model as a well-defined game in [a] graduate students' class, then it [is] not a well-defined model' (p. 234). This test, incidentally, is a practical expression of Shubik's oft-repeated plea that we should in our microeconomic foundations use 'special theories . . . of limited scope, but . . . considerable application' (Shubik, 1970, p. 407) and that this should be an integral characteristic of 'mathematical-institutional-political economy, . . . the joining together of detailed institutional studies, advanced mathematical-economic theory and political economy' (1970, pp. 406–7), which Shubik would like to see as the new wave of the future.[1] This approach is the basis of his critique of what he regards as the 'specious generality', of the supposed 'open sesame' character of classical general equilibrium theory and its modern offshoots, especially those of the *Foundations* (Samuelson, 1947) and *Value*

[1] It is based on Chapter 1 of his important new book, Goodhart (1975), which unfortunately was published after the conference dates.
[2] He is not confident that it will be, however. In his recent *Kyklos* paper (1975), he writes that while his paper 'is in a special sense a survey article in [this field, yet because] mathematical institutional economics is deemed by many to be a contradiction in terms and is regarded by most as a nonexistent subject, the current survey is completed' (p. 545, n. 1).

and Capital (see Shubik, 1970, pp. 413–4). This would also be true of much of the work surveyed in Arrow and Hahn (1971) but it must immediately be added that the authors of the work concerned would be the first to agree: see, for example, Hahn (1973a, 1973b) and pp. 25–40 below. Shubik (1970, p. 415) reminds us that while the general equilibrium approach *assumes* that the price system exists, in oligopoly theory and partial equilibrium analysis its existence is a deduction. Shubik is concerned in his microeconomic foundations to get bargaining, trading, communicating and recontracting *inside* his models. He proposes to use 'the *extensive form* familiar to game theory' (Shubik, 1975, p. 547). He considers that 'the nonco-operative equilibrium solution of Cournot and Nash . . . can be applied to economies with oligopolistic elements and nonsymetric information' (p. 572). Money and financial institutions, the rules of the game and specified disequilibrium behaviour are stressed. The economy is modelled as a series of overlapping and intertwined real and monetary sequences. All these strands of thought had a place in the conference discussions but it really cannot be said that we advanced their concrete applications to any marked degree.

Leijonhufvud's paper on the social consequences of inflation (see pp. 265–312 below) was a by-way from our main considerations. It needs, moreover, to be read in conjunction with the Laidler-Parkin survey (1975); it represents something of a half-way house between their rather hard-line monetarist approach, in the sense of, in the main, approval of models which highlight supply and demand factors for money in relatively competitive markets, and the more institutional, sociological and learning -by-historically-doing approaches as represented, for example, by Hicks (1975a) and Phelps Brown (1975).

Leijonhufvud's analysis is not Laidler-Parkin nor Phelps *et al.*, nor, of course, Friedman. As we have seen, he has now moved away from the Neo-Walrasian model as a means of positive analysis. (It is, on the whole, the Neo-Walrasian model that implicitly backs up the simpler models and econometric specifications in the work on inflation which Laidler-Parkin report most approvingly.) Nevertheless, Leijonhufvud still regards the Neo-Walrasian model as a benchmark, something precise to which other approaches may be referred and by which they may be judged. Moreover, Leijonhufvud is at one with Laidler and Parkin's stress on a detailed examination of the feedback processes of the system, the ranges within which they are likely to be consistent with stable results, and outside of which instability is likely to occur over time, whether it be unemployment, or inflationary pressures, or both. They part company, however, on Laidler and Parkin's insistence that the purely 'economic' factors, summed up in the interrelationships of supply and demand in the labour, goods and money markets of an integrated system, will provide the bulk of the explanation, theoretically and empirically, of the inflationary process. Furthermore, Laidler and Parkin argue that these same factors provide us with the means, again theoretically and empirically, of identifying and estimating the welfare costs of inflation. Leijonhufvud is especially critical of this latter set of propositions; he feels that the factors named fail to pick up the major costs and disruptions of the inflationary process and also lead to our overlooking major causal factors in the process itself.

Hicks (1975a), too, is much more eclectic. The monetarists' diagnosis may be correct in some cases — he outlines the conditions when this is likely to be so (p. 4) — but their's is by no means the only or even the entire story. He therefore puts much more emphasis on at least two other factors, the first of which he calls 'Real Wage Resistance' (p. 5). This is wage-earners' desires not only for 'fairness' *vis-à-vis* those with whom they traditionally compare their earnings but also *vis-à-vis* what they themselves have come to expect in real terms not so much as a level but as a normal *increase* in that level. The second factor is the role of rising import prices. Phelps Brown (1975) finds in the increasing participation of the individual employee who is 'increasingly ready to go it alone', the means with which to implement Real Wage Resistance. This implies a shift of power to the shop floor. It has the corollary of making the traditional national trade union leaders relatively passive followers of their members. If they try to give leads that are unacceptable to the rank and file, they may only succeed in making themselves impotent, as has become increasingly obvious in the United Kingdom over recent years, and as is starting to occur in Australia now. These more institutional, psychological and sociological forces received little sympathy from Laidler and Parkin. Also, though they were received sympathetically in general terms by many participants at the conference, they are only in their infancy as far as their rigorous theoretical modelling is concerned.

Hall's paper (pp. 354–64 below) contains a number of strands that we have already considered, including the literature on models of market organisation with imperfect information.[1] In this area we are concerned with the problem of modelling markets 'whose participants act on the basis of sketchy and incomplete information' (Rothschild, 1973, p. 1283). Obviously, involuntary unemployment and unexpected inflation are likely to be by-products of such markets. Rothschild's discussion concentrates on the derivation of rules which market participants follow when they are out of equilibrium; descriptions of behaviour under these rules and of convergence processes take second place. His main complaint is that too little attention has been given as to *why* people *should* follow the rules (apart from the reason that if they do follow them, an equilibrium will be reached, while if they do not, it will not, a guideline which begs the question as to whether or not *actual* observations are typically observations of equilibrium positions or at least of values of variables which are well on the way to them). For example, Rothschild comments on J. R. Green and Majumdar's 1972 paper establishing the existence of stochastic equilibria in markets buffeted by exogenous disturbances: 'They have established that there is a class of rules

---

[1] This literature has been ably surveyed by Michael Rothschild (1973).

which, if price setters follow them, will lead to stochastic equilibrium. They do not indicate *why* price setters should want to behave this way' (p. 1299, emphasis added). Nevertheless it is Rothschild's view that something substantial has been accomplished in this area and that the way is clear whereby '[a] return to some of the traditional preoccupations of [neoclassical] economic theory will probably lead to a richer understanding of the nature and consequences of market imperfections' (p. 1303), especially with regard to efficiency and welfare. It is at this point that Hall's paper makes its contribution.

Hall draws on his own previous empirical work (Hall, 1972), which has been aptly christened a spare-tyre theory of employment: the notion that when tight labour markets are ruling, overhead labour is kept on when there is a temporary fall in demand, while in slack markets employers are more likely to let labour go, drawing on the resultant buffer stock of re-employables when demand for their product revives. The theoretical question is whether the unfettered market produces the optimum amount of unemployment. The policy conclusion of his paper is one which favours high unemployment benefits rather than low ones, the latter being allied with high employment and tight labour markets brought about by making wage-earners bear most of the cost of being unemployed — which currently is the favoured approach. Unfortunately, the model was shown not to be robust in that its results are remarkably sensitive to small changes in assumptions: see Stiglitz's discussion of the paper (pp. 365–7 below) and Hall's response (pp. 371–2 below).[1]

Streissler's paper (pp. 96–132 below) raises a number of issues which reasserted themselves throughout the conference. His paper relates essentially to what are the macroeconomic constraints on microeconomic behaviour and may they be tackled by use of the traditional device of the representative individual or agent? He is thus concerned with the role of the fallacy of composition in discussing the microeconomic foundations, and the difficulty of aggregation when the average will not serve adequately as a summary measure. He also investigated a theme that recurred at the conference: whether optimisation or overall constraints, or both together, were the final arbiters of the observed behaviour of economic units in a macroeconomic setting.

VI

We are unable to claim more than very modest advances as a result of our conference, a view which explains no doubt the air of general dissatisfaction that pervades the contributions to the final discussion session. We produced no striking new results or breakthroughs — perhaps no one should have

---

[1] Perhaps we should add that Stiglitz gave a virtuoso performance at the session on Hall's paper. He was first, in Hall's unavoidable absence, Hall's spokesman and then, in the opening discussion of the paper, his critic. In the ensuing discussions he alternated the two roles with ease.

expected that we could, for the days when a few could bestride the profession like a Colossus are now well past. Nevertheless, several of the papers provided us with useful overall views of the current state of play (Goodhart's new book, book, 1975 is a splendid detailed supplement to several of them). Others represented useful if marginal nudges into the existing frontiers of knowledge. Perhaps the most satisfactory result was that views in the profession may now be converging together from very different starting points, at least in regard to analytical methods. Ideological and political differences still abound and healthy and vigorous differences were certainly not precluded, as the record of discussion shows. It does suggest that the best minds from different schools of thought may be getting on to the same wavelengths, so that fruitful communication soon may become possible. The pragmatic and undogmatic approach to theory and empirical work, including policy, which our French contributors in particular showed is a very healthy example for others to follow. After all, not to expect too much from any one line of enquiry and to have an open mind that is tolerant of all lines of enquiry is not a bad working rule for social scientists.

REFERENCES

K. J. Arrow and F. H. Hahn, *General Competitive Analysis* (San Francisco: Holden-Day; Edinburgh: Oliver & Boyd, 1971).

A. Asimakopulos, 'A Kaleckian Theory of Income Distribution', *Canadian Journal of Economics*, Vol. 8, No 3 (August 1975) pp. 313–33.

C. J. Bliss, 'Capital Theory in the Short-run' (Buffalo, mimeographed, 1974).

C. J. Bliss, *Capital Theory and the Distribution of Income (Advanced Textbooks in Economics, Vol. 4)* (Amsterdam and Oxford: North-Holland; New York: American Elsevier, 1975).

R. Clower, 'Reflections on the Keynesian Perplex', *Zeitschrift für Nationalokonomie*, Vol. 35, Parts 1–2 (1975) pp. 1–24.

R. Clower and A. Leijonhufvud, 'The Co-ordination of Economic Activities: A Keynesian Perspective', *American Economic Review*, Vol. LXV, No 2 (May 1975) pp. 182–8.

A. S. Eichner, 'A Theory of the Determination of the Mark-up under Oligopoly', *Economic Journal*, Vol. 83, No 342 (December 1973) pp. 1184–200.

A. S. Eichner, 'Determination of the Mark-up under Oligopoly: A Reply', *Economic Journal*, Vol. 84, No 346 (December 1974) pp. 974–80.

A. S. Eichner, 'A Theory of the Determination of the Mark-up under Oligopoly: A Further Reply', *Economic Journal*, Vol. 85, No 347 (March 1975) pp. 149–50.

A. S. Eichner, *The Megacorp and Oligopoly* (Cambridge: Cambridge University Press, 1976).

G. R. Fiewel, *The Intellectual Capital of Michal Kalecki: A Study in Economic Theory and Policy* (Knoxville: University of Tennessee Press, 1975).

S. Fischer, 'Recent Developments in Monetary Theory', *American Economic Review*, Vol. LXV, No 2 (May 1975) pp. 157–66.

L. Gallaway and V. Shukla, 'The Neoclassical Production Function', *American Economic Review*, Vol. LXIV, No 3 (June 1974) pp. 348–58.

P. Garegnani, 'Heterogeneous Capital, the Production Function and the Theory of Distribution', *Review of Economic Studies*, Vol. XXXVII (3), No 111 (July 1970a) pp. 407–36.

P. Garegnani, 'A Reply', *Review of Economic Studies*, Vol. XXXVII (3), No 111 (July 1970b) p. 439.

P. Garegnani, 'Summary of the Final Discussion' in J. A. Mirrlees and N. H. Stern (eds.), *Models of Economic Growth* (London: Macmillan, 1973).

P. Garegnani, 'On a Change in the Notion of Equilibrium in Recent Work on Value and Distribution. A Comment on Samuelson' in M. Brown, K. Sato and P. Zarembka (eds.), *Essays in Modern Capital Theory* (Amsterdam and Oxford: North-Holland, 1976) pp. 25–45.

W. Godley and W. D. Nordhaus, 'Pricing in the Trade Cycle', *Economic Journal*, Vol. 82, No 327 (September 1972) pp. 853–82.

C. A. E. Goodhart, *Money, Information and Uncertainty* (London: Macmillan, 1975).

H. A. J. Green, *Aggregation in Economic Analysis: An Introductory Survey* (Princeton University Press, 1964).

J. R. Green and M. Majumbar, 'The Nature and Existence of Stochastic Equilibria' (Unpublished paper, 1972).

F. H. Hahn, *On the Notion of Equilibrium in Economics. An Inaugural Lecture.* (Cambridge: Cambridge University Press, 1973a).

F. H. Hahn, 'The Winter of our Discontent', *Economica*, Vol. XL, No 159 (August 1973b) pp. 322–30.

R. E. Hall, 'Turnover in the Labour Force', *Brookings Papers on Economic Activity*, No 3 (1972) pp. 709–56.

G. C. Harcourt and P. Kenyon, 'Pricing and the Investment Decision', *Kyklos*, Vol. 29, No Fasc. 3 (1976) pp. 449–77.

J. R. Hicks, 'Mr Keynes' Theory of Employment', *Economic Journal*, Vol. 46, No 182 (June 1936) pp. 238–53.

J. R. Hicks, 'Mr. Keynes and the "Classics"; A Suggested Interpretation', *Econometrica*, Vol. 5, No 2 (April 1937) pp. 147–59.

J. R. Hicks, *Value and Capital. An Inquiry into some Fundamental Principles of Economic Theory* (Oxford: Clarendon Press, 2nd ed., 1939).

John Hicks, *Capital and Growth* (Oxford: Clarendon Press, 1965).

John Hicks, *A Theory of Economic History* (Oxford: Clarendon Press, 1969).

John Hicks, 'Background Paper' (mimeographed, 1973a) pp. 1–3.

John Hicks, *Capital and Time. A Neo-Austrian Theory* (Oxford: Clarendon Press, 1973b).

John Hicks, 'What is Wrong with Monetarism', *Lloyds Bank Review*, No 118 (October 1975a) pp. 1–13.

John Hicks, 'Revival of Political Economy: The Old and the New', *Economic Record*, Vol. 51, No 135 (September 1975b) pp. 365–7.

R. F. Kahn, 'The Relation of Home Investment to Unemployment', *Economic Journal*, Vol. XLI, No 162 (June 1931) pp. 173–98.

M. Kalecki, 'Trend and Business Cycles Reconsidered', *Economic Journal*, Vol. LXXVIII, No 310 (June 1968) pp. 263–76.

J. M. Keynes, *The General Theory of Employment, Interest and Money* (London: Macmillan, 1936).

J. M. Keynes, *The General Theory and After: Part II: Defence and Development. The Collected Writings of John Maynard Keynes*, Vol. XIV (ed. by D. Moggridge) (London: Macmillan, for the Royal Economic Society, 1973).

T. C. Koopmans, *Three Essays on the State of Economic Science* (New York: McGraw-Hill, 1957).

J. A. Kregel, 'Economic Methodology in the Face of Uncertainty: The Modelling Methods of Keynes and the Post-Keynesians', *Economic Journal*, Vol. 86, No 342 (June 1976) pp. 209–25.

D. E. W. Laidler and J. M. Parkin, 'Inflation: A Survey', *Economic Journal*, Vol. 85, No 340 (December 1975) pp. 741–809.

A. Leijonhufvud, *On Keynesian Economics and the Economics of Keynes: A Study in Monetary Theory* (New York and London: Oxford University Press, 1968).

A. Leijonhufvud, 'Maximization and Marshall', 1974–5 Marshall Lectures (forthcoming).

E. Malinvaud, 'Capital Accumulation and the Efficient Allocation of Resources', *Econo-*

metrica, Vol. 21, No 2 (April 1953) pp. 233–68.

E. S. Phelps, *et al.* (eds), *Microeconomic Foundations of Employment and Inflation Theory* (New York: Norton, 1970).

Henry Phelps Brown, 'A Non-Monetarist View of the Pay Explosion', *Three Banks Review*, No 105 (March 1975) pp. 3–24.

Joan Robinson, 'Review of A. Leijonhufvud, *On Keynesian Economics and the Economics of Keynes: A Study in Monetary Theory*, 1968', *Economic Journal*, Vol. LXXIX, No 315 (September 1969) pp. 581–3.

Joan Robinson, *History versus Equilibrium* (London: Thames Polytechnic, Autumn 1974).

Joan Robinson, 'Letter to Editor', *Cambridge Review*, Vol. 96, No 2224 (January 1975a) pp. 91–2.

Joan Robinson, 'The Unimportance of Reswitching', *Quarterly Journal of Economics*, Vol. LXXXIX, No 1 (February 1975b) pp. 32–9.

M. Rothschild, 'Models of Market Organization with Imperfect Information: A Survey', *Journal of Political Economy*, Vol. 81, No 6 (November/December 1973) pp. 1283–308.

P. A. Samuelson, *Foundations of Economic Analysis* (Cambridge, Massachusetts: Harvard University Press, 1947).

M. Shubik, 'A Curmudgeon's Guide to Microeconomics', *Journal of Economic Literature*, Vol. VIII, No 2 (June 1970) pp. 405–34.

M. Shubik, 'The General Equilibrium Model is Incomplete and Not Adequate for the Reconciliation of Micro and Macroeconomic theory', *Kyklos*, Vol. 28, No 3 (1975) pp. 545–73.

P. Sraffa, Contribution to D. C. Hague, 'The Discussion of Professor Hicks's Paper' in F. A. Lutz and D. C. Hague (eds) *The Theory of Capital* (London: Macmillan, 1961) p. 305.

I. Steedman, 'Critique of the critic', *Times Higher Educational Supplement* (31 January 1975) p. i.

J. E. Stiglitz, 'The Badly Behaved Economy with the Well-behaved Production Function' in J. A. Mirrlees and N. H. Stern (eds), *Models of Economic Growth* (London: Macmillan, 1973) pp. 117–37.

J. E. Stiglitz, 'Recurrence of Techniques in a Dynamic Economy' in J. A. Mirrlees and N. H. Stern (eds), *Models of Economic Growth* (London: Macmillan, 1973) pp. 138–62.

T. W. Swan, 'Economic Growth and Capital Accumulation', *Economic Record*, Vol. XXXII, No 63 (November 1956) pp. 334–61.

J. Tobin, 'Keynesian Models of Recession and Depression', *American Economic Review*, Vol. LXV, No 2 (May 1975) pp. 195–202.

J. Tobin and W. Buiter, 'Long-run Effects of Fiscal and Monetary Policy on Aggregate Demand' (Cowles Foundation Discussion paper No 384, December 1974).

A. Wood, *A Theory of Profits* (London: Cambridge University Press, 1975).

1 Keynesian Economics and General Equilibrium Theory: Reflections on Some Current Debates*

F. H. Hahn
UNIVERSITY OF CAMBRIDGE

INTRODUCTION

To many economists Keynesian economics deals with important relevant problems and General Equilibrium theory deals with no relevant problems at all. This view is often the consequence of the ease of learning Keynesian macro-arithmetic compared with reading Debreu. But it also has, alas, an element of truth. This is quite simply that General Equilibrium theorists have been unable to deliver one half at least of the required story: how does General Equilibrium come to be established? Closely related to this lacuna is the question of what signals are perceived and transmitted in a decentralised economy and how? The importance of Keynesian economics to the General Equilibrium theorist is twofold. It seems to be addressed to just these kinds of questions and it is plainly in need of proper theoretical foundations.

In the last fifteen years, starting with Clower (1965) and Leijonhufvud (1968), there has been new work by economists who like and can do theory. The outcome is very encouraging although we are by no means out of the wood and in some instances seem to have got deeper into it. What follows discusses some, but by no means all, of these developments. I have chosen to discuss what I find most interesting. I shall repeatedly have to refer to Keynes and to Keynesian economics. These are sloppy terms and certainly do not imply that I know what 'Keynes really meant'. But I do not know how to avoid this difficulty.

I EQUILIBRIUM

If Keynesian theory is about equilibrium it must be short-period equilibrium. That is, one is concerned with states of the economy which require the

---

*The history of this paper is as follows. In 1974 I delivered an invited address to the Econometric Society meeting at Grenoble on 'Money and General Equilibrium'. The editor of this present volume kindly asked me to make this paper available even though I was unable to attend the I.E.A. Conference. On rereading it in 1976, I found that it did not deal with what I now think most important. I accordingly have completely rewritten it and this paper is the result.

'mutual compatibility' of the actions of rational agents only over a given interval. In particular agents plans over a more distant future are permitted to be incompatible. This then is certainly a world in which many markets for uncertain future deliveries do not exist or are inactive and there is trading and decision-taking at each date. Such a world is speculative in the sense that agents must provide links between the present and the uncertain future by holding assets for the purpose of future exchange. The future is doubly uncertain for not only are future states of the world uncertain but so are the market possibilities which will be available in any given state.

It is only recently that the theory of a short-period Walrasian equilibrium has been rigorously studied, although it has been in the literature for a very long time (see Hicks, 1939; Green, 1973; Grandmont 1976). In its simplest form such a model makes the desired actions of agents depend on current prices and the single valued expectation of future prices. The latter are thought of as generated by past and present price experience. A short-period Walrasian equilibrium is, then, a set of current prices and associated expected prices such that the preferred action of every agent on current markets can be carried out. To show that such an equilibrium exists one needs in addition to conventional postulates certain assumptions concerning the nature of expectations. In particular, the price expectation hypothesis must be compatible with the possibility of different terms of trade between the present and the future which can move both against and in favour of present goods. In addition one needs to suppose that the expectations of different agents are not sufficiently disimilar to allow unbounded arbitrage (see Green, 1973; Grandmont, 1976). If there is money one needs to make sure that in the short-period equilibrium it has a positive exchange value. The above expectation assumptions accomplish that since when properly stated they ensure that money is always expected to have a positive exchange value in the future (see Hahn, 1965; Grandmont and Younès, 1972; Grandmont, 1976). Lastly, if there are debts denominated in money one must ensure that no discontinuities can occur at some admissable set of prices due to bankruptcy (see Arrow and Hahn, 1971). At the end of it all one has an existence theorem. Has it any relevance to Keynesian theory?

Until relatively recently the answer would have been in the affirmative. Indeed the answer would often be that Keynes attempted to show that full employment short-period equilibrium did not exist and that in this he was, under plausible assumptions, wrong. His mistake was attributed to his neglect of real cash balances in influencing the demand for current goods. Therefore Keynesian theory is either not about equilibrium at all or it depends on certain price rigidities, in particular in money wages.

Before I look more closely at these claims it is worthwhile noting that they were made in response to a number of mistakes made over and over again by authors who accepted the short-period Walrasian equilibrium as decisive in the argument but claimed that it did not exist. These claims rested on the 'liquidity trap' and/or on the alleged zero interest responsiveness of investment demand (see Klein, 1950). But in different contexts it had been discovered that 'existence' was at risk only from discontinuous and not from oddly shaped excess demand functions. The purported reasons for non-existence are worthless.

Now the most striking feature of the short-period Walrasian equilibrium approach to Keynesian theory is that it leaves a vast part of the *General Theory* unaccounted for. In particular it makes it impossible to make sense of the Keynesian dependence of agents' choices on quantities as well as on prices (e.g. the consumption function and the demand for money). So if the Walrasian short-period model is the right one, then almost everything in Keynes, and not just the unemployment theory, is wrong. The Counter-revolution is complete. The considerable progress of the last ten years is due to our recognition that the Walrasian short-period model may not be the right one, indeed almost surely is not. That this recognition was so long delayed is partly due to the increased difficulties there are in transcending a well-developed and articulate tradition and partly due to Keynes himself, whose attention to the reconciliation of his micro-theory with his main theory was small and inexpert.

The easiest way of proceeding is, quite provisionally, to consider the case of a given money wage. The Walrasian short-period model is now evidently overdetermined. In what sense then can one speak of a short-period equilibrium with a given money wage? The obvious answer seems to be to remove the condition (equation) that labour markets should clear, but it will not do. For Walras's Law then implies that in this kind of equilibrium at least one market other than that for labour will not clear. But that is not what Keynes proposed. For instance in the long-used *IS/LM* version all non-labour markets clear. There seems no way in which a fixed money wage Walrasian model can make sense of Keynesian unemployment equilibrium. It is here of course that Clower makes his contribution. It is, as I shall argue, not free from faults and he had notable predecesors, in particular Robertson. But it was Clower who took on the Walrasian model on its own terms and made a decisive change.

The basic point is, of course, like much else that is good, very simple. If involuntary unemployment is to be an equilibrium phenomenon then agents must have adjusted all their planned actions to the circumstance that they cannot sell as much labour as they would like. Put in more old-fashioned language, we require the coincidence of *ex ante* and *ex post* in equilibrium states. But this coincidence is now only possible if agents treat their ration of labour as a signal on a par with price signals. That is, to their usual budget constraints we must add the further constraint that not more than a certain amount can be sold. It should be noted that this way of putting the matter is in the spirit of Dréze, Grandmont, Laroque and Hahn (see Dréze, 1975; Grandmont and Laroque, 1976; Hahn, 1976) and not in that of Clower (1965) or Bennassy (1974). The latter make a good deal of the need to use money in exchange when they tell this story. But as I shall argue later money really has nothing intrinsically to do with the matter and indeed, when it is brought to the forefront, leads to muddles.

Even at the cost of some notation it seems convenient to write down the simplest model explicitly. For this purpose I consider an economy which can produce a single good by the aid of this good and labour. The good is perfectly durable if not consumed. The reader will know how to interpret this assumption to make it plausible and will realise that nothing depends on it. Firms issue one-period shares to pay for the quantity of good which they need to produce. At the end of the period (beginning of the next), the share is repaid and all the profit distributed in proportion to share ownership. This rather crazy-sounding postulate avoids complications and leaves everything of interest to us here intact.

Consider household a. The Walrasian budget constraint for the current period is written

$$p \cdot c_a + m_a + \frac{1}{r}b_a + s_a = wl_a + \pi_a + \bar{s}_a + \bar{m}_a + \bar{b}_a\left(1 + \frac{1}{r}\right) \tag{1}$$

Here all prices are in terms of money, c_a = consumption demand and p the price of output, m_a and $\bar{m}_a$ are desired and initial balances respectively, b_a is the number of perpetuities (yielding one unit of money) demanded ($b_a > 0$) and supplied ($b_a < 0$), by a.

Also $\bar{b}_a$ is the endowment of debt ($\bar{b}_a < 0$) or credit ($\bar{b}_a > 0$) while r is the rate of interest on intra-household debt. One interprets s_a as the money value of the demand for shares by a and $\bar{s}_a$ as the current value of shares bought previously and repaid currently. Lastly π_a is the profit entitlement of a, w the money wage and l_a the desired labour supply.

There is also a budget constraint for 'the future'. The money balances, debt and shares demanded today constitute, properly priced, the endowment of the future. Prices for the future are in the mind of the agent and not in the market place. One must also add the profit entitlement of a at the beginning of the future. If π^e, for instance, is the expected profit, that entitlement is $\frac{s_a}{\Sigma s_a}\pi^e$ if in the current period the supply and demand for shares are equal. This can also be written in a different form by writing $s_a = qn_a$ where n_a is the number of shares and q their price. Then if d^e is the expected dividend per share, $d^e n_a$ is the expected profit entitlement. In order to avoid problems with portfolio choices I shall not assume point expectations (but distributions).

Suppose next that a perceives that it cannot sell more than $\bar{l}_a$ units of labour in the current period and expects to perceive a similar constraint $\bar{l}_a^e$ in the future. Then its rational choices are not only constrained by the current and expected budget constraints but also by

$$l_a \leqslant \bar{l}_a \text{ and } l_a^f \leqslant \bar{l}_a^e \tag{2}$$

where l_a^f is planned labour supply in the future. The rational choice of a is taken to result from maximising the expectation of the utility of current and future consumption and leisure. This, as everyone knows, will yield shadow prices for the constraints and in particular $\mu_a \geqslant 0$ for the constraint $\bar{l}_a \geqslant l_a$ such that if l_a^0 is chosen

$$\mu_a(\bar{l}_a - l_a^0) = 0$$

whence $\mu_a > 0$ implies $\bar{l}_a = l_a^0$.

Consider a situation where $\mu_a > 0$, all a. This, of course, implies a given rationing scheme of employment at given prices, etc. Denote summation over a by the omission of the subscript a, (e.g. $x = \sum\limits_a x_a$). Then summing (1) over a one has:

$$\text{If } \mu_a > 0, \text{ all } a{:}p \cdot c^0 + (m^0 - \bar{m}) + \frac{1}{r}b^0 + (s^0 - \bar{s}) = w\bar{l} + \pi \qquad (3)$$

(since perpetuities are bought and sold only by households $\bar{b} = 0$).

Now consider the firms. I shall treat them altogether under the orthodox neoclassical assumptions of the *General Theory*. In the current period output y depends on the stock of capital $\bar{k}$, (there is only one good) inherited from the past and the current employment of labour L. So the current demand for labour is the resultant of maximising $py(\bar{k}, L) - wL$, and the profits which result are available to households owning shares to the value of $p \cdot \bar{k}$ in the current period. I assume that physical disinvestment is not possible, so that if $p \cdot k$ is the value of shares issued currently then $p \cdot k \geqslant p \cdot \bar{k}$. So the new shares help to reduce the old and provide for investment. The choice of k is made by maximising the discounted expectation of $p^e y(k, L^e) + p^e k - w^e L^e - pk$ where $1 + r$ is the discount factor. I do not claim that this is the way the world looks but I claim that it is rather close to Keynes's world.

However, one must pause here to take explicit notice of a serious problem peculiar to sequence economies which, despite the splendid labour of e.g. Drèze (1974) and Hart (1974), is still quite unresolved. The firm is not a person. So what do we mean by the expectations of the firm? Clearly it must be the managers who are meant. But can managers take actions which are independent of those of shareholders? Someone, after all, hires the managers. I need not continue since the difficulty is well known. Until a satisfactory theory emerges all I can do is to look the problem in the face and pass on. But I venture the prediction that we shall have to consider credit rationing (as well as employment rationing) before we are very far on the road to a solution.

Returning to the present story we now suppose that:

$$\mu_a > 0 \text{ all } a \Rightarrow \bar{l} = L^0$$

That is, firms can buy the labour they require if households are rationed in the labour market. So substituting for π in (3) we get

$$p \cdot c^0 + (m^0 - \bar{m}) + \frac{1}{r}b^0 + (s^0 - \bar{s}) = p \cdot y^0$$

and substituting $\bar{s} = p \cdot \bar{k}$ we have

$$p\,[c^0 + (k^0 - \bar{k}) - y^0] + m^0 - \bar{m} + \frac{1}{r}b^0 + (s^0 - p \cdot k^0) = 0 \tag{4}$$

which may be written as

$$p \cdot X_g^0 + X_m^0 + \frac{1}{r}X_b^0 + qX_n^0 = 0 \tag{5}$$

where X_g^0 = excess demand for goods, X_m^0 = excess demand for money, X_b^0 = excess demand for bonds and X_n^0 = excess demand for shares.

Now (5) is the appropriate Walras Law for all values of $(p, r, q, \bar{l})$ and given w and expectation functions for which $\mu_a > 0$, all a; i.e. for which there is involuntary unemployment. As Clower noted, the excess demand for labour will not appear in (5). Also, of course, the actions of households will depend on their ration of labour i.e. on a quantity signal as well as on prices. It is, however, important to understand that I have only written down the half of the story which interests us here. There is another half which would arise at parameter values in which the constraint $L \lessgtr l^0$ would be a quantity constraint on firms. Here $\mu_a = 0$, all a and firms are rationed in the amount of labour which they receive (see Dréze, 1975; Benassy, 1976).

One can now proceed to look for a non-Walrasian unemployment equilibrium. This requires technicalities all similar to those in Grandmont (1976) and I confine myself to brief remarks. First, notice that by the neoclassical firm assumptions one may write:

$$p = g(\bar{l}, w)$$

So, given the money wage w, the unknowns are $(\bar{l}, r, q)$ and in view of (5) there are three independent excess demand relations for the range of household rationing. So solving for $X_i(\cdot) = 0$ ($i = g, m, b, n$), which I suppose to be possible, we obtain $(\bar{l}^0, r^0, q^0)$. If this is to be a real solution we require it to be non-negative and we must see that $\mu_a(\bar{l}^0, r^0, q^0) > 0$, all a. When proper attention is paid to expectational assumptions, etc., there will indeed be values of w for which a non-Walrasian unemployment equilibrium exists. It has all the familiar Keynesian features and in particular agents choices depend on quantities as well as prices. But we have arrived at this point with a fixed money wage.

Before I return to that important matter it will be possible to lay a number of old and new ghosts.

The argument of the simple model, but in fact the general answer we seek, has nothing intrinsically to do with money or any axioms that 'only money buys goods' (Clower, 1965). It is of course true that the model is not one of barter since nothing has been said about any transaction technology. But if a computer costlessly co-ordinated transactions we could replace many by, say, land and work with a fixed land wage.

But there is here so persistent a false trail, first laid by Clower and followed more recently by Benassy (1974), that it is worth making the point in another way. It is argued that involuntarily unemployed labour can only signal its willingness to work but not, until it is employed, its willingness to buy, since an offer of work constitutes a demand for money and not for goods. That is because 'only money buys goods'. But it is a muddle to suppose that in the absence of this axiomatic restriction things would be different. In reality there are many goods. In a barter world a man would not offer his labour in exchange for say some of the sulphuric acid he helps to produce, except on the speculative basis that he could exchange it again. One would expect 'market failure' to be far worse here than in an economy with a medium of exchange (see Ostroy and Starr, 1974). In the fable world of labour and corn this problem would not arise but there would also be no need for a medium of exchange.

It is of course true that Keynes thought of effective demand as demand backed by purchasing power. Since we live in a monetary world this is a convenient and not misleading shorthand for the proposition that in order to actually acquire anything (as distinct from planning to do so), one must have something else, desired by the exchange partner, to give up. In general, then, effective demand and demand differ whenever it is the case that the allocation an agent can reach is smaller than his budget set because of quantity restrictions which he perceives and when his preferred allocation falls into the area where some of the constraints intersect.

However, there is another monetary ghost. Suppose that starting from the equilibrium of our simple model we attempted to have one more unit of employment. If the marginal propensity to save is positive this may be impossible at constant prices, and if the equilibrium is locally unique, the higher employment level will be incompatible with equilibrium. One of the reasons for this is that there are in this economy resting places for saving other than reproducible assets. In our model this is money. But land, as Keynes to his credit understood, would have just the same consequence and so would Old Masters. It is therefore not money which is required to do away with a Say's Law-like proposition that the supply of labour is the demand for goods produced by labour. Any non-reproducible asset will do. When Say's Law is correctly formulated for an economy with non-reproducible goods it does not yield the conclusions to be found in textbooks. As I have already noted Keynes was fully aware of this and that is why he devoted so much space to the theory of choice amongst alternative stores of value.

Money in economic theory always brings out the worst in us. One may take it for granted that in the world exchange is mediated by money. It is one of a number of non-reproducible assets. All such assets must compete with each other as well as with reproducible ones to be held at a positive price. The equilibrium outcome in the labour market is of course not independent of the number of different assets there are and so the existence of money contributes to the outcome. But that, as far as the present story goes, is all. Keynes's view that the rate of return on money (psychic or otherwise) sets a lower bound to the rate of return on any other asset which will command a positive price in equilibrium, does not endanger the existence of Walrasian equilibrium and if the view is correct it affects the amount of unemployment in any fixed money wage non-Walrasian equilibrium but does not affect the theory. There is nothing to suggest that in a world of costless mediation without money, with say a fixed land wage, the story would be different.

So much for the ghosts. But it can now be argued that all that has been achieved is the formulation of a proper concept of short-period unemployment equilibrium with a given money wage. Indeed all one has done is to make explicit the micro-theory which underlies the budget identities and behavioural postulates of generations of macroeconomists. It is easy to replace the postulate of a given money wage with the assumption that it is positively and arbitrarily bounded below and one then is tempted to say that the sum total of Keynesian theory is in this 'price rigidity'. Many textbooks say just that. It is true that, until recently, it was not understood that the set of signals to which agents respond must now include quantities if a proper notion of equilibrium with some fixed prices is to be formulated. But once this is done there is not much left of the 'revolution'. For Keynes's contemporaries were all agreed that lack of 'price flexibility' was responsible for the trouble. I believe there is a good deal more to Keynesian economics than that.

Let us first return to the Walrasian short-period equilibrium. I have already mentioned that there are certain technical requirements if it is to be shown as always possible. The first point to be made is that these requirements are by no means trivial or unimportant. If in the 1930s the computer had to search for the Walrasian equilibrium money wage the search path would have been littered with bankrupt debtors and one needs great heroism to assume that this would have left the computer with continuous behaviour functions. Keynes explicitly refers to this (*General Theory*, p. 264). Next, the history of the economy is given and the conjectured future depends on it and on current events. As current observations depart increasingly from past experience it is not at all clear that it is proper to think of conjectures as continuous in current observations. Moreover, if for instance a much lower money wage than is customary is currently observed the expectational requirement of 'uniform tightness' (Grandmont, 1976) may well be violated. Again Keynes refers to all these points (*General Theory*, p. 269). It is therefore not at all obvious that a short-period Walrasian equilibrium exists for an economy in a given state.

But in thinking of this equilibrium the money stock was taken as fixed and there is no government. If this is rectified one comes to what seems to me a central Keynesian point: a short-period Walrasian equilibrium with fixed money wages but variable government net spending, plausibly exists, while one in which government net spending is fixed but the money wage is the 'unknown' plausibly does not exist. (Later this is strengthened by saying it cannot be reached – *General Theory*, p. 253 – if it exists.) The reasons are that the Walrasian equilibrium will now have prices which are higher and not lower than in the non-Walrasian equilibrium, so that bankruptcies of debtors are avoided. There is also some evidence that marginal productivity schedules are fairly flat. Because the past is given and the future expected to be not too dissimilar, speculative dishoarding will stop spectacularly higher interest rates. All in all no great strain is put on the expectation mechanism. Keynes's point then on this interpretation is not that money wages could not be lower but that it would be better if they stayed where they were. That is, if you are looking for a Walrasian equilibrium you have a better chance of there being something to find if you treat government net spending as an unknown rather than the money wage. Notice that in the Walrasian equilibrium found in this way the given money wage becomes the neoclassical equilibrium money wage.

I now want to make a related point in another way. Consider Patinkin's short-period Walrasian model (Patinkin, 1965). The unknowns can be listed as all prices in terms of labour, cash balances in terms of labour (m/w) and the rate of interest. It follows that one instructs the computer to search for an equilibrium amongst these unknowns. One may clearly fix m or w. But here it departs, so I want to maintain, from Keynesian economics. First, the result depends on the absence of effects from redistribution between debtors and creditors. This in turn depends not only upon an implausible postulate on preferences but upon the very un-Keynesian stipulation that agents have identical point expectations. Second, it is supposed that expectations do not at all depend upon the history of prices before the present moment. If they do, Patinkin's homogeneity postulate is extremely dubious. Nor is attention paid to expectational disorders which are possible and with which Keynes was concerned. So if this familiar model is given some necessary improvements it may easily sustain the conclusion that with a fixed money wage but unknown m an equilibrium can be found, while this is not the case when w is unknown.

Taking the money wage as given, forces new equilibrium concepts to be adopted. Taking expectations seriously, causes us to recognise that the short period depends on an unalterable past and a conjectured future and so also to recognise that short-period Walrasian equilibrium gives rise to new difficulties. Green (1973) and Grandmont (1976) deserve much credit here.

So far I have kept closely to the essentially neoclassical micro-theory of Keynes, but now I want to depart from it. For I want to examine more carefully the claim that the Keynesian theory rests on rigid, i.e. not flexible, money wages. This sentence can be interpreted in one of two ways. One I have just examined and simply says the computer is not allowed to search for a solution amongst all non-negative money wages. The other is that wage-earners actually do not change their money wage. These are of course quite different proposals and the difference has consequences for our notion of short-period equilibrium.

First, notice that if households are rationed in their sale of labour they cannot, evidently, be taken to assume that they can sell what they wish to sell at the going wage. They do not face the world of perfect competition. Second, we notice that since in fact there is no auctioneer – a fact I think widely known by most economists but properly stressed by Iwai (1974) and Benassy (1976) – the decision whether or not to change money wages must be that of some economic agent. If this is the firm then it too cannot be taken to behave like a perfect competitor. In any case as Arrow (1959) pointed out many years ago, perfect competition and prices changing by the decisions of actual agents cannot be reconciled.

Let us stick for the moment to the labour market and think of money wages as being quoted by the sellers of labour. One now needs to supplement the description of the household by a demand curve conjectured by it. This is just like the famous story told by Negishi (1961). The household must have some beliefs as to how its ration of labour would respond to a change in the wage it quotes. If there is an equilibrium it is what I have called a conjectural equilibrium (see Hahn, 1976). That is, it is a state such that actions of agents are compatible and such that, given the conjectures, no price can be advantageously changed by any agent.

Now one can show (see Hahn, 1976), that for certain conjectures an economy can be in conjectural equilibrium which is not the Walrasian equilibrium even if the latter also qualifies as a conjectural equilibrium. More importantly, one can also show (see Negishi, 1974; Futia, 1975) that there are certain examples where in a certain sense locally rational conjectures give non-Walrasian equilibria. Much of this is in its infancy. But sufficient has been done to warrant the following conclusion. If an equilibrium is a state where rational actions are compatible and if amongst possible actions one includes changing of price, then there exist non-Walrasian unemployment equilibria. The wage is neither fixed nor arbitrary nor flexible. It is what it is because no agent finds it advantageous to change it. The invisible hand has ceased before its job is accomplished.

In what sense is unemployment involuntary in such an equilibrium? In the following sense: at the going wage and prices the agent would wish to supply more labour. The wage is not reduced because the conjectured demand curve is not favourable to the agent doing this.

A great deal more work, of course, will have to be done here. The labour market is particularly difficult to study, (i) because normally a man is either employed or unemployed, (ii) because the interests of the employed conflict, and (iii) because there are coalitions and probably a great deal of conventional behaviour. But there is no reason to suppose that the Walrasian equilibrium concept will turn out to be appropriate.

What has just been said of the labour market can be applied to almost all markets. If the economy is not in Walrasian equilibrium then agents must find the hypothesis that they can buy and sell what they like at going prices falsified. They will not persist in these beliefs. Moreover, it is up to them to take action; i.e., they can change the terms on which they offer to trade. This formally puts them into the position of monopolistic competition even if the intrinsic situation is not one of monopolistic competition. All this leads to important departures from Walrasian modes, and Mr Benassy (1976) and Mr Iwai (1974) have been in full cry for some time to the more stately accompaniment of Mr Grandmont and Mr Laroque (1976). In general, agents will be reacting to both price and quantity signals, their expectations will include expectations of quantity constraints and they will need conjectures relating these constraints to the prices they quote.

One can thus argue that the short-period Walrasian equilibrium is not the proper, or at least not the only, benchmark. If that is agreed then even invisible hands which seek equilibria may seek equilibria which we do not like. For instance they are not efficient. So the Keynesian spirit of the thing, namely that there is something for government to do, receives confirmation even before any dynamic processes have been studied. But I think that is all the Keynesian juice there is and I do not think it useful to call each and every departure from Walras, Keynesian. For instance recently there have been investigations of the extreme case where no one ever wishes to change any price as an equilibrium is established purely by rationing (see Dréze, 1975; Grandmont and Laroque, 1976; Hahn, 1976). Almost inevitably such equilibria have been called Keynesian. But they have precious little to do with what Keynes actually wrote. He certainly did not posit fixed prices. Rather the reverse. Nor did he seem to argue that prices change more slowly than quantities, as can be verified in the chapter which tells us why labour cannot control its real wage. It seems to be far less confusing to call such equilibria Drézian or 'French'. We simply have to live with the fact that Keynes never managed to get his micro-theory to mesh properly with the rest of what he had to say.

This leads me to the last point in this section. A picture has emerged in which prices are set at 'the beginning of the period' and the length of the period is then the smallest interval before some price is changed (see Grandmont and Laroque, 1976). This 'fix-price' model does not strike me as very useful but in any case the short period here is not Keynes's short period.

II OUT OF EQUILIBRIUM

In this section I want to talk mainly 'and briefly' about false scents. I have no theory of 'out of equilibrium behaviour' on offer.

Since Leijonhufvud's stimulating book (Leijonhufvud, 1968), which followed on Clower's insight (Clower, 1965), it has become a commonplace to say that Keynesian economics is economics without the Walrasian auctioneer (see, for example, Barro and Grossman, 1971). I do not believe, however, that the cited work logically entails this view nor that the view is very helpful.

In the 1960s a number of non-tâtonnement models of adjustment were studied. Trade took place at 'false' prices and the value at going prices of what was actually bought was always equal to the value of what was actually sold. These models, however, still used the auctioneer. Moreover, during the adjustment process agents were quantity restrained just as they are in the papers which are so popular now. In later versions even Clower's axiom that only money buys goods was included, and still the auctioneer appeared. He did so because no one had the faintest idea how prices are actually changed and because it seemed reasonable to suppose that, when more was known, it would be found correct that prices rose when there were unsatisfied buyers and fell when there were unsatisfied sellers.

Now this last supposition may turn out to be far from correct (see the previous section). On the other hand, we can see that the present cliché is based on a muddle. When people think of an auctioneer they think of a tâtonnement. But the former does not imply the latter. One can agree that Keynesian economics is not about a tâtonnement, which is quite different from the claim that it cannot accommodate an auctioneer. As I have already remarked, Keynes was in no better shape to tell us how prices change in his perfectly competitive world than we are. This then leads to the second observation that economics without the auctioneer requires non-perfect competition economics and not Keynesian economics. Thirdly, the Keynesian non-tâtonnement is not the one which is at present being studied. The assumption in the current non-tâtonnement theory is the rationing of the 'short side' at given prices. Thus if the demand for shoes, before any quantity constraint is perceived, exceeds the supply of shoes then the demand side will be rationed (see Barro and Grossman, 1971; Benassy, 1976). In Keynesian economics suppliers of shoes lose inventories and demands are satisfied. That is, shoemakers will supply more than they planned to do. Anyone who knows the discussion in the 1930s of the multiplier will recognise the story. Yet for some unknown reasons the short side rationing scheme has been christened as Keynesian (see Benassy, 1976; Grandmont and Laroque, 1976).

Of course, the inventory story will only work if there are inventories – the economics of 'depression' was what Hicks called it. Equally clearly, the short side rationing scheme will do for the labour market.

This mistaken interpretation of Keynesian economics goes with a methodology which takes prices as fixed during a short period and misses an important insight into Keynesian economics due to Kaldor (1939). He argued not that prices were fixed because agents think about price only on Mondays, but because 'normal' price expectations combined with inventories prevented prices from changing by much. The argument is straightforward. Anyone encountering an excess demand for what he has to sell could raise prices. But the price is expected to revert to its normal level so either he or others will decumulate stocks. But this means that the current price cannot rise by much. This process Keynesians thought of special significance in the market for loans. Here the expectation of normal interest rates induced the dishoarding of cash which enabled an 'excess demand' for loans to be financed at more or less constant interest rates. No one dreamt of working with models in which the interest rate had already been fixed on Monday.

In a multiplier process the accumulation of inventories was a signal to producers to expand production. However, it is hard to give an interpretation to this under—perfect competition unless one postulates constant returns. If that is done, producers at the 'right prices' simply produce whatever is demanded. Losing inventories is a signal that demand has not been correctly estimated. Many 'mark-up' theories of pricing can be formulated in this way. Indeed, even without constant returns it is possible to use a mark-up mechanism to generate a reasonable theory. Alternatively one can tell a story based on 'perceived demand curves'. Speculative behaviour makes them pretty flat, inventory changes shift them. When there are no inventories to accumulate the story is radically different. In particular, since desired inventories are not in general zero, we are already in a situation with a history of buoyant demand. It is not the situation of the *General Theory*. The short side rationing scheme may here be the appropriate hypothesis.

Recent theorising, however, seems to have been on the right track in arguing that Keynesian dynamics is ill-served by a perfect competition postu-late. In particular the Keynesian investment theory does not seem either helpful or correct. The possibility of bankruptcy is alone sufficient to make of every demand for loan a 'named' demand. That is, every debt differs by the actual borrower. This really is enough to kill perfect competition in the market for loans and leads to a theory of 'self-finance' (see Wood, 1975). The lack of perfect competition in the market for goods requires firms to estimate quantities at different prices. Investment decisions cease to depend on prices only. All this leads to complex models and only economic advisers to govern-ments claim to have the answers. It will be a triumph of accountancy over economics if the simple arithmetic of the multiplier turns out to be correct.

One can certainly now see that the view that with 'flexible' money wages there would be no unemployment has no convincing argument to recommend it. (I am here interpreting this to be a view about dynamics and not 'existence', which I have already discussed). Even in a pure tâtonnement in traditional models convergence to an equilibrium cannot be generally proved. In a more satisfactory model matters are more doubtful still. Suppose money wages fall in a situation of short-run non-Walrasian unemployment equilibrium. The argument already discussed suggests that initially this will lead to a redistribu-tion in favour of profit. The demand for labour, however, will only increase on the expectation of greater sales since substitution effects in the short run can be neglected. If recipients of profit regard the increase as transient (as they sensibly might) their demand for goods will not greatly increase. On the other hand, if wage-earners have few assets their demand will decrease. But that means that producers get a signal to reduce output. Wages continue to fall and prices begin to fall also. Real cash balances increase but expectations about future prices may give a positive rate of return to money. There may be many periods for which falling money wages go with falling employment. Where the system would end up in the 'long run' I do not know.

III   LOOKING BACK

The recent literature for the first time takes seriously the importance of the past and the expected future in Keynesian economics. The first step was therefore a careful study of short-period Walrasian equilibrium. This not unnaturally led to the discovery that certain restrictions are required on the way expectations are formed if existence results are to be possible. It is not clear that there are plausible restrictions. In addition some way is required for a smooth transfer of ownership from a bankrupt debtor. It is not clear that such smooth transfers do take place. So even at this level there is cause for Walrasian anxiety.

But the most interesting development is undoubtedly the change in the requirement for short-period equilibrium. In particular, the study of the given money wage case suggested an equilibrium notion as a snapshot of a non-tâtonnement. That is, one abandons the implausible view that agents consider that they can transact what they wish to at going prices when they in fact find that they cannot. This important line starting with Clower is now developing briskly. It has led some enthusiasts to go to the extreme of fixed price equilibrium and to call that Keynesian. But, of course, there is no good prior reason why agents should treat quantity constraints and prices parametrically. When that assumption is dropped things become more interesting and more difficult. Negishi conjectures appear. So far, except in very special models (Negishi, 1974; Futia, 1975), these have not been treated as the outcome of rational learning. One thinks of them as the outcome of past experience. That may be the right route: the equilibrium of an economy is today what it is because the past was what it was. But much work is required here.

Keynes deserves the credit for forcing one to look sequence economics in the face. He deserves little credit for the rest since he insisted on a purely neoclassical micro-theory. At least this is so at a highly theoretical level. On the other hand if one looks at the sum total of his informal insights one may conclude that all one is doing is to give them adequate theoretical form.

Money in all of this has been a disaster from beginning to end. For a long time it was held that monetary matters are somehow at the root of what is to be learned from Keynes. All sorts of dreadful pronouncements on Say's Law testify to that. The element of truth in this is only that monetary theory requires a sequence economy. But the idea that there would be no unemployment in a barter economy is grotesque. Keynes's own discussion of the consequences of the wage bargain being in money terms only makes sense as a discussion of 'homogeneity' and in any case it was not, as given in that chapter, correct. The 'classical' story being attacked is the corn economy, a 'paradigm' which should not detain one. On the other hand, Keynes fully understood that money was not the only non-reproducible store of value. He attempted to bring the demand for money into a proper theory of portfolio choice and clearly that was the right way of 'integrating' money into real theory. The special properties he claimed to find in the demand for money turn out to make no difference in kind to any theoretical proposition.

That money is of special significance to the non-tâtonnement view of short-period equilibrium seems, as I have argued, simply false. The same conclusion holds for claims that it has this special significance for the multiplier. If we study an economy which is not a barter economy – say a computer-mediated economy – then any non-reproducible asset allows for a choice between employment-inducing and non-employment-inducing demand.

But of course in a monetary economy money is an important non-reproducible asset. It also has one special property amongst assets, namely that it has no uses other than its exchange use. This leads rational agents to care only about real balances. However, once again 'real balance effects' need not refer to money. As prices in terms of land approach zero, land holders become quite wealthy enough to do what is required of them.

These remarks refer only to the pure theory of monetary matters. Of course in actual economies it makes sense to study, say, money wages and not land wages. Keynes, however, knew that for very purely theoretical purposes it made no difference.

Lastly of course there is the view that a certain behaviour of the money stock will ensure a 'natural equilibrium'. There seems to be no theoretical foundations for this.

This leaves at least one important matter undiscussed. That is, of course, macroeconomics, which we think of an an essentially Keynesian invention. The reason for not discussing it is that I have nothing to say. Certainly macroeconomics serves as a good 'simple' model, which many economists feel is what we need. It also no doubt helps in treasuries. But how one is to give it a theoretical foundation I do not know. Whether for instance in discussing investment behaviour one is to think of some 'representative' investor or some particular statistical average seems unresolved. The law of large numbers is perhaps not as applicable to social as to physical phenomena. Think of expectation formation. In addition, macroeconomics seems to suppose that the invisible hand is working smoothly and quickly in allocating resources. It is pretty clear that usable economics will have to be of some sort of macro character. But what sort?

REFERENCES

K. J. Arrow, 'Towards a Theory of Price Adjustment' in A. Abramovitz (ed.), *The Allocation of Economic Resources* (Stanford: University of California Press, 1959).

K. J. Arrow and F. H. Hahn, *General Competitive Analysis* (San Francisco: Holden-Day; Edinburgh: Oliver & Boyd, 1971).

R. J. Barro and H. I. Grossman, 'A General Disequilibrium Model of Income and Employment', *American Economic Review*, Vol. 60, No 1 (March 1971 pp. 82–93.

J. P. Benassy, 'Neo-Keynesian Disequilibrium in a Monetary Economy' (Paris: CEPREMAP, 1974).

J. P. Benassy, 'The Disequilibrium Approach to Monopolistic Price Setting and General Monopolistic Equilibrium', *Review of Economic Studies*, Vol. XLIII(1), No 133 (February 1976), pp. 69–81.

R. W. Clower, 'The Keynesian Counterrevolution: A Theoretical Appraisal', in F. H. Hahn and F. P. R. Brechling, (eds), *The Theory of Interest Rates* (London: Macmillan, 1965).

J. Dréze, 'Investment under Private Ownership: Optimality, Equilibrium and Stability' in J. Dréze (ed.), *Allocation under uncertainty: Equilibrium and Optimality* (London: Macmillan, 1974).

J. Dréze, 'Existence of an Exchange Equilibrium under Price Rigidities' *International Economic Review*, Vol. 16, No 2, (June 1975) pp. 301–20.

C. A. Futia, 'Excess Supply Equilibria' *Bell Telephone Laboratories*, 1975.

J. M. Grandmont, 'A Temporary General Equilibrium Theory' (Paris: CEPREMAP, 1976).

J. M. Grandmont and G. Laroque, 'On Temporary Keynesian Equilibria', *Review of Economic Studies*, Vol. XLIII(1), No 133 (February 1976) pp. 53–67.

J. M. Grandmont and Y. Younès, 'On the Role of Money and the Existence of a Monetary Equilibrium', *Review of Economic Studies*, Vol. XXXIX (3), No 119 (July 1972) pp. 355–72.

J. R. Green, 'Temporary General Equilibrium in a Sequential Trading Model with Spot and Futures Transactions', *Econometrica*, Vol. 41, No 6 (November 1973) pp. 1103–23.

F. H. Hahn, 'On Some Problems of Proving the Existence of Equilibrium in a Monetary Economy' in F. H. Hahn and F. P. R. Brechling (eds), *The Theory of Interest Rates* (London: Macmillan, 1965).

F. H. Hahn, 'On Non Walrasian Equilibria', (University of Cambridge, mimeographed, 1976).

F. H. Hahn and T. Negishi, 'A Theorem on Non-Tâtonnement Stability, *Econometrica*, Vol. 30, No 3 (July 1962) pp. 463–9.

O. D. Hart, 'On The Existence of Equilibrium in a Securities Model', *Journal of Economic Theory*, Vol. 9, No 3 (November 1974), pp. 293–311.

J. R. Hicks, *Value and Capital. An Inquiry into some Fundamental Principles of Economic Theory* (Oxford: Clarendon Press, 1939).

K. Iwai, 'The Firm in Uncertain Markets and Its Price, Wage and Employment Adjustments', *Review of Economic Studies*, Vol. XLI (2), No 126 (April 1974) pp. 257–76.

N. Kaldor, 'Speculation and Economic Stability', *Review of Economic Studies*, Vol. VII, No 1 (October 1939) pp. 1–27.

J. M. Keynes, *The General Theory of Employment, Interest and Money* (London: Macmillan, 1936).

L. R. Klein, *The Keynesian Revolution* (London: Macmillan, 1950).

A. Leijonhufvud, *On Keynesian Economics and the Economics of Keynes. A Study in Monetary Theory* (New York: Oxford University Press, 1968).

T. Negishi, 'Monopolistic Competition and General Equilibrium', *Review of Economic Studies*, Vol. XXVIII, No 77 (July 1961) pp. 196–201.

T. Negishi, 'Existence of an Under-Employment Equilibrium', (University of London, mimeographed, 1974).

J. M. Ostroy and R. M. Starr, 'Money and the Decentralisation of Exchange', *Econometrica*, Vol. 42, No 6 (November 1974) pp. 1093–113.

D. Patinkin, *Money Interest and Prices* (New York: Harper and Row, 2nd ed., 1965).

A. Wood, *A Theory of Profits* (Cambridge: Cambridge University Press, 1975).

2 On Temporary Keynesian Equilibrium*

J.-M. Grandmont and G. Laroque

CEPREMAP, PARIS

INTRODUCTION

One of the fundamental purposes of Keynesian theory is to present a model
of the economy where transactions take place at prices that do not achieve
the equilibrium of supply and demand as the classics understood it. This
implies that, in such a model, short-run adjustments must take place at least
partly by quantity rationing instead of by price movements.

Until recently, the research on Keynesian thinking has been done mainly
within the framework of macroeconomic models pertaining to the neoclassical
tradition. Money wages are assumed to display downward rigidities, and the
labour markets may be equilibrated by quantity rationing (unemployment).
By contrast, prices are supposed to react fast enough on the markets for goods
in order to match supply and demand. Accordingly, economic agents behave
competitively on these markets. It has been shown, within the framework of
this formalisation, that, in some cases (destabilising expectations, the liquidity
trap), there may exist no price system that would achieve an equilibrium of
the economy in the classical sense (see, e.g., Modigliani, 1963).[1] Nevertheless,
according to this line of thought, there is no fundamental difference at the
conceptual level between the neoclassical and the Keynesian models. It is this
neoclassical synthesis that one finds in many macroeconomic textbooks.

After the works of Clower (1965), Leijonhufvud (1968), Patinkin (1949,
1965), the research on this topic has developed in a different direction. The
classical axiom claiming that prices move fast enough in the short run to
match supply and demand is rejected. One is thus led to consider a polar case
of the previous one and to study models which use the 'fixed prices method'
of Hicks (1965). Prices are assumed to be rigid in the short run. The alloca-

*This work was sponsored by the Centre National de la Recherche Scientifique,
Équipe de Recherche Fondamentale en Économie Mathématique (ERA No 507).
Partial support from the Fond National Belge de la Recherche Scientifique is gratefully
acknowledged while J. M. Grandmont was visiting CORE during the acedemic year
1972–3. We wish to thank J. P. Benassy, C. J. Bliss, G. Delange, J. Drèze, F. H. Hahn
and A. P. Kirman for their perceptive comments and suggestions. The paper is printed in
this volume by the kind permission of the editors of the *Review of Economic Studies*, in
which journal and version appeared in February, 1976.
[1] See also Arrow and Hahn (1971) Chapter 14, where the possible influence of
failures is discussed.

42 — Microeconomic Foundations of Macroeconomics

tion is then achieved only by quantity rationing. Therefore, when making
their choices, the agents will take into account the quantitative constraints
that they perceive on the various markets (Barro and Grossman, 1971;
Grossman 1971, 1972a; Solow and Stiglitz, 1968). This conceptual framework seems much richer than the previous one, for it allows one to rationalise
such concepts as the Keynesian consumption function, the accelerator, or the
existence of involuntary unemployment. It also permits us to take into
account such phenomena as the Phillips's curve (Iwai, 1972, 1973).

The foregoing studies were all made either in a macroeconomic framework,
or in a partial equilibrium analysis. It seems therefore useful to re-examine
the issue with the help of modern techniques of general equilibrium analysis.
It is one of the purposes of the present work. This approach was made
possible by the recent research on temporary competitive equilibrium models
(Arrow and Hahn, 1971; Grandmont, 1970, 1974; Green, 1972, 1973;
Sonderman, 1974; Stigum, 1969, 1972) and by some important contributions
to equilibrium theory in the case of price rigidities (Benassy, 1973, 1974; Drèze,
1975; Malinvaud and Younès, 1974; and Younès, 1970, 1973).[1,2] A previous
attempt of this type was made by Benassy (1973), with different techniques.

The aim of this study is to present and compare the neoclassical and neo-
Keynesian models within a unified framework. We shall argue that monopolistic
competition must be a central feature of the Keynesian model. As a matter of
fact, in the neoclassical tradition, prices are determined by the short-run interaction of supply and demand, and the internal consistency of the model does
not force us to make more explicit how prices are set. Once the fixed prices
method is used, the mere logical consistency of the model requires that one
specifies how prices move from one period to the next. It is then surely
logically consistent to specify an adjustment process of prices in the function
of excess demands observed in every period, as in Grossman (1972a),
B. Hansen (1951). We certainly do not want to stick with such a specification,
for it amounts to reintroducing some kind of auctioneering. It is undoubtedly
better to assume at the start that prices are quoted by agents belonging to the
system and revised in every period in the light of the information received on
the past. We shall also emphasise an important feature that seems to have
been underestimated in many previously quoted works, namely, the intertemporal character of production activities and, thus, the importance of
producers' expectations regarding future effective demand in the determination of current wages and employment.

[1] Benassy and Younès assume a fixed price system, while Drèze allows for price
movements. In spite of apparent differences, the equilibrium concepts used by these
three authors are quite similar. The special feature of Benassy's work is to base the
rationing schemes on the agents' effective demands, as in Clower (1965) or Grossman
(1971). In what follows, we shall use the central idea of Drèze's proof and we shall
adapt it to make it closer in spirit to that of Debreu (1956, 1959) for the case with no
price rigidities.
[2] Younès presents an interesting contribution to the study of the optimality properties
of a Keynesian equilibrium in connection with the role of money in the exchange process.

In order to simplify the analysis, we shall consider a rudimentary economy composed of consumers-workers and of firms who exchange among themselves (consumption) goods, labour services and fiat money. In period t, firms combine goods available at the outset of the period and labour services, to produce goods that will be available at the beginning of period $t + 1$. We will exclude from the analysis long-term planning considerations, and thus will not introduce explicitly capital goods. Moreover, there will be no financial system that would enable firms to find external funds. Finally, we shall ignore the possible existence of a stock market or of dividend distribution. The latter restrictions seem unimportant.

We shall study first the neoclassical interpretation of the Keynesian model for such an economy. In this case, all agents behave as price-takers. On the other hand, money prices and wages are free to move at date t to match supply and demand, but money wages cannot fall below some *a priori* given values. When a wage hits its minimum value, the corresponding labour supply is rationed. We shall prove the existence of such an equilibrium with a positive price of money under the assumptions that are commonly used in the study of temporary competitive equilibrium models (continuous price expectations which do not depend 'too much' on the current price system). We shall also show that, under the same assumptions, a competitive equilibrium (i.e., without rationing) exists in this economy when there is no downward wage rigidity. Under some conditions which are weak from the neoclassical point of view, stating essentially that the marginal real productivity of labour services is positive in the domain of feasible allocations, it can be shown that wages must be positive at a competitive equilibrium. It follows that, if all these conditions are satisfied, unemployment would not exist if minimum money wages were low enough.

We shall study in the second part of the paper a Keynesian model with monopolistic competition. To fix the ideas, we shall postulate that prices are fixed by sellers. Accordingly, in the (very) short run, firms choose the prices of their outputs, while workers choose the wages at which they would like to work. These prices are quoted at the outset of period t. Then the adjustment of the markets for goods and labour services is achieved by quantity rationing (money is not rationed). It is important to notice that the agents base their decisions at date t partly on their expectations about the future state of the economy. In particular, firms must forecast the effective demand for their products at date $t + 1$. After having given sufficient conditions for the existence of a short-run equilibrium with rationing, we shall analyse the possible sources of unemployment in this model. We shall find that there are some cases (when the producers' expectations concerning future effective demand are pessimistic) where there may be involuntary unemployment at all positive money wages.[1]

The remainder of the paper is devoted to the formal treatment of the

---

[1] Of course, this does not exclude the case where unemployment is due to 'excessive' wages fixed by the workers.

models, and to a discussion of their respective properties. In Section I we describe the assumptions and concepts that are common to both models. We then examine in Section II the neoclassical version of the Keynesian model, and in Section III, a Keynesian model with monopolistic competition. A discussion of the models, together with suggestions for future research, is presented in Section IV, while all proofs are gathered together in Sections V and VI.

I DEFINITIONS AND ASSUMPTIONS

We gather together in this section, all definitions and assumptions that are used in both models.

We consider an economy at date t. The agents who meet at that date are producers, indicated by j in the finite set J, and consumers-workers indicated by i in the finite set I. They exchange among themselves (consumption) goods and labour services indicated by n in the finite set N, and fiat money. F is the set of goods (produced by firms) and H the set of labour services (offered by households). By definition, $N = F \cup H$ and $F \cap H = \emptyset$. A bundle of goods and labour services is represented by a vector, say $x = (x_F, x_H)$ of R^N, where $x_F \in R^F$, $x_H \in R^H$, and an amount of money by a scalar $m \in R$. The monetary prices of goods and services are denoted by $p = (p_F, p_H) \in R^N$. To simplify, N will also represent the number of elements in the set N. Accordingly, the commodity space is R^{N+1}.

We shall work with positive prices of goods,[1] $p_F \gg 0$, and non-negative wages $p_H \geqslant 0$. In addition, prices will be subject to restrictions represented by non-negative vectors $\underline{p}$ and $\bar{p}$ of R^N, some, or all, components of $\bar{p}$ being perhaps infinite. The admissible set of prices P is then the set of finite prices p such that $p_F \gg 0$, $p_H \geqslant 0$ and $\bar{p} \geqslant p \geqslant \underline{p}$. The presence of short-run price rigidities implies that a market $n \in N$ (but not the money market) may be equilibrated by quantity rationing. Accordingly, a typical agent receives at date t a signal $s = (p, \bar{\zeta}, \underline{\zeta})$ from the market that is composed of the prevailing price system $p \in P$, (the same for all agents), and of the vectors $\bar{\zeta} \geqslant 0$ and $\underline{\zeta} \leqslant 0$ with N components which set quantitative limits to its net demand and supply and may vary from one agent to another. Some components of the vectors ζ may be infinite when no quantitative signal is received by the agent on the corresponding market.

PRODUCERS

We shall choose a very simple representation of production activities. In order to focus the attention on short-run problems, we will neglect the interdependence of short-run and long-run decisions and will limit the firms' planning

---

[1] For all x, y in R^N, $x \geqslant y$ means $x_n \geqslant y_n$ for all n, $x > y$ means $x \geqslant y$ and $x \neq y$, while $x \gg y$ means $x_n > y_n$ for all n.

horizon to one period. In addition, there will be no financial system, nor dividend distribution. Accordingly, the j-th producer's activity in period t is to combine inputs of goods and labour services, represented by $x(t) \in R_+^N$, to get outputs of goods available at date $t + 1$, denoted by $y(t) \in R_+^N$ with $y_H(t) = 0$. Such a representation encompasses storage activities. The production possibilities perceived by the j-th producer at date t are given by a subset T_j of $R_+^N \times R_+^N$. The projection of T^j on the space of inputs R_+^N will be denoted Proj T^j. We postulate[1] for every j:

$(x, y) \in T^j$ implies $y_H = 0$.   (a.1)
T^j is closed, convex.   (a.2)
For every bounded subset B of R_+^N, the set
$\{y \mid (x, y) \in T^j, x \in B\}$ is bounded.   (a.3)

At date t, the j-th firm has an endowment $y^j(t-1) \in R_+^N$ of goods and services that is the result of its production activities in the last period (with of course $y_H^j(t-1) = 0$) and has an amount of money $m^j(t-1) \in R_+$.

The j-th producer must announce at date t a net trade $z(t) = (x(t) - y^j(t-1), m(t) - m^j(t-1))$, with $m(t) \geqslant 0$, in response to the signal he receives $s^j = (p, \bar{\zeta}^j, \underline{\zeta}^j)$. In the light of this signal and of his information on the past, the producer forms expectations about the state of the economy at date $t + 1$, and thus is able to rank all possible net trades. This ranking is described by the *maximum expected profit* $v^j(z(t), s^j)$ corresponding to the net trade z when s^j is perceived by the firm. This function will differ in both models and will be derived precisely in the next sections. It depends on the signal s^j through expectations. Given s^j, the j-th producer will maximise $v^j(z, s^j)$, where $z = (x - y^j(t-1), m - m^j(t-1))$, subject to:

$p \cdot (x - y^j(t-1)) + m - m^j(t-1) = 0$ (i)
$\underline{\zeta}^j \leqslant x - y^j(t-1) \leqslant \bar{\zeta}^j$ (ii)
$x \in \text{Proj } T^j$ and $m \geqslant 0$.   (iii)

The set of optimal net trades is $\zeta^j(s^j)$.

CONSUMERS

For the sake of simplicity, a typical consumer's planning horizon is limited to the next period. Thus the i-th consumer chooses at date t an intertemporal consumption plan $(x(t), x(t + 1))$ in $X^i \times X^i$, where, to simplify, the consumption set X^i is equal to $\{x \in R^n \mid 0 \leqslant x_F, \bar{x}_H^i \leqslant x_H \leqslant 0\}$. This implies in particular that a consumer can survive with no consumption, which is obviously a strong condition. By assumption, for every i,

  (b) *The preferences of consumer i can be represented by a function*

---

[1] Assumptions of this type were used by Sondermann (1974) in a temporary competitive equilibrium framework.

$u^i : X^i \times X^i \to R$ that is continuous and semi-strictly quasi-concave. [1]
Further $u^i(x(t), x(t+1))$ is increasing with respect to $x_F(t)$ and
$x_F(t+1)$, non-decreasing with respect to $x_H(t)$ and $x_H(t+1)$.

We assume that our consumer cannot store goods. Therefore, his resources at date t are only composed of his cash balance $m^i(t-1) \in R_+$. The i-th consumer announces at date t a net trade $z(t) = (x(t), m(t) - m^i(t-1))$ with $x(t) \in X^1$, $m(t) \geqslant 0$ in response to the signal he receives $s^i = (p, \bar{\zeta}^i, \underline{\zeta}^i)$. The set of possible expected consumption plans $(x(t), x(t+1))$ of our consumer depends on his net trade $z(t)$ and on his expectations about the future state of the economy, which are a function of his information on the past and on the signal s^i. The utility function u^i induces through a backward dynamic programming technique a ranking on the set of net trades represented by the *maximum expected utility* $v^i(z, s^i)$, corresponding to the net trade z when the consumer i perceives the signal s^i. As v^i differs in both models, it will be derived precisely in each case in the next sections.

Given s^i, the i-th consumer maximizes $v^i(z, s^i)$ where $z = (x, m - m^i$ $(t-1))$ subject to

$$p \cdot x + m - m^i(t-1) = 0 \qquad \qquad \text{(i)}$$
$$\underline{\zeta}^i \leqslant x \leqslant \bar{\zeta}^i \qquad \qquad \text{(ii)}$$
$$x \in X^i \text{ and } m \geqslant 0. \qquad \qquad \text{(iii)}$$

Constraint (i) is the budget equation; condition (ii) represents the possible rationing constraints; while (iii) expresses the feasibility of the net trade. The set of optimal net trades is denoted $\zeta^i(s^i)$.

EQUILIBRIUM

The concept of equilibrium which we use is that of Dréze (1973). We say that the price system $p \in P$ and the quantitative signals $(\bar{\zeta}^k, \underline{\zeta}^k)$ $(k \in I \cup J)$ define a short-run equilibrium with quantity rationing if there exists $z^k \in \zeta^k(s^k)$ such that:

(E.1) $\displaystyle\sum_{k \in I \cup J} z^k = 0$

(E.2) *For every $n \in N$,*
$$p_n < \bar{p}_n \text{ implies } z_n^k < \bar{\zeta}_n^k, k \in I \cup J \qquad \qquad \text{(i)}$$
$$\underline{p}_n < p_n \text{ or } \underline{p}_n = 0 \text{ implies } \underline{\zeta}_n^k < z_n^k, k \in I \cup J \qquad \qquad \text{(ii)}$$

(E.3) *For every $n \in N$,*
$$z_n^k = \bar{\zeta}_n^k \text{ for some } k \text{ in } I \cup J \text{ implies} \qquad \qquad \text{(i)}$$

---

[1] That is, for every x^1 and x^2 in $X_i \times X_i$, $u^i(x^1) > u^i(x^2)$ and $0 < \beta < 1$ imply $u^i(\beta x^1 + (1 - \beta) x^2) > u^i(x^2)$.

$$\underline{\zeta}_n^k < z_n^k \text{ for all } k \text{ in } I \cup J.$$

$$z_n^k = \underline{\zeta}_n^k \text{ for some } k \text{ in } I \cup J \text{ implies} \qquad (ii)$$

$$z_n^k < \bar{\zeta}_n^k \text{ for all } k \text{ in } I \cup J.$$

(E.4) *For every* $n \in N$, $k \in I \cup J$,

$$z_n^k < \bar{\zeta}_n^k \text{ implies } \bar{\zeta}_n^k = + \infty. \qquad (i)$$

$$\underline{\zeta}_n^k < z_n^k \text{ implies } \underline{\zeta}_n^k = - \infty. \qquad (ii)$$

The equilibrium condition (E.2) says that rationing occurs only when it is no longer possible to adjust the market by means of a price movement. (E.3) prevents rationing of supply and demand at the same time.[1] The additional condition (E.4) says that no quantitative signal is received by an agent on a given market if he is not rationed on that market.[2]

The foregoing definition of equilibrium does not specify how shortages are distributed among agents. Given the present specification of the model, no particular rationing scheme seems more appropriate. One can, however, study the existence of an equilibrium corresponding to a particular scheme. For instance, in the two specifications studied below, it is possible to show without any additional assumption the existence of an equilibrium when the rationing is uniform (all agents rationed have the same net trade), or corresponds to a queue (on a given market, agents are rationed according to some *a priori* given order), or is proportional to effective demand.[3] We shall not pursue further this point.

II THE NEOCLASSICAL INTERPRETATION

We assume in this section that all economic agents act as price-takers. Prices are supposed to react rapidly enough in the short run to match supply and demand, through, for instance, some tâtonnement process. But money wages may display downward rigidities: they cannot fall below some *a priori* given

[1] Without this condition, a no trade equilibrium would always be a solution of the problem. For a derivation of such a condition from more basic axioms, see Younès (1973) and Malinvaud – Younès (1974).

[2] The analysis below applies, with straightforward changes, if one drops the condition (E.4) provided that one assumes that agents always receive quantitative signals on every market involving price rigidities ($\bar{p}_n < + \infty$ or $\underline{p}_n > 0$) even when the constraints on prices are not binding, and when they are not rationed. A solution of this type was implemented by Benassy (1973, 1974).

[3] Effective demand by an agent on a given market is defined as the demand that he would formulate on that market taking into account the quantitative signals received on the other markets, but ignoring the quantitative signal that he may have perceived on that particular market (see, e.g., Benassy (1973, 1974)). Then, proportional rationing means that all agents receive the same proportion of their effective demand on a given market. In order to make this concept meaningful, of course, one has to make assumptions ensuring that effective demands are uniquely defined.

values described by $\underline{p}_H \geqq 0$. Going back to the definition of the set P of admissible prices given in Section I we see that this corresponds to the case $\bar{p} = +\infty$ and $\underline{p} = (0, \underline{p}_H)$. The constraints $p_H \geqq \underline{p}_H$ may be institutionally given (minimum wages law) or may be set by the workers themselves.[1]

It follows from the definition of an equilibrium that, at equilibrium, producers are never rationed in this model ($\bar{\zeta}^j = +\infty$ and $\underline{\zeta}^j = -\infty$ for every j). They base their decisions only upon the current price system and on their knowledge of the past. On the other hand, the consumers are never rationed at equilibrium on the markets for consumption goods ($\bar{\zeta}^i = +\infty$ and $\underline{\zeta}^i_F = -\infty$ for every i), but may receive quantitative signals on the labour markets (some components of $\underline{\zeta}^i_H$ may be finite). Their choices will thus be functions of the current price system, of the quantitative signals received on the labour markets and of their knowledge of the past.

Let us consider the j-th producer who receives the signal $s^j = (p, \bar{\zeta}^j, \underline{\zeta}^j)$. The foregoing argument shows that we can concentrate on the case $\bar{\zeta}^j = +\infty$ and $\underline{\zeta}^j = -\infty$, and thus identify s^j and $p \in P$. The j-th producer's problem is to order all feasible net trades; that is, all $z(t) = (x(t) - y^j(t-1), m(t) - m^j(t-1))$ with $x(t) \in \text{Proj } T^j$ and $m(t) \geqq 0$. In order to do so, the producer has to forecast the signal he will receive at date $t + 1$. Again, since producers are never rationed in this model, he has to forecast only a price system of R^N_+, which is denoted $\psi^j(p)$. Then, the *maximum expected profit* of any feasible net trade $z(t)$, say $v^j(z(t), s^j)$, is by definition the maximum of $\psi^j(p) \cdot y(t) - p \cdot x(t)$ with respect to $y(t)$ subject to $(x(t), y(t)) \in T^j$. As was explained in Section I, given s^j (or $p \in P$) the set of optimal net trades $\zeta^j(s^j)$ is obtained by maximisation of this function $v^j(z(t), s^j)$ under the relevant constraints.[2]

Now consider the i-th consumer, who receives the signal $s^i = (p, \bar{\zeta}^i, \underline{\zeta}^i)$. Here, we can focus the attention on the case $\bar{\zeta}^i = +\infty$, $\underline{\zeta}^i_F = -\infty$. The consumer must order all net trades $z(t) = (x(t), m(t) - m^i(t-1))$ satisfying $x(t) \in X^i$ and $m(t) \geqq 0$. Again, in order to achieve this goal, the agent must forecast the signal that he will receive at date $t + 1$. Since a consumer can be rationed only on the labour markets in this model, his forecast concerns only the price system $p(t + 1) \in R^N_+$ that will prevail, and the maximum amount of labour services that he expects to be able to provide at date $t + 1$, say $\underline{\zeta}^i_H(t + 1) \in R^H$. We shall assume that this forecast depends only on the price system currently quoted, not on the quantitative signals perceived on the current labour markets.[3] This forecast is noted accordingly $\psi^i(p)$, an element

---

[1] But that means that workers then display monopolistic price-making behaviour. We shall see more precisely in section III how to take into account such behaviour.

[2] One obtains the same set $\zeta^j(s^j)$ if one defines $v^j(z(t), s^j)$ as the maximum expected value of the firm at date $t + 1$; that is, the maximum of $\psi^j(p \cdot y(t) + m(t)$ with respect to $y(t)$, subject to $(x(t), y(t)) \in T^j$.

[3] The need for such an assumption comes from the condition (E.4) of the definition of an equilibrium (an agent does not receive a quantitative signal if he is not rationed). This assumption is made in order to avoid discontinuities of expectations when one passes from a state where the agent is rationed to a state where he is not.

of $R_+^N \times R^H$. Then, given s^i, and thus, $\psi^i(p) = (p(t+1), \underline{\zeta}_H^i(t+1))$, the *maximum expected utility* of any feasible net trade $z(t) = (x(t), m(t) - m^i(t-1))$, say $v^i(z(t), s^i)$, is the maximum of $u^i(x(t), x(t+1))$ subject to $(x(t), x(t+1)) \in X^i \times X^i$, $p(t+1) \cdot x(t+1) = m(t)$ and $\underline{\zeta}_H^i(t+1) \leqslant x_H(t+1)$. The set of optimal net trades $\zeta^i(s^i)$ is then obtained by maximisation of $v^i(z(t), s^i)$ under the relevant constraints, as it was obtained in Section I.

AN EXISTENCE THEOREM

Here are sufficient conditions to insure the logical consistency of the model.

THEOREM 1
Assume $\Sigma_j y_F^i(t-1) \gg 0$, $\Sigma_i \bar{x}_H^i \leqslant 0$, $\Sigma_i m^i(t-1) > 0$, *and for every i and j,*

(1) $0 \in \text{Proj } T^j$.

(2) ψ^j *is a continuous function.*

(3) *For every sequence* $p^r \in P$ *such that* $\lim \| p^r \| = +\infty$, $\lim p^r / \| p^r \| = p$, *with* $p_H = 0$, *one has* $\lim \psi^j(p^r)/\| p^r \| = 0$.

(4) ψ^i *is a continuous function.*

(5) *The image of P by* ψ^i *is contained in a compact subset of* $(\text{Int } R_+^N) \times R^H$.

Then, there exists a neoclassical equilibrium with rationing.

Assumption (5) is commonly used in temporary competitive equilibrium models. Together with $\Sigma_i m^i(t-1) > 0$, it makes sure that a 'real balance effect' appears when some prices of goods tend to zero. In the presence of $\Sigma_i \bar{x}_H^i \leqslant 0$, it guarantees that an excess demand appears for r large enough for every sequence p^r that tends to infinity such that $\lim p^r / \| p^r \| = p$, with $p_H \neq 0$. The purpose of assumption (3) is to obtain the same result when $p_H = 0$.[1] This set of conditions implies the existence of a finite equilibrium price system; that is, prevents the price of money from becoming zero.[2]

From (E.3) of the definition of an equilibrium, the foregoing theorem asserts the existence of a competitive equilibrium when $p_H = 0$.[3] It is interesting in that case to have conditions implying that money wages are positive at this equilibrium. To simplify, assume that for every j, the set T^j is defined by a production function F^j taking R_+^N into R_+^N, such that $F_H^j(x) = 0$

---

[1] One can replace (3) by an assumption of substitutability between labour services and inputs of goods to get the same result. Assumption (3) can be suppressed when the firms do not use goods as inputs, that is when $x \in \text{Proj } T_j$ implies $x_n = 0$ for all $n \in F$.

[2] If one accepts an equilibrium with a zero price of money, conditions (3) and (5) can be dispensed with.

[3] For existence theorems in similar frameworks, see Arrow and Hahn (1971), Sondermann (1974), Stigum (1969, 1972).

for all x:

$$T^j = \{(x, y) \in R_+^N \times R_+^N \mid y \leqslant F^j(x)\}$$

Assume further that for all feasible net trades z^j and z^i such that $\Sigma_j z^j + \Sigma_i z^i = 0$, and for every $h \in H$, there exists a producer j such that one of the left-hand partial derivatives $\partial F^j_n / \partial x_h (n \in N)$ is positive. In other words, the marginal physical productivity of labour is always positive on the set of feasible states of the economy. It is then clear that, if $\psi^j(p) \geqslant 0$ for all $p \in P$ and $j \in J$, any competitive equilibrium is such that $p_H \geqslant 0$.

To sum up, we have shown that an equilibrium with rationing involving a positive price of money exists, provided that expectations do not depend 'too much' on the current price system. The purpose of this assumption is to ensure the existence of a real balance effect in the economy. On the other hand, when expectations are strongly influenced by the current price system, one can find non-pathological examples where an equilibrium with a positive price of money does not exist.[1] Thus, this result confirms a conjecture that is often made in the discussion of Keynesian models: there are cases of 'destabilising expectations' where the logical consistency of the classical model (case $p_H = 0$) is not guaranteed. But one sometimes finds in the literature that downward wage rigidities will then restablish the consistency of the system. Theorem 1 shows that this conjecture is false, for we need exactly the same assumptions on expectations with or without downward wages rigidities. The need for assumptions of this type on expectation comes from the very nature of the Walrasian model: the price system is allowed to vary widely (in particular, it may go to infinity) during the tâtonnement process. We shall see later on that such an assumption on expectations is no longer needed when one uses the 'fixed price method'.

The second important finding is that under the assumptions of the theorem, when $p_H = 0$, a competitive equilibrium (i.e. without rationing) always exists, with positive money wages, if the marginal real productivity of labour is positive in the set of feasible states of the economy. The latter condition is not really a restriction, from a neoclassical point of view, in developed economies with enough capital. Thus, we find, as the classics did, that unemployment would not exist in this model if minimum wages were low enough. However, even if one accepts the logic of the model, one cannot claim that minimum wages *should* be decreased for efficiency reasons, for a temporary competitive equilibrium does not in general display any reasonable optimality properties. This is due to the fact that all agents make decisions at date t as a function of their expectations about the future which may be completely false. In particular, it is easily checked that the level of money wages at a competitive equilibrium may be quite low when the producers' *expectations* about the prices of their products are low themselves. This wage level cannot be considered as better than any other.

[1] For an example, see Grandmont (1974).

Finally, we would like to emphasise, after many others, a serious short-coming of the above model, which is related to the interpretation of the constraints $p_H \geq \underline{p}_H$. If one assumes that these constraints describe downward wage rigidities, in which case p_H is equal to the wages that prevailed in the previous period, the model yields the embarrassing conclusion that persistent unemployment cannot be observed with rising wages, which is contrary to the facts. In order to solve this problem, one can consider that p_H is set by the workers in each period and revised as a function of the evolution of the economy. But then, one is led to give to the workers a price-making behaviour. In the same spirit, one should admit a similar behaviour on the part of pro-ducers. It is precisely a model of this kind that we are going to study in the second part of this paper.

III   A KEYNESIAN MODEL WITH MONOPOLISTIC COMPETITION

We now consider a different functioning scheme of the economy. We assume that the agents are no longer price-takers but behave as price-makers. To fix the ideas, we postulate that the agents set the prices of the commodities that they sell. Therefore producers choose the prices of their outputs, while workers choose the wages at which they would like to work. By assumption, the price system which results from these choices is fixed at the outset of the market of date t. This formulation implies that an agent behaves as a price-taker on the markets where he is a buyer. The equilibrium at date t is then achieved only by quantity rationing on the markets for commodities, with the exception of the money market. Thus, the following model must be interpreted as a very short-run model.

The logic of this model leads us to distinguish commodities which are sold by different agents. Accordingly, a commodity is defined by its physical characteristics and by the agent who is able to sell it on the market. The set of goods F is thus partitioned into non-empty disjoint sets $F^j (j \in J)$, where F^j represents the set of products that the producer j can sell on the market. Two goods belonging to F^j and $F^{j'}$ can of course display the same physical characteristics. Therefore, it should be understood in the following that, for all j in J, $(x, y) \in T^j$ implies $y_n = 0$ for every $n \notin F^j$, and $y_n^j(t-1) = 0$ for $n \notin F^j$. In the same spirit, the set H of labour services is the union of the non-empty sets $H^i = \{n \in H \ \ \bar{x}_h^i \neq 0\}$ which are assumed to be pairwise disjoint.

We consider the economy at date t and suppose that the agents already have quoted the prices that they control. Accordingly, the producer j quoted $\bar{p}^j \in R^{F^j}, \bar{p}^j \gg 0$, while the consumer i announced $\bar{p}^i \in R^{H^i}, \bar{p}^i \gg 0$. Going back to the definition of the set of admissible prices P given in Section I, we see that this set reduces to the single point $\{\bar{p} = (\bar{p}^k), k \in I \cup J\}$. The definition of an equilibrium then implies that the agents may receive quantitative signals on every market n in N. But owing to the particular structure of the model, the signals received by the agents at equilibrium may be chosen so as to satisfy the following rules. For any j, one can choose $\underline{\zeta}_n^j = -\infty$ for every $n \notin F^j$, since any feasible trade is such that $z_n^j \geqslant 0$ for such an n. In the same spirit, one can impose $\underline{\zeta}_n^i = -\infty$ for every $n \notin H^i$ and $\bar{\zeta}_n^i = +\infty$ for every $n \in H^i$ for similar reasons. In the sequel, it is always understood that the signals s^j and s^i satisfy these conditions. Finally, it must be noted that, at equilibrium, the j-th producer never buys a commodity $n \in F^j$ from the market, since he is the only one to own such a commodity. If he attempted to do so, he would receive a signal $\bar{\zeta}_n^j = 0$, since all other agents are not buyers of his output.

Let us consider the j-th producer, who receives the signal $s^j = (\bar{p}, \bar{\zeta}^j, \underline{\zeta}^j)$. The producer's choice will depend upon his forecast of the state of the economy at date $t + 1$. For the same reasons as before, we shall assume that expectations do not depend upon the quantitative signals ζ that are perceived in the case of rationing. Typically, the j-th producer has to forecast the price that he will be able to charge for the sale of his products; that is, what will be the *effective demand* for his output, at date $t + 1$? We shall describe this forecast in the following way. For any $y \in R_+^N$ such that $y_n = 0$ for $n \notin F^j$, the number $\rho^j(y) \geqslant 0$ will represent the *maximum* proceeds that the producer expects at date t from the sale at date $t + 1$ of the quantity y. One can imagine that $\rho^j(y)$ is the result of the following process. Given his expectations about the behaviour of the other agents at date $t + 1$, the producer tries to forecast the set of prices $p \in R_+^N$ that will allow him to sell exactly the quantity y at that date, taking into account the possible rationing of the demand. (The only relevant prices are those associated to the goods $n \in F^j$.) One can reasonably assume that this set is closed. On the other hand, if $y_n > 0$ for some $n \in F^j$, the associated component p_n must be bounded, for the product $p_n y_n$ cannot exceed the total wealth of the economy at date $t + 1$. Finally, if $y_n = 0$, the corresponding component p_n may be unbounded: the demand for this good will then be rationed. Under these conditions, there exists always a set $\pi^j(y)$ of prices that maximises the sale's proceeds $p \cdot y$. Then, by definition, $\rho^j(y) = p \cdot y$ for all p in $\pi^j(y)$.[1]

We can now describe precisely the j-th producer's behaviour. Given $s^j = (\bar{p}, \bar{\zeta}^j, \underline{\zeta}^j)$, the *maximum expected profit* of any feasible net trade $z(t) = (x(t) - y^j(t-1), m(t) - m^j(t-1))$, say $v^j(z(t), s^j)$ is by definition the maximum of $\rho^j(y) - p \cdot x(t)$ with respect to y, subject to (i) $0 \leqslant y \leqslant y(t)$ and (ii) $(x(t), y(t)) \in T^j$. The constraint (i) expresses the fact that sales y at date $t + 1$ cannot exceed the available output $y(t)$.[2] As it was described in Section I, given s^j, the set of optimal net trades $\zeta^j(s^j)$ is obtained by maximisation of v^j with respect to $z(t)$ under the relevant constraints. Notice that the choice of an optimal net trade implies the choice of a vector of sales y, hence the choice of prices in $\pi^j(y)$ that will be quoted by the producer at the beginning of period $t + 1$.

[1] This formulation covers the case of 'competitive expectations', when $\rho^j(y) = \bar{p} \circ y$ for some fixed $\bar{p}$. But this case is not very interesting.

[2] We are implicitly assuming 'free disposal' at date $t + 1$.

Let us consider now the i-th consumer, who receives the signal $s^i = (\bar{p}, \bar{\zeta}^i, \underline{\zeta}^i)$. As before, we assume that his forecast is independent of the quantitative signals ζ that are perceived in the case of rationing. The i-th consumer must forecast the prices of goods that will be quoted at date $t + 1$ by the producers, say $\psi^i(t + 1) \in R_+^F$, as well as the maximum amount of these goods that he will be allowed to buy, say $\bar{\zeta}^i_F(t + 1) \in R_+^F$. In addition, our consumer must forecast the effective demand for his labour services at date $t + 1$. For any $x \in R^H$, with $\bar{x}^i_H \leqslant x \leqslant 0$, we shall denote by $\rho^i(x) \geqslant 0$ the maximum income that the consumer expects to receive if he decides to sell at date $t + 1$ the labour services x. This expected income can be justified by the same arguments as in the case of producers.[1] Then, given $s^i = (\bar{p}, \bar{\zeta}^i, \underline{\zeta}^i)$ and any feasible net trade $z(t) = (x(t), m(t) - m^i(t - 1))$, the *maximum expected utility* of the net trade $z(t)$, say $v^i(z(t), s^i)$, is by definition the maximum of $u^i(x(t), x(t + 1))$ subject to:

$$\psi^i(t + 1) \cdot x_F(t + 1) - \rho^i(x_H(t + 1)) + m(t + 1) = m(t). \tag{i}$$

$$x_F(t + 1) \leqslant \bar{\zeta}^i_F(t + 1). \tag{ii}$$

$$(x(t), x(t + 1)) \in X^i \times X^i, m(t), m(t + 1) \geqslant 0. \tag{iii}$$

A term $m(t + 1)$ appears in the budget equation (i). It may be positive for the consumer may be unable to spend all his wealth in period $t + 1$ owing to the rationing of the goods markets (forced savings).

As it was described in Section I, given s^i, the set of optimal net trades $\zeta^i(s^i)$ is then obtained by maximisation of v^i with respect to $z(t)$ subject to the relevant constraints. Here again, it should be noted that the choice of an optimal net trade involves implicitly the choice of a set of wages that will be quoted by the consumer at the outset of period $t + 1$.

AN EXISTENCE THEOREM

We must study the logical consistency of the model.

THEOREM 2

Assume for all i and j,

   (1) $y^j(t - 1) \in \operatorname{Proj} T^j$.

   (2) *The set $Q^j = \{y \in R_+^N \mid \rho^j(y) > 0\}$ is convex, and the restriction of ρ^j to $\bar{Q}^j$ is continuous and concave. If Q^j is non-empty, then for every $y^* \in R_+^N$, with $y_n^* \neq 0$ for some $n \in F^j$, there exists $y \in Q^j$ such that $y \leqslant y^*$.*

   (3) *The function ρ^i is continuous and concave.*

Then, there exists a Keynesian equilibrium.

---

[1] Here again, the case of 'competitive expectations' $\rho^i(x) = \bar{p}_H \cdot x$ for some $\bar{p}_H$, is a particular case of the analysis.

If one looks at the problem defining the producers' behaviour, one finds that a firm which is rationed on all markets may be forced to keep stocks of goods, while being unable to use as inputs the goods of other producers or labour services. We must accordingly assume that the firm can pursue its activities in such a situation. This is done in condition (1), which contains as particular cases the assumptions of 'free disposal', or of costless storage. The assumptions (2) and (3) are there only to guarantee nice continuity and convexity properties of the agents' demand correspondences.

The foregoing result establishes the existence of Keynesian equilibrium for any given system $\bar{p}$ quoted by the agents at the outset of period t. Given the price-making behaviour of the agents, *this price system is endogenous and is entirely determined by the past history of the economy.* But imagine for a moment that we can take $\bar{p}$ as a variable parameter. We can then ask a question that was at the centre of the controversy between classical and Keynesian economists. Does there exist a choice of $\bar{p}$ such that, at the associated Keynesian equilibrium, all markets are cleared in the classical sense; that is, without rationing? In order to give an answer to that query, we must recognise the fact that individual expectations about the state of the market at date $t + 1$ are a function of the prices quoted by the other agents at date t. By analogy with our study of the neoclassical model, it is intuitively clear that, if individual expectations depend 'too much' on the prices that are quoted by the other agents, there may be no choice of $\bar{p}$ that would allow the markets to clear without rationing, as some Keynesian economists conjectured. The important fact to notice is that we need not worry about that to ensure the logical consistency of the Keynesian model as it is formulated here.

We can go further. Assume that there exists a choice of $\bar{p}$ such that all markets clear without rationing. Can we be sure that the corresponding wages $\bar{p}$ are positive? It can be checked that, even when the marginal physical productivity of labour is positive in the set of feasible allocations, there are cases where the clearing of all markets without rationing involves zero wages. It is due to the fact that, in this model, the amount of labour services demanded by firms is strongly influenced by their expectations about the future effective demand for their products. Look at the sets Q^j that are defined in (2) of Theorem 2. To simplify the exposition, assume that they are independent of the current price system $\bar{p}$. It is natural to assume that Q^j is a bounded set for every j. Under reasonable assumptions on the technology T^j, this condition sets an upper bound to the amount of labour demanded by the firm at all prices and wages. Assume on the other hand that there is no disutility of labour so that the (unconstrained) labour supply is constant for all positive wages. It is then clear that, when the firm's expectations are pessimistic (i.e., all points of Q^j are close enough to the origin of R_+^F), there will be unemployment at all positive wages.[1]

---

[1] This argument of course depends crucially on the assumption of an inelastic labour supply; i.e., a labour supply that is bounded away from zero when money wages vary but stay positive. It must be noted that the argument no longer holds in the case of 'competitive expectations' as was shown in section II.

Finally, we wish to remind the reader that, even if there exists a choice of $\bar{p}$ such that equilibrium is achieved without rationing, there is no reasonable ground to claim that this price system is better than another, for the decisions taken by the agents at date t may be based upon wrong expectations about the future course of the economy.

IV CONCLUSIONS

The foregoing analysis suggests that models using the fixed price method are better tools with which to describe the workings of modern economies. The basic axiom underlying neoclassical models is that prices move fast enough in the short run in order to match supply and demand. In order to rationalise this postulate, economists have introduced a fictitious auctioneer who would adjust prices as functions of excess demand on every market. It is hard to find markets which actually function in that way. On the other hand, in fixed prices models, a short-run equilibrium is reached through adjustment of quantities. We have emphasised the fact that, in order to close such models in a satisfactory way, it is better to assume that prices are set by some agents belonging to the economic system and specify the price-making behaviour of these agents. In other words, we were led to introduce monopolistic competition in the model. These two assumptions (monopolistic competition, plus short-run adjustment of quantities) lead to a model which seems much more appropriate to describe the formation of prices which takes place in our economies.[1]

In order to make precise our fixed prices model, we assumed that prices were set by sellers. It is clear that this assumption is quite arbitrary. Indeed, the central question to be answered in subsequent studies of Keynesian models seems to be: how are the prices fixed? It is a difficult problem. It is clear at the outset, however, that any satisfactory answer to that problem should take explicitly into account such elements as information costs, transaction costs, and perhaps more importantly, the cost involved in price quotation. Moreover, the relative sizes of the participants in each market should play a key role in the analysis, this being due to the cost of making coalitions together with the indivisibility of information.

An example may clarify this point. Consider a 'big' seller facing a continuum of small buyers. Assume that these buyers must act individually (i.e., they cannot form syndicates). Assume, on the other hand, that the seller has no information about the identity of buyers.[2] Two extreme organisations of price setting can be considered in this set-up. On the one hand, the seller can quote a single price independent of the buyer. This unique signal then looks like a

---

[1] One can notice that, if the agents have competitive expectations, and if the prices are fixed at their neoclassical equilibrium values, the fixed price model leads to the same allocation as the neoclassical one. In this respect, the Keynesian model appears as a generalisation of the neoclassical one.

[2] This means that the cost of identification of the buyers is very high, which precludes any discriminatory tarification on the part of the seller.

public good and is received by every buyer. On the other hand, one can imagine that every buyer sends a signal (a price) to the seller. If price quotation involves some costs, as it should, it is clear that the first kind of organisation should prevail since it is less costly than the second one. This heuristic argument can be extended to the case of a few big sellers facing a continuum of buyers. Of course it is reversed in the case of a big buyer facing a large number of sellers. In such cases, it seems natural to assume that the big side of the market sets the prices. Then the fixed price method seems quite appropriate.

The method is less applicable when there are only a few participants. In this case, the costs of communication are relatively small. The buyers and the sellers will directly conclude contracts, setting at the same time the exchanged quantity and the price of exchange. The fixed price method cannot deal with these cases, which should be analysed by using the methods of the theory of games.

V   PROOF OF THEOREM 1

The central idea of the proof is borrowed from Drèze (1975).

Choose $\epsilon > 0$ such that $p_n - \epsilon > 0$ for every n such that $p_n > 0$, and define $P_\epsilon = \{\pi \in R^N | \pi_F \gg 0, \pi_H \geqslant \text{Max}(0, p_H - \epsilon)\}$. Thus, P_ϵ is a set containing P. For any $\pi \in P_\epsilon$, let $p(\pi) = (\pi_F, \text{Max}(\pi_H, p_H))$, an element of P. For every j and $\pi \in P_\epsilon$, let $s^j(\pi)$ be the signal $(p(\pi), \bar{\zeta}^j(\pi), \underline{\zeta}^j(\pi))$ where $\bar{\zeta}^j(\pi) = +\infty$, $\underline{\zeta}^j(\pi) = -\infty$. Let $x^* \in R^H$ such that $x^* \ll \bar{x}_H^i$ for every i. For every i and $\pi \in P_\epsilon$, let $s^i(\pi)$ be the signal $(p(\pi), \bar{\zeta}^i(\pi), \underline{\zeta}^i(\pi))$, where $\bar{\zeta}^i(\pi) = +\infty$, $\underline{\zeta}_n^i(\pi) = -\infty$ for every n with $\underline{p}_n = 0$, and, when $\underline{p}_n > 0$,

$$\underline{\zeta}_n^i(\pi) = \begin{cases} x_n^* \text{ if } \pi_n \gtrless \underline{p}_n, \\ \\ 0 \text{ if } \pi_n = \underline{p}_n - \epsilon. \end{cases}$$

Assume in addition that for every n with $\underline{p}_n > 0$, the function $\underline{\zeta}_n^i(\pi)$ is continuous. Finally, for any $\pi \in P_\epsilon$, let

$$\zeta(\pi) = \Sigma_j \zeta^j(s^j(\pi)) + \Sigma_i \zeta^i(s^i(\pi)).$$

Using Walras's Law, we know that $p(\pi) \cdot x + m = 0$ for every $z = (x, m) \in \zeta(\pi)$.

The functions $s^j(\pi)$ and $s^i(\pi)$ being given, it is easy to check that any π in P_ϵ such that $0 \in \zeta(\pi)$ defines an equilibrium with rationing. Conversely, any equilibrium with rationing can be represented in that way by an appropriate choice of the functions $\underline{\zeta}_n^i(\pi)$ for every n such that $\underline{p}_n > 0$.

Remark: One can prove the existence of an equilibrium associated with a specific rationing scheme, by choosing specific forms of the functions $\underline{\zeta}^i(\pi)$. The cases of a uniform rationing and of a queue are straightforward and left to the reader. The case of a rationing proportional to effective demand necessitates a special treatment. In that case, for every n such that $\underline{p}_n > 0$, the function $\underline{\zeta}_n^i(\pi)$ must depend on a new parameter $\tilde{x}_n^i \leqslant 0$, which at equilibrium must equal the consumers' effective supply of labour on that market. More precisely, given $\bar{x}_n^i \leqslant \tilde{x}_n^i \leqslant 0$, the function $\underline{\zeta}_n^i(\pi, \tilde{x}_n^i)$ is equal to x_n^* if $\pi_n \geqslant p_n$, and is linear on the intervals $[p_n, p_n - (\epsilon/2)]$ and $[p_n - (\epsilon/2), p_n - \epsilon]$. It takes the value $\tilde{x}_n^i$ when $\pi_n = p_n - (\epsilon/2)$, and 0 when $\pi_n = p_n - \epsilon$. Given an array $\tilde{x}$ of such $\tilde{x}_n^i$, $\zeta(\pi, \tilde{x}) = \Sigma_i \tilde{\zeta}^i(s^i(\pi, \tilde{x})) + \Sigma_j \zeta^j(s^j(\pi))$ is the set of aggregate net trades corresponding to $\pi \in P_\epsilon$. We assume in that case that preferences are strictly convex, so that the ζ^i are functions. On the other hand, given $\tilde{x}$ and π, one can define the vector of effective supplies of labour by consumers on the markets n such that $\underline{p}_n > 0$, say $\tilde{\zeta}(\pi, \tilde{x}) = (\tilde{\zeta}_n^i(\pi, \tilde{x}))$. Clearly, an equilibrium corresponding to rationing proportional to effective demand is defined by $\pi \in P_\epsilon$ and $\tilde{x}$ such that $0 = \zeta(\pi, \tilde{x})$ and $\tilde{x} = \tilde{\zeta}(\pi, \tilde{x})$. In order to prove the existence of such a couple $(\pi, \tilde{x})$, the argument below needs to be modified only slightly. The details are left to the reader.

Before proceeding to the proof of the existence of such a vector, we establish a few preliminary results. First, one checks easily:

(5.1) *The correspondence* $\zeta^i(s^i(.)) : P_\epsilon \to R^{N+1}$ *is non-empty-, compact-, convex-valued and u.h.c.* [1]

In addition,

(5.2) *Let* $\pi^r \in P_\epsilon$ *be a sequence. Consider*
   (i) *π^r tends to π such that $\pi_n = 0$ for some $n \in F$.*
   (ii) *$\| \pi^r \|$ tends to infinity, $\pi^r / \| \pi^r \|$ tends to π with $\pi_n > 0$ for some $n \in H$.*

If (i) *or* (ii) *is satisfied, then for any sequence* $z^r \in \Sigma_i \zeta^i(s^i(\pi^r))$, *one has* $\lim \| z^r \| = +\infty$.

To prove this result, it is sufficient to show that it holds for one consumer i such that $m^i(t-1) > 0$ in the first case, and such that $\bar{x}_n^i < 0$ in the second (there always exists such a consumer). This can easily be proved, using the techniques of temporary equilibrium analysis. The details are left to the reader.

The above result covers the case where the price system tends in norm towards infinity, but where the relative wages do not tend altogether towards zero. Otherwise, we have to consider the producers' demand to get a similar result.

First one can check easily, using standard arguments:

(5.3) *The correspondence* $\zeta^j(s^j(.)) : P_\epsilon \to R^{N+1}$ *has a closed graph. It is non-empty-, compact-, convex-valued and u.h.c. on the set* $\{\pi \in P_\epsilon \mid \pi_H \geqslant 0\}$.

---

[1] A correspondence α from the metric space X into the metric space Y is A-valued if $\alpha(x)$ has the property A for every x in X. Further α is upper hemicontinuous (u.h.c.) if the set $\{x \in X \mid \alpha(x) \subset G\}$ is open in X for every open subset G of Y.

Then:

(5.4) *Let $\pi^r \in P_\epsilon$ be a sequence such that $\| \pi^r \|$ tends to infinity*
  $\lim (\pi^r/\| \pi^r \|) = \pi$ *with $\pi_H = 0$. Then, for any sequence $z^r \in$*
  $\Sigma_j \zeta^j(s^j(\pi^r))$, *one has* $\lim \| z^r \| = +\infty$.

Proof: Consider such a sequence and a j such that $\pi \cdot y^j(t-1) > 0$. It is
sufficient to show that, for any sequence $z^r = (x^r - x^j(t-1),$
$m^r - m^j(t-1)) \in \zeta^j(s^j(\pi^r))$, one has $\lim \| z^r \| = +\infty$. Were it not true,
one could find a subsequence (same notation) such that (x^r, m^r) converges to, say, $(x, m) \in R^{N+1}$. Let $(x^r, y^r) \in T^j$ be a corresponding
sequence of production plans. For any r, one has $p(\pi^r) \cdot x^r + m^r$
$= p(\pi^r) \cdot y^j(t-1) + m^j(t-1)$, and thus, by continuity, $\pi \cdot x = \pi \cdot y^j(t-1)$
> 0. On the other hand, $0 \in \text{Proj } T^j$ implies that, for any r,

$$\psi^j(p(\pi^r)) \cdot y^r - p(\pi^r) \cdot x^r \geqslant 0.$$

Dividing this inequality by $\| \pi^r \|$ and going to the limit, we get $\pi \cdot x \leqslant 0$,
which leads to a contradiction.

                                                                    Q.E.D.

We now proceed to the proof of the existence of a $\pi \in P_\epsilon$ such that $0 \in \zeta(\pi)$
by adapting standard methods (Debreu, 1956, 1959). Let δ^r be an increasing
sequence of real numbers such that $\lim \delta^r = +\infty$, and $\delta^1 > \underline{p}_n$ for every n.
Consider the sequence of compact, convex sets:

$$P^r = \{\pi \in P_\epsilon \mid (1/\delta^r) \leqslant \pi_n \leqslant \delta^r \text{ for all } n \text{ such that } \underline{p}_n = 0, \text{ and}$$
$$\pi_n \leqslant \delta^r \text{ for all } n \text{ such that } \underline{p}_n > 0\}.$$

From the construction of P^r, the restriction of ζ to P^r is non-empty-,
compact-, convex-valued and u.h.c.. Thus, for a fixed r, the image of P^r by ζ
is contained in a compact, convex subset Z^r of R^{N+1}. For any $z = (x, m) \in$
Z^r, let $\mu^r(z) = \{\pi^* \in P^r \mid \pi^* \cdot x \geqslant \pi \cdot x \text{ for all } \pi \in P^r\}$. To any (π, z) in
$P^r \times Z^r$, let us associate the set $\mu^r(z) \times \zeta(\pi)$. The so defined correspondence
has a fixed point, i.e., there exists π^r in P^r and $z^r = (x^r, m^r)$ in Z^r such that
$z^r \in \zeta(\pi^r)$ and $\pi^r \cdot x^r \geqslant \pi \cdot x^r$ for all $\pi \in P^r$.

We first remark that $x_n^r \geqslant 0$ for every $n \in H$ such that $\underline{p}_n > 0$. For if
$x_n^r < 0$ for such an n, one would have $\pi_n^r = \underline{p}_n - \epsilon$, hence $\underline{\zeta}_n^i(\pi^r) = 0$ for all i,
in which case $x_n^r \geqslant 0$. We next show that $\pi^r \cdot x^r + m^r = 0$. If $\underline{p}_n > 0$ and
$x_n^r > 0$ for some n in H, we have $\pi_n^r = \delta^r$, which is greater than $\underline{p}_n$, and, therefore, $p_n(\pi^r) = \pi_n^r$. It follows that $\pi^r \cdot x^r + m^r = p(\pi^r) \cdot x^r + m^r$, which is
equal to zero by Walras's Law.

Thus the sequence z^r is bounded, since it is bounded below and
$\pi^1 \cdot x^r + m^r \leqslant 0$ with $\pi^1 \geqslant 0$. We can suppose without loss of generality that
the sequence z^r converges towards $\bar{z} = (\bar{x}, \bar{m})$. The sequence π^r is certainly
bounded, otherwise one could contradict (5.2) (ii) or (5.4). Therefore we can
also assume that the sequence π^r converges to $\bar{\pi} \in \bar{P}_\epsilon$. We surely have $\bar{\pi} \in P_\epsilon$,
i.e., $\bar{\pi}_F \geqslant 0$, otherwise one could contradict (5.2) (i). Hence, by continuity,

$\bar{z} \in \zeta(\bar{\pi})$ and

(*) $\bar{\pi} \cdot \bar{x} \geqslant \pi \cdot \bar{x}$ for all π in P_ϵ.

Now, $\bar{\pi}_F \gg 0$ implies $\bar{x}_F = 0$. Next, (*) implies $\bar{x}_H \leqslant 0$ since $\bar{\pi}$ is finite. Consider an n such that $p_n > 0$. We know by continuity that $\bar{x}_n \geqslant 0$. Thus $x_n = 0$ when $p_n > 0$. Consider the next case $p_n = 0$ for some $n \in H$, and $x_n < 0$. That means that there is an excess supply of labour n. But we assumed that the workers' utility functions were non-decreasing with respect to labour services. Thus, we are sure that $(0, \bar{m}) \in \zeta(\bar{\pi})$. Finally, $\bar{m} = 0$ is a consequence of Walras's Law. This completes the proof of Theorem 1.

Q.E.D.

VI PROOF OF THEOREM 2

Here the set P reduces to $\{\bar{p}\}$. Choose $\epsilon > 0$ and define P_ϵ as the cube $\{\pi \in R^N \mid \bar{p}_n - \epsilon \leqslant \pi_n \leqslant \bar{p}_n + \epsilon \text{ for all } n \in N\}$. Also, let $z^* \in R_+^N$ be such that $z_n^* > \Sigma_j y_n^j(t-1)$ when $n \in F$, $z_n^* > -\Sigma_i \bar{x}_n^i$ when $n \in H$. For every $k \in I \cup J$, and any $\pi \in P_\epsilon$, let $s^k(\pi)$ be the signal $(\bar{p}, \bar{\zeta}^k(\pi), \underline{\zeta}^k(\pi))$, where $\bar{\zeta}^k(.)$ and $\underline{\zeta}^k(.)$ are continuous functions satisfying, for every n,

$$\bar{\zeta}^k(\pi) = z_n^* \quad \text{when } \pi_n \leqslant \bar{p}_n,$$

$$= 0 \quad \text{when } \pi_n = \bar{p}_n + \epsilon,$$

and

$$\underline{\zeta}^k(\pi) = -z_n^* \quad \text{when } \pi_n \geqslant \bar{p}_n,$$

$$= 0 \quad \text{when } \pi_n = \bar{p}_n - \epsilon.$$

Define for every $\pi \in P_\epsilon$, $\zeta(\pi) = \Sigma_j \zeta^j(s^j(\pi)) + \Sigma_i \zeta^i(s^i(\pi))$. By Walras's Law, we know that $\bar{p} \cdot x + m = 0$ for every $z = (x, m) \in \zeta(\pi)$. It is easy to check that, given the functions $s^j(\pi)$ and $s^i(\pi)$, a Keynesian equilibrium is defined by $\pi \in P_\epsilon$ such that $0 \in \zeta(\pi)$. Conversely, any Keynesian equilibrium can be obtained in that way provided that the functions $s^i(\pi)$ and $s^j(\pi)$ are properly chosen.

It is straightforward to see that the choice of a net trade in $\zeta^j(s^j(\pi))$ by the producer j involves the choice of vector of sales y at date $t+1$ which belongs to $\bar{Q}^j$, owing to assumption (2) of Theorem 2. It then follows by standard arguments that the correspondence $\zeta : P_\epsilon \rightarrow R^{N+1}$ is non-empty-, compact-, convex-valued and u.h.c.. Let Z be a compact convex set containing $\zeta(P_\epsilon)$. For every $z = (x, m)$ in Z, consider $\mu(z) = \{\pi^* \in P_\epsilon \mid \pi^* \cdot x \geqslant \pi \cdot x \text{ for all } \pi \text{ in } P_\epsilon\}$. The correspondence which associates the set $\mu(z) \times \zeta(\pi)$ to each $(\pi, z) \in P_\epsilon \times Z$ has a fixed point. That is, there exist $\bar{\pi} \in P_\epsilon$ and $\bar{z} = (\bar{x}, \bar{m}) \in \zeta(\bar{\pi})$ such that $\bar{\pi} \cdot \bar{x} \geqslant \pi \cdot \bar{x}$ for all $\pi \in P_\epsilon$. Now, if $x_n > 0$ for some n in N, this implies $\bar{\pi}_n = \bar{p}_n + \epsilon$, in which case $\bar{x}_n \leqslant 0$ by construction of the functions $s^j(\pi)$ and $s^i(\pi)$. In a similar way, $\bar{x}_n < 0$ implies $\bar{x}_n \geqslant 0$. Thus $\bar{x} = 0$. By Walras's Law, $0 \in \zeta(\bar{\pi})$.

Q.E.D.

REFERENCES

K. J. Arrow and F. H. Hahn, *General Competitive Analysis* (San Francisco: Holden-Day, 1971).

R. J. Barro and H. I. Grossman, 'A General Disequilibrium Model of Income and Employment', *American Economic Review*, Vol. 60, No 1 (March 1971) pp. 82–93.

J. P. Benassy, 'Disequilibrium Theory', C.R.M.S. Working Paper (University of California, Ph.D. thesis, 1973).

J. P. Benassy, 'Neo-Keynesian Disequilibrium Theory in a Monetary Economy', *Review of Economic Studies*, Vol. 42, No. 132 (October 1975) pp. 503–23.

R. W. Clower, 'The Keynesian Counterrevolution: A Theoretical Appraisal', in F. H. Hahn and F. P. R. Brechling (eds), *The Theory of Interest Rates* (London: Macmillan, 1965).

G. Debreu, 'Market Equilibrium', *Proceedings of the National Academy of Sciences of the U.S.A.* (Chicago University Press, 1956).

G. Debreu, *Theory of Value* (New York: John Wiley, 1959).

J. Drèze (ed), *Allocation under Uncertainty, Equilibrium and Optimality*, Proceedings of a workshop sponsored by the I.E.A. held in Bergen (London: Macmillan, 1974).

J. Drèze, 'Existence of an Exchange Equilibrium under Price Rigidities', *International Economic Review*, Vol. 16, No 2 (June 1975) pp. 301–20.

J. M. Grandmont, 'On the Temporary Competitive Equilibrium', C.R.M.S. Working Paper (University of California, Ph.D. thesis, 1970).

J. M. Grandmont, 'On the Short-Run Equilibrium in a Monetary Economy' in J. Drèze (ed), *Allocation under Uncertainty, Equilibrium and Optimality* (London: Macmillan, 1974).

J. M. Grandmont and G. Laroque, 'On Money and Banking', *Review of Economic Studies*, Vol. XLII (2), No 130 (April 1975) pp. 207–36.

J. R. Green, 'Preexisting Contracts and Temporary General Equilibrium', (Harvard UP, 1972).

J. R. Green, 'Temporary General Equilibrium in a Sequential Trading Model with Spot and Futures Transactions', *Econometrica*, Vol. 41, No 6 (November 1973) pp. 1103–23.

H. I. Grossman, 'Money, Interest and Prices in Market Disequilibrium', *Journal of Political Economy*, Vol. 80, No 2 (March/April 1972) pp. 223–55.

H. I. Grossman, 'A Choice-theoretic Model of an Income Investment Accelerator', *American Economic Review*, Vol. 62, No 3 (September 1972) pp. 630–41.

B. Hansen, *A Study in the Theory of Inflation* (London: Allen & Unwin, 1951).

K. Iwai, 'The Firm in Uncertain Markets and Its Prices, Wage and Employment Adjust-C.R.M.S. Working Paper (University of California, 1972).

K. Iwai, 'The Firm in Uncertain Markets and Its Prices, Wage and Employment Adjustments', *Review of Economic Studies*, Vol. 41, No 126 (April 1974) pp. 257–76.

A. Leijonhufvud, *On Keynesian Economics and the Economics of Keynes: A Study in Monetary Theory* (New York and London: Oxford University Press, 1968).

E. Malinvaud and Y. Younès, 'Une Nouvelle Formulation Générale pour l'Étude des fondements Microéconomiques de la Macroéconomie' (Paris: INSEE-CEPREMAP, 1974).

F. Modigliani, 'The Monetary Mechanism and Its Interaction with Real Phenomena', *Review of Economics and Statistics*, Vol. LXLV, Supplement No 1, Part 2 (February 1963) pp. 79–107.

D. Patinkin, 'Involuntary Unemployment and the Keynesian Supply Function', *Economic Journal*, Vol. 59, No 225 (September 1949) pp. 360–83.

D. Patinkin, *Money, Interest and Prices* (New York: Harper & Row, 2nd ed., 1965).

R. M. Solow and J. E. Stiglitz, 'Output, Employment and Wages in the Short Run', *Quarterly Journal of Economics*, Vol. 82, No 4 (November 1968) pp. 537–60.

D. Sondermann, 'Temporary Competitive Equilibrium under Uncertainty', in J. Drèze (ed.) *Allocation under Uncertainty, Equilibrium and Optimality* (London: Macmillan, 1974).

B. Stigum, 'Competitive Equilibria under Uncertainty', *Quarterly Journal of Economics*, Vol. 83, No 4 (November 1969) pp. 533–61.

B. Stigum, 'Resource Allocation under Uncertainty', *International Economic Review*, Vol. 13, No 3 (October 1972), pp. 431–59.

Y. Younès, 'Sur une Notion d'Equilibre Utilisable dans le Cas ou les Agents Économiques ne sont pas assurés de la Compatibilite de Leurs Plans', (Paris: CEPREMAP, 1970).

Y. Younès, 'On the Role of Money in the Process of Exchange and the Existence of a Non-Walrasian Equilibrium', *Review of Economic Studies*, Vol. 42, No 132 (October 1975) pp. 489–501.

3 Some New Concepts for the Microeconomic Foundations of Macroeconomics*

E. Malinvaud and Y. Younès

INSEE, PARIS and CEPREMAP, PARIS

INTRODUCTION

It is by now widely accepted that the general competitive equilibrium does not provide the appropriate foundation for the macroeconomic theory of employment or for the study of decentralised transactions that react to some public macro-decisions. But we have no alternative accepted microeconomic model that would provide such a foundation. Important progress has been achieved recently in building up a concept of temporary equilibrium that greatly clarifies the macroeconomics of growth and some problems concerning short-term fluctuations. For unemployment, rationing and similar phenomena this concept is, however, unsuitable since it assumes the formation of prices that clear the markets at each time.

We want to present here an attempt at building a new formalisation that provides a foundation both for the competitive equilibrium of the Walrasian economy and for the underemployment equilibrium of the Keynesian economy. It may, moreover, be appropriate for studying the consequences of given macro-decisions. Our work does not aim at directly providing new insights into the nature of economic phenomena, but rather at finding a fundamental model that helps to unify various lines of theoretical development and may be used for subsequent research in mathematical economics. As is well known, however, the setting up of new formal concepts opens up new vistas and helps to a better understanding of the phenomena.

The genesis of our theory owes much to the queries of Hahn and Negishi (1962), Clower (1965), Leijonhufvud (1967) and many others. At the stage of its formalisation it has been prepared by earlier research due to Younès (1970), Grossman (1972), Drèze (1973), Benassy (1973) and Grandmont and Laroque (1974).

Recent thinking in macroeconomics has emphasised the role played by price rigidities, by the use of money as a counterpart in each transaction and,

*This is a revised version of the paper presented at the conference.

more generally, by various institutional constraints. We must therefore introduce into our basic model from the beginning, these features which the general equilibrium theory, as it is classically presented, cannot take into account. However, we shall not address ourselves here to the questions of knowing why some prices are rigid, why money is almost always used in transactions or why some other institutional arrangements prevail. We want to understand the consequences of these facts; understanding their origin is another problem that we shall not discuss here.

For our purpose the key technical concept of 'type of transaction' will replace that of price. Restrictions will then be imposed *a priori* on the set of types of transaction that may be used by the agents. This replacement will make it easy to deal with price rigidities, with the fact that money is used for payment in all transactions and with many other institutional constraints such as the non-existence of markets for particular commodities.

This replacement being made, we shall remain within the realm of the general competitive equilibrium. Extensions to imperfect competition are feasible, and we shall hint how. Similarly it is rather easy to construct, from the ideas introduced in this paper, a dynamic adjustment process corresponding to our equilibrium concept. But we shall not do it here, as we believe that equilibrium analysis is fully appropriate for dealing with involuntary underemployment and similar phenomena.

The equilibrium concept will proceed from two ideas: (1) in an economy involving many agents, each one of them could freely sell or buy less than he actually does; (2) in order to decide on their transactions, agents co-operate to some degree with one another, but only to a very limited degree.

We shall concentrate our discussion on the study of the newly defined equilibrium as applied to a monetary economy with price rigidities. But other interesting applications of course exist. In order to gain some feeling on what this equilibrium really is, we shall follow two lines of approach.

On the one hand, we shall derive some general properties. We shall first show that all transactions on a given commodity are made at the same price. Commodities will then be divided into three groups depending on whether they turn out to be traded on a 'sellers' market', on a 'buyers' market' or on a 'competitive market'. It will be shown that, in an equilibrium, the price on a sellers' market is kept at its maximum feasible value and on a buyers' market at its minimum. Moreover, when all price rigidities are ineffective, the new equilibrium coincides with the classical competitive equilibrium.

On the other hand, we shall introduce a graphical representation for dealing with the case of full price rigidities in an economy with two individuals and three commodities. This representation will show how the new concept of equilibrium operates in a simple case and will suggest why it is appropriate to the treatment of Keynesian underemployment.

Since this paper aims at being simple and not too technical, we shall refer to our article in French (Malinvaud and Younès, 1974) for complements and some of the proofs. In particular we shall deal here only with an exchange

economy, the generalisation to production raising no fundamental problem.[1]
For the same reason, we shall not consider here the proof given in our French
text and showing that an equilibrium does exist in models that are much more
general than the Walrasian one.

I TYPES OF TRANSACTION IN A MODEL OF THE ECONOMY

If price rigidities and other institutional constraints have not often been
introduced into the classical model of general competitive equilibrium, it is
because this model does not make their introduction easy: it directly deals
with net trades that are the results of many operations. If we want to take
easily into account the institutional constraints, we must explicitly formalise
each operation and obtain net trades as results. This is why we have to start
with a more detailed examination of economic activity than is usually done
in mathematical economics.

(a) By a transaction we mean an operation of exchange concerning various
commodities: specific quantities of some commodity (or commodities) are
obtained, whereas specific quantities of another commodity (or other commodities) are given. Most agents take part in many transactions, so that their
holding of commodities may be very different at the end from what it was at
the beginning.

The common practice in microeconomic theory is to consider only the
overall resulting net trade that may be viewed as leading directly from the
initial to the terminal holding. Detailed consideration of the transaction network through which this overall exchange was realised then appears as
unnecessary.

But institutional constraints, which imply for instance price rigidities or
the use of money as a counterpart for any sale or purchase, limit the set of
transactions that are available for an agent. Whenever such constraints play
an essential part, they must be explicitly introduced in the basic model.
Their introduction raises no real difficulty.

Let there be r commodities indexed by $h = 1, 2, \ldots r$. A transaction of an
agent is a vector u in the commodity space; when positive, the component u_h
defines the quantity of good h that is obtained by the agent; when negative,
u_h has for absolute value the quantity of good h that is given. (For u to be
truly a transaction it should have both positive and negative components, but
we shall not need to stress this fact.)

We may assume that, if a transaction u is institutionally feasible, any
proportional transaction is also feasible; in other words, if institutions do not
rule out the transaction u and if α is any positive or negative number, then
institutions do not rule out the transaction αu. Taking advantage of this

---

[1] The restriction to an exchange economy may appear to be particularly severe when
the foundations of employment theory are involved. We shall, however, hint at the end
of the paper why a phenomenon similar to Keynesian underemployment can occur even
in an exchange economy.

hypothesis, we may build the whole set of feasible transactions from a basic set T of the commodity space.

By definition of T a transaction u is institutionally feasible if and only if there exist a vector t of T and a number α such that $u = \alpha t$. Moreover, in order to avoid ambiguities, T is defined in such a way that no two distinct vectors of T are co-linear. The vectors of T are said to be the *feasible types of transaction*.

(b) The set T will, of course, depend on the kind of problems that the theory aims at exploring. In the *Walrasian economy* any transaction is institutionally feasible; hence T must then be such that any vector u of the commodity space may be written as αt with a t belonging to T. This set might for instance be the unit sphere.

One often considers that any transaction must be an exchange of money against some other commodity. We shall speak of a *pure monetary economy* to characterise such a case. The feasible transactions u then have only two non-zero components: the last one u_r if money is the last good, and some other component u_h. For any t belonging to T we may take $t_r = -1$; if t_h is the other non-zero component, this type of transaction involves the exchange of money against commodity h at price:

$$p_h = \frac{1}{t_h} \tag{1}$$

Indeed, in order to get one unit of h, the agent using a transaction of this type must give $1/t_h$ units of money (if $u = \alpha t$ has its h-component equal to 1, α must be equal to $1/t_h$ and u_r then has precisely this absolute value).

For a pure monetary economy we shall speak of *price rigidities* if the feasible transactions concerning any commodity h are those for which p_h is contained in an interval:

$$\underline{p}_h \leqslant p_h \leqslant \bar{p}_h \tag{2}$$

$$h = 1, 2 \ldots r-1$$

where the minimum and maximum prices, $\underline{p}_h$ and $\bar{p}_h$, are *a priori* given. This definition must be broadly interpreted so that it covers cases in which $\underline{p}_h$ is zero and/or $\bar{p}_h$ is infinite. Following Hicks we may consider the case in which the $r-1$ commodities exchanged against money are divided into two groups: 'fixprice commodities' for which $\underline{p}_h = \bar{p}_h > 0$, and 'flexprice commodities' for which $\underline{p}_h = 0$ and $\bar{p}_h = \infty$.

Restricting the model still further, we may note that the simplest Keynesian theory, that of the multiplier, assumes a monetary economy in which all prices are fixed. We shall then speak of a *multiplier Keynesian economy* to character-ise the case in which $\underline{p}_h = \bar{p}_h$ for all h.

(c) Consider now an individual consumer i (there will be m consumers in the economy, with $i = 1, 2 \ldots m$). We must carefully specify how we shall represent the activity of this individual.

Suppose he enters into n transactions. We may represent these transactions by the vectors u_i^j (with $j = 1, 2 \ldots n$). The component u_{ih}^j then is the quantity of good h that is obtained by individual i in its j-th transaction. His net trade resulting from the n transactions now is the vector z_i defined by:

$$z_i = \sum_{j=1}^{n} u_i^j \tag{3}$$

But, in order to proceed, we must relate each transaction u_i^j to its type. This type may be denoted as t^j, if for simplicity we do not keep an index i that would make the notation heavy but is implicitly assumed. By definition of the types of transaction we know that there is a positive or negative number α such that $u_i^j = \alpha t^j$. This number depends of course on i and on j. For the subsequent argument it will be convenient to characterise it as $\alpha = a_i(t^j)$, even if the notation looks a little heavy at first sight. We shall therefore write:

$$u_i^j = a_i(t^j) \cdot t^j \tag{4}$$

The activity of consumer i is then characterised by the numerical function $a_i(t)$ defined on the subset $T_i = \{t^1, t^2 \ldots t^n\}$ of T.

It would be cumbersome to use two mathematical entities, T_i and $a_i(t)$, for the activity of individual i. But nothing prevents us from extending the definition of $a_i(t)$ to the full set T, it being understood that this function[1] is everywhere zero on the complement of T_i in T. This being done, *the function $a_i(t)$ fully characterises the activity of consumer i.*

Taking (3) and (4) into account we might now express the net trade of i as:

$$z_i = \sum_{t \in T} a_i(t) \cdot t$$

and its h component as:

$$z_{ih} = \sum_{t \in T} a_i(t) \cdot t_h$$

But we shall use instead the simpler notations:

$$z_i = La_i \quad \text{and} \quad z_{ih} = L_h a_i \tag{5}$$

It is then understood that L and L_h are the linear operators expressing how *the net trade z_i of individual i and its h component z_{ih} can be computed from the function a_i, or $a_i(t)$, defining its *activity.*

---

[1] Technically, $a_i(t)$ must be viewed as a 'measure' on T. In all the cases we shall be considering, $a_i(t)$ will be a discrete measure, so that the use of such an entity raises no technical difficulty.

(d) Following the classical tradition we shall assume that individual i has an initial endowment w_{ih} of commodity h, so that his consumption x_{ih} of this commodity will be equal to $w_{ih} + z_{ih}$. It will usually be required that this consumption be non-negative. In particular for the last good, money, the inequality:

$$w_{ir} + z_{ir} \geqslant 0 \tag{6}$$

will express that the individual cannot spend more money than he had either initially and/or has received from his sales; this inequality will therefore replace the classical *budget constraint*.

In order for the individual activities to be mutually consistent and to define a feasible state they must be such that transactions balance. Hence:

$$\sum_{i=1}^{m} a_i(t) = 0 \tag{7}$$

for all $t \in T$

from which the classical equality follows:

$$\sum_{i=1}^{m} (x_{ih} - w_{ih}) = 0$$

for $h = 1, 2 \ldots r$ \hfill (8)

But, and this may be an important difference from the classical formulation, we may want to take into account additional institutional constraints restricting the activity a_i of agent i to belong to some *a priori* given set A_i. For instance, A_i may specify which types of transaction are feasible for i acting as a seller, and which for i acting as a buyer.

In order to root the usefulness of money in the objective fact of the market organisation, we may also argue that transactions take time and that the velocity of money is limited. This may again be formulated as imposing additional constraints on a_i. For instance, in a multiplier Keynesian economy, if consumers must make transactions first on good 1, second on good 2 and so on, we should impose additional constraints in order to take into account the fact that any individual cannot spend for buying good h more money than he had after leaving the market for good $h - 1$.

We shall not introduce in the sequel such additional constraints. But it should be kept in mind that the present approach makes it easy to take them into account.

Finally, there will be for each individual a concave utility index $U_i(x_i)$, i.e. a concave numerical function ranking, in order of preference, the consumption vectors x_i that have components x_{ih}. The function U_i will be taken as strictly increasing with the quantity of money x_{ir}.

The justification for the latter assumption may be formulated as follows. In a short-run framework people must have expectations as to the transactions they will make in the next period. Since transactions take time and the velocity of money is limited, money turns out to have a positive marginal indirect utility, as was shown by Grandmont and Younès (1972).

This remark suggests that our model will be appropriate for dealing with temporary equilibria, i.e. with situations in which present decisions and expectations are simultaneously determined and have to be mutually consistent. It will also be appropriate for analysing future markets problems; the same good available in two different periods will then be considered as corresponding to two different commodities. For instance, one may want to examine a case in which present contracts may concern future transactions on goods as well as present ones, all these transactions being constrained to using money at the date of delivery, and in which, moreover, lending and borrowing transactions on money are allowed. (Future money is then a different commodity from present money, its price being the discount factor.)

II A CONCEPT OF EQUILIBRIUM

In order to study which transactions will finally occur between the agents, we need a new concept that will play a role similar to that played by competitive equilibrium in the Walrasian economy. But we should not start from the idea that, in an equilibrium, each commodity will have the same price in all transactions. This property has to be proved rather than assumed in the general formulation that we are here looking for.[1]

(a) An equilibrium is, of course, a feasible state. Moreover, it must agree with the first idea mentioned in our introduction; namely, that in economies involving many agents each one of them could freely decide to transact less on each type of transaction than he actually does. Notice that this idea rules out situations that have been considered in the literature on games or on imperfect competition. For instance, if an individual wants to buy less of a commodity, he may in such situations have to accept a higher price. We shall come back to this remark later on.

With respect to a feasible state E^* in which individual i has the activity defined by $a_i^*(t)$, we consider that he could have freely chosen any other activity $a_i(t)$ such that:

$$0 \leqslant a_i(t) \leqslant a_i^*(t)$$

for all t for which $a_i^*(t) \geqslant 0$ $\hspace{3cm}$ (9)

$$0 \geqslant a_i(t) \geqslant a_i^*(t)$$

for all t for which $a_i^*(t) \leqslant 0$

---

[1] Indeed, in some cases, which will not be considered here but are presented in our French article, the property does not hold.

In order to express this constraint, we shall subsequently use the short notation:

$$a_i \in I(a_i^*) \tag{10}$$

which must be read as meaning that (9) holds.

The first condition to impose on a feasible state E^* for it to be an equilibrium will then be that, for each i, the activity a_i^* is at least as good as any other activity a_i in $I(a_i^*)$. Let

$$x_i^* = w_i + L\, a_i^* \quad x_i = w_i + L\, a_i \tag{11}$$

then:

(I) *The vector x_i^* maximises $U_i(x_i)$ under the constraints (10) and (11), for all i.*

If we should use only this condition, too many feasible states would usually appear as equilibria. Indeed, in many models the complete absence of transaction, namely $a_i^*(t) = 0$ for all i and t, defines a feasible state and constraint (10) then makes condition (I) trivially satisfied.

(b) We must take into account here the fact that individuals will not stick to a feasible state E^* if they see an opportunity for an additional mutually advantageous transaction. Whereas condition (I) is essentially of a non-co-operative nature, we must introduce a second condition where some degree of co-operation among agents will be recognised.

What should be the most realistic assumption as to the degree of co-operation is, of course, a very delicate question. In this respect a general theory cannot claim to be very realistic, because in fact situations vary considerably from one type of operation to another and from one sector of the economy to another.

We shall here accept the idea that any two individuals can meet,[1] then examine one by one any additional bilateral transaction between them and look to see whether it is mutually advantageous. But we shall assume that they do not push their investigation beyond this point.[2]

An ambiguity might, however, exist about what is meant by 'mutually advantageous'. The first idea that comes to mind is to see whether the additional transaction improves over the activity a_i^* when no other change is brought to this activity. But on reflection this would not lead to a very good definition; for instance when, in a_i^*, individual i was supposed to buy a car from j at a given price and when he finds that he can buy from k an equivalent car at a lower price, he will accept this additional transaction with k but

---

[1] It is, of course, conceivable to deal with partitioned markets in which only individuals belonging to the same subset can meet.

[2] In our French article (Malinvaud and Younès, 1974) we explain why this assumption of bilateralism becomes too stringent as soon as production is taken into account. We then relax it somewhat. In the Appendix to this article we also provide a definition of equilibrium for the case when any kind of additional multilateral transaction is assumed to be examined.

simultaneously withdraw from the previously considered transaction with j, assuming he does not want to hold two cars. When contemplating a new transaction, each individual i will see it as a possible addition not only to a_i^*, but alternatively also to any other activity a_i that he might freely adopt from a_i^*; i.e. to any other activity a_i belonging to $I(a_i^*)$.

A formalisation will now make precise the second condition for a feasible state E^* to be an equilibrium.

Suppose the additional transaction to be of type $\hat{t}$. Consider the activity $\hat{\delta}(t)$ that would consist in the single transaction $\hat{t}$, i.e. the function $\hat{\delta}(t)$ that has value 1 for $t = \hat{t}$ and value 0 for other t. Accepting an additional transaction of type $\hat{t}$ means for i to find a number ϵ and an activity $a_i \in I(a_i^*)$ such that he prefers $a_i + \epsilon\, \hat{\delta}$ to a_i^*; in other words, the consumption vector $x_i = w_i + La_i + \epsilon\, L\, \hat{\delta}$, which is also $x_i = w_i + La_i + \epsilon\, \hat{t}$, gives to $U_i(x_i)$ a value higher than $U_i(x_i^*)$.

Hence, the condition:

(II) *There do not exist $\hat{t} \in T$, a couple of individuals k and l, activities $a_k \in I(a_k^*)$ and $a_l \in I(a_l^*)$, finally a number ϵ such that $a_k + \epsilon\delta$ is preferred by k to a_k^* and $a_l - \epsilon\, \hat{\delta}$ preferred by l to a_l^*.*

(c) The discussion that led to this condition (II) makes it clear that the equilibrium concept here proposed implicitly admits recontracting in the same way as the competitive equilibrium does.

Moreover, condition (II) implicitly requires that, when accepting the additional transaction $\hat{t}$, individual k assumes that this will not change the set $I(a_k^*)$ from which he may freely choose. Such an assumption is valid in large economies where individual k alone has no significant influence on 'the markets'.[1] But it might be very shortsighted in other contexts: for instance, it would induce a monopolist to accept any sale at a price just above his marginal cost and to neglect the fact that this move will usually spoil the demand that prevails at higher prices. Once again, we see that our equilibrium concept is not appropriate for dealing with situations of imperfect competition.[2]

All in all, the degree of co-operation between agents is small in the equilibrium concept that we propose, since at each time it is limited to operations concerning a single type of transaction. This is not surprising since an hypothesis of full co-operation would eliminate such phenomena as under-

[1] More precisely, each agent, being small relatively to the whole economy, can rightly neglect the indirect consequences that a new trade proposal would have on the prevailing contracts, if it were accepted. With the technical concept of type of transaction, this means that each individual, when making a proposal on a given type of transaction, does not have to care about the ultimate consequences of this proposal on the contracts he makes on other types of transaction.

[2] The approach using types of transaction can, however, be conveniently used for covering cases of imperfect competition. For instance, a monopolist, when considering additional transactions, will not deal with types of transaction one by one, as condition (II) assumes, but will take into account simultaneously all types of transaction concerning the good he sells.

employment, which we want to explain. In order to emphasise the predominantly non-co-operative nature of our concept we propose to call it 'strong non-co-operative equilibrium'.

III   SELLERS' MARKETS AND BUYERS' MARKETS

The usefulness of the new equilibrium concept appears in the study of a pure monetary economy with price rigidities, a case of major importance for a proper understanding of macroeconomics. The set T of feasible types of transaction then contains all vectors t having only two non-zero components, one $t_r = -1$ for money, the other t_h being constrained to an interval; i.e. fulfilling conditions (I) and (II).

It is customary, when considering such an economy, to assume that all transactions are made at the same price and some rationing may occur for a good when its price hits either its ceiling, in which case demand may be rationed, or its floor, supply being then possibly rationed. Such properties were explicitly assumed for instance by Drèze (1973), when he proved the existence of an equilibrium under price rigidities, or by Grandmont and Laroque (1974) when they applied this concept to the study of Keynesian underemployment.

Here we do not need to assume these properties. Indeed, they are implied by the equilibrium, as we defined it. Hence our approach seems to be quite powerful for the treatment of an economy with price rigidities.

(a) We shall first show that, in an equilibrium E^* for such an economy, $r - 1$ types of transaction at most will be effectively used, one for each commodity. In other words *all transactions involving the exchange of commodity h against money will be made at the same price p_h^**.

The proof is easy since it is intuitively clear that the property follows from condition (II). Indeed,[1] suppose that, for a given commodity g, trades are carried out at two distinct prices p_g^0 and p_g^1 (types of transaction t_g^0 and t_g^1) and let, for instance, p_g^0 be smaller than p_g^1. Consider two individuals k and l such that k sells at price p_g^0 and l buys at price p_g^1; formally: $a_k^*(t^0) < 0$ and $a_l^*(t^1) > 0$. Let p_g^2 be any price which is intermediate between p_g^0 and p_g^1 (the nature of the constraint (2) makes it clear that this price is institutionally feasible). Let δ^0, δ^1 and δ^2 be the elementary activities consisting just in the exchange of one unit of money against respectively $1/p_g^0$, $1/p_g^1$ and $1/p_g^2$ unit of good g.

If ϵ is positive and sufficiently small:

$$a_k = a_k^* + \epsilon \frac{p_g^0}{p_g^2} \delta^0 \tag{12}$$

belongs to I (a_k^*) since $a_k(t) = a_k^*(t)$ for all $t \neq t^0$ and $a_k^*(t^0) < a_k(t^0) < 0$.

---

[1] The proof is given here in full so that, without referring to our French article (Malinvaud and Younès, 1974) the reader may see how one can work with condition (II).

Similarly:

$$a_l = a_l^* - \epsilon \frac{p_g^1}{p_g^2} \delta^1 \tag{13}$$

belongs to I (a_l^*). Activity $a_k - \epsilon \delta^2$ is preferred by individual k to a_k^* since it gives him precisely the same quantity of all good h except for money of which he gets more: $\epsilon(p_g^2 - p_g^0)/p_g^2 > 0$. Similarly $a_l + \epsilon \delta^2$ is preferred by individual l to a_l^*. But this is contradictory to condition (II).

(b) In order to keep this paper simple, let us assume that in E^* all commodities are effectively traded. Hence precisely $r - 1$ types of transaction are used: one for each good except money. Let t^h be the type used on the market for h (this depends on E^*, but the notation t^{h*} would be cumbersome). Let δ^h be the corresponding elementary activity.

We shall say that *individual i is rationed on the market for good h* if he does not buy or sell as much as he would like at the ruling price p_h^*. Formally, this will be the case if there is a number ϵ_i and an activity $a_i \in I(a_i^*)$ such that $a_i + \epsilon_i \delta^h$ is preferred by i to a_i^*. Condition (I) and the usual convexity assumption makes it obvious that $\epsilon_i \cdot a_i^*(t^h) \geqslant 0$, which means that, if rationed in an equilibrium, a buyer would like to buy more not less; similarly, a rationed seller would like to sell more.

Moreover, using condition (II) again, one may easily prove that, if two individuals k and l are simultaneously rationed on the market for the same commodity, they cannot act one as a buyer and the other as a seller.[1] More precisely, the numbers ϵ_k and ϵ_l showing the existence of rationing must have the same sign.

Hence the commodities can be divided into three groups:
those for which no individual is rationed, their markets being then said to be 'competitive';
those for which some individual is rationed, but none of the sellers is; hence we may speak of sellers' markets (all the numbers ϵ_i showing the existence of rationing are positive);
and finally those for which some individual but no buyer is rationed, these being the object of buyers' markets.

The fourth group in which some buyers and some sellers would be rationed for the same commodity is necessarily empty in an equilibrium.

(c) One may expect that *on a sellers' market transactions are made at the maximum price that is compatible with the price rigidities*, i.e. at $\bar{p}_h$. Similarly on a buyers' market the minimum price $\underline{p}_h$ is used for the transactions.

The proof can indeed be given for the case in which the utility functions U_i are continuous quasi-concave and the individual consumption vectors x_i^* are interior to their respective individual domains of feasibility. Once again condition (II) provides the basic reason for the result.

---

[1] This follows from the proof of the more general Proposition 4 of our French article (Malinvaud and Younès, 1974).

Indeed,[1] let us assume that the price p_h^* is smaller than $\bar{p}_h$ for some commodity h traded on a sellers' market. Let t^* and t be the two types of transaction on h for which prices p_h^* and $\bar{p}_h$ respectively are used. Let δ^* and $\bar{\delta}$ be the corresponding elementary activities.

Let k be one of the individuals for which rationing occurs: there exists a positive number ϵ_k and an activity $a_k \in I(a_k^*)$ such that $a_k + \epsilon_k \delta^*$ is preferred by k to a_k^*. Since the utility function U_k is continuous, there exists a positive number ξ, smaller than ϵ_k, such that:

$$\bar{a}_k = a_k + \epsilon_k \delta^* + (\bar{\delta} - \delta^*) \tag{14}$$

also is preferred by k to a_k^*. But $\bar{a}_k$ gives the same global net trade $L\bar{a}_K$ as the new activity:

$$\bar{a}_k = a_k + \epsilon_k \hat{\delta} \tag{15}$$

where $\hat{\delta}$ is the elementary activity using the price $\hat{p}_h$ defined by:

$$\frac{\epsilon_k - \xi}{p_h^*} + \frac{\xi}{\bar{p}_h} = \frac{\epsilon_k}{\hat{p}_h} \tag{16}$$

Hence, $\hat{a}_k$ is also preferred by k to a_k^*.

The price $\hat{p}_h$ is a weighted harmonic mean of the price p_h^* and $\bar{p}_h$; it is therefore compatible with the price rigidities. Consider now any seller l and the activity

$$a_l = a_l^* + \epsilon_k \frac{p_h^*}{\hat{p}_h} \delta^* \tag{17}$$

It belongs to $I(a_l^*)$ if ϵ_k is chosen small enough, which is always possible. Moreover $a_l - \epsilon_k \hat{\delta}$ leads to precisely the same consumption as a_l^* for all commodities except money, for which it gives a positive surplus·

$$\epsilon_k \left(1 - \frac{p_h^*}{\hat{p}_h} \right) \tag{18}$$

Hence $a_l - \epsilon_k \hat{\delta}$ is preferred by l to a_l^*.

We have found the type of transaction $\hat{t}$ (on which the elementary activity $\hat{\delta}$ operates), the number ϵ_k, the two agents k and l, and finally the two activities a_k and a_l which contradict condition (II).

IV THE COMPETITIVE EQUILIBRIUM

We may now consider a little more closely the case *when all markets are said to be 'competitive'* according to our previous definition. We shall see that in this case *the new concept of equilibrium boils down to the classical competitive equilibrium.* This result is interesting in itself.

---

[1] This proof also is given in full here.

Indeed, the Walrasian model assumes that, for each good, there exists an auctioneer who fixes the price. This state of affairs is not satisfactory because either the auctioneer is said to be a purely fictitious agent, or else the model describes not a competitive economy, but market socialism with centrally determined prices. On the contrary, our concept of equilibrium is defined without introduction of any other agent than the individual traders.

In this respect our approach is similar to the theory of the core that was developed in the 1960s and dealt with the economy as being a sort of co-operative game. The difference comes from the fact that we assume only a very limited degree of co-operation among the individual agents.

In order to prove the equivalence in this case between our equilibrium and the classical competitive equilibrium[1] we shall show that the consumption vector x_i^*, which is allocated to individual i in equilibrium E^*, does maximise $U_i(x_i)$ under the budget constraint:

$$p^* x_i \leqslant p^* w_i \tag{19}$$

The property, indeed, holds if the utility function U_i is quasi-concave and differentiable and if x_i^* is interior to the domain of the vectors x_i that are feasible for i. This short section will be devoted to proving the property.

We shall proceed in demonstrating successively:

(i) For all h, the following equality holds:

$$p_h^* = \frac{U_{ih}'(x_i^*)}{U_{ih}'(x_i^*)} \tag{20}$$

where U_{ih}' is the derivative of U_i with respect to x_{ih}.

(ii) The vector x_i^* maximises $U_i(x_i)$ subject to:

$$p^* x_i \leqslant p^* x_i^* \tag{21}$$

(iii) The following equality holds:

$$p^* x_i^* = p^* w_i \tag{22}$$

The conjunction of properties (ii) and (iii) is, indeed, the property we are looking for.

In order to prove (20) let us assume that, for some h, for instance:

$$p_h^* < \frac{U_{ih}'(x_i^*)}{U_{ih}'(x_i^*)} \tag{23}$$

Consider the elementary activity δ^h as consisting in spending one unit of money to buy commodity h at price p_h^*. Let ϵ be an infinitely small positive number and consider replacing activity a_i^* by $a_i^* + \epsilon \delta^h$. The consumption of

---

[1] Hence, we shall show that, under the conditions specified, a 'strong non-co-operative equilibrium' is a 'competitive equilibrium'. The converse property also holds, even more generally.

h will increase by ϵ/p_h^* and the consumption of money decrease by ϵ. Hence, the variation of utility will be:

$$\epsilon \left[\frac{U'_{ih}(x_i^*)}{p_h^*} - U'_{ir}(x_i^*) \right] \tag{24}$$

which, according to (23), will be positive. Hence, replacing a_i^* by $a_i^* + \epsilon\delta^h$ is advantageous for i, which contradicts the assumption according to which individual i is not rationed. This completes the proof of (i).

It is well known that (ii) follows for (i) as soon as the utility function is quasi-concave (see, for instance, Malinvaud, 1972, Section 2.8). Therefore we now need only to prove (iii).

The equilibrium requires that the sum of $x_i^* - w_i$ for all i is the zero vector. Hence, if (22) does not hold for some individuals, there is at least one of them for which:

$$p^*x_i^* < p^*w_i \tag{25}$$

Let us consider such an individual.

Differentiability of U_i together with (20) immediately shows that, when (25) holds, $(1 - \epsilon)x_i^* + \epsilon w_i$ is preferred by i to x_i^*, the positive number ϵ being taken as sufficiently small. Consider now $a_i = (1 - \epsilon)a_i^*$; it clearly belongs to $I(a_i^*)$; it gives precisely the consumption vector $w_i + (1 - \epsilon) La_i^* = (1 - \epsilon)x_i^* + \epsilon w_i$, which is preferred to x_i^*. The existence of activity a_i then is a contradiction to condition (I). This completes the proof of (iii).

V UNFILLED DEMANDS AND SUPPLIES

In an equilibrium under price rigidities we expect that some individuals will be rationed. Some demands and supplies will not be fulfilled. We must, however, carefully distinguish between those and the excess demands or supplies that, according to the classical theory, are supposed to appear out of equilibrium.

The distinction has already been made several times in the recent literature about Keynesian theory. It clearly appears on a graphical representation that is appropriate for the case of full price rigidity and will be used in the next section for discussing the non-optimality of equilibrium.

Let us consider the case of a monetary economy with three commodities ($r = 3$) and fixed prices $\bar{p}_1$ and $\bar{p}_2$ for the transactions of respectively commodities 1 and 2 against money (this is what we called a multiplier Keynesian economy). In the three dimensional commodity space the vectors x_i that can be reached by individual i are constrained to belong to a plane containing the initial endowment vector w_i. Let, in Figure 3:1, the extremity of vector w_i be represented by point P. The consumption vector that can be reached by i belongs to the triangle $A_1 A_2 A_3$ that is supposed to be orthogonal to the price vector $(\bar{p}_1, \bar{p}_2, 1)$.

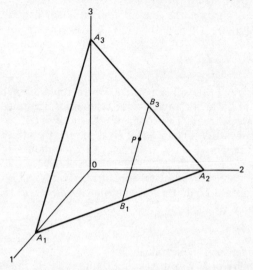

Fig. 3:1

The following discussion will be carried on by reference to this triangle. Before looking at it more carefully, let us remark that, from the initial position P, making transactions on commodity 1 will mean moving along the segment $B_1 B_3$ containing P and parallel to $A_1 A_3$: from P toward B_1 for a purchase, from P toward B_3, for a sale.

Suppose now that at some stage consumer i has the allocation represented by point M in Figure 3:2, which is drawn in the plane of triangle $A_1 A_2 A_3$. In

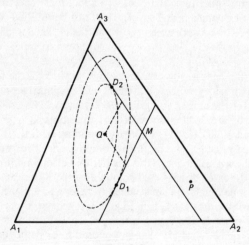

Fig. 3:2

this plane, the contour lines of U_i can be drawn: two of them actually are and point Q is supposed to be the best point for i. The classical excess demand vector would be MQ. But, according to the present theory, the unfilled demand expressed on the market for commodity 2 will be represented by vector $M D_1$ because, when forming this demand, the individual does not know whether he can sell more of commodity 2 than he does in M.

We have therefore two unfilled demand vectors MD_1 on the market for 1 and MD_2 on the market for 2. The sum of these two vectors generally differs from the excess demand vector MQ.

The reader may like to consider the case in which M would coincide with point D_1. There would then be a zero unfilled demand for 1 and an unfilled supply of 2. If, however, the latter would meet a demand from some other individual, then the demand of 1 by i would be reduced.[1]

VI   A FIXED PRICE EQUILIBRIUM

In the case of three commodities, two consumers and fixed prices the triangle of Figure 3:2 may play a similar role to that of the Edgeworth's box in the classical theory. Indeed, if prices were not fixed, the transposition of Edgeworth's box to the case of three commodities and two consumers would be a parallelepiped that could be drawn on the three-dimensional Figure 3:1. The vertex O' opposite to the origin would have as co-ordinates the sums of the initial endowments of the two consumers for each of the three commodities.

Any point M in the parallelepiped would represent a feasible distribution of commodities among the two consumers, the vectors OM and $O'M$ defining respectively the consumptions of the first and second consumers. Since prices are fixed, considering the intersection of this parallelepiped with the plane $A_1 A_2 A_3$ will suffice for a representation of the consumption vectors that may be related after some trading at these prices had taken place.

Figures 3:3, 3:4 and 3:5 are drawn in this plane. For simplicity only a part of the interior of the triangle $A_1 A_2 A_3$ is represented. The point P corresponds to the case of no trade. The lines PR_1 and PR_2 are drawn from P respectively parallel to $A_1 A_3$ and to $A_2 A_3$. Any point on PR_1 to the right of P will be achieved through trading of commodity 1 against money. The first consumer will then be selling commodity 1 and the second will be buying this commodity.

With respect to Figure 3:2 the complication arises from the fact that two sets of contour lines must now be drawn one for each individual. If these individuals are denoted as i and j, the best point in the plane will be Q_i for i and Q_j for j. In Figures 3:3 to 3:5 one contour line is drawn for each consumer and it is assumed for simplicity that other contour lines are homothetic with the one drawn.

---

[1] What is called here 'unfilled demand' is also called elsewhere 'effective demand' whereas the classical excess demand is often referred to as 'notional demand'.

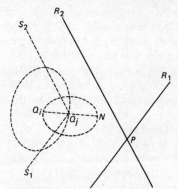

Fig. 3:3

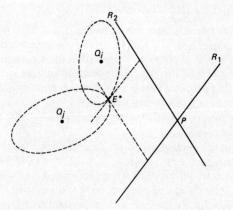

Fig. 3:4

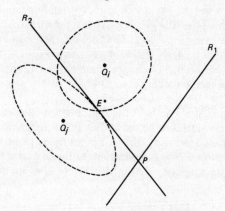

Fig. 3:5

These figures are interesting from several points of view. First, they show how the new equilibrium concept operates when price rigidities are effective. Indeed, the unique equilibrium is Q_j in Figure 3:3 and E^* in Figures 3:4 or 3:5.

In Figure 3:3, conditions (I) and (II) are of course met in Q_j for consumer j, since Q_j is his preferred feasible point. Condition (I) is also fulfilled for consumer i, since moving from Q_j in the directions PR_1 or R_2P would decrease U_i. Hence Q_j is an equilibrium in which individual j is not rationed, whereas i is rationed on both commodities, as a buyer for commodity 1 and as a seller for commodity 2. The market for good 1 is a 'sellers' market', the market for good 2 a 'buyers' market'.

No other point of Figure 3:3 can be an equilibrium. Indeed, points in the quadrant bounded by $S_1 Q_j S_2$ do not fulfil condition (I) for individual j. ($Q_j S_j$ and $Q_j S_2$ are respectively parallel to PR_1 and PR_2.) Any other point does not fulfil condition (II).

Similarly we can see that, in Figure 3:5, the unique equilibrium is E^*. Any point on the left of PR_2 is ruled out by condition (I) applied to consumer i: in such a point this consumer would demand some of commodity 1, but in the region left of PR_2, the utility U_i everywhere increases in the direction PR_1; reducing the demand for commodity 1 is therefore preferred by i. For a similar reason applied to consumer j, any point to the right of PR_2 is also ruled out. Points above E^* on PR_2 would violate condition (I) for consumer j since U_j decreases from E^* to R_2. Points below E^* on PR_2 would violate condition (II) because an additional purchase of commodity 2 by j from i would benefit both consumers.

In this equilibrium E^*, consumer i is rationed on both markets: he would like to sell some quantity of commodity 1 at price p_1, whereas he is not selling any; he would also like to sell more of commodity 2 at price p_2. Consumer j is rationed on the market of commodity 1 that he also would like to sell; but he is not rationed on the market for commodity 2. The markets for both goods are 'buyers' markets'.

The reader may now check by himself that E^* is also the unique equilibrium in Figure 3:4 (the two dotted straight lines passing through E^* are respectively parallel to PR_1 and PR_2 as well as tangent to the contour lines). Individual i is then rationed on commodity 2 and individual j on commodity 1. Again 'buyers' markets' exist for both goods.

It is worth noting now that the uniqueness of equilibrium is special to the case of two individuals and that *our theory is not specific in general as to the rationing scheme that will prevail.* Indeed, let us consider Figure 3:3 again but assume that there are four individuals: i, j, i' identical to i and j' identical to j. We then represent the activities of i' and j' in the same way as were respectively represented the activities of i and j. The equilibrium still requires that the consumption vectors of j and j' be both equal to $O'Q_j$. But the consumption vectors OM and OM' of i and i' do not have to be equal; they are only required to be such that $OM + OM' = 2\,OQ_j$ and M or M' be in the quadrant bounded by $S_1Q_jS_2$ but not beyond the limit where U_i would decrease in the direction Q_jS_1 or Q_jS_2. For instance, individual i might be non-rationed, with his consumption vector equal to OQ_i as long as individual i' would be sufficiently rationed for his consumption vector to be ON.

Figures 3:4 and 3:5 also disprove a false conjecture. One might have thought that any equilibrium is 'second best' when trade is restricted to agree with the given prices p_1 and p_2. This would mean that the equilibrium would be Pareto-optimal among all feasible states restricted to belong to the plane of Figures 3:3 to 3:5. (Such a state was called a p-optimum in Younès (1970).) But this is obviously not the case in the last two of the three cases considered, since from E^* there exists a trade that involves the three commodities, agrees with the prices p_1 and p_2, and is beneficial to both consumers. Individual i ought both to sell commodity 1 and to buy commodity 2. But the two transactions must be simultaneous in order to be mutually beneficial. Their realisation would require more co-operation between the two agents than we assumed to exist.

The type of inefficiency that Figures 3:4 and 3:5 exhibit goes beyond the one resulting from price rigidities. It is tied with the fact that money has to be used as a counterpart in each transaction and that transactions are concluded independently of one another. It is a basic feature of Keynesian underemployment, a feature that was well discussed in the recent literature.

VII   INVOLUNTARY UNEMPLOYMENT

At this stage the reader may have to strain his intuition a bit. Indeed, we want to use the preceding figures in order to suggest why the new concept of equilibrium provides an appropriate microeconomic foundation for understanding involuntary unemployment. Even though there is no production in the model of this article, the basic reasons for the underemployment phenomenon are already present.

Let us then relabel commodity 1 as 'goods' and commodity 2 as 'labour'. Let us say that individual i is the 'worker' and individual j the 'capitalist'. In Figures 3:3 and 3:4 the worker is selling labour and buying goods, whereas the capitalist is selling goods and buying labour, as they should do. On the market for labour the capitalist is not rationed but the worker is, so that we may speak of involuntary unemployment.

There is, however, an important difference between the two figures. In the first one, given the prices and the wage rate, the capitalist will never find it interesting to hire more labour. We may then speak of 'classical underemployment' because the situation is reminiscent of the one that was in the mind of the classical economists in the early 1930s: wages, they thought, were too high for firms to find it profitable to produce more.

In Figure 3:4, on the contrary, the capitalist does not buy more labour because he cannot sell as much as he would like to do. The situation is typical of 'Keynesian underemployment', because in such a situation, if the demand for goods were higher, the firms would hire more labour quite independently of any change in prices and wage rates.

Of course one should not insist too much on the interpretation of the examples given here: the absence of any production makes the model inappropriate for a full understanding of Keynesian equilibrium. But one sees how the bridge is made with the approach advocated for instance by Benassy (1974). The reader may then refer to Grandmont and Laroque (1974) in order to find a fuller analysis of unemployment in a Keynesian economy with production.

VIII FURTHER DEVELOPMENTS

Two other applications of the concepts introduced here may be briefly mentioned.

On the one hand, one may argue that an inefficient equilibrium may exist, even with flexible prices, because of the peculiar types of transaction that are permissible. The simplest example is given by a state where two among the agents have no money left and would improve their utility by an exchange bearing on other goods than money. In a pure monetary economy, whether competitive or oligopolistic, the exchange is not institutionally feasible.

For instance, let us consider again a three-good monetary economy and a state in which the first two individuals have no money, other individuals being fully satisfied with their allocations. If the marginal rates of substitution between goods 1 and 2 are not the same for individuals 1 and 2, an exchange exists that would be profitable for both. For instance, consumer 1 ought to have more of good 1 and consumer 2 more of good 2. But in a pure monetary economy the exchange cannot occur as long as the transactions are concluded independently of one another, because individual 1 has no money to buy commodity 1 and individual 2 no money to buy commodity 2.

On the other hand, in planning problems one often will have to work with equilibria of economies where the market structure is incomplete. For instance, in decisions under uncertainty, the planning agency may have to fix some prices. In order to decide about these prices, the agency ought to determine, for each state of nature, the non-Walrasian equilibrium that would follow from the values given to the prices. Alternatively, when some well-organised markets are lacking, such as future markets, the planning agency may want to provide quantity signals in order to give firms some idea about the extent of the future demand for their products. (This has been alleged as a rationalisation for 'French planning', see Malinvaud (1965), for instance.) Under such an organisation the equilibrium will again be non-Walrasian.

Finally, let us note that, corresponding to our equilibrium concept, one might define equilibria without assuming recontracting. For instance, in a pure monetary economy, one might assume that consumers visit markets successively in a given order. When contracting on the market for a good they take into account expectations about the contracts that they will conclude on the markets to be visited later. Since often some expectations will prove false, the equilibrium without recontracting will usually differ from the equilibrium assuming recontracting, in which by hypothesis those expectations are fulfilled.

REFERENCES

J.-P. Benassy, 'Neo-Keynesian Disequilibrium Theory in a Monetary Economy' (Paris: CEPREMAP 1973, revised 1974).
R. Clower, 'The Keynesian Counterrevolution: A Theoretical Appraisal' in F. H. Hahn and F. P. R. Brechling (eds), *The Theory of Interest Rates* (London: Macmillan, 1965).
J. Drèze, 'Existence of an Equilibrium under Price Rigidity and Quantity Rationing', Core Discussion Paper (Louvain 1972, revised 1973).
J. M. Grandmont and G. Laroque, 'On Temporary Keynesian Equilibrium', (Paris, CEPREMAP 1973, revised 1974).
J. M. Grandmont and Y. Younès, 'On the Role of Money and the Existence of a Monetary Equilibrium', *Review of Economic Studies,* Vol. 29 (3) (July 1972) pp. 355–72.
H. I. Grossman, 'Money, Interest and Price in Market Disequilibrium', *Journal of Political Economy,* Vol. 80, No. 2 (March/April 1972) pp. 223–55.
F. H. Hahn and T. Negishi, 'A Theorem on Non-Tâtonnent Stability', *Econometrica,* Vol. 30, No 3 (July 1962) pp. 463–69.
John Hicks, *Capital and Growth* (Oxford: Clarendon Press, 1965).
A. Leijonhufvud, 'Keynes and the Keynesians: A Suggested Interpretation', *American Economic Review,* Vol. LVII, No 2 (May 1967) pp. 401–10.
E. Malinvaud, 'Interest Rates and the Allocation of Resources', in F. H. Hahn and F. P. R. Brechling (eds), *The Theory of Interest Rates* (London: Macmillan, 1965).
E. Malinvaud, *Lectures on Microeconomic Theory* (Amsterdam: North Holland, 1972).
E. Malinvaud and Y. Younès, 'Une Nouvelle Formulation Générale pour l'Étude des Fondements Microéconomiques de lay Macroéconomie', Note soumise au Séminaire d'économétrie de R. Roy et E. Malinvaud (Paris: 1974).
Y. Younès, 'Sur une Notion d'Équilibre Utilisable dans la Cas où les Agents Économiques ne sont pas assurés de la Comptabilité de Leurs Plans', Note soumise au Séminaire d'économétrie de R. Roy et E. Malinvaud (Paris: 1970).

Appendix

Equilibrium with Multilateralism

It is perhaps useful to define our concept of equilibrium in a more compact way, in order to see exactly what are the messages that are sent and how each agent behaves in view of the messages sent by other agents. However, it is not without interest to evaluate the huge quantity of information which is exchanged at the competitive equilibrium when it is defined without an auctioneer. We shall assume that useful trades may be multilateral and, in order to simplify, that T is finite.

We wish to cast our equilibrium concept in the general frame of processes for the exchange of information and contract proposals between agents. Let us first describe this general frame.

We know that, in an economic organisation, agents differ with respect to their possibilities of action, their initial information and their preferences. There is, moreover, a set of possible messages or proposals m; we call it M. At each time s, each economic unit sends messages to others. Consider economic unit k at time s. Given its initial information (e_k) and messages received at time $r < s$ from others (m_r^k), it makes its provisional plan b_s^k according to some rule:

$$b_s^k = g^k (m_{s-1}^k, m_{s-2}^k \ldots, m_0^k; e_k)$$

Then it sends messages $^k m_s$ according to a rule:

$$^k m_s = f_s^k (m_{s-1}^k, m_{s-2}^k, \ldots, m_0^k; b_s^k; e_k)$$

At the end of the process (at time S), according to some rule, provisional plans are transformed into 'real' plans (a) which have to be compatible:

$$a^k = \Phi(b_S^1, \ldots, b_S^k)$$

Let us now consider our concept of strong non-co-operative equilibrium in an exchange economy. For each consumer i, we start from an activity a_i^*. First, we take each type of transaction separately. Thus, given a type of transaction $\hat{t}$, let us contemplate the set of all measure $q_i^{\hat{t}}$ which are possible for i and which are of the form:

$$q_i^{\hat{t}} = a_i + \epsilon \hat{\delta}^t$$

where ϵ is a real number and $a_i \in I(a_i^*)$. Moreover, among this set of measures $q_i^{\hat{t}}$, let us choose those which are better than a_i^*; that is to say, such that:

$U_i(w_i + Lq_i^{\hat{t}}) \geqslant U_i(w_i + La_i^*)$. Let us consider the measures d_i^t, such that

$$\begin{cases} d_i^{\hat{t}}(t) = q_i^{\hat{t}}(t) & \text{if } t = \hat{t} \\ d_i^{\hat{t}}(t) = 0 & \text{if } t \neq \hat{t} \end{cases}$$

where $q_i^{\hat{t}}$ belongs to the set defined above. Let us note $D_i(a_i^*, \hat{t})$, this set of measures $d_i^{\hat{t}}$ which are concentrated on $\hat{t}$.

Let us note $I(a_i^*, \hat{t})$ the set of all measures $a_i^{\hat{t}}$ concentrated on $\hat{t}$ such that $a_i^{\hat{t}}(t)$ is the $\hat{t}$-component of measure $a_i \in I(a_i^*)$, which is possible, and such that

$$U_i(w_i + La_i) \geqslant U_i(w_i + La_i^{*\hat{t}})$$

where $a_i^{*\hat{t}}$ is the best activity among all measures which are possible, belong to $I(a_i^*)$ and have zero as their $\hat{t}$-component.

Finally, let us note $B_j(a_i^*, \hat{t}) = D_i(a_i^*, \hat{t}) \cup I(a_i^*, t)$. Thus, for each t, $B_i(a_i^*, t)$ is the set of the contract proposals made by i along t, when he considers the activity a_i^*. It is clear that when he is at a_i^*, consumer i says that he accepts first all contracts along $\hat{t}$ which are better than $a_i^*(\hat{t})$, second all contracts along $\hat{t}$ which imply less intensity than $a_i^*(\hat{t})$ but are better than 0.[1]

Let us note J_{it}^* the set of individuals $j \neq i$ such that sign a_{jt}^* = sign a_{it}^* and J_{it}^{*c} the set of other individuals (excluding i). Let us further define as $S_i^t[a)_{i}($ the set of all measures a_i^t that are concentrated at t and such that:

$$a_i^t + \sum_{j \in J_{it}^{*c}} \bar{a}_j^t + \sum_{j \in J_{it}^*} a_{jt}^* = 0$$

where

$$\bar{a}_j^t \in B_j(a_j^*, t)$$

Let us finally define as $S_i[a)_{i}^*($ the set of all a_i that are feasible for i and such that:

$$a_i = \sum_t a_i^t$$

where[2]

$$a_i^t \in S_1^t[a)_{i}^*($$

[1] It is clear that each agent, being small relatively to the economy, does not take into account, when he makes a contract proposal along a type of transaction $\hat{t}$, the effect of this contract proposal, if it is accepted by others, on the contracts already made by him along other types of transaction.

[2] When T is not denumerable, it is better to define $B_i(a_i)$ in a slightly different way, because in this case its elements would be measures which are not σ-finite: see our paper in French (Malinvaud and Younès, 1974).

We can then pose the following *definition*:

A 2-uple (z^*, a^*) is a strong non-co-operative equilibrium relatively to T if:

(1) $a = (a_i^*, \ldots, a_m^*)$ is feasible for T and for each i we have: $z_i^* = La_i^*$

(2) For each i, a_i^* maximises $U_i(w_i + La_i)$ among all a_i such that
  $a_i \in S_i[a]_{i(}^*$.

Discussion of the Paper by Professor Malinvaud and Mr Younès

Professor Sir John Hicks opened the discussion by recalling the I.E.A. Conference on the theory of capital at Corfu sixteen years earlier, when it fell to Professor Malinvaud to introduce Sir John's paper, and the gratitude which he there felt to Professor Malinvaud for his understanding of what he had then had to say. He hoped but was not sure he would now be able to reciprocate He admitted that he did not find his and Mr Younès's paper easy. With the new mathematical economics he had to think several times before he saw what was meant. Then he often found himself saying 'But that was quite obvious!' He had a good deal of that feeling about the first half of the paper. As he understood it, they were engaged on the construction of a new theory of competition, which would be wider than the Walrasian theory, but would include the Walrasian theory as a special case. They hoped the extensions would make it possible to include 'Keynesian unemployment' as another special case. Whether that was in fact achieved would no doubt be one of the major issues the conference would wish to discuss.

Sir John Hicks pointed out that when we were solely concerned with the theory of multi-good exchange in the Walrasian manner, there were three basic assumptions which enabled Walras and Walrasians to suppose that in a competitive system a 'Walrasian equilibrium' would be established. These were:

(1) prices were flexible
(2) recontract was permitted
(3) 'full' facilities for triangular trade were provided.

These assumptions were explicitly mentioned in the Malinvaud-Younès paper, but (2) was apparently not one the authors wanted to drop. The particular extensions with which they concerned themselves arose from dropping (1) and, more briefly discussed, (3).

Most of the paper was concerned with (1). Suppose we maintained the other assumptions, but rejected the assumption of price flexibility, what happened? We had to decide just what we were to put in its place. What the authors assumed was that there were some products with maximum and minimum prices, in terms of some numéraire, so that these prices were constrained, by some external authority, to lie between the prescribed limits. There were then three possibilities for each such commodity:

(1) that the price was at its maximum;
(2) that it was at its minimum;
(3) that it lay between the maximum and the minimum.

It was clear that if the 'Walrasian' price lay between the prescribed maximum and the prescribed minimum, for each commodity, there would be no reason (granted the other assumptions) why a Walrasian equilibrium should not be attained. If we were to get a different result, some of the price constraints must be *effective*.

The case in which just one price constraint was effective was familiar; it was part of the regular stock-in-trade of neoclassical economics. If it was a minimum price that was effective, supply at that price would exceed demand; buyers could buy all they wanted to buy at that price, but sellers would find that some part of what they wanted to sell would be left on their hands. If it was a maximum price that was effective, demand would exceed supply; sellers could sell all they wanted to sell at that price, but buyers would be 'rationed'. (Sir John Hicks protested against the word 'rationing' in this connection, for it obscured the practically and theoretically important question of whether the 'short' supplies were distributed randomly or on some plan.) This direct effect of price constraints was rather elementary; the non-Pareto-optimality of the resulting distribution was also rather obvious.

When more than one price was constrained the position became more complicated. Sir John Hicks thought that the ingenious diagrams developed by the authors to deal with the case of two controlled prices were helpful; but he expected that they were no more than the tip of an iceberg and that the authors' paper in French provided a more general theory. He would himself have liked to see the indirect effects of fixed prices developed further, for there was no doubt that this was a practically important problem. For example, the imposition of a maximum price for common cheese could cause some disappointed customers to shift to uncontrolled superior varieties.

Sir John Hicks then turned to assumption (3), which he himself found more interesting and relevant to the Keynesian application which the authors wanted to make. He explained that he found it impossible to believe that the phenomena he had been discussing had anything to do with 'unemployment equilibrium' in the sense of Keynes. He thought he could say that with some authority, greater in a sense than that of Sir Austin Robinson or Dr Moggridge, since when one had sat on a pin one had a livelier sense of its reality than those who had not done so. His own *Theory of Wages* (1932) took full account of the unemployment of labour which resulted from fixed relative prices, but he knew from experience that his book was always regarded, by Keynes and his circle, as altogether pre-Keynesian, and that was how he had come to regard it himself. So he was sure that Keynes had thought he was talking about something different.

In later work the position had become confused because it had become conventional in expositions of Keynes to start from a version in which prices were fixed, allowing for flexible prices only subsequently. This was convenient, but it gave a very inadequate representation of Keynes. Keynes had worked in wage-units because he regarded the money wage as variable, and even in terms of wage-units he admitted flexible prices of products.

Therefore it was in the other direction, that indicated by assumption (3), that the Keynesian explanation of Keynesian unemployment was to be found. As there were several passages in the paper which dealt with this assumption, Sir John Hicks enlarged upon it, first summarising some of what he had written in 'The Two Triads' in his *Critical Essays in Monetary Economics*.

There he had started from the simplest form of exchange, bilateral exchange. This was insufficient to establish a Walrasian equilibrium even with flexible prices. Some means for triangular trade had to be found. The simplest form of triangular trade was *indirect barter* — the appearance of merchants who bought not in order to satisfy their own wants, but to sell again. Indirect barter was, however, not necessarily efficient, for it might mean no more than that 'market transactions have begun to coagulate into little knots of triangular trade, knots that need not be in any contact with one another. In order that

the market should be completed, the knots must be brought into contact'.
That was where money came in.

It could be a commodity money, one of the commodities traded being
treated as a numéraire; but this was in practice highly inconvenient, so almost
if not quite from the dawn of history traders had been looking for better ways
of doing their dealings than handing over bags of metals. Thus the logical
evolution of the market tended in the direction of something more sophisticated
He had distinguished two main types of sophisticated system which were the
chief and perhaps the only logical possibilities, a Clearing system and a
Banking system; elements of both survived in existing monetary institutions.

When one worked out either system in detail, considering how people
would actually have to behave in order to work it, one realised that each of
them depended upon some degree of trust or *credit*. That could easily get
left out of mathematical models, but in practice it was essential; it was
certainly on that level that Keynes was thinking.

So the way Sir John Hicks read Keynes was as follows. There was unemployed labour. The workers who were unemployed would be willing to
buy the things they would produce if they were employed; why was their
potential demand ineffective? The answer was not lack of money, for the
money would do no good unless it got into the right hands, but lack of
credit. One had to distinguish two cases:

(1) that in which there existed unsold stocks of the goods which the
     unemployed would like to buy;
(2) that in which there were no such stocks, only unused capacity.

In the former case a sufficient injection of consumer credit might absorb the
surplus stocks, which would restore the liquidity or credit-worthiness of
businesses, and so enable production to recover. This was *not* a fixprice
process; some of the most obvious instances of surplus stocks occurred in the
case of staple commodities with highly flexible prices. In the latter case, where
there were no surplus stocks, direct credit to producers would be necessary.
In either case, in a free market economy, it was a restoration of confidence,
expressed in a flow of credit, that was required. Sir John felt sure that this
was the kind of world of which Keynes was thinking. A Walrasian model, so
long as that contained nothing more than a commodity money, just did not
measure up to it.

Sir John Hicks hoped that his straying from the paper would prove to be
an example to others. The conference was one with a central topic, but it was
a topic which branched out: when one was at the end of the branches, it was
easy to forget the central trunk. We would need to be reminded, all the time,
of the relation between the topic of each particular paper and the central
issue.

Professor Davidson said that what he found difficult in most general equilibrium models was the lack of a sense of time. As Marshall had said, time was
the essence of all economic problems. Referring to Sir John Hicks's suggestion
of merchants who make markets, Professor Davidson pointed out that there
were two types of merchants and two types of markets. Merchants operating
in spot markets made those markets by creating liquidity. The other type of
middleman, a trader who was a link in the one-way non-integrated chain from
raw material to final product, often operated as an order-taker in forward

markets. Prices were flexible in spot markets; but the rigidity in contracting for forward delivery forced stickiness of prices in forward markets. Professor Davidson suggested that Keynes had had these two markets in mind and said that he himself found them difficult to introduce into a general equilibrium system. He proposed that we kept the two types of market separate in our discussions, in order to avoid semantic problems.

With reference to Sir John Hicks's point that creation of consumer credit could reduce unemployment, he said that he assumed that Keynes thought it quite possible that even at full-employment income and with readily available cheap consumer credit there could be a lack of effective demand. This sort of problem was difficult if not impossible to handle in a general equilibrium system, but he thought that it could be handled in a Marshallian system where the two types of markets, spot and forward, existed side-by-side.

Professor Stiglitz did not believe that the distinction between general equilibrium and partial equilibrium was so important, since the difference was that the latter took into account only some of the total number of interactions between variables in the system.

He agreed with the distinction between intertemporal trades and atemporal trades: if there was no temporal element in the system, there would be no triangular trade. Triangular trade tended to break down because it required trust or faith in the future and the enforcement of contracts. Related to this problem of introducing intertemporal trades in a general model was the problem of explaining the process of price adjustment: one wanted to analyse the flexibility or rigidity of prices rather than make it an assumption of the model. He gave two examples of these problems: the fact that the heterogeneity of labour could cause employers to use the price of labour as an indicator of its quality, and the difficulty of a firm in deciding whether a lack of demand for its products was a relative price phenomenon or a macro-economic phenomenon.

Professor Shubik first replied to Professor Stiglitz that in any model with a financial system the distinction between general equilibrium and partial equilibrium was absolutely crucial. In general equilibrium 'the books always balanced'; but working in a partial equilibrium framework guaranteed that one would never need to reconcile the books. He then said that he found the Malinvaud-Younès concept of equilibrium somewhat special. He believed that what they really had in mind was a one-period non-co-operative Markovian equilibrium point. By using such a definition of equilibrium they denied themselves much of the possibility of describing time-flexible readjustment processes, which depended on the structure of previous historical information. He illustrated this with the example of an individual borrowing from his bank. The banker would be readier to lend without enquiry as to the individual's past history to an individual who owned, say, 1000 shares of I.B.M. than to an individual with no assets. In other words, there could be previous information states which were germane to the dynamics of the credit mechanism.

He hoped that Sir John Hicks and/or Professor Malinvaud would enlarge upon the distinction between money and credit; he pointed out that the fundamental problem in developing a financial microeconomics was to make operational mathematically the concepts of money, credit and confidence.

Professor Negishi pointed out that in the Malinvaud-Younès paper only the nominal amount of money was in individuals' utility functions. This could be justified only if the real amount of money was calculated in terms of future prices which were assumed constant and inelastic with respect to current prices. He wondered how many of the authors' results would hold if current prices were introduced into the utility functions.

Mr Younès intervened to explain that Professor Malinvaud and he thought that in general equilibrium models the problem of exchange was not usually captured in a sufficiently realistic way. The classical theorem of the existence of a price vector such that if all agents act independently and take the price vector as given there is a set of plans which are coherent and Pareto-optimal, left open the question of where the price vector comes from. Surely, the theory of the core and co-operative equilibrium established under certain conditions the equivalence of the core and market equilibrium. Although up to now the auctioneer had remained an essential agent in a non-co-operative framework the authors' approach allowed them to cast the Walrasian equilibrium concept in a non-co-operative framework without an auctioneer. One could, therefore, have a general equilibrium theory without an auctioneer, and starting from the notion of contract proposals one could enlarge the theory to take into account price rigidities and institutional arrangements which forbade certain types of transactions.

With respect to the introduction of constraints *Professor Frey* pointed out that in the real world fixed quantities were more important than fixed prices. Furthermore, sometimes both prices and quantities were fixed, and sometimes there were also inconsistencies due to the constraints being imposed by different institutions. Professor Frey also doubted the validity of the authors' assumption that if a transaction was institutionally feasible any proportional transaction was institutionally feasible.

Professor Shubik said that he was in quite strong agreement that it was worth exploring quantity as an independent variable. One of the difficulties was that in the microeconomic theory of markets starting with Cournot we had so far explored only one limit process, when there were in fact three limit processes:

(1) What happens to the structure of trade in the markets as the number of individuals increases?

(2) What happens to the structure of trade as the number of time periods increases?

(3) What happens to the information structure as both the number of individuals and the number of time periods increase?

Implicitly the general equilibrium model and modifications to the general equilibrium model assumed rather than deduced limiting behaviour. Sometimes one could get away with it; on other occasions one 'throws out the baby with the bathwater'. He thought that in the Malinvaud-Younès paper half of the baby had been thrown away. He suggested that there was a link between general equilibrium theory, oligopoly theory and macroeconomics, and illustrated his point with the Cournot duopoly model. If one passed to the limit on number of competitors in a reasonable way, one ended up with a competitive price system, the partial equilibrium equivalent of a general equilibrium result. What happened in the process was that although the model depended on the details of the market structure the going to the limit 'washed out' the market structure details. Although the model looked as though it had come from an institution-free theory, it was not in fact such a theory.

Dr Goodhart supported Professor Shubik: one had to make clear the information structure of a model. He wondered where the additional constraints added to the Walrasian general equilibrium model came from. They must come from more fundamental information deficiencies. The constraints in the model should follow from the information structure assumed.

Professor Streissler pointed out that in the structure of the Malinvaud-Younès model there remained a certain co-operative element: individuals told one another what their contract offers were. An essentially Keynesian point, and an essential point of many microeconomic models, was that individuals tried to be cleverer than the market, speculating in the hope of an economic gain. Macroeconomic problems arose when many individuals all tried to be cleverer than the market and did not communicate their intentions to one another in order to avoid frustration of their intentions. An important example was holding cash, which was a way of not telling others that one wished to buy later. By assuming that all contract proposals were communicated, one changed the information structure of the model.

Professor Leijonhufvud intervened to ask to what extent price stickiness was the key to our problems in the area of the microeconomic foundations of macroeconomics. In the 1930s, when there was heavy unemployment, prices fell rapidly; this did not cure unemployment; instead it undermined everyone's credit-worthiness. When starting from a general equilibrium model and considering how to allow representation of disequilibrium situations, the only way to proceed would seem to be to make prices sticky; neo-Walrasian theory pointed us towards fixprice constructions as the first stage of enquiry. If one took a simple partial equilibrium model, say Marshall's supply and demand diagram, the equilibrium point satisfied two conditions simultaneously: at the given transactions price, the quantities demanded and the quantities supplied were equal in the aggregate; and at the given rate of output, the valuations of the marginal quantum made on the two sides of the market are equal. The fixprice approach consisted in giving up the first of these two and focusing on the consequences of inconsistent planned quantities (valued at the same fixprice by all); this enabled one to retain the general framework of the neo-Walrasian theory of exchange without much modification. By giving up instead the second condition, a different brand of simple disequilibrium analysis would be posited for investigation: the consequences of inconsistent valuations of the same aggregate quantity. This approach was equally deserving of the attention of theorists. Having previously attempted to interpret the *General Theory* in terms of the first approach, Professor Leijonhufvud had belatedly come to recognise that the second was Keynes's. Ultimately, we must learn to handle rigorously an analysis that did without both conditions. Meanwhile, Professor Leijonhufvud felt that the fixprice alternative was unduly monopolising attention.

Dr Nuti thought that if our object was the understanding of the nature of unemployment equilibrium, it was very important to realise that one could not consider labour as just the *n*th commodity in the system; he found this a slightly disappointing aspect of the Malinvaud-Younès paper. He pointed out that there were important institutional differences between labour and other commodities. From a physical point of view, labour was a perishable commodity: it was only by means of embodying it in production that one could speculate in labour. Furthermore, he thought that any piece of economic analysis that did not allow for the fact that one cannot buy a worker would not take us closer to understanding Keynesian economics. He regarded that as the greatest drawback of the general equilibrium approach; he also thought that if one acknowledged that there could not be a forward market in labour, one did not need a new microeconomic foundation of the type offered by Professor Malinvaud and Mr Younès. He himself was satisfied with the framework of Hicks's *Value and Capital*, Books IV and V, where there were no forward markets for any good except money.

Professor Davidson suggested that what made labour different from other commodities was an institutional fact, the absence of slavery. There was a forward market in labour, albeit a defective one. He went on to explain that those economists who do not regard general equilibrium as just something more general than partial equilibrium had in mind two kinds of models, general equilibrium and historical models. He claimed that the former model required recontracting. If one wished to talk about the problems connected with, say, liquidity, one would have to use an historical (calendar time) Marshallian model.

Sir John Hicks disagreed with Dr Nuti's suggestion that the peculiar properties of labour were the fundamental cause of Keynesian underemployment. Slave economies had existed with Keynesian disequilibrium properties, working under capacity, which corresponded to unemployment in a non-slave economy. He believed that the problems of information and uncertainty were much more important.

Professor Asimakopulos asked whether Professor Malinvaud and Mr Younès assumed perfectly or imperfectly competitive markets in their model?

Professor Nell raised the question whether results obtained in a pure exchange model could be extended to the case of production. Taking the case of forming a uniform wage rate as an example, in a simple model with two producers each consuming his own product while using that of the other as a means of production, and assuming fixed coefficients of production, one party's gain would be the other's loss. Each did a different kind of work, yet they were interdependent, and there appeared to be no easy way to determine the relative worth of their respective labours. Until this was done, however, the price system would be indeterminate. Moreover, it could be shown that adding the producers' respective utility functions would not help: solutions might or might not exist. If they did not, then the model was in obvious trouble; but if they did, there was no reason to suppose that the only solutions would be ones in which the wage rate, or rate of net earnings to labour time, would be equal for the two producers. In short, wages might not be uniform. Furthermore, the solutions need not, and normally would not, be compatible with the initial endowments. The trouble lay in the fact that the Walrasian model possessed no institutional detail. To establish a uniform wage, there had to be a market for *abstract* labour, labour in whatever field or area simply measured by time and valued according to the training and other resources invested in it. But for this, as both Marx and the American institutionalists had recognised, there had to be institutions which compelled some people to work for others. Roughly speaking, this entailed social classes and private property; the Walrasian framework was not rich enough to encompass these.

Dr Sweeney agreed with Professor Stiglitz that the question of flexibility or fixity of a price should be an endogenous variable in a model. While some markets, such as financial markets, did have flexible prices, others tended to have different prices over space, transactions and transactors at the same point in time; these characteristics depended on information states and the costs of acquiring information. He thought that one might want to investigate models in which Professor Malinvaud and Mr Younès's first theorem, that all transactions were made at the same price, need not always hold.

At this point *Professor Stiglitz* rose to defend general equilibrium theory against its critics. Although he agreed that the particular general equilibrium model under discussion had many restrictive assumptions and implications which were hard to accept, it was an admirable attempt to work within and improve upon a consistent model by loosening its assumptions. Criticisms of general equilibrium models had mostly been that there remained much to be done, not that what had been done was mistaken or misguided. One aspect that had been repeatedly touched upon was the information structure of the models. To deal with these problems, some 'general equilibrium' models had worked with price distributions rather than a single price; others had explained quantity-dependent prices, for example rationing, in terms of the heterogeneity of commodities and/or loan contracts.

Professor Koopmans seconded Professor Stiglitz's point. Professor Malinvaud and Mr Younès's paper made important progress in formalising some phenomena which previously did not find a place in formal theory. The fact that the results seemed obvious was not an objection to introducing them, as one needed to make them formal in order to make further progress.

Professor Davidson thought that the question of the information structure was a question of how one envisaged calendar time. It was not only history that was important but also the future, which was created when people made decisions. The insurance framework was not adequate; Knight's distinction between risk and uncertainty was relevant. With respect to single-price models, he referred to Kaldor's 'Speculation and Economic Stability' (*Review of Economic Studies*, 1939) which gave seven conditions for the existence of a spot market. Professor Davidson believed that general equilibrium models, as opposed to historical models, could never explain Keynesian unemployment, because they could not relax the gross substitution assumption; Keynes had said that one of the essential properties of interest and money was that not all commodities (including money) were substitutes.

Professor Stiglitz suggested that the Malinvaud-Younès model illustrated some of the advantages of having a general equilibrium model. One of the most interesting results was the non-Pareto-optimality of the equilibrium. If there were only two commodities the market with fixed prices would be constrained Pareto-optimal; the non-optimality arose when there were more than two commodities. Since if one constrained relative quantities rather than relative prices, for instance in a model of the stock market, one could show that the many-commodity model was not Pareto-optimal, he wondered if there was a general result here.

Professor Streissler questioned whether Dr Sweeney's remark that flexible prices went together with equal prices for all transactors was factually correct Oligopoly prices were inflexible and equal; real estate prices were flexible and unequal. The great difficulty in general equilibrium models was that they did not deal with the question of how different prices came about.

Professor Spaventa doubted whether the discussion of whether general equilibrium models were better than partial equilibrium models had anything to do with Keynesian economics.

Professor Izzo wondered whether the involuntary unemployment that Professor Malinvaud and Mr Younès mentioned in their paper was really involuntary, since Keynesian involuntary unemployment occurred when not enough demand for goods was forthcoming to absorb the full-employment supply of goods.

Professor Segura suggested that the way in which money was introduced in the Malinvaud-Younès model was not the best one. The two reasons for money offered by the authors were the limited velocity of circulation and the fact that transactions took time: neither explanation made room for uncertainty and/or transactions costs which would be better reasons for the inclusion of money in the individual utility functions.

Professor Malinvaud and Mr Younès then replied to the speakers. Discussing the role of fundamental theory, *Professor Malinvaud* said that he thought that the intention was to base our analysis on a consistent set of concepts and axioms. In the process one often found things that were obvious but that had not hitherto been incorporated into a logical model; the work of building theoretical foundations was to define a logical model into which these things would fit. In the area in which he and Mr Younès had been working he thought the approach could illuminate at least two problems. In the case of equilibrium with price rigidities, other economists had assumed that all transactions took place at the same price which would be the minimum feasible price in a buyers' market and the maximum feasible price in a sellers' market; he and Mr Younès had derived these properties from a more general definition. In the case of Keynesian underemployment, which was not due to excessive real wage rates but to lack of effective demand for firms' outputs, this type of underemployment could be found as an equilibrium in a model with price rigidities.

In reply to Dr Nuti's suggestion that we needed only to recognise the absence of the relevant futures markets to explain unemployment of labour, Professor Malinvaud asked on what basis would we analyse the behaviour of an economy without these markets? One motive for his and Mr Younès' work had been to analyse such a situation in a formal way. He agreed that they had made great simplifications; in particular, they had not taken into account imperfect competition and the reasons for the existence of institutional constraints on transactions. They had also used the concept of a minimum price as a simplication of the fact that in a situation of excess supply prices did not adjust sufficiently rapidly to restore equality between demand and supply. They could take constraints on relative quantities into account, as Professor Stiglitz had suggested, but Professor Malinvaud had not really thought over this suggestion.

Mr Younès first answered Professor Negishi's question about the inclusion of prices in the utility function: they had assumed that each agent formed expectations about contract proposals for each type of transaction, rather than expectations of prices. In reply to Sir John Hicks's question as to whether recontracting was possible, he said that they could in principle take it into account, but they could also obtain an equilibrium without recontracting in their model. With respect to the problems of the exchange of information and of the nature of competition assumed, Mr Younès explained that they need not have assumed that any agent could make contract proposals to every other agent, so that it was possible to assume that agents did not all have the same information and thus to obtain an equilibrium with many prices in one segment of the economy. Similarly, the competitive framework was not essential, though if one assumed the existence of monopoly the convexity assumptions needed to derive a fixed point theorem might not hold. Finally, in reply to Sir John Hicks's and Professor Stiglitz's queries about multilateral exchange, Mr Younès said he thought that there was an easy way to obtain a non-Walrasian equilibrium. Assume an economy in which there were three goods and three agents, in which money had to enter into all transactions (involving two goods only), and that two of the three agents had no money at some point. Even with flexible prices you would not get a Walrasian equilibrium, unless you allowed agents the possibility of obtaining credit.

4 What kind of Microeconomic Foundations of Macroeconomics are necessary?

Erich Streissler

UNIVERSITY OF VIENNA

I A SURVEY OF THE PROBLEM

To begin with, it is easier to state what the microeconomic foundations of macroeconomics should *not* be. Basically the whole discussion about the need for a microeconomic foundation of macroeconomics is the expression first of a revolt against, and then of a partial return to, figures of thought symbolised (for me) by the Marshallian concept of a *'representative firm'*.[1]

It is general knowledge how one goes about analysing an aggregate via the concept of the representative individual. If you wish to know what happens to the whole take a representative, i.e., an average individual, analyse its optimising action and then inflate the result by an appropriate factor — possibly unity, as in the case of price — to derive the corresponding result for the whole.

This analysis assumes that differences between or, more precisely, *variances* of individuals as to the causal economic variables do not influence the affected variables in a significant way.[2] Probabilistically speaking it is assumed that one can predict the parameters of the population from a (fictitious) sample of unit size, an assumption which is only correct if the variance between individuals in the sample space is insignificant.

When are variances insignificant in an operational sense? Even the most embattled 'old' microeconomist would have conceded that by the method of examining a (fictitious) representative individual we arrive at conclusions only true on the average. We estimate a *mean value* around which there might be variation. But this need not be the only error of our estimate.

Variances enter significantly into the macroeconomic result when either microeconomic decisions have already been taken and thus the decisions to

---

[1] For the definition of the concept see Marshall (1890) p. 317 ff.

[2] Furthermore, interactions between individuals are also thought not to influence the aggregate. For these very reasons there is a long-standing tradition of scepticism towards aggregates in the Austrian School of Economics, going back to Menger: see Menger (1871) Chapter 2, paragraph 4, p. 74 ff., which is sceptical on the usefulness of the concept of national wealth as a measurement of welfare; Hayek, (1968) p. 5 ff.; Morgenstern (1972), pp. 1163 ff, 1184 ff.

be analysed are different according to whether the variable on which they depend is a point variable or whether it is a distributed variable (this is the point of much of the New Microeconomics);[1] or, if the true macroeconomic average is in itself functionally dependent on the variance between individuals, differing with the value of intra-individual variation (a point made long ago by Theil).[2] So our first question in establishing a macroeconomic result from microeconomic deductions has to be: *do variances between individuals enter significantly in the two ways just described[3] into the macroeconomic result?*[4]

The 'old' analyst of the representative individual tended to conceive of the economic problem as one of *unconstrained* individual optimisation. In spite of well-known earlier achievements it was only the Hicks—Allen revolution[5] of the 1930s (a revolution which might have sailed under the title, the microeconomic foundations of microeconomics) which made it generally understood that rational economic decisions are constrained optimum problems. The elaboration of the theory of constrained optimisation has made it clear that not infrequently the constrained optimum may become a *corner* solution. A second question (which is partly an important sub-question of the first) in the realm of the microeconomic foundations of macroeconomics therefore has to be: *does already the very existence and further the distribution, the variance of constraints between individuals, enter significantly into the macroeconomic result?* (The term constraint is used in this paper in a wide sense: it relates to an economic variable which is, relatively, so inflexible or so uncontrollable that it appears to be an appropriate simplification of a mathematical model to postulate it as an invariant limitation for admissible solutions to the problem in question.)

As is very well understood by now, the old analysis of the representative individual assumed instantaneously available, costless and complete information of the decision taker and consequently his *lack of uncertainty*. The rationalisation for this assumption — if rationalisation there was — followed again the same train of argument as was put forward with respect to interindividual differences: by analysing decisions under certainty we arrive at an average result which holds true even for uncertainty. (Sometimes an even more unguarded conclusion is put forward. We can tell what happens under certainty; we do not know what happens under uncertainty; therefore it is best to assume that the same thing happens under uncertainty as under certainty.)[6]

[1] See Phelps, *et al.* (1970).
[2] Theil (1954).
[3] I tried to make the point of the decisive importance of variances for economic analysis and that this point had always been recognised by the Austrian School in my inaugural lecture in Vienna, (Streissler, 1969a) and the accompanying mathematical model on a special topic, (Streissler, 1969b).
[4] For an example where they do see Appendix A.
[5] See Allen and Hicks (1934) pp. 52 ff, 196 ff; Hicks (1939) Part I.
[6] In the *first* edition of Sohmen (1961, p. 46) the author comes dangerously close to stating this fallacy. The passage is wisely omitted from the second edition.

Our third question therefore has to be: *Does lack of information and uncertainty in microeconomic decision-taking affect the macroeconomic result?* Through the influence of the New Microeconomics it is by now so well known that this is indeed so that I shall concern myself very little with a still further elaboration of this problem in my paper. But one important consequence of uncertainty has, to my mind, not received adequate recognition: *it is from uncertainty that individual constraints derive much of their importance.* Because of uncertainty an individual *assumes* his actions to be constrained in a certain way though they would not be so if information were less restricted.

If extreme uncertainty exists as to the value which a goal variable, an optimand, will take, it seems 'natural' for the individual to assume that increments of the goal variable in question (e.g., profit per unit of output or marginal utility), will take more or less the same value over a considerable range. The total goal variable is then monotonically rising over this range (an assumption all the more plausible as it even holds true in the face of quite considerable miscalculation of, or under still weaker assumptions on the true increments to, the goal variable). If an upper boundary constraint falls within this range we are then − basically due to uncertainty − always faced with a corner solution at this constraint. The optimiser, who is uncertain as to the value a goal variable is likely to take over the range of another variable and who knows only that the goal variable rises monotonically over *part* of this range, tends to assume that it reaches its maximum at the upper boundary of this range.[1] If the constraint moves within the range of the goal variable specified above, the resultant economic changes are then 'only' due to changes in constraints. *Under conditions of extreme uncertainty a macroeconomic result may therefore 'solely' depend upon the average value of and the variance between individuals of a variable which may be thought of as a constraint of behaviour given certain side conditions of this behaviour.* Apparently no more microeconomic foundation is necessary to a macroeconomic statement than reflections on this constraint. (For a mathematical illustration of this statement see Appendix A). Without further microeconomic analysis, we then derive macroeconomic statements; e.g., of the kind: Supply creates its own demand; for all income (the budget constraint) is always spent. Or: An increase in credit supply increases investment, for entrepreneurs, starved for credit (the constraint on their investment behaviour), always lap it up and use it to enlarge plant.[2]

It might be argued that I have just made a more general point, not

[1] This is, I think, *one* possible explanation of the rationale behind sales maximisation. It is assumed that in the long run profits − a variable known in advance with great uncertainty − are maximal with maximum sales.

[2] This, to my mind, is the foundation of Hayek's trade cycle theory. See, for example, Hayek (1929). For a closer examination of certain aspects of that theory see Streissler (1969c), p. 245 ff., here p. 250 ff. It is interesting to note that, basically, Hayek uses a *macroeconomic* approach with an even simpler microeconomic foundation than Keynes, whom Hayek castigated for the meagreness of his microeconomic foundations. See pp. 117−8 below.

necessarily dependent upon uncertainty at all; for the goal variable, even if correctly known with certainty, might in fact be increasing over its whole relevant range up to the (old and new) constraint. In some degree this is true. But then we still have to ask why individual constraints do have the stringency they frequently appear to have. Why does the Hicks—Allen reformulation of the microeconomics of consumption point at the budget constraint in the sense of an income constraint when, at least in the short run, it might be very sensible for the individual to borrow or otherwise to dis-save from accumulated wealth? Interestingly enough, this question is seldom raised, perhaps because it is so evident that, from its very definition, income[1] must be the constraint on (individual and aggregate) consumption in the long run. For the corresponding problem of entrepreneurial expenditure the question why credit should be a limiting variable for investment at all has, in fact, frequently been raised. If ventures are profitable relative to a general equilibrium criterion of admissible profitability it should, after all, be immaterial whether they are self-financed or credit-financed. In fact, credit rationing does occur because the *risk* for the leader *increases* the more a given borrower increases the share of his capital which is borrowed;[2] and that is the same as saying that the rate of return on a given venture is partly due to chance and therefore uncertain as to its exact outcome. More important still, this uncertainty is estimated differently by different individuals. Why else should it frequently happen that an entrepreneur would be willing to undertake a certain venture while potential creditors are unwilling to put up the money? This can only happen because of 'a *variety* of opinion about what is uncertain'.[3] The entrepreneur may either be better informed about the *ex post* probability distribution of returns of the venture or simply more optimistic in forming his subjective probabilities *ex ante* (or both); the creditors are either less well informed about the *ex post* probability distribution of returns or more pessimistic in their subjective probabilities *ex ante* (or both). *A credit constraint* (and even the short-run income constraint on consumption) *is basically due to inter-individual differences of opinion and thus to uncertainty.* One individual imposes a constraint (in a wider sense) upon another individual; i.e., confronts him with a supply curve which at a certain point becomes very inelastic, because the first individual thinks that the probability is rapidly mounting that the second individual might involve him in a loss.

Some might say credit constraints are due to a *lack of trust* between creditors and debtors.[4] This is a fruitful approach, for where there is complete trust of the creditor in the debtor, that is to say both complete trust in the informed judgement of the borrower with regard to investments and

[1] See Hicks (1939, Chapter XIV). On p. 173 of that volume one of the basic income concepts is defined as 'the maximum amount which can be spent over a period if there is to be an expectation of maintaining intact the capital value of prospective receipts.'
[2] See Hayek, (1969) p. 274 ff., here p. 282 ff.
[3] Keynes (1936), p. 172.
[4] See Shubik (1970).

complete trust in his ability to honour his obligations, no credit rationing occurs: as with the borrowing of very large corporations, on the one hand, and of banks and perhaps the borrowing of some governments, on the other. (The Austrian experience, where for centuries the State has been credit rationed, makes me hesitate to include *all* States in the list of the completely trusted or trustworthy debtors).

Many constraints are *quantitative* constraints. To consider such constraints (and to consider constraints on prices which may be bid or asked) is equivalent to the assertion that *not all information relevant* to the economic decision-taker is transmitted *by a freely variable price system*. Or to put it in another way: a quantitative constraint means that, at some point, the relevant price to an individual rises to infinity in spite of the fact that the shadow price for the whole system might remain finite. The price schedule as plotted against the quantity shows a discontinuity at that point. (Realistically we would have to weaken this statement somewhat, saying that at a certain point a price schedule rises 'very' steeply; closer examination will show that no 'constraint' is really absolute.) This is the situation as seen from the angle of, so to speak, the 'constrainee'. From the point of view of the 'constrainer' (e.g., in the case of credit from the point of view of the bank which ceases to lend) we could say that an individual for some reason finds it advisable not to vary its price; i.e., *not to use the price system* for 'rationing'. In assuming a constraint we shall have to examine very carefully why this should be so.

The final assumption of the 'old' microeconomic analyst of the representative individual is that the optima planned by the individuals can be realised within a global constraint *without conflicting* with one another: a realisable configuration of results is planned *ex ante*. In reality economic plans very frequently are in conflict with one another.[1] It would therefore be a very tenuous microeconomic base of macroeconomics to try to derive macroeconomic results from *ex ante* microeconomic optima which prove to be non-viable. For this reason Clower has argued in his dual-decision hypothesis[2] that demand functions planned for expected incomes must be thought of as constrained by actually realised incomes if these fall below those expected. It can be argued that they are also constrained by actual prices being larger than expected; i.e., real incomes falling below their expected levels for given levels of nominal incomes.[3] In fact, doubts about the usefulness of any elaborate microeconomic foundations to macroeconomics may stem from the opinion that individual plans are frequently in conflict with global constraints. Our last question in deriving the microeconomic foundations of macroeconomics therefore has to be: *Are individual optimising plans incompatible to a serious degree?*

In incompatibility of individual plans, once again a constraint becomes of

---

[1] This point has been made above all in the game-theoretical literature, particularly by Shubik. See e.g. Shubik (1973).

[2] See Clower (1969) p. 270 ff., here p. 287 ff.

[3] See Streissler (1972a) p. 39 ff., here p. 43 ff.

the first consequence, this time a *global constraint.* If, e.g., the sum of the individual demand plans always outruns achievable total supply, why bother with them at all? Why not construct a purely macroeconomic theory of this very total supply, a theory essentially of a moving constraint (this would appear to have been the recipe of much of growth theory). In an important sense global constraints are experienced by individual decision-takers as *constraints which the actions of others impose upon their own attempts at optimisation.* A whole branch of the microeconomic foundations of macro-economics seems to be totally missing: a systematic investigation of the question *to what extent which types of economic plans will in situations of conflict be more fully realised than others and why.* Part of this investigation must concern itself, e.g., with the 'rationing rules'[1] resorted to if demand exceeds the current supply streams.

Due to the incompatibility of plans constraints enter the picture in a second and no less important way. After all, individuals learn from the fact that their planned optima frequently will not be achievable; this experience is psychologically frustrating and leads — by definition — to suboptimal economic results. Individuals will therefore try to formulate *secondary plans* which already envisage what should happen if the primary plans prove to be unachievable to a certain extent. Entrepreneurs whose profits are smaller than expected will have built up credit lines in order to finance a certain investment as planned or will have financial assets to sell or even cash (more realistically: time deposits) to decumulate;[2] or they might postpone invest-ment for some while; or they might switch to a less ambitious investment programme. The attempt to realise primary plans under uncertainty (or rather the adverse aspects of uncertainty) thus frequently entails the building up and holding of reserves. Thus, in order *not* to experience the immediate impact of the full constraint imposed upon the optimising behaviour of the individual decision-taker by the consequences of the decisions of others, the decision-taker hedges in order to circumvent this primary constraint. These outlets planned for because of the probability of planning wrong in the first place are, however, again of the nature of constraints, of *secondary* con-straints: cash reserves, other financial assets, credit lines, stocks, free capacity, order books (waiting room for customers) etc. They constrain the admissible amount of changes in plans or limit the changes in data which can be ignored in the pursuit of a given plan. *Uncertainty thus leads to a cascade of con-straints.* In trying to determine macroeconomic consequences it may frequently be more fruitful to analyse this complex hierarchical structure of constraints than to try to derive macroeconomics from the frequently un-realised primary *ex ante* individual plans.

[1] This is recognised, e.g., in Sweeney (1974) p. 56 ff.
[2] The question of how unexpected shortages in receipts impinge upon the plans for finance of production and investment has been analysed by Rose (1957) p. 111 ff., and Laufer (1970) p. 290 ff. Recently Akerlof (1973) p. 115 ff., has analysed differences in spending decisions for intended and unintended accruals and disbursals of money.

In concluding this initial survey it should finally be pointed out that economic decisions are not infrequently reached without any attempt at optimisation at at all. (This is much more the case with respect to *unimportant* or routine economic acts and, furthermore, such acts where there is no mechanism for the exclusive survival of the fittest individuals.) We have to recognise that not only the gathering of information but also the attempt to formulate an optimising plan may be costly to most individuals. In a wider sense we may even call non-optimisation optimal: aspects of economic behaviour are defined where one need not bother or where one follows a simple rule of thumb.[1] With such behaviour, *constraints* provide the *only* microeconomic basis of macroeconomic results. Rules of thumb frequently embody certain constraints to inactivity or routine behaviour (e.g., do not replenish stock as long as it does not fall below a certain level). In order not to become dangerously large, areas of non-optimisation are frequently defined by a constraint (e.g., spend a *given* amount of pocket money without bothering on what). Constraints in areas of expenditure without an attempt at item by item optimisation have much the same significance as in areas of extreme uncertainty (in fact uncertainty and a lack of an attempt to optimise may be correlated). While with uncertainty it may be *impossible* to assign a precise value to a goal variable, with a lack of optimising behaviour one does not even *attempt* to do so.

As a microeconomic foundation to macroeconomics, *constraints* on behaviour are the *last resort* of the economist where individual optimisation has been reduced or is lacking. But even in the case of optimising micro-economic behaviour we are faced with optimisation under uncertainty, which from the point of view of the isolated decision-taker frequently is already initially constrained and which may further be constrained by competing and conflicting plans of others. For one reason or another constraints on individual behaviour can thus provide both the best and the analytically simplest micro-economic foundation of macroeconomics. This does not mean that they may not be a treacherous foundation. When resort is taken to analysis by con-straints, their average value and their variance, it must always be shown that it is the constraints that matter most in the particular case. Analysis by con-straints frequently takes the form of assuming a corner solution. It must always be demonstrated that the corner solution, and not an interior solution, is alone relevant.

II   CONSTRAINTS AS FOUNDATIONS OF MACROECONOMIC STATEMENTS IN THE HISTORY OF ECONOMIC ANALYSIS

To some it may appear strange to stress the importance of constraints on behaviour as a type of microeconomic foundation of macroeconomics. But it

---

[1] Simon (1957) stresses (p. 196 ff. and p. 241 ff.) 'bounded' and 'approximate' rationality under uncertainty. Rules of thumb are a variant of this kind of sub-optimisation.

is strange only from the so-called 'neoclassical' viewpoint (in a very restricted sense) and there, in fact, only from the viewpoint of two of the three branches of the marginalist revolution: from the Marshallian and the Walrasian. The third branch, the Austrian School, had always stressed the differences between individuals, the degree of uncertainty for the planner, and the great probability of the faultiness of individual plans.[1] In the latter respect it has been supported by the *ex ante—ex post* analysis of the Swedish School, linked to the Austrian tradition through Böhm-Bawerk's pupil Wicksell. As I have tried to show, these are aspects from which one can easily arrive at a stress placed on constraints. Historical proof of this can be seen in Hayek's monetary theory of the business cycle.

A different approach to an emphasis on constraints arises both from late mercantilist and especially from classical economics. In the eighteenth and the first three-quarters of the nineteenth century economic literature relied heavily on constraints on individual behaviour as an explanation of macro-economic results.

It is interesting to contrast, e.g., the different interpretation of competition in the classical and the neoclassical period of economic thought. Perfect competition to the neoclassicist in the Marshallian tradition means individual optimisation under certainty and under the condition of an infinitely elastic demand schedule as viewed by the single firm. It is thus a conscious striving to achieve the best possible outcome within the area of choice. Given the further assumption of increasing costs optimisation leads to unique economic results. (In a wider sense we might of course even call the given market price — the consequence of anonymous economic actions of other entrepreneurs and of consumers — a constraint on the behaviour of the perfect competitor). In the classical view, most forcefully expressed by Marx, competition is seen as constraints (consciously perceived), which are imposed on the given entrepreneur by the actions of the competitors. His range of choice is narrowed by his competitors' to a single point. Under static conditions this may well be the same as the unique solution of the neoclassical fable. Nevertheless the difference remains that the one model sees competition as *individual* optimisation possibly constrained as to the admissible value of certain variables; the other, as a result of social constraints imposed upon individual action by a *social system* (the survival of the fittest).

The adherence to one or the other concept of competition leads to different conclusions when total demand in an industry changes, especially when demand increases. Under the classical model competitors in principle do have the power of price setting. They are *potential* price setters. They are only constrained from using this power in 'normal' situations of constant demand (or of demand changing at a constant rate equal to the increase in productive capacity). If demand accelerates they become conscious that competition has declined and that they are now able to exercise their dormant powers of

[1] See Streissler (1969a, 1973) p. 160 ff.

increasing their prices. (Translating the same thing into the neoclassical story: they would learn that their individual demand schedule had become less than perfectly elastic.) They learn that demand accelerates and that consequently their prices setting power increases because customers tell them that they could not be supplied at ruling prices by competitors: Customers ask whether a given competitor does still stock commodity X; or whether an order for that commodity can be accepted by him.

Thus, working from the classical assumption of constrained behaviour and of changes in constraints it becomes much easier *to explain price changes* than in the standard neoclassical case which has to resort to the reputedly Walrasian figure of the auctioneer. Arguing in the classical tradition one has, however, to recognise that non-price information is used by entrepreneurs as well as information condensed in prices — a more catholic view on informational data processed, not at all repugnant to classical thought. The quantitative data used by entrepreneurs are, though, a dangerous source of double counting (a point which will be elaborated presently) and so also a source of planning error.

Considering the central role of market prices in economic theory it is very curious how little systematic thought has been devoted to the analysis of the *process of formation* of such market prices. Richard Cantillon who, because of his stress of the importance of the informational contents of markets, should altogether be considered a 'founding father' of the New Microeconomics, is one of the very few authors who present a model of market price formation,[1] though even his model is admittedly very sketchy. In a localised produce market on a certain market day potential buyers and sellers form a provisional estimate of the quantities which might be demanded (Cantillon says: of the 'money' offered; i.e., of *effective* demand). Thus once more non-price information is resorted to. The first price offers and bids are made, presumably by those who consider themselves best informed. Each new price agreed upon is then constrained more and more, in a sequential chain, by the prices of the sales already made: the price sequence converges to a unique market price due to the constraints that the prior actions of competitors impose upon the bargaining set of the later sales.[2] Such a model well describes certain modern markets where a 'fixing' of price takes place. (We are not told what happens in the case where the value of the market price, to which the series converges, is 'wrong' in the sense that it does not clear the market; in another model of Cantillon the price sequence moves down approximately along the demand curve as the most eager customers, those willing to offer most, are served

---

[1] Cantillon (1931) Part I, Chapter 4, pp. 10–12.

[2] Note that this reduction of price indeterminacy in a *time* sequence, as more and more *transactions* are made during a (short) market period, is similar to but not quite the same thing as the reduction of price indeterminacy as more and more *competitors* enter the market analysed in modern game-theoretical literature. The latter limiting process is already the foundation of the price theory of Menger. See Menger (1871) Chapter 5, especially p. 206 ff.

first, those holding back being served at lower prices.)[1]

The most extreme criticism of a naïve derivation of macroeconomic conclusions from microeconomic phenomena can also be found in the mercantilist
and early classical tradition. The first to voice this criticism was, of course,
Bernard Mandeville.[2] If macroeconomic consequences differ qualitatively and
totally from what is planned microeconomically (in his treatment above all:
if socially advantageous macroeconomic consequences are derived from
morally reprehensible microeconomic acts) then it might be better to start
out with a system analytically wholly macroeconomic from the very beginning.
Or, at least, it is necessary to contrast microeconomic plans and their macroeconomic consequences: social outcomes are 'the results of human action but
not of human design', as Ferguson stated and Hayek frequently quotes.[3]

Marx, of course, was an author who dwelt largely on this contrast between
individual design and social consequences. The attempt, e.g., by each and
every entrepreneur to increase his sum total of profits by investment may,
according to Marx, by its macroeconomic consequences (over-investment)
lower the profits for all.[4] A similar example is afforded by the so-called
'paradox of competition'[5] and other economic cases of what in game-
theoretical literature is called the prisoners' dilemma. In a market of monopolistic competition it may be to the advantage of each entrepreneur separately
to lower his price (he increases profits due to an increase in his market share),
while, if all follow suit and cut their prices too, profits are decreased for the
whole industry. All these contradictions or paradoxes are basically due to the
fact that the individual considers his optimisation problem as unconstrained
while, in fact, a global constraint due to similar actions of others exists. If
this global constraint is recognised by the individuals it supplies the rationale
of collusive action.

III   HA YEK'S MONETARY MODEL OF THE BUSINESS CYCLE: A CASE STUDY IN QUANTITATIVE CONSTRAINTS OR THE NON USE OF THE PRICE MECHANISM

As has already been pointed out in the first part of this paper, Hayek's
monetary model of the business cycle provides an instructive example of a
macroeconomic model where the microeconomic foundation is a constraint.
This model shall therefore be analysed *in extenso* here; not because I think it
to be of direct explanatory value under presently prevailing economic conditions, but because of its methodological interest. Certain modifications of
it can, however, also yield insights of immediate contemporary relevance.

---

[1] Cantillon (1931) Part II, Chapter 2.
[2] Mandeville (1714).
[3] See e.g. his article with this title in Les Fondements Philosophique des Systèmes
Économiques; Textes de Jacques Rueff et Essais Rediges en Son Honneur, E. M. Claassen
(ed) (1967) p. 98 ff.
[4] See Marx (1969) p. 337 f.
[5] Stützel (1958) p. 3.

Hayek's model appears to be the following: the 'natural' rate of interest or, as I would say, the rate of profit on capital or, in Keynesian terminology, the marginal efficiency of investment, varies strongly over the business cycle. More precisely, the 'natural' rate of interest should be taken to be the demand price of financial capital or of credit by entrepreneurs, given a certain rate of profit for their present investment (from which they deduct some kind of risk premium). This demand price for capital provided from outside the firm is important to entrepreneurs because they finance investment mainly with borrowed funds (an essential feature of the original Hayek model): entrepreneurs are unable to finance their investment *ex ante* out of profits, but only *ex post* out of quasi-rents.

The *market rate of interest*, on the other hand, varies little over the cycle. The market rate of interest is the supply price of credit by the banks.

Thus the demand price and the supply price, the price offered and the price bid, for the same commodity in the same market differ; and they differ by more than a broker's fee, a difference which would be an everyday occurrence explainable purely by information and transaction costs. Whenever for some reason or other we find an economic problem where supply price and demand price diverge for long periods, a constraint becomes the decisive explanatory element. This is so at least when the supply price is *below* the demand price; in the opposite case sales become zero. (In our case in the slump, when the 'natural' rate of interest is *below* the market rate, entrepreneurs would not borrow from the banks, which would only loan to other types of individuals, e.g., owner occupants as house builders or the State.)

The divergence of the supply and the demand price is the 'Austrian' feature of Hayek's model (a feature taken from Wicksell, himself a pupil of Böhm-Bawerk). For the founder of this tradition, Menger, had stressed the possibility that supply and demand prices might differ.[1]

The rest of Hayek's story is quickly told. In the upswing, when the demand price of credit is above the supply price, the entrepreneurs invest to the hilt of their credit rationing (they must be rationed by the banks because of the disequilibrium in price). As the boom progresses, banks, for reasons easily explainable in terms of microeconomic optimisation (as will be shown below) can no longer extend their volume of credit. Investment programmes cannot be completed unless 'savings' increase or, more precisely, unless deposits with the banks increase, enabling them to extend their volume of credit. (All this could also be formulated more dynamically in terms of deviations from growth paths with constant growth rates.) The non-completion of investment projects leads to business failures and thus to the slump. (Such non-completion of projects is not very likely and does, in fact, occur only in the case of speculative housing booms. I have maintained that Böhm-Bawerk and Hayek basically described Viennese housing investment cycles of the 'Ringstrasse'

[1] See Streissler (1973a) p. 170 ff; (1973b) p. 164 ff, here p. 169 ff.

period.) Apart from the fact that for the investing entrepreneur it may be an error to rely upon a prolongation of credit, that he may be in error as to the length of the rise in the rate of profit, in error as to the amount of increase of demand which will be his share,[1] and in error as to the amount of investment of his competitors,[2] the model is evidently well founded microeconomically on the side of the investing entrepreneurs. Boom and slump, on the other hand, are caused by the behaviour of the banks, the villains in Hayek's picture. And they are precisely the villains because their microeconomic behaviour does *not* fit in with macroeconomic equilibrium. It is to the examination of their behaviour, therefore, that we now turn.

We first note that the non-completion of investment projects, very important to Böhn-Bawerk and Hayek, and even credit rationing by the banks, are in fact inessential frills of the model. The essential point is simply that in the interest rate — quantity of credit demanded (or supplied) — plane of the credit supply curve of the banks is a *flat* curve (see Figure 4:1). We have to assume that the cyclical shift in the rate of profit is a shift in a demand *schedule*, negatively inclined as is usual with demand schedules. Credit-dependent investment then shows large quantitative variations over the business cycle: due to the fact that the demand curve for credit shifts much (*large* variations in the rate of expected profit) while the flat credit supply curve shifts little; even an investment credit market without credit rationing would oscillate over the cycle around a flat ellipse. The credit market for investment purposes would in the sense of Hicks be more nearly a *Q*-market than a *P*-market,[3] a market equilibrating more via quantitative than via price changes. (Note that this Hayekian vision is exactly, so to speak, the reflected image of the Keynesian system, where the financial markets, though somewhat differently conceived, are price equilibrating, all *other* markets being *Q*-markets.)[4] The essential feature of the model is thus the non-use of price as a parameter of action by the banks (for good reasons, as will be shown).

The credit supply schedule becomes so flat because of the ability of the banks to increase their credit creation with rising interest rates in the sense of a demand price (or in the boom) and their declining ability (or willingness) to create credit with declining interest rates (or during recession). Without credit creation the supply schedule of finance out of voluntary household saving would be much steeper: larger variations of interest would choke off excessive

---

[1] The overestimation of the demand increase in a market being supplied at full capacity utilisation arises in a perfectly rational way: a customer turned down by one supplier because of lack of further productive capacity shops around with very many other suppliers, who are all likely to turn him down for the same reason. Finally he may find someone able to meet his demand. Thus the *one* customer is counted many times: all the entrepreneurs register him as *their* potential customer not recognising that he is just as likely to be the potential customer of their competitors.

[2] See, especially, Richardson (1960).

[3] Hicks (1956) p. 139 ff.

[4] This is Hicks's interpretation of the Keynesian system in Hicks (1956).

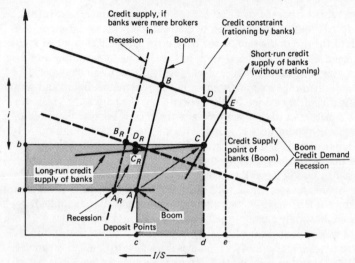

Figure 4:1   Hayek's Credit Market

quantitative upward variations of investment and stimulate investment in the
downswing (see the curve *AB* in Figure 4:1). Thus the *magnifying effect of
credit intermediation causes instability.* By rationing credit, banks in fact
mitigate their dangerous effects on the economy by *reducing* the quantitative
upward variation of investment: see investment level *Dd* relative to investment
level *Ee* in Figure 4:1. The steeper supply curve of savings of ultimate savers
is not relevant for entrepreneurs because ultimate savers do not invest directly
in firms for reasons of information costs and costs of administration. It would
be very costly for savers to find profitable enterprises in need of credit at a
certain moment of time. It would be costly to control such a direct loan. It
would be costly to gather in many small savings for the ultimate investor.
These costs are taken from the shoulders of savers and investing firms by the
banks which reduce them socially by being specialised agents. (To put it on
Shubik's terms: depositors 'trust' banks but they do not trust entrepreneurs.)

What needs thorough investigation in Hayek's model is thus only the
pricing behaviour of the banks at both ends of their business: both in taking
in deposits and in loaning out credit.

If the market rate of interest varies little over the business cycle this must
mean that the deposit rate at which the banks take in deposits also varies little.
In fact the demand schedule of banks for deposits appears to be nearly completely flat; or to be more exact, it appears to be flat for *small* deposits. For
the small depositor has (because of the transaction and information costs
sketched above) no alternative but to loan to the bank. In times of great
demand for commercial credit, banks tend to increase, more or less clan-
destinely and secretly, the deposit rate for large deposits relative to small

ones: they practice monopolistic price differentiation with a view to the different competitive strength of their depositors. But why do they not increase the deposit rate all round? The answer is simple: the potential volume of *new* deposits which might be attracted and which would form the basis for new loans by the banks, is always small in relation to *old* deposits; any rise in the deposit rate for *all* deposits (old and new) would thus be an inordinately expensive way of attracting new deposits.

When the interest rates on old loans are fixed by contract (and by the very nature of banking they must always be fixed for a longer period than those on deposits) while the interest on old deposits is raised, this might entail a loss out of all proportion to the gain achieved from the new loan possibilities due to an attraction of new deposits. More precisely: the marginal loss on old loan contracts due to an increase in deposit rates which would just balance the marginal gain from an increase in new loan possibilities would coincide with so tiny an increase in the deposit rate that because of the considerable cost of changing the price (the deposit rate) and the need to make it a discrete number on small loan contracts (the interest rate seems to vary here by $\frac{1}{8}$ per cent as the smallest step) it is *optimal* under most circumstances *to hold the deposit rate constant*.

Thus we meet with another quantitative 'constraint': the 'inability' to change price — more precisely, the non-optimality of doing so — places the banks under a quantitative restriction as to the amount of deposits attracted by them. This is due to the fact that a price change primarily aimed at changing a flow or a small increment to a stock would also affect the price of a vastly larger stock as a whole.

This kind of constraint occurs quite frequently. It is, e.g., at the core of many types of substitution between factors. Entrepreneurs frequently argue that the reason for substituting machines for labour is the non-availability of labour. They thus argue in terms of a quantitative restriction, not a price-sensitive labour supply schedule as envisaged by most economists. Economists on the other hand usually see the reason for substitution in relative price changes. Who is right? Both are, but the entrepreneurial argument points to the more central fact. Substitution frequently means that a certain type of labour ('non-available' to the firm) is replaced: e.g., a new brick-baking oven is intended to economise on labour in extreme heat.[1] With rising living standards workers become more and more reluctant to work in conditions of extreme physical inconvenience. But, so the usual economist's argument runs, they would be willing to work under such conditions (at least for a few years) if only paid sufficiently well! True enough. But this, at least after some time, would mean a very steep increase in their wages relative to those of other types

[1] The example of the brick oven is taken from an international co-operative study of economic research institutes on the diffusion of technologies. The Austrian version of this study was published as: *Die Ausbreitung neuer Technologien — Eine Studie über zehn Verfahren in neuen Industrien* (Österreichisches Institut für Wirtschaftsforschung (1969)).

of employment in the firm. Now workers in general have very marked views on a 'just' wage structure, which in fact means the traditional, the past wage structure. An increase in the wages of workers labouring in extreme heat creates a strong pressure for wage increases all round in order to preserve 'just' – i.e., traditional – wage differentials. If wages have to be increased all round simply because of the shortage in a certain type of labour then, indeed, filling the quantitative gap for this type of labour by wage variation becomes enormously expensive. If wages are increased only for the type of labour in short supply costly industrial strife would ensue. Thus the only way out is substitution because of a 'purely quantitative' constraint on a certain type of labour. The constraint arises because of the need to change the *increment* to a total *without consequences* to the total and the inability of the employer to practice price differentiation within this not quite homogeneous total.

We have seen that it is perfectly rational for banks not to vary the deposit rate of interest and thus to be faced with a relatively more inelastic loan supply. But why do the banks not vary their lending rate; or rather why do they vary it so little? After all, keeping the borrowing rate fixed need not imply that the same pricing policy should also work on the other end of the banking business. In fact, according to the theory of monopoly pricing we should expect that, whatever shape the supply schedule has, in cases of an increase in demand the monopolist's own supply schedule would be steeper; i.e. it would be optimal to increase his profit margin. And in certain expectional circumstances – not analysed in Hayek's model – such a reaction does in fact occur. The sharp restriction of credit by the German Bundesbank in 1973–4 made the German banks bid up deposit rates quite sharply, contrary to the above analysis for normal situations; and the banks handed on these increases to their customers with a vengeance; i.e. they increased their profit margins as well. Why is such a behaviour of the credit market so rare?

This is so for two reasons. On the one hand, *banks*, in contrast to manu-facturing enterprises, can create their own product; i.e. credit, 'out of thin air': they have the ability to multiply financial media. Thus they must not only look at the restrictive effect a price increase has on the demand for the credit which they, as it were, merely hand on from their depositors. They must look also at the restrictive effect of an interest increase on the *additional* credit which they can create over and above new deposits; this being their most lucrative business, as they do not have to pay a deposit rate on this additional credit. Their supply schedule is thus much flatter than it would be if they were only (monopolistic) credit brokers. And it is so particularly at the moment when investment demand increases most. For this, as will be shown, is the very moment of the cycle when the credit multiplier has increased and is at its peak. On the other hand, commercial banks operating on the Con-tinental system also hold a large amount of *securities*, especially bonds. The bond rate is closely linked to the commercial loan rate. When the banks push the commercial loan rate to its maximum they make a capital loss on their

bonds and other financial assets. Accounting procedures force them to consider such a capital loss as equivalent to a current loss. Thus, additional
profits due to a higher loan rate would be balanced by losses on bond value
and other similar capital losses, an effect similar to one shown for deposit
rates, which limits loan rate variation to a minimum. The effect of its loan
rate variation on bond values is for any single bank, of course, only of the
nature of a distant repercussion. But bankers have long been trained to
collusive behaviour: more than other entrepreneurs they abhor action which
might be advantageous for a single individual but would be disadvantageous
to the whole, if others follow. And it is rational for bankers to act more
collusively than other entrepreneurs: bankers depend upon assistance from
other bankers in moments of crisis, when they change from being suppliers of
to being customers for credit. Those banks which, in an attempt to increase
their particular profit, have not stuck to the code of good behaviour of
bankers, are liable to be let down in a crisis by their colleagues, so that they
incur a great increase in risk if they attempt to turn an extra profit in any
unusual way.

How is it that the credit (or money) multiplier increases in the early boom
simultaneously with an increase in investment demand, so that this higher
demand can be met at loan rates which change little? The credit multiplier
depends negatively on the ratio of cash transactions to other monetary transactions, on the one hand, and also negatively on the amount of reserves which
the banks either are legally required to hold or hold voluntarily for reasons of
safety. In the situation which Hayek described (still prevailing to this day in a
country like Austria) wages are largely paid in cash while profits are not; and
correspondingly consumption goods are purchased against cash while export
goods or investment goods are paid for by drafts on a deposit account. Thus
in a beginning boom, when profits rise faster than wages and the investment
and export stream rises relatively to the consumption stream, the money
multiplier increases because the same number of units in the monetary base
can support a larger volume of M_1. The money multiplier falls, of course, if
legal reserve requirements increase; and, as we have seen in the case of Germany
in 1973–4, things can then change completely. Voluntary reserve requirements, on the other hand, decline during a boom. They depend, on the one
hand, upon the probability that the reserve risk, against which they are held,
materialises. In a boom this risk declines. Sharp withdrawals of deposits
become less likely, new deposits flow in because of the increase in business,
the payment morale of creditors improves and entrepreneurs appear to be
better risks altogether. On the other hand, reserves depend upon the cost
incurred, if the reserve risk materialises. But the cost of emergency loans from
other banks again decreases during a boom. And, finally, reserves are econ-
omised because of the higher profitability of or the greater quantitative
demand for loans. All this changes as the boom proceeds. Banks have thus to
diminish their loans (at least relatively to a normal rate of expansion) as the
boom proceeds and, as far as they do increase the loan rate at all, they

increase it in the later phases of prosperity. Thus credit becomes scarcer and more expensive as the boom proceeds and the expectation of financing investment to completion is, according to Hayek, frustrated.

The salient features of Hayek's monetary model of the business cycle are therefore two quantitative constraints due to the total lack of variation, or at least due to an insufficient variation of price: the constraint of depositors placed upon the banks and the constraints of credits imposed by the banks on investing entrepreneurs. I have tried to show that both these constraints can be explained by rational neoclassical optimising models. But then, after all, many will say there is no difference between action ruled by individual optimisation and that ruled by constraints. The constraints are no real barriers to behaviour but self-imposed outcomes of optimising. Yes and no. I have attempted to explain constraints fully. But in a world of uncertainty a full re-examination of traditional ways of behaviour − in themselves in *general* well founded in rational action − is not undertaken in every case. Generally optimal behaviour hardens into rules of thumb: one just 'knows' that action is best thought of as constrained in a certain way. Certain possible parameters of action are no longer fully investigated, certain limited and limiting dimensions are considered as immutable. The normal decision-taker in 'normal' times suboptimises under certain constraints. The theorist can therefore also limit his analysis to simpler models. He will not only gain simplicity. He will frequently also predict better than the theorist of 'full-optimisation' because constraints hardened into rule-of-thumb quasi-taboos will frequently be operative, even when fully rational behaviour − 'radical' re-examination of an optimisation problem − would counsel action to break down the constraints.

Let us wind up this re-examination of Hayek's model, which in many aspects appears archaic, by pointing briefly to a variant of it which still works in present-day Austria. In Austria, as in most modern countries, the largely credit-using and credit-starved industrial entrepreneur is a thing of the past. Entrepreneurs nowadays finance their investment mainly out of profits. Profits, however, do not only take the place of the credit offered by the banks, according to the original Hayek model; in a certain sense and for new institutional reasons they themselves imply a new type of credit. In Austria businessmen are allowed to write off investment in machines in normal times to the tune of 55 per cent to 60 per cent in the first year, depending upon whether the machine is installed in the second or first half of the year. At present (1974−6) the write-off for tax purposes is even 80 per cent to 85 per cent. At marginal tax rates of 51 per cent for corporations and 62 per cent for unincorporated enterprises this means that, relative to normal depreciation, entrepreneurs get a *tax credit* of some 30 per cent to 50 per cent of gross investment and of some three to four years' duration on the average; and this is a loan which they can force out of the State (provided they earned profits to the corresponding amount) by merely filing their tax declarations, a loan for which they pay 0 per cent interest. Thus the loan interest at which entrepreneurs borrow is a *mixed* interest rate (opportunity rate of loaning out profits, instead of investing, commercial interest on commercial loans, if any, and zero interest on the State loan). This mixed rate is certainly *below* the 'natural' rate or the rate of profit. Once more we have a constraint model; but now a constraint simply defined by the tax law. (The tax credit is limited by the sum invested, by the size of profits, by the tax rate and the write-off allowances.) But this credit proves reliable for the entrepreneur in contrast to credit-financing through the banks: there is no danger of not being able to complete 'structures', once started. The terms of the tax credit cannot be varied *ex post.* Thus there is no danger of a boom being cut short because of the inability of banks to prolong credit.[1]

Naturally such a tax policy causes overinvestment, at least when profits are high, relative to the increase in demand. Excess capacity accumulates because the supply or loan rate of interest (one hesitates to call it the 'market' rate) is kept permanently below the demand rate. Excess capacity accumulated in Austria during the 1960s. But this also meant that, during the years 1970–4, Austria was able to grow more quickly than Germany, by more than 2 per cent per year on the average, or altogether by a 'big jump' of 14 per cent just *because* of this excess capacity. (Austria gained export market shares.) Here is an interesting moral. At least *if* a strong boom comes along, as it did in the early 1970s, individual optimisation evidently *underestimates* investment profitability. It does so for two reasons: first, because it is usually *'cautious'* about the opportunities the next boom will offer and, second, because the profit-creating effects of *complementary* investment of other forms are always underestimated individually. A constraint mechanism can appear socially more rational than unperturbed individual optimisation.

As the State has become the lender of 'first resort', so the commercial banks have in fact become lenders of 'last resort'. As is usual with banks they practice preferential rules as between certain types of customers in apportioning credit. In a boom the industrial entrepreneurs need some residual credit to finance investments. As they rank first in preferential order they lap up most of the credit available. Small enterprises are 'rationed' and in fact receive very little credit then. This is rational bank behaviour, as small loans are more costly (while loan rates are not differentiated much between loans of different size). Small enterprises, however, need a larger share of credit in financing investment than large enterprises; for to them investment is a much 'lumpier' stream relative to profits. This demand is satisfied during recession. Then, when industrial credit demand falls, banks nearly force loans on the victims of their rationing: on small enterprises and, interestingly enough, on the State. Thus credit rationing works so as to compensate and even out the business cycle. When big industrial investment drops (which is indirectly largely State-financed), small entrepreneurial investment and direct public investment take its place.

[1] For the full consequences of this kind of investment policy see Streissler (1972b) p. 49 ff.

Thus credit constraints can be a very efficient mechanism for switching off demand streams with *either procyclical* (the Hayek case) *or anticyclical effects* (the present Austrian case). The Austrian system is, of course, not the first system to work a successful strategy of credit switching with a constraint. Economic historians stress that the legal maximum rate of interest at 5 per cent in Britain during the Industrial Revolution was such a system.[1] The State was allowed to offer any interest rate it pleased. So during wars it got all the credit by bidding up rates, while private individuals were debarred from taking credit by their legal inability, strictly enforced, of paying the going rate of interest. Peace worked the complementary switch towards productive investment at falling(!) interest rates. A judicial system of either a quantitative constraint or of a constraint on the admissible prices can thus even be a sound foundation for macroeconomic policy.

IV   THE KALDOR MODEL OF DISTRIBUTION: CONSTRAINT VIA REPERCUSSION OF THE UNKNOWN ACTION OF OTHERS

The previous case study of the microeconomic foundations of a macro-economic model highlighted above all the importance of quantitative constraints due to the inadvisability or legal inadmissability of using the price mechanism as an instrument of control. Let us briefly turn to another well-known model in order to discuss the importance of constraints placed on the individual decision-taker by other decision-takers in a like position.

As my second case study I shall take the Kaldor model of distribution, Kaldor (1955–6); or rather a variant of it. Kaldor's model has received much praise and much criticism.[2] All the criticism is, however, directed at its presumably *long-run* and purely *full-employment* nature. Now there certainly exists a long-run version of the Kaldor model, which fits in with many other well-known features of growth models.[3] But to my mind, the basic application of the Kaldor theory of distribution should be as a *short-run* model. For it is Keynesian in essence and I was always led to believe that Keynesianism is the economics of those of us who think they will be dead in the long run; and it is essentially derived from a national income *identity*, which holds for the short run as well as for the long run. Kaldor, of course, expressly came out against a short-run, non-full-employment interpretation of his model:

> The principle of the Multiplier . . . could be alternatively applied to a determination of the relation between prices and wages, if the level of output and employment is taken as given, or the determination of the level of employment, if distribution . . . is taken as given . . . the Keynesian technique . . . can be used for both purposes, provided the one is conceived as a short-run theory and the other as a long-run theory.[4]

[1] See, for instance Pressnell (1960) p. 178 ff., here 180 f., p. 184.
[2] See for many others Johnson (1973) p. 199 ff.
[3] See, for instance, Pasinetti (1962) p. 267 ff.; Morishima (1969) p. 36 ff.
[4] Kaldor (1955–6) p. 94. Full employment is explicitly assumed on p. 95.

Now if the discussion of the short-run Phillips curve has taught us anything at all, it would surely be that these two aspects do not exclude each other: short-run adjustment in an economy with some spare capacity works *both* via employment and via distribution. And such a short-run version of Kaldor's model of distribution, in and out of full-employment, appears to me to be more interesting from the point of the constraints on individual action implied; while the long-run version is not interesting as a constraint model. A short-run version of the Kaldor model of distribution is an analysis of the *deviation* of the actual outcome of distribution from the distributional situation expected in or planned for by individual optimising; i.e., a model of planning *error*. In this modest role it is thus *complementary* to a long-run theory of planned distributional change, fully compatible with a marginal productivity theory of distribution (for those who believe they cannot do without such a theory). The essential point of such a model is, perhaps, best brought out by Marx (1969, p. 648), who used it long before Kaldor: 'Um mathematischen Ausdruck anzuwenden: die Größe der Akkumulation ist die unabhängige Variable, die Lohngröße die abhängige, nicht umgekehrt', a causal relationship explicitly said by Marx to hold for the 'Krisenphase des industriellen Zyklus'; i.e., in the short-run and in states of underemployment. That in a circular flow model the *sole* causal chain runs from investment to profits, as Marx puts it, is, perhaps, again an overstatement of the case. Let us be more modest: while − via individual optimisation − profits (though perhaps past profits or future profits: there is room here for a recursive model) determine investment, investment at the same time also determines (present) profits. Or to put it still differently: from the point of view of finance, entrepreneurs, acting collectively, have a greater ability to finance investment than appears to each acting in isolation; additional investment partly creates its own profits.

According to national income theory this profit-creating propensity is, of course, not merely a feature of private investment, but also of a budget deficit (regardless of whether it is due to additional public investment or additional public consumption or merely to lower tax receipts) and finally also of a balance of trade surplus. I think the whole point is, in fact, best brought out by looking at the identity

$$I_{pr} + (I_{st} - S_{st}) + (Ex - Im) \equiv S_w + S_c \tag{1}$$

(I: Investment, S: Saving, Ex: Exports, Im: Imports, sub-indices, pr: private, st: of the State, w: of wage earners, c: of capitalists).

Assuming that private investment *can* be varied independently (the central assumption) and making in addition the purely preliminary assumptions, in order to make the point more clearly,

$$\frac{d(I_{st} - S_{st})}{dI_{pr}} = \frac{d(Ex - Im)}{dI_{pr}} = \frac{dS_w}{dI_{pr}} = 0 \tag{2}$$

we get

$$dI_{pr} = dS_c \qquad (3)$$

If we make the further assumption that capitalist consumption is not affected by increased profits, then the *whole* additional private investment (in this verbal explanation we assume the change to be *positive*) creates not only its own savings according to the usual multiplier analysis, but also additional profits to exactly the same extent. While the absolute increase in profits is in that case equal to the absolute increase in investment, the profit *share* would only increase to the same extent as the investment share if these shares had been equal to start with (which is approximately true for my country, Austria, both shares being not far from one-third).

In order to show that this extreme version of the Kaldor model is only an improbable and not an impossible model, the strong set of assumptions (2) could with some effort be rationalised. Let there be some free capacity in the investment goods sector so that additional demand for investment goods could be met from home production, which is only dependent on home materials. Then there need be no effect on the balance of payments. The budget receives no additional tax inflow from the higher incomes created by investment: if investment rises, businesses are not taxed on extra profits and workers work overtime, overtime pay remaining untaxed (both close to actual fact in Austria). Workers consume all additional income on home consumption goods: their savings function is kinked at the initially expected income, falling to zero for higher (windfall) incomes. Similarly the entrepreneurial savings function is kinked in the other direction, rising to unity for any unexpected additional profits.

All these are somewhat weird assumptions. They make it clear that in actual fact there will be *compensatory* movements working *against* a change in private investment, both in the budget deficit (especially via higher tax returns) and in the balance of trade (especially through higher imports but possibly also through lower exports). Furthermore, the savings of workers will increase with higher income. Yet it is both theoretically likely and empirically observable that, in terms of nominal income, there will be no full compensation of increased investment on the left-hand side of equation (1); and as wages are in the short run much stickier than profits and the rate of savings out of wages is much stickier than that of savings out of profits (windfall profits being mainly saved), any remaining increase on the left-hand side of (1) due to an increase in investment will raise profits more than wages. Basically the model is thus nothing but a statement on the *relative* degrees of stickiness of behaviour; and so, of course, are all models dichotomising economic magnitudes into 'variables' and 'constants': constants, realistically interpreted, are simply the stickier variables.

Economic magnitudes can be 'constants' (sticky variables) for two reasons: either because the determining variables of optimising behaviour do not change (this should be read as to include wilful inertia) or because behaviour underlying the constants is strongly constrained. The variant of the Kaldor model of distribution here presented is above all such a model of the varying restrictiveness of constraints. On the one hand, entrepreneurial investment behaviour is nowadays much less constrained than household consumption behaviour (if it were the other way round we would be back in the classical world where savings determine investment). There are two reasons for this: firms have much easier access to credit than households (large loans to firms are cheaper to administer for banks than small loans to households), so that it is easier for them to surmount their budget constraint in the narrower sense; and, second, firms with some price strategic latitude (oligopoloid or monopoloid firms) are able to vary their 'income' (profit) by individual action, while households can normally vary their income only collectively, and that means with a lag. These are the reasons why the model starts out from the 'independent' variation of investment.

Exports and public expenditure are only slightly more constrained than private investment. Therefore they rightly fall into the same category. Foreign demand is largely autonomous relative to home demand and can thus vary independently relative to the latter; and the State has resort to credit just as easily as firms and the same ability as firms to change its income (via tax changes). The *balance* of trade and the budget *deficit* are already more con- strained in their independent variation than exports and public expenditure: additional exports, to a considerable degree, create their own additional imports and additional public expenditure its own tax back-flow. Thus private investment rules the roost. While wage income is more constrained than profits, savings out of wages are sticky for another reason: here the optimal savings ratio is probably not influenced strongly by changes in income, a statement which is a variant of Keynes's 'psychological law'. At the heart of the Kaldor model is the *ability of entrepreneurs to vary expenditure relative to income and the unwillingness or inability of households to do the same.*

A different insight into the constraint structure behind the Kaldor model can be gained by looking at the *pricing behaviour* of firms. Here the model points to the constraints imposed by *other firms* on the optimising behaviour of each firm; or rather the conditional probability basis of this optimising. Under certainty each firm would (given certain concavity and regularity con- ditions) work at the unique price optimising its profit. But on closer inspection this is just a *conjectural* point *assuming* certain supply and demand behaviour of *other* individuals. This is not a Keynesian point but was in fact stressed in implicit criticism of Keynes by the presumably neoclassical Hayek (1937, p. 174 ff). Without knowing the investment behaviour of other firms, their complementary or substitutive investment, the marginal efficiency of capital or the return on investment of a given firm cannot be calculated; neither can the profit share or the rate of profit. When prices are (relatively) increased in the boom this is so because entrepreneurs believe that limitations on their pricing behaviour have diminished (the demand curve has been raised). 'Boom' pricing will be profitable, if individuals, especially entrepreneurs, all increase demand in step; while divergent behaviour relative to an expansion in demand is more constraining. Price increases in step are the more likely to succeed because of their usual motive: they are meant to finance additional investment; and to the extent that all entrepreneurs share this motive and all are investing simultaneously and without delay, this pricing behaviour is likely to prove profitable *ex post*. Price increases may even be unexpectedly profitable, because expansion of demand in step also lowers costs because of a better utilisation of capacity. Expectations that constraints — placed by others upon one's own elbow room in pricing — will be raised can thus yield a good explanation for a macro-economic theory of price *change*, which is always, to a considerable degree, price change under uncertainty. To put it simply: because of changes in the stringency of constraints there are periods when one feels one has to keep commodity prices (given cost prices) fixed and others where one feels one might with impunity change them.

Such a theory of price change under uncertainty is frequently confused with the primitive idea that entrepreneurs *determine their profits by* an in-variable mark-up on cost. It has frequently been pointed out that mark-ups are not at all as fixed as entrepreneurs try to make them out. But much more important: mark-ups can be only calculated on *conjectural* cost. Quite a larger part of cost, especially of course in wholesale and retail trade, the typical fields of mark-up pricing behaviour, is, however, determined by the *speed of sale*: interest charges on carrying inventory, carried, storage and spoilage costs, etc., are time-dependent. If the speed of sale declines this can drastically lower profit in spite of a 'constant' mark-up on conjectural (wrongly estimated) cost. If sales follow a probability distribution in which the variance of the sales stream over time is a positive function of its mean, it can be shown that a falling sales' speed not only lowers *average* profit but also *increases* the *variance* of profit for each individual firm, thus doubly increasing the likeli-hood of a loss.[1]

As the last discussion has already shown, it may be a useful device to mirror the unforeseen raising and lowering of constraints on behaviour imposed by other individuals by a probability distribution of events, especially for long-run models. (See also Appendix B.) Individual optimisa-tion then corresponds to the mean of the probability distribution *without* a variance, while the full model — possibly shifting the relevant mean — has to embody the appropriately specified variances. Models embodying a stochastic process are therefore frequently the appropriate microeconomic foundation of a macroeconomic analysis.[2]

We have so far discussed a short-run variant of the Kaldor model of

---

[1] I have elaborated this point with the use of several stochastic models in Streissler (1974a) p. 33 ff.

[2] I have been stressing this point since Streissler (1969a, 1969b).

distribution in situations where some free capacity is available; now to the limiting case of full employment and full capacity. What if in this state spending plans do not harmonise but exceed the producable total? Optimising behaviour of all individuals does not tell us what would happen then. Evidently not all plans can be realised; and underfulfilment of plans will sometimes be more, sometimes less, noticeable.

But which plans are more likely to be fulfilled? Again, the answer is: this depends on the degree of constraints on behaviour of the individuals imposed by others or, as I like to put it in that context, the hierarchy of plans[1] determines which plans are to be fulfilled first or (relatively) to the fullest. The model again points to investment plans as the plans 'most likely to succeed'. Entrepreneurs can not only vary investment plans more easily than households can vary their consumption plans, they can also in cases of full or near full employment *realise* their investment plans more easily than households can realise their consumption plans. By raising prices they can keep down real consumption (at least relatively to its steady growth path) and thus make room for an increase of the real investment share: booms are frequently marked by a less than average growth of real consumption and a more than average growth of consumption prices. Thus modern entrepreneurs with some price-strategic latitude (oligopoloid and monopoloid firms) and with some help from the banks can, in situations of full employment, impose more binding constraints on households than vice versa; and by doing so they also change the short-run picture of distribution.

We make one final note on the Kaldor model. In the long-run version of Pasinetti (1962)[2] it is pointed out that it is illogical to assume that workers save out of the profit income (which accrues to them because of their previous savings) at the *capitalists'* savings rate; they should do so at their proper workers' rate. This is, however, not necessarily so because of the constraints imposed upon them: perhaps the workers, as far as they become part-time capitalists, are *forced* to save like capitalists out of their profit income; i.e., they are given no other choice. This is institutionally so if they invest in the shares of corporations. Corporations have not only the historic function of acting as *collecting points* of capital but also that of acting as its retaining vessel: by taking the decision about the amount of profit to be withdrawn from the firm out of the hands of the individual investors, they ensure a higher rate of retention of profits; and especially so when profits rise fast during a boom but are needed for extra investment. If workers do not constitute the majority of shareholders they may thus have no decisive say in the amount of retained earnings and will have to acquiesce in the saving decisions of their 'purely' capitalist brethren.

[1] See Streissler (1972) p. 49 ff.
[2] For empirical evidence that in the post-war world they did indeed do so, see Streissler (1969d) p. 164 ff.

V   THE REPERCUSSIONS OF PROBABLE CONSTRAINTS ON INDIVIDUAL OPTIMISATION

The knowledge that the outcome of individual action depends upon the actions taken by others and is constrained by them has important repercussions on individual behaviour itself. Individuals prepare in advance for the likelihood of making forecasting errors and consequently of making decisions later revealed as suboptimal. They prepare in advance for the likelihood that some others are going to make grievous errors of judgement.

To run an enterprise with a certain amount of free capacity in normal times, or, if the firm is able to shift the burden upon the customer, to run a business with an order book, a waiting list of customers, is evidently a consequence of a basic residue of unpredictability in demand. The prevalence of extreme full employment assumptions in economic theory would seem to show that it is still not sufficiently understood that no good macroeconomic theory can neglect such factors making for a certain leeway of the economy or its ability to accomodate unforeseen changes.[1] Apart from the nowadays tiny amount of stocks necessary because of a *known* divergence in production and demand dates (formerly this proportion was of greater importance because of the mainly agrarian character of economies), stocks and monetary balances for transaction purposes also serve to cushion against the 'random' variations in demand and possibly also in supply.

What seems, to my mind, least well understood is that in situations of uncertain demand and supply (in other words nearly always) optimisers experience a need to formulate *secondary plans* in case their primary plans meet a constraint, the likelihood of the occurrence of which is foreseen. Most reserves in physical as well as in financial terms try to remove a constraint and are thus due to such a precautionary formulation of secondary plans. Solely due to secondary plans is the use of credit lines. No sensible entrepreneur will e.g., formulate investment plans without specifying what kind of finance is to be resorted to if the expected amount of profit needed to meet the requirements of finance does not fully materialise. Today, contracts often have open-ended price clauses. No sensible entrepreneur will fail to specify what should be done in order to meet greater liabilities if the price turns out to be higher than originally expected. A macroeconomic analysis has to take account of the likely average amount and likely distribution of errors in the primary plans, especially of entrepreneurs, and the likely nature of and distribution of secondary plans (and their consequences).

To my mind, the worst mistakes in the formulation of an appropriate macroeconomic theory are here made in the evaluation of short-run global restrictive measures of economic policy. The ability to carry through one's plans even in adversity and consequently the prerequisite reserves are 'luxuries', goods in increasing demand with mounting income per head. This implies that in rich countries global demand restrictions are at first fended

---

[1] This has been elaborated already long ago in Hart (1951).

off by the falling back on reserves: with economic growth the lag up to the time at which continued demand restriction becomes effective is constantly increasing. Thus the ability of the government to impose constraints on expenditure, the knowledge of citizens that governments have this ability, and with rising incomes their desire and ability to arm themselves against restrictions frustrate the effectiveness of this very policy-imposed macro-economic constraint. More precisely, the hedges against the bite of demand restriction by fiscal policy are a cause of the stop-go nature of much of present policy. Demand restriction has to be imposed for long periods until it becomes effective; when it does so (reserves being exhausted and the need to replenish them rising) the whole accumulated restriction erupts in a sharp even cumulative setback of the economy. The same is true of restrictive credit policy. Here, existing credit lines are used up to the hilt and time and savings deposits are withdrawn. Thus current expenditure, which has already been planned for, is hardly diminished. The banks, however, become all the more unable to finance any *new* projects and future plans; so expenditure, after some time, is liable to drop off sharply and suddenly: See Streissler (1972).

One of my former collaborators, Nikolaus Läufer (1970, p. 290 ff.), has built a model of secondary plans in the form of a *plan revision matrix*. It is very similar to an input—output matrix specifying what percentage of an excess demand manifesting itself in one market is switched around to other markets and becomes excess demand there. Thus the unexpected excess demand (the error) in one market (as input) 'produces' (so to speak as output) excess demands in the same (inflexible behaviour) or in other markets (flexible behaviour).[1] The liquidity preference theory − e.g., in the interpretation of Rose (1957, p. 111 ff.) − would imply that an unexpected excess demand in the investment market (as input) would create a secondary plan (as output) which keeps excess demand in the investment market constant (one does not permit one's investment plans to be disturbed by lower profits) and runs down monetary balances (creates excess demand in the money market) by an *equal* amount, while the loanable funds theory according to that author would imply a secondary plan also keeping excess demand in the investment market constant but creating an excess demand in the market for bank credit (or for bonds) to an equal amount (e.g., running down credit lines). The exact pattern of these plan revision or switch coefficients, taken in conjunction with the price sensitivity of the excess demands (or the sensitivity of prices to excess demands), determines the stability of an economy's reaction to unexpected displacements from equilibrium. Läufer shows that, if one linked either the extreme liquidity preference model or the extreme loanable funds model to the price sensitivities empirically found in Germany in 1950−67, this would in both cases result in an unstable adjustment process. Thus economic stability is crucially dependent upon the

---

[1] A similar analysis, stressing a 'second round' utility maximisation of asset holding, is sketched in Rader (1972) p. 310 ff.

distribution among individuals of secondary plan behaviour in response to constraints experienced and of the distribution of these evasive or assertive actions between markets. To my mind, the reason why many global equilibrium models show instabilities as their result, while actual economies are apparently much more stable, appears to lie in the canny mixture of evasive and assertive actions of individuals in reality, once the constraints of the plans of others on their own plans bite while the models are devoid of representations of such adaptive behaviour.

A second type of planning in expectation of planning mistakes is *speculative* behaviour. Speculative balances are always held in the hope of profiting from the mistakes of others. They are either held because one thinks oneself cleverer than the 'market' (i.e., the reflection in a price of a weighted average of the expectations of others); or they are held because one hopes to profit either from the lack of knowledge of the market price by a seller or his need to sell below it in distress sales. Both if one hopes to profit from a rise in price of a stock held by oneself but not held by others and if one hopes to profit from distress sales by others, one assumes that the actions of others are more constrained than one's own: speculation to a large extent depends upon the *distribution* of constraints between persons. It *always* depends upon *either* the differences in expectations between individuals *or* differences in their constraints on the ability to act according to their expectations. 'It is interesting that the stability of the system and its sensitiveness to changes in the quantity of money should be so dependent on the existence of a *variety* of opinion about what is uncertain', Keynes (1936, p. 172) sums up his characterisation of the stock market as a speculative market.

It is frequently forgotten that speculative markets can never be correctly explained as long as the differences of expectations and of constraints as between individuals are neglected. For instance, Mill's (1848, Book IV, Chapter 11, §4, 5) model (revived by Friedman (1953, p. 174 ff) of the stabilising nature of profitable speculation may have many flaws:[1] but it certainly has the one very simple flaw that it assumes *one* single type of speculator. Insiders can very well thrive upon the elimination of outsiders by behaving in such a way as to destabilise markets. In fact, outsiders need not even be eliminated. Contrary to the most hopeful proponents of flexible exchange rates[2] the foreign exchange markets under that system appear to show very little tendency towards stability. To my mind, this is so because with fluctuating exchange rates exporters and importers are frequently tempted or even forced to enter as *part-time* speculators in the foreign exchange markets (perhaps the State, which cannot go bankrupt, underwrites their flutter). They are constrained from becoming full-time speculators by the amount of time and attention they can profitably devote to exchange rates and also by a lack of credit resources. Hopefully, they will make their

[1] See especially Farrell (1966) p. 183 ff.
[2] For instance (apart from Friedman) see Sohmen (1961) Chapter 3.

profit on their commodity sale, their normal business. As a group, they can thus support a constant loss on their 'speculative' sideline without going to the wall (the State may share in their 'charity' sideline). Speculators can find a constant source of gain, even if they destabilise the market.

Speculation depends upon differences in behaviour. It is therefore representative of a class of economic phenomena where in a sense there can be no microeconomic foundation to macroeconomics. In a sense all microeconomic models of speculation[1] and even microeconomic models of the optimal inventory type[2] assume that the actor can benefit from being cleverer than the rest without affecting their actions significantly. At least he can benefit from a fixed institutional set-up, given transaction charges, e.g., for macroeconomic purposes such models may be extended by assuming that there are small specialised groups acting in the way described. By their very nature these models must, however, break down when they are extended equally to everybody. (At the very least we have then to ask whether an equilibrium reflecting a certain type of behaviour of all individuals can be found.) Though it may be just conceivable that everybody *thinks* he is brighter than everybody else − in which case we build a model of constantly frustrated expectations − a model which assumes that everybody in fact *is* brighter than everybody else would belong to that important and not at all empty set of economic models: the logically impossible ones.

VI   OCCAM'S RAZOR AND INDIVIDUAL OPTIMISATION

The need for a substructure of macroeconomic models built upon a foundation of individual optimisation is often argued. It is asserted that only the aggregation of individual optima can yield determinate macroeconomic results. To my mind, this chain of reasoning, offered as a methodological rule without exception, shows important flaws. On the one hand, it is not at all certain that the individual behaviour of those who stay throughout within the decision group on which the economic aggregate depends over time determines the value of that aggregate; it can very well be that the *inflow and outflow of individuals* into and out of the decision group in question has a much greater effect. But even where individual behaviour in an approximately constant decision group is decisive, much more general types of regular behaviour within this group can, together with a constraint, explain the same result as that derived from rational individual optimisation. The principle of Occam's razor would then counsel the relegation of the rational optimisation model to a more modest role: it makes a certain macroeconomic theorem didactically plausible, while its likely predictive accuracy has to be derived from a survey of other types of behaviour, from which it would also (or would not) result.

The importance of the inflow and outflow of individuals into decision

---

[1] I have tried to construct such a model in Streissler (1973) p. 164 ff.
[2] Typically for instance the well-known model of Baumol (1952) p. 545 ff.

groups has been stressed by Steindl.[1] By a complicated derivation of the
relevant probability distributions he shows that measures of concentration of
employment or of production within an industry depend at least as sensitively
upon the rate of entrance of new firms and the rate of 'mortality' of firms as
upon the growth experience of firms, once they are in an industry. A similar
argument applies to the derivation of many income elasticities of demand
from time-series data. They can depend much more upon the inflow of new
customers, which is correlated with a rise in the *general* level of income, than
upon the purchase behaviour of old customers, who either buy larger quantities or buy more frequently, depending upon a rise in their individual
incomes. In a similar vein Hickman (1959, p. 535 ff) has argued that the
accelerator can be derived by looking at the percentage of firms experiencing
growth or in other words the inflow and outflow of individuals into the class
of the growth firms.

The venerable 'law of demand' — quantitative demand of a good falling
with a rise in price — has been proved in uncountably many ways with the
help of numerous formalisations of rational choice behaviour of the individual
consumers. These endeavours have certainly been fruitful in illuminating
many aspects of economics. But for the central question to be proved the
assumption of rational choice is not even necessary; it is a candidate for
Occam's razor.[2] If we wish to derive the negative slope with respect to price
of a demand curve not compensated for the real income effect of a price
change (and that is, after all, the only type of demand curve we observe in
practice) the budget constraint alone can take the main load of the argument.
With a rise in price of commodity A and constant nominal income that is
fully spent (or with a constant average savings rate) a formerly chosen bundle
of commodities including A can no longer be chosen: a *smaller* quantity of
some commodity has to be purchased. To this basic fact, solely due to a
constraint, we have then only to link some assumption about behaviour
ensuring that the decline in consumption will affect *not only other* commodities than A, the price of which has risen. *One* such assumption is the
usual model of rational substitution. But we could also assume that the
decision-taker keeps constant the *proportion* of the quantities purchased of
each commodity; be it that he has a habitually fixed relative consumption
bundle or be it that he acts only on impulse, buying quantities haphazardly
till his budget is exhausted, a behaviour which would yield the same result of
fixed proportions for the average of consumers: see Figure 4:2. In this simple
case all purchases decline proportionately, the quantity purchased of commodity A being affected by its price rise just as much as all other purchases.
(The uncompensated price elasticity of the demand curve for A is negative,

[1] Steindl (1965) p. 57, p. 70 ff; (1968) p. 295 ff.

[2] Similarly it can be proved that a unique equilibrium price corresponding to the
competitive price can be established in a market where no firm maximises but if a
variable exceeds a certain constraint to the 'non-action' box merely follows very simple
decision rules. See Rothschild (1973) p. 1283 ff., especially models by Winter.

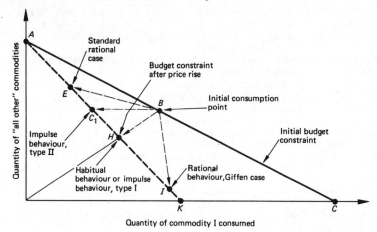

Figure 4:2   Budget Constraint and The 'Law of Demand'

though here the compensated elasticity is zero.) Another model of impulse behaviour yields an even stronger result: if the consumer purchases haphazardly always 'a pound's worth' of anything that takes his fancy, then, with a rise in price of commodity A alone, all other purchases will on an average stay constant in quantity; for there still is the same amount of (nominal) pounds to be scattered around. The quantity of A purchased will, however, decline in strict proportion to the price rise[1] (unitary absolute uncompensated price elasticity). A practically unlimited number of other models of arational consumer behaviour could be constructed, all of course crucially dependent upon the budget constraint, and all yielding, practically indistinguishably, the 'law of demand'.[2]

This proves a final important point: when a certain meso- or macroeconomic result can be derived from a certain set of assumptions on individual optimisation, empirical verification of this meso- or macroeconomic result must never be construed as to be evidence for the prevalence of that type of individual optimising behaviour, from which it just happens to have been accidentally derived in that one theory.

REFERENCES

G. A. Akerlof, 'The Demand for Money: A General Equilibrium Inventory – Theoretic Approach', *Review of Economic Studies*, Vol. XL (1), No 121 (January 1973) pp. 115–38.

R. G. D. Allen and J. R. Hicks, 'A Reconsideration of the Theory of Value', Part I, *Economica*, New Series, Vol. 1 (February 1934) pp. 52–75; Part II (May 1934) pp. 196–219.

[1] See Becker (1962) p. 1 ff: (1963) p. 505 ff.
[2] See Streissler (1974b) p. 1086 ff., here p. 1090 ff.

W. J. Baumol, 'The Transactions Demand for Cash: An Inventory Theoretic Approach', *Quarterly Journal of Economics*, Vol. LXVI, No 4 (November 1952) pp. 545–6.

G. S. Becker, 'Irrational Behavior and Economic Theory', *Journal of Political Economy*, Vol. LXX, No 1 (February 1962) pp. 1–13.

R. Cantillon, *Essai sur la Nature du Commerce en Général, 1755* (English translation (H. Higgs, ed.), Macmillan, 1931).

J. F. Chant, 'Irrational Behaviour and Economic Theory – A Comment', *Journal of Political Economy*, Vol. LXXI, No 5 (September/October 1963) pp. 505–10.

R. W. Clower, 'The Keynesian Counter-revolution: A Theoretical Appraisal', in R. W. Clower (ed.), *Monetary Theory* (Harmondsworth: Penguin, 1969).

M. J. Farrell, 'Profitable Speculation', *Economica*, New Series, Vol. XXXIII, No 130 (May 1966) pp. 183–93.

M. Friedman, *Essays in Positive Economics* (Chicago University Press, 1963).

A. G. Hart, *Anticipation, Uncertainty and Dynamic Planning* (Chicago University Press, 1951).

F. A. von Hayek, *Geltheroie und Konjunkturtheorie* (Vienna: Hölder-Pichler-Tempsky, 1929).

F. A. von Hayek, 'Investment that Raises the Demand for Capital', *Review of Economics and Statistics*, Vol. LIX, No 4 (November 1937) pp. 174–7.

F. A. von Hayek, *Der wettbewerb als entdeckungsverfahren* (Kiel: Institut für Weltwirtschaft, 1968).

F. A. von Hayek, 'Three Elucidations of the Ricardo Effect', *Journal of Political Economy*, Vol. LXXVII, No 2 (March/April 1969) pp. 274–85.

B. G. Hickman, 'Diffusion, Acceleration and Business Cycles', *American Economic Review*, Vol. LIX, No. 4 (September 1959) pp. 535–65.

J. R. Hicks, *Value and Capital. An Inquiry into Some Fundamental Principles of Economic Theory* (Oxford: Clarendon Press, 2nd ed., 1939).

J. R. Hicks, 'Methods of Dynamic Analysis' in *Twenty-five Economic Essays in Honour of Erik Lindahl* (Stockholm: Ekonomisk Tidskrift, 1956) pp. 139–51.

H. G. Johnson, *The Theory of Income Distribution* (London: Gray-Mills, 1973).

N. L. Johnson and S. Kotz, *Distribution in Statistics, Continuous Univariate Statistics*, Vol. I (Boston: Houghton-Mifflin, 1970).

N. Kaldor, 'Alternative Theories of Distribution', *Review of Economic Studies*, Vol. XXXIII, No 60 (1955–6) pp. 83–100.

J. M. Keynes, *The General Theory of Employment, Interest and Money* (London: Macmillan, 1936).

N. K. A. Läufer, 'Liquidity Preference and Loanable Funds, the Theory of Neutral Revision Behaviour', *Zeitschrift für Nationalökonomie*, Bol. XXX, HEFT 3–4 (August-December 1970) pp. 291–308.

B. Manderville, *The Fable of the Bees or Private Vices, Publick Benefits* (D. Garman (ed.) (London: Wishart, 1934).

A. Marshall, *Principles of Economics* (1890, Variorium Edition, C. W. Guillebaud, ed., London: Macmillan, 1961).

K. Marx, *Das Kapital* (Hamburg 1867; Berlin: Marx-Engels – Gesamtausgabe, 1969).

C. Menger, *Grundsätze der Volkswirtschaftslehre* (Vienna: Braumuller, 1871).

J. S. Mill, *Principles of Political Economy* (London: Parker, 1848).

F. Modigliani and R. Brumberg, 'Utility Analysis and the Consumption Function: An Interpretation of Cross-section Data', in K. Kurihara (ed.), *Post Keynesian Economics* (New Brunswick: Rutgers University Press, 1954) pp. 388–436.

O. Morgenstern, 'Thirteen Critical Points in Contemporary Economic Theory: An Interpretation', *Journal of Economic Literature*, Vol. X, No 4 (December 1972) pp. 1163–89.

M. Morishima, *Theory of Economic Growth* (Oxford: Clarendon Press, 1969).

L. L. Pasinetti, 'Rate of Profit and Income Distribution in Relation to the Rate of Economic Growth', *Review of Economic Studies*, Vol. XXIX, No. 81 (1962) pp. 267–79.

E. S. Phelps, *et al.* (eds), *Microeconomic Foundations of Employment and Inflation Theory* (New York: Norton, 1970).

L. S. Pressnell, 'The Rate of Interest in the Eighteenth Century' in L. S. Pressnell (ed), *Studies in the Industrial Revolution*, presented to T. S. Ashton (London: Athlone Press, 1960), pp. 178–214.

T. Rader, *Theory of General Economic Equilibrium* (New York: Academic Press, 1972).

G. B. Richardson, *Information and Investment – A Study in the Working of the Competitive Economy* (London: Oxford University Press, 1960).

H. Rose, 'Liquidity Preference and Loanable Funds', *Review of Economic Studies*, Vol. XXIV, No 64 (1957) pp. 111–19.

M. Rothschild, 'Models of Market Organisation with Imperfect Information: A Survey', *Journal of Political Economy*, Vol. 81, No 6 (November/December 1973) pp. 1283–308.

M. Shubik, 'A Theory of Money and Banking in a General Equilibrium System', Research memorandum No 48, of the Institute of Advanced Studies (Vienna: July 1970).

M. Shubik, 'The General Equilibrium Model is the Wrong Model and a Nonco-operative Strategic Process Model is a Satisfactory Model for the Reconciliation of Micro and Macro-economic Theory', Cowles Foundation discussion paper No 365 (November 1973).

A. H. Simon, *Models of Man – Social and Rational* (New York: Wiley, 1957).

E. Sohmen, *Flexible Exchange Rates, Theory and Controversy* (Chicago University Press, 1961).

J. Steindl, *Random Processes and the Growth of Firms – A Study of the Pareto Law* (London: Griffin, 1965).

J. Steindl, 'Size Distributions in Economics', *Encyclopedia of the Social Sciences*, Vol. XIV (1968), pp. 295–300.

G. J. Stigler, 'The Economics of Information', *Journal of Political Economy*, Vol. LXIX, No 3 (June 1961) pp. 213–25.

E. Streissler, 'Structural Economic Thought – On the Significance of the Austrian School Today', *Zeitschrift für Nationalökonomie*, Bol. XXIX, HEFT 3–4 (August/December 1969a), pp. 237–66.

E. Streissler, 'A Stochastic Model of International Reserve Requirements during Growth of World Trade', *Zeitschrift für Nationalökonomie* Bol. XXIX, HEFT 3–4, (August/December 1969b), pp. 347–70.

E. Streissler, 'Hayek on Growth: A Reconsideration of his Early Work' in E. Streissler *et al.* (eds), *Roads to Freedom, Essays in Honour of Friedrich A. von Hayek* (London: Routledge & Kegan Paul, 1969c) pp. 245–85.

E. Streissler, 'A Reexamination of the Haavelmo-Bias in the Least Squares Estimation of the Keynesian Consumption Function', *Metrika*, Vol. XIV (1969d) pp. 164–82.

E. Streissler, 'Monetäre Unsicherheitstheorie bei Menger und Keynes', in G. Bombach (ed.) *Studien zur Geldtheorie und Monetäre Ökonometrie* (Berlin: Duncker & Humblot, 1972a), pp. 39–60.

E. Streissler, 'Investment Stimulation and the Hierarchy of Individual Plans', in W. Schmitz (ed.), *Convertibility, Multilateralism and Freedom, Essays in Honour of Reinhard Kamitz* (New York and Vienna: Springer, 1972b) pp. 49–65.

E. Streissler, 'To What Extent was the Austrian School Marginalist?', in R. D. Collison Black, A. W. Coats and C. D. W. Goodwin, *The Marginal Revolution in Economics – Interpretation and Evaluation* (Durham, North Carolina: Duke University Press, 1973a) pp. 160–75.

E. Streissler, 'Menger's Theories of Money and Uncertainty – A Modern Interpretation', in J. R. Hicks and W. Weber (eds), *Carl Menger and the Austrian School of Economics* (Oxford: Clarendon Press, 1973b) pp. 164–89.

E. Streissler, 'Verteilungstheorie ausserhalb der Neoklassischen Preistheorie', in G. Bombach *et al.* (eds), *Neue Aspekte der Verteilungstheorie* (Tübingen: Mohr–Siebeck, 1974a) pp. 33–42.

E. Streissler, 'Konsumtheorien', in *Handwörterbuch der Absatzwirtschaft* (Stuttgart: Pöschel, 1974b) pp. 1086–103.

W. Stützel, *Volkswirtschaftliche Saldenmechanik – ein Beitrag zur Geldtheorie* (Tübingen: Mohr-Siebeck, 1958).

R. J. Sweeney, *A Macro Theory with Micro-Foundations* (Cincinnati: South-Western, 1974).

H. Theil, *Linear Aggregation of Economic Relations* (Amsterdam: North Holland, 1954).

Appendix A

The life-cycle hypothesis of consumption assumes that total income over the life-cycle is fully consumed. During working life savings are accumulated which are then fully spent during retirement. If the population is stationary and income streams over time conform to expectations, no macroeconomic savings would result in equilibrium. No accumulation of wealth to be handed over to future generations takes place.[1]

This reasoning has a flaw in its microeconomic foundation. Under the principle of collective risk a *large* group of individuals acting *together* can plan their savings and dissavings for periods conforming to the *average life expectancy* of the population as a whole. But a *single* individual can never do so rationally; for the probability is large that he might live for *longer* than the average, in which case he would be reduced to penury. He could rationally pursue either of two courses of action: he could either plan to accumulate during working life a sum which would allow him to consume up to his *maximum possible age*, say 100 years (just as in Stigler's model of search[2] not the average, but an *extreme* value of a distribution, in this case the age distribution, is microeconomically relevant); or he could *revise* his consumption-saving plans with *every year* actually lived, which also changes his life expectancy. In the latter case when entering working life at, say, 25 years of age he would start to accumulate a fund which would tide him over till the end of his life expectancy at the age of 25 of, say, 70 years. Once he reaches the age of 26 he has to *step up* his savings a fraction, for now his life expectancy is, say 70·05 years. If he actually reaches retirement age of, say, 65, he can spend his fund up to, say, age 75, his life expectancy at age 65. With every year lived his life expectancy increases, in very old age in fact by about half a year for every year lived, which then is a very substantial proportion of his total remaining life expectancy. Such a savings plan, involving *changing conditional probabilities*, would *explain* the rising saving propensity of old people which we find empirically.

Under both these assumptions of individual optimisation additional wealth accrues to future generations, *in spite of the fact that no individual plans to save for posterity*. This is due to the savings, not yet used up, of people who *expected* to live longer than they actually do. In both cases the actual amount of macroeconomic savings depends upon the *mortality distribution* in the population as a whole.

[1] See, for instance, Modigliani and Brumberg (1954) p. 388 ff.
[2] Stigler (1961) p. 213 ff.

Appendix B

Macroeconomic statements can sometimes be derived solely from a consideration of the mean value and the variance of constraints linked to a very simple decision rule.

Take the following situation: an individual plans to have a fixed outflow per period. He is, however, constrained to achieve this outflow unless he has a corresponding inflow during this period of at least to the same amount. For instance a fixed expenditure is planned which cannot be achieved if the income during the period falls short of planned expenditure. Calling the actual outflow (expenditure) d, the planned expenditure d^*, the expected inflow (income) y^*, and the actual inflow (income) y, we would then observe the following behaviour pattern:

$$d = y \quad \text{for } y \leqslant y^*; d \leqslant d^*$$

$$d = y^* \text{ for } y \geqslant y^*; d = d^* \tag{1}$$

Now assume that the actual inflow (income) y is not a point variable but one obeying a continuous probability density function $f(y)$. The average expenditure D of a 'representative' individual from infinitely many would then be:

$$D = \int_{\infty}^{y^*} yf(y)dy + y^* \int_{y^*}^{+\infty} f(y)dy = m - \int_{y^*}^{+\infty} (y - y^*)f(y)dy \tag{2}$$

where m is the mean of the inflow (income) probability distribution. (If we admit only positive values of inflow the lower boundary of integration would be zero; but this does not change any of the following results.) Note that the average outflow (expenditure) D falls short of the average inflow (income) m. Denote by S, or average 'saving' per individual, this difference ($S = m - D$) and by s the average 'savings' rate with respect to income

$$\left(s = \frac{S}{m} = 1 - \frac{D}{m} \right).$$

Now to bring out the point to be established more sharply let us assume that *average* inflow (income) is *correctly foreseen* ($y^* = m$) and a fixed expenditure of the same amount planned ($d^* = m$). No savings would accrue in this case if income were a point variable. But as it is distributed in our model and thereby constrains expenditure in part we get positive savings of the following size:

$$s = \frac{1}{m} \int_{m}^{+\infty} (y - m)f(y)dy = \frac{\delta}{2m} \tag{3}$$

where δ is the mean absolute deviation from the mean. This is so because:

$$\delta = -\int_{-\infty}^{m} (y-m)f(y)dy + \int_{m}^{+\infty} (y-m)f(y)dy \qquad (4)$$

$$\int_{m}^{+\infty} (y-m)f(y)dy = -\int_{-\infty}^{m} (y-m)f(y)dy \qquad (5)$$

$$\int_{-\infty}^{+\infty} yf(y)dy - m\int_{-\infty}^{+\infty} f(y)dy = m - m = 0$$

The absolute mean deviation is a measure of variation in the wider sense. For many distributions (for instance for all Pearson type distributions) it is, furthermore, linked parametrically to the variance.[1] Thus the contention immediately follows: *Even if planned expenditure is fixed at the correctly foreseen level of income a greater variation of income – and thus a greater variance also of the constraining part of income – will lower relative expenditure.* In the simple model given, a greater variation of income (higher mean absolute deviation) without a change in mean income or with a change in mean income correctly foreseen and adjusted to increases the savings rate.

With suitably skew probability distributions of incomes even Keynes's 'psychological law' of an increasing savings 'propensity' with rising (average) income can be derived without psychology, but only from constraints. This can be done in two ways:

(I) If a rise in income leads to an *underestimation* of that average income to which the fixed expenditure is adjusted, a rise in the savings rate with rising income will result for all those distributions, where the mean absolute deviation from the mean is *proportional* to the mean (the savings rate thus being unaffected by correctly foreseen average income changes). For with underestimation nobody will save less and everybody who has a higher income than the underestimated average, at which expenditure is fixed, will save more: so that the savings rate, invariant for correct foresight, will be raised. This will be the case, for instance, if income is distributed either according to a gamma-distribution $g(y)$ or the exponential distribution $h(y)$:

$$g(y) = a^2 y e^{-ay} \quad (6a) \qquad\qquad h(y) = be^{-by} \qquad (6b)$$

$$s_g = \frac{\delta_g g}{2m_g} = \frac{2}{e^2} \quad (7a) \qquad\qquad s_h = \frac{\delta_h h}{2m_h} = \frac{1}{e} \qquad (7b)$$

(II) Even for *correct* foresight and *full adjustment* of planned expenditure

[1] See Johnson and Kotz (1970) p. 15, 20.

to a higher average income a higher savings rate results for the Pareto distribution $p(y)$, which is frequently applied to income analysis (though here, of course, to chance income receipt per period):

$$p(y) = \frac{ck^c}{y^{c+1}}; \quad \delta_p = \frac{2k}{c-1}\left(1 - \frac{1}{c}\right)^{c-1}; \quad m_p = \frac{ck}{c-1}; \quad c > 1 \tag{8}$$

$$s_p = \frac{1}{c-1}\left(1 - \frac{1}{c}\right)^c = \frac{m-k}{k}\left(\frac{k}{m}\right)^{m/m-k} \quad (m = m_p \text{ for short}) \tag{9}$$

$$\frac{dsp}{dc}\frac{c}{sp} = cln\frac{c-1}{c} < 0 \tag{10}$$

The elasticity of the savings rate with respect to the parameter c, of which — with given k, the minimum income — mean income is a monotonically falling function, is negative. Thus in our constraint model with a Pareto income distribution the *savings rate rises with rising average income* correctly adjusted to.

Discussion of the Paper by Professor Streissler

Dr Sweeney opened the discussion by saying that he found it a pleasure to introduce Professor Streissler's fine paper: not only was it very interesting, but it evoked memories of the Austrian teachers under whom he had studied. The paper demonstrated the historical continuity in economic thought and also the use of knowledge of the history of the discipline as a tool to advance it. He wanted to begin with what he thought were the most important contributions of the paper.

Professor Streissler had stressed 'keeping our eye on the ball'; that is, on the constraints in the system that 'really bite'. He had given two extended examples of what he meant by constraints and how they worked. In Hayek's monetary model of the business cycle the equilibrating function of price was unused: the interest rate charged by banks on credit was relatively constant, so when demand for it was great, credit had to be rationed. Professor Streissler emphasised two aspects of this example: first, the credit rationing mechanism — a constraint mechanism — was the key to understanding Hayek's effort; second, Professor Streissler argued that empirically the credit rationing assumption 'fitted' well enough for Austria. Thus the investigation of 'biting' constraints was a possible technique for analysing the fundamentals of a given author's macroeconomic theory; in addition, empirical investigation to discover the 'stringent' constraints on an economy could possibly show what deserved to be placed at the core of a macroeconomic model of a given economy.

What Professor Streissler was urging was the development of an art, rather than the application of a technique. For example, extending the theory of the neoclassical firm under conditions of certainty was by and large the application of technique; the art lay in choosing the application, the elegance in use of the technique. Professor Streissler's argument that economists might well profit from a search for key constraints provided no paradigm as to how best to do this.

This was especially so because Professor Streissler had a quite catholic view of constraints. Dr Sweeney wished Professor Machlup were present, for it might then be appropriate gently to chide one Austrian for neglecting another's sound advice to put indices on a word when it was used with several different meanings. He had counted eight different ways in which Professor Streissler had used the word 'constraint'. With respect to this catholicity two examples on the third page of the paper [p. 98] were revealing. The first was the derivation of one version of the maxim 'Supply creates its own demand' from individuals' budget constraints and the accounting principle that the sum of the values of the excess demands equalled zero. The only behavioural content of this example was the assumption of non-satiation; and even this could be avoided with the fiction of 'disposal activities'. The next sentence, however, referring to the Hayek model went: '. . . an increase in the supply of credit increases investment, for entrepreneurs, starved for credit (the constraint on their behaviour), always lap it up and use it to enlarge plant'. This was dependent on the *behaviour* of both demanders and suppliers of credit.

The familiar problems regarding accounting identities and 'supply creates its own demand' could mostly be settled on logical grounds, for example, the recognition that income-constrained excess demands were not the same as Walrasian excess demands. Professor Streissler's second example, based on Hayek, held potential for much the same sort of logical pitfalls as his first: given non-zero excess demand for credit, in what sense were other excess demands zero or non-zero and what was the relationship between, say, the Walrasian excess demand for money and the credit-constrained demand? Beyond this were the *empirical* problems of determining if credit rationing was binding, and if so in the *stringent* way Professor Streissler rightly required for it to take centre stage?

Dr Sweeney thought that we could use these two examples to get some insight into Professor Streissler's insistence that we ought to reduce the emphasis on full-blown microeconomic modelling in looking for the foundations of macroeconomics. In his concluding section on Occam's razor Professor Streissler had argued that the downward-sloping demand curve could be derived from individuals' budget constraints plus any of a host of behavioural assumptions (some of which might seem irrational). Thus one apparently did not need the superstructure of utility maximisation, revealed preference, etc. However, although anyone doing policy research knew that frequently nothing beyond a downward-sloping demand curve was needed for a fairly robust conclusion, the explanation of the downward-sloping demand curve for factors of production, to, say, non-mathematical undergraduates could be rather difficult *even with* a maximising superstructure.

Dr Sweeney admitted that some economic propositions were intuitive: for example, that the increase in quantity demanded was larger for a price cut the longer the given cut was maintained; but he wanted to add two *caveats*. First, in formal derivation of a proposition interesting and surprising implications could often fall out along the way. Second, and much more important, the central proposition of a theory (including a simple theory reasoning from constraints) might be difficult or impossible to test because of, for instance, data limitations. If we were lucky we might be able to test subsidiary propositions of the theory in order to discriminate between competing theories. It would be a pity not to erect the superstructure necessary to glean such subsidiary information. Dr Sweeney did not think Professor Streissler would disagree with this as he had called for rigid checking to see that constraint theories were accurately getting to the heart of the matter, and this would often call for theoretical elaboration. He thought that in so far as Professor Streissler was merely urging us to eschew elaboration for its own sake, we ought *as macroeconomists* to agree (though we might well derive some satisfaction from elaboration *per se*).

Dr Sweeney then turned to those matters where he had stronger disagreement with Professor Streissler. The 'petrified man' of the price-taking representative firm under perfect competition was not a 'straw man', but he was one whom time had passed by and ossified to preserve for historians of thought. The price-taking assumption had to go in the new microeconomics – the auctioneer was dead. The perfect certainty assumption was sometimes still useful *if* recognised as a mere device for some limited purposes. The representative firm should, however, stay. He recalled Professor Machlup's longstanding contention that economic theory was intended to give comparative static predictions, not precise maxima. Thus perfect certainty assumptions *need* not be bad and the representative firm could be rehabilitated as a device giving the qualitative comparative statics for all firms. (The question of to what extent such findings could be aggregated was crucial to whether macroeconomics was viable but that was the topic of other papers.) He agreed with Professor Streissler that firms' reactions to others' behaviour and the variance in that behaviour was important, but he thought this *could* be handled by reasoning with the representative firm.

Dr Sweeney said that he had ambivalent feelings about Professor Streissler's treatment of the stochastic nature of the model. Though agreeing with Thomas Hardy that chance is the 'warp and woof of life', he was not convinced that there was a meaningful sense in which massive increases in uncertainty improved constraint-theorising's ability relative to more detailed modelling. He was not sure that one could usefully think of reserves, inventories, etc., as possible constraints that might become effective, in the same category as credit rationing or the budget constraint. In an optimising model inventories were *chosen* as *ex ante* optimal; if the process were repeated a large number of times they would be judged *ex post* as appropriate if decisions had to be made in advance for all periods. Might not this sort of constraint just be an instance of 'Decision-making is hell under uncertainty', and not the key considerations we should look for? In fact, once we moved beyond a single key constraint such as credit rationing, to discuss the many ramifications of a stochastic world, it seemed that any clear-cut distinction between full optimisation models and constraint theorising became very fuzzy, perhaps no more than the formal *versus* the informal.

In a similar vein of doubt Dr Sweeney could not be sure whether at points the paper's argument went too far regarding constraints imposed by competitors' actions. The first mention of such a so-called *global constraint* (on p. 100) was in the context of 'Are individual optimising plans incompatible to a serious degree?', where he agreed that we needed more work on 'a systematic investigation of the question to what extent which types of economic plans will in situations of *conflict* be more fully realised than others and why'. But on p. 105 it was noted that 'if this global constraint is recognised by the individuals it supplies the rationale of collusive action'. Dr Sweeney would not like this insight about global constraints to be used to justify macroeconomic theory being made to depend on or be concerned with such facts as 'if you ate less beefsteak there would be more left for me' and 'if there were fewer economists, I would be better off' — examples of mere pecuniary externalities in the price-taking and price-searching spheres respectively. Furthermore, perhaps the best grasp we had on such situations of *conflict* was the very complex modelling of game theory, introduced to economists by von Neumann and Morgenstern. The usefulness of this tool for the present problem was demonstrated by Professor Streissler's own reference to it.

With regard to global constraints, Dr Sweeney also thought there was much insight in considering cases where, for example, the demand for output was larger than could be filled in the short run and some desired investment plans were frustrated. This provided a very important constraint on the intertemporal behaviour of the entire system. Americans had tried inflation with this sort of positive excess demand (under the Johnson administration) as well as inflation where there was no such constraint on investment (under the Nixon and Ford administrations): the behaviour of the system was in many crucial respects different depending on whether this constraint was binding on investment or not (in which case there might be unintended investment which could be viewed as a different sort of constraint). Not only had we to be careful of using this constraint in theorising, we had also to spend some serious effort on optimising models to show how results differed depending on whether the constraint was binding or not.

Dr Sweeney also disagreed with Professor Streissler about the efficiency of financial markets, particularly regarding flexible exchange rates. He thought financial markets tended to work very efficiently, particularly regarding the pricing and distribution of currently outstanding assets. For United States domestic capital markets, the theory of efficient markets and its testing were by no means completed, but the results were strongly in favour of efficiency. In foreign exchange markets, the theory and testing were less advanced. The major conceptual point was that in an efficient market a country's (detrended) exchange rate should do a 'random walk', which would produce the very kind of day-to-day oscillations that Professor Streissler offered as evidence of how unsatisfactory the current float had been. Dr Sweeney admitted that some spot and forward exchange markets showed some evidence of inefficiency, but their nature and extent and whether they were due to government policy was unclear; paradoxically, any tendency of the rate to return to a central value was evidence of *in*efficiency, contrary to Professor Streissler's evaluation. In this work a major methodological break-through was that if domestic capital markets passed the random walk statistical tests, then simple buy and sell rules based on the timepaths of prices performed less well than simply buying into the market and holding; and vice versa. In exchange markets the series could pass either test and still fail the other.

Dr Sweeney suggested that the really exciting frontier for the new micro-economics was at the juncture of macroeconomic and international phenomena, efficient markets, and rational expectations. Work was already going on concerning interest rate behaviour and the integration and efficiency of labour markets; he would not want to see Professor Streissler's excellent paper marred by the slighting of this area.

He concluded that the paper offered both many useful insights and opportunities for differing opinion and interpretation; he hoped that the discussion would concentrate on both aspects of the paper.

Professor Green echoed this hope. Professor Streissler had rightly emphasised that in moving from microeconomics to macroeconomics we tended to leave out such factors as the existence of global constraints upon investment and the implications of uncertainty for the individual micro-economic relations. However, he seemed at some points to be suggesting that in macroeconomic theory we needed to say only that investment was determined; here Professor Green hoped it would still be relevant to start with the microeconomic relations as well as taking into account global con-straints and uncertainty. There were, after all, a number of alternative useful ways in which one could reproduce the market behaviour of consumers; the global budget constraint was not the only determinant.

Professor Shubik challenged Dr Sweeney's view that the available evidence supported the efficient market hypothesis. That might be true for international money markets but it was not true for stock markets. As examples he gave the 3 to 8 per cent spread on over-the-counter dealings on the New York stock market, in some instances a 200 to 300 per cent spread between the family's and the tax collector's valuation of the stock of a closely held corporation held by a deceased member of the family, and the rapid rise in the value of a stock on the announcement of a takeover bid. These markets were probably relatively efficient in their reaction to a combination of information and control, but they were still efficient only in a limited sense. He thought that some of our concepts of a free competitive market needed reconsideration.

Professor Spaventa thought that Professor Streissler's paper dealt to a large extent with composition fallacies and was therefore a useful contribution to the subject of the conference. He was, however, puzzled by Professor Streissler's two examples. With respect to the Hayek model he disputed Professor Streissler's statement (p. 110) that banks could create credit 'out of thin air': that was certainly not true for a single bank even if it was true for the banking system as a whole; he also thought that the statement about the determinants of the credit multiplier (p. 111) ignored the reserve behaviour of individual banks. As for Kaldor's model, that could be used in several ways; but this was the first time the Professor Spaventa had seen it applied to distribution at less than full employment. He found the assumptions about the balance of payments and the government deficit (pp. 115–7) rather curious: they reminded him of the Cambridge New School!

Dr Nuti discussed the notion of the representative firm. Professor Streissler had dismissed the Marshallian notion that the economy or industry was a large-scale replica of the representative firm as a possible microeconomic foundation of macroeconomics; but there was an alternative, Kaldorian notion of the representative firm, where the firm was regarded as a small-scale replica of the economy. The demand curve facing the firm was then a function of the firm's output level via the multiplier process. This notion thus took into account constraints but it failed to say how firms perceived their position in the economy. A general wage increase was seen as an increase in cost and not as an increase in the potential demand for output. Once we shifted from the microeconomics of the representative firm to a microeconomic picture that took into account the macroeconomic constraint, we ended up with something that was not of much use because it had nothing to do with individual economic behaviour.

Professor Parkin raised three points. First, on the question of the extent to which we needed to concern ourselves with the distribution of characteristics across individuals, there was already a body of empirical literature, which at least could give some clues as to the importance of this question. In the area of the demand for money and other financial assets he was not aware of any serious problems from ignoring distributions. In areas such as price and wage setting empirical work had failed to find strong systematic effects from distributions.

Second, with respect to the notion of the representative firm, it seemed to Professor Parkin that simple-minded commonsense considerations led us to start from the idea that many individuals were to be regarded as price-takers and as capable of putting through their plans. This was not true of all individuals: when there was underemployment 95 per cent of individuals were working the desired forty-hour week, but the rest were not working at all. The macroeconomic approach that proceeded as though we could treat the individual household or firm as representative was leading us astray. He cited Barro and Grossman's 'A General Disequilibrium Model of Income and Employment' (*American Economic Review*, 1971) as an example. It would be better to work with aggregates that were linear combinations of a Walrasian group and a Keynesian group of individuals; the latter group would be larger the further the economy was away from equilibrium.

Third, what level of aggregation should we regard as the level for which macroeconomics was designed? Professor Streissler's Hayekian example applied to the Austrian economy under fixed exchange rates; would the world economy be a better level of aggregation for macroeconomics?

Professor Streissler said that he found Dr Sweeney's summary excellent and perceptive. It was true that there were several different kinds of constraints in his paper. On the question of flexible exchange rates he referred to his 'Stochastic Model of International Reserve Requirements During Growth of World Trade' (*Zeitschrift für Nationalökonomie*, 1969), where he had derived the observed distribution from behavioural assumptions. He was not questioning that flexible exchange rates did not create an efficient allocation, but whether they would be marked with stabilising speculation. Dr Sweeney was correct in saying that individual optimisation models were richer and better, but he had himself only claimed that one must not turn the model around; for example, one must not deduce from a downward-sloping demand curve that individuals were utility-maximising.

With regard to Professor Spaventa's criticism, Professor Streissler claimed that the individual banker did create credit 'out of thin air', although to a lesser extent than the banking system as a whole. Individual bank reserves depended on the probability distribution of cash inflows and outflows, so that what was true of the banking system as a whole was true to some extent for an individual bank.

He agreed with Professor Parkin's idea of plan fulfillers, but not with the idea that plan non-fulfillers were rare: as an Austrian he was used to the fact that plans were not always fulfilled. As to the distribution of characteristics over individuals, his own empirical work led him to believe that they were important, but there was a shortage of statistical information on distributions.

Professor Davidson intervened to suggest that constraints were a question of contracts; for example, debt constraints and wage constraints. Since there were certain types of goods, e.g., fixed capital and consumer durables, that could not be consumed in a single income period, and therefore had to be financed, financial market contracts spanning several periods of calendar time and financial market structures became very important as constraints. These varied over countries and over time. The institutional rules under which the 'market makers' operated created constraints. A market would remain a liquid market as long as everybody believed prices were not perfectly flexible but moved in an orderly manner; market makers needed buffers to maintain orderliness. In the market for placements where there was a need to balance the flow of new issues to finance investment and the flow of new demand for placements out of savings, speculation was important and could be destabilising. In this market the price was determined by bulls and bears, so that if the price was stable over time both the bulls and the bears were being disappointed, and if the price was moving in one direction or the other at least half the market was being disappointed. Professor Davidson therefore raised the question: would we *want* a steady price in that market?

With respect to the representative firm, *Professor Malinvaud* pointed out that if we were not satisfied with that methodology, it might be for two reasons:

(1) The microeconomic analysis was not satisfactory;
(2) the aggregation problem was not properly dealt with.

The microeconomic analysis was often not satisfactory because the model of the firm was a very simplified one that had been built in order to study something else. For example, the neoclassical model was not suitable for deriving an investment function for a short-term business cycle macro-economic model. To deal with the aggregation problem we should study the behaviour of a firm taking due account of all the features of the situation and maybe even of the interdependencies of the action of the particular firm and the actions of other agents. Once we had done that, we should look at the macroeconomic consequences of the fact that many firms were acting under circumstances that were similar in some respects but different in others.

This diversity of situation at the microeconomic level was not a justification for saying that there could be no microeconomic foundation of macroeconomic analysis; he had been surprised to read Professor Streissler's statement (p. 123) that 'Speculation depends upon differences in behaviour. It is therefore representative of a class of economic phenomena where in a sense there can be no microeconomic foundation of macroeconomics'. Instead diversity should be incorporated in the model.

Aggregation often turned out to be very important but, since the aggregation problems tended to be specific to each problem, there was not much to be learnt from a general study of aggregation in the way of a justification for particular macroeconomic laws. On the contrary, when one looked at the justification for, say, the macroeconomic investment function, it was important to derive it from a study of the microeconomic situations of firms in a variety of situations.

Professor Malinvaud also wondered exactly what Professor Streissler meant by global constraints. Professor Streissler had said that the individual considered the optimisation problem as unconstrained while there was a global constraint, but Professor Malinvaud thought that one type of global constraint *was* taken into account in existing microeconomic analysis, namely those that were imposed by the market, the result of action of other individuals. Were there any other global constraints? If the individual was not aware of the constraints, could they affect his behaviour?

Professor Streissler replied that the global constraints were the market constraints. Sometimes they entered into individuals' calculations; sometimes they did not. To Professor Malinvaud's first criticism, Professor Streissler replied that if there were different expectations, one had to build a multi-sector model. The problem was that we had no good theory of how to choose the sectors and very little theory about how different expectations arose.

Professor Harcourt raised two points about Kaldor's model of distribution. Using the Kaldor model as a one-commodity model hid Kaldor's essential point that the process by which the system reached full employment depended on there being a differential rate of growth of investment goods and of consumption goods. Therefore, one needed at least two representative firms, one producing consumption goods, the other producing investment goods. Kaldor himself had obscured this. Kaldor had also been ambivalent as to whether his model was short-period or long-period, full-employment or not. He had wanted to have full employment, but this had caused difficulties. It was also an unnecessary constraint, because there were some quite rich and illuminating models of distribution which had dropped the constraint of full employment. Professor Harcourt said that in Keynes's *General Theory* as well as in the *Treatise on Money* there was a macroeconomic theory of distribution as well as a theory of the level of activity. *Professor Streissler* replied that he had used the Kaldor model because of his experience of Austria which since 1960 had had full employment but less than full capacity production. The Kaldor model corresponded to his experience in forecasting in that situation where if one underestimated investment one underestimated profits too; the Kaldor model showed that if investment or exports were higher than anticipated the gains went mainly to profits. The conditions for this were that the investment share varied more easily than the consumption share and that savings propensities had a certain amount of stickiness; Professor Streissler thought these were reasonable assumptions to make in the short run.

Professor Izzo asked why Professor Streissler had said (on p. 99) that credit rationing was due to differences of opinion. He was also puzzled by the connection in Professor Streissler's Hayekian model between the commercial loan rate and the bond rate. Did not firms have the possibility of going into the bond market and raising funds so that if there was rationing of bank credit then it was possible for them to raise money in the bond market? He was dubious also about the statement that when there was a balance of payments surplus the monetary base was increased faster than when there was a balance of payments deficit; he did not think evidence supported that proposition.

Sir John Hicks suggested that the proposition was true under the pre-1914 international gold standard. By the 1920s central banks were ceasing to behave in that way, but it was possible that in days of world inflation the pre-1914 behaviour might recur, albeit for different reasons than before 1914.

Professor Asimakopulos thought that Professor Streissler did not understand Kaldor's distinction between the short run and the long run, which Kalecki had made very emphatically. He was disappointed to see that Professor Streissler had accorded only a modest role to this theory of distribution.

Professor Henin, referring to Professor Parkin's remarks, considered the case where macroeconomic relations could be viewed as linear combinations of two different kinds of microeconomic relations, those constrained by quantity rationing and those free of this kind of constraint. For example, *a posteriori* aggregate demand was the sum of employed and unemployed consumers' demand, but *a priori*, in an uncertain world, this status variable — to be employed or unemployed — was a random variable. He therefore wondered to what extent one could consider macroeconomic relations as mathematical expectations and how one could specify the relation between prior demands and posterior effective demand.

On the dispute between Professors Streissler and Spaventa about bank credit, *Dr Goodhart* introduced Professor Tobin's argument that there was nothing particular about banks creating credit since other financial institutions created credit too. Any financial institution had to attract funds from the public by offering certain services. The feature that did distinguish banks from other financial intermediaries was the special constraints that monetary authorities imposed on them. This raised the question of why banks should be the only non-natural utility which the authorities tended to constrain. His own partial explanation was that the social cost of bankruptcy was in the case of banks greater than the private cost.

Professor Leijonhufvud suggested that there were two ways to look at Professor Streissler's paper: one was to sum it up as recommending that we back away from otpimisation as the framework for representing individual behaviour; the other that we ought to recognise that the constraint structure on individual experiments needed to be richer and more complicated if we wanted it to be relevant to macroeconomics. He thought that we had so far discussed only the more congenial second point. He himself thought there were good reasons for taking a second look at optimisation itself; in particular, using the optimisation framework required the acceptance of very stringent information requirements. For example, a transactor with an n-dimensional budget constraint needed to know all the terms of the constraint. Therefore, when one used the optimising framework one had to put in all the information the individual agent would need to solve his maximising problem; if it was in a temporal setting then one had a model where all the decisions were made in the beginning and thereafter the individuals lived out a plot that had already been written. In order to have sequential decisions in the model, we had to reintroduce ignorance; that is, information that the individual would only obtain later. He thought that we ought to consider the option of pulling back from the methodological requirement always to represent individuals' actions as part of an optimally chosen time path.

Professor Frey, pointing out that economists explained individual behaviour by (a) preferences and (b) constraints, suggested that economists should concentrate as much as possible on constraints, simply because there was an economic theory of constraints; for example, the budget constraint following from the circular flow of money. On the other hand, economists had no professional knowledge about why and how preferences arose and changed. There had been some attempts at the explanation of preference changes, for example by C. von Weizsäcker, 'Notes on Endogenous Change of Tastes' (*Journal of Economic Theory*, 1971) but they had not been very successful. As there was up to now no appropriate theory of preference formation, economic theory ran the danger of tautological statements such as 'people's behaviour changed because their preferences must have changed'.

Professor Negishi agreed with Professor Streissler that constraints were very important, but he thought that as far as Keynesian situations were concerned the most important constraint to be considered in microeconomic theory was the constraint of effective demand. Perhaps we should really be talking about the macroeconomic foundations of microeconomics! It was true that this effective demand constraint was not properly taken account of in Walrasian microeconomics under perfect competition, but in the field of imperfect competition this kind of constraint had been taken account of, even in neoclassical economics, particularly in the kinked demand curve theory of oligopoly.

Professor Spaventa intervened to point out that the discussion was showing the truth of Dr Sweeney's remark that we had to define constraints. What was not a constraint for one agent might be a constraint for another agent. In the context of his Kaldorian model Professor Streissler seemed to consider as a constraint that additional exports tended to create additional imports and additional public expenditure to increase tax revenue; neither was always true.

Professor Marty suggested that even if the utility maximisation model required too much information it did have the advantage of having welfare implications. If we had only constraints and no preferences in microeconomic theory, we would have no welfare theory. It was possible that we needed a new welfare economics; for instance we wanted to know whether involuntary unemployment really was involuntary.

Sir John Hicks thought that not enough distinction had been made between constraints and changes in constraints; no one who had worked on consumer demand theory would doubt that it was changes in constraints that one was really considering.

Replying to the discussants, *Professor Streissler* agreed with Professor Leijonhufvud that we should look again at optimisation; in his paper he had tried to show why there could be reasons not to use the price system. On the other hand, he tended to favour Professor Henin's suggestion that you might have a two-stage model: first a long-run theory and, as a second stage, the short-run deviation in a probabilistic sense from that. For example, we might have a long-run theory of distribution together with his short-run interpretation of the Kaldor model. However, he had doubts whether it was possible that the random deviation from a long-run path might not have repercussions that changed the long-term path, so that it would not logically be possible to have a two-stage analysis.

He disagreed with Machlup's view cited by Dr Sweeney that models should be built so as to yield comparative statics conclusions. He thought this factual statement was in fact wrong; it assumed in effect that the initial conditions of a differential equation did not influence the final result. One had to allow for the fact that an individual's awareness that he might make errors could cause him to anticipate errors and make provision to fulfil his plans even if he made errors.

In reply to Professor Izzo, he first said that credit rationing could be interpreted as depending on differences of opinion: a potential lender did not lend to a borrower when they had different opinions about the borrower's venture. Second, commercial loan rates and bond rates of interest did not influence each other in Austria where individual firms were not allowed to go to the bond market, which was mainly a government bond market. Third, his statement that the balance of payments determined the money supply was meant as a long-run statement; like Sir John Hicks he had in mind something like the gold standard system.

Finally, he said he still believed that there were differences between banks and other financial intermediaries. Banks handed on the demand deposits of their customers to their borrowers. In that sense they did not create credit, but if they handed on more than they had received in deposits the banks, and the banks alone, could create something out of nothing.

5   Examples of Production Relations Based on Microdata*

Tjalling C. Koopmans
YALE UNIVERSITY

I   INTRODUCTION

The view has been expressed by many that a meaningful capital theory can and should be developed without ever defining an aggregate capital index. A fine prototype of this approach is Malinvaud's now classical paper of 1953. The same banner has been unfurled, though not with full identity of views, in Cambridge, England and in Cambridge, Massachusetts.

With princely unconcern econometricians have continued to fit aggregate production functions approximating an aggregate output index, for an economy or a sector, by a function $F(L, K)$ of aggregate labour (L) and capital (K) input indices. When the matter of the logical foundations for such a construct is raised, words such as 'parable' or 'metaphor' are pressed into service.

Coexistence of logically unconnected or even incompatible approaches makes for a rich science. Part of this richness lies in the challenge to find points of view that may tie together what appear to be competing approaches. This paper does not attempt to arrive at a definite stand on the issue of capital aggregation. Its more modest purpose is to select a few pieces of work in the literature that have a bearing on the problem, to describe their principal ideas in a summarising way, and to comment on such insights as they may give in the problem of aggregating production relations. The selection is avowedly subjective, and leaves out some important contributions already extensively discussed in the literature.

There are two other self-imposed constraints. One is the acceptance of that shadowy notion of perfect allocation that is subject to two seemingly opposite interpretations: that of perfect markets guided by complete information and perfect foresight, and that of perfect planning possibly guided by appropriate shadow prices. This constraint is adopted on the hunch that aggregation is simpler within it than without it, while what is learned in this way may still be a worthwhile starting point for the study of more complicated situations. The constraint is applied to that part of the economy whose aggregation is under discussion, and not necessarily to the rest of the economy. It may also

*Research supported by grants from the National Science Foundation and the Ford Foundation. I am indebted to Katsuhito Iwai and Herbert Scarf for valuable comments.

be applied to the future under conditions showing that it could not have held in the past.

The second constraint arises from a preference for the notion of elementary processes as the building blocks from which production relations are constructed. In the simplest case each process is defined merely by the ratios of inputs to outputs in any utilisation of the process. Use of this simple linear case implies an assumption of constant returns to scale within any one process, possibly subject to an upper bound set by a capacity limit. The assumption of a finite number of processes has the advantage that the micro-data that describe technology in detail often are of this nature. Also, algorithms for marshalling such data to answer broader questions are available. Finally, cases of joint production can readily be included in this way. Generally speaking, however, the discrete representation of processes is more suited for the industrial sector than for agriculture. In the latter case, the differentiable production function normally employed for aggregate relations may well be the appropriate form to represent a family of elementary processes that allows continuous substitution of one factor of production for another. Production relations in which the two forms are combined may, of course, be most appropriate in some cases.

In Section II we reason from a given size and composition of the capital stock available to each productive unit and held constant during the single period considered. The object of the analysis is to derive the production function in the space of current inputs and outputs implicit in efficient utilisation of its 'own' capital stock by each unit. The characteristics of these stocks find expression in the shape of the production locus, but do not explicitly appear as variables. In this context, therefore, the term aggregation refers only to the fact that one production relation for the whole is derived from a number of simpler relations for the parts. There is no attempt yet to reduce the number of variables by the formation of suitable index numbers. Rather, the number of relations is reduced to one, using the assumption of internally efficient utilisation (or in some cases non-use) of the individually controlled parts of the capital stock.

In Section III the size and composition of the total capital stock do explicitly appear in the model, and can change over time. However, the attention concentrates on the search for a capital stock that if initially given does not change (is 'invariant') as a result of optimisation of the production path for capital goods and consumption goods over an infinite horizon. Implied in this optimisation is that not only the use of individually controlled parts of the capital stock, but indeed the size, composition, allocation and use of the total stock are optimally chosen in a sense to be defined in Section III. The ideas of Section III are presented with the help of a simple example.

Section IV discusses how such an invariant capital stock may depend on the discount factor for future utility flows that enter into the optimality criterion for paths over time. While normally a larger discount factor (a smaller discount rate) is associated with a larger invariant capital stock, a simple example of the reverse relationship is given.

Section V is an Addendum following the S'Agaro conference, in order to elaborate on statements made in the discussion in response to comments and questions by a number of participants. In particular, the Addendum indicates that, in a counter-intuitive example of an invariant capital stock that is larger when the discount factor is smaller, that invariant stock is not unique, is not stable under small changes in the initial capital stock, and is bracketed by two other invariant stocks each of which is stable.

II ONE-PERIOD PRODUCTION RELATIONS

Consider a period short enough so that the size and composition of the stock of fixed capital can be regarded as given and constant within the period. The discussion concerns itself with an aggregate or *whole* that may be interpreted as a branch of industry, a sector of the production economy, or the entire production system of an economy. We are looking for a procedure that derives the 'short-run' production function for the whole from production possibility data associated with the *parts* (pieces of equipment, departments, plants, firms, or branches of industry) that together make up the whole. In keeping with the short-run point of view, we allow (but do not insist on) an interpretation in which the possibility of transfers of capital goods between parts during the period is ruled out.

The *locus classicus* is a beautiful brief paper by Houthakker (1955). Variants of his procedure were developed by Levhari (1968) and K. Sato (1969). A fuller and more systematic treatment is given by Johansen (1972) in an important book in which the various production function and supply function concepts are defined, are related to each other, and to empirical data.

Houthakker, Johansen and Levhari represent the production possibilities inherent in the capital stock of any given part by a *process vector* in the space of input and output commodity flows. Besides indicating the ratios of inputs and outputs by the ratios of its components, the process vector is given a length expressing the absolute inputs and outputs corresponding to full-capacity use of the capital stock for that part. Then, as long as the capital stock is held constant, the collection of process vectors, one for each part, is all one requires for the derivation of the short-run production function for the whole. Information about the physical composition of the capital stock available to each part and the processes involved in its production are needed only at a later stage of analysis, where changes in the capital stock are introduced.

We have argued above that, in regard to industrial production, it seems more suitable to treat the number of parts represented by process vectors as finite, but often large. Houthakker, Levhari and, in his Chapters 3, 4, 5, Johansen, approximate this discrete collection of vectors by an infinite number of process vectors arranged in a smooth frequency distribution over the entire space of inputs and outputs, or over some sub-set of this space that may be of lower dimensionality. This has the advantage that each individual process may be thought of as operating only at a level of 1 or 0.

Here I shall use a finite number of process vectors, as is done by Johansen in his first exposition of the short-run production function (Section 2.4) and in his applications to the Swedish wood pulp industry (Section 8.7) and the Norwegian tanker fleet (Chapter 9). As already explained, let in this case the *capacitated* process vector $a^j \equiv (a^j_1, a^j_2, \ldots, a^j_n)$ represent inputs and outputs under full utilisation of the capital stock of that part. A scalar *utilisation factor* x_j can then be applied to the process vector a^j to represent the input and output flows at feasible activity levels by the scalar product

$$x_j a^j \equiv (x_j a^j_1, x_j a^j_2, \ldots, x_j a^j_n), \qquad 0 \leqslant x_i \leqslant 1.$$

Figure 5:1 illustrates the construction of the short-run production function in the simplest case of one input and one output. This case could serve as a first approximation for a collection of base-load power plants burning clean coal (if we include labour with the capital stock). Process vectors a^1, a^2, a^3, a^4 might represent plants of increasing age with decreasing 'efficiency' of conversion of fuel into electric energy. In this simple case the

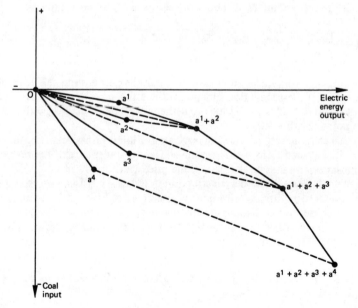

Fig. 5:1   Short-run aggregated production function for four electric power plants

short-run production function is represented by the broken straight line connecting the successive partial sums $0, a^1, a^1 + a^2, \ldots$, of the given process vectors taken in order of decreasing 'efficiency' of conversion. Under a regime of maximisation of net revenue from current operations of the whole, a gradual increase of the ratio of the output price to the input price will trace out the production function. Intervals on the relative price axis will correspond to points $a_1, a_1 + a_2, \ldots$, where the production function has a kink, and relative prices characteristic of successively less efficient pieces of capital will correspond to segments on which these pieces are taken into use in the same order.

If there are $m > 2$ inputs and outputs and n processes, there is no natural linear order of the subsets of processes successively taken into use, and there are price vectors which permit more than one process to be efficiently taken into partial use simultaneously. The construction then is as follows.

Let T (for 'technology') denote the set $\{a^j \mid j = 0, 1, \ldots, n\}$ of all capacitated process vectors a^j, where $a^0 \equiv 0$ (the origin). For any subset T' of T (including T itself but excluding the empty set) let $a(T')$ be the sum

$$a(T') \equiv \sum_{a^j \in T'} a^j$$

of all process vectors of T'. Then the feasible set in the space of commodity flows is the convex hull H of the set of vectors $a(T')$ for all T'; that is,

$$H \equiv \left\{ \sum_{T' \subset T} x(T') a(T') \mid \sum_{T' \subset T} x(T') = 1, x(T') \geqslant 0 \text{ for all } T' \subset T \right\},$$

the set of all convex-linear combinations of all the partial sums $a(T')$. Finally, the graph F of the production function is the efficient boundary of H; that is, the set of those points h of H such that the only point $h + \epsilon$ of H with $\epsilon \geqslant 0$ is the point h with $\epsilon = 0$.

In this case, as output prices increase and/or input prices decrease, the order in which additional processes are started up under current net revenue maximisation depends on the path in the price space followed.

A diagram illustrating this construction in the case of three processes and three goods (two outputs, one input) is given here as Figure 5:2. A similar diagram for the case of two inputs and one output is given by Johansen (1972, p. 17) in projection on the input space, with isoquants drawn in to indicate increasing output levels.

III   A CAPITAL STOCK INVARIANT UNDER OPTIMIZATION OVER TIME

In Section II simplicity was bought by the assumption of a fixed capital stock and a fixed technology for its utilisation. In the present section, in which we

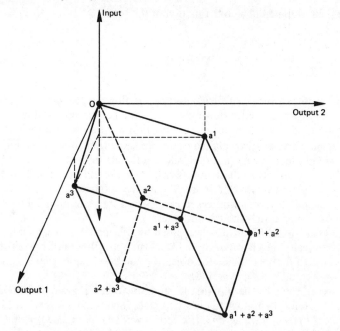

Fig. 5:2 Short-run aggregated production function for three plants with one input and two outputs. (a^2 is not on the efficient production locus.)

consider an intertemporal model of an entire economy, we shall continue to assume a fixed technology, not only in the utilisation of capital goods in production, but also in the production of the capital goods themselves. However, we shall treat changes over time in the capital stock as entirely feasible. We also assume absence of institutional barriers to the transfer of capital goods from one control to another. The process notion therefore no longer implies allocative control over a fixed capital stock associated with each part. The process thus becomes a more purely technological concept, in which capital goods are now represented by coefficients for capital inputs required by the process.

We shall also strengthen the assumption of efficient use of resources to one of intertemporal optimality, defined by specifying some suitable social objective function over time. As explained already, this construct can be regarded as a simulation that yields a first approximation either to a centrally planned and managed economy, or to the course over time of a market economy that manages to sustain reasonably full employment. In the latter case the interpretation of the assumed intertemporal preferences is an implicit rather than an explicit one. In both cases, the simulation takes a rosy view of the working of the simulated economy.

We shall utilise an objective function of the form

$$U \equiv \sum_{t=1}^{\infty} (\alpha)^{t-1} u(y^t), \quad 0 < \alpha < 1.$$

Here y^t denotes a vector of final consumption flows of the various consumables in period t, $u(y)$ the utility flow associated with a consumption flow of y per unit period,[1] and α a discount factor[2] per unit of time, applied to future utilities and assumed given and constant. Consumption goods as well as capital goods are produced using processes selected from a finite collection of processes. The inputs to these processes include the utilisation of capital goods and the consumptive use of resource flows such as labour, minerals, clean air. Total available flows of resources in each period are again assumed fixed over time (for simplification though not realism).

The grand and difficult problem posed by this model is to associate with any (historically) given initial capital stock an optimal path (if one exists); that is, a path that maximises the objective function U among all feasible paths over an infinite time period.

However, some further provisional simplification can again be bought by first asking only the following question: *Does there exist a capital stock which, if put in the place of the given initial stock, will be reproduced precisely at the end of each period as a result of the optimisation?* If so, such a capital stock can be regarded as being in equilibrium with the technology, the resource constraints, and the preferences, both intertemporal as given by α, and within each period as given by $u(\cdot)$. We shall refer to such a stock as an *invariant optimal capital stock.*

For the basic case of a single good in the double role of capital good and consumption good, our question has been fully answered by Ramsey (1928) and his followers.[3] If the output flow of that good produced by a fixed labour force is a strictly concave function of the available capital stock, then there is a *unique* invariant optimal capital stock. It has been called the golden rule stock modified by discounting. Its dependence on the discount *factor* α is also well known: As α increases (hence the discount *rate* $\rho = (1 - \alpha)/\alpha$ decreases), the invariant stock increases and approaches the golden rule stock proper as $\alpha \to 1$, hence $\rho \to 0$. It is readily computed from the value of α and the form of the production function, by requiring the marginal productivity of the good as capital in terms of the good as an output flow to be equal to ρ. Hence, it does not depend on the shape of the utility function. Finally, for any α, $0 < \alpha < 1$, and any positive initial capital stock, a unique optimal

---

[1] $u(y)$ is assumed differentiable and concave.

[2] $(\alpha)^t$ denotes α raised to the power t, in contrast with the use of superscripts t as time labels in y^t, and in x^t, z^t below.

[3] For a more recent exposition see Koopmans (1967), in which other literature is also cited.

capital path exists which approaches the modified golden rule stock as time proceeds.

Matters are more complicated for an arbitrary number of commodities. An analysis of the general case involving any finite numbers of processes and of the three types of goods (i.e., capital, consumption, resources) is given by Hansen and Koopmans (1972) from both the theoretical and computational points of view, with references to earlier work. Here we consider in some detail an example with *one* capital good, *one* resource and *two* consumption goods. It is hoped that such an exploration will bring out some of the economic content and implications of the concept of an invariant optimal capital stock more vividly than can the theorems and algorithms regarding the general case. While the presentation is self-contained and uses only elementary calculus, some unproved statements are supported by the reference cited.

We shall assume that the single-period utility function $u(y_1, y_2)$ is defined for all $y_1 \geqslant 0, y_2 \geqslant 0$, increases strictly with each of the two consumption flows, y_1, y_2 (nonsaturation), is strictly concave and continuously differentiable. As to the constraints, Table 5:1 gives the input and output coefficients

TABLE 5:1

Technology Matrix for an Intertemporal Model of Production

Notations for coefficient vectors			Activity levels x_i and technical coefficients			Availabilities and total 'outputs' $\geqslant$	
			x_1	x_2	x_3		
f_1	f_2	$f_3 =$	$-a_1$	$-a_2$	$-a_3$	$-z^1$	capital input
			b_1	b_2	b_3	z^2	capital 'output'
-1	-1	$-1 =$	-1	-1	-1	-1	labour
d_1	d_2	$0 =$	1	0	0	y_1	cons. good '1'
			0	1	0	y_2	cons. good '2'

for the four goods for each of three processes. The symbols a_j, b_j, x_j, y_i, z^t represent non-negative scalars. The technical coefficients a_j, b_j are independent of time by assumption. The coefficient vectors are normalised so as to specify a unit input of the single resource (labour, say) for the unit activity level of each process. Also, the units of the two consumption goods are chosen so that one unit of labour is required to produce one unit of either good. As to timing, labour and consumption can be regarded as flows during the period. In those parts of the reasoning in which we consider only one period at a time, no time label will be attached to the x_j, y_i. Capital input is required to be available at the beginning of each period for use during that period. Capital output becomes available at the end of each period. Since capital input and output for a given period may differ, a time superscript t is attached to the symbol z whenever needed.

Capital 'output' represents the sum of (already used) capital released for possible use in the next period and new capital goods produced during the period. In principle one should consider two capital goods constructed from the same blueprint but with different lengths of prior use as different capital goods. For simplicity, for the processes $j = 1, 2$, interpreted as producing consumption goods only, we specify $a_j > b_j$ to simulate loss of effectiveness of the capital good by a constant geometric decline per period in its quantity, regardless of the rate of use. In this case the specification $a_3 < b_3$ is essential for an increase or even constancy over time of the capital stock to be compatible with a positive level of consumption. The symbols f_j, d_j are abbreviated notations for the corresponding column vectors of order two for the coefficients of capital goods and consumption goods, respectively. These symbols are used mostly in the diagrams.

The first line of the table expresses the feasibility constraint

$$-a_1 x_1 - a_2 x_2 - a_3 x_3 \geqslant -z^1$$

which says that capital in use during the period cannot exceed the amount available at its beginning. The other constraints can be read off accordingly. The entire set of constraints remains the same at all times, and can be read as applying either to the first period, or to any nameless future period. To apply it to a specific period, say the tth, superscripts t are attached to the x_j and y_i, and $t - 1$ is added to the superscripts of z^1, z^2.

Note that the only variable occurring in the constraints for two successive periods, say those with labels t, $t + 1$, is the variable z^{t+1}. This, together with the additive form of the objective function, makes it possible to carry out the optimisation of the entire future path (starting with any prescribed initial stock z^1) in two stages. In the first stage all values z^t for $t = 1, 2, \ldots$, are held fixed at arbitrary jointly attainable levels, and the attention is directed towards maximising the term $\alpha^{t-1} u(y^t)$ within each period by choice of the x_j^t, y_i^t, subject only to the constraints for that period. The result is a value

$$\max_{x^t, y^t} \alpha^{t-1} u(y_1^t, y_2^t) \equiv \alpha^{t-1} \psi(-z^t, z^{t+1}), \text{ say,}$$

that depends only on the initial and terminal capital stocks of that period. The second stage then consists in maximising

$$\bar{U} \equiv \sum_{t=1}^{\infty} \alpha^{t-1} \psi(-z^t, z^{t+1})$$

subject to the given initial stock z^1 and such constraints on the pairs (z^t, z^{t+1}), $t = 1, 2, \ldots$, as are implicit in those of Table 5:1.

While our focus is on initial stocks z^1 that in the second stage yield constant optimal paths $z^t = z^1$, $t = 2, 3, \ldots$, it will help if we do not yet specify $z^t = z^{t+1}$ in describing the first stage. Reverting to the nameless-period notation of Table 5:1 we therefore now take both z^1 and z^2 as given and possibly different, and drop the factor α^{t-1}. The first observation then is that optimality requires

$$y_1 = x_1, \quad y_2 = x_2,$$

because any slack in the consumption of either good would unnecessarily diminish the utility $u(y_1, y_2)$.

Our procedure for analysing stage one will be to compare the maximal utility flow, $\psi(-z^1, z^2)$, for the given z^1, z^2, with that attainable flow, to be denoted $\varphi(-z^1, z^2)$, that results if each of the three other constraints is tentatively required also to hold with strict equality,

$$-a_1 x_1 - a_2 x_2 - a_3 x_3 = -z^1$$
$$b_1 x_1 + b_2 x_2 + b_3 x_3 = z^2$$
$$-x_1 - x_2 - x_3 = -1.$$

We shall call these the no-slack constraints for capital input, capital output and labour, respectively. The domain of definition of $\varphi(-z^1, z^2)$ then is that set of points $(-z^1, z^2)$, to be denoted $\mathscr{Q}$ below, for which a non-negative solution (x_1, x_2, x_3) of the no-slack constraints exists.

We choose our example such that the 3×3 matrix of coefficients of the x_j is non-singular, solve for x_3 from the third equation and substitute the resulting expression in the other two equations, obtaining

$$-(a_1 - a_3) x_1 - (a_2 - a_3) x_2 - a_3 = -z^1$$
$$(b_1 - b_3) x_1 + (b_2 - b_3) x_2 + b_3 = z^2,$$

with a non-singular 2×2 matrix. Ignoring non-negativity constraints, these equations define a 1:1 linear mapping from the points (x_1, x_2) to the points $(-z^1, z^2)$.

The non-negativity of the activity levels $x_j, j = 1, 2, 3,$[1] and the identity of the x_j and y_j allow us to enter the level curves (indifference curves) of $u(y_1, y_2)$ in the closed positive quadrant of the (x_1, x_2)-plane (see Figure 5:3). We recall for later use some elementary mathematical verities. Since the derivatives

$$u_1(x_1, x_2) \equiv \frac{\partial u}{\partial x_1}, \quad u_2(x_1, x_2) \equiv \frac{\partial u}{\partial x_2},$$

---

[1] For $j = 3$ the constraint now takes the form $x_1 + x_2 \leqslant 1$.

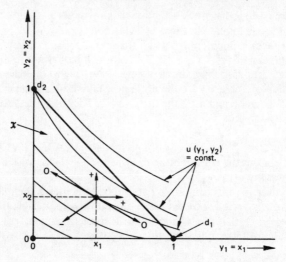

Fig. 5:3   Level curves of the single-period utility function

are positive in all points of the quadrant, there is in each point (x_1, x_2) a tangent to the level curve of negative finite[1] slope. This tangent partitions the set of all directions out of the point (x_1, x_2) into three sub-sets. As illustrated by arrows labelled +, 0, or − in Figure 5:3, in all directions (δ_1, δ_2) leading from (x_1, x_2) to points 'above' the tangent the directional derivative

$$\left(\frac{du(x_1 + \lambda\delta_1, x_2 + \lambda\delta_2)}{d\lambda}\right)_{\lambda = 0}$$

of u is positive; in the two directions along the tangent that derivative is zero; in all directions to points 'below' the tangent the derivative is negative. The origin is 'below' the tangent.[2] Finally, an implication of the strict concavity of u should be noted. Proceeding from (x_1, x_2) along a straight line in any direction with a non-positive directional derivative in (x_1, x_2), the function will monotonically decrease along the entire feasible segment of that line. In particular, the maximum of $u(x'_1, x'_2)$ among points (x'_1, x'_2) of the tangent in (x_1, x_2) is reached uniquely in (x_1, x_2).

The no-slack constraints for labour allow us to represent the set of attainable activity vectors (x_1, x_2, x_3) by the closed triangle $X \equiv X(0, d_1, d_2)$ with vertices $0, d_1, d_2$ in the space of (x_1, x_2) only, since $x_3 = 1 - x_1 - x_2$. The mapping $(x_1, x_2) \leftrightarrow (-z^1, z^2)$ in turn transforms this triangle into the triangle $\mathscr{Z} \equiv \mathscr{Z}(f_1, f_2, f_3)$ in the space of $(-z^1, z^2)$ – see Figure 5:4. The triangle $\mathscr{Z}$ represents the set of all those pairs $(-z^1, z^2)$ that are both attainable

---

[1] Our assumptions about $u(., .)$ imply that the axes are not tangent to any level curve.
[2] Whenever $(x_1, x_2) \neq (0, 0)$.

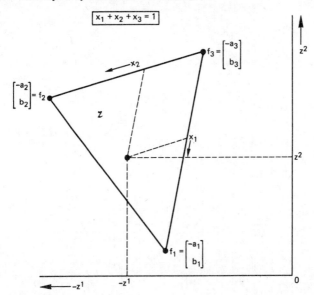

Fig. 5:4   Attainable set $\mathscr{L}$ in the capital input and output

and consistent with the added no-slack constraints. Any point in this triangle simultaneously represents the pair $(-z^1, z^2)$ by reference to the rectangular co-ordinate axes of $-z^1$ and z^2, and the pair (x_1, x_2) by reference to a skew co-ordinate system defined within the triangle by placing the origin in f_3 and unit points on the two axes in f_1 and f_2. Transferred to the new (x_1, x_2)-co-ordinates defined on $\mathscr{L}$, the level curves of $u(x_1, x_2)$ now also serve as level curves for the function $\varphi(-z^1, z^2)$ mentioned above (see Figure 5:5). This function is then defined on $\mathscr{L}$ by

$$\varphi(-z^1, z^2) \equiv u(x_1, x_2) \quad \text{whenever } (x_1, x_2) \leftrightarrow (-z^1, z^2).$$

It represents the utility attained in the given period with initial and terminal capital specifications $(-z^1, z^2)$ if each of the five constraints is forced to hold with equality. Because of the linearity of the mapping φ inherits the continuous differentiability and the strict concavity of u.

The function $\varphi(-z^1, z^2)$ so defined in $\mathscr{L}$ is not necessarily the same, even within $\mathscr{L}$, as the function $\psi(-z^1, z^2)$ defined earlier in the entire set of feasible $(-z^1, z^2)$. The difference within $\mathscr{L}$ is that $\psi(-z^1, z^2)$ is the maximum attainable utility under constraints permitting slacks, whereas $\varphi(-z^1, z^2)$ is the unique utility level that is attainable — hence optimal — under constraints that rule out all slacks. Since narrowing the constraint set cannot increase the maximum attainable utility we must have

$$\psi(-z^1, z^2) \geqslant \varphi(-z^1, z^2)$$

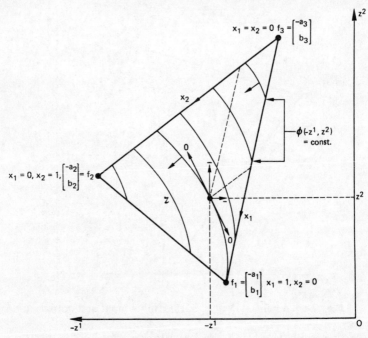

Fig. 5:5   Test of no-slack constraints for capital input and output

in all points $(-z^1, z^2)$ of $\mathscr{Z}$. On the other hand, we must have

$$\psi(-z^1, z^2) = \varphi(-z^1, z^2)$$

in all those points $(-z^1, z^2)$ of $\mathscr{Z}$ in which the maximum utility attainable und
constraints permitting slacks is in fact attained for the unique no-slack activity
vector $(x_1, x_2) \leftrightarrow$ the given $(-z^1, z^2)$. We shall now examine for each of the
three constraints under what conditions this is the case.

Let $(-z^1, z^2)$ be a point in the interior of $\mathscr{Z}$. Taking first the two capital co
straints, we assume that the no-slack constraint for labour is satisfied. Then a
slack of $\delta^1 > 0$ in capital input would mean that out of a stock z^1 made
available only $z^1 - \delta^1$ is used in production. Similarly, a slack of $\delta^2 > 0$ in
capital output would be to produce $z^2 + \delta^2$ but hand on only z^2. For either
of these and any combination of them to decrease utility, it is sufficient[1] for

---

[1] In the configuration of Figure 5:5, where the new origin f_3 for the (x_1, x_2)-co-
ordinate system is 'above' and 'to the right of' the point $(-z^1, z^2)$, it is necessary and
sufficient that these derivatives are non-positive (not both can be zero), thus allowing a
vertical or a horizontal tangent. See the implication of strict concavity of u discussed
above.

the two derivatives

$$\varphi_1(-z^1, z^2) \equiv \frac{\partial \varphi}{\partial(-z^1)}, \qquad \varphi_2(-z^1, z^2) \equiv \frac{\partial \varphi}{\partial z^2},$$

to be negative. Figure 5:5 illustrates that this implies a finite negative slope

$$s \equiv -\frac{\varphi_1(-z^1, z^2)}{\varphi_2(-z^1, z^2)} = \left(\frac{dz^2}{d(-z^1)}\right)_{\varphi = \text{const.}}$$

for the tangent to the level curve of φ in the point $(-z^1, z^2)$.

We now turn to the no-slack constraint for labour, which we examine assuming the no-slack constraints for capital to be satisfied. Let the amount of labour in use be changed from 1 to

$$x_1 + x_2 + x_3 = 1 - \epsilon, \qquad 0 < \epsilon \leqslant 1$$

allowing a slack of ϵ. We choose a particular small value of ϵ and treat the above equation as defining a new experimental equality constraint on labour. This defines a new mapping between the new activity levels $\tilde{x}_1, \tilde{x}_2$ and the capital specifications z^1, z^2, according to the equations

$$-(a_1 - a_3)\tilde{x}_1 - (a_2 - a_3)\tilde{x}_2 - a_3(1 - \epsilon) = -z^1$$
$$(b_1 - b_3)\tilde{x}_1 + (b_2 - b_3)\tilde{x}_2 + b_3(1 - \epsilon) = z^2.$$

But then those values $\tilde{z}^1, \tilde{z}^2$ of the capital stocks that would have produced the present consumption flows $\tilde{x}_1, \tilde{x}_2$ in the absence of any labour or capital disposals are related to the specified flows z^1, z^2 by

$$-\tilde{z}^1 = -z^1 - \epsilon a_3, \qquad \tilde{z}^2 = z^2 + \epsilon b_3.$$

It is these values that are to be tested in relation to the level curves of the function φ in Figure 5:5. This is done in Figure 5:6, where the dashed line connecting the interior point $(-z^1, z^2)$ of $\mathscr{L}$ with $(-\tilde{z}^1, \tilde{z}^2)$ is drawn so as to be parallel, in slope and direction, to the line $0f_3$ connecting the origin of the $(-z^1, z^2)$-plane with the point $f_3 = (-a_3, b_3)$ representing the capital-producing process. Therefore, for any slack in labour use to be non-optimal, the following condition on the directional derivative in the direction $(-a_3, b_3)$ is both necessary[1] and sufficient,

$$\left(\frac{d\varphi(-z^1 - \lambda a_3, z^2 + \lambda b_3)}{d\lambda}\right)_{\lambda = 0} = -a_3\varphi_1(-z^1, z^2) + b_3\varphi_2(-z^1, z^2) \leqslant 0.$$

Since we assume capital slacks to be non-optimal, φ_1 and φ_2 must be non-positive, which precludes $\varphi_2 = 0$. Therefore the condition just obtained is

[1] The necessity is achieved by the inclusion of the = sign, on the strength of the strict concavity of φ.

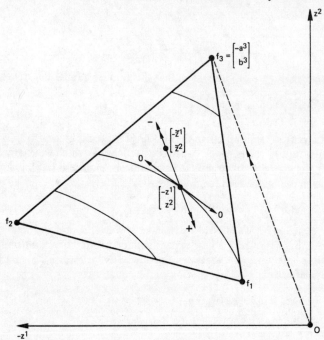

Fig. 5:6   Test of the no-slack constraint for labour

equivalent to the slope condition

$$s(-z^1, z^2) \equiv -\frac{\varphi_1(-z^1, z^2)}{\varphi_2(-z^1, z^2)} \gtreqqless -\frac{b_3}{a_3},$$

as illustrated in Figure 5:6.

We have now derived condtiions on the non-optimality of slacks by testing the effect of the no-slack constraints one or two at a time while assuming the other(s) to be satisfied. Due to the differentiability and strict concavity of φ, the conditions so obtained can be combined to form one condition on the non-optimality of any combination of non-negative slacks in the three constraints with $\delta^1 + \delta^2 + \epsilon > 0$, that leaves the resulting point $(-z^1 + \delta^1 - \epsilon a_3,$ $z^2 + \delta^2 + \epsilon b_3)$ in $\mathscr{Z}$. In terms of the slope $s \equiv s(-z^1, z^2)$ of the tangent to the level curve of φ in $(-z^1, z^2)$ that comprehensive sufficient (necessary)[1] condition then is

$$-\frac{b_3}{a_3} \lesseqqgtr s(-z^1, z^2) < (\lesseqqgtr) \ 0.$$

---

[1] See footnote 1 on p. 156.

Finally, in all interior points $(-z^1, z^2)$ of $\mathscr{Z}$ in which the comprehensive sufficient condition is satisfied we must have, as explained above,

$$\varphi(-z^1, z^2) = \psi(-z^1, z^2).$$

Therefore, the level curves of φ and ψ coincide in that part of $\mathscr{Z}$ in which the sufficient slope condition is satisfied. Moreover, in those points, we can look upon the negatives

$$q^1 \equiv -\varphi_1(-z^1, z^2), q^2 \equiv -\varphi_2(-z^1, z^2), r \equiv a_3\varphi_1(-z^1, z^2) - b_3\varphi_2(-z^1, z^2),$$

of the directional derivatives used in testing for the tightness of the capital and labour constraints as non-negative shadow prices associated with the corresponding inputs and outputs. These prices are expressed in units of marginal utility discounted to time $t = 1$.

For all points $(-z^1, z^2)$ of $\mathscr{Z}$ for which the no-slack conditions are met, stage one, the discussion of optimisation within single periods for which $(-z^1, z^2)$ is given, has now been completed. It will turn out that the stage one analysis for this subset of $\mathscr{Z}$ is sufficient for our present exploratory purpose.

We are therefore now ready for stage two, the search for invariant optimal capital stocks. We now want to examine points $(-z^1, z^2)$ for which $z^1 = z^2 = z$, say. In the diagrams these points are denoted

$$f = (-z, z) = z \cdot (-1, 1) \equiv z \cdot e,$$

that is (see Figure 5:7), points of the line $\mathcal{L}$ through the origin and of slope -1. Again, we first limit our search to points $(-z, z)$ in which the reproduction of $z^2 = z$ from $z^1 = z$ is achieved optimally without slacks. This limits the search first of all to points of the segment $\mathscr{S}$ in which $\mathcal{L}$ intersects $\mathscr{Z}$. Since by previous assumptions about the a_j, b_j the points f_1, f_2 are 'below' $\mathcal{L}$, f_3 'above' $\mathcal{L}$, the segment $\mathscr{S}$ intersects $\mathscr{Z}$ in its interior. It is the segment $\mathscr{S}$ minus its end points in which we shall now search.

Secondly, we shall at first use the slightly more restrictive sufficient slope condition

$$-\frac{b_3}{a_3} < s(-z, z) < 0.$$

for the within-period optimality of the no-slack activity vector $(x_1, x_2) \leftrightarrow (-z, z)$.

Assuming that such a point $(-z, z)$ exists we must now find a test whether the maximisation of

$$U = \sum_{t=1}^{\infty} \alpha^{t-1} \psi(-z^t, z^{t+1})$$

subject to $z^1 = z$ and the within-period constraints for each period is achieved by $z^t = z$ for all $t > 1$. Trimming our sails once more, we shall first study a

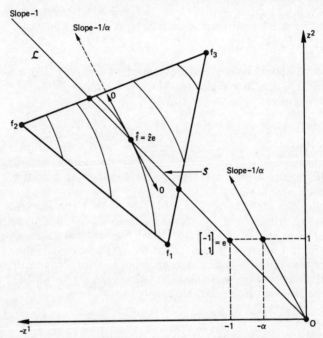

Fig. 5:7   Condition for an invariant optimal capital stock in an interior point of $\mathscr{Z}$

weaker test, necessary but perhaps not sufficient, obtained by specifying

$$z^1 = z = z^3 = z^4 = \ldots,$$

which leaves only z^2 free to vary. We then need to consider only the maximisation of

$$V \equiv \psi(-z, z^2) + \alpha\psi(-z^2, z)$$

with respect to z^2. Finally, since u and therefore φ have continuous first derivatives, the present slope condition is satisfied also in a neighbourhood $\mathscr{N}$ within $\mathscr{Z}$ of the point $(-z, z)$. Therefore, restricting z^2 further such that both $(-z, z^2)$ and $(-z^2, z)$ are in $\mathscr{N}$, we are in fact maximising

$$W \equiv \varphi(-z, z^2) + \alpha\varphi(-z^2, z).$$

The test then is whether the maximum of W within $\mathscr{N}$ is attained for $z^2 = z$. For this to occur, it is necessary that

$$0 = \left(\frac{dW}{dz^2}\right)_{z^2 = z} = \varphi_2(-z, z) - \alpha\varphi_1(-z, z),$$

or, equivalently,[1]

$$s(-z, z) = -\frac{\varphi_1(-z, z)}{\varphi_2(-z, z)} = -\frac{1}{\alpha}.$$

It has been proved elsewhere[2] that this necessary condition for the maximality of U in the constant programme $z^t = z$ is also sufficient. Figure 5:7 illustrates the construction. *One scans the points of $\mathscr{S}$ to find one or more points where the slope of the level curve of φ has the value $-1/\alpha$ for the given α. Any point in the interior of $\mathscr{Z}$ satisfying this 'slope condition' represents an invariant optimal capital stock, to be denoted $\hat{z}$, provided* the prescribed slope $-1/\alpha$ itself meets our present 'no-slack' slope constraint[3]

$$-\frac{b_3}{a_3} < -\frac{1}{\alpha} = s(-\hat{z}, \hat{z}).$$

The 'slope condition' for an invariant capital stock we have found has a natural interpretation in terms of the shadow prices q^t, r^t associated with the constant programme $z^t = \hat{z}$. The condition specifies

$$q^2 = \alpha q^1, q^3 = \alpha q^2, \ldots, \text{so } q^t = (\alpha)^{t-1} q^1, t = 2, 3, \ldots,$$

a geometric decline in marginal utility of the invariant capital stock $z^t = \hat{z}$, in the ratio α per period equal to the discount factor prescribed by the objective function U.

The condition $q^2 = \alpha q^1$ extends to the end points of $\mathscr{S}$ and to points of $\mathcal{L}$ for which an associated optimal activity vector involves slacks. It also generalises to similar models with any number of capital goods, resources and consumption goods. In these cases, q^1, q^2 are to be regarded as vectors of shadow prices (dual variables). Where these vectors are not uniquely determined, the condition $q^2 = \alpha q^1$ requires only that one can find values q^1, q^2 within the permissible joint range of (q^1, q^2) that meet the condition.

IV THE RELATION BETWEEN THE DISCOUNT FACTOR AND AN INVARIANT OPTIMAL CAPITAL STOCK

In the preceding Section III, the element of intertemporal preferences was introduced by a discount factor α applicable to future *utilities*. At the end of the Section it was found that, if an invariant capital stock is indefinitely maintained, that same factor α also applies in the definition of shadow prices of *goods*. The reason is simple. As long as the capital stock, the consumption vector, and the one-period utility function $u(\cdot, \cdot)$ do not change over time, the same holds for the *marginal utilities of the goods* in question. Therefore the discount factor for utilities equals that for goods in this case.

[1] Since not both, hence neither, of φ_1, φ_2 can vanish in $(-z, z)$.
[2] Hansen and Koopmans (1972).
[3] We do not need to reiterate the constraint $s < 0$ because the specification $0 < \alpha < 1$ requires that $s < -1$.

It is of interest to study the relation between the discount factor α and the associated value or values of the invariant capital stock $\hat{z}(\alpha)$. This may be defined as the set of compatible pairs $(\alpha, \hat{z}(\alpha))$. This notion is applicable equally to the perfect market interpretation and to the perfect planning model. Its principal weakness in either case is the disregard of technical change. A second weakness is the circumstance that for a historically given initial capital stock, even without further technical change, continued growth towards an attractive invariant capital stock is likely to be, in most if not all existing economies, the first recommendation of the criterion U on which the concept rests. For most policy problems knowledge of the characteristics of the near-future segment of that path is the most urgent requirement.

However, we have to crawl before we can walk, and walk before we can run. It is hoped that an analysis of the relation between α and $\hat{z}(\alpha)$ may add precision to intuitions and ideas with a long history in economic theory. It may also turn out to be a useful preparation for the more difficult problems associated with a path that chases a capital stock which itself is in a moving equilibrium over time with changing technology, changing resource availability, and changing momentary and intertemporal preferences.

Figure 5:8 illustrates that there can easily be more than one invariant capital stock for a given value of α. The diagram exhibits two distinct points of $\mathcal{S}$, both labelled $\hat{f}(\alpha)$, with identical slopes $-1/\alpha$, and between them a third

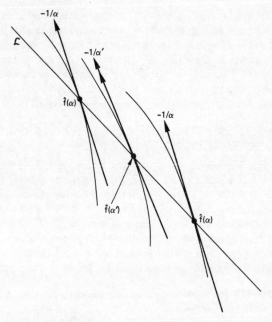

Fig. 5:8   Case of more than one invariant capital stock for a given α

point $\hat{f}(\alpha')$ with a different slope $-1/\alpha'$, where $\alpha' > \alpha$. Such a pattern is entirely compatible with strict concavity of the function $\varphi(-z^1, z^2)$.

Figures 5:9 and 5:10 illustrate that this cannot occur if the two consumption goods are *normal* goods. By this I mean that, for any fixed positive relative prices p_1, p_2, the utility-maximising consumption pair y_1, y_2 attainable within a given budget b at those prices increases strictly in both components as b increases. In that case the absolute value of the slope

$$| s^*(y_1, y_2) | \equiv \frac{u_1(y_1, y_2)}{u_2(y_1, y_2)}$$

of the level curve of u in the point (y_1, y_2) increases if y_2 increases with y_1 held constant and decreases if y_1 increases with y_2 constant. Therefore, if one follows any straight line with negative slope such as $\overline{d_1 d_2}$ in Figure 5:9, the absolute slope of the level curve increases as y_2 increases (and hence y_1 decreases at the same time). Choosing $\overline{d_1' d_2'}$ in such a way that by the mapping $(y_1, y_2) = (x_1, x_2) \leftrightarrow (-z^1, z^2)$ it transforms into the segment $\mathcal{S}$ in Figure 5:10, we find that $\hat{z}(\alpha)$ increases as α increases. The interpretation is that a higher discount factor (a lower real interest rate) is associated both with a higher equilibrium capital stock per worker and with a proportionately higher consumption of the good '2', which is more capital-intensive in its production than good '1'. In contrast, in Section V we shall consider the counter-intuitive case of decreasing $\hat{z}(\alpha)$, where a higher discount factor is associated with a smaller invariant capital stock and, indeed, a lower utility level in each period.

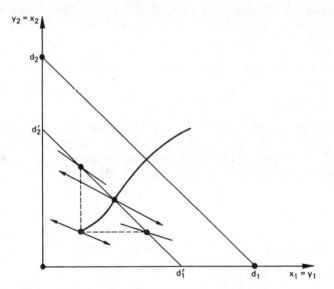

Fig. 5:9 Slopes of level curves of the utility function for normal consumption goods

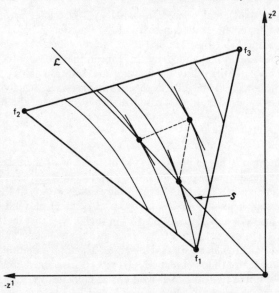

Fig. 5:10   The invariant stock increases with α when both consumption goods are normal

In that case the more capital-intensive good '2' is superior[1] to good '1'.

For the present case of normal consumption goods, we shall describe without full proof the $(\alpha, \hat{z}(\alpha))$ pairs for α and/or z at the end points of their permitted ranges. If, as in Figure 5:11 on p. 165 $s(-z, z)$ reaches its algebraic upper bound -1 in some point $(-\hat{z}(1), \hat{z}(1))$ of $\mathcal{S}$ interior to $\mathcal{Z}$, then

$$\hat{z}(1) \equiv \lim_{\alpha \to 1} \hat{z}(\alpha)$$

is an analogue of the (undiscounted) golden rule capital stock of the one-sector model. Values $z > \hat{z}(1)$ then cannot occur as invariant capital stocks for any permitted value of α. If as in Figure 5:12 the slope $-1/\bar{\alpha}$ of φ at the (boundary) point $(-\bar{z}, \bar{z})$ of $\mathcal{Z}$ with the highest attainable value $\bar{z}$ of z satisfies

$$-\frac{b_3}{a_3} < s(-\bar{z}, \bar{z}) \equiv -\frac{1}{\alpha} \leqslant -1,$$

then $\bar{z}$ is an invariant stock for the following set of values of α,

$$\hat{z}(\alpha) = \bar{z} \quad \text{for} \quad \bar{\alpha} \leqslant \alpha \leqslant 1.$$

---

[1] At least in a neighbourhood of the set of consumption vectors $\hat{y}_1(\alpha)$, $\hat{y}_2(\alpha)$ associated with the pairs $(\alpha, \hat{z}(\alpha))$ in question.

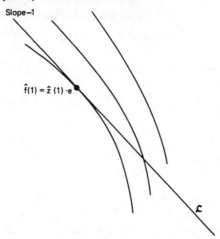

Fig. 5:11   Limiting invariant stock for $\alpha \to 1$

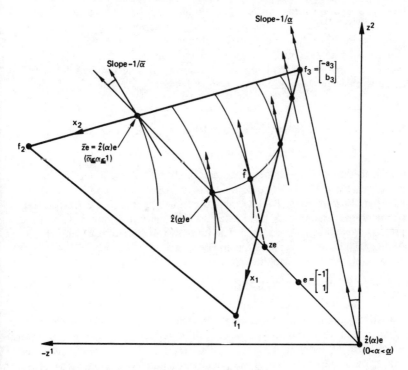

Fig. 5:12   Locus of the invariant capital stock for $1 > \alpha > 0$

Most intriguing is the situation for the lowest value

$$\alpha = \underline{\alpha} \equiv \frac{a_3}{b_3}$$

of α permitting within-period optimality without labour slack in combination with the corresponding invariant stock of $\hat{z}(\alpha)$, if a stock satisfying the 'slope condition' exists for that $\underline{\alpha}$. In Figure 5:12, this $\hat{z}(\underline{\alpha})$ is in the interior of $\mathscr{Z}$. It could also be the lower end point z of $\mathscr{S}$. In either case, the same value $\alpha = \underline{\alpha}$ can also be associated with any stock z in the range

$$0 \leqslant z \leqslant \hat{z}(\underline{\alpha})$$

in the role of an invariant stock for that $\underline{\alpha}$, with unemployment increasing as z decreases.

Figure 5:12 shows for any given such z the determination of the *unemployment* $\epsilon = 1 - x$, say, where $x = x_1 + x_2 + x_3$ is the remaining *employment*, both measured in a total-labour-force unit. It is now preferable to give up the principle underlying Figure 5:4, the representation of (x_1, x_2) and $(-z^1, z^2)$ by a single point referred to two different co-ordinate systems. If we were to insist on maintaining this principle in the presence of unemployment, we would have to use a co-ordinate system of (x_1, x_2) that moves, level curves and all, with the axes remaining parallel to themselves but the origin in the point $(-a_3 x, b_3 x)$ sliding along $\overline{Of_3}$ in step with the employment x. It is simpler to retain the old origin f_3 for the co-ordinate system of (x_1, x_2). Using z as a parameter, and denoting the corresponding employment and activity levels by

$$\hat{x}(z), \hat{x}_1(z), \hat{x}_2(z), \qquad 0 \leqslant z \leqslant \hat{z}(\underline{\alpha}),$$

these quantities are determined with the help of a displaced vector

$$(-\tilde{z}^1, \tilde{z}^2) \equiv (-z, z) + (1 - x)(-a_3, b_3)$$

similar to that used in the tightness test for the labour constraint. For given z and variable x, the point so defined moves from $(-z, z)$ along a straight line of slope $-b_3/a_3 = -1/\underline{\alpha}$. To determine the value $x = \hat{x}(z)$ of x corresponding to the given z one extends this line, if possible, until it is tangent to an (undisplaced) level curve of $\varphi(-z^1, z^2)$. The value of x at the point of tangency $\hat{f} \equiv \hat{f}(z) \equiv (-\tilde{z}^1(z), \tilde{z}^2(z))$, say, is the desired $\hat{x}(z)$. The values of $\hat{x}_1(z), \hat{x}_2(z)$ are read off from the mapping relation

$$(\hat{x}_1(z), \hat{x}_2(z)) \leftrightarrow (-\tilde{z}^1(z), \tilde{z}^2(z)),$$

taken in the reverse direction. If no tangency points exists, $(-\tilde{z}^1(z), \tilde{z}^2(z))$ is a boundary point of $\mathscr{Z}$. Which one it is, is determined by rules similar to those applicable in the end points of $\mathscr{S}$. As to the latter, if in no point of $\mathscr{S}$ interior to $\mathscr{Z}$ there is a tangent to $\varphi(z^1, z^2)$ of slope $-1/\alpha$, then the boundary point $(-\underline{z}, \underline{z})$ of $\mathscr{Z}$ on $\mathscr{S}$ nearest to the origin will take the place of $(-\hat{z}(\underline{\alpha}), \hat{z}(\underline{\alpha}))$ in the above description, and will also serve as a no-slack invariant capital stock for all α such that

$$-\frac{1}{\overline{\alpha}} \leqslant -\frac{1}{\alpha} \leqslant s(-z, z).$$

How does the ratio a_3/b_3 come to have such an important role as a critical value $\underline{\alpha}$ of the discount factor in the present problem? The answer lies in a connection between the present model and the von Neumann model obtained from Table 5:1 by discarding all but the first two constraints. Since process '3' has the highest ratio b_j/a_j of capital output to input among the three processes, the requirement of fastest capital growth implicit in the von Neumann model can be met only by shifting all labour from the production of consumption goods to that of capital goods – a feat easier in the so truncated model than in reality. A counterpiece to this observation arises in the present model. If impatience rises, hence the discount factor sinks, below the critical value $\underline{\alpha}$,

$$0 < \alpha < \underline{\alpha} \equiv a_3/b_3,$$

then the only invariant capital stock in existence is the null stock,

$$\hat{z}(\alpha) = 0, \quad \text{with } \hat{x}_j(\alpha) = 0, \quad j = 1, 2, 3.$$

At the precise point $\alpha = \underline{\alpha}$, a whole family of invariant capital stocks z, $0 \leqslant z \leqslant \hat{z}(\alpha)$, and associated employment levels $\hat{x}(z)$ varying continuously from 0 to 1, maintains the connectedness of the set of all points $(\alpha, \hat{z}(\alpha), \hat{x}_j(\alpha), j = 1, 2, 3)$ in 5-dimensional space.

Figure 5:12 illustrates the dependence of $\hat{z}(\alpha)$ on α and shows one particular possible geometrical form for the family of $\hat{x}(\underline{\alpha})$ associated with $\alpha = \underline{\alpha}$. Figure 5:13 exhibits a corresponding curve for the dependence of the $\hat{x}_j(\alpha), j = 1, 2,$

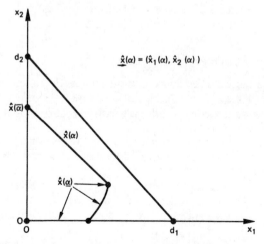

Fig. 5:13   Locus of the associated consumption vector for $1 > \alpha > 0$

on α in the (x_1, x_2)-plane, again with a one-parameter family of points for the value $\alpha = \underline{\alpha}$.

V   ADDENDUM:[1] INSTABILITY OF THE INVARIANT CAPITAL STOCK IN THE COUNTER–INTUITIVE CASE

So far we have only asked for a capital stock *invariant* under optimisation. We now raise the question of *stability* of an invariant capital stock under small perturbations of the initial stock. An invariant optimal capital stock will be called *stable* (under optimisation) if optimal paths starting from initial stocks in some neighbourhood of the invariant stock will converge over time to that invariant stock.

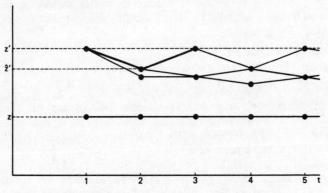

Fig. 5:14   Stability test for invariant capital stock z

Figure 5:14 illustrates a simple heuristic (non-rigorous) test of the stability of an invariant optimal (scalar) capital stock in one important case. It is based on properties of the function

$$W \equiv W(z^1, z^2, z^3; \alpha) \equiv \varphi(-z^1, z^2) + \alpha\varphi(-z^2, z^3)$$

that go beyond those studied above in connection with the test of invariance of an initial stock $z = z^1 = z^3$. Recall that the latter test confirms the invariance of such a z if the maximum of W with respect to z^2 is attained when also $z^2 = z$. Let this be the case.

The heuristic test of stability then applies in the case where, for all z^1 and z^3 in a neighbourhood $(z - \epsilon, z + \epsilon)$ of z, the value $\hat{z}^2$ of z^2 that maximises W is a strictly increasing function both of z^1 and of z^3. While this, let us say, *strong smoothness* condition on W may seem arbitrary, it becomes more natural if we think in terms of a class of functions W which, in the limit for smaller and smaller time units, permits a smooth transition to a continuous time variable.

---

[1] As indicated at the end of Section I, this Addendum was added after the Conference.

To apply the stability test to the invariant stock z, let $z < z' < z + \epsilon$, and now take $z^1 = z' = z^3$ and write $\hat{z}'$ for the value of z^2 maximising $W(z', z^2, z')$. The strong smoothness condition then requires that $\hat{z}' > z$. The stability test then says that,

$$
\left.
\begin{array}{l}
z \text{ is stable if } z < \hat{z}' < z' \\[1.5em]
z \text{ is unstable if } \quad z' < \hat{z}'
\end{array}
\right\} \quad \text{whenever } z < z' < z + \epsilon.
$$

To be conclusive the test would also need to be applied symmetrically to all z' with $z - \epsilon < z' < z$.

Figure 5:14 illustrates by heavy lines a case where the stability test is met by a z' with $z < z' < z + \epsilon$. The thin lines give plausibility to the test by suggesting a limiting process converging to the optimal path from an initial stock $z^1 = z'$ by alternately holding the capital stocks constant in odd-numbered and even-numbered points of time while optimising at all other points. The convergence follows from the strong smoothness condition.

So far the discussion has been concerned with the stability of a capital stock $z \equiv \hat{z}(\alpha)$ invariant for a given value of the discount factor α. We shall now show that the same test also answers the question whether, for a discount factor α' slightly larger (or smaller) than α, we have the intuitive case where the corresponding invariant stock $z' \equiv \hat{z}(\alpha')$ is also larger (smaller) than z, or the counterintuitive case where $z' < (>) z$.

The conditions defining z and z' are

$$W(z^2) \equiv \varphi(-z, z^2) + \alpha\varphi(-z^2, z) \text{ is maximal for } z^2 = z,$$

$$W'(z^2) \equiv \varphi(-z', z^2) + \alpha'\varphi(-z^2, z') \text{ is maximal for } z^2 = z'.$$

Necessary and sufficient conditions for these to hold are, respectively,

$$\varphi_2(-z, z) - \alpha\varphi_1(-z, z) \quad = 0,$$

$$\varphi_2(-z', z') - \alpha'\varphi_1(-z', z') = 0.$$

The stability test involves a third function of a W-type, viz.,

$$W^{(\prime)} \equiv \varphi(-z', z^2) + \alpha\varphi(-z^2, z'),$$

and, is, on account of the strict concavity of $W^{(\prime)}$, equivalent to

$$
z \text{ is } \begin{bmatrix} \text{stable} \\ \text{unstable} \end{bmatrix} \text{ if } \left(\frac{dW^{(\prime)}}{dz^2}\right)_{z^2 = z'} = \varphi_2(-z', z') - \alpha\varphi_1(-z', z') \begin{bmatrix} < \\ > \end{bmatrix} 0
$$

for $|z - z'| < \epsilon$. But then, since this expression vanishes if α is replaced by α', and since φ_1 is positive, we find that z is stable if $\alpha < \alpha'$, unstable if $\alpha > \alpha'$. Note that these are precisely the intuitive and the counter-intuitive case, respectively, with regard to the direction of change of the invariant capital stock when the discount factor is changed.

To illustrate the implications of this finding (see Figure 5:15), assume that the counter-intuitive behaviour of $\hat{z}(\alpha)$ applies throughout the interval $\mathscr{S}$ of Figure 5:7. Let as before $\underline{z}$, $\bar{z}$ denote the capital stocks corresponding to the lower and upper end points of $\mathscr{S}$, and $\bar{\alpha}$, $\underline{\alpha}$, respectively, the corresponding discount factors. Then $\underline{z} < \bar{z}$, $\underline{\alpha} < \bar{\alpha}$, and $\underline{z} = \hat{z}(\bar{\alpha})$, $\bar{z} = \hat{z}(\underline{\alpha})$ are invariant capital stocks for the discount factors shown, provided $\underline{\underline{\alpha}} \geqslant \underline{\alpha} \equiv b_3/a_3$. Now take an α with $\underline{\alpha} < \alpha < \bar{\alpha}$, and study the dependence of the optimal path z^t on the prescribed initial value z^1. Then, if by chance $z^1 = \hat{z}(\alpha)$, the path z^t continues on the constant level of the unstable invariant capital stock $\hat{z}(\alpha)$. If $\underline{z} < z^1 < \hat{z}(\alpha)$, by however little, z^t decreases until the level $\underline{z}$ is reached, whereupon the path continues at that level. Likewise, if $\hat{z}(\alpha) < z^1 < \bar{z}$, the path increases until it becomes constant at the level $\bar{z}$. In fact, $\underline{z}$ is a stable invariant stock $\hat{z}(\alpha')$ for all α' such that $\underline{\underline{\alpha}} \leqslant \alpha' < \bar{\alpha}$, and $\bar{z}$ is a stable stock for all α' such that $\underline{\alpha} < \alpha' \leqslant 1$. Hence, under the present assumptions, the end-points $\underline{z}$, $\bar{z}$ are prototypes of empirically meaningful invariant capital stocks, while $\hat{z}(\alpha)$ is a freak, a knife-edge occurrence. Its only conceivable empirical significance is a signal that for z^1 in a neighbourhood of $\hat{z}(\alpha)$ the many features of reality not expressed in an otherwise acceptable model will influence the outcome of the toss of a coin.

Iwai (1975) has confirmed the heuristic reasoning of this Addendum by a rigorous application of stability analysis that examines the behaviour of

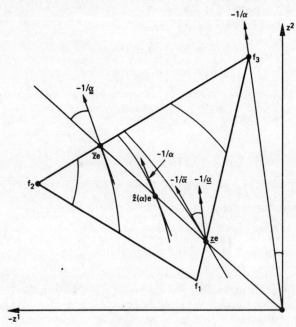

Fig. 5:15   An unstable invariant stock $\hat{z}(\alpha)$

second derivatives of the function $W(z^1, z^2, z^3; \alpha)$ for the z^t in a neighbourhood of an invariant capital stock $\hat{z}(\alpha)$. His analysis also includes the case where strong smoothness of W is not assumed. It can then happen that, for some $z^1, z^3 > \hat{z}(\alpha)$, the value of z^2 maximising W satisfies $z^2 < \hat{z}(\alpha)$. In such a case optimal paths can oscillate between values above and below $\hat{z}(\alpha)$, with stability not governed by the criterion found above.

REFERENCES

T. Hansen and T. C. Koopmans, 'Definition and Computation of a Capital Stock Invariant under Optimization,' *Journal of Economic Theory*, Vol. 5, No 3 (December 1972) pp. 487–523.

H. S. Houthakker, 'The Pareto Distribution and the Cobb-Douglas Production Function in Activity Analysis,' *Review of Economic Studies*, Vol. XXIII, No 1, (1955–56) pp. 27–31.

K. Iwai, Unpublished memorandum (1975).

L. Johansen, *Production Functions* (Amsterdam-London: North Holland Publishing Co., 1972).

T. C. Koopmans, 'Intertemporal Distribution and "Optimal" Aggregate Economic Growth,' Chapter 5 in W. Fellner, *et al.*, *Ten Economic Studies in the Tradition of Irving Fisher* (New York: Wiley, 1967) pp. 95–126.

D. Levhari, 'A Note on Houthakker's Aggregate Production Function in a Multifirm Industry,' *Econometrica*, Vol. 30, No 1 (January 1968) pp. 151–4.

E. Malinvaud, 'Capital Accumulation and the Efficient Allocation of Resources,' *Econometrica*, Vol. 21, No 2 (April 1953) pp. 233–68.

F. Ramsey, 'A Mathematical Theory of Saving,' *Economic Journal*, Vol. 38, No 152 (December 1928) pp. 534–59.

K. Sato, 'Micro and Macro Constant-Elasticity-of-Substitution Production Functions in a Multifirm Industry,' *Journal of Economic Theory* Vol. 1, No 4 (December 1969) pp. 438–53.

Discussion of the Paper by Professor Koopmans

Professor Shubik, after admitting that he would have preferred Professor
Koopmans to introduce his own paper because he felt both that he would
have been a better discussant and that it was slightly incestuous for colleagues
from the same institution to praise each other's papers in public, read a few
passages from the paper [pp. 144–6] which explained succinctly
what the paper was about. While Section II discussed one theory of production
associated with the work of Houthakker and Johansen, where production was
represented by process vectors, in Section III the capital stock problem under
optimisation over time was considered. Here the modelling was explicitly
dynamic, with a standard utility function, a linear function of the discounted
future income stream, and the discount factor was a natural time preference
factor. The 'golden rule' notion was discussed and the work of Ramsay and
others referred to, but the purpose was quite clearly to push beyond the
already known results. In other more technical papers Professors Koopmans
and Johansen had looked at the many goods case, with n processes and three
goods; in this paper there were one capital good, one resource and two consumption goods. Professor Koopmans had shown that this particular problem
could be reduced by making a mapping from the inputs on to the initial
capital stock and the capital stock at the end of each period. Once one had
done that one was faced with a dynamic programming problem. With the aid
of some extremely ingenious diagrams Professor Koopmans had not only been
able to present the full model but to put it into two dimensions and illustrate
several surprising results. In particular, even in this simple model there was
not necessarily one invariant capital stock. Furthermore, a new and counter-
intuitive result appeared: as the discount rate approached unity, it was possible
to have a case where the capital stock was reduced. This would not occur if
the consumption goods were normal goods. In other words, if given the price
vector, increasing the budget constraint led individuals to purchase more of
all goods, then there would be a unique invariant capital stock.

In Professor Shubik's opinion the paper had the same elegance and
precision as the *Three Essays on Economic Science* and Professor Koopmans's
other works. The extension from one-dimensional dynamics to two- or more-
dimensional dynamics was clearly one of the key problems in the development
of a satisfactory theory of economic dynamics; and it was also clearly
extremely difficult. The most important question in terms of aggregation was
whether when we became explicitly disaggregative in a dynamic model we
had any hopes of showing under what conditions the more aggregative models
would be sufficient. This particular analysis gave us one set of conditions concerning normal goods.

In Professor Shubik's considered opinion, the paper was illustrative of the
extreme distance between careful microeconomics and macroeconomics. It
was a classic example of thorough microeconomic modelling and because of
its thoroughness and precision there was little need for debate concerning the
conceptual foundations of the model. Furthermore, the model did not claim
to do any more or less than it set out to do. In particular, there was no
discussion of the capital stock profile (one had only to think of financial considerations to realise that at least forty to forty-five years was probably
relevant in the description of the capital stock in any major economy). We

might suspect that a great amount of economic dynamics depended upon the profile of the capital stock. This model could not deal with that aspect of dynamics. Furthermore, the model was primarily technological, so that in the nature of the model the question of whether the economy being modelled was centralised or competitive was finessed. There was no financial structure; and there was also implicit within the model the concept of perfect foresight. This list of lacunae was not an attack on the paper, but an indication that there were in fact hundreds of problems in the reconciliation of macro-economics and microeconomics. The importance of this paper was the care taken in describing and delimiting the territory it covered. It was always important to try to display the frailties and ambiguities in one's models; indeed the great benefit of mathematical economics was that it called for a precision which if used skilfully enabled people to spot the items left out of a model much more quickly than if one had 300 pages of philosophical dis-course. In contrast there were some mathematical economics writings where the straitjacket of the mathematics killed ideas too early. One of the real con-tributions that Professor Koopmans had made was that his paper provided an example of how to use mathematics and to communicate in a parsimonious manner what particular pieces of a problem were being tackled so that one could both immediately raise questions as to what had been left out and immediately see the value of the analysis that had been included.

Professor Davidson, although believing that within its logic the paper was quite excellent, wished to compare it with Keynes's capital theory (*The General Theory of Employment, Interest and Money*, Chapter 16). Keynes did not mention 'production functions'; he said that a capital theory should be able to explain such things as scarcity and redundancy of capital and positive and negative rates of return. Could a model such as Professor Koopmans's show us a possible equilibrium situation where production is undertaken by rational entrepreneurs while the aggregate stock of capital is earning a negative rate of return (e.g., the Great Depression)? If it did not, was there something wrong with the real world or something wrong with the applicability of the model?

Professor Stiglitz pointed out that the contribution of this paper as opposed to many other papers in the same area was that it took only one capital good but many consumption goods and illustrated some of the so-called perver-sities that had arisen in the context of many capital goods. In other models it was generally the case that as the rate of interest rose the price of the capital-intensive good would rise and normally lead to a reduction in the demand for this capital good and hence a fall in the demand for capital; in this model if consumption goods were inferior it was possible that because of the income effects if the price of capital goods increased the demand for the capital-intensive good increased and hence the demand for the capital stock would increase.

At this point *Professor Koopmans* drew attention to a correction he had made. After some discussion *Professor Stiglitz* continued by suggesting that since the model could be interpreted as a descriptive model of a competitive economy as well as a planning model, one might want to ask whether the patterns of consumption out of interest and wages might be different. Could one obtain the same kinds of perversities with a wider range of utility functions? Many of these results had been established in the context of models with more than one capital good; i.e. in the literature on reswitching and the Ruth Cohen *curiosum*.

Professor Malinvaud agreed with Professor Stiglitz that it was interesting that there was no simple necessary relationship between the interest rate and capital intensity even in the very special framework of the invariant capital stock. Economists had looked for this simple relationship, one of the main propositions of neoclassical economics, for a century; but now it was generally recognised that the property did not always hold. Professor Malinvaud had himself worked on the problem in a model with only one capital good, two commodities (a durable good and a perishable good), and labour. He had looked at the stationary efficient programmes assuming constant technology and constant labour force, and found that in this programme there was not a necessary one-one relationship between the interest rate and capital intensity. Thus in the debate between the two Cambridges, Cambridge U.K. had been right on this point. However, he did not think the consequences were very profound. The situation where theory cannot fully support intuition had arisen before in economics, with respect to, for example, downward-sloping demand curves or cost-of-living indices. Whether intuition is right then becomes an empirical question. Most demand curves are in fact downward-sloping.

Professor Spaventa drew attention to the resemblance of the counter-intuitive case in Professor Koopmans's model to the 'transformation problem'. The attempt to establish a unique relationship between labour values and prices and between rate of surplus value and rate of profit broke down, even without joint production, exactly when a change in the consumption basket entailed the consumption of two commodities moving in opposite directions.

Professor Green asked whether Professor Koopmans could indicate the relevance of his paper to the aggregation problem?

Professor Asimakopulos asked the meaning of the discount factor. Did it apply to capitalists or to workers?

Dr Nuti thought that the most attractive feature of Professor Koopmans's paper was that the mathematical conditions for the relationship between the interest rate and the value of capital to be perverse were spelled out in very clear and understandable economic terms. He did not think, however, that the result obtained meant that we could dismiss capital intensity reversal as a curiosity, for several reasons:

(1) Even if there was only one capital good, this perversity could arise because of something unusual on the preference side.
(2) If we looked at cross-section data involving several countries, each country having different preferences, or if we looked at time series where preferences changed in an unforeseen fashion, we could still observe a perverse relationship between the interest rate and the capital stock.
(3) While most of the literature had focused on stationary economies, a zero growth rate was just as arbitrary as a growth rate of, say, 2·79. Once we enlarged the universe of economies to include steady growth rate economies, we had no reason to expect any systematic relationship between the interest rate and the capital stock. This was not due to any perversity of preferences or of technology.

The implication was that it was not just a question of the relationship between the interest rate and the capital stock. It was a question of the relation between output per man and capital per man. Again, one had no reason to expect that a multi-sector model would behave as a one-sector model in this respect, for there were at least three effects determining the relationship in value terms: the Wicksell real effect of interest rates on the choice of technique, the Wicksell price effect of interest rates on the relative values of various commodities, and the composition effect of the growth rate on the relative proportion of capital goods and consumption goods in the economy. The resultant of these three forces would not necessarily be a well-behaved relationship between capital per man and output per man. Dr Nuti disagreed with Professor Malinvaud's suggestion that it was only an empirical question. Even if data suggested a perfectly normal relationship there was no reason to suppose that it involved any substitutability between capital goods; the question could not be settled empirically. He also emphasised the meaning of the apparently harmless assumption of perfect foresight: it was equivalent to, and as heroic an assumption as, that of perfectly malleable capital goods.

Professor Harcourt also thought that there was a difference between the phenomenon of Giffen goods and the relationship that had for a century been thought to exist between the rate of profits and the capital stock of a capitalist economy. The latter problem was more important. Referring to the symposium in the *Quarterly Journal of Economics*, February 1975, on Joan Robinson's 'The Unimportance of Reswitching', Professor Harcourt pointed out that in the reswitching debate the two groups antagonistic to neoclassical economics had also been antagonistic to each other. One group usually used the Ricardian strong case, long-run equilibrium comparisons; the other group were, like Professors Stiglitz and Hahn, trying to analyse out-of-equilibrium processes occurring in actual time; the failure to keep the three groups separate had led to many confusions in the debates.

Professor Frey thought that a more proper analogy than Giffen goods was that between aggregation in capital theory and aggregation in preference theory. There was in both cases heterogeneity, of capital goods and of preferences respectively. The theoretical discussion had in both cases proceeded in almost the same fashion, in seven consecutive steps:

(1) The profession was unaware that there was an aggregation problem.
(2) An Impossibility Theorem was proved under special and restrictive assumptions. In capital theory there were at this stage the various contributions by Joan Robinson and Pasinetti; in preference theory the famous contribution by Arrow. After some resistance the profession accepted the possibility that there might be an aggregation problem.
(3) Conditions were sought under which *no* paradox arises. For example, it was proved that if there was a linear wage rate-rate of profit relationship there arose no perversity in capital aggregation.
(4) Monte Carlo studies were undertaken to find out the *probability* of occurrence of a paradox. It was, for example, shown that if there were three voters and three issues (and all preference distributions were equally likely) the probability of no majority winner was only approximately 7 per cent, but rose quickly with the number of votes and issues. Verbal communications seemed to indicate that analogous research was under way in capital theory.

(5) Empirical studies were undertaken looking for instances of paradoxes. In preference theory there were some observations in the case of university elections (Niemi) and the United States Congress (Riker). In capital theory there were very few studies in this direction so far.

(6) At this stage established theory pointed out that its foundations were really unaffected if such paradoxes arose. Neoclassicists stressed that the correct approach to capital theory was disaggregative, and that the use of aggregate capital and aggregate production functions was at best a useful approximation. In the field of preferences it had even been said that paradoxical outcomes were welcome, because they made the exploitation of the minority by the majority impossible (Buchanan).

(7) Finally, the most general theorems were formulated and there was some consensus in the profession about the whole aggregation problem. Preference theory might in this respect be more advanced: Kramer ('On a class of equilibrium conditions for majority rule', *Econometrica*, 1973) had proved that the conditions required for individual preferences to be aggregated were extremely restrictive. It should, therefore, be accepted that the paradoxes of preference aggregation were a fact of life; Professor Koopmans's contribution seemed to point in the same direction with respect to capital.

Professor Shubik raised two points. First, he asked Professor Koopmans where he thought the next fruitful directions were. Second, he disagreed with Professor Frey's remarks about preference aggregation. To prove Arrow's impossibility theorem one had to accept a lot of assumptions. In Professor Koopmans's model there was in the utility function implicitly a social welfare function, but we should like to disaggregate the utility function as well as the production process. The problem in putting in more than one utility function in the model was that one would have a set of parallel dynamic programmes, on which very little work had been done. However, there did exist one or two mathematical handholds, and Professor Shubik conjectured that in the next two or three years economic insight would improve mathematical methods, for he believed that there was often an interaction between the substantive insights in a subject and the development of the appropriate mathematics.

Professor Koopmans explained the correction that he had made to his paper as circulated. Once corrected, the model showed that in the 'perverse' case the invariant capital stock was unstable. He then replied to the comments that had been made.

On the way in which the ideas could be developed further in relation to the aggregation problem, he had the following suggestions. Even in this very simple model the discount factor entered as a parameter, on which depended the invariant capital stock and other variables such as the consumption vector and the resource bundle used. If we eliminated the discount factor we would have a relation between the invariant capital stock, the resource use vector and the consumption vector. We might then be able to proceed by defining index numbers of capital, of resource use and of consumption, in which the shadow prices could be used as weights. In this case we could get some approximation to the curvature of the production surface and we could derive estimates for the various elasticity concepts to be constructed from the basic data of technology and preferences. Recent algorithmic developments in connection with finding a fixed point, due to Scarf and others, might also help here, making it possible to introduce the capital stock profile, as Professor Shubik wished.

Professor Davidson's point that the rate of return might change even with a constant technology was pertinent, but the concept of an invariant capital stock was not in that particular compartment of conceptualisation and theory. However, some of Houthakker and Johansen's work that he had referred to might bear on that question.

Professor Koopmans was in full agreement with Professor Malinvaud that the question of 'perversities' was an empirical one. He hoped that we would find empirically that the perversities were not important. He also agreed with Professor Spaventa that perversities could arise from several causes. In reply to Professor Asimakopulos, Professor Koopmans said that he had not been working at the level at which one could assign discount factors to workers and capitalists separately. Although aware of the difficulties, he had used the rate applicable to the social welfare function, because one had to work one step at a time. There was much more work to be done: the ultimately more important realistic formulation would have to take into account the way society is made up of different groups with different economic functions and behavioural parameters and the effect of that on the decision processes. He agreed with Dr Nuti that further work could be done on the three effects which Dr Nuti had mentioned; he also thought that his model could be adjusted to take into account a non-zero growth rate. But he hoped that the perverse relationship in his model was just a curiosity and could be ignored. He had been relieved to find in the symposium to which Professor Harcourt had referred that Joan Robinson and Samuelson apparently agreed on the unimportance of reswitching because he had earlier decided not to study that problem very hard.

Professor Stiglitz was in the unusual position of agreeing with Dr Nuti and disagreeing with Professor Malinvaud about the empirical nature of the question in hand. The available models left out enough of the relevant characteristics of the economy such as the presence of technical change and the existence of natural resources, that one could not test their validity empirically. Furthermore, he found it difficult to see in what interesting sense these models were of steady states. They analysed the question: Given an initial capital stock, what is the optimal growth path? Professor Stiglitz doubted whether this gave much insight into the behaviour of a system in which there were natural resources and technical change. He also raised a methodological point: how could one decide whether something was important or not? One of the consequences of the development of a higher standard of theory was that we were now able to generalise and one result was the disappearance of theorems that were true in a more restrictive world; he gave two examples in consumption theory.

Professor Nell raised the question of whether if in Professor Koopmans's model we had two or more capital goods, used in each other's production, there was not a difficulty in moving from one activity level to another, because this might necessitate special investment to build up the fixed capital stock in one of the industries? If the stock of fixed capital goods were assumed fully utilised at the initial activity level, where would the additional capacity for the new activity level come from, in those sectors that produced more in the new situation? And what would happen to the underutilised capacity in those sectors that produced less, since capital goods were not transferable?

Professor Koopmans agreed that the real problem was where to go from the historically given capital stock, but that was a much more difficult problem, both analytically and computationally.

Professor Malinvaud said that he was facing a dangerous coalition of Dr Nuti and Professor Stiglitz. He was not going to go into that subject further, because it would be too difficult; it would be the subject of a conference on the empirical foundations of macroeconomics. He added that Dr Nuti and Professor Stiglitz might not qualify for that conference!

Professor Shubik thought that all present realised that economics in the broad sweep of the subject did not really deal with equilibrium positions but with tendencies to equilibrium. Although it was probable that no economy had ever reached equilibrium, this did not mean the analysis of tendencies towards equilibrium was not worthwhile. It was a good methodological device to start with the simple non-stochastic case and then to add an exogenous stochastic element. In Professor Koopmans's model a random variable would get rid of the knife-edge equilibrium.

Professor Henin believed that models should be specified much more for empirical work; in particular, we should depart from comparative dynamics and introduce actual adjustment processes in historical time. Then the difference between the points of view of, say, Professors Malinvaud and Stiglitz would become less important. The empirical debate would also probably become less connected with the theoretical debate. For example, the lack of regularity in the relation between interest rates and capital intensity was well known to be connected with multiple rates of return at the microeconomic level, but nobody finding an empirically low interest-elasticity of investment demand would use this as an explanation. Professor Henin also pointed out that Houthakker's 1955 paper showed that macro-economic relations were not always more perverse than microeconomic ones.

6 Aggregation Problems of Macroeconomics

H. A. John Green

UNIVERSITY OF KENT AT CANTERBURY

I INTRODUCTION

It is clear that macroeconomics, by its very nature, involves aggregation.[1] The questions I seek to investigate in this paper are: With what aggregates should macroeconomics be concerned? How should these aggregates or macro-variables be related to the micro-variables from which they are derived? I shall be concerned with the 'short-run' rather than with problems of economic growth.

These questions, of course, can be answered only on the basis of a view of the purpose or purposes of macroeconomic analysis. I would argue that as economists we are interested in macroeconomics because the ultimate aggregates it seeks to explain (typically, for example, in the short run employment, prices, and national income and its distribution) are of profound interest to everyone. For the direction of movement of any one of these aggregates is likely to affect everyone, or at least broad groups of people, in the same way. In answer to my first question with regard to this type of aggregate (which I shall call 'final variables'), it is required to select and construct aggregates which give to the citizen an indication of his own likely well-being, and which may in principle be inserted in the policy-maker's objective function.

The other variables in a macroeconomic model are included because of their role in determining the values of the final variables; I shall call these variables 'auxiliary'.[2] The appropriate aggregation procedure for auxiliary variables (which would typically include, for example, the quantity of money and the rate of interest)[3] is determined by the wish to explain or predict the values of the final variables satisfactorily.

It is possible for a final variable to appear as an independent variable in an equation explaining the value of an auxiliary variable or of another final

---

[1] 'The term 'macro-economics', introduced by Ragnar Frisch in 1933, applies to the study of broad aggretates, as opposed to the decision-taking procedures of individuals which is [sic] the subject-matter of micro-economics' (Allen, 1956, p. 1).

[2] The distinction between final and auxiliary variables is not the same as that between 'targets' and 'instruments', nor between 'exogenous' and 'endogenous' variables. It is a distinction stemming from differences in appropriate aggregation procedures, and owes much to Malinvaud (1956).

[3] See below, p. 192, footnote 1.

variable (e.g., the price level may appear in a system of equations explaining wages), so that the two sets of variables may not be disjoint. But in other cases the two variables may be similar rather than identical, and call for different aggregation procedures (e.g., income may be a final variable, but disposable income, or perhaps a partly disaggregated disposable income, may be an appropriate independent variable in the explanation of consumption).[1]

A final question is: What type of model are we considering? Is it an econometric model for prediction purposes? Is it a model designed to test, in so far as this is possible in economics, the relative merits of alternative hypotheses? Or is it intended for classroom exposition? The answer will have an important bearing on the type and degree of aggregation to be employed.

These preliminary considerations will determine the organisation of the more detailed discussion of aggregation problems in macroeconomics. Thus Sections II, III and IV are concerned respectively with final variables, auxiliary variables and types and sizes of model, and an attempt is made to draw some of the threads together in Section V.

II FINAL VARIABLES

Though real national *income* is the most usual summary measure of economic well-being and performance, most of the theoretical work on its significance has in fact been concerned with real *consumption*. It has been known for some time that extreme caution must be exercised in drawing conclusions about welfare changes from conventional measures. If income is always redistributed in a lump-sum fashion so as to maximise a social welfare function, then we can draw inferences from index numbers of total consumption exactly as if they related to a single individual (Samuelson, 1956). If there are no restrictions on the distribution of income, but all individuals have identical preferences with indifference surfaces homothetic to the origin, a comparison of index numbers of total consumption which would tell us, if they related to a single individual, that he was better off, would imply for society a 'potential improvement' in the sense of a uniform outward shift of the utility-possibility surface (Samuelson, 1950). The same conclusion may be drawn if, at any set of prices, individual Engel curves are linear and parallel for all distributions of income that occur (Gorman, 1953; Nataf, 1953). If the proportional distribution of income is constant, and the preferences of individuals are homothetic with reference to the origin but not necessarily identical, then an index-number change which would tell us that an individual was better off would imply that every individual was better off (Nataf and Roy, 1948).

If the implied social indifference curves are homothetic to the origin there is, along any ray from the origin, a natural measure of real consumption which is invariant to the bundle of goods actually chosen. Fisher and Shell (1972) have argued that if tastes change it is the current indifference map that should

---

[1] See below, p. 187.

be used in any comparison of present and past consumption, and that (whether or not the current indifference map is homothetic) the ratio of present to past real consumption should be measured as the ratio of the minimum expenditures necessary, at current prices, to attain the indifference curves on which the present and past bundles of goods lie. Thus if in Figure 6:1 the indifference curves drawn are from the current map, the ratio of current consumption (A) to past consumption (B) would be measured as OD/OE.

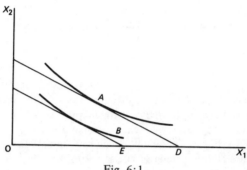

Fig. 6:1

In view of the lack of theory as to how far departures from the strict satisfaction of the conditions for the existence of social indifference surfaces lessen the usefulness of index-numbers of real consumption (and of the corresponding price-indices which are used to deflate money consumption), observers may derive varying measures of comfort from their estimates of the degree of optimality or variability of the distribution of income or of the similarity or homotheticity of tastes. I am myself more disturbed that the foregoing analysis is exclusively concerned with *consumption*. Even if we disregard the problems of evaluating public goods and services and the complex of factors which have come to be known as the 'costs of economic growth', it is impossible to omit in the context of this paper a problem which is close to the traditional concerns of macroeconomics — namely the treatment of investment in a measure of real national income.

A man's income has been defined as 'the maximum amount he can consume in a week and expect to be as well off at the end of the week as he was at the beginning' (Hicks, 1939). If we measure national income as $Y = C + pI$, where p is the price of capital goods in terms of consumption goods, then Y exceeds the amount that could be spent on consumption while leaving K intact unless p is constant (Green, 1964, p. 90). Thus in Figure 6:2 Y as measured is OA, while the maximum output of consumption goods consistent with zero net investment is OB.

But even if p were independent of the allocation of resources between consumption and investment (or we could measure national income as OB

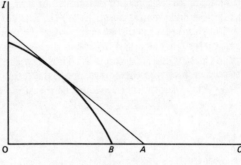

Fig. 6:2

rather than O*A* in Figure 6:2), two economies with identical transformation
frontiers between *C* and *I* might have different marginal productivities of
capital. The economy with the higher marginal productivity of capital could
have a rate of interest sufficiently higher to make the values of *p* the same in
the two economies, but would be unambiguously better off in terms of
present and future consumption (Samuelson, 1961).

Samuelson draws the conclusion that what is required is a measure of
'wealth' rather than of 'income', and in principle this is undoubtedly the case.
An alternative is simply to treat real consumption and real investment as
distinct final variables, entering separately into the objective functions of
policy-makers, without trying to combine them into a single figure.

If one adopts this course there remain two problems. The first is the
measurement of real investment. I do not mean here to re-open the question
of 'maintaining capital intact', but rather to ask in what conditions two
different batches of heterogeneous capital goods should be regarded as con-
stituting equal quantities of capital or investment.

The second problem is that, even if we refrain from combining *C* and *I* in a
single measure of *income*, the overall levels of *output* and labour productivity
of an economy are useful final variables. When consumption and investment
are regarded as produced goods, there appears to be no similar argument
against combining them in a single measure.[1]

To take the second problem first, one would like to be able to take the
location of the transformation curve attained as the basis for measuring output. Thus if there is a movement along a given transformation curve from *A*
to *B* in Figure 6:3, so that the value of *C* + *pI* increases from O*D* to O*E*, it
would be necessary to apply the appropriate 'deflator' to *Y* (dividing it by
O*E*/O*D*) so as to keep the measure of output constant: see Fisher and Shell
(1972).

But even in the most favourable conditions, where labour and homogeneous, malleable capital are optimally allocated among industries, a change

[1] I owe this point to conversations with my colleague Professor C. M. Kennedy.

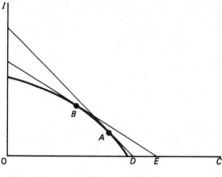

Fig. 6:3

in the total amount of labour or capital will cause the transformation curve to tilt unless the production functions in the individual sectors are identical. Otherwise an increase in K could shift the curve in Figure 6:4 from AB to DE, and an increase in L to FG.

But as I said earlier, I am concerned in this paper only with the 'short run'. I shall not interpret this as meaning that the stock of capital is strictly constant; to do so would exclude from consideration any effect of investment on output, and would leave us no way of measuring investment except in terms of consumption forgone. But I shall *not* make the 'long-run' assumption that capital is optimally allocated among industries.

In this case it is impossible for the transformation curves not to tilt. If we confine ourselves to the consumption and investment sectors,[1] with production functions $C(K_C, L_C)$ and $I(K_I, L_I)$ and assume that labour is optimally

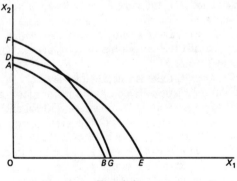

Fig. 6:4

[1] I shall not discuss the aggregation problems involved when many consumption goods and capital goods are produced with many kinds of capital goods and of labour. I believe that the basic principles are to be found in this section of the paper and in section IV below.

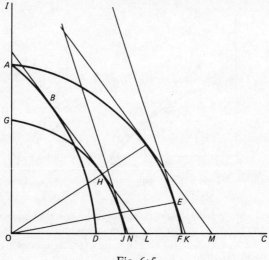

Fig. 6:5

allocated between K_C and K_I (which means in this case only that it is fully employed) an increase in K_C alone must shift the transformation curve from *ABD* to *AEF* in Figure 6:5. But how then is output to be measured?

Consider a map of transformation curves based on *AEF* and constructed by changing all resources (L, K_I and the new value of K_C) in the same proportion. If the two production functions are homogeneous of the same degree these transformation curves (*GHJ* is one of them) will be homothetic. Output was initially at *B* and is now at *E*. If the prices at *B* had ruled with the new transformation map, and goods of the same value as *B* had been produced, production would have been at *H*. $C + pI$ has risen in the ratio OK/OL. This must be corrected for the change in p by the deflator, which multiplies it by $OM/OK = OL/ON$, so that real output has risen in the ratio $OM/OL = OK/ON$: see Fisher and Shell (1972).

The measure of output, then, is a deflated value of $C + pI$, the deflator depending on p and the shape of the current transformation surface. As to the measurement of investment, let us now take optimal allocation of labour to mean an allocation which maximises $C + pI$ given K_C and K_I. We can then draw on the work of F. M. Fisher (1965, 1969) and others for the conditions in which an aggregate capital stock exists. They are that there exist functions $A_C(K_C)$ and $A_I(K_I)$ such that the production functions are identical and homogeneous of degree one in labour and the transformed capital variables:

$$C = F[A_C(K_C), L_C]; \quad I = F[A_I(K_I), L_I].\tag{1}$$

When labour is optimally allocated the marginal product of labour in C will be p times that in I, so that the ratio of $A_C(K_C)/L_C$ to $A_I(K_I)/L_I$ will depend on p. Thus:

$$C + pI = (L_C + L_I) f \left[\frac{A_C(K_C) + g(p) A_I(K_I)}{L_C + L_I} \right]. \qquad (2)$$

The measure of the capital stock is:

$$K = A_C(K_C) + g(p) A_I(K_I). \qquad (3)$$

In the Cobb-Douglas case, with capital exponent α, $g(p) = p^{1/\alpha}$, and in general $g'(p) > 0$.

Suppose now that a unit of K_C and a unit of K_I (hitherto unspecified) cost equal amounts in terms of consumption goods forgone. Then as p increases the weight given to K_I in the capital index increases, and the ratio of the marginal products of (money) capital and the ratio of the rates of profit move in favour of the investment goods industry. Investment in the industry with the higher rate of profit may tend to change p, and the relative prices of K_C and K_I, in an equilibrating direction, but so long as we do not assume capital to be optimally allocated the conditions for capital aggregation are extremely stringent. And we cannot, of course, differentiate Y or output with respect to K to obtain the rate of profit!

But, of course, output is determined by many things, some of which may have a claim to be treated as final variables in their own right: the amount of labour employed (or the labour force times the fraction employed)[1] and its productivity (dependent on the stock of capital, the state of technology, the efficiency of resource allocation between firms and 'X'-efficiency within firms: see Leibenstein, 1966).

But even if real consumption and investment, employment and productivity are all increasing, the figures may conceal redistribution between significant groups of people. The shares in $C + pI$ of labour and property income (the latter, together with Y itself, presenting even more formidable difficulties in times of inflation) are a major indicator of distribution, and may differ significantly between sectors. And I would retain the price index of consumer goods as a final variable because of its significance to those whose money incomes are fixed or predictable or controllable by policy (e.g., pensions)

My list of final variables therefore consists of real consumption and investment, real output (perhaps distinguishing employment and productivity), the shares of wages and profits (perhaps distinguished by sectors) and an index of consumer prices.

III AUXILIARY VARIABLES

It is not my intention to set out a macro-model to explain the values of the final variables selected in the previous section. Rather I shall draw attention

---

[1] In what its proponents call the 'new micro-economics', visible employment is important for the rational allocation of *time* by members of the labour force: see Phelps *et al.* (1970).

in this section to a number of aggregation problems (usually referred to as problems of 'aggregation over individuals') which arise in any such model.

The standard problem can conveniently be illustrated by the case of consumption (Theil, 1954; Green, 1964). Let individual consumption be a function of individual (disposable) income: $c_i = f_i(y_i)$, and let the aggregate dependent variable (one of our final variables after deflation) be defined as the sum of individual consumptions: $c = \sum\limits_{i=1}^{n} c_i$. If the aggregate independent (or auxiliary) variable is taken as the sum of the individual incomes ($y = \sum\limits_{i=1}^{n} y_i$), and there is no restriction on the distribution of the y_i's, then it is well known to be necessary and sufficient for c to be a function of y that the individual consumption functions are linear with equal slopes. But if there are restrictions on the distribution of income, the conditions are broader. Suppose that:

$$c_i = \alpha_i + \beta_i y_i \ (i+1, \ldots, n), \tag{4}$$

and that in any period y_i differs by an 'error' ϵ_i from a 'normal' proportion δ_i of y. Then:

$$y_i = \delta_i y + \epsilon_i, \quad (i = 1, \ldots, n), \tag{5}$$

where, of course, $\sum\limits_{i=1}^{n} \delta_i = 1$, $\sum\limits_{i=1}^{n} \epsilon_i = 0$. From (1) and (2):

$$c = \sum\limits_{i=1}^{n} c_i = \sum\limits_{i=1}^{n} (\alpha_i + \beta_i y_i) = \sum\limits_{i=1}^{n} \alpha_i + \sum\limits_{i=1}^{n} (\beta_i \delta_i) y + \sum\limits_{i=1}^{n} \beta_i \epsilon_i. \tag{6}$$

c is an exact function of y if and only if $\sum\limits_{i=1}^{n} \beta_i \epsilon_i = 0$. This will be so if:

(a) $\beta_i = \beta$, all i, since then $\sum\limits_{i=1}^{n} \beta_i \epsilon_i = \beta \sum\limits_{i=1}^{n} \epsilon_i = 0$.

(b) $\epsilon_i = 0$, all i.

(c) $\beta_i \neq \beta_j$ for some i and j and $\epsilon_i \neq 0$ for some i but $\sum\limits_{i=1}^{n} \beta_i \epsilon_i = \sum\limits_{i=1}^{n} (\beta_i - \bar{\beta})(\epsilon_i - \bar{\epsilon}) = 0$.

The necessary and sufficient conditions for exact aggregation are therefore that either, (a) all marginal propensities to consume are equal; or (b) the distribution of income is exactly determined; or (c) (a) and (b) are false but the co-variance of β_i and ϵ_i is zero. This last means, roughly, that in each year those who have (for them) unusually high incomes are evenly distributed between those with high and low marginal propensities to consume, and similarly for unusually low incomes.

Recent theories of the consumption function imply that consumption may respond differently to wage income and property income. There would then be more than one independent variable in the equation, but the aggregation conditions are easily adapted. These theories, however, also place great weight on *expectations* of future income, and theories of investment and wage and price determination assign an important role to expectations of output, interest rates, wages and prices. The usual procedure in empirical work is to take the expectation as a weighted sum of previous values of the variable in question. But *whose* expectation is being measured? The question has not, so far as I know, been considered from the point of view of aggregation.

Expectations involve uncertainty, and a way of looking at uncertainty that lends itself to a standard treatment of the aggregation problem is the 'State-preference' approach. To illustrate, suppose that there are S States of the world and n individuals, and that individual i believes with certainty that his wage income will be W_{si} in State s, and attaches the subjective probability π_{si} to State s. Thus individual i's expected wage income is:

$$E_i = \sum_s \pi_{si} W_{si} \tag{7}$$

Is it possible to define aggregate probabilities π_s which sum to one such that:

$$E = \sum_s \pi_s W_s? \tag{8}$$

The obvious method is to define:

$$E = \sum_s \sum_i \left(\pi_{si} \frac{W_{si}}{W_s} \right) W_s \quad \left(\sum_i \frac{W_{si}}{W_s} = 1 \right), \tag{9}$$

and we then seek the conditions under which:

$$\sum_s \sum_i \pi_{si} \frac{W_{si}}{W_s} = 1 \tag{10}$$

Let the average subjective probability for State s be written:

$$\alpha_s = \frac{\sum_i \pi_{si}}{n} \tag{11}$$

and define:

$$\beta_{si} = \pi_{si} - \alpha_s \tag{12}$$

Plainly $\sum\limits_s \alpha_s = 1$ and $\sum\limits_s \beta_{si} = 0$ for all i.

Let the average share of individual i over all States be written:

$$\gamma_i = \frac{\sum\limits_s W_{si}}{\sum\limits_s W_s} \tag{13}$$

and define

$$\delta_{si} = \frac{W_{si}}{W_s} - \gamma_i \tag{14}$$

Plainly $\sum\limits_i \gamma_i = 1$ and $\sum\limits_i \delta_{si} = 0$ for all s.

It follows that:

$$\sum_s \sum_i \pi_{si} \frac{W_{si}}{W_s} = \sum_s \sum_i (\alpha_s + \beta_{si})(\gamma_i + \delta_{si})$$

$$= 1 + \sum_s \sum_i \beta_{si}\delta_{si}, \tag{15}$$

so that expectations can be aggregated if and only if:

$$\sum_s \sum_i \beta_{si}\delta_{si} = 0 . \tag{16}$$

There are three conditions (strongly reminiscent of those on pp. 186–7 above) in which (16) is true:

(a) For each s, $\beta_{si} = 0$ for all i, so that all individuals attach equal subjective probabilities to any given State.

(b) For each i, $\delta_{si} = 0$ for all s, so that any given individual receives the same share of total wage income in each state.

(c) For some $i, s, \beta_{si} \neq 0$ and for some $i, s, \delta_{si} \neq 0$ but (16) holds. This means that there is no systematic tendency for any individual whose share is (for him) unusually high (or unusually low) in a particular State to attach a higher or a lower subjective probability than other individuals to that State.

A somewhat neglected point concerning aggregation over individuals (or firms) was first made by Grunfeld and Griliches (1960). They estimated the total investment of a number of firms by two different methods:

(a) by expressing the total investment of all the firms as a function of their total market value and the total value of their plant and equipment;
(b) by adding the estimates obtained by expressing the investment of each firm as a function of its own market value and the value of its plant and equipment.

They compared the two coefficients of multiple determination:

(a) $R_a^2 = 1 - \dfrac{s_a^2}{s_y^2}$: $\quad s_a^2 = \mathrm{Var}\left(y - [a + b_1 x_1 + b_2 x_2] \right)$

(b) $R_c^2 = 1 - \dfrac{s_c^2}{s_y^2}$: $\quad s_c^2 = \mathrm{Var}\left(\sum_s [y_s - (a_s + b_{s1} x_{s1} + b_{s2} x_{s2})] \right)$

where: $y = \displaystyle\sum_s y_s$, the sum of the dependent micro-variables;

$s_y^2 = \mathrm{Var}\, y$;

$x_i = \displaystyle\sum_s x_{si}$ $(i = 1, 2)$, sum of the independent micro variables x_{si}.

It turned out that $R_a^2 > R_c^2$, so that total investment was 'better' predicted by the aggregated model than by adding the predictions from a disaggregated model. There was a somewhat inconclusive discussion of the conditions for such a result to occur, but the explanation favoured by Grunfeld and Griliches is that the values of the dependent micro-variables were influenced by the values of the *macro-*, as well as of the micro- independent variables. That is to say, the investment plans of a firm were affected by the state of the economy as a whole, as well as by its own fortunes. This implies that the individual micro-equations are mis-specified. Neglect of this possible mis-specification weakens the force of the simulations of Orcutt, Edwards and Watts (1968), which lead them to argue in favour of disaggregated models; nor is this point made in the analysis of their results by Aigner and Goldfield (1973).

In sectors other than the investment sector this mis-specification may take different forms. It may be that the dependent micro-variables are affected by estimates of, or information about, the values of the *dependent* macro-variables. This would be the implication, for example, of the 'bandwagon' and 'snob' effects of Leibenstein (1950) in the theory of consumption. And information about the beliefs of others (as conveyed by changing odds at a racetrack, or movements of share prices) may lead to a move of individual subjective probabilities in the direction of greater uniformity. I would conjecture that in all these cases the argument for aggregated relationships would be strengthened, though the formal analysis has not (to my knowledge) been carried out.

Our discussion of aggregation over individuals and firms in this section has so far been lacking in specific references to the financial and wage-price equations of macro-models. As to the former, the assumption of the absence of 'distribution effects' when, for example, the quantity of money changes can, of course, be justified only by an appeal to the standard aggregation conditions at the beginning of this section (Leijonhufvud, 1968, pp. 114–15), though of course when there is an unmistakable redistribution between debtors and creditors the assumption of constant distribution is abandoned.

There are recent theoretical developments relating to the financial and wage-price sectors which make it worthwhile to develop the conditions for aggregation a little further in a particular direction (Green, 1964, pp. 63–7). Let us assume that the individual micro-equations are identical (except perhaps for a constant additive term). If in addition they are *linear*, then as we have seen the only aggregate independent variable we need is the sum (or the mean) of the micro-independent variables.

If there is a single independent variable and the micro-equations are identical and *quadratic*, or identical and non-linear and the distribution of the independent micro-variables is normal or lognormal, the sum of the dependent micro-variables will depend on the mean and *variance* of the independent micro-variables. If there are several independent variables, the means and variances of all of them will appear in the quadratic case. In the general non-linear case, if the density functions are *independently* normally or log-normally distributed, only their means and variances will appear; but co-variances will enter if the distributions are not independent.

Even if the micro-equations of different individuals are not identical, the sum of the dependent micro-variables may depend only on the means and variances of the distributions of the independently normally or log-normally distributed independent micro-variables in certain conditions. Suppose that individual consumption depends on income and a 'taste' parameter; then if tastes are distributed independently of income, the conclusion just stated follows. (This is a generalisation of our standard condition (c) on p. 186 and 189 above; it was used by Friedman (1957, p. 18) and emphasised by Malinvaud (1956, pp. 122–3).

There may frequently be a case on aggregation grounds, therefore, for including second moments of probability distributions in aggregate equations. The case may be reinforced on grounds of economic analysis if, for example, one is an adherent of the mean-variance approach to portfolio selection. A recent view of behaviour in the labour and product markets places emphasis on the divergence, real or imagined, between wages and employment, prices and sales, experienced by an individual worker or firm and experienced elsewhere. This may constitute an additional argument for including a measure of dispersion in aggregate equations (Phelps *et al.*, 1970, esp. pp. 212–3 by G. C. Archibald).

IV TYPES AND SIZES OF MODEL

The position we have now reached is that a number of 'final' variables have been selected, their number and nature determined by the fundamental questions we wish our macro-model to answer. The question of aggregation over individuals has been discussed with regard to equations determining the values of final and auxiliary variables. There remains the question of the *size* of the model – the *number* of auxiliary variables to be included.

I begin, as in the last section, by reporting on the standard conditions for treating a group of variables as if they were a single variable. This can be done if:

(a) their prices always move proportionately (because, for example, they are perfect substitutes in demand or supply); this is Hicks's 'composite commodity theorem' (Hicks, 1939);

(b) their quantities always move proportionately (Leontief, 1936);

(c) the group of commodities is 'separable' in a utility or production function. There are many definitions of separability (Goldman and Uzawa, 1964), but the only one with the properties most commonly assumed when variables are grouped, namely that the 'price' of the aggregate is a function of the prices of the component variables, that the 'quantity' is a function of the quantities of the component variables, and that the product of the 'price' and the 'quantity' is equal to total expenditure on the group of goods, is 'homogeneous' separability (Gorman, 1959). This means that it is possible to replace the group of variables in the utility or production function by a number which is a function of a function homogeneous of degree one in the variables in the group.

The appropriate size of model depends, as was suggested earlier, on its purpose. If the purpose is to predict the values of a set of final variables like that discussed in Section II above, the work of W. D. Fisher (1969) is of relevance. Consider the reduced form of a model expressing the values of m endogenous variables as functions of n pre-determined variables. Define a loss function:

$$L = (y - \hat{y})' \, C(y - \hat{y}), \tag{17}$$

where y and $\hat{y}$ are respectively vectors of actual and forecast values of endogenous variables and C is a positive semi-definite symmetric matrix representing the significance of errors (and possibly also their interactions) to the investigator. Fisher considers reductions in the number of endogenous variables, or of predetermined variables, or of 'corresponding' sets of both types of variables (e.g., outputs and final demands of the same group of goods in input-output analysis) and their effect on L.

To apply this technique to a short-run macroeconomic model of the type we are contemplating, we should first reduce its reduced form still further by solving for the final variables in terms of the pre-determined variables, and then consider reducing the number of pre-determined variables by replacing subsets of them by some (presumably linear) function of their values. For each of the $n(n-1)/2$ ways of reducing the number of predetermined variables by one the change in L can be calculated, and the one which increases L by least is said to be the best. In Fisher's experiment with the Klein-Goldberger model, every grouping of predetermined variables *increased* L; is there, one wonders, no counterpart to the Grunfeld-Griliches effect?

With small sample sizes, the number of distinct explanatory variables is limited by consideration of the number of degrees of freedom, so that groupings have to be made. If we ask which of the variables cash, demand deposits,[1] time deposits, short-term bonds, long-term bonds and equities should be combined, aggregation theory tells us to look for assets whose prices or quantities move proportionally, or which form a homogeneously separable group in the utility functions of wealth-holders. Fisher's loss function may also be of assistance, permitting as it does judgements like: '. . . very little cost will be entailed by proceeding down to four subsets by continued mergers, but a very large increase in cost will occur by proceeding down to three' (W. D. Fisher, 1969, p. 45).

A second type of model attempts to discriminate (in so far as this is possible in economics) among alternative hypotheses. While the work of Jorgenson (1971, for example) on the determinants of investment appears to raise no profound methodological issues, an attempt by Friedman and Meiselman (1963) to compare the success of two models in predicting national income was severely criticised. The models represented the ultimate in aggregation; each had a single explanatory variable: 'money' in one case and 'autonomous expenditure' in the other. Ando and Modigliani (1965) question the relevance of the exercise, recognising no obligation to choose between two such hypotheses, particularly as neither 'independent' variable is exogenous to the economic system. Friedman and Meiselman (1965) reply that those 'economists who regard monetary changes as primary' make the 'empirical judgement' that they are 'critical in the sense of being in practice the primary source of change and disturbance' (p. 761).

---

[1] Those who believe the 'welfare costs of inflation' to be of quantitative significance may object to my treating the quantity of money throughout as an auxiliary rather than a final variable.

Finally, by an 'expository' model I mean one designed to emphasise the distinctive characteristics of a particular view of the operation of the economic system. The number of distinct variables is governed by the wish to facilitate comprehension. In one recent instance the aggregative structure of two alternative macroeconomic models has been claimed as critical. I refer, of course, to the comparison by Leijonhufvud (1968) of the 'income-expenditure' model with his own view of Keynes's system. He argues that capital goods and consumption goods should not be aggregated because of the importance attached by Keynes to changes in their relative prices. He would combine money with short-term bonds and capital goods with long-term bonds on the grounds that: 'In Keynes's thinking, the dichotomy of "short" vs. "long" overrode in importance all other distinctions between properties of stores of value' (p. 149). I look forward to a textbook version of the Keynesian model aggregated along these lines – though given the view of Leijonhufvud and others of adjustment mechanisms in the Keynesian system, such a model would differ from the income-expenditure model in more than its aggregative structure.

V CONCLUSIONS

In preparing this brief survey I have formed the impression that the conditions in which, when constructing a predictive or expository short-run macroeconomic model, it is desirable partly to disaggregate what I have called the 'auxiliary' variables, are well understood. (It is perhaps worth adding that second moments of probability distributions may be a useful form of aggregate.) As for the final variables, a good deal is known about consumption as an aggregate; indeed, the conditions for the existence of social indifference curves are, in a formal sense, the conditions for the existence of a system of social demand functions – though the existence of the former does not remove the need for indicators of income distribution as final variables.

But there appear to be unresolved (and perhaps insoluble) difficulties in the definition of aggregate real income, investment and capital. I have argued that if we are unhappy with $C + pI$ as a measure of income, and believe Samuelson's 'wealth' to be unmeasurable, then we must treat real investment as a distinct final variable. Yet in the short run – where we must surely assume that capital is not optimally allocated over sectors – an aggregate production function with an aggregate capital stock requires (unless we are willing to assume that the quantities or prices of the components of the capital stock move proportionally) that the sector production functions have an identical structure. And the aggregate capital stock itself then has the property that the weights given to its components in the aggregate depend on the relative prices of the outputs they help to produce.

REFERENCES

D. J. Aigner and S. M. Goldfield, 'Simulation and Aggregation: A Reconsideration', *Review of Economics and Statistics*, Vol. 55, No 1 (February 1973) pp. 114–8.

R. G. D. Allen, *Macro-Economic Theory* (London: Macmillan, 1967).

A. Ando and F. Modigliani, 'The Relative Stability of Velocity and the Investment Multiplier', *American Economic Review*, Vol. 55, No 4 (September 1965) pp. 693–728.

F. M. Fisher, 'Embodied Technical Change and the Existence of an Aggregate Capital Stock', *Review of Economic Studies*, Vol. 32(4), No 92 (October 1965) pp. 263–88.

F. M. Fisher, 'The Existence of Aggregate Production Functions', *Econometrica*, Vol. 37, No 4 (October 1969) pp. 533–77.

F. M. Fisher and K. Shell, *The Economic Theory of Price Indices* (New York: Academic Press, 1972).

W. D. Fisher, *Clustering and Aggregation in Economics* (Baltimore: 1969).

M. Friedman, *A Theory of the Consumption Function* (Princeton University Press, 1957).

M. Friedman and D. Meiselman, 'The Relative Stability of Monetary Velocity and the Investment Multiplier in the United States, 1897–1958', in E. Cary Brown *et al.*, *Commission on Money and Credit, Stabilization Policies* (Englewood Cliffs, N.J.: Prentice-Hall, 1963).

M. Friedman and D. Meiselman, 'Rejoinder', *American Economic Review*, Vol. 55, No 4 (September 1965) pp. 753–90.

S. M. Goldman and H. Uzawa, 'A Note on Separability in Demand Analysis', *Econometrica*, Vol. 32, No 3 (January 1964) pp. 387–98.

W. M. Gorman, 'Community Preference Fields', *Econometrica*, Vol. 21, No 1 (January 1953) pp. 63–80.

W. M. Gorman, 'Separable Utility and Aggregation', *Econometrica*, Vol. 27, No 3 (June 1959) pp. 469–81.

H. A. J. Green, *Aggregation in Economic Analysis* (Princeton University Press, 1964).

Y. Grunfeld and Z. Griliches, 'Is Aggregation Necessarily Bad?' *Review of Economics and Statistics*, Vol. 42, No 1 (February 1960) pp. 1–13.

J. R. Hicks, *Value and Capital* (Oxford: Clarendon Press, 1939).

D. W. Jorgenson, 'Econometric Studies of Investment Behaviour: A Survey', *Journal of Economic Literature*, Vol. 9, No 4 (December, 1971) pp. 1111–47.

H. Leibenstein, 'Bandwagon, Snob and Veblen Effects in the Theory of Consumers' Demand', *Quarterly Journal of Economics*, Vol. 64, No 2 (May 1950) pp. 183–201.

H. Leibenstein, 'Allocative Efficiency vs. "X-efficiency" ', *American Economic Review*, Vol. 56, No 3 (June 1966) pp. 392–415.

A. Leijonhufvud, *Keynesian Economics and the Economics of Keynes* (New York: Oxford University Press, 1968).

W. W. Leontief, 'Composite Commodities and the Problem of Index Numbers', *Econometrica*, Vol. 4 (1936) pp. 39–59.

E. Malinvaud, 'L'Agrégation dans les Modèles Économiques', *Cahiers du Seminaire d'Econométrie*, 4 (1956) pp. 69–146.

A. Nataf, 'Sur des Questions d'Agrégation en Économétrie', *Publications de l'Institut de Statistique de l'Université de Paris*, 2 (1953).

A. Nataf and R. Roy, 'Remarques et Suggestions Relatives aux Nombres – Indices', *Econometrica*, Vol. 16, No 4 (October 1948) pp. 330–46.

G. H. Orcutt, H. W. Watts and J. B. Edwards, 'Data Aggregation and Information Loss', *American Economic Review*, Vol. 58, No 4 (September 1968) pp. 773–87.

E. S. Phelps *et al.*, *Microeconomic Foundations of Employment and Inflation Theory* (New York: Norton 1970).

P. A. Samuelson, 'Evaluation of Real National Income', *Oxford Economic Papers*, New Series, Vol. 2, No 1 (January 1950) pp. 1–29.

P. A. Samuelson, 'Social Indifference Curves', *Quarterly Journal of Economics*, Vol. 70, No 1 (February 1956) pp. 1–22.

P. A. Samuelson, 'The Evaluation of "Social Income": Capital Formation and Wealth', in F. A. Lutz and D. C. Hague (eds), *The Theory of Capital* (London: Macmillan, 1961).

H. Theil, *Linear Aggregation of Economic Relations* (Amsterdam: North-Holland, 1954).

Discussion of the Paper by Professor Green

Professor Cochrane introduced Professor Green's paper with a brief overview of it. Consistently with his *Aggregation in Economic Analysis* (Princeton University Press, 1964) Professor Green had chosen to concentrate on the 'technical aspects' of the microeconomic foundations of macroeconomics that we describe generically as *the* aggregation problem. Perhaps if this conference had occurred a few years earlier or if a slightly different, more empirically-oriented, sub-set of the profession had been present, the issues raised and the points made by Professor Green would have been the major ones of the conference. We might have found ourselves concentrating on the logical and technical difficulties of aggregation *in general* rather than focusing on *exchange* – that is, on prices, market periods, Keynes *versus* Keynesians, incompletely cleared labour markets, and the nature of money within alternative theoretical market frameworks. Professor Green was interested in two questions: (1) With what aggregates should macroeconomists be concerned? (2) How should these aggregates or macroeconomic variables be related to the microeconomic variables from which they were derived? To answer these questions, he had first distinguished between 'final variables' and 'auxiliary variables'. Final variables 'give to the citizen an indication of his own likely well-being, and . . . may in principle be inserted in the policy-makers' objective function'. The appropriate aggregation procedure for auxiliary variables was 'determined by the wish to explain or predict the values of the final variables satisfactorily'. Professor Green emphasised that the nature of 'final' and 'auxiliary' variables in a given piece of macroeconomic analysis would depend upon the *use* to which the analysis was meant to be put, and suggested a three-fold teleological division of macroeconomic models: (1) econometric models for prediction or policy-making; (2) models designed for hypothesis testing; and (3) pedagogical models. Professor Green had then presented a section on final variables, a section on auxiliary variables, a section on types and sizes of variables, and a concluding section in which the main threads were drawn together.

Professor Cochrane then made some *specific* points about the paper:

(1) Professor Green referred to the Grunfeld-Griliches point about aggregation over individuals ('Is Aggregation necessarily bad?', *Review of Economics and Statistics*, 1960) as 'a somewhat neglected point'; Professor Cochrane questioned this. Also, economists interested in the technical problems which were lumped together under the umbrella phrase 'aggregation problems' might be gratified to know that the topic was of substantial current interest in other areas, particularly demography and genetics. Researchers in both fields were producing growing bodies of literature on what Professor Parkin had referred to yesterday as the 'stylised facts' to be drawn from populations of subjects.

(2) Professor Green might have placed a bit more stress on the fact that his analysis in Figures 6:1–6:5 was based on the assumption of full utilisation of resources.

(3) The third section on auxiliary variables was not really about auxiliary variables, but about some general problems of aggregation.

(4) Professor Green did not address himself *at all* to what may be, even for

some of the points he was making, an important technical distinction: he never mentioned the difference between what might be called 'census' aggregates, for example the G.N.P. deflator, and 'sample' aggregates, for example the consumer price index. This was a distinction which would be of less interest to theoreticians than to practitioners, but it was a distinction that we should not overlook in any discussion of the econometrics of the microeconomic foundations of macroeconomics.

(5) Professor Green *did* discuss some of the issues accompanying the fact that the purpose of a model and the appropriate level of aggregation were interrelated, but he did not say enough about differences arising from *understanding* versus *prediction*. For example, if we wished to *predict* real national consumer spending, a linear regression equation with real national disposable income might be sufficient to give us what we wanted, but if a *correct* specification of a *family's* consumption function was one with both the family's real disposable income and real disposable income for the nation as a whole, we could not interpret our regression coefficient as a proper estimate of the marginal propensity to consume. Our regression coefficient would exaggerate the true marginal propensity to consume. We would have learned nothing about household behaviour; we would have prediction, not understanding. Professor Cochrane would have preferred to have seen more about this problem in Professor Green's paper.

(6) When discussing national income (Y) as a single measure of economic well-being and performance, Professor Green mentioned two problems of using C and I in the policy-makers' objective function rather than the sole variable Y, but he did not mention a third problem, the advantage of getting policy-makers to *specify* the functions; that is, to give some indication of their marginal rates of substitution. In the discussion of Professor Streissler's paper the previous day, a great deal had been said about constraints. What many economists seemed to be unaware of was that in the past few years applied mathematicians had made substantial strides in the area of decision making in the absence of fully specified objective functions. For example, one class of solution currently attracting a great deal of attention among operations researchers was decision-making when the arguments of a utility function were given and the algebraic *signs* of the first partials were given, but the function itself was unknown. This sort of approach, along with control theory, should increase the realism of macroeconomic models, as it provided a way of circumventing the problems accompanying the giving of a choice-theoretic foundation to macroeconomic analysis and necessitated careful analysis of all relevant *constraints*. (See J. L. Cochrane, 'Optimal Macro-Economic Policies', *Economic Journal*, 1975.) The rich and growing literature which Professor Cochrane associated with, for example, Kenneth MacCrimmon, P. L. Yu, Milan Zeleny, Werner Dinkelbach, Bernard Roy, Jean Marie Blin and Peter Fishburn, was based on the proposition that individual preference functions, especially for individuals or collections of individuals making 'public' decisions — from portfolio managers for pension programmes to open-market committees of central banks — were virtually impossible to specify. Psychological journals contained many case studies of the difficulties inherent in obtaining the trade-offs or weights in such functions. Whether

it was the case of teams of physicians systematically weighing certain symptoms differently in the morning than in the afternoon when diagnosing a given ailment, or of portfolio managers whose weights assigned to risk and rate of return varied systematically with the average yield on corporate securities, it had been shown that one phase of orthodox microeconomics, the *separation* of the 'technical' and 'subjective' sides of neoclassical analysis, did not square with reality. Applied mathematicians had found ways to get round these problems, and economists needed to learn from them.

Professor Cochrane then turned to two more *general* issues. First, Professor Green considered macroeconomics as used by three classes of users: students, economists testing hypotheses, and economists producing forecasts and explanations for personal pleasure and enlightenment of the public and national policy makers. Throughout the paper Professor Green viewed 'final variables' as the traditional aggregates; employment, prices, and national income and its distribution. He neglected the extraordinary surge in demand by regional and provincial units of government as well as by private financial and industrial enterprises to be incorporated into a national econometric model. This class of macroeconomic modelling had brought in its train some peculiar aggregation problems. The difficulties that Professor Cochrane had seen facing such organisations as the Governor's Office of South Carolina, which had a major forecasting contract with Data Resources Inc., and the textile firms using Chase Econometrics's services were rather interesting. The macroeconomists working on these models had a tendency to be innocent of State and municipal finance or of the basic problems which were the everyday meat of the public accountant. The types of 'aggregation problems' a Chase econometrician was liable to run into when integrating the American cotton textile industry or the United States aluminium fabricators into their national models could be answered most readily by going to a book such as R. H. Parker and G. C. Harcourt (eds.), *Readings in the Concept and Measurement of Income* (Cambridge University Press, 1969). In short, there was a gap between a growing class of users and the economists. Macroeconomic models were no longer solely for scholarly or recreational purposes at universities or for central banks and finance Ministries. Corporate finance committees and State budget and control boards needed the macroeconometrician. The need was being filled, but there were *economics* problems requiring solution.

Secondly, there was the bearing of the *political* aspects of national economic policy on aggregation. Professor Green rightly concentrated on the *users* of macroeconomic models, but neither Professor Green nor anyone else at this conference had mentioned the *level of aggregation itself* as a policy variable. We generally neglected to view the appropriate degree of aggregation as an economic variable to be determined by politicians or by politicians disguised as economists. To exaggerate to make the point, every economic decision and every economic event left a portion of society better off, worse off or unaffected. The impact of the economic issues of the day could be measured in many ways. The level of aggregation could wash out, disguise or fudge (*or it could illuminate*) the winner-loser nature of economic events and decisions. It seemed to Professor Cochrane that a high degree of aggregation, for example, was often politically convenient and that economists (but not politicians) failed to recognise this.

Professor Cochrane illustrated his point by an internal policy debate which had occurred in the United States a few years earlier. In June 1967 the Chairman of President Johnson's Council of Economic Advisers was at the very bottom of his despair over the general vacuum in American economic policy. The war in South-east Asia was raging. The Federal budget was out of control because the President continued to ask Congress for Defense Supplementals while not pressing for tax increases, owing to his fear that to ask for tax increases would cause drastic cuts in his domestic programme as well as a full-scale legislative debate about his military adventure. The administration's incomes policy of voluntary wage-price guideposts was nearly moribund by late 1966. Gardner Ackley decided that the United States might have to move towards a formal incomes policy which would be, in his words, 'essentially a form of indicative planning'. Ackley personally sketched out one programme and how such a programme could be put into operation. Essentially he called for tripartite negotiations of *specific* wage and price targets for each year to be obtained through a series of *confrontations*. The targets would be numbers not ranges. They would be set 'at a level of aggregation in all cases higher than the individual industry. Thus the targets would not become or replace individual bargaining' (Gardner Ackley, 'Outline of an Incomes Policy', C.E.A. Microfilm, Roll 70, Johnson Library, Austin, Texas, 3 July 1967). That is, the *level* of aggregation became a policy issue; Ackley was trying to flank the potential opposition of the industrial unions in order to make his plan palatable to an important administrative constituency. Ackley's proposal excited many of the economists both formally and informally linked to administration policy-making. Walt Rostow and Wassily Leontief, for example, had been strongly lobbying the U.S. government for years, to abandon the

$$Y = C + I + G + X$$

statistical categories of the Council of Economic Advisers crypto-Keynesian analytical framework, since they thought that the Council's approach larded over rather than illuminated critical *structural* aspects of the economy. The Ackley proposal, which was never made policy although it was debated at the highest levels of government for six months, required *dis*aggregation, which was attractive to Rostow, Leontief and others. But one main issue throughout the six months of debate was the *proper* level of aggregation. What level of aggregation would reconcile the continued performance of traditional duties by existing institutions, which must politically be accepted as data, on the one hand, with the requirement that a major increase in central government economic direction of wages, prices, production and income distribution might be necessary for the existing government to stay in power? That is, in actual practice, the appropriate level of aggregation was a *political* and not an economic question.

Professor Cochrane ended by quoting from a reaction to Ackley's proposal by an economist (Clopper Almon of the University of Maryland):

> It is undoubtedly a good idea initially to limit the *published* targets to the income and price side for only the major producing sectors. But the soul of this operation is the *discussion*, not the publication, which could be

prepared by the Council in a week or so. The success of those discussions will depend upon getting high-level participants, posing the problems in the concrete terms which . . . [business leaders and union officials] can think about, and making the sessions informative for them through thoroughly researched presentations. I trust you agree, . . . [since] you suggest that the operation needs about fifty professionals. But such discussions can no more be limited to the incomes side to the exclusion of the product side than a discussion of lungs can be limited to breathing out to the exclusion of breathing in. Without one, the other stops. Any businessman asked about the reasonableness of a proposed 'G.N.P. originating' will — after learning what on earth it is he's being asked about — immediately begin to ask questions about sales, implied profit margins, his investment needs, and the like. If the staff cannot help him fill in the rest of the picture, I'm afraid not much will result from the discussion save some resentment over being asked questions out of context.

Not only must staff work be done on the product side of the accounts as well as on the income side, it must also be done with some amount of industry detail. Only we economists can discuss G.N.P. endlessly; everybody else soon inquires about its components.

The need for detailed preparation is even more pressing in the pricing field. The Council has a reputation for dealing with prices at only two levels. It writes at the G.N.P.-deflator level but swings into action at the pork-bellies level. The need for a way to bridge this gap would, I should think, become painfully obvious in any formal discussions with industry.

As you may recall, the French have to use about 65 sectors in their discussions though they use only 30 in the published plan. The Belgians use about 30, as do the Dutch in their plan. It would seem to me that 30 might be a good compromise between the need for concreteness in discussion and the desire to avoid criticism for attempting [central] planning. Such criticism, however, is more likely to prove a spectre haunting civil servants and academicians than to be a real obstacle posed by business, at least if my sample of companies is indicative. You may recall that the . . . [Office of Business Economics] published in 1958 [input-output] table with many qualms about charges of providing details for government planners. Yet the only criticism it has received from business . . . is for not publishing *more* detail [Clopper Almon to Gardner Ackley, C.E.A. microfilm, Roll 70, Johnson Library, Austin, Texas, 13 July 1967].

Professor Malinvaud pointed out that we had to distinguish the level of aggregation to be used for public debates from the level to be used in our professional work in our preparation for those debates. The two things raised different issues. He agreed that politicians had their own way of proceeding, but that was not a new matter. The difficult question for us was to find the proper level of aggregation when we were preparing our economic advice or when we were trying to make good forecasts. One difficulty was that we really had no principle as to the proper level of aggregation. When we looked at the problem in practice one was inclined to say like Leontief that the aggregation was always too coarse. On the other hand a detailed model would not have the data to fit it, and also ran the risk of getting out of hand. As a practical economist Professor Malinvaud said that he never knew what to do and was glad of advice from others.

Professor Henin thought it might be useful to introduce a further distinction, when aggregating over individuals, between the case where the number of individuals was great and no one of them could affect the outcome, and the case where the number of individuals was small. The important peculiarity of the first case was that it would in general be possible to find out the law of distribution of the relevant characters among individuals and to take that explicitly into account in the process of aggregation. The shapes of the mathematical structure of the microeconomic relations could depend as much on the law of distribution of characters among the population as on the shape of the microeconomic relations. Examples could be found in the work of Houthakker on production functions ('The Pareto Distribution and the Cobb-Douglas Production Function in Activity Analysis', *Review of Economic Studies*, 1955) and of Karl Borch on aggregation of demand functions ('Effects on Demand of Changes in Distribution of Income', *Econometrica*, 1953); a special case occurred when variances entered macroeconomic functions. In the other case, there would not in general exist a stable distribution of relevant characteristics, so that the strong assumptions of identity, linearity and independence were necessary for the existence of a meaningful macroeconomic relation. If these assumptions could not be made, then we had to use an explicitly microeconomic approach or to content ourselves with approximations.

Sir John Hicks asked for an explanation of the Grunfeld-Griliches point: was it a matter of empirical testing? *Professor Green* replied that it was; moreover, these data had been previously used with some success in the prediction of investment by the individual firms. *Professor Malinvaud* intervened to point out that the 'paradox' might be explained by mis-specification of the microeconomic relations. Alternatively, one might accept a microeconomic model as it was stated and a macroeconomic model that followed by summation, on the understanding that the procedure used to deal with the microeconomic data was not fully efficient; if one replaced the procedure by a fully efficient procedure one would find a better fit using the microeconomic data. The procedure that had been used on the microeconomic data in the Grunfeld-Griliches experiment was to fit each one of the twenty equations separately on time series. An efficient procedure would be to allow for the fact that the deviations for the particular firms were correlated among themselves for the same year, by estimating the correlation matrix at the same time as the microeconomic coefficients before aggregating. Zellner had done this and solved the 'paradox'.

Professor Henin said that the agreed with Professor Malinvaud: he thought that the macroeconomic relation would be a correct specification only in very special cases, like those of full rigidity of perceived relative income by consumers or of perceived market shares by firms.

Professor Green replied that he did not find the Grunfeld-Griliches point a 'paradox'. The implication for microeconomic behaviour of the existence of aggregate constraints was an important one. He wished to withdraw the conjecture that he had made on p. 190, but he would still be surprised if the

Grunfeld-Griliches effect turned out to be an illusion. *Professor Malinvaud* said that he had used the word 'paradox' because the Grunfeld-Griliches paper was not only reporting an experiment on data. It was mainly a theoretical analysis starting from a given theoretical model, namely that microeconomic units' behaviour fitted a linear regression equation; in this theoretical framework and on the assumption that the specification was correct, the answer had been given that aggregation was not always necessarily bad.

Dr Nuti raised the question of whether when we were looking for a measure of welfare we should deduct from income the leisure time forgone in the process of production. If so, how should we calculate the replacement cost of the leisure lost in the production process? Should we deduct the entire amount of earned income from a notion of income as an aggregate measure of welfare? Or should we take into account some element of rent in the transformation of leisure into consumption by means of labour?

Professor Green agreed with Dr Nuti that we should take leisure into account. In Section II of his paper he had taken the simplest model, which excluded leisure. Barna had once argued that one could take productivity rather than consumption as the measure of welfare. With respect to Professor Cochrane's third point, he agreed that Section III was not only about auxiliary variables. The distinguishing feature of that Section was that he had at no point assumed that the aggregation process was in any way helped by the satisfaction of any optimal allocation conditions, whereas in the attempt to aggregate the final variables of consumption and investment he had assumed, particularly in the case of consumption and partially in the case of investment, that there was an optimal allocation which facilitated the process of aggregation. He had hoped that some of the discussion would focus on this question, particularly the aggregation of production.

Professor Davidson asked why should we want to aggregate? He thought that for policy purposes we only needed to understand employment trends, purchasing power and the distribution of value added in gross terms. Net income was a theoretical conundrum which gave pleasure to economists but was unimportant for policy purposes and business decisions. Welfare economics was something that economists worried about more than anyone else did. Purchasing power was not command over quantities of utility, but was either the power to buy goods and services for consumption in a given community or the power of money to command units of human effort. For policy purposes one had to decide which of these standards to use — either a commodity standard or a labour standard.

At this point *Professors Asimakopulos* and *Green* had a brief and inconclusive discussion on the meaning of the marginal productivity of capital.

Professor Streissler admired Professor Green's paper very much for stressing the point that you must not look for an aggregate which worked for all questions; each question implied its own aggregation. To his mind the paper said that the weighting scheme behind the aggregation changed for different questions. Aggregation schemes were very important; for example, in Austria trade unions and entrepreneurs were interested in keeping the distribution of income constant, so that there was intensive discussion of the neoclassical concept of the share of wages in the national income, and rises in wages had been made equal to the average increase in productivity. A difficulty was that this could be true only under certain conditions. It was not true that if every wage increased by the same percentage as aggregate productivity there would be no increase in total wages that was higher than the increase in productivity, because there was always a shift of workers to higher productivity sectors.

Professor Streissler thought that this was probably the most important aggregation problem, but there were other problems not stressed in the paper. Gorman had stated that aggregation of capital was impossible because capital was used with different information by different individuals. Closely linked to this problem, though conceptually different, were the changes in the optimal specialisation of factors which were usually interpreted as demand shifts. In Austria economists and others had been astonished that people could produce in 1970 with the same capital a greater output than had been expected: people had found they could use their capital goods more productively than before. Other examples were a revaluation of the exchange rate, where there was a change in the value of capital and labour, and in interwar Austria, which was left with the civil servants and bank employees of the former Austro-Hungarian Empire — the value of the labour force fell, so that there was a very low level of national income. Professor Streissler suggested that the current British economic situation was similar.

Sir John Hicks made two points:
(1) The transformation curve in Professor Green's paper was frequently referred to as though it were a production frontier; Sir John doubted whether it was. What we really wanted were curves which connected the possible outputs which were attainable with the initial organisation; that was a question of positive economics and could not be deduced from technical data.
(2) It was difficult to ignore the public sector and the balance of payments. Even if one left them out, there remained a question that he hoped would be discussed, the general question of when did we seriously lose information by aggregating? One certainly lost information when one added an unreliable figure to a reliable one, and thus obtained a figure which purported to give information which it did not in fact provide. This was surely the case with our conventional macroeconomic aggregates; for example, we could say more about the volume of industrial output than we could about the volume of services.

Professor Stiglitz pointed out that in some cases we should deal with probability distributions rather than with numbers. In other words, when we simply added means we were losing much information associated with the separate probability distributions. The conventional aggregation problems were mainly about aggregation of numbers, not about probability distributions. One of our problems was that the kinds of theories which were formulated were precise aggregation theorems; the gist of the results was, not surprisingly, that we could almost never aggregate. We did not know much about the errors that arose. Could we get some approximation theorems saying that provided certain conditions were satisfied the losses were related to certain properties of the functions we were dealing with? We also often did not know all of the economic structure that we would like to know; aggregates often hid relevant aspects of the structure. Two examples were the unemployment statistics — which if broken down by area, race, etc., might give us a better picture of the unemployment problem — and monetary aggregates. In the latter case, where macroeconomic issues were involved, Keynes had in effect aggregated short-term assets with cash and long-term bonds with equities. This would not satisfy the aggregation theorems discussed in Professor Green's paper, and in the aggregation much of what was crucial in the economy was left out, but Keynes did get some results! (Laughter.)

Professor Green thought that Sir John Hicks's first question was of the greatest importance. He also agreed with Professor Stiglitz that we needed some approximation theorems. He had said that in his book in 1964 but not much had in fact happened in that area. Franklin Fisher had, however, not only discussed the question of the extent to which the aggregate production function failed to exist if the conditions failed to be satisfied by a certain amount of error, but had also produced theorems about being able to approach a production function when one had a drastic failure of the conditions to be satisfied ('Approximate Aggregation and the Leontief conditions', *Econometrica*, 1969). The work of Walter Fisher had the notion of costs of aggregation as one reduced the number of variables by, say, combining two into one.

With respect to Professor Cochrane's comments, Professor Green did not wish to add to Professor Malinvaud's remarks. He agreed with Professor Streissler about the difficulties of defining the average wage for the purpose of wage and price policies. He had deliberately refrained from saying anything about the objective function itself. In answer to Professor Henin, he said that he thought that even if there was basically an absence of aggregation bias, the co-variance was more likely to vanish the more individuals there were in the market. Contrary to Professor Davidson he thought it would be difficult to define a satisfactory measure of consumption unless it was based on the concept of utility.

Professor Davidson disagreed: there was, he said, a representative basket of goods in any community. *Professor Green* asked what happened when the basket changed? *Professor Davidson* replied that he would be more worried about comparing utilities over time than comparing baskets over time. In the case of money, economists had some very strange views about what they were aggregating. When he was a biochemist he was taught that one should never define something by example. Yet in economics, money tended to be defined by example rather than by its properties (e.g. Friedman defining money via M_1, M_2, M_3, etc.), rather than by properties (as Keynes had done in Chapter 17 of *The General Theory*). *Professor Green* accepted the problem of changing preferences. On the other hand, if one adopted Lancaster's goods-characteristics approach then preferences among characteristics might be more stable than preferences among goods.

Finally, Professor Green said that, as Professor Cochrane quite rightly pointed out, he had been dealing with the simplest possible case. It seemed to him likely that if one had this kind of aggregation difficulty in defining output and capital in the simple case than it would be more difficult in more complex cases. He did not deal with the question of utilisation: in drawing transformation curves in Figure 6:5 he was assuming full employment of capital and labour. He could not take into account all of Professor Streissler's points because he had assumed labour to be homogenous. With respect to capital,

changes in the relative price of two goods would change the proportions of
the two kinds of capital in the capital aggregate. He was in fact very
pessimistic about the aggregation of capital, and inclined to think of at least
two sectors.

Professor Malinvaud turned again to the aggregation challenge for a macro-
theorist. Aggregation was hardly ever justified, except in rather narrow cases
which were not often found in actual fact. Most of the time our macroeconomic theory therefore lacked the rigorous justification that we should
like to find in microeconomic analysis. Considering this unfortunate fact,
what did we do? The profession was divided between people who followed
one or other of three strategies:

(1) Never work with macroeconomic theories. (It was indeed pleasant to
    remain pure from the sin of macroeconomic confusion by behaving in this
    way, but none the less, as Professor Green had reminded us, the questions
    we asked were often about final variables which were of an aggregate
    nature. So we could not really avoid macroeconomic theories.)

(2) Look for direct justification of macroeconomic theories. (This could only
    be empirical. But experience had shown us that the facts were too complex
    or the information too poor for us to go very far along these lines. The
    historical school of the nineteenth century came to the conclusion that
    there were no economic laws because they believed they had to look at
    history alone. Professor Malinvaud saw no hope that within the foreseeable
    future we could really base our macroeconomic analysis on pure
    empiricism.)

(3) Stop being a purist and accept some compromise. (We had to work with
    poor theoretical justification and poor data and bring the two into contact
    in the best possible way. Those who followed this strategy should have
    the respect of the rest of the profession and should not be under strong
    attacks from people who said that their logic was insufficient. All sciences
    had used rigour as a relative notion, and in macroeconomics the level of
    rigour to which we could pretend was still admittedly very low. Professor
    Malinvaud believed that nevertheless the accumulation of knowledge
    achieved during the past two decades provided a reasonable justification
    for the third strategy.)

Professor Shubik added a postscript. He thought that we must distinguish
advocacy, advice and introspection. The way statistics were presented differed
in each case. The reporting of economic statistics in large-scale organisations
was an art form in itself, providing much scope for presenting the same set of
basic data to reach opposite conclusions. This could be done without violating
scientific objectivity because there was rarely if ever a consensus on measurement. The statistics we have depend upon advocacy; economic advisers while
not necessarily advocates had a difficult problem of persuasion if they were
to be heeded. Introspection was the least responsible and most pleasant role
where economists could talk to one another, preferably in pleasant hotels,
with good wine, and objectivity and majesty, surveying the sweep of time and
the advancement of science, without having to worry about the economy
per se.

7 The Role, Functions and Definition of Money*

C. A. E. Goodhart
BANK OF ENGLAND

I DEFINITION

Money can be and has been defined in many ways. For statistical purposes
the stock of money is often defined in terms of certain clearly distinguishable,
but analytically arbitrary,[1] institutional dividing lines. Since the dividing line
between monetary and non-monetary assets is, perhaps, arbitrary, (e.g.,
whether or not term deposits at banks, or savings banks, or other financial
intermediaries should be included), the choice of assets to be included in the
definition of money may be taken on pragmatic and empirical grounds. For
example, money might be defined as that set of liquid financial assets which
has both a close correlation with the development of the economy, and which
is potentially subject to the control of the authorities. Attention then becomes
focused on the fluctuations of that set of assets giving the clearest indications
of the development of the economy and of the authorities' efforts to influence
that development.

Such a pragmatic approach, selecting the definition on the basis of *ex post*
statistical correlations, leaves one no wiser about the role of money.[2] Why
should the statistical construct, the stock of money, vary in certain predictable
ways with the level of economic activity? Why is it held at all? To answer
such questions it is necessary to begin by enquiring what particular functions
money fulfils.

A standard economic approach to defining a particular commodity, or
industry, is to examine the cross-elasticities between it and other potential
substitutes, in this case between monetary and other assets. Only if such

---

*Most of this essay is a redraft of Chapter I of my *Money, Information and Un-
certainty* (London: Macmillan, 1975). I am most grateful for comments and suggestions
from A. D. Crockett, D. E. W. Laidler, J. Melitz and M. J. Thornton, but neither they,
nor the Bank of England, bear any responsibility for the views which I have set out here.

[1] Among the statistical issues which require decision in order to reach a definition of
the money stock are the following: What is a bank? What is a deposit? Are the sight and
short-term liabilities of public sector institutions, such as the Post Office and Local
Authorities, to be included in the money stock? Are non-resident holdings of domestic
money balances to be included, or resident holdings of foreign money balances?

[2] Among papers discussing the appropriate method of defining money, see Friedman
and Schwartz (1969), Yeager (1968), Laidler (1969), Melitz and Martin (1971).

cross-elasticities are low, can one claim to have identified a separate economic entity. Only if such cross-elasticities between monetary and non-monetary assets are low will there be a close correlation between the growth of the money stock so defined, and will this growth be subject to the control of the authorities. Otherwise the process of substitution, either on the demand or the supply side, would weaken the empirical links between movements in the stock of money and in money incomes.

But this approach also is essentially *ex post* descriptive, showing where the breaks in the chain of substitution have come, rather than explaining what are the special, peculiar functions of money that make it separably distinguishable. So if one probes further to ask why there should be such low cross-elasticities between money and other assets, it is necessary to enquire what are the special functions of money.

II FUNCTIONS

The main functions of money are that it serves as a medium of exchange and a means of payment.[1] As such it must, by definition, be a store of value, and, in general, it proves most efficient to treat it as the unit of account. In much of the earlier literature the terms 'medium of exchange' and 'means of payment' were used virtually interchangeably and treated as synonymous. More recently, however, the distinctions between these concepts have been stressed. For example, Melitz has argued[2] that certain specialised means of payment are not general media of exchange. Thus he cites the basic primitive examples: the tribute, the bride price, and the 'blood price'. For example, a transfer of a certain number of cows for a wife might conclude the transaction; cows in this case would be a means of payment, but cows need not necessarily also be generally used in trade and markets. On this basis Melitz argues that the function of providing a medium of exchange is the crucial function of money. No doubt there are many particular transactions involving specialised means of payment; e.g., peppercorn rents, and such specialised means of payment would not be included in any definition of money. Nevertheless, an asset with the property of serving as a *generalised* means of payment, capable of completing the payment in a wide range of trades and markets, would be accepted as a monetary asset.

The functional definition of money as 'a generalised means of payment' is different from, and narrower than, the concept of an asset as a 'medium of

[1] Particular forms of money may provide certain specialised functions; for example, only certain coins can be used to operate a pay telephone box. Similarly, however, cars and trains serve the same transportation function and for some purposes we might want to define a 'transportation services' good. But for other purposes we will want to distinguish between cars and trains. The same argument can be applied to money. We define it above as providing a 'means of payment' service, but for some purposes we may want to distinguish currency and demand deposits with banks.

[2] Melitz (1974) especially Chapter 2.

exchange'.[1] A medium of exchange includes those assets, or claims, whose transfer to the seller will commonly allow a sale to proceed. The distinction is that when the seller receives a medium of exchange, which is not a means of payment, in return for his sale, he will feel that he still has a valid claim for future payment against the buyer, or even more generally against some other group on whom the buyer has provided him with a claim.[2] As Shackle has insisted, 'Payment is in some sense final'. Many – perhaps even most – transactions are, however, carried out on a credit basis, trade credit, or a personal charge account at the store. Such credit does represent a medium of exchange, but not a means of payment.

This distinction is important because the conditions that will require a medium of exchange are more general and wider than those that will generate a means of payment. It is, therefore, possible to specify the functions of a means of payment in an economy rather more precisely. In fact a medium of exchange will be desirable in any economy with a time dimension. Because of differences between people in tastes, endowments, etc., exchanges will occur. Because of the existence of time, these deals will not all take the form of contemporaneous exchanges of goods or services; i.e., barter. So the process of exchange must involve the extension of credits and debits; i.e., there will be a medium of exchange through which current goods will be exchanged for future claims to payment. But in a world of certainty, without transactions costs, there is no reason why the ultimate payment need be made in the form of a specialised means of payment. Person A could sell goods to person B at time 1, confident in the knowledge that his claim[3] on goods in return will be met by a transfer from person C at time $t + n$, while B may extinguish his debt by selling services at some other time to some other person.

In such an (Arrow-Debreu) world of certainty the whole time path of the economy is effectively determined at the outset with both present and all future markets cleared at known relative prices. No one can default on an obligation, or purchase goods and services which over the course of time exceed the value of the goods and services which he can proffer in return, through the employment of his initial endowment of physical and human

[1] This distinction has been emphasised by Shackle, for example, in his comments (Shackle, 1971) on Clower's paper at the Sheffield seminar on money in 1970, reported in Clayton, Gilbert and Sedgwick (1971) pp. 32–4.

[2] Misunderstandings arise because terms such as means of payment and medium of exchange may be defined differently, or not defined at all. I have, I think, here defined the term medium of exchange somewhat more broadly than Melitz and Yeager, for example, who do not draw the same distinction between media of exchange that are means of payment and others that are not. Nevertheless I believe such a distinction to be useful.

[3] These claims will bear an interest rate dependent on the real forces of time preference and time productivity, even in a world of complete certainty. For an excellent analysis of interest rates under conditions of certainty, see Hirshleifer (1970) Part I.

capital (plus transfer payments). Under these circumstances everyone knows
to whom to send his products and where to pick up his own consumable
goods in return. As Meltzer noted in a discussion on the subject of 'Is There
an Optimal Money Supply?':[1]

> ... in the economy under discussion all market exchange ratios are known,
> all price changes are correctly foreseen and the only service of money is to
> serve as an inventory. In the economy, why can't the inventory gap be
> closed by holding verbal promises to pay, produced whenever they are
> required without any trips to the bank?

*So the main function of money, defined as a specialised means of payment,
is to meet and alleviate problems of exchange under conditions of uncertainty,
for otherwise a generalised claim on future goods would suffice.* In a world of
certainty market exchange ratios (i.e., relative prices) are fixed at the very
outset of the system, in period 1. From then on activities, production, consumption, proceed along pre-arranged lines. Whenever all market activity can
be collapsed in this way into the initial period, there will be no need for money.
Such a condition is, of course, unrealistic. Nevertheless perfect certainty is
not the only state in which all market activity could, in theory, be simultaneously arranged in the initial period. If marketing transactions were costless
(and required no time to complete), then in principle it would be possible for
the members of the economy to prepare themselves for *all* possible uncertain
outcomes by exchanging claims on contingent commodities (i.e., a claim for
x units of good y if state of the world z should occur).[2] Transactors can, in
these circumstances, arrange their affairs to take into account all possibilities
at the outset. Exactly as in the case of a certainty economy, all market
decisions, all relative prices (for each possible path of the economy) could be
fixed in the first period.[3] Although consumption and production take place
over time, all planning and decisions on the allocation of resources, all market
activity, could still be collapsed into the first period. Whichever path the
economy took, depending on uncertain developments such as weather,
technology, etc., the pattern of transfers of resources and goods could have
been predetermined. Such an economy can be described as having a certainty-
equivalent form.[4] In such an economy, presumably, no money would be
needed, because people would know in advance, for each possible path of the
economy, what transfers of goods and services would take place, and also
that such transfers would satisfy the conditions that ultimately everyone had
obtained equal value in goods and services for those that he had sold.

---

[1] Meltzer (1970) p. 452.

[2] See Hahn (1973).

[3] If marketing processes were costless, presumably it would be possible to arrange for
tâtonnement, recontracting marketing arrangements which would allow this. In practice,
of course, marketing involves participants having to make commitments, either
simultaneously or sequentially, which cannot be recontracted. This will, in general,
prevent all marketing decisions being taken in the first period.

[4] See, for example, Hirshleifer (1970) Part II.

Yet the assumption of a world of uncertainty without transactions costs is so strained that it soon runs into practical difficulties.[1] For example, what happens if some of the transactors are dishonest? Perhaps it would be possible to cope with this by widening the set of states of the world still further to encompass the various subjective probabilities of whether each of the other various transactors would honour his contracts.[2] But there are in any case, even without worrying about honesty in dealing, a virtually infinite number of possible states of the world in any future period, let alone sequence of periods, and to establish a complete set of contingent prices — and transfers at such prices — for all goods and services in all such states is clearly impossible. It would take for ever. Time is a scarce resource also, and the use of time represents an opportunity cost.

It is also arguable that it is superfluous to specify both uncertainty and transactions costs as necessary conditions for the existence of money,[3] since uncertainty will entail transactions costs.[4] Certainly transactions costs mainly, if not entirely, reflect the cost of obtaining information (i.e., of reducing uncertainty). Costs are involved in learning the demand and supply schedules for tradable goods of others in the economy, and in discovering the prices bid and offered. Setting up physical markets, which in itself involves a resources cost, is a means of trying to reduce such search costs. Once a seller has made a sale he will need information, either on the honesty and worth of the purchaser — should the purchaser offer deferred payment — or on the value and characteristics of the asset or good offered in exchange; which of course leads on directly to the specialised role of money as a device for simply providing the requisite information necessary to consummate an exchange.

In a world of certainty there is no need for the physical existence of markets or for money. So uncertainty, a condition which would also seem to

---

[1] Even though in this context we are *not* including among transactions costs those transportation expenses that must be incurred, even in a certainty world, in shipping goods from *A* to *B*.

[2] Though this might lead, perhaps, to the reintroduction of 'money' into an economy of this form, if, for example, all commodities were subject to physical decay and some transactors were regarded as more trustworthy than others. Then under conditions of subjective uncertainty over honesty it might be of general benefit to arrange for payment in the liabilities of the trustworthy transactor.

[3] These conditions of uncertainty and transactions costs are, it may be interesting to note, exactly the same as Coase regarded as required to establish a rationale for the existence of firms, see Coase (1937). Otherwise the functions of a firm, essentially the organisation and combination of factors of production for the provision of certain goods and services, could have been undertaken through the market mechanism.

[4] If, as suggested, transactions costs are a function of uncertainty, it is not entirely logical to investigate systems of uncertainty without transactions costs or of certainty with transactions costs. Yet there has been some interest in such hypothetical situations, especially in the case of uncertainty without transactions costs. Studies of the other situation, where there are transactions costs but no uncertainty, are less common; indeed it does seem to represent an even more artificial and less interesting framework. Nevertheless some analyses of an economy of this kind have also been attempted, for example, by Starrett (1973).

imply the existence of transactions costs, is a necessary condition for a monetary system, defined as one which normally uses some specialised means of payment to implement exchanges. Is uncertainty also a sufficient condition to require a monetary system?

The answer is probably not, if the roles of the various participants in the social system can be established with sufficient central direction and coherence. There are usually, for example, no monetary transactions within a monastery. To take a somewhat wider example, once a contract has been agreed between employer and employee, the employer can, within the terms of that contract, direct the employee to allocate his labour services first on this project, then on that. No money passes hands in the often long intervals between pay-days. The price mechanism is *not* being used to ensure that the worker is so employed at every moment of the working day as to equate his marginal revenue product with his wage.[1] The allocation of resources in such cases is by central direction, rather than through the price mechanism. This may be because it would be too costly or technically impossible to use the price mechanism (how, for example, would one monitor the marginal productivity of workers, or indeed of university teachers or bankers from hour to hour?). Such central direction, whether democratic or coercive, could, however, be easily extended to control the allocation of goods and services, even where the price mechanism could, in principle, be used. No money would then be required in that area of activity.

In a system where the role of each participant is laid down by agreement and/or by custom, for example in the family, or the commune, or in religious communities, transactions between individuals generally do not take the form of exchanges of stores of value. It would represent an inefficient way of achieving the goals of the group, as any allocative benefits of a monetary system would be outweighed by the extra marketing and transactions costs in these cases. Indeed considering the very large range of our activities in any day, most of which in principle could be organised through the price mechanism and involve monetary transfers, it is remarkable what a very large proportion are internalised in social groups such as the firm,[2] or the family, or even informal groups of friends.

Nevertheless the complete suppression of the price mechanism, and the allocation of goods and resources by direction, somehow organised internally, would require a more authoritarian society than most people would desire, particularly since the difficulty of maintaining harmony in any group beyond

[1] See Coase (1937) and also Alchian and Demsetz (1972) for a discussion of this point.
[2] Oliver Williamson (1971) noted that 'Internal resource allocation can be regarded both as a market substitute and an internal control technique'. As the unitary firm expands, however, the internal information network becomes overloaded with resulting control loss. In order to cope with this, firms tend to develop multi-divisional forms which make more use of the price mechanism and monetary transfers to allocate resource between divisions. Allocation of resources between the constituent quasifirms of the multi-divisional firm is based on objective financial results separately calculated rather than on subjective information on relative productivity, as in the case of the unitary firm.

some small size is notorious. Therefore in any such system the wishes of some of its members would tend to be overridden. These problems imply that in the majority of those cases which involve relationships between large numbers of participants, economic transactions must be seen to be to the personal advantage of each individual, rather than adding to the social welfare of the group.[1] Apart, therefore, from the technical problems involved in trying to organise the allocation of goods and services through central direction, the use of the price mechanism, markets and money reflects a preference by individuals to exercise individual choice in their economic context rather than to participate (voluntarily or involuntarily) in some group plan. In this context, therefore, the price mechanism, markets and money are jointly complementary social institutions for transmitting and economising on information.[2]

III INFORMATION

Given a system in which exchange transactions take place between individuals, each seeking to maximise his own personal welfare — though each may obtain utility or lose it through seeing others better off, through benevolence or envy — the question then becomes how can each individual assess when a transaction will be to his advantage? This is largely a matter of the adequacy of information. If you have no information about the behaviour of the opposite number to a transaction — e.g., a casual purchaser at your stall — then the risk that he would abscond or default, if he does not pay on the spot, is high. The only way to minimise risk sufficiently to enable a trans-action to go forward to the benefit of both is to exchange physical stores of value.[3] If, however, the seller has more information about the buyer — e.g., a

[1] It is partly a question of perception. The distribution of welfare in a competitive free-market system is arbitrary, without ethical content, and certainly violates the wishes of some of the members. But it has the advantage of not requiring conscious agreement, and seems to distribute welfare by act of God rather than of authority: whereas in an uncertain decentralised and complex world it is very hard to obtain an altruistic consensus.

[2] Several economists seeking to explain the existence of money consider that the development of a monetary economy results from the availability of transaction economies in a marketing context; see, for example, Clower (1971) p. 20, Brunner (1971), pp. 7–13, Niehans (1969). This is certainly an important element in the story, but it is not the main key. In their approach the prior existence of markets is assumed, and the underlying cause of transactions costs not given sufficient consideration. Both markets and money derive essentially from the same need to overcome information costs.

[3] 'One way or another, we must see to it that nobody can get something for nothing' (Niehans, 1969 p. 707). Also see the section on 'Trust, Rationality and Noncooperative Solutions' in Shubik (1973). He notes that
'As the general equilibrium model of the economy is nonstrategic' [i.e. participants do not have trading strategies], it is natural for a modeler to implicitly ignore the problem of how strangers in a market economy can trade together efficiently and more or less impersonally with a minimum need for trust. When the economy is modeled as a non-cooperative game, this problem must be faced. If individuals trust only cash and there is no banking system, then although it is highly likely that optimality in trade cannot be attained without credit, at least all trades that are made are made for immediate value received by both parties [pp. 36–7].

local farmer comes to buy at the stall — so that there is both information on his balance sheet position and sanctions against default[1] (e.g., by informing all the other traders), then the seller may be prepared to exchange his goods for credit, involving, perhaps, an interest payment. The debtor will, however, still have to extinguish this debt in due course by the transfer to the creditor of a store of value acting as a means of payment.

If market information improves still further, so that there is complete, or virtually complete, information on the standing and behaviour of all the participants, then there is no need even for bilateral clearing of debits and credits.[2] Instead we have returned virtually to a certainty-equivalent world, in which transactions will give rise to credit and debit balances which can be settled multilaterally without the need for a monetary asset as a means of payment. The extent to which transactions in any economy are settled by exchanges of stores of value, or by bilateral credit arrangements, or by multilateral credit arrangements (non-monetary sub-systems), depends on the availability of information on the parties to each transaction. The proportion of transactions settled through monetary exchanges will, however, rise with the growing complexity and dispersion of the economy, because of the greater likelihood of *not* having adequate information on the behaviour of the counter party to the transaction, and will decline with the development of methods to increase the information available about the participants. Seen in this light credit cards are, of course, an information augmenting device. Reductions in the use of money, as a means of payment, depend on increases in personal information.[3,4]

If however, the extent of personal information on the credit standing of the prospective purchaser is not adequate, transactions will only take place on the basis of a physical exchange of stores of value. If this involves the exchange of one good for another, say apples for haircuts, this is described as barter. It is sometimes said that barter requires a joint coincidence of wants and endowments,[5] finding a person with apples wanting a haircut meeting up with a barber who is feeling that he might appreciate an apple. Certainly there

---

[1] On this point see Ostroy (1973). Ostroy's key point is that 'Sellers, by requiring payment in money, are guaranteeing a steady flow of information such that the monetary authority, and it alone, is able to monitor trading behaviour.'

[2] Thus the degree to which 'the bilateral balance requirement' holds, c.f. Niehans (1969), is a function of information. With little information it holds both by transaction and time. As information increases the time constraint will be loosed. With full information the requirement will cease to hold at all.

[3] Peretz (1971) p. 353 has noted that 'Cash is basically a decentralised information system; possession of cash is an indicator of entitlement to resources to the holder, and to those who sell to him; but cash itself provides no means of centralising (and then analysing) information about all holders and all transactions.'

[4] The efficient working of non-monetary systems in general depends on the availability of, and access to, personal information. In so far as the provision of personal information is regarded as a potential infringement of freedom, it follows that money, and the development of a monetary system, is a pre-eminently liberal institution.

[5] 'The well-known problem of a barter economy reflects the necessity for a double coincidence of wants before any exchange can take place and the resulting high search

would normally be little likelihood of finding such a joint coincidence of wants and timing, even when the process is facilitated by the development of markets which provide an occasion for all prospective buyers and sellers to assemble in one place. Indeed the search costs involved in overcoming the need for a joint coincidence of wants are so considerable that barter rarely takes that form.[1] Instead one or other of the parties to the deal will take in exchange a good which he does not want himself with a view to subsequent resale with the intention of moving towards his desired position through a chain of sales and purchases.

It is, therefore, possible to overcome the double coincidence of wants if one of the parties to the deal will accept in payment some good that he does not directly want. But why should he do so? He is still left holding a good, which he wants to sell, and with wants, which he should like to satisfy, and he still faces uncertainty whether, and on what conditions, he can market his new good.

One answer is that there are some goods which have a broader and more stable market than others. If a person is offered salt, or corn, or cigarettes in payment for some sale, he is more likely to find a wide group of transactors, offering a large variety of products, wishing to buy this product at a reasonably stable price, than if he was offered a fishing rod, or roses, or a bowl of goldfish. Thus there will be a tendency for people to move towards the general use of one or more goods (assets) as a common means of payment, in order to avoid the inefficiencies of barter, in a system where uncertainty requires the use of means of payment.

Following the analysis of Brunner (1971, pp. 7–19),[2] such inefficiency derives mainly from two sources. First, the length of the transaction chain necessary to complete the desired exchange (of good A for good X) will commonly be elongated by barter (in order to overcome the double coincidence of wants and time in a barter context), and, second, each link in the chain involves uncertainty. Assume a chain of the form $ABC \rightarrow X$. When making each step the participant has to assess the quality and value of the good offered in exchange. In this case to get from A to X the participant either has to bear considerable risk or obtain a good deal of information (on the characteristics and marketing prospects) on goods B, C, etc. If then a good can be found which embodies desirable informational qualities, there

---

costs which this implies. A problem which has not received as much attention is that a barter economy also involves the necessity for a double coincidence of timing of transactions' [Perlman, 1971, p. 234].

[1] Except, perhaps, among schoolboys swapping treasures. Even then it is noticeable how some frequently used, standardised treasure, such as marbles or football cards, becomes the common basis for exchange and valuation, and, moreover, is prized for its use in exchange. Even if my son already has a Leeds United picture, he will welcome another for its swap value.

[2] See also, Brunner and Meltzer (1971), where they develop their ideas further. This is, in my view, the best article on the uses and nature of money to be found in the literature.

will be a tendency to use it as the counterpart of all trades both to reduce the length of the transactions chain and to limit the extent of uncertainty involved at each step.

There are two main bits of information which people need to learn about goods if they are to accept them as a step in their transactions chain.[1] First, has the object got satisfactory physical characteristics? Think of the difficulties of using cars or furniture as money! Second, are there satisfactory marketing outlets for the object where it can be swapped on? It will be easiest to use as money an object whose precise physical attributes do not require continuous and skilled checking, (otherwise each transaction will necessitate the cost and time involved in checking out the state of the means of payment as well as the object being sold), and whose acceptance is guaranteed.

There have been two common forms of answer adopted by societies to the problem of finding some standard means of payment, embodying sufficient information to make it generally acceptable without detailed physical checking. The first has been to use objects, of varying intrinsic use value – sometimes very little – which also symbolise some esteemed abstract value – often status, prestige, power. If your standing in the group is determined by the number of cows, pigs or cowrie shells you possess, rather than the precise physical state of these objects, then they can be accepted in payment irrespective of minor physical differences between them, so long as they count recognisably as a member of the set possessing the desired value. The second has been to have some external authority provide the information, on the monetary object, by stamping it or marking it in a manner that signifies information to potential users about the characteristics of the object.

[1] Niehans has shown that, under certain assumed conditions, some commodities with relatively low transactions costs may emerge 'automatically' as means of payment, as a result of optimisation processes to minimise transaction costs: 'The adoption of money requires neither law nor convention, nor can it be attributed to an "invention"; it is simply the effect of market forces.'

In my view, however, Niehans's commodity, which becomes used as a means of payment, is not *initially* to be described as money, any more than any other commodity. After a period during which it begins to be used as a means of payment, this process will, however, alter the information about its characteristics, in particular of the existence of satisfactory markets where it can be swapped on. This accretion of information will result in falling transaction costs for this commodity, and turn it into a general 'means of payment', *money*. Thus the development of money by this route should be seen as a dynamic process, not settled by relative transaction costs at a point of time.

In practice, however, the main transactions costs would seem to be related to information costs. So exogenous factors affecting such information (the role of the State, religion, custom, conventions, etc.) are likely to be as, or more, potent than physical characteristics in determining what is used as money. On this point, see Niehans (1969) and also a further development of a similar approach in Niehans (1971).

The view that money emerges spontaneously as a result of market forces has a long intellectual history. As Melitz (1974, p. 115, n. 15) notes, Karl Menger stressed this hypothesis, and offers a useful bibliography of the early history of this doctrine (traced back to John Law, 1705) in Menger (1950) Appendix J, pp. 318–9.

There has long been a debate between those who argue that the use of currency is based essentially on its symbolism of the *power* of the issuing authority (Cartalists) — i.e., that currency becomes money because the coins are struck with the insignia of majesty, not because they happen to be made of gold, silver or copper — and those who argue that the value of currency depends on the intrinsic value of the metal, with the role of the authorities (e.g., minting) restricted to the nevertheless vital function of providing the necessary information[1] on the characteristics of the metal in the currency (Metallists). The substitution of unbacked fiat, paper money for metallic coin as the main component of currency during this last century provides support for the Cartalist view that the monetary essence of currency *can* rest[2] upon the power of the issuer and not upon the intrinsic value of the object so used.[3]

In any case this line of analysis leads on naturally from a survey of the general conditions required for the establishment of a standard means of payment to the particular history of the development of currency, and subsequently of banks and of demand deposits as a means of payments. But this is not the place to pursue this historical and institutional development.

IV ROLE OF BANK DEPOSITS

Instead I should like to end this essay by considering certain questions about the monetary role of bank deposits in the light of the distinction, which has been emphasised earlier, between a means of payment and a medium of exchange. In general, though not of course universally,[4] people accept that

---

[1] Precious metals in an unworked state have only been used as a means of payment in exchanges under very special circumstances — e.g., in the various gold rushes in California and Klondike — and, even then, the picture, immortalised, for example, in film by Charlie Chaplin, of merchants and bartenders weighing and checking the gold dust before accepting it in payment suggests that payment in unworked precious metals has more in common with barter than with a monetary payment.

[2] Paper money may serve as no more than a claim, a ticket, to metallic currency, or other assets, of intrinsic value. As long as people trust the redemption pledge, the paper will circulate, because it is more convenient than coin in many ways, without the issuer having any necessary State power. There are many examples of this. On the other hand, after the collapse of the gold standard, most national paper currencies became pure inconvertible, fiat money, unsupported by any convertibility clause.

[3] There are definite overtones of this debate in some recent arguments about the reform of the international monetary system. There are those who would seek to base the international monetary system upon some object, gold, with characteristics that might make it a suitable monetary object, and those who recognise that, *au fond*, the establishment of an international monetary system must be based on the realities of international politics and power.

[4] There is the well-known inn motto, 'We have an agreement with our bank. We do not cash cheques, they do not sell beer'. People without bank accounts may stipulate payment in cash since the transfer costs of cashing a cheque may be relatively high for them. Cash payment may be demanded in order to avoid any records of the transaction being kept; e.g., to facilitate tax evasion.

the transfer of credit to their current account (demand deposit) at a bank represents a satisfactory final payment. But the means of payment is the actual transfer on the banks' books, whereas the medium of exchange at the time of the sale (the transaction) takes the form of writing out a cheque, an order to the bank to make this transfer.

It is sometimes overlooked that handing over a signed cheque to the seller of a good does *not* complete the payment; it is not a means of final payment in the sense that handing over currency, or the transfer of other goods (barter), does represent a means of payment. A cheque merely represents an order to a third party, the banker, to complete the final payment to the creditor. The process of payment through the banking system, put into motion by drawing the cheque, therefore involves several credit relationships, requiring the establishment of a state of personal trust dependent on adequate information. This is not the case with payment by barter or, perhaps, with currency, whose value, though, does reside in the public's confidence in the continuing power of the issuing authority.

In order to accept payment by cheque, the crucial information which the seller needs is whether the bank, to whom the order is addressed, will honour the payment order.[1] This does not depend solely on the state of the payer's current account credit balance. As Shackle (1971, p. 33) has noted, 'I cannot write a cheque on my deposit account, but I can write one on my current account which, even if that account is empty, will be honoured if covered by my deposit balance.' In addition, 'A man can just as well make a payment by increasing his overdraft (if he has his banker's permission to do so) as by reducing a credit balance.'

Even if the drawer of the cheque is completely sure of the value of payment orders which the banker will honour (and he often may not be), the payee does not possess this information. Unlike the transfer of currency, or barter, the payee is, in a sense, extending credit to the payer until the cheque has been cleared.[2] Indeed the distinction between accepting a cheque and accepting trade credit is not entirely clear-cut. Both involve the extension of credit until final payment is completed.

The use of cheques, as a medium of exchange, to set in motion the payment for a transaction by transfers within the banking system does, therefore,

---

[1] Moreover the experience of the Irish bank strikes, during which the banks were shut for several months, suggests that the inability of a bank to honour such an order immediately, in this case because of physical constraints, will not prevent the use of cheques as a medium of exchange, as long as the payee is confident that the payer, or some intermediary endorser, will in due course be able, if required, to make payment in legal tender. During these strikes cheques circulated with multiple endorsements, as they had done in the nineteenth century. There is a very interesting unpublished paper on this episode by A. E. Murphy, (Murphy, 1972).

[2] In practice the payee's account will be credited with the value of the cheque paid in while in transit. This reduces the cost to the payee of the extension of credit to the payer, but as long as there remains a finite probability of the cheque bouncing – i.e., until it is finally cleared – the process still essentially involves an extension of credit.

involve certain credit relationships which are virtually absent when currency is used in payment. This qualitative distinction has aroused, at different times, three separable, but related, questions about the monetary role of bank deposits. First, cheques may sometimes be declined as a medium of exchange, either because the payee does not want to accept payment in the form of a transfer to his credit within the banking system, or because the payee does not trust that acceptance of the cheque will, in fact, provide the stated credit transfer. On these grounds, particularly before the banking system is fully mature and established, it may be argued that bank current account deposits do not count as money at all.[1]

Second, since the acceptance of cheques is akin to the acceptance of trade credit, in that both involve some extension of credit, it has been argued that a bank balance, which is in a sense an immediately available unused credit facility, is fulfilling basically the same function as any other source of unused credit, which could be used as a medium of exchange. On this argument the definition of 'money' would have to be widely extended to cover overdraft facilities, trade credit facilities, loan facilities from all sources.[2]

Third, a bank customer does not have to hold a positive current account (demand deposit) balance, in order to have his order to complete the payment honoured by his bank. Payment may be made from unused overdraft facilities[3] or by a semi-automatic transfer from time deposits. The means to complete the requisite payment may be established by holding time deposits or by having access to unused overdraft facilities in a bank. On these grounds it may be argued that the definition of money, while not encompassing all credit facilities, should at least include all bank deposits and, perhaps, unused overdraft facilities with banks.

The first question is pragmatic. It is certainly true that under some conditions payment by cheque may be refused, but then under other conditions payment by cheque may be much preferred to payment in currency. You will not be allowed to pay your taxes by dumping a lorry load of pennies in the front lobby of the Inland Revenue. There are dangers, of loss or theft, in carrying high value notes, so most large transactions (at least those that are legal) are carried out in preference through cheque payments. Even by the

---

[1] In the nineteenth century this was a subject of considerable dispute, being, for example, one element in the celebrated debate between the Currency and the Banking Schools in the United Kingdom. On this point, see Laidler (1972) especially pp. 172–7.

[2] This argument is favoured by Laffer (1970). He argues that 'the empirical counterpart of the classical concept of money must include unutilised trade credit available along with demand deposits and currency'. Clower (1971, p. 18) also agrees that trade credit should be included in the definitions of money.

[3] Examination of the variations in bank 'float' suggest that in the United Kingdom, where reliance on overdrafts is widespread, about 60 per cent of items in transit will result in a reduction in gross deposits and about 40 per cent will lead to an increase in advances. The proportions are, however, not very clearly determined. In other countries, where overdrafts are less used, a higher proportion of payments will be made from deposit balances.

end of the nineteenth century the greater bulk of total transfers, in value terms, passed through the banking system.[1] People in fact do generally accept that a credit transfer to their current account with banks represents final payment, and that makes current accounts a means of payment. If people widely accepted transfers to their accounts with other financial inter-mediaries, such as building societies, as a form of final payment, this would make such accounts serve *de facto* as money.

The second issue arises from a confusion between the general need for instruments to serve as a medium of exchange and the more specialised role of money as a means of payment. There is, indeed, no fundamental difference between accepting a cheque or accepting any other form of credit as a medium of exchange allowing the transaction to take place. The fundamental difference occurs later, when the transmission process initiated by drawing the instrument has been completed. When the current accounts of the payer and payee have been respectively debited and credited by their banks, the payment is completed; nothing further needs to be done. When trade credits and debits are written in the books, or when loans have been negotiated to finance the original payment, an obligation remains to be settled; the process is not completed.[2]

Similarly the argument that unused bank overdraft facilities serve as a means of payment fails on the same grounds.[3] If *A* owes *B* money, but gets *C* to pay *B*, then *A* has merely substituted a debt to *C* for a debt to *B*. At some stage the debt has to be paid off. *B* may regard the transfer as completed, but it is not, since *A* has yet to make the final payment. Whether *C*, who steps in to finance *A*'s payment to *B*, is a person, a bank, or some other financial intermediary is irrelevant.[4]

A much more difficult question is whether to include time deposits with

---

[1] See the survey by Kinley (1901).

[2] For a somewhat similar approach to the definition of money, see Newlyn (1962) especially Chapter 1; (1964) especially pp. 334–9. However, in addition to the above condition that the transfer of the asset must complete the payment for the payer and payee, Newlyn also requires 'the consequential adjustments in the financial system [to] have a zero sum'. This seems unnecessarily restrictive; for shifts in the composition in which the public prefer to hold their money balances will cause adjustments in the financial system. See the criticism of Newlyn's approach by Friedman and Schwartz (1969).

[3] In addition there is the practical, operational problem of obtaining adequate estimates of the total of unused credit facilities. It is dubious whether this is possible even in principle. Attempts by Laffer (1970) to do so were remarkable for their heroism.

[4] The individual payer (person or company) may feel that it makes little difference to his basic economic position whether he pays any particular debt by running down his bank balance or by drawing on his overdraft or trade credit. I would not deny that such credit facilities may be regarded as quite close substitutes for money balances. This has an immediate implication for applied, empirical studies of the demand for money; the rate of interest on such liabilities (advances, trade credit) should enter the demand function as well as the rates obtainable on alternative assets. Indeed I do not think it possible, or useful, to interpret recent United Kingdom monetary developments without paying

banks, along with current accounts, in the definition of money. Although the process may be somewhat more costly and time consuming, holders of time deposits can use these to make payments. The transfer of funds from A and B by debiting A's time deposit and crediting B's current account will complete the payment for both A and B.[1]

There would seem no very strong basis on theoretical grounds for excluding time deposits from the definition of money. The issue should perhaps, be again decided on pragmatic grounds. If the turnover of current accounts is much higher than that of time deposits, one could conclude that there is a real difference in the usage of these assets as a means of payment. The degree to which the various types of deposit serve as money could be calculated approximately by the figures for relative turnover.[2] Unfortunately in the United Kingdom such data are not available, but in Holland monetary assets are indeed classified on the basis of their relative turnover. Even though it might be possible to construct a theoretically preferable monetary series, with assets entering weighted by their relative turnover, this would inevitably seem an artificial and complex concept. In the meantime it is probably best to think

---

explicit attention to the differential between the yield charged on advances and offered on time deposits.

Nevertheless I do believe that there is a substantive difference between holding as of right a means of payment, and a contingent – even if promised – access, at some uncertain interest rate, to a means of payment. Assume for the moment that banks were encouraged by the monetary authorities to expand overdraft facilities considerably. Would the demand for money fall equivalently; would it fall at all?

Yeager (1968, p. 51) presents another argument that overdraft facilities cannot be money, because, although a close substitute for money at the individual level, any attempt to draw on such facilities in the aggregate will cause a rise in interest rates, a non-neutral financial disturbance. This argument troubles me, because it is equally true that a shift by the public between cash and bank deposits will cause a non-neutral financial disturbance. If so, this line of reasoning either falls or forces one to restrict the definition of money to cash alone, which I would not be prepared to accept.

[1] The banks' balance sheet position will have altered. But it will also alter, and more drastically, if A pays B by cheque and B draws the money out of the bank in cash. A shift in the composition in which the public holds their money balances between cash, current accounts, and time deposits may have major consequences for the financial system, but this fact is hardly relevant to the question of what assets serve as means of payment.

[2] Laidler (1969) addresses the same question, whether time deposits should be counted as part of the money stock. He agrees that the test should be empirical and pragmatic. My preferred test, however, is to examine whether time deposits do serve as a means of payment; his preferred test is to examine whether current accounts and time deposits appear to be close substitutes in econometric studies of demand for money functions. The two approaches are quite closely related, (i.e., if time deposits are not used as a means of payment they are less likely to be a close substitute for current accounts), but they might give somewhat differing results.

Nevertheless, as Laidler has suggested to me in correspondence, perhaps the proper way to define money, when one has an imperfect and incomplete theory of it, is dependent upon the particular problem under discussion and might legitimately differ between problems.

of the total of currency and bank demand deposits as an operationally useful approximation to the total means of payment in the economy, on the grounds that most surveys show a very much higher turnover for current accounts than for time deposits.

REFERENCES

A. A. Alchian, 'Information Costs, Pricing, and Resource Unemployment' in E. S. Phelps, *et al.* (eds) *Microeconomic Foundations of Employment and Inflation Theory* (New York: Norton, 1970).

A. A. Alchian and H. Demsetz, 'Production, Information Costs and Economic Organization', *American Economic Review*, Vol. LXII, No 5 (December 1972) pp. 777–95.

K. Brunner, *A Survey of Selected Issues in Monetary Theory* (Reprint No 2 of the Research Project in Monetary Theory at the University of Konstanz, 1971).

K. Brunner and A. H. Meltzer, 'The Uses of Money: Money in the Theory of an Exchange Economy', *American Economic Review*, Vol. LXI, No 4 (December 1971) pp. 784–805.

R. Clower, 'Theoretical Foundations of Monetary Policy' in G. Clayton, J. C. Gilbert and R. Sedgwick (eds) *Monetary Theory and Monetary Policy in the 1970s: Proceedings of the 1970 Sheffield Money Seminar* (Oxford: Clarendon Press, 1971).

R. H. Coase, 'The Nature of the Firm', *Economica* (New Series), Vol. IV (November 1937) pp. 386–405.

M. Friedman and A. J. Schwartz, *A Monetary History of the United States 1867–1960* National Bureau of Economic Research (Princeton University Press, 1963).

M. Friedman and A. J. Schwartz, 'The Definition of Money', *Journal of Money, Credit and Banking*, Vol. 1, No 1 (February 1969) pp. 1–14.

F. H. Hahn, 'On the Foundations of Monetary Theory', in M. Parkin and A. R. Nobay (eds) *Essays in Modern Economics* (London: Longman, 1973) pp. 230–42.

H. Hino, 'Disequilibrium Dynamics with Keynesian Agents: An Expectation Theory of Unemployment and Inflation' (Rochester, mimeographed, 1974).

J. Hirshleifer, *Investment, Interest and Capital* (Englewood Cliffs, New Jersey: Prentice-Hall, 1970).

M. W. Holtrop, *Money in an Open Economy*, Publication No 17 of the Netherlands Institute of Bankers and Stockbrokers (Leiden: Stenfert Kroese, 1972).

G. A. Kessler, 'Monetary Analysis and Monetary Policy' in M. W. Holtrop, *Money in an Open Economy*, Publication No 17 of the Netherlands Institute of Bankers and Stockbrokers (Leiden: Stenfert Kroese, 1972).

D. Kinley, 'Credit – Currency and Population', *Journal of Political Economy*, Vol. 10, No 1 (December 1901) pp. 72–93.

A. B. Laffer, 'Trade Credit and the Money Market', *Journal of Political Economy*, Vol. 78, No 2 (March/April 1970) pp. 239–67.

D. E. W. Laidler, 'The Definition of Money', *Journal of Money, Credit and Banking*, Vol. 1, No 3 (August 1969) pp. 508–25.

D. E. W. Laidler, 'Thomas Tooke on Monetary Reform', in M. Peston and B. Corry (eds) *Essays in Honour of Lord Robbins* (London: Weidenfeld & Nicolson, 1972) pp. 168–86.

D. E. W. Laidler, 'Information, Money and the Macroeconomics of Inflation', *Swedish Journal of Economics*, Vol. 76, No 1 (March 1974) pp. 26–41.

J. Melitz, *Primitive and Modern Money* (Reading, Massachusetts: Addison-Wasley, 1974).

J. Melitz and G. Martin, 'Financial Intermediaries, Money Definition and Monetary Control', *Journal of Money, Credit and Banking*, Vol. 3, No 3 (August 1971) pp. 693–701.

A. H. Meltzer, Discussion on the question 'Is There an Optimal Money Supply?', *Journal of Finance*, Vol. XXV, No 2 (May 1970) pp. 450–3.

C. Menger, *Principles of Economics*, translated and edited by James Dingwall and B. F. Hoselitz (New York: Free Press, 1950).

A. E. Murphy, 'The Nature of Money – with particular Reference to the Irish Bank Closure' (Dublin, mimeographed, 1972).

W. T. Newlyn, *The Theory of Money* (Oxford: Clarendon Press, 1962).

W. T. Newlyn, 'The Supply of Money and its Control', *Economic Journal*, Vol. LXXIV, No 294 (June 1964) pp. 327–46.

J. Niehans, 'Money in a Static Theory of Optimal Payment Arrangements', *Journal of Money, Credit and Banking*, Vol. 1, No 4 (November 1969) pp. 706–26.

J. Niehans, 'Money and Barter in General Equilibrium with Transaction Costs', *American Economic Review*, Vol. LXI, No 5 (December 1971) pp. 773–83.

J. M. Ostroy, 'The Informational Efficiency of Monetary Exchange', *American Economic Review*, Vol. LXIII, No 4 (September 1973) pp. 597–610.

D. Peretz, 'Thirty-five Years of Change for the Financial System', *Futures*, Vol. 3, No 4 (December 1971) pp. 349–56.

M. Perlman, 'The Roles of Money in an Economy and the Optimum Quantity of Money', *Economica*, Vol. XXXVIII, No 151 (August 1971) pp. 233–52.

E. S. Phelps, *et al.* (eds) *Microeconomic Foundations of Employment and Inflation Theory* (New York: Norton, 1970).

G. L. S. Shackle, *The Years of High Theory: Invention and Tradition in Economic Thought 1926–1939* (Cambridge University Press, 1967).

G. L. S. Shackle, Discussion on 'Theoretical Foundations of Monetary Policy' by Robert W. Clower in G. Clayton, J. C. Gilbert and R. Sedgwick (eds), *Monetary Theory and Monetary Policy in the 1970s: Proceedings of the 1970 Sheffield Money Seminar* (Oxford: Clarendon Press, 1971) pp. 32–4.

M. Shubik, 'Commodity Money, Oligopoly, Credit and Bankruptcy in a General Equilibrium Model', *Western Economic Journal*, Vol. XI, No 1 (March 1973) pp. 24–38.

D. A. Starrett, 'Inefficiency and the Demand for "Money" in a Sequence Economy', *Review of Economic Studies*, Vol. XL, No 124 (October 1973) pp. 437–48.

O. Williamson, 'Managerial Discretion, Organisation Form, and the Multi-division Hypothesis', Chapter 11 in R. L. Marris and A. B. G. Wood (eds), *The Corporate Economy* (London: Macmillan, 1971).

L. B. Yeager, 'Essential Properties of the Medium of Exchange', *Kyklos*, Vol. 21, No Fasc. 1 (1968) pp. 45–69.

Appendix

Money and Disequilibria

In a world of certainty there would be no undesired unemployment, no disequilibria arising from incorrect and inconsistent decisions. Everyone would know from the outset the underlying distribution of wants on the one hand and skills and resources on the other. Each individual would be able to select an optimal life plan of activity and expenditures consistent with equilibrium, which would entail working as long as the marginal utility, in the form of wage and work satisfaction, was greater then or equal to the marginal costs in leisure opportunities forgone. People might be 'resting', but they would be doing so by preference.

In the world of uncertainty there is neither the information nor the equilibrating mechanisms available to allow equilibrium to be achieved. Decision-makers have to respond as best as they can to very limited information. If sales should fall, producers have to guess whether it would be better for them to lower their offered prices or to cut back on output. But, if some individual worker should find that he could not retain, or obtain, some particular job, which would provide him with greater prospective rewards than in other alternative jobs, why would he not offer his labour at a lower rate, as long as that still leaves him better off than in any alternative occupation? Clearly unions will strive to prevent this happening, since the possibility of competitive bidding down of wage rates by aspiring entrants would limit their own ability to select that combination of relative wage and size of industry that they prefer. But even in a non-unionised industry the transactions costs of dealing with each worker separately suggest that wages will tend to be held at standardised, common, fixed levels with occasional quantum-jump readjustments, rather than being perfectly flexible. In such cases workers may well not be able to find jobs, even in non-unionised occupations, despite being prepared to accept wages below the going rate. Because of the learning process involved in becoming part of a productive team, the value to an employer of a long-standing, trained employee is considerably greater than is the case with a new entrant. A job seeker will be unlikely to replace an existing worker by offering to accept a slightly lower wage.

So in an uncertain world, with imperfections in the market, transactions costs, information costs, etc., people will often be unable to obtain the work of their choice, even though they would be prepared to take that job at less than the going rate. This social problem is considerably accentuated by the specific nature of human capital. A worker is usually trained in some specific skill, with a considerable investment outlay in terms of time and money. The difference between the wage that a skilled worker would get if only he could obtain a job requiring that skill and his alternative prospects in the pool of unskilled workers may be very considerable. Again a worker will have developed specific attachments to his place of work, housing, schools, friends, etc. Even if a reasonable job can be found in some new area at a distance, an unemployed worker may prefer to risk his chances of finding one nearer home.

Phelps, *et al.* (1972, especially Part I)[1] liken the choice facing the unemployed man to an investment decision. By remaining unemployed and continuing to search for better jobs, the unemployed man foregoes current income, from the job vacancies currently available, in the hopes of enjoying a larger income in future from the job that he may secure by searching and waiting. He should continue to hold out as long as the present expected value of the returns to waiting, adjusted for risk, is greater than, or equal to, the costs involved.[2]

In an economy with perfect certainty foreseen changes in the pattern of wants would call forth smooth adjustments in the movements of factors of production between different uses. There would be no wastage of unemployed resources in the midst of want. But uncertainty leads to error, particularly in the extent of specific capital investment in infrastructure, equipment and human skills, which remain dependent for full utilisation on the continued, uncertain prosperity of some particular activity. Modern unemployment theory thus identifies uncertainty and information failures as the fundamental causes of disequilibria and factor unemployment.

Now the theme of the main section of this paper was that money, defined as a generalised means of payment, provides the necessary information to allow the continued functioning of a complex, decentralised economy. If so, it would surely seem to follow that, if unemployment (and disequilibria) is caused by information failures while the monetary system works essentially as an information-enhancing system, then the *existence* of money[3] should

---

[1] See, also, Phelps (1970), Alchian (1970).

[2] In this sense unemployment is a chosen state, and the choice is subject to the process of rational decision-making. Yet the analogy with investment provides too comfortable a connotation, for the term investment is generally connected with growth and expansion. For the unemployed worker it will usually be a choice between evils, to accept now a worse job, perhaps in a distant community, or to wait in unpleasant straits for the uncertain possibility of getting a better job in due course; though both the economy and the unemployed worker may well be better off if he does not immediately accept the first job offered but assesses as best as possible the prospects of obtaining better jobs.

[3] It is important to distinguish between the *existence* and the operation of a monetary system. There is no doubt that the monetary system can be mismanaged (as can fiscal policy, or international monetary policy, or other important aspects of economic life) in such a fashion as to lead to serious economic disturbances. Friedman and Schwartz (1963) attribute most of the responsibility for disturbances in the economy to monetary mismanagement. Laidler (1974) within an analytical framework similar to that adopted here, has shown how excessive monetary expansion generates inflation. Be that as it may, the question which we are asking here is *not* whether mismanagement of monetary policy within an already functioning monetary system can lead to disequilibria, but whether the very existence of a monetary system will result in *additional* disequilibria.

lead to a reduction in the prevalence of unemployment and disequilibria. The institution of money is a device for the provision and extension of additional information in a complex, decentralised economy. As the economy expands from a small tribal group, in which everyone knows everyone else, to a vast, *impersonal* industrial system, the increase in uncertainty is inevitable. In truth, the uncertainties in a modern, decentralised system are *so* great, that it could not function unless institutions had developed to provide the additional information-flows necessary.

The possibilities for disequilibria arise from lack of information within a decentralised economy. Uncertainty is inherent in the structure of this economic society; money is a device for mitigating that uncertainty. Without the information-flows obtained by the use of money (or by some alternative or equivalent informational system), the system could not function. Even with the advantages accruing to the economy from the use of money, the uncertainties are still so pervasive that maladjustments and unemployment occur.

A monetary system is, therefore, a necessary adjunct for the development and expansion of a decentralised economy. But the institution of money, which allows such decentralisation within the economy, is then sometimes blamed for the disequilibria which subsequently arise. Indeed this view that the existence of money should reduce disequilibria within a given economy, or allow the greater expansion of an economy with no extra disequilibria resulting, does not seem to be generally accepted within the literature.

Consider the following two quotations. The first is by Kessler; in Kessler (1972) he wrote:[1]

Holtrop's monetary views are based on the recognition, already stressed by J. G. Koopmans in 1933, that J. B. Say's law of markets does not hold in a money-using economy. In a barter economy every supply of goods implies a demand for goods. This rigid connection between supply and demand ceases to exist when money is used in exchange for goods. It is only in a money-using economy that 'pure demand' (reine Nachfrage) can exist, i.e., a demand for goods that is not met by a corresponding supply. This is the case when the purchasing power for the demand for goods is not derived from current income but from the creation or dishoarding of money. Conversely, there may be a shortfall of demand (reine Nachfrageausfall) when income from production is 'lost' in destruction or hoarding of money. It is no exaggeration to say that in all his studies Holtrop explicitly or implicitly endeavours to draw logical conclusions from the view that monetary factors are at the root of macroeconomic disturbances such as price inflation and overfull employment in case of excess demand and underemployment in case of a shortfall in demand.

[1] This appeared in Holtrop (1972) and was reissued as Reprint No 1 of De Nederlandsche Bank.

Similarly Shackle (1967) argues that disequilibrium is a *monetary* phenomenon. Thus he writes:

Now when, instead of an equilibrium model, we suppose one where each producer must decide what size of output to produce and offer, of his own kind of product, on the basis of his mere *conjecture* of the demand curve facing him, there is nothing to ensure that the revenue (price times output) resulting from this offer will be, in the event, the amount which his decision assumes. Nonetheless if all today's conjectural income is intended, by those who expect it, to be spent on today's products, the total of revenue will necessarily, in the event, equal the total of these conjectural incomes, and a shortfall of one person's revenue below his expectation will be exactly compensated by an excess of others' revenue above their expectations. Thus in the model or assumed system where the only acceptable means of purchasing today's products is other of today's products, *total* demand and supply in value-unit terms are necessarily equal. It is only when we introduce a *substantive* means of purchase, one which does not merely *represent* today's products but exists or arises in its own right, *outside* the list of products, that total demand and total supply can be unequal. It is *money* which destroys the necessary, inevitable equality which they have in a barter or virtual barter system. Money, of course, could not do so in the general *equilibrium* system, where indeed its independent existence would be meaningless and any role beyond that of unit of account non-existent. If we cared to construct a general equilibrium system where 'money' entered on the same footing as current products, the system of simultaneous equations determining this equilibrium would have to specify the conditional intentions in respect of spending or accepting money, and the enlarged system would still show an equality of that total of demand and supply which included offers and demands for money. For in a general equilibrium system we suppose that each action-chooser has full relevant knowledge, provided for him by the equilibrating mechanism whatever its precise nature and mode of working. Inequality of total demand and total supply, to be logically possible, requires the presence and the play of both *ignorance* and *money*. Ignorance in the real world, there is indeed: ignorance of the future. And money is that institution which permits *deferment* of specialised, fully detailed choice [pp. 90–1; italics in original].

There would appear, therefore, on the face of it to be some contradiction between these two views; the first that the existence of money, by breaking the link between the demand and supply of goods and services inherent in a barter system, allows the development of disequilibria; and the second that money provides essential information services, which should serve to lessen disequilibria and inefficiencies within a complex economy. My own opinion is that, whereas the monetary system *can* be mismanaged so as to exacerbate disequilibria, the existence of money actually reduces disequilibria and in-efficiencies, and allows the development and expansion of a much more complex and decentralised economy.

For example, a change in tastes, or a shift in supply conditions, may bring about just as much, or more, maladjustment in a barter economy as in a monetary economy. Whether the economy had a barter, or a monetary, exchange technology, car producers faced with a fall in demand (i.e., with a fall in the amount of food and services offered in exchange for cars) — perhaps because the running costs of cars were rising in real terms — would have to decide whether to accept a lower price for existing output, or to withold some output (involuntary stock building) from the market. If the producers' reservation price is such that some current output goes into stock-building, the producers will then probably decide to cut output in the subsequent period. They will then have spare time (short-time working and unemployment), which they may fill with searching for an alternative, or secondary, occupation. If their training in car production endows them with specific human capital, the return from alternative unskilled occupations may be far below their usual incomes, and they may well be reluctant to move to other available jobs.

The main argument of those who claim that the institution of money is responsible for disequilibria is, I think, that its existence facilitates the separation of the decision to save from the decision to invest. This separation is, of course, a central feature of economic growth, but equally it does entail greater dangers of instability within a decentralised economy.

Even so, while the separation of the decision to invest and to save does require the existence of some financial instruments, this does not necessarily entail the presence of a *monetary system*, though no doubt a well-functioning monetary system is conducive to the development of financial instruments and financial intermediation. Consider, for example, an instrument promising to pay the bearer a certain bundle of goods (X oranges, Y apples, Z bottles of wine, etc.) at time t in exchange for q per cent of those same goods now. Investors could borrow, and savers could lend, through the medium of such instruments, even in an otherwise barter society (though the transactions costs would be high).

Assume that suddenly households decided to save more. Current demand would go down, so at existing production rates stockbuilding would rise. This *could* be financed exactly at current interest rates since the increased demand to finance stocks would be matched by an increased demand for future goods. But this would not happen in practice. Each individual producer would be faced with the fact of a reduction in present demand. He would be in no position to know whether this was due to a shift in demand away from his particular product, to a preference for future goods relative to present goods, or whatever. Under such circumstances he would hardly be likely to raise *ex ante* investment to the same extent as *ex ante* saving has increased. The basic reason is that each producer (in a multi-good, multi-producer economy)[1, 2] cannot be confident that the fall in current demand for his individual product represents an increase in future demand for his own product.

Perhaps this difficulty could be avoided in some large part by encouraging each borrower to denominate financial instruments just in terms of his own product, whether goods, services or labour. This, of course, transfers the uncertainties to the saver, who will not know whether he will want or be able to re-sell the particular future good offered. Presumably this would raise interest rates, and reduce both saving and investment, even though it would probably lessen the likelihood of general disequilibria.

Basically these problems are caused by the increased uncertainties that result from the separation of investors and savers. Investors do not know whether the future demand for their products will be sufficient to justify current borrowing, and savers do not know whether they will want (or be able to re-sell) any particular products at some future date. This separation, and the ensuing uncertainties, may be facilitated by the presence of a developed financial system, and within it by the existence of a monetary system, but this is hardly enough to claim that the institution of money, defined as a generalised means of payment, is a necessary constituent of economic disequilibria.

---

[1] A more centralised – single producer – economy should be able to avoid certain forms of disequilibria which arise from the inconsistent decisions of independent decision-makers within a decentralised economy; thus totalitarian States should manage to eradicate unemployment. But the more fundamental problem of obtaining, processing and reconciling information on the economic desires and capabilities of members of the economy remains. In a totalitarian, centralised economy individual wishes have less outlet. The centralised economy may, therefore, avoid certain forms of disequilibria but usually at the cost of functioning less efficiently to satisfy the real wants of its members.

[2] In a single-good economy there could only be the one good in the financial instrument based on goods, so that each producer would know that additional saving by households now would have to re-emerge later as effective demand for current production being stockpiled. In a system of this kind it can be shown that the introduction of money would allow disequilibria: see Hino (1974). I doubt the value of this exercise to a wider understanding of the role of money, since it is not at all clear why money should be introduced into a one-good economy, nor that any of the main conclusions would hold in a multi-good economy.

Discussion of the Paper by Dr Goodhart

Introducing the paper, *Dr Grandmont* said that it was partly concerned with
the proper definition of 'money'; the starting point of the analysis was that
money served as a generalised means of payment. Dr Goodhart distinguished
between a means of payment which, when received by a seller, completed the
transaction, and a means of exchange. According to his definition,

> A medium of exchange includes those assets, or claims, whose transfer to
> the seller will commonly allow a sale to proceed. The distinction is that
> when the seller receives a medium of exchange, which is not a means of
> payment, in return for his sale, he will feel that he still has a valid claim for
> future payment against the buyer, or even more generally against some
> other group on whom the buyer has provided him with a claim.

Such a definition of the function of money excluded all assets which involved
the extension of credit until final payment was completed, such as trade
credit, cheques and the like. It led to the natural conclusion that money must
include cash and bank demand deposits. Although time deposits might serve as
a means of payment, Dr Goodhart proposed to exclude them from the
definition of money 'on the grounds that most surveys show a very much
higher turnover for current accounts than for time deposits'.

Dr Goodhart's analysis of this point was clear and elegant; Dr Grandmont
felt, however, that a definition of money had no sound basis when the use to
be made of that concept was *not* specified, and this was not done in the paper.
He believed that Dr Goodhart in fact agreed, since he wrote (p. 219, n.2),
'perhaps the proper way to define money... is dependent upon the particular
problem under discussion and might legitimately differ between problems'.
Dr Grandmont wished to add that in his view the problem which motivated the
search for an appropriate definition of money must be an empirical one. Most
theoretical issues in monetary economics could be handled, at least in principle,
by using a model of the economy which did not involve any aggregation of
the monetary sector. For instance, such questions as: Why do people hold
monetary assets that do not yield direct utility? or, What is the precise meaning
of the quantity theory of money or of the theory of optimal cash balances?,
could be studied without worrying about an appropriate definition of an
aggregate called 'money'. If this view was correct – that is, if the need for a
definition of an aggregate called money came from a particular empirical
problem – then this problem had to be clearly specified before one began to
talk about the proper definition of money. This was not done in this paper,
and Dr Grandmont expected that in the course of the discussion Dr Goodhart
would clarify this point.

Dr Goodhart was also concerned with two important theoretical issues of
monetary economics which were independent of the problem of finding an
appropriate level of aggregation of the monetary sector: first, the conditions
that were required in an economy for the establishment of a generalised
means of payment; and second, the role of such a means of payment in connection with the existence of disequilibria.

The survey of the general conditions required for the establishment of a
standard means of payment given by Dr Goodhart was brilliant and clear. The

main point, which was well known, was that in large and complex economies transactions costs and uncertainties associated with barter exchange were very great and the institution of monetary exchange reduced these costs. While this intuitive argument showed clearly what should be done if we wanted to formulate it precisely in microeconomic models, it was difficult actually to do it. Dr Goodhart's criticism of some recent attempts to study this point with the help of models involving transactions costs but no uncertainty was, there- fore, too harsh. Dr Grandmont agreed with Dr Goodhart that uncertainty entailed transactions costs which mainly reflected the cost of obtaining information; that is, of reducing uncertainty. But Dr Goodhart had con- tinued:

> If, as suggested, transactions costs are a function of uncertainty, it is not entirely logical to investigate systems of uncertainty without transactions costs or of certainty with transactions costs. Yet there has been some interest in such hypothetical situations, especially in the case of uncertainty without transactions costs. Studies of the other situation, where there are transactions costs but no uncertainty are less common; indeed it does seem to represent an even more artificial and less interesting framework.

Dr Grandmont disagreed with this last point. In view of the difficulties that one faced in the study of systems operating under uncertainty, he believed that the study of systems with certainty and transactions costs was an interesting and promising *starting* point. The recent work of Hahn, Starr, and Starret, among others, on the theory of general equilibrium with sequential trading and transactions costs but no uncertainty had already given us deeper insights into the nature of inefficiencies entailed by barter exchange and how they could be lessened by the introduction of low transactions costs commodities, such as money. Dr Grandmont believed that further progress could be made along these lines.

The second important theoretical issue that Dr Goodhart had discussed was the role of money in relation to the existence of disequilibria. He had con- trasted two views that could be found in the literature on this topic. The first view, which he had presented at length, was that 'money provides essential information services, which should serve to lessen disequilibria and inefficiencies within a complex economy'. The second view was described in the appendix to the paper and amounted to saying that 'the existence of money, by breaking the link between the demand and the supply of goods and services inherent in a barter system, allows for the development of disequilibria'.

Dr Grandmont suggested that this apparent contradiction came from the fact that the proponents of these two views were reasoning with the help of implicit models with drastically different assumptions; the conflict was resolved if one reasoned within the framework of a single model. When one claimed that money reduced disequilibria and inefficiencies, one was implicitly comparing the allocation of goods and services which would result from a barter exchange process where transactions costs were great, with the allocation which would result from a monetary exchange process where transactions costs were relatively low. On the other hand, economists claiming that money allowed the development of disequilibria were comparing the result of a monetary exchange process with an hypothetical situation where barter could take place *without incurring transactions costs.* The last line of reasoning was clearly unwarranted. Once the large transactions costs associated with barter exchange were reintroduced into the picture, there was no contradiction between the two views.

Professor Davidson commenced his intervention by reading from K. J. Arrow and F. H. Hahn, *General Competitive Analysis* (Oliver and Boyd, 1971), Chapter 14.

> The terms in which contracts are made matter. In particular, if money is the good in terms of which contracts are made, then the prices of goods in terms of money are of special significance. This is not the case if we consider an economy without a past and without a future. Keynes wrote that 'the importance of money essentially flows from it being a link between the present and the future', to which we may add that it is important also because it is a link between the past and the present. If a serious monetary theory comes to be written, the fact that contracts are indeed made in terms of money will be of considerable importance [pp. 356–7].

> The example is sufficient, however, to show that if we take the Keynesian construction seriously, that is, as a world with a past as well as a future and in which contracts are made in terms of money, no equilibrium may exist. [p. 361].

He wished to rephrase these two statements. If we were going to have a microeconomic foundation compatible with macroeconomics, then we had to take into account the fact that the economy had a past as well as a future. Dr Goodhart had gone a long way in illustrating the line to take. He had pointed out that until we had shown that cross-elasticities were low we did not even have a definition of commodity money. Keynes had defined money similarly in *The General Theory of Employment, Interest and Money*, Chapter 17. Friedman had claimed that Keynesians said that money had a high elasticity of substitution with other assets; in Friedman's own model there were in fact no durable goods because there was no line between elasticities.

Dr Goodhart had said that we did not know enough to look at empirical estimates of elasticities; we had to consider the functions and properties of money. Two of the functions were, said Professor Davidson, the means of discharge of money contracts and the provision of liquidity. In *The General Theory* Keynes had said that these two functions required specific elasticity properties and had insisted that any good that did not have these elasticity properties could not maintain its liquidity. As for the means of settlement, that would depend on the law relating to contracts, and would be different in different countries. The 'gold clause' in the United States was a good example; also, the problem of international money was partly a problem of how international contracts were enforced and who enforced them.

Professor Davidson took the view that we should not begin our analysis by imagining reasons why money should be invented. We should start from the fact that we had a real world monetary economy; if we had a non-monetary economy there would be no involuntary unemployment even if there was uncertainty. Trade credit could not become money because it could not discharge contracts. Could a clearing system for private debts become money? Drawing on Sir John Hicks's *Critical Essays in Monetary Theory*, Professor Davidson said one would need: (1) private debt to be denominated in the means of settlement of contracts; (2) general accessibility to the clearing system; and (3) confidence that uncleared debts could be converted into the means of settlement instantaneously. These conditions were implied in Dr Goodhart's paper (pp. 212–3). We could justify three types of asset-holding: the holding of money or undated purchasing power; the holding of placements which might be debts or titles and which were dated purchasing power, with the possibility of resale; and the holding of physical assets, which had dated utilities and expected date of purchasing power and where in the extreme case resale was impossible or at least very costly. The last group of assets had no liquidity.

With respect to the Appendix to Dr Goodhart's paper, Professor Davidson raised the question of what Keynes had meant by unemployment. He said that peanuts could never be money in Keynes's world because that commodity did not have the right elasticities; peanuts could only be money in a general equilibrium model. Money had the properties described in Chapter 17 of *The General Theory* and that led to unemployment.

Professor Nell wished to take up one of the many points that Professor Davidson had made and to ask a question of both Dr Goodhard and Dr Grandmont. In his remarks on Professor Malinvaud and Mr Younès's paper Sir John Hicks had distinguished three Walrasian assumptions that might be questioned: price flexibility, recontracting, and opportunities for multilateral exchange. Professor Malinvaud and Mr Younès had examined the first and the third, but not the second. His own question was: In the case where we were examining money as a means of settlement, did it make sense to do so by means of a general equilibrium model in which there was universal recontracting? Should one not consider the analysis of money in the context of a model in which we explicitly dropped recontracting?

Dr Goodhart replied that his answer was 'Yes'. *Dr Grandmont* agreed that if we looked at the real world the use of money partly came from the fact that we had a relation with everybody in the market. At the formal level, however, one could look at the Malinvaud-Younès concept of equilibrium; Dr Grandmont reported a result which was related to Professor Nell's question. If one assumed that one had, say, rigid prices and that recontracting had to take place through monetary exchange, then one could show that if there were a large number of agents the only allocation which was stable in the sense of the core was the allocation given by the Malinvaud-Younès equilibrium. At this formal level, the use of money in a process of exchange was perfectly compatible with free competition and free contracting. Dr Grandmont conjectured that by enlargement of the theory of the core one could get the same result if one assumed that one agent could recontract with only a few agents around him. It was perfectly compatible to have a model where money was used as a means of settlement and to have free recontracting in that model.

Professor Malinvaud reminded us that Edgeworth had introduced the recontracting hypothesis. We did not have any good justification in reality for that hypothesis; the only reason we used it was that it made for a clear theory and a theory which was, he thought, useful for interpreting some facts. If we dropped recontracting, we had a messy theory which we could not get much out of. Perhaps it was a point of scientific honesty that the theorists drew the attention of the reader to the fact that recontracting had been assumed and that therefore some aspects of reality could not be dealt with.

Professor Shubik thought that Dr Grandmont and Professor Malinvaud had made a false analogy between two totally different theories. The whole Edgeworth construction was totally non-monetary in form. Furthermore, twenty years had been spent unsuccessfully trying to get money into the core model. We could not succeed because money happened to involve externalities. The externalities were markets, which were the means to interlink trading strategies; this meant rather strict limitations on the strategy spaces of individuals. The correct *alternative* way to begin if we wanted a well-defined formal model was to take Cournot's model. This had the property that it provided a way to define a simple model in which trade had to take place through a market and in money without recontracting. The particular model would involve bidding quantities of money for any particular commodity; it would have a different characteristic function and core from Edgeworth's model except in the limit. Shepley and Shubik had explored this model.

Professor Marty asked whether the existence of money was compatible with the assumption of a one-commodity world? There had been a proliferation of money and economic growth models a few years ago, when he had pointed out that there was no money in the Tobin and Johnson models; he now believed that the models had *no room* for money, and that the attempt of Patinkin and Levhari as well as his own previous work to incorporate money in a one-sector one-commodity model was fundamentally misguided.

Professor Stiglitz suggested that the Tobin and Johnson models were like Samuelson's consumption-loan model because money was a store of value in these models; *Dr Goodhart* asked why we needed a store of value in these models? This prompted a three-cornered discussion between him and Professors Marty and Stiglitz on the subject.

Professor Izzo intervened to say that he sympathised with the critics of these models. He went on to point out that present general equilibrium models with money excluded investment and accumulation. Recent disequilibrium models were built on the assumption that we had a difference between notional and effective demands, but as far as he knew there was no analysis of investment decisions, which were made autonomously; he did not think that we could properly analyse the working of a monetary economy without considering this fact. With reference to the problem of the Appendix to Dr Goodhart's paper, the risk concerning a single commodity could be ignored because people could take out insurance or have a balanced portfolio. The real problem concerned the future course of economic activity and rates of interest.

Professor Leijonhufvud noted that Dr Goodhart's paper at several points relied on the Brunner-Meltzer article, 'The Uses of Money: Money in the Theory of an Exchange Economy' (*American Economic Review*, December 1971). He had two comments:

(1) That article had made a plausible case that a barter system would evolve to a point where only a sub-set of goods would be used as media

of exchange. But it did not go beyond making that plausible; it did not, for example, prove that this medium of exchange sub-set would tend to shrink to a 'very few' goods or a single good. Nor did it develop the concept of means of payment beyond that of goods serving exchange-intermediary functions in indirect barter exchange regimes. There were other problems in the article pertaining in particular to the definition of the marginal rates of substitution used to characterise the behaviour of agents.

(2) Professor Leijonhufvud wanted mainly to consider the general approach of the Brunner-Meltzer paper rather than how it was executed. Its starting-point was the question: What goods will serve as moneys? To go directly for the definition of 'M' was an approach that came naturally to empirically-oriented quantity theorists. Yet, it was questionable whether this was a promising way to proceed. To adopt the prior conception of 'money' as a set of assets with special characteristics might be to start on a false trail. The Friedman—Schwartz survey (Part I of their *Monetary Statistics of the United States*, New York, 1970) had shown how inconclusive had been the attempts to arrive at clearcut theoretical criteria for whether particular assets do or do not belong to the set 'M'.

It might be more promising to start with the notion of a payment mechanism and enquire as to the purposes for which it would exist. The main purpose, Professor Leijonhufvud suggested, was to police the behaviour of agents, by providing an institutional mechanism to check their honesty; if the system were to work, agents must not be allowed to get away with more than they are entitled to. In a standard neo-Walrasian general equilibrium model the agents were bound only by a budget constraint where the planned intention to supply certain goods to a certain value was enough to back up the simultaneously planned demands for goods to be purchased. Clower and others had tried to work from that starting point by introducing a 'prior possession constraint': it was not enough for an agent to go to the market and announce his intention or promise to sell something of equal value to someone else in order to obtain the goods he desired. He had to have evidence of a prior social entitlement arising from a prior sale. In other words, individuals had to have income before expenditure to make their demands effective. 'Prior possession' could be regarded as a particularly restrictive variant of the more general notion of 'accountability constraints'. By studying how accountability is maintained in the system, Professor Leijonhufvud suggested, we might hope eventually to reach a better understanding of how trade credit arrangements and collateral requirements, bankruptcy laws and legal tender provisions, overdraft and Giro banking practices, credit cards and centralised clearing arrangements, and various forms of transferable or non-transferable deposits 'fit into' a monetary system. We might then be in a position to look at a particular system in order to discover which asset stocks play the most important roles in the operation of the payments mechanism and what the most relevant concept of 'M' might be for econometric purposes.

Dr Goodhart said that he had indeed been hoping to start many of the hares that had got under way in the discussion; for example, the question of whether money was a disequilibrium concept. But he wished to answer one point raised by Dr Grandmont and Professor Leijonhufvud, namely the question of whether money should only be defined with respect to a particular problem. They had argued that one need only consider an economy with a certain given set of institutions such as banks, currency, etc., and then within this economy one could simply look at the relationships between these assets and preferences and see if one could establish an equilibrium. Why was that not sufficient? Dr Goodhard felt that only when one was dealing with a short-run situation, in which it could be assumed that institutions were given, was that approach valid. He had in fact been concerned with the problem that the structure of the economy did not remain constant over time, that assets, relationships and institutions changed. When one was considering the question of structural reform and the process of development of the economy, one had to consider assets in terms of more fundamental definitions and to ask what kinds of services one expected a monetary good to be providing for individuals. In other words, he was concerned with a long-term structural problem.

Professor Shubik said that he was in complete agreement with the approach of Dr Grandmont and Professor Malinvaud, of formally modelling certain institutions to see what one could get out of the model. He was also in agreement with Dr Goodhart, for he did not regard the two approaches an antithetical. He suggested that we were on the verge of a new and strange subject, *mathematical institutional economics.* The question of money was a systemic problem, and that was one reason why he had always talked about money and financial institutions. He would prefer to talk about money, other financial instruments, and financial institutions; and to adopt the approach of starting with a formal economic model and seeking where rules of the game, which could be interpreted as institutions, would be called for by the mathematical structures.

One place where the institutions were called for by the mathematics could be seen very simply by starting with a simple financial general equilibrium trading model. Here there were many assumptions that did not hold in the real world: it was assumed that there was no gap between expenditure and income; however, an individual might spend at one time period but receive his income in the next time period. This could be described mathematically by requiring all goods to be traded in markets with a one-period lag between receipts and payments. However, one would then have to have a *float* to finance the first period's expenditure. If there was no trust except in the State, coin could be used to cover the float. If further credit needs required a bank then in a truly dynamic model bankruptcy and bank failure laws would have to be specified. At this point Professor Shubik mentioned his simple criterion for monetary models: if one could not play one's model as a well-defined game in one's graduate students' class, then it was not a well-defined model. He went on to point out that once one did not assume perfect foresight in one's model, one had to have very conservative banks or bankruptcy laws. He believed that the major gaps in existing monetary theory were the unsatisfactory roles for the float, perfect foresight, bankruptcy and insolvency. In an economy without trust the relatively natural way to introduce money was to assume that fiat money financed the first period float and bank money financed the intertemporal needs for credit. Thus one needed two types of paper in a general equilibrium system: one without and the other with a rate of interest.

Finally, on the question of the link between macroeconomics and micro-economics, Professor Shubik said that he favoured a very simple, strict model of a microeconomic monetary system where everybody had to sell everything every time period. In the real world a great number of people made their particular economic gains by disguised wealth; many economic transactions were undisclosed capital gains or losses, of which frequently the losses were exposed and the gains disguised. Probably only 50 per cent or 60 per cent of the most sophisticated economy was monetised. For mathematical simplicity, for accounting honesty, and for an understanding of the control individuals had in a monetary economy, he advocated the other extreme from the Edgeworth model, namely a model where nobody was in control of his own assets. In an Edgeworth-type general equilibrium barter economy the ownership conditions were described by a vector of real resources held by an individual; in a totally-monetised Cournot-type economy, ownership would be defined differently, namely that ownership of a vector of resources at time t meant entitlement to the monetary income to be received in time $t + 1$ from the sale of that vector of resources at time t.

Professor Davidson intervened to say that the income which had to be earned before expenditures were made was truly related to endogenous expenditure. Kalecki had used this in his theory because he wanted to assume that profit recipients finance current consumption out of last period's profits. Nevertheless, as long as production took time and labour was willing to sell its efforts by entering into forward contracts for a period which exceeded the period of production, and as long as institutions existed which would permit financing out of future income in some way, there was no necessary require-ment that one financed expenditure out of past income. This was where liquidity and financial institutions came in. The monetary economy was different from a Cournot society. Real world institutional rules permitted financing of only certain future income streams and if in the aggregate there were people who currently earned income and did not want to purchase (or order for future delivery) reproducible goods, and if they had a kitchen sink in which to keep their current income claims, there would be unemployment equilibrium. This kitchen sink would always be money; if there was no asset that had a zero elasticity of production, people would invent one.

Professor Davidson then repeated his earlier argument that what made spot markets were market makers, another institution. This was where con-fidence and liquidity came in. Middlemen or market makers in spot markets had to have inventories of money and goods, and it was necessary to have an institutional rule that if they ran out of stocks they had preferential access to the monetary authority who would restock them with money for short periods of time. Macroeconomics had two sorts of markets, flexprice and fixprice, of which the former were spot markets and the latter were forward markets, where the price was fixed by the duration of the money contract.

Professor Stiglitz thought that Dr Goodhart's paper had raised some very interesting issues, one of which was the proper criteria for comparing monetary and non-monetary economies. If we considered the two functions of money which were emphasised in the paper, namely as a source of some of the problems that generated unemployment equilibrium, and as a medium of exchange, our views of the function of money were radically altered when we formulated the appropriate models. With respect to the medium of exchange we had the possibility that there was no reason to show that we needed money as a method of facilitating exchange. Credit of one sort or another could serve all the functions of money in a world with perfect certainty. When one realised this, statements that money was required as a medium of exchange and that demand depended on income were hard to interpret. Professor Stiglitz did not believe that there was any theory of money in Keynes's writings on the transactions demand for money, because to create a theory of money one would have to formulate a theory that money could perform this function and credit could not: that would need factors such as bankruptcy and lack of information. Although it was clear that much more work in modelling this formally was needed, Dr Goodhart's paper suggested that it was a deeper problem than a matter of putting *ad hoc* constraints into a general equilibrium model.

The second aspect of money stressed in the paper raised the question that we had been addressing when discussing Professor Malinvaud and Mr Younès's paper. Which were the really crucial assumptions of those we conventionally made in trying to formulate a macro-equilibrium theory of unemployment? Professor Malinvaud and Mr Younès had pointed out that price-inflexibility without money could generate similar results; Dr Goodhart had also pointed out that money was not crucial. If there was a lack of information a firm would have to make decisions as to future contracts in the face of an uncertain demand; that could lead to the same kind of problems. This was an area which needed more precision and more information but there was clearly something here of considerable importance.

Professor Stiglitz raised two other brief points:

(1) On the question of methodology, why did we want to define money? Why was this not just an empirical question? Dr Goodhart was right in saying that we were concerned about the structure of the economy. One of the theoretical directions that we could have pursued was to look at the question as an aggregation question: what kind of restrictions on utility functions would lead to particular aggregates having particular properties? If we aggregated money and short-term assets, there must be a separability theorem involved; we could, therefore, look at the assumptions necessary for the theorem to hold. As for the notion of liquidity, the term lent itself to confusion, and Professor Siglitz was not sure that it added much to our understanding.

(2) An empirical way of isolating what we ought to include as money was to look at rates of turnover. If a bank had a non-linear return function of the magnitude of the deposits, one could arbitrarily call one part of the function demand deposits and the other part time deposits; these would have different rates of turnover, but that would tell us nothing about whether the deposits were close substitutes.

Dr Nuti was not sure that the distinction between money as a medium of exchange and money as a means of payment was a really useful distinction. According to Dr Goodhart's paper, the set of means of payment included cows or peppercorn rents which extinguished an obligation, the set of means of exchange comprised the things which enabled a person to be a partner in an exchange without extinguishing obligations, and the intersection of the two sets was money. Was this more helpful than looking at means of payment and means of exchange as the same thing? With respect to primitive economies, where cows might be used as 'money', economic anthropologists referred to 'special purpose money': there were different spheres of exchange within the economies and different means of payment in those spheres. With respect to peppercorn rents, the peppercorn was not really a means of payment; it was a zero price to all intents and purposes. As for more substantial instances, while there was a difference between cheques and currency in that the latter extinguished an obligation, a note might be forged, and then it would not extinguish obligations; a dud cheque was no different from forged currency. While Dr Goodhart said that unused overdraft facilities were not a means of payment, there was the possibility that an individual paid cash and then rushed to his bank to obtain more cash on his overdraft facilities; Dr Nuti suggested that the exchange was not at an end in this case.

Sir John Hicks was glad that Dr Goodhart had made it clear that the fact that the money operated normally within a legal system was absolutely vital, but he thought that Dr Goodhart had driven this point a bit too hard. What in fact happened in advanced societies was that money operated in terms of habits and customs that had built up within the legal framework; the effective money supply depended upon the habits as well as the legal framework. This was relevant to the point that one was both working within a given system and thinking of changing the system. Sir John was not altogether convinced that considering some generalised concept of money was helpful when one was considering changes: the importance of the distinction between the legal system and the customs within it was shown by the fact that in some historical cases legal changes had had much less effect than had been expected because they did not operate on the habits and customs. Sir John also agreed with Dr Nuti about overdrafts; he thought that in Britain where the overdraft system had been carried to considerable lengths people treated increased overdrafts as money, and that Dr Goodhart's distinction was in that respect legalistic.

Professor Green disagreed with Dr Goodhart's exclusion of unused overdraft facilities from the quantity of money. In a country in which overdraft facilities were not available, a loan from a bank increased the borrower's deposit (so that Dr Goodhart would include it), but the debt was not 'finally' settled until the bank loan was repaid (so that he would exclude it). The dilemma could be resolved only by including both such a bank loan and unused overdraft facilities as part of the quantity of money.

On the question of the empirical definition of money, *Dr Sweeney* pointed out that the quantity theory of money had had some considerable empirical success. He feared that many economists would not accept Dr Goodhart's definition of money as a generalised means of payment because it would not turn out to be empirically successful. Sir John Hicks and Professor Davidson had talked about institutions and laws differing across countries; the answers to the question of whether M_1 or M_2 worked better in terms of predictive power also differed across countries. But since *transmission* in the quantity theory rested at present on the weak reed of the real balance effect, which applied only to reserve money, we needed microeconomic foundations which

would explain the fact that Friedman and others had found that several
different definitions of money were empirically successful.

Professor Parkin, having himself been labelled as a monetarist, pointed out
that Dr Goodhart's paper was not concerned with the monetarist debate. That
debate was a debate that was essentially empirical and concerned rules of
thumb that might or might not help in short-run stabilisation problems; in
that context he was prepared to search empirically for stable money-demand
functions. Microeconomic foundations might also show whether stable
money-demand functions could exist. The literature which started with
Edgeworth and which modelled the demand for existing assets with fairly
well-defined characteristics, led naturally to simple individual optimisation
experiments in which we took as given certain market prices and a certain set
of information. Much of the observed empirical instability of certain
monetary aggregates could be explained in terms of changes in transactions
costs, etc. This literature should not be ignored, and Professor Parkin wished
to see an integration of partial equilibrium analysis with general equilibrium
analysis, for that might give us some clues as to why some assets existed and
were held.

Referring to Dr Goodhart's point that within a world of certainty there
was no need for the physical existence of markets or money, *Professor Shubik*
suggested that this raised a point about precision in modelling. We could
create a perfect certainty model in which everybody trusted the government
and nobody trusted each other: 'In God we trust; all others pay cash'. This
economy would have to use money. In order to make the point that it was
not necessary to have uncertainty to introduce money, Professor Shubik then
gave us an example of a game for his graduate students. Having stated what
the market and the rules for trade were, he would introduce fiat money or
'green chips' and perhaps, 'blue chips' or bank money. If we had two types
of chips, there were four types of models we could play with:

(1) A market with full trust, no need for chips: i.e. barter; this gave us the
    classical model for cores, general equilibrium, etc.;
(2) Green chips issued at the beginning with trade only in chips and no
    credit: here the feasible set of trades might limit Pareto-optimality;
(3) Green chips issued by an outside bank which posted explicit laws about
    how to obtain and pay back chips: here optimality may be achieved with
    any level of inflation or deflation;
(4) Green chips and blue chips: in this instance optimality could be achieved
    but inflation depended on the rules of issue.

If you introduced elementary uncertainty, you would immediately have eleven
logically different models; you would then have to build a three-stage model
with an individual move, a bank move, and a market move. As Dr Goodhart
had observed, the laws and the markets were essentially the rules of the game
and the specification of the processes.

Professor Shubik agreed with Professor Davidson about the impossibility
of monetising everything. The point was, however, that a robust market
theory had to distinguish the cases of many individuals in the market and of
few individuals in the market. In finance there was the concept of a thin
market: no adequate theory for the functioning of financial structures with
thin markets exists. The idea of monetisation of individual assets was also not

new. In Chile when every landowner understated the asset value of his land, the government introduced self-assessment for tax purposes, with a buy-sell clause attached. The question of the realistic valuation of assets was another problem in financial theory with which we had to deal.

In reply to the discussants, *Dr Goodhart* said that there had been two main themes in the discussions and in his paper. First, there was the question of whether consideration of the conditions for the existence of money should make one reassess the structure of the models that one was analysing. Here he felt that the discussion had been satisfactory and well summed up by Professor Stiglitz. Second, could one establish a general definition of money working from these conditions for its existence? Dr Goodhart's feeling was that the assessment of Sir John Hicks and Dr Nuti was that he had probably failed to do so: perhaps money could *only* be defined in a particular context.

8 Some Issues on Firm Behaviour in Light of Microeconomic Foundations of Macroeconomics

J. Segura

INTRODUCTION

Until some decades ago nobody thought that there was a lack of continuity between micro- and macroeconomics. The neoclassical world functioned very smoothly from an aggregate point of view because only real variables mattered, and short-run maladjustments were considered as nothing more than the temporary illnesses of a wealthy system. But since the 1930s even a superficial observation of the actual world raised serious doubts about the smoothness of economic systems and how they react to partial diseases. Roughly speaking, short-comings between micro- and macroanalysis may be summarised into two broad groups:

(a) The micro-Walrasian cosmos is not able to give us a valid explanation with which to understand a macro-Keynesian world characterised by equilibria with various degrees of unemployment and even with permanent disequilibria due to the downward rigidities of money wages and prices. The missing link is an explanation of short-run disequilibrium dynamics.

(b) Aggregate models of growth are not able to explain the facts of an actual growth process. They usually analyse smooth economies with flexible technologies and point out the equilibrium characteristics of an ideal system working, sooner or later, at constant speed. The missing link is an explanation of long-run disequilibrium dynamics.

In this paper I shall discuss some alleged solutions, the object of which is to overcome this lack of continuity between micro- and macroeconomics from the point of view of the behaviour of the firm, which means that I shall not discuss any explanations concerning the demand side or consumer behaviour. In the first part I shall deal with some theories or hypotheses that try to explain short-run disequilibria. In the second part, the discussion is focused on long-run dynamics and therefore deals with growth models. The last part is a brief sketch of a possible integration of both kinds of disequilibria. The main conclusions are:

(1) Both neoclassical and behavioural paradigms are useful as short-run explanations of disequilibrium dynamics.

(2) Although the expectations hypothesis points out a very important market imperfection, it is a loose explanatory device in long-run dynamics.

(3) The basic shortcoming between micro and macroeconomics in long-run disequilibrium analysis is the treatment of technical progress. Neoclassical and managerial paradigms are useless as a microeconomic foundation of an analysis of technical progress.

(4) A behavioural paradigm that is able to include some basic Schumpeterian ideas on innovation and development would be the best framework to deal with long-run dynamics. It also provides a solid basis for short-run disequilibria when combined with an adequate theory of price determination.

I   SHORT-RUN DISEQUILIBRIUM DYNAMICS

The neoclassical firm is a pure, abstract concept that is impossible to understand when taken out of its original framework: general competitive equilibrium analysis. In this context the single firm is no more than a decision criterion that is able to collect enough information from the market place. Due to this fact the neoclassical paradigm cannot explain directly problems related to actual decision processes *inside* the single firm. With perfect information, an instantaneous response to demand changes and perfect markets, the excess demand hypothesis:

$$\dot{p} = F(D - S) \qquad F' > 0$$

avoids any kind of disequilibrium dynamics. Prices react to changes in D and/or S at a high speed and they always reach the levels which clear markets. Two ways are open to change this picture: to provide a substitute for the neoclassical single firm paradigm, or to introduce some kind of imperfections in the market.

From the point of view of a new paradigm there are two well-known alternatives: managerial and behavioural theories. Managerial models may be roughly defined as models that expand the number of decision variables included in the maximand of the firm and/or use additional constraints upon the optimisation process. In a general sense it may be sustained that these models are richer and more explicative than the traditional profit or present value maximisation ones, but the cost of this broader explicative power is a decrease in precision, even in a static framework.[1] Many of the comparative static relationships between prices, outputs, employment, wages and so forth cannot be deduced from a very simple managerial model of the Williamson type including three strategic variables. This weakness is much more evident when we try to analyse the single firm's true dynamic properties: stability

---

[1] As has been pointed out, managerial models cannot be included in a general equilibrium model, at least at the moment. This could be another criticism (although not a very strong one) in our context.

conditions, dynamic links between sales and advertising outlays, and so on, depend crucially on rather special and rigid assumptions with respect to second and third derivatives of utility and costs functions. Furthermore, the more perfect and complex is the paradigm the less is its proper generalisation to the whole industry system. And, finally, a rigid paradigm — managerial or neoclassical — is not able to explain asymmetrical reactions, i.e., downward rigidities and upward flexibilities, unless we introduce either *ad hoc* constraints or imperfections in the market place. It seems more useful to me to use the latter alternative rather than *ad hoc* rules.

Behavioural models are characterised by the fact that decision rules depend on the specific environment in which the single firm acts. This fact makes room for both changes in decision rules over time and the introduction of observed facts such as specific rules of thumb. The first point could be a very important one in long-run dynamics and the second allows us to introduce asymmetrical behavioural rules for specific purposes. But, once again, the latter could be done at a lower cost by introducing imperfections through the market mechanism. Therefore, we must keep in mind behavioural theories for long-run dynamic purposes but in the short term we must concentrate our efforts on market imperfections.

Market imperfections may be introduced in at least two ways. One comes from traditional oligopoly theory and the other through direct elimination of some Walrasian postulates, more specifically the assumption of costless or perfect information.

The acceptance of imperfect information produces a temporary monopolistic and/or monopsonistic power of the firm. We can analyse the effects of this transient power using the simplest paradigm: present value maximisation. It is important to note that in this context competition may be supposed atomistic although not perfect. Every firm is assumed not to be strong enough to determine or change sector prices in either commodities or factor markets. But the single firm faces a short-run decreasing demand curve for its product and/or a short-run increasing supply function of its primary inputs.

Now, with imperfect information in hand, we must return to our original problem: the explanation of dynamic disequilibrium in which unemployment can last for many periods of time. In this context unemployment might mean two different, although related, things:

(i) buffer stocks at microlevels which imply idle commodities or intermediate inputs;

(ii) labour unemployment considered as not voluntary.

The case for buffer stocks can be studied easily by supposing that the single firm faces a stochastic demand schedule. This means that the excess demand hypothesis can be applied but taking into account the observed rather than the actual demand. In this case the individual firm which experiences a demand increase of x per cent will only partially adapt its production when considering a fraction of the x per cent: the observed one. This is similar to translating price dynamics into a theory of learning which comes through some kind of adaptive expectations: see Gordon and Hynes (1970).

It is very easy in this context to demonstrate the existence of a Phillips-like relationship between the rate of change in prices and the level of buffer stocks. Starting from an equilibrium position with stocks at level S^e, a positive and exogenous increase in demand will raise prices. If this increase is repetitive some positive rate of inflation will appear. In the short run this positive rate of inflation will reduce the level of buffer stocks due to the fact that only a part of this increase in prices is taken into account in the firm's calculations. This is so because part of the future expected prices depends on past prices and part on newer and higher ones. Therefore, the short-run effect will be a decreasing relationship between $\dot{p}$ and the rate of change of stocks. But when the total price increase in every period is taken into account, the single firm will accept a positive rate of inflation as permanent and will restore its level of buffer stocks. If this permanent increase in demand is produced by a continuous increase in money supply we will reach a well-known monetarist proposition: a short-run Phillips-like relationship between the rate of inflation and buffer stocks (unemployment) and a long-run inelastic trade-off between both variables.

Leaving the commodities market and moving on to the labour market, a neoclassical world with imperfect information is apparently able to explain the existence of temporary dynamic disequilibria. The basic reasoning is well known after Phelps (1967), Friedman (1968) and Alchian (1970): an increase in aggregate demand makes it profitable for firms to reduce vacancies and offer higher money wages than before. Unemployed workers searching for a new job will begin to receive higher money wage offers that, due to the lack of information, are considered as better offers than before in real terms. In other words, unemployed workers think they have found better wages instead of average ones with respect to the new money wages distribution. Consequently, the unemployed will accept new wages and become employed and, therefore, as a short-run result, these new wages will reduce unemployment. But after a while, new employed people realise that higher prices provoked by the original increased demand call for real wages as low as before when they refused to be employed and looked for a job. When expectations about future prices catch up to higher money wages, newly employed workers will quit their jobs and unemployment will go back to its original level.

Theoretical improvements of this basic idea coming from the demand side of the labour market have accepted the excess demand hypothesis when taking into account not only unemployment rates but vacancy rates as well. The Phelps wage differential (see Phelps *et al.*, 1970) paid by every single firm in order to fulfil vacancies at a higher rate, plus the introduction of prices and/or wages adaptive expectations, results in the well-known conclusion that the Phillips curve is valid only in the short run when expectations about inflation rates are not fully anticipated.

The kind of disequilibrium dynamics summarised above is only short run. In the long run, supply side considerations win and real variables reach their full-employment levels which are determined only by pure real factors such as labour productivity, individual trade-offs between work and leisure, the rate of growth of labour force and structural levels of information. The Phillips-like relationship vanishes because there is one, and only one, optimal or natural level of unemployment.

Although these explanations have been ameliorated in many ways, see Phelps and Winter (1970) on commodities markets and Mortensen (1970) and Lucas and Rapping (1970) on the labour supply side, I feel that the very centre of the discussion has been correctly summarised above. In both kinds of markets there exists a temporary monopolistic power for every single firm due to the lack of information. Single firms do not fully exploit temporary power in the short run because:

(a) in labour markets they will find it impossible to fulfil vacancies at the rate they want to;

(b) in commodity markets they will lose part of their share.

In both cases firms use their monopolistic power to offer lower money wages and higher commodity prices than those of pure competitive firms, but in the long run there is a return to 'normal' levels although firms will retain some excess capacity and some excess vacancies due to the desire for more flexible future adjustments to changes in demand.

There are a few things that I feel would be worth raising about the analysis summarised above related to imperfect information and expectations hypothesis as a source of short-run disequilibria.

(A) Can we properly speak about a truly dynamic disequilibrium analysis? The final objective of the hypothesis discussed above is to demonstrate that in the long run everything will be all right, and this can be done only if we accept that there is some kind of steady state that could be reached in the long run. First of all, steady states are exactly the opposite of disequilibrium dynamics. As Joan Robinson pointed out some decades ago, steady states imply perfect foresight or perfectly accomplished expectations, which means that basic variables must have been in their long-run equilibrium positions for quite a few periods. But this being true, basic variables must have been for far more than a few periods in their equilibrium levels, and therefore back to the infinite.

This is in my opinion a definite criticism. The microfoundation of macroeconomics must be able to explain long-run dynamic disequilibria if we want to have a theory properly called theory. However, if we are only interested in short-run disequilibrium, the expectations hypothesis could be a reasonable device to count for it.

(B) Another powerful criticism applied to the labour market comes from Tobin (1972): the expectations hypothesis fails to differentiate between two opposite kinds of economic forces which simultaneously affect the level and rate of change of money wages. First, there is an equilibrium component which equals the labour productivity rate of growth. Second, there is a disequilibrium component coming from inter- as well as intrasectorial shocks. Although at an aggregate level the rate of vacancies could equal the unemployment rate, permanent disequilibrium flows among individual labour markets can explain a long-run Phillips curve.

This criticism can be easily translated into an application to commodities markets: although the $\dot{p}$ value could be perfectly foreseen in the long run, changes in demand for some commodities compensated by changes in the opposite direction for others can sustain the aggregate demand at the same level, but these intrasectorial inflows produce a negatively sloped Phillips relationship between the rate of inflation and the idle commodities level. This will be a very important factor in markets with highly heterogeneous commodities — *i.e.*, capital goods markets — because the plurality of prices makes it more profitable to wait for better offers (see Nichols, 1970).

(C) The existence of costs inherent in changing jobs is not enough to explain short-run disequilibria in the labour market. These costs must be different for employed and unemployed workers if because, for example, these costs are not higher for employed people, a temporary cut in wages is more likely to be accepted without quitting jobs.

Although the theoretical explanation of short-run disequilibria is quite lucid and points out some microeconomic forces behind markets avoided in the basic Phillips analysis, the whole expectations hypothesis relies crucially upon a postulate which is, at least, doubtful: that workers find it more profitable to look for a new job while being unemployed rather than looking while keeping their jobs. Unfortunately, turnover rates in actual labour markets do not sustain this assumption, and it is easy to accept the fact that turnover rates for countries not highly industrialised are even less consistent with the expectations hypothesis. In commodities markets that criticism does not apply because the equivalent assumption is really true: it is less costly to make short-run adjustments through buffer stocks than through changes in output plans.

(D) It is impossible to generalise the expectations hypothesis in order to explain long-run maladjustments or permanent disequilibria. It is true that, as Ross and Watcher (1973) point out, the stability of expectations depends on the forecasting horizon and, as the latter increases in length, expectations are smoother and the Phillips-like relationships more stable. However, at the same time any kind of adaptative expectations must reach a stable pattern sooner or later if variables which matter change following some kind of temporal law. Even a constantly increasing speed of variation will be caught by adaptative expectations, because in this case the lagged parameters will depend upon the rates of growth of the relevant variables. Therefore, the learning process described by any kind of adaptive expectations will reach a stable equilibrium unless authorities or external shocks act in a crazy way.

Perhaps the most important point of emphasis is that all of these models are based upon the fact that imperfect information produces a temporary imperfection in firms' behaviour, but a transient imperfection calls only for temporary disequilibria and not for permanent disequilibria. If the basis of short-run maladjustments can be properly explained through temporary monopolistic power, it seems rather obvious that a permanent oligopolistic structure would be able to explain long-run disequilibria. If we accept this point we enter in the old and very well known field of traditional oligopolistic pricing.[1]

As we all know, the neoclassical paradigm cannot deal with a generalised theory of oligopolistic behaviour due to the variety of assumptions we can make regarding oligopolistic reactions to changing conditions. Here, once again, is a field in which behavioural models of the firm can give us an explanation of the real world. First of all, we must agree upon the fact that profit or present value maximisation remains as the most important target of the single firm, but behavioural hypotheses give room for some kind of 'lazy' behaviour which justifies the maintenance of the *status quo* as a second objective. Both aims call for some kind of theory based upon barriers to entry. From the point of view of present value, to avoid newcomers will usually imply raising future profits. From the point of view of an easy life, prices settled at an intermediate level between competitive and monopolistic prices allow durable agreements. If we like, it is not impossible to complete this picture with imperfections such as stochastic demands, myopic foresight, etc. In any case, it is easy to obtain a model for pricing determination basically dominated by technology and costs considerations, with permanent excess capacity, changeable decision rules and non-symmetric price flexibility. Although we will not enter into a detailed discussion, the basic frame of reference would be Sylos-Labini's theory of industrial pricing (Sylos-Labini, 1967, 1974).

What is the outcome of the above discussion? In my opinion the following points are the most relevant:

(i) the neoclassical paradigm remains as powerful as any other in explaining short-run disequilibria. At the same level, some behavioural kind of paradigm accepting permanent oligopolistic structures allows us to obtain similar results without utilising *ad hoc* assumptions;

(ii) a lack of perfect information is a fruitful hypothesis if and only if we are interested in short-run disequilibria. Transient monopolistic and/or monopsonistic power calls for temporary disequilibria;

[1] Throughout the expectation hypothesis discussion I had not made any criticism of the 'adjustment cost' theories which are closely related to it. This is due to the fact that expectations do not always need the separability assumption that adjustment cost analysis requires and which is a very strong criticism of it.

(iii) expectational hypothesis may be used in short-run horizons; however, in that case, we must add some complementary hypothesis in order to explain permanent disequilibria; the expectational hypothesis forbids the study of growth and long-run disequilibrium dynamics;

(iv) taking the above into account, Sylos-Labini's theory of price determination plus some kind of informational imperfections in labour markets seems to be the best framework for analysing short-run disequilibria and, at the same time, avoiding the shortcomings between short- and long-run dynamics; this obliges us to make room for some Tobinian intersectorial shocks and/or an endogenous determination of labour productivity related to long-run behaviour of wages.

II LONG-RUN DISEQUILIBRIUM DYNAMICS

Three forces explain the dynamic motion of economic systems: changes in demand, changes in primary input endowments and technological progress. Changes in demand are related to the income distribution and the propensity to save of the economy, a subject which I have cautiously avoided throughout this paper. The second element, factor endowments, must be divided into two parts: the labour force which is supposed to grow at an exogenously given rate; and capital accumulation, which depends on both the availability of funds and capital needs. These needs change over time due to the growth of the labour force and to technical change. It is not difficult to agree that technical change is the most important force in any development process, an idea shared even by Solovians.

If our main interest is focused on the microeconomic foundations of macrotheory, the first critical point to analyse is the theoretical roots of neoclassical technical progress analysis at the level of the individual firm. First of all we must remember two characteristics of the neoclassical paradigm which, in my opinion, destroy any kinds of fruitful technological change analysis:

(a) every firm acts in the same way as any other single firm due to its strictly defined objective: present value maximisation;

(b) every firm receives exactly the same amount and quality of information.

(a) plus (b) mean that every firm will react in the same way to external challenges; i.e., to changes in technological possibility sets.

Within the neoclassical paradigm there is no room for a differentiated behaviour, for the chosen techniques will always be those which are expected to minimise average long-run costs. Every change in technique will be managed in the same way for every single firm, and all of them choose *the* best technique as soon as possible (a fact that depends on obsolescence and depreciation but that, in the long run, does not create differences in single-firm behaviour).

Under these conditions all firms absorb new technologies in the same way and at the same speed, and their technological behaviour can be represented by changes in the static production function through some temporary trend

linked to or representative of a constant rate of introduction of technical
improvements. This implies an additional hypothesis, namely that technical
improvements appear in the system continuously. Although this is not a basic
hypothesis, it has played an important role in neoclassical analysis of technical
progress. If innovations were introduced by discontinuous shocks into the
system, we would face discontinuous jumps in the firms's production function.
Every jump would need some time to be absorbed, and long-run paths of the
single firm would every now and then display some breaks, and some
characteristics of aggregate growth processes in neoclassical analysis would
disappear. If we try an *ex post* description of technical change the assumption
of a constant and slow rate of introduction of improvements would be an
admissible device, but if we focus our interest on explaining the actual process
of technical change, it seems to me that this constant rate is an indispensable
hypothesis.

Allow me to take one further step. If we accept the neoclassical view of
technical progress, the rather obvious fact is that the whole of individual
behaviour can be summarised in an aggregate production function.[1]

The theoretical framework summarised above signifies that no technical
change can destroy equilibrium conditions. New technologies are introduced
smoothly and absorbed in the same manner. This neoclassical paradigm is the
main reason why growth models have usually displayed one of the following
characteristics: equilibrium growth and/or steady state and mechanical rules.

Economic history does not present the basic features of equilibrium growth
processes, which are self-contradictory even with short-run disequilibrium
dynamics. The central point of the discussion in that field is the equilibrium
concept itself and its relevance in a dynamic context, a subject exhaustively
and very recently discussed (see Hahn, 1972 and Koopmans, 1974). Although
I shall not discuss the theme it is rather obvious that dynamic equilibrium as a
situation of perfectly fulfilled expectations and self-repetitive values or rates
of change of basic variables makes a fruitful dynamic analysis difficult. If there
is motion in a system it is basically due to the necessity for adjustments to new
situations. This implies true disequilibria. In an equilibrium growth model
nobody has any reason to be dynamic and therefore the movement along the
path has very little theoretical meaning, if any.

The case for steady states is slightly different because, as Hahn (1973) has
pointed out, these states are nothing more than reference points. However, we
must emphasise the significance of steady states. If they try to be descriptive
tools, we must reject them, first, because our world does not display the
stylised characteristics of steady states; second, because an aggregate model
of growth based only on supply side considerations is not able accurately to

[1] I shall not discuss capital theory problems related to aggregate production functions.
I do not believe in aggregate production functions but, as an explanatory device, we may
suppose that a vintage function avoids problems related to the heterogeneity of capital
goods and even is able to include embodied technical progress, two assumptions far from
being fulfilled.

describe a capitalistic growth process. Microeconomic investment decisions are taken by private capital owners and do not guarantee a permanent appropriate level of effective demand with which to fulfil full employment dynamic paths. Even a planned economy could not be described by these models due to both balance of trade and balance of payments constraints. Nevertheless, a growth model without any kind of stable long-run path in the absence of external shocks must be inappropriate, because its internal feed-back mechanism is explosive, a fact which is against empirical evidence. Therefore, steady states are useful as reference points both because they guarantee some desirable internal properties of growth models and because they point to paths which fulfil static efficiency allocation requirements. However, as a conclusion we must keep in mind the fact that a path of continuous equilibria or constant long-run rate of growth for life cannot describe the actual behaviour of a modern economy.[1]

What are the facts of the actual growth process which the neoclassical paradigm does not take into account? In my opinion there are at least two at the microeconomic behavioural level:

(a) different firms choose techniques with different criteria even when facing both the same technological set and informational stimuli; as a result, firms do not always choose the most efficient technique;[2]

(b) one firm's access to innovations is different from the others.

We may feel tempted to answer the above criticisms in a very easy manner: the neoclassical paradigm is flexible enough to absorb almost every imperfection. However, this is not enough to recognise and explain the fact that firms follow rules which differ as between firms. The basic rigidity of the present-value maximisation paradigm — as well as any other kind of managerial paradigm — is that it is a fixed and unique target and, therefore, may be only accomplished with one specific strategy. Moreover, the alleged flexibility of the neoclassical paradigm is responsible for the interpretative indeterminancy that it exhibits. As Nelson (1973) has recently summarised, the United States historical series can be interpreted both as a result of a Hicks-neutral technical progress with elasticity of substitution equal to one, or with an elasticity inferior to unity and labour-saving technical progress. In both cases the technical progress term is quantitatively quite different. Therefore, flexibility really signifies indeterminancy.[3]

Accepting this criticism, which are the basic points if we try to explain a growth process properly? I feel that two aspects are fundamental:

---

[1] Multisectorial models are not necessarily steady-state ones but in the long run every individual sector grows at a constant rate or presents an explosive dynamic path. On the other hand, optimal growth models are normative, therefore have scarce explicative power, if any.

[2] A fact that could perhaps be partially explained in terms of X-efficiency instead of the purely technological one.

[3] The neutrality concept in itself is due to neoclassical analysis. As an analytical tool I think it is not relevant, although it serves to epitomize a past phenomenon.

(i) a firm's behaviour paradigm able to include different reactions and strategies when facing the same set of events;

(ii) an aggregate growth theory that allows us to localize and explain sources, channels of diffusion and actual effects of technological progress, and which makes room for permanent disequilibria growth paths.

From the point of view of the single-firm paradigm, I feel that the best possibility is the behavioural paradigm. First, it excludes the managerial and neoclassical paradigms. Second, only behavioural paradigms can include different reactions to the same environment coming from different firms. Firms that use the same technology for quite a long period of time while realising that there are more powerful techniques available, firms that do not innovate or research due to the consumer's preference for specific brands, firms that want a quiet life, and so on, are actual behaviour rules only explicable in terms of a behavioural paradigm. In fact, different responses could come from differing managerial ability. It is rather surprising that neoclassical theory recognises this element as the most difficult factor to change even in the long run but, at the same time, does not introduce any kind of differentiated behaviour among firms. The neoclassical solution is a very Malthusian one: entrepreneurs who are worse than average disappear and their places are occupied by average or better than average managers.

From the point of view of (ii) we need at least two additional elements. The first one is a theoretical structure which allows us to differentiate between embodied and disembodied technical progress due to the fact that both kinds of improvements have quite different effects on the economic system. Embodied technical progress increases labour productivity and usually requires higher rates of accumulation in order to be fully absorbed as well, so as to sustain an expanded rate of growth. Disembodied technical change also increases labour productivity but mainly through a generalised saving in primary input requirements due to better organisation, quicker absorption of new techniques and so on. Therefore, we must concentrate our effort upon explaining the effects of embodied technical progress which, for most of the time, is treated as an exogenous factor in growth. The second element to be included in our theory is a hypothesis which justifies discontinuous technical shocks in the growth process. This is due to the necessity for permanent long-run disequilibria and also to the fact that this is the only way in which changes in labour productivity cannot be foreseen, introducing a new short-run disequilibrium element of a permanent nature.

It seems to me that Schumpeterian ideas about economic development, technical change and innovations formulated in his *Theory of Economic Development* (Schumpeter, 1936) are the best frame of reference from which to introduce these qualifications in a growth theory which tries to explain actual facts. Schumpeter's idea of competition as a fight among entrepreneurs, some of whom are aggressive and look for innovations while others are more imitative, makes room for different behaviour patterns even by firms which start from identical positions. Some other Schumpeterian hypotheses about the kinds of firms which are more dynamic, or about temporal trends in concentration due to returns to scale in research and innovation activities, are not necessary and must be more cautiously admitted: see Fisher and Temin (1973). The second idea from Schumpeter is the cumulative character of innovations which demonstrates how technological improvements appear from time to time in large groups and not smoothly throughout time. This second basic hypothesis has a very important advantage: it allows an evolutionary explanation of technical change. Both hypotheses combined can give an adaptative interpretation of an actual growth process.

When a 'group' of innovations is exogenously introduced into the system, the technological possibility set broadens for every firm. In an oligopolistic industrial environment firms have different reactions to this change in conditions because of both their unequal technical possibilities in the original situation and their different behavioural rules for innovating, searching, and so on. The system breaks its growth path through the non-regular introduction of new embodied technologies which spread over the economy with more or less stochastic patterns. Additionally, breaking the *status quo* signifies in itself an incentive to innovate. New techniques change the relative position of every single firm, its market share, its rate of profit, and so on. Although many firms do not absorb new technological possibilities from the beginning of the process, a broader disequilibrium derived from the 'group' of innovations makes them look for a new adjustment. This group of embodied innovations creates opportunities for disembodied additional innovations which are easier to produce and apply domestically, and that could be necessary in order to absorb the original embodied technologies due to scarcities of primary inputs. This implies a second and more spread out shock into the system.

Although I believe in the fruitfulness of this idea, I am also aware of its main difficulty: its formalisation. As far as I know the only formalised model which includes some basic characteristics of Schumpeterian analysis (although not his second hypothesis about 'groups' of innovations) is the Nelson and Winter simulation model (Nelson and Winter, 1973). I do not believe that this is the right place to discuss the model, but I do believe that, appealing as it is, it has two doubtful points. First, the Markov process used is only one of the many that can be employed in that context, and therefore one could think that its objective is to build up a theoretical construction in order to find an *ex post* explanation of the United States historical series (a criticism similar to the one raised by Nelson (1973) himself against the neoclassical analysis). Second, capital is considered as an homogeneous aggregate, and that point links with capital theory problems. Nevertheless, the basic idea of formalising a behavioural paradigm as a three-number vector (two technological ratios and the capital stock) plus the assumption about innovations and their introduction linked to a concrete level of profits, is quite interesting and deserves further consideration.

III   CONCLUSIONS

To quote Koopmans (1974, p. 328), 'In a world of continuing but only dimly foreseeable change in technology and in preferences, the notion of equilibrium disappears, but that of adjustment process remains'. This quotation, taken from a general equilibrium analysis context, points out the care with which the term 'equilibrium' must be used. The neoclassical paradigm of the single firm was originally created to explain both equilibrium and static efficiency properties of an atomised system. Nowadays it is able to include some kind of short-run adjustment processes but, nevertheless, I think it is not able to deal with long-run dynamics in an actual growth process. If we accept that technical progress is the main explicative variable of any growth process, the theoretical micro-economic neoclassical treatment of it must be considered at least as inadequate. A simple and unique target, plus identical reactions for every firm, plus a smooth absorption of innovations make room for nothing more than a textual translation of static efficiency conditions to a dynamic environment. This could be useful as a planning device but not as an explanation of the actual world. Do we have any alternative? My answer must be yes.

From a short-run point of view, the behavioural paradigm, applied to an oligopolistic industrial structure might be able to explain: (a) non-clearing market prices; and (b) asymmetries in wages and prices responses to changes in demand. Sylos-Labini's explanation of industrial pricing derived from barriers to newcomers is a good framework with which to account for reservation prices, price rigidities and permanent excess capacity.

In addition to that we must complete short-run disequilibrium analysis with partially endogenous determination of labour productivity which would create the basic link between short-and long-run behaviour. Changes in labour productivity could be explained in a twofold way: (a) through a long-run relationship between the rate of change of wages and of labour productivity in both directions; and (b) through external technological shocks generated by embodied technical progress coming from abroad.[1] This second point makes room for a 'dimly foreseeable change in technology' which calls for an adjustment process in which technology itself is used as an adjustment factor through induced and disembodied technical change domestically generated.

This adjustment process could be introduced through a behavioural paradigm which incorporates basic features of the Schumpeterian hypotheses about innovations and their diffusion, and makes a permanent reorganisation of firms and sectors necessary. This last point will generate Tobin-like intra-sectorial disequilibrium shocks.

I must accept the important criticism that this is not a formalised model, but I feel, like Pasinetti (1973, p. 367), that 'by reducing all economic

---

[1] The exogenous character of embodied technical progress is an acceptable hypothesis for countries not highly industrialised.

problems to questions of rational behaviour in the face of scarcities, it seemed that economists became prisoners of a narrow way of thinking . . . the more complicated the problems, the more aritificial in order to fit into schemes'.

REFERENCES

A. A. Alchian, 'Information Costs, Pricing and Resource Unemployment' in E. S. Phelps, *et al.* (eds) *Microeconomic Foundations of Employment and Inflation Theory* (New York: Norton, 1970).

F. M. Fisher and P. Temin, 'Returns to Scale in Research and Development: What does the Schumpeterian Hypothesis Imply?', *Journal of Political Economy*, Vol. 81, No 1 (January/February 1973) pp. 56–70.

M. Friedman, 'The Role of Monetary Policy', *American Economic Review*, Vol. 58, No 1 (March 1968) pp. 1–17.

D. F. Gordon and A. Hynes, 'On the Theory of Price Dynamics', in E. S. Phelps *et al.* (eds) *Microeconomic Foundations of Employment and Inflation Theory* (New York: Norton, 1970).

F. H. Hahn, *On the Notion of Equilibrium in Economics: An Inaugural Lecture* (Cambridge University Press, 1973).

F. H. Hahn, 'Summary of the Final Discussion', in J. A. Mirrlees and N. H. Stern (eds) *Models of Economic Growth* (London: Macmillan, 1973).

T. C. Koopmans, 'Is the Theory of Competitive Equilibrium with It?', *American Economic Review*, Vol. 62, No 2 (May 1974) pp. 325–9.

R. E. Lucas and L. A. Rapping, 'Real Wages, Employment and Inflation', in E. S. Phelps *et al.* (eds) *Microeconomic Foundations of Employment and Inflation Theory* (New York: Norton, 1970).

D. T. Mortensen, 'A Theory of Wage and Employment Dynamics', in E. S. Phelps *et al.* (eds) *The Microeconomic Foundations of Employment and Inflation Theory* (New York: Norton, 1970).

R. R. Nelson, 'Recent Exercises in Growth Accounting: New Understanding or Dead End.', *American Economic Review*, Vol. 63, No 3 (June 1973) pp. 462–8.

R. R. Nelson and S. G. Winter, 'Neoclassical *vs.* Evolutionary Theories of Economic Growth: Critique and Prospectus', *Economic Journal*, Vol. 84 No 336 (December 1974) pp. 886–905.

D. A. Nichols, 'Market Clearing Conditions for Heterogeneous Capital Goods', in E. S. Phelps *et al.* (eds) *Microeconomic Foundations of Employment and Inflation Theory* (New York: Norton, 1970).

L. L. Pasinetti, 'Summary of the Final Discussion' in J. A. Mirrlees and N. H. Stern (eds) *Models of Economic Growth* (London: Macmillan 1973).

E. S. Phelps, 'Phillips' Curves, Expectations of Inflation and Optimal Unemployment over Time', *Economica* (New Series), Vol. 34, No 135 (August 1967) pp. 254–81.

E. S. Phelps, 'Money Wage Dynamics and Labour Market Equilibrium' in E. S. Phelps *et al.* (eds) *Microeconomic Foundations of Employment and Inflation Theory* (New York: Norton, 1970).

J. A. Schumpeter, *Theory of Economic Development* (Cambridge, Massachusetts: Harvard University Press, 1936).

P. Sylos-Labini, 'Prices and Wages: A Theoretical and Statistical Interpretation of the Italian Experience', *Journal of Industrial Economics*, Vol. 15, No 2 (April 1967) pp. 109–27.

P. Sylos-Labini, *Trade Unions, Inflation and Productivity* (Saxon House, Hampshire: D. C. Heath, 1974).

J. Tobin, 'Inflation and Unemployment', *American Economic Review*, Vol. 62 No 1 (March 1972) pp. 1–18.

Discussion of the Paper by Professor Segura

Professor Nell, after briefly summarising the paper, made the following comments. His general observation was that Professor Segura's theoretical ambitions overreached the analytical framework he apparently accepted. In particular:

(1) To replace the concept of the representative firm there were several directions in which one could proceed. For example, one could take account of the different kinds of firms in legal terms; or one could take account of the differences between firms in economic terms, such as the differences between multi-product firms and single-product firms; or one could take account of the fact that some firms, notably multi-national firms, operated in several different legal and monetary environments. But some of these took us further outside the neo-classical framework than Professor Segura seemed to go. In particular they led to a discussion of the manipulation of preferences and technology by corporate interests.

(2) A second set of questions arose with respect to growth: here Professor Segura had questioned the equilibrium concept; that is, the idea that on the equilibrium growth path the agents making the decisions about investment, etc., found themselves satisfied with the outcome of their decisions. He had also questioned the relevance of the steady state as a descriptive notion. Professor Nell though that these were both worth-while questions to raise but he wanted to know what could be put in place of such well-known concepts. If we rejected equilibrium had we to accept disequilibrium? If so, could we speak of a determinate disequilibrium? Perhaps one could, more to the point, perhaps one should, but Professor Nell wished to know how.

(3) One suggestion to replace the steady-state notion to which many people paid lip-service was to be found in the work of Schumpeter and of Marx: instead of considering growth one considered the addition of new products and new sectors. If we had an input-output matrix we talked about the addition of the new products and new processes and sometimes we talked about the elimination of a product or process; in the Marxian tradition we were usually talking about the imbalance between agriculture and industry. But it occurred to Professor Nell that a rejection of equilibrium growth on the one hand, and a questioning of the significance of steady-state growth on the other, suggested, almost by elimination, this third pattern of analysis. The question then was: Could we develop the analytical tools to examine this and what implications did it have for our traditional questions? Professor Nell suggested one implication: we could incorporate phenomena which had been difficult to take account of while using our traditional tools. For instance, there had been the difficulty of defining initial endowments given the existence of, say, uranium, which had no value until the discovery of atomic energy.

(4) Professor Segura's remarks about Schumpeter's work could lead one to raise some questions about the approach we should adopt in connection with technical change. If we were to follow Schumpeter in considering

the conflict between businesses as the means by which technology was introduced irregularly and in accordance with the position of firms, their differential access to technology and their different strategies for their development, could technology be taken as independent of the preferences, plans and strategic objectives of the firms themselves? It was an important characteristic of many microeconomic models that technology was either given or assumed independent of the economic process, just as on the demand side preferences were taken as given or at least independently developing. This approach might run into difficulties if we took a Schumpeterian or Marxian position.

(5) The Schumpeterian view also had welfare implications and implications concerning investment. The welfare implications were obvious, but with respect to investment, investment of the market-breaking variety might be productive from the point of view of the individual firm but much less productive in the aggregate. Professor Nell was reminded of the first page of Marshall's *Principles of Economics*, where Marshall spoke of the significance of the length of time that a person spent at his employment and how the place where he was employed was an important influence in all the decisions of his life. This suggested that there was an important link between the kind of technology and the development of the preferences and economic acts of those who worked in that system; it suggested further that one could not separate preferences from technology when one was looking at long-run development.

Professor Parkin addressed himself to the part of Professor Segura's paper which dealt with the so-called 'new microeconomics' of Phelps *et al.*, *Microeconomic Foundations of Employment and Inflation Theory* (1970). That particular development in the literature had been designed essentially with two purposes in mind: the first was to provide a choice-theoretic underpinning of the equation of the Phillips curve; the second was the specifically empirical problem of finding a choice-theoretic explanation of the observed behaviour of aggregate excess demand; i.e. of the stylised facts of the Phillips curve. Professor Parkin thought that literature did that job tolerably well. At the same time it made some predictions about economic phenomena which were not its central purpose. Professor Parkin wished to see the problem of evaluation of that literature more centrally attacked, for a major prediction with respect to individual households' choice of labour supply and of output demand in the Mortensen and Phelps–Winter analyses was that people could never be in involuntary situations; that made the analyses singularly unsuitable for analysing the macroeconomic questions with which this conference was concerned. Barro and Grossman had pointed out in their forthcoming book, *Money, Employment and Inflation* (Cambridge University Press, 1976) that one needed adjustment costs along with some measure of uncertainty or some stochastic element in order to get involuntary behaviour in the system; this could be used as a starting point for explaining involuntary household behaviour. Professor Parkin also found two other aspects of the 'new microeconomics' difficult to accept: namely, the wage and price equations in the econometric models had either no theoretical underpinnings or only the Mortensen-Phelps–Winter analysis, which did not fit in with the rest of the models; and there was no theory of the demand for capital and labour, since firms were assumed to be price-takers or quantity-choosers.

With respect to the distinction between the steady state and equilibrium in Professor Segura's paper, *Professor Harcourt* asked why was a steady state not necessarily an equilibrium? *Professor Nell* responded that a steady-state expansion was an expansion along a path where on the supply side the aggregate output which was to be invested in each period was produced exactly in the proportions required for reinvestment; this was independent of aggregate or microeconomic considerations on the demand side.

Professor Henin emphasised the necessity of a better understanding of firms' behaviour for the macroeconomic analysis of imperfectly competitive capitalist economies where much of economic power belonged to firms. Referring to recent French work in the field, he thought that we had to consider the price, investment and financing decisions as intrinsically linked and forming together the kernel of microeconomic behaviour relevant for macroeconomic equilibrium. Standard neoclassical theory did not provide us with a comprehensive and integrated theory of firm behaviour; only in a world of perfect competition and no uncertainty could separation theorems such as the Modigliani–Miller theorem hold, and then every decision variable could be related directly to exogenous variables, as in a just-identified model. 'Advanced neoclassical theory' which incorporated imperfect knowledge, adaptive or rational expectations and/or adjustment costs was a significant improvement over traditional analysis, but it suffered from a lack of integration of financial variables, which was a serious limitation because of the empirical importance of growing indebtedness of United States and European firms and the necessity of stabilising it in the near future.

Professor Henin suggested that one concept which could explain a firm's behaviour was 'organisational slack', which implied that at 'equilibrium' constraints were not binding. Disequilibrium resulted in firms facing additional constraints; allowing for constraints to be effective without being binding avoided the unduly mechanistic consequences of a multiplication of constraints. Organisational slack was related to the 'degree of constraint' firms faced. This 'degree of constraint' would vary with the business cycle and according to stabilisation policies; some empirical evidence on this was available in an econometric study of a sample of French firms in 1962–6 (J. F. Echard and P. Y. Henin, 'Une Etude econometrique de la decision d'investir et des structures financières dans l'entreprise privée: Essai d'analyse typologique et causale', *Economie et societié*, 1970).

Professor Spaventa suggested that although Professor Shubik had said on the previous day that economists, when in conference, should be concerned neither with advice nor with advocacy but with introspection, he wondered, having read Professor Segura's paper – with the critical part of which he very much sympathised – whether there was much room for introspection left in the field of the theory of the firm. The theory, or rather theories, of the firm had occupied a very proud place in economic analysis, but they were now seen to have been an endless series of rationalisations of yesterday's behaviour, which proved inadequate to explain today's, not to speak of tomorrow's behaviour. They were, to paraphrase Joan Robinson, a series of 1:1 maps of a territory which changed under our eyes. Professor Shubik's advocacy of introspection had been a plea for microeconomics as the right point of departure for economic analysis, but Professor Spaventa doubted whether the theory of the firm could represent a useful point of departure. Perhaps we ought to recognise that, after all, macroeconomics had made considerable steps forward in spite of the conspicuous lack of a widely acceptable theory of the firm.

Professor Asimakopulos was pleased that Professor Segura had favoured an oligopoly theory of the firm but was disappointed that in summing up his discussion of some of the neoclassicals, Professor Segura had said that the neoclassical paradigm remained as powerful as ever in explaining short-run disequilibria. He disagreed because of the neoclassical emphasis on the competitive firm and its assumption that variations in demand would be reflected in variations in price rather than in output. With respect to Professor Segura's discussion of the requirements for a growth model, he pointed out that the analysis omitted factors that were important in the real world; for example, government. The model might be explosive in the absence of such factors, so that one could not argue that the observed lack of explosion in the system meant the satisfaction of the stability conditions. With respect to technical progress, Harrod had introduced 'Harrod-neutral' technical progress in his non-neoclassical model because that type of technical progress was required in order to permit the possibility of an equilibrium growth path where entrepreneurial expectations were fulfilled. This equilibrium path was the steady state.

The first page of Professor Segura's paper reminded *Professor Cochrane* that Professor Leijonhufvud, in one of his 'Two Postscripts' to *Of Keynesian Economics and the Economics of Keynes* (Oxford University Press, 1968), had made a point which economists seemed to have overlooked. Professor Leijonhufvud had argued that a viable synthesis of 'classical' theory and Keynes's theory had not been achieved because the *dual* role of the price mechanism had not been made clear by potential synthesisers. The information function and the incentive function must operate together to *co-ordinate* the plans and activities of individual transactors so that they become consistent in the aggregate. The classical writers had developed a theoretical apparatus in which both roles were performed efficiently and the system functioned 'automatically'. In particular, the general equilibrium model of Walras was (and remained) an excellent and admirable exposition of this efficient performance. Walras, influenced by Newtonian mechanics, developed a scheme 'admirably suited to the study of the *incentive* function of prices', but it was a clockwork model – 'a strictly deterministic, Newtonian mechanism in which prices perform the functions of levers and pulleys'. Keynes, according to Professor Leijonhufvud, did not reject the incentive side of the short-run model, but did reject the information side. Keynes emphasised *uncertainty* (as opposed to risk) in the *General Theory*, which is what one would expect the author of *A Treatise on Probability* to have done.

The essence of cybernetics was communication and control. It was very difficult to develop formal models incorporating both anticipations and realisations. To circumvent the analytical difficulties associated with the question 'How does *ex ante* become *ex post*?', economists had resorted to what Professor Leijonhufvud had called 'expedient assumptions'. Professor Leijonhufvud had viewed Keynes's *General Theory* as an unsuccessful attempt to turn economists away from their 'clockwork', mechanistic mentality toward an emphasis on the cybernetic quality of economic systems.

Professor Stiglitz was disturbed by the tension in the discussions about the notion of equilibrium. We both recognised the role of imperfect information and wanted to use the notion of perfect foresight in a non-stochastic form; if we wanted to work with imperfect information and simultaneously talk about systematic factors we had to form some notion of stochastic equilibrium. Most of the objections to traditional equilibrium analysis would not apply to stochastic equilibrium models. In such models individuals would often regret the decisions which they had made but they would still have made the correct decision in the light of the information available to them at the time of decision. Most of the 'new microeconomic' models had focused on only one aspect of the unemployment situation, namely the short-run adjustment frictional unemployment. The stochastic equilibrium framework, on the other hand, could explain some unemployment of the involuntary variety, for example, if there was heterogeneous labour, or the consequences of the implicit risk-sharing in some labour contracts, or the short-run unemployment arising from a lack of people with specialised training that firms required. More generally, in a world of imperfect information it was not obvious that the notions of competition that we had been using were appropriate. Perhaps one should look at the fundamental equilibrium notions, and consider whether there was free entry or a sufficiently large number of participants to enable a Nash—Kornai equilibrium to exist.

Professor Streissler said that he frequently thought that it was necessary to build a theory of disequilibrium economics, but, as Professor Machlup had forcibly told him, that was a very imprecise term. Concepts of equilibrium were useful in clarifying the things one disliked about equilibrium. For example, what was the difference between historical development and equilibrium? There could be several different equilibria and the path taken by a system to reach an equilibrium might change the equilibrium, so that there was no uniqueness of equilibrium. Was the idea of stochastic equilibrium related to this problem? Historical development might mean that the initial conditions did not allow the attainment of equilibrium; that is, the equilibrium was unstable and we could not be certain that it was ever attained. Or it might mean that convergence to a unique equilibrium existed but the system took so long to come close to the equilibrium path that we could not be certain that a new random shock would not occur before the system was close to the equilibrium path, which would be changed by the shocks. For example, one could assume a commodity market which did not converge to a uniform price, one where there was no regular market established and there were only brokers between people who dealt only occasionally in the market.

Professor Shubik found himself in sentimental agreement with Professor Segura's paper, for several reasons. First, there was really not much satisfactory dynamic oligopoly theory. Second, firms probably conformed fairly closely to the law of administrative convenience, considering primarily their suppliers and employees rather than their stockholders and the tax collector. Third, oligopoly theory and the theory of the firm in general had been implicitly concerned with both markets and money. The concept of a market was implicit in partial equilibrium analysis, in the Marshallian analysis as well as in

Cournot's analysis, unlike Edgeworth's analysis which ignored the institutional structure of the market. Professor Shubik was interested in the problem of embedding an oligopoly model into a closed economy model; this was very much related to monetary theory because without money the oligopoly system would not have enough strategic freedom. Finally, he remarked that non-co-operative behaviour was more general than the behaviour covered by competitive equilibrium and took into account non-symmetric information conditions, whereas without symmetric information the competitive equilibrium was not well-defined.

Replying to the discussion so far, *Professor Segura* said he agreed *partially* with Professor Parkin, but he was not sure how conclusive the empirical evidence was with respect to short-run disequilibrium phenomena. It demonstrated the predictive power of models which included some kind of adaptive expectations hypothesis, but this did not necessarily mean that the expectational hypothesis had to be maintained as the most useful explanatory device for short-term disequilibrium phenomena. Momentary adjustment could be explained in terms of a present value maximisation target but this was not necessarily the best device for explaining short-run disequilibrium dynamics. Professor Segura explained that when he had been talking about equilibrium analysis in his paper he had been talking about momentary equilibrium analysis; and when he had been talking about steady states he had been talking about situations in which expectations were fulfilled. Steady states were, of course, equilibrium states.

Professor Segura agreed with most of Professor Asimakopulos's points. There was in fact no reason why he should not agree, since Professor Asimakopulos had strengthened his own criticisms of the neoclassical paradigm. In talking about Harrod-neutral technical progress, he had been trying to say that the neutrality concept was not designed to explain how technical progress was introduced in an economy. As for the self-correcting mechanism in growth models, he held an 'intermediate' position. From a theoretical point of view he preferred growth models with some kind of self-correcting mechanism, but the studies of stability of growth paths were not satisfactory because the period needed for self-correction was extremely long, and even when stability was proved this did not guarantee that before time went to infinity the model did not display perverse or absurd results. Professor Segura also agreed with Professor Cochrane about the necessity of introducing feedback mechanisms into economic models, but he was not sure that the solution was a 'biological' theory of the firm; he did not at present find Kornai's ideas a good starting point.

With respect to Professor Nell's comments, Professor Segura explained that he believed that behavioural paradigms, which considered the firm as formed by different groups with partially contradictory aims, were the only ones which could take into account all the observed facts about modern firms. Like Professor Nell, he did not believe that technology and preferences were independent of each other. The problem was that it was difficult formally to take account of the interdependence. Some notion of X-efficiency rather than allocative efficiency might perhaps be a good framework to try to deal with this problem. In his paper technology had only been partially given. He had assumed that embodied technical progress came from abroad and disembodied technical progress was domestically produced. This was a reasonable assumption for economies where research and development expenditure was low. He did not believe that the neoclassical analysis of embodied technical progress was satisfactory; it did not explain actual research and development, and it also did not take account of the fact that disembodied and embodied technical progress had different effects upon the economic system.

Sir John Hicks raised some more general issues. The theory of the firm was one of the most sensitive issues in the microeconomic foundations of macroeconomics and there was a sharp divergence between the microeconomic and the macroeconomic assumptions usually made in this field. But Sir John believed that the situation had to be accepted, and was indeed defensible, for we always had to consider the purpose for which our economic theory was designed. Furthermore, economic phenomena were immensely complex, so that usefully to deal with any particular problem involved drastic simplifications and omissions. The factors that could be omitted differed from problem to problem. In regard to Marshall's representative firm, Marshall's theory had been intended to deal with what was now a historical problem: namely, what factors determined the average size of firms in different industries? The example in Marshall's day was the cotton industry, where in the spinning and weaving sections of the industry firm sizes differed. The issues we had to concentrate on now were different. Simplifications for the short-run macroeconomic analysis might well be different from those suitable for long-run analysis, just as simplifications for microeconomic and macroeconomic analysis might well differ. One simplification was a division of an economy into fixprice and flexprice sectors.

Professor Leijonhufvud wished to second Sir John Hicks and put in a plea for us to minimise our ambitions. He was himself concerned primarily with the short-run problems of co-ordinating economic activities in the system. The fact that there were millions of agents and of alternative activities made the system complex; he thought that the relevant question of dealing with firms in such a system was: How simple-minded a theory of the firm can we get away with? Certain commonly employed simplifications, he suggested, should probably not be countenanced:

(1) we could not hide all the firms in an aggregate production function;
(2) the notion of 'perfect competition' taken from static analysis belonged in statics and could not be used in macro without modification;
(3) the conventional lack of budget constraints on firms in general equilibrium analysis was unsatisfactory; and
(4) pure flow models of the firm, ignoring physical and financial working capital, were inadequate also in the short run (when one might perhaps allow the assumption of 'constant' fixed capital).

His own preference was for simple feedback models of the firm rather than elaborate expectational models of maximising behaviour under *ad hoc* assumptions about expectations. He had a strong preference for models where all that agents were assumed to know were things that the model dictated that they would know if they remembered at all what had happened to them. In other words, all they knew about demand and market conditions should be things that they knew from memory and from *ex post* data. In process analysis, one could *not* assume, for example, that imperfect competitors just 'know' their demand curves. A specific example of the problem of adapting standard microeconomic theory to the requirements of macroeconomic theory was that if we moved from the competitive model of the firm in general equilibrium analysis to the analysis of competitive firms in systems where markets did not clear all the time, we needed some reasonably simple analysis of how competitive firms behave in disequilibrium. One way that had sometimes been suggested was to treat the firm as a 'temporary monopolist' and to use the static monopoly model to represent its disequilibrium behaviour; this seemed to Professor Leijonhufvud to be a most misleading conception. A disequilibrium situation did not endow the competitive firm with (rent-earning) 'monopoly power'; rather, when the market did not clear, the agent would be subject to additional constraints that were not binding in the special case of equilibrium. Since the agent was more constrained than he would be in the standard equilibrium model, his information requirements were greatly increased. A genuine monopolist might operate in a stable enough environment to be able to obtain useful information on the position and elasticity of 'his' demand curve (information that the 'perfect competitor' in equilibrium did not require). But for the competitor in disequilibrium, the demand curve facing him was apt to shift before he could be confident of knowing even a single point on it.

Professor Davidson believed that there were only two types of economic model: general equilibrium models and historical models. The meaning of equilibrium was different in the two types. Patinkin had rightly pointed out that in a general equilibrium model Keynes could not have been talking about equilibrium unemployment. But that was not true in an historical model. Equilibrium in a general equilibrium model means all markets clear; in an historical model equilibrium is used in the sense that over a period of calendar time if the *same* conditions prevail no one changes his market behaviour. Professor Davidson claimed that Keynes had three models in *The General Theory*, Chapter 5: a static model and a dynamic model, which were both dated models, and an expectational model. *Sir John Hicks* interposed: suppose that we were to say that a study of equilibrium was one in which some dependent variables were at least temporarily unchanged over time, would that be what Professor Davidson was trying to get? *Professor Davidson* said that it was. Hahn's definition of equilibrium in his Inaugural lecture essentially did not allow for learning-by-doing. Keynes had in Chapter 5 of *The General Theory* talked about the difference between expectations and their realisation; he had believed that the world was not static, that expectational variables were not completely endogenous.

Professor Izzo referred to the current macroeconomic theory of investment where the level of investment was explained by aggregating over firms whose investment decisions were analysed essentially on the basis of models such as those of Jorgenson, Gould, and Lucas. These models tried to explain the lag structure in the investment process and how it was possible that monetary and fiscal policy influenced the lag structure and the choice of investment decision. He wished to know what Professor Segura thought of these models; in particular, whether he thought that they were satisfactory explanations of the lag structure. He himself felt that they faced a problem of explaining the formation of expectations and their influence on investment decisions.

Professor Marty intervened to enquire as to the questions we were trying to ask. Were we asking what was the proper microeconomic theory of the firm to explain macroeconomic disequilibrium *à la* Keynes in the short run, in which the stock of capital was fixed? Or were we asking what was the proper theory of the firm for explaining the long-run growth of output per man? We could have either demand-oriented theories (e.g. Robinson, Harrod) or supply-oriented theories (e.g. Meade, Chicago); all these growth theories had deficiencies: for example, technical change was exogenous and Harrod-neutral. Sometimes one tried to patch them up with induced technical change *à la* Kennedy. But when Professor Segura said that the oligopoly model was more appropriate, was that for short-run or long-run growth explanation? Professor Marty agreed with Sir John Hicks that theories of the firm might be a reflection of the study of historical development, but he would like to see some concrete historical empirical evidence, other than this list of possible cases, that the degree of oligopoly was an important variable influencing growth rates across countries at a particular time or the growth rate of a particular economy over time, or alternatively that growth would affect market structure.

Professor Segura agreed with Professor Leijonhufvud that the notion of temporary monopolistic power did not explain short-run disequilibria and was not a useful theory. With respect to Professor Davidson's intervention, he did not have any comments to make except that he did not believe in expectational theories. Like Professor Izzo he did not think that the lag structure was the best way in which to explain the investment function. There was a problem of aggregation of individual firms' investment functions, which was perhaps the most controversial step in capital theory. He agreed with the Italian and Cambridge school that the lag structure might be used for forecasting purposes but was not appropriate for explaining why the investment process was going on. Professor Marty's question was, he thought, really important. But in his paper he had only been trying to demonstrate how some actual facts of both short- and long-run disequilibria *might* be explained by a very simplified model in which the actual growth process depended on technical progress and in which the determination of labour productivity played a central role in accumulation and distribution. This model would apply to a 'second-rate' country for which one could accept the assumption of exogenously given embodied technical progress.

Professor Malinvaud pointed out that Professor Segura's paper led us to consider whether and how we ought to and could introduce non-economic factors as explanatory factors in macroeconomic analysis. In the paper there was the idea that behavioural paradigms would be useful for analysing short-run equilibrium and perhaps also long-term equilibrium; there was also the idea of the role of the Schumpeterian entrepreneur. Perhaps we could benefit from contributions from other sciences. In the past many economists, particularly those critical of the 'classical theories', had taken the position that in order to understand macroeconomic phenomena we ought to introduce such considerations. When Professor Malinvaud had himself worked on an empirical study of the growth of the French economy he had had to raise the question whether when we took into account economic factors we were leaving out phenomena which might affect or complement the economic factors. For example, was there a particular reason for improved entrepreneurship? Or was there a particular reason for increased intensity of work by workers? He had tried to get answers from sociologists, but they had not been very helpful; was there any prospect of a better collaboration in the future from people working on micro-sociological phenomena?

Professor Streissler pointed out that Professor Segura had raised the difficulties of formulating a Schumpeterian model of inventive diffusion. One of his own research students had recently formulated such a model; with a determinate rate of spread of information on technical progress technical progress was slower than if one assumed instantaneous access to information about technical progress. In stochastic models where the spread of technical progress varied stochastically over time the spread took place more slowly. This was one case where the introduction of the variance changed the mean of a variable.

Professor Parkin wondered whether when Professor Segura said that he objected primarily to the analyses in the Phelps volume because of their long-run implications he meant that he objected to the fact that any long-run equilibrium model did not possess any unemployment other than voluntary search activity. In the short run in those models unemployment would be voluntary but people might still be disappointed in their expectations; in the long run people would only be engaged in voluntary activities *and* would not be disappointed in their expectations. Did Professor Segura believe that we should be searching for models where involuntary unemployment existed as a long-run phenomenon? If so, what empirical evidence should Professor Parkin be looking for? What empirical evidence could he produce to persuade Professor Segura otherwise? With respect to the remarks of Professor Leijonhufvud and Sir John Hicks, Professor Parkin sympathised with the view that we ought to be simple-minded in this area. But he did not regard simple-mindedness and lightweight analysis as synonymous; we might need some heavyweight analysis. He also asked what Professor Segura meant by saying that he did not believe in expectational models. Expectations could be isolated and used, for example, by Carlson and Parkin ('Inflation Expectations', *Economica*, May 1975). Finally, he said that he was not sure that Sir John Hicks's fixprice-flexprice distinction was helpful, that it did not provide a dichotomy where there was really a continuum. In the 'new microeconomic' literature prices responded to excess demand and expectations of price change; this included the two extreme cases of fixprice and flexprice.

Sir John Hicks replied that he believed that all models were simplifications and that we had to be prepared to throw away some things when we were dealing with one question, others when dealing with other questions. He also thought that the old-fashioned distinction between growth and fluctuations was still quite a useful one.

Professor Parkin suggested that we had currently got into a mess in the real world by misguidedly distinguishing between short-run and long-run stability problems.

Professor Leijonhufvud said that he was not offering a new trick but an example of an old trick, Marshall's trick, that he would like to see used more often. Marshall had used it, for example, in his theory of competitive supply. In the simplest version, the industry output would be auctioned off each

period and that was how prices were formed. Each individual firm knew its
particular expenses curve and thus its supply price for different rates of output; it would display an interative behaviour, utilising the *ex post* observations
of market price, in groping for its equilibrium output from market day to
market day. The representation of its behaviour would be:

$$q_1 = h[p^s(q_0) - p_0] + q_0$$

$$q_2 = h[p^s(q_1) - p_1] + q_1$$

. . . and so on.

The consecutive actions taken as steps in this iterative routine $- \Delta q_0 = q_1 - q_0$
being an example — were not here segments of an optimal time-path planned
ex ante. The behaviour pattern might be characterised as 'satisficing converging
on maximising'. The alternative assumption, of course, was that at the end of
the first day the firm formed an expectation of tomorrow's price and maximised on the basis of that expected price to choose its output rate for
tomorrow.

Professor Spaventa asked Professor Parkin whether he envisaged price
behaviour as a continuum. Was there any empirical evidence that there was
a gap between, for instance, nationally competing firms and internationally
competing firms?

Professor Davidson claimed that since some firms produced for the market,
while other firms produced to contract, there was bound to be a dichotomy
of types of markets, namely spot *versus* forward markets.

Professor Parkin replied that there was a continuity of contract lengths, so
that there was a continuity as far as price adjustments to excess demand
were concerned.

Sir John Hicks said that he was not suggesting that this distinction was a
complete description of the working of any actual economy nor did he wish
to deter Professor Parkin from making his empirical investigations. He had
merely suggested that it was a useful simplified model which seemed to cover
the facts.

Finally, *Professor Segura* replied to Professor Parkin that when he had
said that he did not believe in expectations, he meant that he did not believe
in adaptive expectations in the short run; that is, a process of learning-by-
doing which always reached an equilibrium unless there were 'permanent'
shocks. This was not a good explanatory device in the long run, although it
could be a good device for forecasting purposes. Professor Segura said that
nobody knew anything like a 'long-run natural equilibrium'.

9 Costs and Consequences of Inflation*

A. Leijonhufvud
UNIVERSITY OF CALIFORNIA

1 INTRODUCTION

One approach to the microeconomic foundations of macroeconomics problem takes the frame and the components of standard 'neoclassical' theory as the given starting point. One asks what can be used and what needs modification for purposes of representing the movement of a macro-system through time and into a future that is in some respects unknowable. The aim is to define and, if possible, solve the analytical problems that emerge at the levels of individual conceptual experiments, market experiments, and general equilibrium experiments. I have pursued this approach in other recent papers[1] but am running into diminishing returns.

An alternative approach is to start from the other end with some 'applied' problem, preferebly one of such importance that no macroeconomist can really afford to dodge it, and consider the difficulties that arise in trying to handle it in a 'reasonable' way with standard micro-theoretical tools. From this viewpoint we get a different critical angle on the problems requiring solution if micro- and macro-theory are to be made to mesh. This is the approach taken in this paper.

The 'practical' macro-question to be considered here is that of the social costs and consequences of inflation. A new view of the welfare costs of inflation has emerged in the last ten or fifteen years. It trivialises the cost of inflation. This new view is undergirded by essentially 'neoclassical' theoretical constructions and may, indeed, be regarded as a by-product of work primarily oriented toward seeking neoclassical foundations for macro-theory. In the analytical exercise that is central to this view, inflation is treated as a foreseen tax on money balances and its costs are seen to lie in the productive and transactional inefficiencies induced by such a tax. Even a quite high rate of inflation will not imply a very sizable tax as taxes go in modern mixed economies; the inefficiencies that it may induce will be correspondingly trivial.

*I am thankful to Armen Alchian, Robert Clower, Ben Klein, John McCall and Sidney Afriat for comments and obliged to declare them free from responsibility. Financial support of the Liberty Fund is gratefully acknowledged.
[1] Leijonhufvud (1974, 1974–5).

Some economists will feel that this work has helped us put the undesirability of inflation into proper perspective by dispelling old and murky myths about its dangers. To those, my topic will not seem a promising avenue towards a fuller understanding of the trouble we are having with microeconomic foundations.

It should thus be obvious and shall in any case be openly admitted that my choice of topic is predicated on the prior conviction that in advocating or letting go unopposed this new view of inflation we have been guilty of profound and appalling naïveté. I fear that the spreading influence of the new view is dangerous in so far as it directly or indirectly influences policy.

The new view on inflation is not altogether unassailable on its own terms. But the questions about it that may be raised strictly within the neoclassical framework are probably not the important ones. Neoclassical theory − or, more precisely, its scope − is itself at issue. The social consequences of inflation most germane to 'wise' conduct of economic policy may fall largely outside its purview. For this once, I do not think inside ('immanent') criticism is the tack to take. This paper wilfully refuses obedience to the neoclassical rules of the game. We begin by taking an 'institutionalist' view of monetary exchange.

The institutional approach has, of course, its own limitations. One cannot be perfectly 'general' (i.e., refer to all times and all places) and still retain content. The time-space 'reference co-ordinates' that I have had in mind in writing this paper are (i) the last ten years or so, and (ii) the United States. Similarly, the term 'inflation' in the title is not to be read as denoting a theoretically defined 'pure' concept but as referring to inflationary processes 'like' the one of recent years.

II   AN INSTITUTIONALIST SKETCH OF MONETARY EXCHANGE

> *Whether the true idea of money, as such, is*
> *not altogether that of a ticket or counter?*
> ──── Bishop Berkeley, *The Querist*

Some of the questions on the present theoretical agenda are much older than the current movement to provide microeconomic foundations for macrotheory: Why do people hold money? Why is the set of goods serving as means of payment so small? Why are 'indexed' contracts so uncommon? Etc.

One approach to these questions starts by interpreting the mathematical structure of a standard general equilibrium model as representing a multilateral 'barter' system. One then seeks precise formulation of realistic assumptions about information imperfections and transactions costs that can be shown to lend a 'monetary' transactions structure to the G.E. model. It is not part of my aim to criticise this research, much of which I find interesting and promising.

The point to be made here is simply that these conceptual experiments should not be given historical interpretations. The proposition that 'barter is costly and inefficient' will no doubt be part of any explanation of the 'use of money'. That 'the inefficiency of barter *leads* to the use of money', would, however, be false as an historical generalisation. Monetary exchange systems have not evolved out of non-monetary exchange ('barter') systems but out of non-exchange systems. Both intertemporal and cross-cultural comparisons show us that in the spheres of economic activity where monetary exchange does not prevail, neither do we find predominantly 'private' property rights, commercial contracting, and organised markets. (These are however institutional features presumed by the 'non-monetary' G.E. model.) We will still expect to find a fairly extensive division of labour but the institutional arrangements – the systems of rights and obligations governing the activities of individuals – devised to ensure that the community can depend on the benefits from the division of labour will be different in kind. 'Custom and Command', in the terms of Classical Economics, or 'Reciprocity and Redistribution', in those of Anthropology – not barter exchange – are the alternatives to monetary exchange.[1] The development of monetary exchange is, consequently, part of a complex evolution of institutions. Perhaps the best short statement is Wesley Mitchell's famous passage:[2]

> When money is introduced into the dealings of men, it enlarges their freedom. . . . By virtue of its generalised purchasing power, money emancipates its users from numberless restrictions upon what they do and what they get. As a society learns to use money confidently, it gradually abandons restrictions upon the places people shall live, the occupations they shall follow, the circles they shall serve, the prices they shall charge, and the goods they can buy.

In largely non-monetary economies, important economic rights and obligations will be inseparable from particularised relationships of social status and political allegiance and will be in the same measure permanent, inalienable, and irrevocable.[3] Assurance of stability of the economic order is sought in tying economic functions to social roles that carry particular rights and duties *vis-à-vis* particular individuals or groups. In monetary exchange systems, in contrast, 'the value to the owner of [his human capital or] a physical asset derives from rights, privileges, powers, and immunities against society generally

[1] All I can do at this point is to provide a personally favoured select list of 'further reading': J. S. Mill (1909) Book II, Chapter IV; F. H. Knight (1965) Chapter 1; Dalton (ed) (1968) esp. Dalton's Introduction); Hicks (1967, Chapter 9; 1969); Michael Polanyi (1969).

[2] W. C. Mitchell (1953). For a summary of Mitchell's views and further references to his writings, cf. Friedman (1952).

[3] Feudal land-rents, for example, cannot be 'decomposed' into a rental price on land 'plus' a tax on the cultivator of it; nor can the overlapping rights and interlocking obligations of a peasant, of other village members, of the manorial lord, and of the sovereign with regard to a particular piece of land be disentangled in terms of modern notions of 'ownership'.

rather than from the obligation of some particular person.'[1] And, paraphrasing J. S. Mill, 'competition is the governing principle of such contracts' as leave particular agents with a debt-claim relationship.

Neoclassical theories rest on a set of abstractions that separate 'economic' transactions from the totality of social and political interactions in the system.[2] For a very large set of important problems, this separation 'works' — since we are usually dealing with monetary exchange systems. But it assumes that the events that we make the subject of conceptual experiments with the neoclassical model of the 'economic system' do not affect the 'socio-political system' so as to engender repercussions on the economy of such significance as to invalidate the institutional *ceteris paribus* clauses of that model.

It is not 'in the nature of things' that this assumption necessarily holds. There can be no epistemological guarantee that interactions between the 'economic', the 'political', and the 'social spheres' of the system we study will be negligible. Double-digit inflation *may* label a class of events for which the assumption is a bad one. The neoclassical conceptual experiment of a steady-state inflation, which in time becomes accurately foreseen, and to which 'everything adjusts' — *except* property rights, contract forms, and the organisation of markets[3] — is at the very least a most instructive exercise. But that does not suffice to make it a good theory. It is a long-run theory. But its institutional *ceteris paribus* assumptions may not hold approximately true for that long.

We should at least keep an open mind to this disturbing possibility. We do not now have the empirical knowledge to rule it out. It may be the case that in the world we inhabit, before the 'near-neutral' adjustments can all be smoothly achieved, 'society *un*learns to use money confidently' and reacts by restrictions on 'the circles people shall serve, the prices they shall charge, and the goods they can buy.'[4] If such reactions are in fact endogenous to the social system, we mis-identify the consequences of inflation to the extent that we regard them as fortuitous 'political' events exogenously impinging on 'the economy'.

*

Mitchell uses the term 'money' in a sense so broad as to cover not just all of

[1] Cf. Burstein (1963), p. 105.

[2] Exactly what all these abstractions are and what conditions will allow them validity, we are not very clear about. We are content to live with the correspondingly hazy definition of the boundaries between economics and other social sciences for, I think, the simple reason that most of the time our work is shaped by the 'economic method' we use — and letting 'the way economists think' establish the limits to our 'territorial imperative' will almost always be good enough.

[3] E.g., the line between legal and 'black' markets.

[4] Historical processes are not reversible. The paraphrase of Mitchell here is not intended to convey some silly suggestion of a return to feudalism or even mercantilism. It is intended to convey the judgement that an analysis of inflation that does not attempt to take political feedback on the economic process systematically into account is, in contemporary jargon, 'irrelevant.'

money and banking but also the 'Legal Foundations of Capitalism' (J. R. Commons) and even the psychological attitudes and calculating modes of decision-making that go with life in a society where the range of alternatives subject to the common measuring-rod of money is very wide. But something need be said also about how 'money', in the narrow sense of 'M', fits into such an institutionalist schema.

The stability of any social order requires (i) an exhaustive and consistent allocation of rights to economic resources, and (ii) rules for the transfer of these rights and means for keeping track of the legitimate succession to them. Disputes over the possession of rights, where the legal entitlement of the parties cannot be tracked down or otherwise 'fairly' determined, must as far as possible be avoided — since the residual method of settling conflicts will be the use of force.

In monetary exchange systems, the problem of keeping track takes a particular form. The 'typical' basic forms of wealth are defined in terms of rights and immunities *vis-à-vis* 'society in general'. Transactors have discretion in what they choose to sell and buy and whom they choose to sell to or buy from. The institutional problem is to ensure that no one takes more out of the system than he puts in, so that everyone is assured of being allowed to appropriate resources from the rest of society 'equal' to what he has contributed to others.

Hawtrey's insistence that every transaction generates a claim and a matching debt is helpful here in leaving all questions of settlements temporarily open. The first problem is the measurement of debts and claims. We may assume them to be recorded at the prices in terms of unit of account agreed upon by the parties. In the simplest multilateral exercise, we would have only 'real' transactions — involving the transfer of a physical asset, real good or service (or the forward contract for such a transfer) — to consider. Assuming 'rules' allowing no financial transactions or the running of financial surplus and deficits, a purely 'imaginary money',[1] tied to no real *numéraire* good, could perfectly well serve as unit of account. The conceivable ways of 'policing the rules' are legion.

As an illustration, suppose we find a short closed loop in this system where repeatedly real resources are transferred from A to B, from B to C, C to D, and from D to A, and all links in the chain happen to be quoted by the two parties at the same value in terms of 'imaginary money':

(1) We might decide to run a central social bookkeeping office charged with keeping the respective balance-sheets of A, B, C, and D continuously up-to-date by adding on the debts incurred and claims gained in each period. The object is simply to check that each balance sheet continues to balance. If accurate addition is cheap enough to come by, we could as well let the balance sheets go on lengthening indefinitely. Going through the motions of extinguishing debts would be superfluous.

---

[1] Luigi Einaudi (1955).

(2) We might feed all debits and credits arising from resource transfers into a computer programmed to hunt for 'closed loops' and to wipe out all debts and claims (up to the largest common numerator) in all such loops found. Shrill bells should sound and red lights flash whenever the computer ends its daily exercise with a residue of net claims, etc. With this system, debts are systematically 'extinguished', putting less of a burden on central archives, but they are not 'paid.' None of the goods in the system is identifiable as the 'means of payment'.

(3) A social abacus might be cheaper than a central computer. We might issue little pellets, 'tickets or counters' (called 'Berkeleys'), pronounce them legal tender and instruct every transactor to keep 'paying' them out until his debts are zero. We could leave A, B, C and D alone to agree on how many Berkeleys extinguish a debt of one 'imaginary' unit or we could try to help them out. Record-keeping and computational requirements will be drastically simplified by the expedient of handling 'counters' around; even people who had trouble with arithmetic in primary school can participate.

(4) We could allow any transactor able to acquire the trust of the others to issue I.O.Us. (in 'Berkeley's') and have them handed around (or transferred between agents on his books) instead.[1] If experience tells us that people sometimes misplace their trust, we might intervene to force the 'bank' regularly to extinguish its I.O.Us. or stand ready to do so in either 'our B's' or real goods.

(5) Some transactor might be designated as a 'credit card company' which allows others that it trusts to register the debts and claims arising from resource transfers between them on this company rather than on one another. The method or methods for extinguishing these debts and claims, we might leave to the company unless it proves prone to misplace its trust.

In a system where some mix of these (and perhaps other) arrangements is in operation, it is quite possible that we might find an empirically stable demand function for a suitably defined 'M'.[2] Securing its micro-theoretical foundations does not appear an easy task, however. Putting 'real M' in utility-functions, for example, leaves one with a residue of fearful doubts; and proposals to reduce the marginal utility of M to zero seem of uncertain import.

The above sketch has not provided conditions assuring the stability over time of the relationship between 'Berkeley's' and the imaginary accounting unit (I.A.U.). Changes in the relation of B to I.A.U. would, however, be of relatively limited concern as long as we deal with systems where the accounts receivable and payable carried over through time are small or zero, as assumed above.[3]

[1] Cf. Hicks (1967), Chapter 2.
[2] At least as long as arrangements (1) and (2) or variants and permutations thereof do not come to dominate the others entirely.
[3] Horrible penalties for those found feigning the bishop's graven image on the counters

Nor is a stable relation between the I.A.U. and some 'composite basket' assured by the sketch as far as we have carried it. The 'I.A.U.-value' of the basket could be any positive number. It is interesting, however, that between Charlemagne and the French Revolution the drift of the *libra* was rather slow[1] and, more to the point, without dramatic discontinuous jumps. Comparative static models, defined to exclude 'money illusion',[2] will provide no reasons to expect this. Yet, it is possible for an 'imaginary money', without secure real anchorage, to drift slowly enough so as to preserve its usefulness for economic calculation of the advantages of alternative courses of action (and, apparently, retain some − ill-understood − superiority over 'composite basket' contracting units). But this, it would seem, could only be the case if agents faced with the task of setting prices today seek help in the memory of yesterday's prices; i.e., find value in 'precedent'.[3]

A sketch of this sort will have to leave many loose ends. Here, they are beyond counting. But we resolutely turn our backs to all that, hanging on to but one strand − that our various social bookkeeping devices have not been shown capable of 'keeping track' in systems that allow nominally denominated debts and claims to remain outstanding from one 'period' to the next.

III INFLATION AND THE LAW

Mankind presumably has put more intellectual effort and ethical reflection over the centuries into the creation of the law than has as yet gone into social benefit-cost analysis. If, then, repeated rounds of gradually improved social

---

or otherwise manufacturing 'money' have been historically helpful. Sovereigns and legislators usually end up exempt, however, leaving them with the capability of appropriating resources from the private sector by 'money' issue. The consequences of such 'inflation taxes' should not be very serious however − as long as they do not also succeed in enforcing a fixed relation between the unit of legal tender and the unit of account in general use.

[1] Cf., Einaudi (1953) *passim.*

[2] The term 'money illusion' is used here with apologies. Recent changes in professional usage have made it virtually useless as a technical term. Originally, it referred to individuals with a tendency to be fooled by currency reforms shifting the decimal point on all nominally denominated contracts or misers with an irrational passion for nominal money. This concept is trivial but clear-cut and useful. Later, in the Keynesian debate, the term came to be used with reference to the behaviour of transactors lacking complete information on their alternatives of choice. (Cf. Leijonhufvud, 1968, especially pp. 384−5). More recently still, in the literature on neoclassical monetary equilibrium growth models, some writers have used it to refer to agents who fail accurately to *foresee* the rate of inflation. This last step should signal general abandonment of the term.

[3] Cf. Hicks (1970) p. 19:

In imperfect markets prices have to be 'made'; they are not just 'determined' by demand and supply. It is much easier to make them, in a way that seems satisfactory (because it seems fair) to the parties concerned, if substantial use can be made of precedent; if one can start with the supposition that what was acceptable before will be acceptable again.

cost calculations for inflation keep repeating the answer that it is relatively trivial, it gives one pause to note that the law is helpless to assure justice in inflations.

Because of this impotence of the law, inflations tend to accelerate the secular tendency of most Western countries to move away from the Rule of Law toward Rule by Men. Associated therewith, we expect to observe a tendency for the dominant popular conception of social justice in democratic societies to shift from Equality under the Law towards Income Equality. The first of these conceptions focuses on the evenhanded application of the rules governing social and economic activities irrespective of the identities of individuals and of the social status they occupy, etc. The second focuses on the *ex post* real outcome of individual economic activity.[1]

The two linked tendencies are, of course, subject to divergent value judgements. Some would cheer them on, others wish that they could be braked, halted, or even reversed. Here we are concerned to argue only that the strength of these tendencies will be associated with inflation and, consequently, that this association should be considered in assessing the consequences of inflation. One note might be added to this: namely, that inflations, even as they speed up the process, are likely to make orderly and coherent evolution in the directions indicated more difficult to achieve.

The law is helpless to assure that a just real outcome is restored to contracts concluded in nominal terms. That is so for rather simple reasons. The expectations about the rate of inflation in prospect[2] that the two parties originally held cannot be objectively ascertained after the fact.[3] The only 'evidence' for what they then were would be what the two contending parties now allege and it, of course, is useless to the courts.

No independently defined measuring rod suggests itself as a standard of

---

[1] In order to get on with the topic, this paragraph had better be left as is — patently inadequate. Two references to cover my escape: Hayek (1973) and Rawls (1971). The basic opposition between Hayek's emphasis on 'spontaneous orders' and Rawls's equally evident 'constructivism' need not, as far as I can see, produce a clash in the context of this section (the Appendix would be another matter — but there I will avoid the issue).

[2] Here and elsewhere we make use of '*the* rate of inflation' *as if* both parties to a contract would define inflation, with regard to their own best economic interests, in terms of money-price changes of *strictly identical* composite baskets.

This fudge seems unavoidable if we are to go ahead with the argument. *But* — could this condition ever be exactly fulfilled (while leaving room for gains from trade between the two)? Assume two agents with identical, homothetic consumption tastes. If they are to trade, there must be division of labour (or differential endowments) between the two. No price will be more significant to their respective economic interests than that of the good that is the object of their specialisation of labour. The prices of what they sell must be included in the respective welfare calculations . . . and we are in trouble.

[3] Note that the economist studying the 'distribution effects' of inflation on the basis of data on the net monetary creditor or debtor position of transactors or groups will be in the same boat. The work of Armen Alchian and Reuben Kessel (reported in numerous articles) of some fifteen years ago is subject to this uncertainty. The solidity of the inferences drawn depends on that of the assumption that both parties expected price stability at the time their contracts were negotiated.

justice. Measures of the inflation that has taken place over the term of a contract cannot be imposed as a standard *ex post*.[1] If both parties initially expected 5 per cent inflation (in the price of some agreed-upon composite basket) and the actual rate was 10 per cent, a court using the actual rate to recompute a contract would fix a debtor loss of 5 per cent as the legally enforced outcome. By simply enforcing the contract in nominal terms as written, the result would be a creditor loss of 5 per cent relative to the original intentions of the contract. If, on the other hand, both parties had expected a 15 per cent inflation, a 10 per cent actual rate means that the debtor loses 5 per cent if the contract is settled without dispute; if a court were to adjust the contract by adding on the actual inflation the resulting debtor loss would be 15 per cent.

The parties may have had discrepant expectations about the rate of inflation in prospect. In that case, it will be impossible in pure principle to find an adjustment coefficient such that, when applied to what the contract says, one succeeds in realising the expected real outcome for both parties.

Finally, there will be a class of contracts in existence of which it is true that the parties would never have been able to come to terms − i.e., would not have found any mutual gains from trade in prospect − had their expectations (correct or not) about the future inflation rate originally been in agreement.

Consequently, the law refuses to recognise inflations as a source of 'unjust' outcomes. If suit were brought claiming that the legitimate expectations of one party to a contract (e.g., a United States Savings Bond) have been defeated by inflation, such a suit would be thrown out of court. The price-stability fiction − 'a dollar is a dollar is a dollar' − is as ingrained in our laws as if it were a constitutional principle. Indeed, it may be that no 'real' con-stitutional principle permeates the law as completely as does this manifest fiction. Inflations (or deflations) end up being ranged with those Acts of God for which parties are not held accountable. But this is not because jurists have mis-identified the potentate responsible. It is because the law cannot tangle with 'him', whoever he is.

To see this in proper perspective, one should realise how very wide is the range of contingencies with regard to which the law will adjudicate. The out-comes of any individual's efforts are contingent upon the present and future behaviour of others. The law seeks to provide a stable framework of social interaction within which people can form expectations about the outcomes of their actions sufficiently firm, if not precise, to allow them to plan their conduct accordingly. It does so, in the first place, by making certain broad classes of behaviour permitted or forbidden, in the penal code, to everyone. For a socio-economic system dependent upon a very high degree of specialisa-tion of labour this will not suffice. The 'rules of the economic game' (in the

---

[1] Some such standard may, in effect, be imposed *via* legislated price controls or incomes policies − but the courts would and could never do it (which is a sidelight of sorts on what incomes policies imply).

game-theoretic sense) must be given a more detailed, consistent structure or else the 'positive sum' capable of being realised will be very modest and less than reliable. One system of design to accomplish this is to constrain the 'strategies' of individual players or groups by restrictions of the type referred to by Mitchell. Individuals whose economic effort depends for its result on the behaviour of 'the shoemaker' are provided the assurance that he will *have to* 'stick to his last' . . . and his son after him, etc. The other system of design, of course, is that which provides the legal frame of 'monetary exchange systems'. One of its principal features will be provision for 'free' contracting between parties. If your welfare is significantly dependent upon the behaviour of shoemakers, you contract with *a* shoemaker – depending upon the potential competition of other shoemakers to prevent him from holding you over the barrel. To work reasonably well, therefore, this system of legal design requires competition as a 'governing principle of contract'. It also requires dependable 'money' if people are to be 'emancipated from restrictions on what they do and what they get' and be let loose to do as they please. The vast, overwhelming majority of contracts will specify receipt of 'general purchasing power' as the main right of at least one of the parties.

One of the dominant concerns of the law in an exchange system must then be to ensure the dependability of contracts. How is this to be done? It is a tempting but most naive notion to envisage a system of law that *guarantees* (in some sense) to everybody the realisation of the expectations held when the contract was concluded.[1] This is impossible even as just a general model of approach (e.g., with 'scaled-down' guarantees – '90 per cent as a minimum', or whatever). Some of the reasons are obvious – in particular, the omnipresence of a class of contingencies outside the control of the community as a whole: 'Acts of God' and the behaviour of people outside the law's jurisdiction (OPEC). And, of course, people may and will sometimes expect more than they can get in any case. But the problem with outcome-guarantees is more fundamental than that.

It would not work even in a 'closed system' – i.e., a system 'closed' off from the wars, pestilences, and natural disasters of a wrathful Deity and the greed of foreigners alike. For the expectations of parties can never be made either to mesh perfectly with one another or to match all conceivable contingencies – putting aside the inconceivable ones that none the less materialise.[2]

---

[1] Proponents of guaranteed real income schemes for everybody had better give some thought to the underlying rationale of the structure of inherited law in this respect. In Britain, during the autumn of 1974, there was some public debate of universal real income guarantees (by 'indexing') as a notional device for snapping out of the 'cost-push' syndrome. Some commentators envisaged guaranteeing the present real living-standards of the population – at a time when the United Kingdom trade-deficit amounted to 10 per cent of national consumption. This might be the simplest recipe for hyperinflation and unreconcilable social strife ever invented.

[2] I am, of course, denying any 'jurisdiction' to Arrow-Debreu contingency market models in the present realm of discourse. Hopefully, it is superfluous to elaborate on this. My indebtedness to the works of Ronald Coase and Steven N. S. Cheung will, on the other hand, be evident in what immediately follows.

The recorded terms of a contract will *never* reveal the original expectations of the parties 'in their entirety' (whatever that might be made to mean); nor will they ever anticipate all relevant contingencies and specify outcomes pre-agreed upon for each. In part, the expectations held will be left unstated for the simple reason that the parties will often wish not to reveal to each other how they intend to 'profit from the deal'. But, more fundamentally, their expectations will in general not be completely structured; innumerable contingencies will be unanticipated, and not in the sense of being assigned a low or zero probability, but in the sense of not envisaging the situation that would arise, if and when they materialise, in the specifics of its behavioural structure. Expectations with regard to such contingencies are left 'unformed'. Contracts fail to state them not because of their 'unspeakable avarice' (though that might often be a decent reason) but for reasons of a more Wittgensteinian profundity: 'Whereof one cannot speak, thereof one must be silent.'

The contingencies capable of significantly affecting the outcome to contracting parties will never be exhaustively enumerated. Again, one may explain this by reference to the 'cost' of letting the fine print run on indefinitely. And this would be a true statement – no contract will explicitly cover all those contingencies that can be envisaged, for it does not pay to do so. But, beyond that, the conditions of human understanding will not allow for the anticipation of every relevant contingency.[1]

Economists, I firmly believe, need to do a great deal of further work in this direction. If we are ever going to get a firm grasp of what isomorphisms we may claim to obtain between our models and the real system, we need to understand much better than most of us now do *how* the law seeks to reduce the uncertainties of human condition to (literally speaking) 'manageable proportions' and, more importantly, *why* its solutions to this are structured in a particular way. But here we must leave off without attempts to transcend the naïveté with which the problem has been sketched above.

The point for present purposes is this: The set of contractually unspecified contingencies where the law will step in to adjudicate the outcomes to parties is almost infinite. But it is not exhaustive. 'Changes in the Value of Money' are left out.

In adjudicating disputes,[2] the courts will, in effect, make a determination of what expectations the parties could *legitimately* entertain. The case will be settled so as to satisfy everybody's legitimate expectations, in this sense. Most

---

[1] The actual economic 'game' that people find themselves 'playing' has vast arrays of the 'pay-off matrix' blank *ex ante*. Entire dimensions of the outcome space are left unspecified (also in the probabilistic sense). What the parties *will know* about most of the 'blanks' of the matrix, however, is that, if that is where they find themselves ending up, the courts will adjudicate; i.e., will provide an *ex post* definition of what the rules should have been understood to have been. They will expect, moreover, that such a ruling will most often, though not invariable, 'make sense' to them. More importantly, they know that they will not end up deadlocked in an irreconcilable conflict.

One of the dimensions of the matrix should be reserved for changes in the value of money. Along that dimension, the above observations do not hold.

[2] My indebtedness to Hayek (1973, *passim*) will be evident here.

often, this will be done by reference to precedents. A court will not hesitate to invoke precedents of which each party is and was manifestly totally ignorant. And it will make new law where no precedents are to be found. In so doing, it may argue from consistency with existing law, advancing the particular decision, as it were, as a novel 'lemma' to long-established laws. More significantly, for our purposes, it may adjudicate a case without precedent by reference to general communal conceptions of what is and is not 'fair', and hold the parties responsible for understanding and sharing these social conceptions. Among unprecedented cases, it is those with regard to which the public does not hold certain 'Truths to be self-evident', that the law normally would find it most difficult to cope with.

Yet, inflations — apart from hardly being unprecedented — are not like that. They are 'unfair' — 'everyone knows that'. No social convention could be stronger and more universally shared. But the law is impotent. The next section attempts a preliminary analysis of the behavioural implications of this fact.

*

One subject has been ignored: 'indexation'. It is potentially a large one. I have little to say on it, except that I do not believe it gives us a way out.

The law is utterly permissive with regard to indexed contracts, escalator clauses and the like.[1] It will only recognise and enforce nominally defined debts and claims, it is true, but it will allow the parties very wide latitude indeed in specifying mutually agreeable formulae whereby this nominal sum is to be computed.

Having emphasised, first, the impotence of Justice in inflations and, now, the permissiveness of the Law with regard to stable purchasing power clauses, one can only go on to suggest that there are deeper problems to indexation than is revealed by recent discussion.

For 'indexation' persists, of course, in failing the market test[2] long after the force of any initially prevalent social convention of 'money illusion' type must have been dissolved. Even the most ardent proponents of indexing schemes are usually looking for government to take the lead and put it into effect. But why are not governments, saddled with the borrowing requirements common today and given their record of printing money to 'redeem' debt, forced by the competition of the private sector to rely on index-bonds?

---

[1] Many countries do, however, prohibit index contracts. It may be that in most cases such prohibitions are of old standing, going back to an age when sovereigns were struggling to establish their own coinage as a dominant money. Lending the powers of the law to the enforcement of private agreements concluded in contracting units that do not correspond to the payment unit of government issued legal tender would entail a self-imposed constraint on the sovereign's ability to rely on inflationary finance in a pinch. But in Finland the prohibition is recent, having been imposed following the abandonment of the celebrated Finnish experiment with indexation.

[2] Cf. Klein (1974).

We have seen some spread of escalator-clauses in labour contracts. That only makes the situation more odd, however, since these are of short term[1] – short enough, generally, for models of 'foreseen inflation' to possess some measure of putative relevance.

The fact that the system does not spread by itself, one must suppose, probably contains a few lessons for macroeconomists habituated to index-deflated 'real magnitudes' as variables of scientific analysis. If transactors found no problem in finding a mutually agreeable composite basket, and saw no novel and potentially serious risks from using it, is it at all plausible that the system should not spread rapidly in the present age?

The mutually agreeable basket is not necessarily a problem so trivial as to be swamped by perception of the uncertainty of inflation rates. Even in the simplest case of the 'pure consumption-loan' between two parties of identical, homothetic, time-independent tastes, we might expect to find some wrangling over the virtues of Laspeyre *vs.* Paasche and over 'the' rate of interest which should go with one or the other. Where the specialisation in production of at least one of the parties is part of the *raison d'être* of contracts, things get murkier. Suppose, both 'shoes' and 'apples' are in the composite basket used in comprehensive indexation of contracts. If the apple harvest fails badly, the shoe-producer finds himself obliged to increase wages. The apple harvest would not normally be a business risk that much concerned him. If demand shifts from shoes to apples and apple prices promptly go up, the shoe-producer might have to raise his own price in face of falling demand.[2] And so on.

With regard to the use of indexation to provide not just predictable prices and wages but predictable incomes, the work of S. N. Afriat shows that use of one common index number to scale up nominal income proportionally will not leave the real income distribution among income classes unaffected. In general, a different 'marginal price index' should – in fairness – be used for each income-class and even that will fail to take care of individuals with atypical tastes in a given income-class.[3]

When the law draws a line between legitimate and 'illegitimate' expectations of contracting parties, the result is, as we have indicated, a line between contingencies for which a party can and cannot seek redress at court. Inherited law thus embodies a 'choice' of the adverse contingencies that parties must accept without recourse as well as of profitable outcomes that they need not share. Since the system as a whole does not possess 'certainty in the aggregate', the law must necessarily contain some set of rules allocating risks in this manner. The particular rules that we have inherited might have a functional

---

[1] Such short-term employment contracts will not be affected by the capital gains provisions of tax-law. It may be that it is chiefly the tax law that inhibits the development of longer term index contract markets. I doubt, however, that this could be the whole story.

[2] The point is Klein's.

[3] S. N. Afriat (1975).

basis. If so, it is one ill-understood by the economics profession at the present time. In any case, it is clear that private parties contracting on an index basis will thereby (a) redefine the sets of adverse and favourable contingencies for themselves, and (b) within the former set give novel definition to the sub-set for which some measure of redress can be sought. And, to repeat, they are not doing it.

There remains the question: Suppose everybody did, what would be the systemic consequences? Until we gain a better understanding of the considerations sketched above, we cannot hope to get a full answer to this one. But the point forcefully made in a recent paper by Davidson and Kregel suffices, in my opinion, to settle the question of the desirability of trying to bring it about. It would, they argue, 'institutionalise' and give legal force to unitary elasticity of price-expectations. A system where expectations generally had this property would, as Hicks pointed out long ago, be on a knife-edge at best. Any small disturbance increasing one price could set 'the price level' going up without end. And monetary restriction, Davidson and Kregel add, could then only serve to break virtually every index-contract in existence.[1]

IV   THE SOCIAL AND POLITICAL CONSEQUENCES OF INFLATION

In 1919, Keynes began a short piece on inflation by paraphrasing Lenin as having declared that 'the best way to destroy the Capitalist System was to debauch the currency'. And Keynes agreed: 'Lenin was certainly right. There is no subtler, no surer means of overturning the existing basis of Society . . . .'[2] So, we have two thinkers with some influence on our times concurring that inflation is not to be trifled with. This sweeping judgement that they shared obviously differs not just in degree but in kind from that of those latter-day students of the problem who seek the social cost of inflation in the effects of a predictable tax on money balances.

But appeal to 'authority' does, of course, exactly nothing to elucidate the issues for us. Indeed, to the extent that these are scarecrow authorities to some people, it may confound the issues. Besides, neither man has a spotless record as a social scientist. We are obliged to ask whether they knew what they were talking about. And if at the time they did, does it still apply to the world of the twentieth century's last quarter? Keynes, for example, was much preoccupied with the effect of inflation on the saving habits of the Victorian middle and upper classes. The bourgeoisie of the nineteenth century is no longer with us. So it is not at all obvious that Keynes's and Lenin's *obiter dicta* have any bearing on how the social consequences of inflation in the 'mixed economies' of our age are to be assessed.

Keynes, moreover, can be pretty discouraging: 'The process [of inflation] engages all the hidden forces of economic law on the side of destruction, and does it in a manner which not one man in a million is able to diagnose.'[3] Any

[1] Paul Davidson and Jan A. Kregel (1975).
[2] Cf. Keynes, *Essays in Persuasion*, (1972), pp. 57–8.
[3] Ibid.

individual is entitled to the claim of being one in a million – in some respect. But not in this one. This famous line is quoted here only to lodge the complaint that the United States is short of the 200-odd experts on the 'Social Consequences of Changes in the Value of Money' that, on Keynes's reckoning, we are entitled to.

What may be attempted at this stage, given how the whole problem area has been neglected in recent decades, can be little more than to state some of the questions that need to be attacked.

The social cost calculations of the output-loss attributable to inflation have had the dominant share of economists' attention in this area in recent years. It seems natural to start from them, therefore. Two sets of questions suggest themselves. First, have they the 'strictly economic' effects of inflation right? Second, are the redistributive consequences of inflation correctly derived and are they then appropriately weighed on an acceptable scale of redistributive justice?

From the given state of the debate, these are the 'natural' questions to pursue. They are questions that certainly may not be avoided in any attempt to assess the social consequences of inflation. But natural or not, I submit that they do not now belong on top of our agenda. The assumption that, once the output-loss (if any) attributable to inflation has been estimated and taken into account, the Social Consequences of Inflation end with its redistributive incidence may be the single most serious stupidity to which economists are prone when discussing inflation.

In trying to think analytically about the question, we would do well to concentrate, to begin with, on a thought experiment that puts all the problems of the *ex post* redistributive incidence of inflation to one side. There will be an incidental benefit in so doing for, once those problems are brought on to the agenda, emotive political and ideological considerations inescapably impinge on our thinking. It is important that we direct our attention away from such divertissements, for as long as this can legitimately be done, and on to questions of the behavioural implications that flow from the experience of inflation. Its redistributive consequences are *not* the 'final outcomes' of inflation; there are the further questions of how people experience them, of how their perceptions of society are thereby affected, and of how they adapt their behaviour in society as a consequence. And these *may* be the most important questions of them all; whether that is so or not, they *are* the questions that can put us on the trail of what Lenin and Keynes were talking about.

In order to set aside the immediate redistributive consequences, therefore, let us proceed 'as if' we were dealing only with a set of individuals that are 'representative' in the limited (and somewhat peculiar) sense that their *ex post* redistributive gains and losses cancel each other out in approximately the same way as for the economy as a whole.[1] To illustrate: For all I know, I may be

---

[1] For reasons already given in the last section, it is very doubtful indeed that we would be able to ascertain who exactly belongs to this set and who does not. But – no matter. . .

such a 'representative' individual. I am being swindled on my life insurance
and my pension but am getting a sizable stream of ill-gotten gains on my home
mortgage. Suppose these things cancel.

Does that mean that for people in this 'representative' position inflation
does not matter? Of course not. How silly ever to think so. That *ex post* real
net worth may happen to be unaffected does not mean that such an individual
is living in the 'same world' as provided by a regime of price stability. His
socio-political attitudes will not be unaffected, unless he is uncommonly
obtuse; his behaviour will change and adapt, unless he is 'irrational'.

What are for such an individual the most salient facts about inflation sum
up to the sadly trite cliché: *Two wrongs do not make a right.* You may
happen to come out even, as the dice fall, but the game is not inherently fair.
At no point in time do its rules make sense. Besides, 'the House' will switch
them on you without warning. (That in a society with progressive income
taxes, the House also takes a cut we here ignore.)

We can see that substitutions among patterns of socio-economic activities
in two broad directions are indicated:

IV: A

Being efficient and competitive at the production and distribution of 'real'
goods and services becomes less important to the real outcome of socio-
economic activity. Forecasting inflation and coping with its consequences
becomes more important. People will reallocate their effort and ingenuity
accordingly.

The relative significance of two types of capacity for adaptation to
changing conditions have changed. The product designer who can come up
with a marginally improved or more attractive product, the production
manager who in a good year is capable of increasing the product per man
hour by a per cent or two, the vice president of sales who might reduce the
real cost of distribution by some similar amount, etc., have all become less
important to the stable functioning and/or survival of the organisations to
which they belong. Other functions requiring different talents have increased
in importance: the vice president of finance with a talent for so adjusting the
balance sheet as to minimise the real incidence of an unpredictable inflation
rate is an example. But the 'wise guy' who can do a good job at second-
guessing the monetary authorities some moves ahead is the one who really
counts. Smart assessment of the risks generated by the political game comes
to outweigh sound judgement of 'ordinary' business risks. Other roles will
gain in importance also (for reasons that we will come to). Among them is
the lawyer capable of finding ways to minimise the impact of sudden new
governmental interventions and that of the 'operator' who is quick to spot
ways of making profit (or avoiding loss) from new subsidy, quota, or price
control schemes.

In short, being good at 'real' productive activities — being competitive in the ordinary sense – no longer has the same priority. Playing the inflation right is vital.

Perhaps, we had better consider these to be primarily 'economic' rather than 'social' consequences. One had better not presume that their social aspects are negligible. But philosophising on what effects on the 'quality of life' in society may follow from changing the relative rewards of 'hard work' and 'huckstering' seems neither inviting nor promising. If we postpone these considerations until we come to the Economic Consequences of Inflation we will at least find the jargon in which to talk about them more comfortable.

One exception has to be made, however. The most important of the effects of this type will straddle the boundary between 'economic' and 'socio-political' consequences no matter how we choose to draw that line. It concerns the great majority of workers. They, too, are put in a situation where individual effort and performance at work have become a less effective way of augmenting or just maintaining family real income. The increases in wages that an individual could hope to gain in any given year through bonuses or upgrading of his job classification, etc., are of little consequence in a double-digit inflation. Collective action becomes correspondingly more important. He will have to put increasing reliance on his union.

Since the United States has a lower proportion of workers unionised than most Western countries, the 'theory' that puts the 'blame' for inflation on union 'militancy' has gained less currency in the United States than elsewhere. This should be to the country's advantage in trying to address its problems rationally, since this 'cost-push theory' basically misidentifies the forces at work, making *the* 'cause' for inflation out of what is a predictable *consequence* of inflation; namely, observably increasing union activism.[1] In any case, we should note that the association between high inflation and union activism, out of which has been conjured the inflation theory most 'popular' in some other countries, is observable also in the United States. Unions will not only bargain harder and more frequently, they will also lobby more energetically and continuously in Washington and in State capitals. This brings us to our second set of observations about the behavioural adaptations that we expect to find.

IV: B

People will rely relatively less on private contracts and relatively more on political compacts in trying to ensure for themselves a reliable frame for their economic lives.

Inflation, and particularly a ragged inflation, renders private agreements

---

[1] While this should be to our advantage in trying to understand the processes in which we are caught up, it is one that we squander by simply going witch-hunting among big business and food-chain middlemen, etc., instead. The natural sciences have got rid of 'animism' all the way down through primary school but 'social animism' still is a far, far way from falling into general disrepute.

less reliable in their outcome. Inflation also renders private agreements less 'agreeable' — shall we call it? — in the simple sense that the fact that both parties initially entered into an agreement 'voluntarily' carries much less of a guarantee that it can be carried out amicably and without rancour than is the case in a regime of stable prices.[1]

The 'economic interest' of individuals goes beyond consuming food, clothing, shelter, health care, entertainment, and so on. We all strive to control our fates, to shape our lives, and to gain some sphere of relative autonomy in the midst of a world which 'in the large' is quite beyond our control. Most of us are conscious that the trouble with unemployment and with poverty lies less in the reduced size of the 'consumption basket' — which at other times and in other places has allowed people to live content and with dignity — than in the loss of control and autonomy in this sense that individuals experience. Were it otherwise, a programme of adequate hand-outs could eradicate the social problem — a barbarous presumption.

In a regime of unstable money, it is *not* rational for people to rely on private contracts and agreements to the same extent as in a stable money regime. The substitute instrumentality is political.[2] We expect people to use their votes and lobbies increasingly to help ensure for themselves a predictable real income. Such activity may take the form of demands on the government itself for adjustment of taxes, for transfer payments, for 'free' or subsidised government-provided services. Less obviously perhaps — but more importantly, probably — we expect our 'representative' individual to rely less on competition and contractual agreements and more on legislated or administered regulation to control and constrain the activities of those other groups and agents in society on whose present and future behaviour the outcome of his own efforts most significantly depends.

The following observations seem pertinent in relation to this substitution of public political for private economic ways of goal-seeking:

(i) Consider the polity as a feedback regulated machinery. If our political institutions allow unemployment to grow, the feedback will be in unmistakable clear text: You'd better do something about unemployment or else . . . ! If they err on the side of inflation, there will be widespread and general complaining abour rising prices to be sure, but that diffuse message is quite drowned in the rising babble of *specific* demands and *concrete* proposals from *identifiable* interest groups — to compensate *me*, to regulate *him*, to control *X*'s prices, and to tax *Y*'s 'excess profits', etc., etc.

---

[1] Cf. Hicks (1975): '. . . direct economic loss and (very often) loss of temper as well'.

[2] In less developed countries, a slowing down or reversal of the movement out of the 'subsistence sector' and into the 'market economy' may be the more feasible adaptation. In highly developed industrial economies, to withdraw into economic activities the outcomes of which are largely not contingent upon what others do will not be a relevant option for any significant number of people. It is ignored here. The process of economic development is not reversible — which is not to say that a developed economy could not unravel and come apart at the seams.

The political demands triggered by unemployment are to reduce unemployment; those triggered by inflation are for the most part not obviously identifiable as 'instructions' to stop inflating. There is an informational bias to the process.

(ii) Inflation-induced political activities are not likely to be 'neutral' in their budgetary implications. The 'representative' individuals whose undeserved losses are balanced by ill-gotten gains might be expected to lobby rather earlier and rather harder for compensation for their losses than for taxation of their gains. There is then a bias towards deficits to the political game of trying to re-redistribute the redistributions *via* governmental budgets. Growing deficits will make it harder to brake the inflation down even as the realisation that it does after all have deleterious social consequences spreads. And the economy generating the taxes is not going to get better at it from the proliferation of regulations and controls — even if these were not often half-baked as such interventions go, but fully studied, carefully considered, and intelligently implemented.

(iii) The efficiency of the polity as a 'productive organisation' should also be considered, however. Is it, perhaps, subject to laws of diminishing marginal returns to input of 'issues'? It seems more than likely that inflation-induced politicking is overloading our political institutions. There are limits to what they can handle intelligently and wisely in any given session. Inflations create more 'wrongs' than legislatures can put 'right'.[1]

Much has been made in American media of the legacies of Vietnam and Watergate as explaining the obviously mounting ill-temper of public debate, and impatience with 'the system'. How big a part of the story these events make is impossible to tell. But it is simply foolish not to note that the same phenomena are prominent in other countries, such as Britain, who were not involved in the Vietnam War and have had no Watergate but who have also failed to control inflation.

(iv) The overloading of political institutions is exacerbated by another factor. Inflation will unsettle a number of political compacts and compromises reached in the past.[2] Consider minimum wages, for example. Economists are apt to think of the erosion of minimum-wage barriers to the employment of the young and of minority groups as a reminder that 'there are good things about inflation too'. But our professional disapproval of minimum-wage laws is not really to the point as long as the basic distribution of economic-political

[1] In early 1975, President Ford attempted to get action on his own proposals by portraying the present Congress as a 'do-nothing' Congress. He was rebuked by a Congressional leader who pointed out that the 94th Congress had already at that time passed a far greater amount of 'significant legislation' than was passed by any of the Congresses where Gerald Ford was Minority House Leader. The number of 'significant changes' per year in the laws governing a country would be an odd index to choose for either 'wise' government or 'health' of the polity. That number in any case is rising. But is there any indication whatsoever that our political institutions are thereby catching up with the demands for 'Justice, Now!'?

[2] Again, cf. Hicks (1970).

interests and the ways in which we have constitutionally agreed to let them take expression are as they are. All it means is that the lobbying, log-rolling, and so on will have to be done over again. With minimum wages we expect this to happen regularly, predictably, and in short order. But presumably this is not always the case. Issues regarded as long settled may be irrelevant in elections; politicians make no promises relating to them, and groups with a significant interest in them decide how to vote on other grounds. When such compacts come unstuck, the political 'equilibrium' of which they were part will not necessarily be quickly reformed. Rights and privileges won in constitutionally fair political contests become more impermanent. Thus, the polity too becomes less reliable in delivering the goods.

Private economic contracts, we know, will be concluded for shorter contract terms, and, even so, be more uncertain as to their real outcomes. Both statements can be made also for political agreements.

(v) The law and the political agreements in force embody the rights and privileges, immunities, duties and obligations that constitute the framework of social order within which individuals live their social lives and pursue their economic goals. A totally inflexible framework prevents such necessary adaptations to the social order in a changing world and will ultimately break. A totally 'flexible' one is not a social order at all. Some measure of basic continuity must be present, must be maintained. One cannot treat *all* the laws and political compacts as perpetually 'fresh' issues, up for renegotiation or open to fundamental reform in every season. This is so not so much because 'change' will thwart particular individuals or groups in achieving their goals (whatever they may be and whatever we may think of them). It is rather because some continuity is necessary for any individual to 'make sense' of his social setting, to be able simply to *set* goals for himself and his family and to formulate plans to work towards them. The rights, immunities, and obligations with which one goes to bed at night must be there in the morning and not found unpredictably reshuffled or a meaningful social existence becomes impossible.

Any society must strike and maintain a balance between conservatism (in the literal sense) and reformism.

There is a third bias to the inflationary process viewed in terms of its socio-political rather than 'purely' economic consequences that should be pointed out in this connection. Consider once again the hypothetical individual who is 'representative' of society at large in that his gains and losses from inflation balance. As long as the economic machine continues to turn out the goods in roughly the same volume, his consumption standard, etc., will not be impaired. He is suffering undeserved losses and will identify certain institutional arrangements as the instrumentalities whereby this has occurred, certain groups or organisations as the 'privileged' recipients of the corresponding gains, and certain immunities of the law as barring restitution. He will side with others seeking reform of one or more of these features of the inherited social order which he sees as having combined to produce a manifestly unjust outcome.

In the nature of the case, the set of institutional arrangements that produce his ill-gotten gains will not be (completely) the same. Those members of society that directly or indirectly are paying for his inflationary gains will be out to reform a different set of laws and political compacts.

When inflation gets into double digits by a good margin, one thus has to expect that virtually all the institutions providing the framework of economic order will in this way come under attack. To some extent, of course, they always are — there will always be critics with some following among dissatisfied groups. But normally most such 'movements' will be ineffective; at any rate, we expect only a very few of them to make significant headway at any one time. Great inflations, however, are capable of letting loose a social epidemic of effective but uncontrolled and incoherent pressures for institutional change.

For where could we expect the defenders of continuity to come from? Whence the reserves of 'countervailing powers'? Ordinary, decent, honest people will not stand up for the laws and institutions producing the gains they know to be ill-gotten.[1] Conscience forbids it and conscience, despite impressions to the contrary, is a widespread attribute. Our 'representative' individual, who has so far come out even, is not likely to defend his ill-gotten gains when they come under political attack by others; he is more likely to respond by redoubling his efforts to remove the sources of his own losses.

The 'representative' citizen will, on balance, be on the attack against, not on the side of the defence of, the inherited order.

(vi) All of the above concerns the 'rational', relatively deliberate and unemotional adaptations that people are apt to make to the experience of a rapid, but ragged inflation. But to assume that the degree to which they maintain their deliberate rationality is itself unaffected by the process runs counter to the most casual observation. The process is ill-understood by everybody; it is controlled by nobody; relatively few people will know themselves to benefit systematically, predictably, and lastingly from it. But the notion that 'somebody is behind it', somebody who is in control and who is doing it for profit will be almost inescapable to a great many people. The habit of confusing the allocation of 'blame' with the description and explanation of historical processes is almost universal. Thus public opinion increasingly acquires paranoid overtones. Opinion-making entrepreneurs make careers from such suspicions. The legislation process itself cannot remain — does not remain — entirely uninfected by irrational expressions of social strife.

V INFLATION AND RESOURCE ALLOCATION

Observations about the 'purely economic' effects of inflation — or, more accurately perhaps, about the state of our knowledge regarding them — are collected in this section. They are collected under three sub-headings; it will be obvious that these are not exhaustive of the issues. In this section, we

[1] Cf. Keynes (1972), especially pp. 68–9.

attempt to retreat in good order — hopeful of avoiding a rout — to within the boundaries of standard economic theory. Constructive discussion requires that we now obey the neoclassical 'rules of the game' — more or less.[1]

Some remarks on the relationships of neoclassical constructions to what has gone before may aid in transition:

(1) The standard model treats the economy as a subsystem whose interactions with the rest of the socio-political system may be ignored for the purpose at hand. The definition of protected property rights, permitted and enforceable contract forms, the kinds and extent of political intervention, are treated as parametric. The good x_i is x_i and stays x_i and that is that.

(2) The model leaves no room for the production manager, product designer, distribution expert, *et al.*, to whom we made reference in the last section. It represents a world without need for people whose Sisyphean job it is to try to keep you on the minimum cost curve, judge where the demand-curve is at, keep things 'running smoothly' when somebody falls sick or the coffee-machine breaks down. The 'efficient loci' are there for anyone to see and you will not drift off them if nobody pays attention.

(3) It is at least unclear whether money is needed as a means of payment on a regular basis. Transactors apparently hold it as a buffer-stock against unplanned, temporary deficits in their balances of payments on current account but the representation of the system leaves the possibility open that most debts incurred might be extinguished by the delivery of (arbitrary?) baskets of non-monetary goods.

(4) 'Money' is not needed as an aid to economic calculation. Convex production sets and convex preferences meet for a coolly tangential kiss — hygienically separated by the Cellophane of a hyperplane — without such mercantile intermediation. A huge steel corporation, say, can be just as efficiently run by calculating all values in terms of apples as the numéraire (and will, as we have seen, not be embarrassed by ending up a profitable fiscal year with a rather long position in apples).

(5) Since transactors are good at solving n-dimensional decision-problems simultaneously under 'uncertainty', they make no use of other devices for simplifying calculation either. In particular, they have no need for Hicksian 'precedents'. Of course not all the constructions of standard theory represent worlds in which memory is of no use and the global equilibrium is recomputed from freshly gathered information in a daily before-breakfast *tâtonnement*. Memory, even if limited to the some-

---

[1] In my 'Maximization and Marshall', Leijonhufvud (1974—5), I recently forswore the use of the term 'neoclassical' arguing that the conceptual differences separating Walrasians, Marshallians, and Mengerians are of greater significance to the microfoundations of macroeconomics debate than are whatever common denominators 'neoclassical' might refer to. So much for New Year resolutions. Here I need a broad blanket to cover standard micro-constructions of all sorts and, soggy as it is, 'neoclassical' will do.

what non-vertebrate capacity of storing no more than some half-dozen lagged G.N.P. terms, may well be essential to the formation of transactor's 'expectations' in such models. But *ex post* values of observed variables do not enter into the decision-rules that agents use to guide their actions *given* these perceptions of their opportunities.[1]

Fair enough. Now what is there left to say about inflations?

A: PRICE ADJUSTMENT PROCESSES AND PRICE SIGNALS

The first thing to say, surely, is that we know very little about how inflations work their way through the economy. Our empirical knowledge is scant,[2] which becomes less surprising once one notes that the theoretical work needed to lend it analytical structure has been neglected, too. The neoclassical monetary general equilibrium growth model has inflation as 'near-neutral' as makes no difference. The Austrian tradition has inflation associated with systematic and serious distortions of the price system and hence of resource allocation. It is difficult to see that we have the empirical knowledge that would discriminate between the two. My own 'hunch' with regard to present-day conditions would be that the price distortions are apt to be less systematic than in the Austrian view but none the less serious. There is no good evidence for this view either. The procedure of arriving at indirect measures of 'real G.N.P.' by index-deflation of money value data gives us little indication of how sizable the losses might be.[3] But we might entertain the hypothesis that, when 'everybody' complains of being worse off in the face of reportedly unchanged real *per capita* G.N.P., they may be right. The more popular hypotheses adducing epidemics of 'money illusion' or spontaneous outbreaks of mendacious greed are not necessarily true.

---

[1] In 'Maximization and Marshall', Leijonhufvud (1974–5), I interpret the role of the 'constant marginal utility of money' assumption in Marshall's theory of consumer behaviour along the lines hinted at in the text. Last period's MU_M – an *ex post* magnitude and hence a 'constant' – is used by the consumer to simplify his n-dimensional decision-problem and achieve what he hopes to be a good approximation of the optimal outcome. Assuming cardinal, additive utility, the reliance on MU_M makes possible sequential decisions on purchases following the thumbrule to buy if and as long as:

$$(MU_X/MU_M) = P_x^d > P_x$$

Inflation will obviously wreak havoc with this decision procedure.

[2] So scant that one is more than usually indebted to Phillip Cagan for his recent pamphlet, Cagan (1974).

[3] E.g., if we move people from 'real productive activities' into 'inflation huckstering' (or price control bureaucracies, etc.) at unchanged salaries, 'real G.N.P.' might show no significant change. Suppose, for example, that the new price-controller's best efforts are precisely stalemated by the corporate manager newly assigned to precisely this task. The work of both may, to a first approximation, end up counted as 'real service output' measured by their G.N.P.-deflated salaries.

How does the price-rise process work through the system? It depends on what type of markets we are talking about.[1]

For securities and commodities traded on the organised exchanges the usual 'auction' model is probably good enough. So these we pass over with the observation that, in the United States, the prices of (the not very oil-intensive) basic food-stuffs have in the last years severed a long, close association with the other components of C.P.I. and wandered off on their own, while individual markets — meat, sugar, etc. — show rather uncommonly severe 'hog-cycling, patterns.[2] It is not the case that everything is well in our 'flexprice' markets.

For most manufactured goods, we have 'fixprice' markets. For such market, 'my story' — obviously both impressionistic and incomplete — would go as follows.[3] An original increase in monetary demand, increases rates of sales and reduces inventories faster than anticipated. Prices, I assume, are most often not put up at this stage. Some producers may have 'sticky' prices simply because they are wary of the competition; others will prefer to 'stick' because they hope over the medium-run to cash in on hitherto unexploited increasing returns. Orders to restock are passed backwards through the chain of inter-mediate goods producers, leading to inventory reductions at these levels. At various places down the line we finally run into producers who find them-selves unable to expand output at constant cost. Now, price-increases begin to be passed forward through the same maze of interlocking customer-supplier chains. The demand-impulse comes back on the rebound as 'cost-push'. Cost increases that a supplier can be confident he has in common with his com-petitors will be passed on in fairly short order — also, I assume, by sellers who, if assured of a permanently higher turnover, would find their present prices very profitable. Reservation-wages of labour will react in the same way to cost-of-living increases. We observe 'mark-up pricing' in operation.

We know little about the overall lag-time of this process. How much 'inflation' is still in train at some date following the termination of the demand-impulse will be almost impossible to predict. This matter was probably rather badly misjudged around 1964—5 in the United States and reaction-patterns have undoubtedly adapted to the experience since that time.

Presumably, the process of inventory depletions running backward and price increases passing forward does not proceed at uniform speed between sectors and industries. In some lines of business, moreover, the practice will be to adjust prices in fairly small steps at fairly frequent intervals; in others, to use a larger step-size with longer intervals of posted 'fixprice'.

---

[1] The following discussion owes obvious debts to Sir John Hicks, particularly his recent *The Crisis in Keynesian Economics* Hicks (1974). In a fuller treatment, I would lean more than is here done on P. Davidson (1974).

[2] I am indebted to my colleague Larry Kimbell for driving home this point to me — with striking statistical illustrations.

[3] The basic 'plot' is due to Armen A. Alchian and William R. Allen (1967, pp. 86ff). Cf. also P. Cagan (1974) especially pp. 2–7. and 21–6.

Consequently, even if the inflation were balanced, it works its way through jerkily. At double-digit rates (on some smoothed average), one may expect sizable price increases on some sub-set of goods to be announced every week. What are the implications? They can hardly be discussed without at least bending the 'rules of the game' a bit.

First, of course, it becomes a bother to keep up with it all. Scale-economies will affect who does and who does not try hard to do so. Traders expecting to transact large quantities will invest considerable resources in keeping track of prices. (Still, one would not expect a 10–20 per cent inflation to be 'enough' to call forth inflation-trading specialists in large numbers – *die Gulaschbaronen* are not yet prominent amongst us). Most households will not try to maintain their stock of price-information at the 'quality' they normally desire – even as they spend more effort at it. If beef prices go up in every odd-numbered week and potatoes every even week, sensible beef-and-potato eaters will resign themselves to a constant proportions diet that is non-optimal every week – and curse the statisticians who assert their real income is unaffected by it all.

Perhaps that sort of thing is not important. But another proposition, I feel, is: *Transactors will not be able to sort out the relevant 'real' price signals from the relative price changes due to these inflationary leads and lags.* How could they? Messages of changes in 'real scarcities' come in through a cacophony of noises signifying nothing . . . and 'sound' no different. To assume that agents generally possess the independent information required to filter the significant messages from the noise would, I think, amount to assuming knowledge so comprehensive that reliance on market prices for information should have been unnecessary in the first place. Some adjustments in resource allocation that are needed will not be made. Some will be made that should not have been. Between the omissions and commissions, the vector of effective excess demands is distorted and the 'hunt' for the G.E. solution vector goes off on false trails.

Transactors will gradually lose all firm conception of where the equilibrium neighbourhood for relative prices lies. Setting prices and determining reservation wages becomes a more difficult problem – and also a problem that no longer 'makes sense' in the way it used to. We may safely assume that, even in more stable times imposing less pressing short-run information requirements, agents have not been used to consider the problem in n dimensions. Rather, your own past price was used as the main 'precedent' to be revised in the light of new information on changes in demand and on developments in a relative small set of markets – for the main inputs and substitute products. With prices 'popping all around' and in irregular sequence, such a partial 'Marshallian' method makes less and less sense – the pot in which all its *ceteris paribus* presumptions have been thrown together is boiling furiously and cannot be ignored.

Consider the task of somebody put in charge of price control. When is it safe to freeze relative prices? Not right now is always the answer. Could they be regulated by some 'rule of proportion' relating them to prices obtaining in a less discoordinated state at some date in the past? What date? Obviously, there never is a particularly 'good' one to pick. Yet, price-controllers *invariably* find themselves making decisions based on changes from some past date or dates — although the economic theory they learned at school probably never featured decision-making based on precedents. Economic agents 'at large' will have more and better information than, but possess no secrets of efficient decision-making not accessible to, price controllers.

What 'value' — in some 'real' sense — is the rest of society willing to pay for one's marginal product? We lose track of what can be expected. In the process, conceptions of what is 'fair' also dissolve.[1] In their original choice of specialisation, producers are guided by expectations of what real rewards society accords this role in the overall division of labour, what frequency of unemployment might be expected in it, how this is affected by seniority, and so on. The role is voluntarily chosen and most people are, actually, fairly well acculturated to the understanding that the real reward is not socially guaranteed if tastes change or someone comes up with a better way to make a mousetrap. The irregular changes in the real purchasing power of nominal income that occur in a ragged inflation cannot be traced to such understandable changes in what the rest of society will accord you.

We will tend to end up, therefore, with symptomatic struggles over 'fair shares'. It is not necessary to postulate that people's envy is excited by inflations to explain this. It suffices to note that the normal basis for making (reservation) price-decisions and forming income expectations has badly eroded. People are forced to look around for some reasonably simple, even though inferior, guideline. What one used to earn relative to others is it.

Beyond this point we cannot go without ending up back in Section IV. We have bent the neoclassical rules of the game here but to bring in the further complications to efficient adaptation by transactors that political feedback will cause would be to break them entirely.

B: THE FISHER EQUATION

In the models, from which it is argued that the cost of inflation is relatively trivial, the Fisher equation plays a crucial role. A full discussion of the questions surrounding this relation would ramify into all corners of monetary theory.[2] Here, I want to take up only one question. Letting $\dot{p}^e$ stand for $(1/P)(dP^e/dt)$, the relation is normally written

$$i = r + \dot{p}^e, \tag{1}$$

where i is the observed, nominal market rate of interest and r, called 'the real

---

[1] Cf., once again, Hicks (1970).
[2] Touching, for example, on several of the core issues that separate the modern monetarists from all the various macro-traditions (e.g., Mises-Hayek; Lindahl-Myrdal; Robertson-Keynes-Hicks) that accord Wicksellian themes a prominent role.

rate', is interpreted as the real return facing savers and the real opportunity cost of funds to investors.

It would be much preferable, I believe, if our convention were to write it instead as follows:

$$(r_i^e + \dot{p}_i^e) = i = (r_j^e + \dot{p}_j^e),\qquad\qquad(2)$$

where i and j denote individual contracting parties. We are dodging the additional formalism required to distinguish risk-classes and time-structures of contracts. We should think of (2) as referring to the market for a particular type of contract.

The first requirement for efficient allocation of a good is always that a single price should rule in the market. It is such an analytically trivial proposition that we get in the habit of passing quickly to more intriguing exercises in welfare theory.

Here, we may assume that *competition* establishes a unique value of i. If all individuals (somehow) perceived the same real rate in prospect, then trading in this market would go on until, at the margin of the positions taken, inflation-expectations were uniform – to put it very roughly. If inflation-expectations were uniform to begin with, then competitive trading would go on until perceived marginal real rates of return were equal. If we find it difficult to justify one *or* the other of these two assumptions, we cannot conclude that competition will produce $r_i^e = r_j^e$ and $\dot{p}_i^e = \dot{p}_j^e$ as separately holding conditions. But, presumably, one would like to establish some such proposition as part of one's case for the 'near-neutrality' of (foreseen) inflations.[1]

Consider, first, the assumption that a common perception of real rates of intertemporal transformation is autonomously given. For a Crusonia world – does the plant still flourish on the South Side of Chicago? – this makes sense. Only use of money and inflation do not. Perhaps, it might be stretched to Fisher's paradigmatic two-period case, where a homogenous present good is subject to a diminishing marginal rate of transformation into a physically identical future good. Accepting the assumption in that context amounts, however, to assuming that the pricing-process works as if 'dichotomised'. A single input, single (but transformed) output case might still do, at least if it is also point-input, point-output. But multiple stream-inputs, multiple stream outputs makes computation of 'real rates' virtually impossible to conceive of[2] – unless, of course, fixed relative prices at a constant rate of depreciation of money were (somehow) guaranteed. But that would be the second case.

---

[1] We say 'presumably' and 'some such' here because, intuitively sensible as the notion seems, it appears almost impossible to give it precise analytical formulation for the general case. Some of the difficulties are hinted at below.

[2] The economic historical literature on late-medieval, early Renaissance developments in accounting and the 'rationalization' of business methods and on the innovations in business organisation that such (*necessarily*) 'monetary calculation' made feasible is very instructive in this context.

I can see no 'mechanism' that we could plausibly adduce which would tend to bring inflation rate expectations into conformity. If we assume a world which has already been experiencing an unvarying rate of x per cent for a generation or two, one has to agree that it is plausible people will expect it to continue — unless they learn of developments that might threaten the institutional arrangements of this peculiar 'monetary standard'. The analysis of this possibility is useful for various theoretical benchmark purposes. But surely one might justifiably postpone taking it seriously as a theory of how the world behaves until such time as somebody actually brings the trick off? Here, at any rate, it is simply left aside. Without it, it is still plausible that there will be some substantial degree of conformity with respect to the inflation rate in prospect for the more immediate future — i.e., that people will share some general auto-correlation notion: 'Things won't change much overnight'. But beyond that, what can we say?

While acknowledging that more theoretical work is needed, my own tentative position is as follows. Future inflation rates are not to be drawn from one of Nature's Urns. Decision-makers can hardly assume that current observations are drawn from some 'normal distribution'. What the rate will be five or ten years down the road is 'uncertain', but it is not uncertainty in that domain of their 'natural' expertise where transactors have learned to make (implicit) probability judgements. Farmers cope with uncertain harvest outcomes. In speaking theoretically of 'decision-making under uncertainty' as a general rather than specific skill we tend to blind ourselves to important aspects of behaviour. To have learned to manage rationally despite the vagaries of weather, however, will not leave much experience applicable to coping with the consequences compounded from the vagaries of voters in future elections, of legislatures and governments, and of Central Bank responses to the contingencies that the polity produces. Nor do 'rational expectations' models provide assurance. They require an underlying, relatively swift and sure 'survival of the fittest' process anchored in relatively stable conditions of 'real scarcities' for their results to be plausible.[1] Do we have something of the same sort governing the price level?

Benjamin Klein has discussed this matter in terms of the theory of monetary standards.[2]

(1) With the old gold standard, it was 'rational' to expect (roughly speaking) reversion of the price level back to its old level following a rise or decline.

(2) From the mid 1930s through to the early 1960s or so, 'rational expectations' (for Americans) might have been to count on the monetary authorities to revert to a zero rate of change 'as soon as feasible'.

[1] E.g., the type of process we adduce in explaining to students why refraining from 'destabilising speculation' has survival-value in commodity markets.
[2] Klein (1974).

(3) Klein refers to the situation of recent years as one of a 'purely fiduciary standard'. This is a fair description — *but* how would one describe the operating 'rules' that would govern the 'probability distributions' of future price levels?

I would not even try.[1] My impression is that the international monetary 'system' has for some time been in a period of unstructured experimentation and 'innovation'. Whether this will converge to a stable institutional arrangement and, if so, what it will be like seems obscure indeed — if for no other reasons than that those doing the innovating do not understand what they are tampering with or know what their criteria of design should be.

In the United States, a transactor might listen to those economists who argue that policy should not be employed to reduce inflation, but at most to stabilise it. If he believes they rule the world, he will get unity as the lower bound to the elasticity of his price-level expectations.[2] Another transactor, looking back over the past ten years, might be more impressed with the fact that the Fed will still, whenever unemployment is 'tolerable', listen to Congressional complaints of 'high' (nominal) interest rates and take the chance to deflate. If we surveyed people's expectations about *the* price level' in 1980 — assuming that they are tolerant enough to answer such a 'dam'-fool question' — and found them bimodally distributed, who is 'irrational'?

The most plausible conjecture, I submit, is that perceived 'real rates' are not brought into line so that 'capital' is being misallocated all over. Question: Would this be favourable to the employment of labour?

Integrating the analysis of 'ragged' price-rise processes (spot and forward) from Sub-section A with that of intertemporal allocation under conditions of non-uniform inflation-expectations is left as 'an exercise for the reader'.

C: THE DEMAND FOR FLEXIBILITY

With a tax on 'money', we expect people to substitute into longer placements

---

[1] The type of 'uncertainty' envisaged in most standard economic models of decision-making under uncertainty may be illustrated by a game of dice. We know the properties of the mechanism generating the probability distribution of outcomes. If the agent does not know it — the dice may be biased, say — a Bayesian learning model may still be used to model his adaptive behaviour. For most economic decisions, the game of chess may, however, be the better source of appropriate metaphors. Here we cannot exhaustively specify all the possible alternative future positions in a game. Consequently, the 'actuarial calculus' cannot be applied to the decision-problems of the game (cf. also p. 275 and footnote 1 above).

Consider then major business decisions, the outcomes of which are crucially dependent upon the future rate of inflation, and which have to be made in a setting where no rules, ultimately constraining the rate of money creation, are accepted as 'constitutionally binding' by the legislature and monetary authorities. Observed inflation rates are not 'drawn' from a probability distribution generated by a law-abiding mechanism. The appropriate metaphor for this case, I suggest, is that of playing 'chess' in the presence of an official who has and uses the power arbitrarily to change the rules — i.e., a man who may interrupt at move 14 with the announcement: 'From now on bishops move like rooks and *vice versa* . . . and I'll be back with more later.'

[2] Cf. again, Davidson and Kregel (1974).

and to reduce non-interest earning accounts receivable. With nominal contracts more uncertain, we expect people to substitute into 'real' assets. The first-mentioned tendency would operate endogenously to accelerate inflations. If this has been happening, increasing 'velocity' has had less to do with it than expected. With regard to the second tendency, stock-markets have not been noticeably firmed up by inflation.

When the future becomes more 'uncertain', but the risk that increases is not a simple 'actuarial' one, we expect people to avoid long-term commitments in favour of more 'flexible' positions.[1] You steam slow waiting for the fog to lift (and sound your bullhorn a lot). The demand for flexibility is expressed by going 'short *and* nominal'.[2] Thus, this tendency will tend to counteract the two mentioned earlier.

That resource allocation will be affected is obvious. We will not elaborate on it. Flexibility is brought up here because I believe it ranks in significance with the two topics already discussed, not because I have anything new to say in general terms. Instead, two pieces of 'casual empiricism' plus a comment:

(a) In the United States, short rates have been plummeting since the summer of 1974. Long rates are staying up. We expect short rates to move with greater cyclical amplitude than long rates. Yet, this time there may be a bit more to it. First, the weakness of long markets is properly appreciated only when the uncommonly short average duration of the massive Federal debt is recognised. Secondly, the fall in the short rate is to some extent deceptive. Many corporations (and New York City) have had their credit-ratings written down (Aaa to Baa, etc.). Reports in the press indicate that underwriters are hardly to be found for floating Baa bonds. Some borrowing demands are being rationed out. These prospective borrowers are missing from the supply side of bond markets. Lenders are going for short *and* safe placements in this kind of market. The fall in interest rates gives an exaggerated impression of all-around 'credit ease'.

(b) In Britain, during the autumn of 1974, the inflation rate was close to 20 per cent. Yet, much of the banking system was at or beyond the 'prudential limits' conventionally deemed safe. The corporate manufacturing sector and much of agriculture were in bad liquidity straits with serious immediate cash-flow problems. Banks were unable to render further help which would require additional long lending against short borrowing. Meanwhile, the government was running a deficit such as to give a borrowing requirement corresponding to 10 per cent of

[1] For the concept of 'flexibility', cf. A. G. Hart (1951). Long neglected in macrotheory, the concept is brought to prominence and the necessity of its inclusion in our tool-box driven home in Hicks (1974) Chapter II.

With a 'simple actuarial risk', I mean in the text to refer to cases where Hart's 'compounding of probabilities' is not needed.

[2] This is what Janeway has been talking about in commercials for savings and loan institutions that have much upset American economists.

G.N.P. while, at the same time, the 'fiscal drag' from inflation was proving *negative* (and sizable). With a rate of investment lower than desirable, the country was running a balance of trade deficit equal to 10 per cent of national consumption, mostly financed by 'petro-money' inflows so short as to increase the strain on banks. Money and liquid assets were piling up in the 'personal sector' and in the portfolios of such institutions as Oxbridge colleges and insurance companies — 'earning' their holders *obviously* negative real rates. No positive *and* safe real rates were perceived. Alternative placements would include lending to transactors to whom banks would not lend or purchase of shares in corporations whose equity might be expropriated by government as a condition for assistance with ready cash.

A rather different picture from the Quantity Theory of balance inflations where one expects to find 'dollars burning holes in *every* pocket'! An economist, ignorant of the rate of inflation, taking a look at the 'real' situation by sectors of the British economy would see it as in dire need of 'reflation'.

In a 1973 article (Leijonhufvud, 1973) I outlined what was there (none to happily) termed a 'corridor hypothesis' of the adjustment capabilities of (monetary) market economies. In brief, I proposed that within some range around its 'equilibrium' time-path, such systems will tend to exhibit predominantly self-stabilising properties of the basic type that neoclassical models presume. Outside the corridor, on the other hand, (Keynesian) 'effective demand failures' would increasingly impair the ability of market homeostats to get the system back on course. Two subsidiary hypotheses, proposed in this paper, about system behaviour outside the corridor seem relevant here:
  (i) we should expect to observe the emergence of distribution effects loosening the normal empirical relationships among monetary aggregates and between them and aggregate demand; this would be associated with increasing spreads between interest rates on safe and risky claims and with increasingly prevalent rationing of borrowers with low or deteriorating credit ratings;
  (ii) in such situations, monetary policy action should be expected to be less effective than normally — and particularly if operated against the current of a contrary fiscal policy.
This 1973 paper was written, out of ivory-tower mental habit, with prolonged large-scale unemployment as the problem foremost in mind. I would now like to add to it the claim that the *Gestalt* of the theory sketched there is one that will accommodate discussion of double-digit inflation — including that stage of it where unemployment still stays safely within the 'single digits'.

VI CONCLUDING REMARKS

I have attempted to point out a number of issues that appear to me germane to the task of providing microeconomic foundations for macro-theory. Still other issues are implicit above. An attempt at systematic summary and assessment would seem to little purpose here. Readers who have actually survived to this point might, I hope, agree.

Some concluding remarks on the 'attitude' of the writer may save time in discussion. It will have emerged that I am (again) critical of general equilibrium theory and 'neoclassical' models more generally and on several counts. Among those others who share my critical view (and would add to them), some will ask why one should bother with these branches of theory at all.

When faced with methodologically profoundly difficult problems of 'relating' — never mind 'integrating' — branches of economics that for long periods have developed along separate and independent lines, the easiest posture to take is outright and wholesale rejection of one approach or the other. Almost always, I strongly believe, this will prove 'too easy' a way out. Epistemologically sophisticated and convincing cases why this or that aspect of reality can, in pure principle, not be captured *via* some particular approach will not often be much to the point. Such philosophical 'impossibility theorems' have a bad track record in the history of science. All too often, 'some damn fool' will go ahead and do it anyway and clean up his methods, or have others so it for him, afterwards.

In any case, this writer has never come close to considering 'junking' neo-Walrasian constructions. If I have been more harpingly critical of this branch of theory than of any other, it is because in its highly developed modern form it gives us something *precise* to refer to. Although my own 'beliefs' about how real world economies behave cannot be adequately represented by current neo-Walrasian models, I find that — for my 'personal use' — they provide, as it were, clear *benchmark* reference motions that I would not do without. I do not expect other critics to share this mental habit, nor is there any point in attempting to convince them that they should.

The result, of course, of trying to hang on to achievements gained by as yet methodologically incompatible approaches will be a bit of a muddle. It is easily productive of sundry analytical tangles that will be merely tiresome to others. There is no wonder at all that many economists will see the incentives to plump for one exclusive approach.

This paper is a good muddle. It will have been evident to the reader that it draws on Marshallian, Austrian, and Institutionalist as well as Neo-Walrasian sources. The predominantly critical tone towards the last mentioned branch of economics is due, in the author's mind, simply to disproportionate reliance — with attendant diminishing marginal returns symptoms — on this branch in recent discussion of the paper's topic.

The time for deciding what approach to economics should be it, I believe, is not yet. Probably pretty far off, in fact. Meanwhile, we need all the help that we can get. Drawing from disparate traditions for 'insight' means that one still accords legitimacy to 'intuitionism' in economics, even as some of its branches develop so as to increasingly resemble some sort of science.

Hence, there is still in my view an important element of 'art' in economics.

With regard to the very broad problems in particular, one is obliged to 'play it by ear'. Whether the 'chord' of Marshallian, Austrian Institutionalist, and Neo-Walrasian 'notes' struck here makes acceptable 'harmony' to others, I do not know. Yet, in trying to understand the consequences of inflation, one should, I believe, search for some such balance.

REFERENCES

S. N. Afriat, 'The Marginal Price Index Method, Parts I and II,' University of Ottawa Department of Economics, Research Paper No 21 (1975).

A. A. Alchian and W. R. Allen, *University Economics* (Belmont, California: Wadsworth, 2nd ed., 1967).

M. L. Burstein, *Money* (Cambridge, Massachusetts: Schenkman, 1963).

P. Cagan, 'The Hydra-headed Monster: The Problem of Inflation in the United States' (Washington, D.C.: American Enterprise Institute, 1974).

G. Dalton (ed.) *Primitive, Archaic and Modern Economies: Essays by Karl Polanyi* (Garden City, New York: Doubleday, 1968).

P. Davidson, 'Disequilibrium Market Adjustment: Marshall Revisited', *Economic Inquiry*, Vol. XII, No 2 (June 1974) pp. 146–58.

P. Davidson and J. A. Kregel, 'Keynes's Paradigm: A Theoretical Framework for Monetary Analysis' (New Brunswick: Rutgers University: mimeograph, 1975).

Luigi Einaudi, 'The Theory of Imaginary Money from Charlemagne to the French Revolution' (translated from 1936 original by G. Tagliacozzo) in F. C. Lane and J. C. Riemersma (eds) *Enterprise and Secular Change* (London: Allen & Unwin 1953) pp. 229–61.

M. Friedman, 'The Economic Theorist', in A. F. Burns (ed.) *Wesley Clair Mitchell: The Economic Scientist* (New York: National Bureau of Economic Research, general series No 53, 1952) pp. 237–82.

A. G. Hart, 'Risk, Uncertainty, and the Unprofitability of Compounding Probabilities', in W. Fellner and B. F. Haley (eds) *Readings in the Theory of Income Distribution* (Philadelphia: Blakeston, 1951) pp. 547–57.

F. A. von Hayek, *Law, Legislation and Liberty*, Vol. I (London: Routledge & Kegan Paul, 1973).

John Hicks, *Critical Essays in Monetary Theory* (Oxford: Clarendon Press, 1967).

John Hicks, *A Theory of Economic History* (Oxford: Clarendon Press, 1969).

John Hicks, 'Expected inflation', *Three Banks Review*, No 87 (September 1970) pp. 3–21.

John Hicks, *The Crisis in Keynesian Economics* (Oxford: Blackwell, 1974).

J. M. Keynes, *Essays in Persuasion* (*Collected Readings*, Vol. IX) (London: Macmillan, 1972).

B. Klein, 'The Social Costs of the Recent Inflation: The Mirage of Steady "Anticipated" Inflation' in *Carnegie-Rochester Conference Series*, Vol III (Amsterdam: North-Holland Publ. Co., 1976).

F. H. Knight, *The Economic Organization* (New York: A. M. Kelley, 1965).

A. Leijonhufvud, *On Keynesian Economics and the Economics of Keynes* (New York: Oxford University Press, 1968).

A. Leijonhufvud, 'Effective Demand Failures', *Swedish Journal of Economics*, Vol. 75, No 1 (March 1973) pp. 27–48.

A. Leijonhufvud, 'The Varieties of Price Theory: What Microfoundations for Macrotheory' U.C.L.A. Discussion Paper No 44 (January, 1974).

A. Leijonhufvud, 'Maximization and Marshall', 1974–5 Marshall Lectures (forthcoming).

J. S. Mill, *Principles of Political Economy* (London: Longman, 1909).

W. C. Mitchell, 'The Role of Money in Economic History' in F. C. Lane and J. C. Riemersma (eds) *Enterprise and Secular Change* (London: Allen & Unwin, 1953) pp. 199–205.

M. Polanyi, 'The Determinants of Social Action' in E. Streissler (ed.), *Roads to Freedom: Essays in Honour of F. A. von Hayek* (London: Routledge & Kegan Paul, 1969) pp. 165–79.

John Rawls, *A Theory of Justice* (Cambridge, Massachusetts: Belknap Press, 1971).

P. A. Samuelson, 'Comment' in B. F. Haley (ed.) *A Survey of Contemporary Economics*, Vol. II (Homewood, Illinois: Irwin, 1952) pp. 96–8.

P. A. Samuelson and R. M. Solow, 'Analytical Aspects of Anti-inflation Policy', *American Economic Review*, Vol. L, No 2 (May 1960) pp. 177–94.

J. J. Spengler, 'Social Science and the Collectivisation of *Hubris*', *Political Science Quarterly*, Vol. LXXXVII, No 1 (March 1972) pp. 1–21.

Appendix

Inflation and the Economists: Critique

I

About ten years ago, our collective confidence in what economists could accomplish in the area of stabilisation policy crested and we were not reluctant to tell anybody who would listen what we could do. The policy record (in the United States) since that time has been thoroughly lamentable, featuring mounting inflation and a 'stop-go' pattern of policy response of increasing severity.

II

Five times the American public has been promised a campaign to end inflation:

    (1) the 'Art of Central Banking' credit crunch of 1966;
    (2) the 'Keynesian' tax surcharge;
    (3) the 'monetarist' crunch of 1969–70;
    (4) the price freeze of autumn 1971 plus the price control 'stages';
    (5) the 1974 biggest crunch of them all.

Rounds (2) and (4), in one sense, should not count. They were interludes during which the monetary system was stoked up for a resumption of worse inflation. In another sense, they do count, namely, as parts of the pattern showing our policy-institutions consistently failing to deliver on ballyho'ed promises. The public has come increasingly to doubt that policy-makers will persevere with their stated policy-intentions and that standard fiscal and monetary policy instruments can do the job. Quite apart from exogenous complications (OPEC, etc.) therefore, our situation has become steadily more difficult to manage:

    (i) anti-inflationary policy becomes more difficult and costly to conduct, and the lags in its effects more tricky to predict, when you are playing it 'against' a public that does not believe its goals will be realised. Stabilisation policy is easier to conduct when the private sector regards the stated policy-intentions as good, strong predictors of the future state of affairs.

    (ii) The mistakes of past years have constantly buffeted the system every which way. The economy is today (spring 1975) in a more disorganised state than at any time since 1950 or so. We know a fair amount about how the economy behaves in the neighbourhood of 'full' employment and with reasonably stable prices. We cannot have at all the same confidence in our knowledge about how it will behave and will respond to

policy actions in the present situation. Our accumulated store of
quantitative information is less reliable for purposes of extrapolative
forecasting.

Round (5) — the harsh monetary restraint of last year (1974) — is now
regarded by some media commentators as having 'licked inflation' at last.
They cite the sharply reduced rate of increase particularly of the wholesale
price index in the last couple of months. Not many economists share the
view, even as we look forward to more months of the same as efforts to
reduce inventories and weak commodity markets continue. The last downward kick of the whip-saw has simply been the hardest kick so far — plunging
us into serious recession. The policy machine has already been put into reverse
and is picking up maximum steam in the opposite direction. We have yet to
see how a $80-billion deficit will be financed. The second half of 1976
and 1977 should tell whether 1974—5 was when we snapped out of inflation
or was 'merely' another phase in a time-pattern of divergent oscillations. I
think the odds are on the latter.

III

Economists have not controlled events, of course. One can tell this deplorable
story as a sequence of hard-to-handle exogenous disturbances combining with
abnormal obstacles to the formulation and execution of a consistent, coherent
stabilisation policy — Peruvian sardines conspiring with Arabian shieks to
make things difficult; first a President intent on 'guns *and* butter', then one
inattentive because of Watergate; a Congress too preoccupied with Vietnam
or Watergate to produce the right fiscal policy with short enough lags; and,
of course, the *always* accursed Fed. The 'full' story of the last ten years would
be a very complex tale indeed; obviously, having that tale told right would be
useful. But the trouble with a complex tale is that one cannot draw a simple
Moral from it.

Could it be that through this tangled web of events there runs a skein of
systematic error in policy-response? If so, why — and why not earlier? And, if
we systematically fail to do things right, does the economics profession have
any part of the responsibility?

It may be that simple Morals follow only from outright Fables. Perhaps
my impressions add up to no more than a Fable.

IV

It has become a widespread view among American professional economists
that the economic costs and social dangers of inflation tend to be grossly
overestimated by the general public and among policy-makers, particularly in
relation to the social costs and dangers of unemployment.

I disagree with this 'New View'. Indeed, I am apprehensive that the
undesirability of inflation is, if anything, underestimated by politicians, media

commentators, and the public. Hence, as an economist, I am quite untypically fearful of inflation. In any scientific field, the untypical view is most likely to be quite wrong.

But the economics profession as a whole has not done its homework on inflation. We have little in the way of well-validated knowledge about inflationary processes, such as the one of the last decade, and of their economic, social, and political consequences. Theoretical analysis and empirical research alike have been neglected — presumably *because* of the attitude that inflation is not such a serious social problem. The New View just is *not* on solid ground. Where science is ignorant, one does not get at Truth by attitudinal surveys among scientists.

The general type of statement with which I want to take issue may be exemplified as follows:

(a) 'For the purpose of abating inflation it will almost never be worth incurring any non-trivial increase in aggregate unemployment.'

(b) 'If the action required to reduce the inflation rate by 10 per cent will increase the unemployment rate by 1 per cent (for t quarters), it ought not to be done.'

(c) 'It is always better policy to stabilise the ongoing inflation rate (whatever it happens to be) than to reduce it, since the latter alternative will always create some unemployment.'

Some economists hold opinions adequately paraphrased in this manner. A probably far greater number see an obvious, serious, known social cost to unemployment while recognising that, in terms of present-day economics teaching, the costs and dangers of inflation appear uncertain, intangible and possibly trivial. The feeling that it would be irresponsible to countenance incurring known costs for benefits considered 'speculative' in nature and unknown in extent makes the policy pronouncements of this latter group for all practical purposes of the same import as the advice of those who express opinions, such as those paraphrased, with conviction.

V

The policy-making institutions are endogenous to the system the behaviour with which we are concerned. A change in the perceived ratio of the costs associated with inflation relative to those associated with unemployment will change the response-pattern of the policy-making 'sector' and thereby the dynamic behaviour of the system as a whole. A reduction in the perceived ratio of inflation to unemployment 'damages' will imply a tendency for the historical 'stop-go' pattern to change towards longer, harder 'go'-phases and shorter, more hesitant 'stop'-phases; it would make you more prone to use your major, proven policy instruments to keep employment high and to try doubtful, *ad hoc* measures to hold inflation down, 'hoping for the best'. It also brings with it a tendency toward more myopic, short-horizon decision-making on policy. The cost of unemployment that comes first to mind is that of the output irrevocably lost *right now*, whereas the benefits of price stability are those of a lasting regime. The politick 'Short View' tends to take precedence over the statesmanlike 'Long View'. You go hard for the best feasible policy-outcome *this* year and cross next year's bridges when you come to them.

Changes of this sort in the pattern of policy response can, of course, suffice to change significantly the dynamic behaviour of the system. They could account for the emergence of gradually divergent policy-oscillations around an underlying trend of mounting inflation in a system previously showing much more 'favourable' behaviour. Is this what has happened? To make a convincing case that it is would admittedly be very difficult.

A change of the ratio of perceived costs would in any case not be the whole story. Lack of policy co-ordination and an inappropriate allocation of responsibilities for 'national goals' among Congress, the Executive and the Federal Reserve has also been part of it. There was no significant alteration in these institutional arrangements in the early 1960s, however. Yet, their weaknesses did not show up in such a serious way earlier. The new attitude towards the costs of inflation, on the other hand, was gaining ground in the economics profession from the early 1960s on.

VI

Now, I 'feel' that the New View on inflation is 'unsound' and would use the same word for the various statements about the 'ratio of social costs' or the 'social marginal rate of substitution' between the two ills of unemployment and inflation. I say 'unsound' rather than 'wrong' because it is unclear whether the categories 'true' or 'false' are pertinent to them. It is no less unclear, moreover, whether categories of ethical judgement or of political preference, etc., apply to their appraisal.

They are statements of a sort that is difficult to debate. What kind of propositions are they? What are their basis? Where do they come from? The last of these questions looks easiest.

VII

The notion of a stable Phillips Curve is gone. By now, everybody's P.C. shifts and tilts and loops, now clockwise, now counterclockwise — and goes north by east when the Gods are against you. The original idea has evaporated. But it has left us a curious legacy — the empty space where it used to be. And we stay there, spinning perilous confusions in it.

The original problem was to explain the rate of change of money wages. Suppose, like other prices, they move in response to 'excess demand'. How measure it? Unemployment must surely reflect 'excess supply' of labour. Suppose observed unemployment to be a stable proxy for the theorist's concept of 'excess supply'. A resonable hypothesis that deserves a try. Phillips tried it and thought the results encouraging enough to warrant further pursuit of the general approach. But the hypothesis was falsified in the same paper where it was advanced. The 'loops' in the data and the vertical scatter at low unemployment showed that the two variables were not related by a (single-valued) function.

In a famous paper, Samuelson and Solow (1960) used a P.C. regression as the basis for a discussion of the policy-maker's 'Dilemma' — he cannot have price-stability and a tolerable level of unemployment at the same time. This Dilemma discussion set the context in which the P.C. became popularised, quickly gaining entry to the textbooks and from there into the financial pages.

The change in the perception of the Phillips-curve construct that this came to entail was of considerable significance. The Dilemma discussion tentatively treated P.C. regression results, in effect, as information about an 'opportunity set' facing policy-makers. Although this seems a natural enough extension of Phillips's attempt to predict the rate of wage-inflation from unemployment data, the opportunity set notion turned developments onto a completely new track. To non-economists the notion had tremendous appeal — the P.C., in this version, promises to dispense with the need to learn a lot of 'technicalities' of inflation and unemployment theory, wrapping up what you need to know about both subjects in one neat package. But economists too were influenced — much of subsequent research and discussion has been in pursuit of the opportunity set P.C. rather than 'merely' wage-inflation prediction.

The change in the perception of the P.C. has had two effects:

(a) It entirely changes the research question. Finding what variables will give a good proxy for the excess supply of labour and thus provide an equation predicting wage-inflation is one research task. Finding a stable reduced form relating inflation and unemployment is a completely different one. One task may be feasible and promising and the other a fool's quest. In any case, they are not the same. Much of the later P.C. literature strikes one as confused in this regard.

(b) It recast the theory of stabilisation policy as a 'choice problem' exercise in the conceptual space given by the two axes of P.C.

With (a), we will not concern ourselves. The entire tangle of problems referred to as the 'P.C. controversy' is irrelevant to what follows. We will be concerned with (b) only.

VIII

The inflation rate and the unemployment rate are considered as 'outcomes' of policy. To alternative policy programmes under consideration there will correspond combinations of the two forecast ('for next year') with more or less accuracy. The locus of these combinations is thought of as an opportunity set boundary for policy-makers. It may shift, tilt, etc., but at any given date, there it is.

The habit of thinking of any consciously undertaken action as requiring if it is to be intelligible, a preference ordering over the alternative 'outcomes' now takes over. Where there is an 'opportunity set' there must be 'tastes'. Otherwise, how could one decide at all? So a preference ordering with the 'outcomes' of alternative policy actions as its arguments must exist. Except for being defined over 'bads' rather than 'goods', why should it not have all the same general properties that give stability, convexity, etc., to a consumer's utility-function (for, say, apples and oranges)? Except, of course, that this one ought, in a democratic society, to be a 'social welfare function' — i.e., a hypothetical preference ordering over alternative 'states of society' that does not represent the policy-maker's own interests and sympathies but is derived, somehow, from similar preference orderings held by individual members of society.

Voilà. We have managed to squeeze a very complex question of what is a 'wise' course of policy for a nation into a two-dimensional conceptual space (with, let us say, the unemployment percentage on one axis and the rate of CPI (inflation) on the other). And we have partitioned the problem 'neatly' into questions of feasible 'opportunities' and of appropriate 'tastes'.

What are the consequences of accepting this conception of the problem and of purveying it in public places?

The practical consequences we have experienced and are still experiencing. But leave that aside. What twist will acceptance of the conception give to the work and discussions of economists?

The partitioning of the problem complex into questions of 'opportunities' and of 'tastes' appears very nearly to be a partitioning between questions about which one makes, respectively, 'positive' and 'normative' statements. Suppose we take it that way.

Then the economist will tend to think of his strictly professional responsibilities as confined to the determination of the 'policy options'; i.e., to the tasks of forecasting. On this side of the partition, where positive statements rule, the disciplined Popperian process of Conjectures and Refutations will operate.

Having defined the rest of the problem for himself as 'a matter of preferences' he will tend to ignore the *factual consequences* of inflation and unemployment as subjects of research. Value judgements he knows to be statements irreducible within economics itself. Economic enquiry halts where it runs up against normative propositions and does not trespass on the ground beyond them.

Since the political process does not in fact grind out a social welfare function, no one knows what it is. For an economist who looks at this as 'a matter of preferences', it is by that token also a matter on which 'everyone is entitled to his say' including, of course, he himself. At the same time, however, to such statements about what 'should be' done will apply that part of the professional credo which runs: *De gustibus not est disputandum.* Here, then, we do not necessarily expect to see a Popperian process in operation.

So when economists earnestly lecture students, newspaper readers or members of Congress on what the public good dictates with regard to the inflation-unemployment trade-off to be made next, what they say may not have been through any crucible of Popperian criticism. But they are likely to get a serious and attentive hearing anyway. Many people will defer to some degree to our opinions on the rather natural assumption that, selectively filtered through personal value judgements as these normative recommendations may be, what has been thus filtered must still be a much more detailed, objective knowledge of what inflation and/or unemployment *'means'* than laymen would possess. But is not such deference quite misplaced?

'Values' and 'knowledge' will be conflated in what they hear and read, all right. But how they are fused and how they might be disentangled is obscure. And when their expression takes the form of an indifference map in P.C. space, who is to distinguish shoddy ethics and sketchy knowledge from their genuine, warranted counterparts?

IX

The unclear fusion of values and knowledge poses a nasty predicament for whoever thinks he sees 'unsound' views gaining ground. To join debate means to get oneself entangled in the 'rules of the game' associated with this entire conception. There seems to be no avenue by which the 'real issues' can be reached that does not lead first through a quagmire of 'ideology' and what not. Fastidious aversion to mud on your face will put you on the sidelines. So one wades in.

For example: In 1973 (say), someone who had retired on a private pension in 1966 or thereabouts had already been taken for one-third of his life's savings. Stabilising the inflation rate as it was going would mean that he could only look forward to more of the same. At the same time, the unemployment rate was high but the average duration of unemployment was not yet such as to cause a substantial fraction of the unemployed to exhaust their rights to unemployment compensation. 'Cyclical' or 'non-structural' unemployment is to the individual a temporary status; he is partially compensated for it through transfer payments; he may possibly have options for investing in human capital that are profitable during the period when forgone current earnings are reduced; he may by his own subsequent efforts 'undo' some of the loss of his lifetime earnings, and so on. None of which — one is quick to add — makes his unemployment a matter of social indifference. The man on a private pension shrinking in real purchasing power will not see his current real income loss reversed; he is not compensated for it; he is beyond the age where learning additional skills or working harder will get him back 'nearly' to his pre-inflation wealth-positions.

And so on. Hopeless, isn't it? These two hypothetical individuals are not the only ones affected. They are not 'typical'. Even if they were, such arguments could not lead to conclusions with which any decent person will be compelled to agree. They cannot settle what our social value judgements 'ought to be'.

Still, as matters stand, it is *not* pointless to pursue such discussion. On the contrary, reluctant as we will be to get into such a compromising, unscientific tangle, such debate cannot be dispensed with. For it will reveal to others (and remind us) of two things. First, it will reveal the immense, tangled complex of factual consideration − meaning the fates of individuals − relevant to any responsible judgement *and* how little we know about that. Second, it will make clear to everyone that there is *no* simple, coherent, widely acceptable ethic − or, indeed, party platform − such as to enable us, once the factual consequences are taken into account, to derive general (and time-independent) guidelines of the type 'one unemployment percentage point is as bad as *x* inflation points'.

In an older tradition of scientific enquiry, that posed *Wertfreiheit* as an approachable even if unreachable ideal, the economist was obliged to keep his social values to himself and out of his work. This conception no longer rules even in the natural science fields from which it was at one time presumed to have been imported. The 'right' to state and argue for one's social value judgements is now no longer challenged. But this 'right' may be on the way to something more − to becoming a privilege with which to cloak sketchy analysis, casual empiricism, and shallow thinking on questions of gravity to the common weal − and with which to shield the basis for judgements from critical scrutiny.

X

Since disputing over tastes is so fruitless, one is tempted to try another tack. Professional training may 'pervert' an economist's attitudes to social questions to some degree, but they are naturally shaped very largely by the same influences that operate on everybody else. If disputing these attitudes is pointless and/or illegitimate, those critical of them are tempted into sociological reflection to 'explain' them instead. For example:

(i) In some not too sharply defined sense most economists are egalitarian at heart. Do we think, implicitly, of the pensioneer (again) as someone who, if he 'really' has a lot to lose from inflation, must by that token be 'pretty well-to-do'? And of the 'working classes', who risk unemployment, as *prima facie* poor? Does the reluctance to put a brake on inflation stem in part from a vague feeling that anti-inflationary measures amount to 'regressive' economic policy? If so, are the generalisations about the groups affected behind that presumption sound ones? Or, are we concerned, in this illustration, with groups that, since they differ in age, differ also in their respective ratios of inflation-taxed net worth to relatively inflation-proof human capital? And, if it were the case that letting inflation rip is indeed the progressive' thing to do, is it also the constitutionally and politically sound way to go about the redistribution of wealth?

(ii) The memory of the horrors of the Great Depression of the 1930s still runs deep in the American polity — which, until now, has not experienced serious inflation. But the economics profession is probably the particular repository of this tribal memory of large-scale unemployment — it is ingrained in assistant professors that were not born then in ways they are hardly aware of. (Meanwhile the intellectual immigrants from Continental Europe who so greatly contributed to the flowering of economics in the United States, and who *had* experienced serious inflations first-hand, have moved out of influence in Academia into retirement — promptly to be swindled out of their retirement income by inflation. Do their still active colleagues sometimes send them a grateful thought?) The view that unemployment is the worst of all social ills is the lesson American economists have drawn from the 1930s. Their advice on the unemployment-inflation trade-off is heavily influenced by it. And that advice is contributing to impoverishing the retirement years of that very generation which suffered through the unemployment years of the 1930s (and then went to war).

(iii) We used to assume that equities and other real assets were inflation-proof. One lesson of the last several years is that human capital is virtually the only reasonably reliable store of value in periods like the present. Is it just coincidence that active academics (*not* the emeriti), media commentators and 'intellectuals' in general think the rest of society makes too much fuss over inflation as a social problem? Or is it perchance the case that these groups — who conduct the public debate on social, economic, and political issues — are composed disproportionally of individuals on whose personal experience the consequences of inflation are not brought home with full force? The real value of top-grade 'intellectual' human capital is insensitive to inflations and, for that matter, unless complemented by strong political convictions, to changes in political regime. Over the last century, the 'intellectual classes' have a sorry record of toying with revolutionary notions. On occasion, the 'man in the street' will show a ready appetite for them. Ordinary people who would, on such occasions, rather keep the hell out of the street will feel differently.

XI

The last ten years have brought a spreading realisation among economists that subjective value judgements on the relative social undesirability of inflation and unemployment are not good enough and that the presumed objective components of the policy recommendations made need be brought out in the open. One result of this has been a number of simple social benefit-cost (or, rather, comparative social cost) calculations on inflation and unemployment. The early examples of this brand of Political Arithmetick have produced numerical results that, on the face of it, strongly *support* the most complacent attitude about inflation: it takes an inflation rate well into double digits or even near triple digits to equal the social cost of 1 (additional) per cent of unemployment.

Such 'objectification' of the issue compels adoption of a common unit of social cost-measurement; this, of course, is unnecessary when the problem is left in 'preference space'. The results obtained depend overwhelmingly on the choice of measuring-rod for social cost that has been made. For unemployment, the choice has been the national product loss attributable to the market inactivity of the unemployed. At first sight, this may seem a 'natural' measure for the social cost of unemployment. A second look is less reassuring. In any case, this choice necessitates measuring the cost of inflation also in terms of 'output loss' – a less obvious notion. What is thus quantified as the cost of inflation is some estimate of the productive and transactional inefficiencies associated with attempts to economise on the holding of money balances that will be induced by the negative real rate on money during inflations. This, of course, turns out to be a modest number. To the extent that inflation does not affect the size of the 'G.N.P. pie' annually turned out by the economy, it is considered to have zero social cost.

This social cost concept, then, is drawn from a social welfare function into which 'distributive justice' arguments do not enter in the sketchy, implicit, and haphazard way in which they tend to be present in expressions of 'social preferences'. On the unemployment side, the 'output-cost' is the same whether the unemployed receive compensation or not. It is similarly invariant to the time that individuals spend in an unemployment pool of given size. If one individual is 'voluntarily' unemployed and full of hope that he can do better than the employment opportunities immediately open to him while another individual in despair and resentment sees no better alternative than criminal activity – the measure of 'social cost' is the same. On the inflation side, the neglect of all other consequences than aggregate output-loss may be given a semblance of respectability by assuming (a) that redistributive losers *can* be compensated, or (b) that they *will* be compensated, or (c) that, as the inflation is or becomes foreseen, transactors will be able to safeguard themselves so as to make compensation irrelevant. None of these (including the first one) is sound on the face of it. What particular mix of the three is relied upon in these cost-calculations is not always clear. The questions left dangling are without end: How is the probability of receiving or the ability of obtaining compensation distributed among losers? What is the probability that compensation will be paid by gainers? What institutional mechanisms exist or can be conceived to carry out re-redistribution? By what methods are the gains and losses to be ascertained and accurately measured? How are the skills required to conduct one's affairs successfully in an inflationary regime distributed in society? And assuming all these things to be known and settled, can we evaluate the results as if they were 'final outcomes'? Or do, perhaps, further social consequences flow and economic implications follow from these 'given' results?

Economists who have tried their hand at this sort of Political Arithmetick have not claimed anything more than rough-and-ready first approximations. The suggestion is rather that this type of 'objectification' of 'social preferences' gives us a starting-point for a Popperian Growth of Knowledge process of successive rounds of improved conjectures and more sophisticated refutations. Some work along this line, starting from one or another specific criticism, has been attempted. It has led to no more than trivial adjustments in the 'numbers'. What it *has* demonstrated is that the earliest such calculations were rough-ready-*and-robust* with regard to model specifications and estimating methods — which is to say, it has demonstrated that the initial choice of 'output-loss' as the commensurable unit completely dominates the results.

For societies in which 'Man lives by G.N.P. alone', is motivated in his conduct only by the collective total of G.N.P., and where it does not matter who gets it, by what rules, or through what institutional mechanisms, we can take it as firmly established that inflation is a trivial social problem. Further efforts to refine and adjust these estimates are superfluous. One may accept the result mentioned as an 'arithmetical certainty'.

Given what we have thus learned, it strikes one as odd — funny, even — that historians have all but invariably been so very harsh in their judgement of those statesmen and potentates who have presided over major inflations through the ages and that they have given such 'inflated grades' to currency reformers and restorers of monetary stability. One infers that, as usual, historians have not had the right model. Having now learned better, thanks to modern quantitive methods, one must earnestly hope that our leaders will not be afflicted with an old-fashioned concern for those posthumous reputations that historians administer but will let their conduct be soundly guided by nought else than their prospects in the next election.

XII

I know I have not lived up to customary standards of rational, objective discussion so far. I feel compelled to take up these 'issues', but I *cannot make sense of them.* Not being able to make sense of what I am talking about cramps my style.

The benefit-cost arithmetic is not my basic problem. It is the more general, underlying Social Welfare Function conception — of which these 'output-loss' calculations represent a class of crudely 'objectified' special cases — that does not make sense.

Two axes metred in apples and oranges; their relative market price; the budget of an individual; his fruity tastes; a budget-line, a convex indifference curve, a tangency point — and on to a 'rational' solution to an economic problem. These are the notions that we have, by some analogy, transferred lock, stock and barrel into the conceptual space of the Phillips diagram. Inflation and unemployment are 'bads' rather than 'goods' but, *mutatis mutandis*, one naturally expects a 'rational' solution to stabilisation policy to pop out of this thing, if it is only handled right.

It is then disturbing that the policy-record does not strike one as more 'rational' since this conception took hold than it was before. Perhaps the analogy needs checking? Consider:

(i) The polity is not 'like' an individual consumer. The Crusoe metaphor, always far-fetched, fails us totally, for example. Or should we write a New Chapter? Wherein Robinson takes a house-cure for idleness, gets that sinking numéraire feeling and imposes a ceiling price on apples in terms of oranges and follows it up with an excess profits tax on oranges?

(ii) Inflation and unemployment are not 'like' apples and oranges — unless, perhaps, we are thinking of Discordia's golden apple (which may have been an orange — a tomato? — also a matter of dispute).

(iii) Are inflation and unemployment in the 'social welfare function' (S.W.F.) as indices of social discord and political unrest, perhaps? At least, such a version reminds us of the uneven incidence of costs and benefits and hence of the presence of conflicting individual interests. If A and B have directly opposing interests on a given issue, we do not ordinarily proceed by supposing that sundry conditions for the aggregation of their 'tastes' are fulfilled so that a collective utility function for the social group AB can be formed, which is then optimised to resolve the conflict.

Aggregation does not make sense. But, then, neither does the notion that individuals have preference functions that, in addition to the usual arguments, include the rate of change of some price index and the national average unemployment rate. There is nothing to aggregate in the first place. But what kind of S.W.F. is it that is not built up by some specified aggregation procedure from the valuations of individuals? How do we 'legitimise' it?

(iv) Leave legitimacy aside and consider whether this could be some dictator's utility-function. It had better be a dictator confident in his own caprice — for transitivity, convexity, etc., will not go very far towards putting together a guiding Principle of Justice. But no matter — the thought experiment allows us to ask whether there might exist an underlying general welfare theory, too complex and costly in its information requirements to be implemented but in the operational version of which unemployment and inflation serve as 'proxies' for the 'real arguments' — regrettably poor proxies, perhaps, but the best that can be done. Our dictator should be 'knowledgeable', therefore, and able to keep track of every subject's fate.

We should start from detailed state-descriptions of the system. The dictator's utility-function is defined over such States. The elements of a state-description would reflect 'how individual subjects are doing'. Not in terms of their own utility, however, but in terms reflecting their unemployment and inflation experience *separately*. Otherwise, the notion of a S.W.F. defined over unemployment and inflation 'proxies' is lost from the start.

Consider unemployment first. Imagine a vector of some millions of elements, one for each working-age, able-bodied, sound-of-mind subject. Put a '1' for employed and a '0' for unemployed. We might suppose our dictator to be ranking all such vectors and his ranking to be transitive and all that. We now notice, however, that he is neglecting the duration of unemployment, the probability of re-employment tomorrow, the distinction between 'voluntary' and 'involuntary' unemployment – and many other things. So we should proceed to remedy these errors and omissions. Unfortunately, every step we take in this direction will carry us further away from a state-description for which a count of the unemployed could be a 'proxy'. It becomes clear, in fact, that the unemployment rate is if anything worse as a proxy for the relevant welfare consequences than it is as a predictor of money wage changes. So let us drop it and turn to inflation.

Here we might, as a first step, imagine a matrix where each column-vector gives the balance sheet of a subject household. Again, let the dictator know 'how much he likes' any state thus described. Consider the matrix as our operand. Some certain inflation-rate – say, 10 per cent on C.P.I. – will be our operator. Applying operator to operand, we obtain a state transformation resulting in a new matrix. (Use of a price index, rather than individual prices, fudges the transformation, of course.) The new state has a different value to the dictator. Note, however, that we do not and cannot assign 'utility' to the operator – the inflation rate; it is associated with *changes* in the value of the S.W.F. Note also that this association is *not a stable one.* Apply the same operator repeatedly and the successive transformations obtained are *not* the same. Nor can we have any guarantee that the process will settle down, after a limited number of steps, to repeated identity-transformations in such a way that evaluation of such steady states will serve as an acceptable approximation to the 'utility' of the entire process. It may not settle down ever.

(v) In the single consumer example, the apples and oranges are 'final' and 'ultimate' consumer goods. He eats them and they are finished with. Bygone fruits are bygones and leave no lasting rot in the system. Tomorrow we start all over again with essentially the same decision-problem.

Inflation and unemployment are not 'like' apples and oranges in this respect either. With them you do not 'step into the same river twice'. Troy was never the same after Discordia's apple has been 'redistributed'.

They have further consequences. The behaviour of our dictator's subjects adapts to the experience. He needs to keep track also of another matrix (of individual 'behaviour coefficients') and evaluate the transformations that it undergoes as well. As a particular historical process unfolds, he will find, moreover, that the original matrix of balance sheets needs to be supplemented with additional information – for the property rights and contract forms that underlie its definition are themselves being transformed.

But here we may as well cease and desist, for it is clear that wherever such a search for the ultimate arguments of a S.W.F. of 'true generality' might end up, the observed inflation rate will be utterly and totally hopeless as an 'intermediate variable' in any reasonable procedure for evaluating such irreversible historical processes.

XIII

'The social welfare function is a concept as broad and empty as language itself — and as necessary.'[1] Perhaps. With any given language, though, we need some set of injunctions: 'Whereof one cannot speak . . .' etc.

The concepts of the 'New' welfare economics at one time did useful service in identifying the dangers lurking in the 'Old'. Yet, in contexts such as the present one, what makes the S.W.F. notion survive — except fascination with its inexhaustible shortcomings, so many of which will look potentially remediable?

The Samuelsonian 'necessity' of imagining a S.W.F. follows only from prior acceptance of the 'necessity' of conceptualising any problem of policy in choice-theoretical terms. Of the concepts of choice-theory we may also say that they are 'as broad and empty as language itself. . .' etc. Again, misuse of the language needs to be guarded against. Naïveté about the definition of the 'outcomes' of choice may, as we have seen, set this engine of analysis to producing the most appalling muddles. But there are more serious questions to consider beyond such abuses. Is a choice-theoretical formulation always the *sine qua non* for 'rational' conduct of policy? The 'choice' may be between irreversible historical processes that we ill understand and which we can control only to the extent that a rodeo rider controls the Brahma bull. Squeezed into the apples and oranges frame, the world is portrayed 'as if' understood and subject to precalculated control. When the 'as if' clause hides *more* in the way of unrecognised distortion than of probabilistic approximation of the situation, the 'constructivist error' is afoot. And that way lies the 'Collectivisation of *Hubris*.'[2]

We should be on guard against the type of mentality we are cultivating, or we will end up with students trained to translate human drama into jargon: Assume a young man named Oedipus X; his utility-function is quadratic, his opportunities strictly convex, and so, naturally, he . . . .

---

[1] Quoted from Samuelson (1952), p. 37.
[2] Cf. Spengler (1972).

Discussion of the Paper by Professor Leijonhufvud

Commenting on Professor Leijonhufvud's paper, *Professor Davidson* began by recalling the story that Gerald Shove once said 'Maynard has never taken the twenty minutes that is necessary to understand microeconomics'. Such stories underlay the widespread belief that Keynes did not have a proper micro-economic foundation for his macroeconomics, and therefore the continuing delusive search by our profession to find a 'new micro-foundation' which was compatible with Keynes's underemployment equilibrium phenomenon. This might, in part, explain why we were meeting here thirty-nine years after *The General Theory*.

Professor Davidson went on to say that Keynes, was, however, an excellent microeconomic theorist. He had developed a full-blown theory of markets which was an extension of Marshall's analysis where calendar time was specifically taken into account. Keynes's theory of markets, though not perfect, was an 'in calendar time' theory through which, as he indicated on p. 293 of *The General Theory*, he had hoped 'to escape from this double life' of a separate microeconomic theory of value unrelated to a macroeconomic theory of employment, money and price level and 'to bring the theory of prices [and output] as a whole back to close contact with the theory of value'. In his *Treatise on Money* especially Volume II, pp. 140–7, Keynes had spelt out his theory of markets and market institutions in great detail. In *The General Theory*, especially Chapter 6 and its appendix, as well as Chapters 11, 14, 17, 19 and 20, his micro-market theory was again spelled out in some detail (though marred by some typographical errors in the formulas). His microeconomic theory was even more obvious in the variorum of drafts of *The General Theory* which had now been published in Volume XIV (*sic*) of *The Collected Works of John Maynard Keynes*. Keynes not only presented his microeconomic theory but proclaimed it superior to others. In the *Treatise on Money* (p. 140) he had presented an equation

$$pq = xy$$

which he claimed other theories of short period price had neglected, and without which these other theories were defective. This simple equation permitted stock and flow market equilibrium to be related in a single equation. Again in a footnote on p. 55 of *The General Theory*, in his chapter on definitions, Keynes declared others had incomplete micro-theories for they inappropriately ignored user costs 'in problems of the supply price of a unit of output for an individual firm'. In sum, Keynes's microeconomic foundations had been explicitly developed from Marshallian economic theory, by looking at the relation of supply price *vis-à-vis* demand price.

Professor Leijonhufvud's paper might appear to an unsympathetic reader (who believed that general equilibrium was *the* micro-theory) as a collection of shrewd, unco-ordinated and sometimes wrong-headed ramblings, for these *obiter dicta* did not, to Walrasian eyes, have a consistent microeconomic foundation. To some at this conference this paper might appear to be poor old Axel muttering political economy (full of value judgements) in his beard. The paper might even be relevant but it did not really fit into the well-articulated Alice in Walrasland inhabited by general equilibrium theorists; and

Professor Leijonhufvud's own comments on p. 271 of his paper and Section XII of his Appendix might appear to lend support to this view. But Professor Davidson claimed that to understand the Keynesian Revolution, one could not ignore the Marshallian calendar time price theory at its core. He thought Professor Leijonhufvud's comments were well grounded on Marshall—Keynes microeconomic theory of markets as social and economic institutions, and he wanted to present an oversimplified view of this framework and to demonstrate that Professor Leijonhufvud's main propositions were based on these Keynes microeconomic foundations.

He described Keynes's micro-theory as follows: Keynes's microeconomic analysis might not be perfect (it might not even be correct) but it was the compatible foundation on which he had built his *General Theory*, as anyone who had carefully read his chapters on units, on definitions, and on the essential properties of money should know. Furthermore, one's choice of macroeconomic policy issues and conclusions was often dependent upon which micro-theory one used as his foundation. It was fatuous, for example, to evaluate incomes policies from a Walrasian perspective in which prices (including factor prices) provided signals to economic agents about allocative efficiencies of the effects of their decisions. If, on the other hand, different choices occurred in different calendar time sequences over different Marshallian periods, with inventory adjustment and changing lengths of queues providing signals, an incomes policy could be properly evaluated.

In Keynes's micro-foundations, for any good two markets existed at any point of time.

(1) Spot markets were 'stock' markets and reflected Marshall's market period analysis for a representative 'produce-to-market' entrepreneur. Such markets involved transactions for delivery at a date less than the gestation period of production so that supply was fixed by the inherited stock. This was the Monday Morning Market of a Patinkin world, where as Sir John Hicks had pointed out in his *Value and Capital* (p. 129) the connection between Mondays was never made. In Figure 9:1, D_1 was normally conceived as the demand of final buyers for the needs of week 1, but in a full treatment D_1 should also include the reservation demand of sellers when the 'week' involved a time period less than the

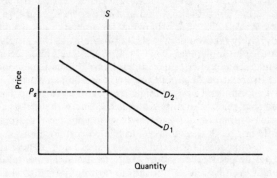

Fig. 9:1

gestation period of production. All prices such as p_s represented the equilibrium price vector of spot prices which under the usual background assumptions was Pareto-efficient. If the demand of final buyers increased in week 2 to D_2 then price adjusted 'instantaneously' in this *flexprice* Market. (This was true *only* if one ignored the reservation demand of sellers and how they reacted to an increase in the demand of the public.) If, however, sellers had the function of maintaining 'orderliness' — as in financial spot markets — and if sellers assumed that the increase in final buyers' demand was temporary, they might reduce their reservation demand to stabilise p_s. Thus the *flexprice* view of spot markets ignored the institution of 'market makers' whose function might be to make a continuous orderly market.

(2) Forward or flow supply markets for producible goods represented Marshallian short-run phenomena, for a representative 'produce-to-contract' entrepreneur. If forward markets for producible goods were well-organised and competitive with well-advertised prices associated with future delivery dates, then producers could operate as neoclassical 'price-takers' and maximise profits. In the real world of manufactured, branded goods, such forward markets were not well-organised and were made by producers themselves via their holdings of shelf inventories. (Prices in forward markets for non-reproducible goods depended wholly on speculation of future spot prices.)

In Figure 9:2 d_1^e represented the entrepreneurs' expectation of the demand of the public for next Monday's market, while s represented the traditional

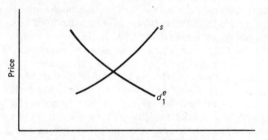

Rate flow associated with a given delivery date

Fig. 9:2

Marshallian flow supply schedule based on Keynes's 'wage unit' cost of production approach. (In the real world, in a non-integrated chain, most production occurred via a produce to forward contract basis. Marshall's spot market — his fish market analysis — was hardly representative of the most real world production markets.) Following Keynes's theory of markets we could integrate Figures 9:1 and 9:2 in Figure 9:3 and suggest that any point of time (say Monday of week 1) final buyers could either buy spot at a price of p_s^1 or put in an order to buy forward (delivery later in the week at the gestation date) at a price of p_f^1. If the good was scarce, $p_s^1 > p_f^1$ as the spot price rose to a premium sufficient to encourage some buyers to place orders for forward delivery.

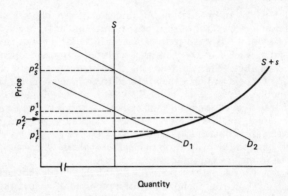

Quantity

Fig. 9:3

If final demand was higher than D_1, say D_2, the spot price would 'instantaneously' rise to p_s^2, an increase which was directly proportional to the increase in demand. (If this was occurring throughout the economy, this was what Keynes called *Commodity Inflation* which resulted in capital gains.) The forward price would increase from p_f^1 to p_f^2 only if the elasticity of supply was less than infinite as long as the height of the s curve was unchanged; i.e., as long as the money wage relative to productivity ('the wage unit') was sticky and sellers did not expect an increase in user costs. Thus an increase in demand, in Keynes's micro-theory, inflated spot prices, but might not affect prices of newly produced goods in the near future if the elasticity of supply tended to infinity and money wages were sticky. (The latter would be true if labour had contracted forward and the duration of the wage contract exceeded the duration of the gestation period of production.) If, however, the money wage rose relative to productivity (or the profit mark-up increased) then the s curve would shift up leading to what Keynes termed an *Incomes Inflation*.

In the case of non-reproducible goods (i.e., non-reproducible via the use of labour inputs) only spot markets might exist, or if futures markets did occur their price was based on current expectations of future spot prices of these goods. Thus for non-reproducible goods, we had a bootstrap theory of value. For most reproducible goods, however, both spot and forward markets would exist, at least conceptually. Professor Shubik had quite rightly reminded us that many spot markets might be very thin or even notional.

Professor Davidson claimed that such a micro-theory underlay Professor Leijonhufvud's *obiter dicta*, for several reasons:

(1) As Professor Leijonhufvud had argued (pp. 266–7) institutions were important, especially in understanding the law of contracts in the various spot and forward markets. What gave money liquidity was the institution of contracts in money terms for forward delivery, especially long-duration wage contracts. For if the current spot price jumped, if wage contracts remained intact, this would induce inelastic expectations about costs of production (and therefore prices) of goods to be delivered at the gestation date.

(2) Since there were overlapping *seriatim* forward contracts in money terms,

the value of scarce producible goods were grounded in their costs of production as long as buyers were willing to wait for delivery. Thus what gave value was not 'precedents' as Professor Leijonhufvud claimed (p. 271) but 'the wage unit' and the willingness to wait.

(3) Professor Leijonhufvud's continual emphasis on the connection between inflation and the law was, he thought, fundamentally correct. The law of contracts in nominal terms was what gave money its liquidity. Contracts were an institutional device to help man face an uncertain future. Production took time. Employment contracts and forward sales contracts in money terms were the institutional devices used by the 'free market' to maintain wage and price orderliness or wage-price controls over time. Businessmen abhorred what general equilibrium theorists loved, namely recontracting. When the law of private contracts broke down so that the duration of the labour contract shortened to less than the gestation period of production, then no entrepreneur would take a 'long position' in production, and only spot markets would remain. Thus a social contract was necessary when the institution of private contracts broke down, so that production could be undertaken.

(4) It was, he thought, essential that the law refused to recognise inflation in enforcing contracts, since production took time and someone had to contract in money terms if production was to occur — unless we were going to have either a completely centralized and/or a non-monetary economy. As Keynes had pointed out on the first page of his *Treatise on Money*, money and contracts were intimately related.

(5) Fully anticipated inflation would mean the immediate increase in D_1 to say D_2 in Figure 9:3, as such anticipations increased the marginal efficiencies of all durables. Thus fully anticipated inflation would have an instantaneous impact on all spot prices leading to a *Commodity Inflation*.

(6) Indexation would result in an increase in the wage unit if any random shock touched off a change in D_1 or S in Figure 9:3. The result would be to transfer a Commodity Inflation into an Incomes Inflation by changing the height of the s curve. Thus, as Professor Leijonhufvud had pointed out, indexation (if the lag was short) would institutionalise an elasticity of expectations of unity, thus precariously balancing a money economy on a knife-edge of potential instability. In his classic study on the *Economics of Inflation*, Brescioni-Turroni had presented dramatic evidence that the increase in indexing in Germany during the latter half of 1922 and most of 1923 had permitted the economy to settle down to an almost constant rate of inflation of 400 per cent per month. Such indexed contracts did not stabilise the economy: they led to the breakdown of all production commitments and the collapse of the monetary economy.

Dr Sweeney pointed out that he had heard Professor Davidson use the word 'money' in two different contexts, money interest and money wages: it seemed to him strange that 'money' was used only as an adjective rather than as a major, if by no means sole, explanation of inflation. He agreed with Professor Davidson about the effects of indexation.

Dr Nuti pointed out that although it had been said on the previous day that whatever the process by which an economic system had become a monetary system it was very hard to get out of once money was introduced, there *was* a way to get out of the monetary system, namely by indexation. With respect to the German hyperinflations, although there had been monetary expansion, the fact that Germany had lost a large part of its productive capacity to France might have been relevant too.

Professor Parkin thought that it was difficult to know where to begin when commenting on Professor Leijonhufvud's paper because it contained so much material; at the same time he had felt some irritation, because he had had to keep making connections with earlier literature. Professor Leijonhufvud had been unwilling to adopt the distinction between an inflation which was anticipated and one which was not. Although there might be no such thing in the real world as a fully anticipated inflation, it was, thought Professor Parkin, a useful analytical device. Much of the literature that Professor Leijonhufvud had criticised did not in fact trivialise the costs of inflation, even though it dealt only with the costs of anticipated inflations.

The central clue of Professor Leijonhufvud's paper that Professor Parkin liked very much was the notion that when there was a rapid inflation in progress, prices would be jumpy, and relative prices would be changing all the time, providing an incentive to wasteful activity. But concerning the costs of inflation, Professor Leijonhufvud's approach had been too negative in the light of the accumulated literature. Professor Parkin believed that the message of the 900 articles he had read over the last year for a survey article (Laidler and Parkin, 'Inflation: A Survey', *Economic Journal*, December 1975) was that there was probably a fairly predictable demand function for money which had a relatively low interest-elasticity. That had implications for the transmission mechanism from changes in the money stock to nominal output. A large amount of empirical work had looked for the proximate causal connections between inflation anticipations, excess demand, and the rate of wage and price change, and had provided fairly definite results for the American and British economies. The literature which had approached the problem from the view that social-pressure type factors were crucial was entirely conjectural. These findings together with a stable demand function for money led to the prediction that inflation was generated by variations in the stock of nominal money. But we still had to worry about the supply of money, in other words the behaviour of governments. On this Professor Parkin liked what Professor Leijonhufvud had said in his paper, but wished that he had put it into the context of the recent work on inflation. One could analyse the costs and benefits to the government of inflation and associated variables: it seemed apparent that governments had been taking advantage of the lag in inflation to create booms before elections; it was also apparent that governments had been aiming for a level of unemployment that was inflationary.

Professor Frey approved of Professor Leijonhufvud's approach which tried to see inflation not merely as a purely economic matter, but as a phenomenon which had to be analysed within a broad socio-political context. He made two critical remarks:

    (1) When Professor Leijonhufvud analysed the impact of inflation on the
        political process, he omitted to mention the costs of *stopping inflation*,

which might be very heavy. Inflation could serve as a rather efficient 'social mollifier'.

(2) Professor Frey agreed with Professor Leijonhufvud that economic theory should move away from being *only* traditionally neoclassical, but he believed this for reasons different from those that Professor Leijonhufvud had given. The naïvely individualistic approach should be abandoned, and the ideas of economists such as Boulding, Leibenstein and Kornai should receive more attention. Furthermore, it was not true that once one entered the socio-political sphere one left neoclassical economics: there was a large body of literature, namely non-market economics and the economic theory of politics, in which rigorous neoclassical theory *might* be applied to socio-political problems. In fact, it had been usefully applied to the interrelationship of inflation and political processes. One example was the so-called election and popularity functions, which were in Professor Frey's view the nearest one could get to an *empirical* estimation of the welfare effects of inflation and unemployment in a democracy. These empirical studies (for example, Kramer for the United States, Goodhart and Bhansali for the United Kingdom, Frey and Garbers for Germany) had shown that there was a significant effect of both inflation and unemployment on election outcomes and government popularity. Professor Frey wished that Professor Leijonhufvud had included these and other empirical and theoretical results of the economic theory of politics in his analysis.

Professor Spaventa missed any mention of international economics, at the conference in general and in Professor Leijonhufvud's paper on inflation in particular. Although he did not have completely definite ideas about the precise causation of recent phenomena he was quite sure that the inevitable collapse of the international monetary order which had ruled us until the end of the 1960s had much to do with the predicaments which concerned Professor Leijonhufvud. He was aware that the international side of the problem could not be dealt with in purely economic terms, but since Professor Leijonhufvud had made a special effort to take a wider look at the problems of inflation, Professor Spaventa was disappointed that his reference to international problems should be confined to the whims of Arabian sheikhs and Peruvian sardines. In every European country the external component of inflation had been remarkably large. Was this merely a feedback or was there not something more important, in the shape of exogenous factors, and were not such exogenous factors partly due to international monetary causes? International monetary disorder was still with us, and suggestions for more co-operative solutions had been dismissed. The longer-run danger we were now facing was that of ever more frequent wild fluctuations of the terms of trade between primary commodities and manufactures as a result of inflations and recessions in the industrialised world. This was due to the inherent contradictions of the present system. Unless we set about trying to correct these contradictions the quotation from Lenin in Professor Leijonhufvud's paper might turn out to be correct!

Professor Streissler was not sure whether Professor Leijonhufvud's contribution applied to low-digit inflations. What was the critical point on the inflation scale? In Austria Professor Streissler had witnessed two-digit inflations which had changed absolutely nothing in the real world. While Professor Leijonhufvud seemed to suggest that there was much less un- certainty when there was *no* inflation, Professor Streissler pointed out that entrepreneurs also had difficulty in making decisions in non-inflationary situations during rapid economic growth. As a trained lawyer, he also did not entirely agree with the meaning which Professor Leijonhufvud had given to the idea of the rule of law. The main point of the rule of law was the freedom of contract; laws usually only stated that it was not legitimate for one party to a contract to try to get the better of the other party to the contract in a reprehensible way. The fact that index clauses were not used was a case of *caveat emptor.*

Professor Jané-Solá agreed with Professor Frey that inflation and its solution were more than economic problems but social and political ones, as Professor Leijonhufvud had pointed out. On the subject of indexation, there had been much discussion in Spain recently, in which he and Professor Segura had been involved. The main question under discussion had been whether indexing was an instrument of the Left or of the Right. In France, for example, Socialists and Communists were in favour of full indexation; in Spain Professor Segura thought that indexing was an instrument of the Right, while he himself believed that indexation would benefit workers and fixed-income receivers. He would be interested to know Professor Leijonhufvud's opinion.

Professor Marty thought that Professor Leijonhuvud's interesting paper was marred by its attack on the 'inflation tax' analysis, since that analysis did not trivialise the cost of inflation but rather condemned the use of monetary expansion to raise real resources for the government as an inefficient form of taxation. He reminded us of the positive propositions that this literature had substantiated through detailed empirical work; he believed these were of the first moment in understanding the causes of inflation as well as its welfare costs:

(1) The primary cause of inflation was an expansion of the nominal money supply, which had its roots in a government budget deficit. The way this increase in the money supply worked its way through the system affecting first real output and then, with a lag, prices was, as Professor Leijonhufvud had pointed out, worthy of more detailed empirical analysis.

(2) There was no evidence that the system was unstable in the sense that with a steady rate of monetary expansion price rises tended to accelerate.

(3) Under the heroic assumption that the rate of price change was fully anticipated and that all contracts and institutions except money were indexed, it was possible to determine the rate of monetary expansion at which the revenue from monetary creation was maximised and to determine the welfare costs, which could be measured by deadweight loss triangles.

Although inflations were *not* fully anticipated, and institutions did not adjust, one should not just throw up one's hands at the heroic nature of the assumption and label this analysis trivial, because it was *part* of the story of inflation and it gave hints as to where to expand the analysis. In the first place, the assumption of fully anticipated inflation was a strong one, implying that everyone held the same point expectation of inflation with zero variance. The triangle measures of welfare loss did not make sense when the variance term was changing or when the actual rate was not equal to the expected rate of inflation. Perhaps some extension of mean-variance analysis was needed to get a grip on this important aspect of inflation. Further, how did one aggregate the probability distributions of different individuals? Thus it was the assumption that the actual was equal to the expected rate of inflation that was the distressing one; this was surely because it was when this assumption was violated that people went short and held liquid assets at negative interest rates. But the really interesting question was whether things changed systematically when we deviated from a stable price level. What was so magical about the number zero that constant prices were more desirable than some anticipated price trend? Was it easier to anticipate constant prices? Was there any rational expectations model which told us that the confusion between relative and absolute price changes was less when the rate of monetary growth validated a constant price level as compared to any steady rate of monetary growth?

Professor Marty then considered the policy choices that are open to us if we have an excessive inflation rate. Suppose that we tentatively accept the natural unemployment rate hypothesis. Then if the authorities are attempting to validate a level of unemployment below the natural rate, we will have accelerating inflation. Alternatively, suppose we are at the natural unemployment rate with the actual rate of inflation equal to its expected rate. The welfare costs at this point are only partly measured by the inefficiency of the payment matrix. To claim this is the whole story *is* to trivialise the cost of inflation; even though the actual inflation rate is equal to the expected rate *now*, it was not when some contracts were written. As Professor Leijonhufvud rightly insisted, there was an overhang of history. The authorities could try to lower the inflation rate, but this would result temporarily in a loss of output and employment. The natural rate 'scenario' would have us weigh this temporary loss of output against the benefits of a permanently lower inflation rate, and this weighting depended upon the social rate of time preference: the lower that was, the more heavily the gains from steady-state lower inflation would be weighted as compared to the temporary unemployment.

There was, however, reason to doubt that this scenario captured the salient choices facing the authorities. For it treated the loss of output and employment as temporary and assumed there were no hysteresis effects. Professor Leijonhufvud, although he had rightly stressed the overhang of history in the case of inflation, had treated unemployment differently; he had written,

'Cyclical' or 'non-structural' unemployment is to the individual a temporary status; he is partially compensated for it through transfer payments; he may possibly have options for investing in human capital that are profitable during the period when forgone current earnings are reduced; he may by his own subsequent efforts 'undo' some of the loss of his lifetime earnings, and so on. None of which — one is quick to add — makes his unemployment a matter of social indifference.

Remembering that an unemployment rate of, say, 8 per cent implies a much higher rate for blacks and other minority groups and for new entrants to the labour force, Professor Marty was less sanguine about the reversible effects of unemployment. When employment was low, some loss of human capital might well be irreversible. Symmetrically, during periods of tight labour markets (for example during the Second World War) an upgrading of skills occurred with unskilled labour moving into semi-skilled and skilled grades; also unions became more willing to loosen entrance requirements. We needed more detailed empirical evidence on the effects of unemployment and the reversibility of these effects.

Professor Nell seconded Professor Marty. He also raised three points:

(1) He questioned the monetarist theory of inflation as an instrument for analysing inflations. There were very unequal rates of price increase in different sectors and unequal rates of increase of a general price index compared with a general increase of wages; and a divergence between the rate of increase of a price index and the rate of increase of a wage index was a classic cause of changes in distribution. This had been analysed by such people as Kaldor and Joan Robinson, and it played an important part in their theories of distribution. Professor Nell thought it was worth calling attention to that and pointing out that sometimes the changes we described as consequences of inflation might be related to a shift in distribution which was related in turn to a process of adjustment of aggregate demand.

(2) One might consider a similar kind of shift in the relations between sectors; Professor Nell suggested that one should consider some of the effects which we described as inflation as relative price changes. There were rigidities in the economy; for example, fixed capital was employed which could not very easily be replaced. Policy changes and exogenous shocks led to pressure on fixed capital. This was a simple and obvious point but in thinking about microeconomic foundations we should take into account the fact that we were dealing with short-run phenomena and did not have malleable capital.

(3) With respect to the social and political consequences of inflation, Professor Nell thought that Professor Leijonhufvud perhaps ought to consider whether or not the social and political consequences which he mentioned would be different if he crossed out the word 'inflation' and replaced it with 'relative price change'; for example, a change in the relative price of oil. Any major economic change had social and political consequences: were the consequences described by Professor Leijonhufvud peculiar to inflation? We were perhaps led to overlook the fact that a relative price change in an important commodity could have significant social and political consequences by our simple theories of supply and demand, which were based on unrealistic assumptions of easy substitutability.

In answering the queries of Professors Streissler and Spaventa, *Professor Leijonhufvud* agreed that his paper had been rather full of references to the situation in the United States and that, as Professor Spaventa had pointed out, he had confined his discussion to the consequences of inflation internal to a country. He had been aware of that; it reflected concerns that he had had prior to writing the paper; having chosen a rather 'institutionalist' approach to the subject, he had found it impossible in the last revision to erase the references to the United States; it would not do to pretend that the analysis in it was 'general' enough to apply to countries with quite different institutional arrangements.

Professors Marty, Parkin and others had raised a set of interrelated questions: Did he (Leijonhufvud) intend to deny the possibility of steady-state foreseen constant-rate inflation? Could it really be argued that the variance between individuals of expected inflation rates was necessarily larger for a 10 per cent inflation than for a zero rate? What was so special about price stability? Did not that in the end become pure mysticism? Professor Leijonhufvud pointed out that in his paper there had been several statements to the effect that the anticipated inflation model was a useful contribution, particularly as an analytical benchmark case, but would acknowledge that beyond that he had given short shrift to it. He did not want to give this piece of modelling undue prominence in the discussion of actual inflations as long as we did not have a clear and dependable policy-recipe for bringing about a state of, say, a 10 per cent foreseen inflation rate (and saw that recipe actually being used). It would be rather silly to deny this case as a possibility. But in terms of (his subjective) probabilities, he would argue that in order to settle the economy on a 10 per cent foreseen inflation path (where the main effects are due simply to the tax on base money), just keeping the inflation-rate at about 10 per cent for a few years was not enough. If people were to extrapolate that rate with confidence five, ten or twenty years into the future, something like a *monetary constitution* — a set of easily-understood rules seen by the public to be binding on the central bank and on politicians temporarily in power — would be needed. In other words, we would require a new monetary standard with the peculiar property of guaranteeing 'stability' around a 10 per cent average inflation rate.

A second reason for not giving the model prominence was that if we supposed that the task of setting the system on such a constant-rate de-preciating standard had been somehow accomplished, then in such a situation it ought, as far as he could see, to be the case that a currency reform switching the system from a 10 per cent to a 0 per cent rate of depreciation should be just as easy and just as 'neutral' as a currency reform that moved the decimal point on everything nominal one or two steps to the left. If one could issue one new Franc for every 100 old Francs without much ado, could one not just as well issue 'new dollars' appreciating at 10 per cent a year relative to 'old dollars' without sending the system into a major depression? Professor Leijonhufvud would tend to regard this thought-experiment as an informal, judgmental test-case for the empirical relevance of the foreseen inflation model. If the model were descriptive of current conditions, then — or so it would seem to him — such a currency reform should solve all our problems.

With respect to the critical remarks by several participants which raised the question of the causes of inflation, Professor Leijonhufvud wished to plead the title of his paper: he had intended to separate the issues into the causes *versus* the consequences of inflation and to discuss only the latter. In this connection, Professor Parkin had objected to his characterisation of our knowledge as 'scant'; Professor Leijonhufvud did not wish to side with those agnostics who 'felt' our knowledge of the causes of inflation was scant. As for bringing in the breakdown of the international monetary system, and also the behaviour of governments to explain the causes of inflation in individual countries, as requested by Professor Spaventa and Professors Parkin and Frey respectively, his answer had to be that, though he recognised the importance of these things, he could not see his way to incorporating them without making his paper even longer than it already was.

In reply to Professor Davidson, Professor Leijonhufvud said that he had not argued that 'Value' depended upon precedents, but only that reservation prices in the short run would be set using precedent as a source of information. He had appreciated Professor Marty's raising some of the questions which he had expected to face from Professors Phelps and Tobin, had they been able to attend. Professors Marty and Nell had found in his paper a perceptible attitude of ruthlessness towards unemployment and its social incidence. But 80 per cent or so of his previous work had concentrated on involuntary unemployment and he would not now turn about to trivialise that phenomenon. On the social costs and the incidence of unemployment he had nothing new to say: his views were probably much the same as everyone else's. It was the 'New View' on the costs of inflation that had concerned him and which he wanted to discuss. Having paid the devil his due, he (Leijonhufvud, that is) wanted to pay attention also to the deep blue sea.

In the Appendix to his paper he had stressed the way in which the rules of professional discussion had been narrowly drawn by putting the entire discussion into the Phillips curve framework. As a consequence, it had become almost impossible to turn to the analytical and empirical issues concerning the consequences of inflation without first trudging through a quagmire of 'social welfare judgements'. One simply had to be resigned to some of that mud sticking.

Professor Leijonhufvud agreed with Professor Nell that much of what he had to say about the social and political consequences of inflation could be said about any major shock to the system; indeed, his main point had been that inflation had to be classed among such major disturbances; if that point was granted, he would be satisfied.

He also agreed with Professor Streissler that uncertainty was always present and that miscalculation of individual prices could be of more importance to individual agents than the effects of double-digit inflation. One of the problems with indexation was that two agents might find it difficult to agree on one basket of goods as the unit of contract because they specialised on the production side and would want to give their respective outputs a high weight in the composite basket; the 'relative price noise' in the system during rapid inflation could aggrevate this problem. However, Professor Leijonhufvud thought it inadequate to talk about decision-making under uncertainty as though it were a generalised skill. There was a distinction between ordinary business risks, where outcomes might be drawn from a stable distribution obeying the 'law of large numbers', etc., and the uncertainties to be faced in trying to 'second-guess' the monetary authorities. Herbert Simon had pointed out that it was impossible to model the play of a good chess-player using the standard decision-theory framework so that a computer could simulate his play; inflation had some aspects which were more analogous to the uncertainties faced in playing chess than to the risks in choosing lottery tickets. Indeed, without a binding monetary constitution, one of the consequences of inflation was to put agents into a decision-making situation similar to that which would be faced if one were playing chess while someone stood by with the power to impose erratic changes in the rules of the game and was exercising that power at erratic intervals while the game was in progress!

Professor Davidson, referring to Professor Parkin's comments about fully anticipated inflations, raised the question of why people held financial assets which *ex post* had negative real rates of return, and said that Keynesian theory could explain that. In *The General Theory*, pp. 160–1, Keynes had said that people would not hold real assets in their portfolios because they wanted liquidity and the possibility of resale in spot markets. (There was a market-maker in spot markets but not in the markets for fixed capital goods.) In a real world monetary economy, even in a period of inflation there are economic agents who wish to store current income claims without committing them-selves to purchase a specific good at a specific future date. Such agents seek liquid stores of value; i.e. low carrying cost durables which can be readily resold in spot markets. Since market-makers do not exist for most spot markets in real assets such as fixed capital, such durables do not possess liquidity; hence fixed capital goods are considered inferior stores of value by precautionary economic agents desiring liquidity even if the real rate of return on such real assets exceeds the rate of return on liquid financial assets (even if the latter returns are negative).

Commenting on the appendix to Professor Leijonhufvud's paper, *Professor Koopmans* said that inflation and unemployment clearly affected different groups differently; he agreed with Professor Leijonhufvud that optimisation was not appropriate for analysing this. One needed what one could call 'impact indices' for each of the different groups affected by a policy which struck a balance between the two phenomena. Having been impressed as a newspaper reader by the political weakness of a number of governments in countries with parliamentary representation in recent years, Professor Koopmans had asked himself whether there was a connection between that and the phenomenon of inflation, since in this situation a government was very vulnerable to threats of withdrawal of support depending on the policies it pursued. There was an element of a trap in such a situation because while it might be in the common interest to work out a compact the situation did not make that easy to bring about. He suggested that the analytical need in order to achieve such a compact was for economists to provide each party or pressure group with as accurate an assessment of alternative policies, in terms of their effect on all concerned, as could be produced. When it came to aggregation, the most pressing need was aggregation over time for the individual or the group rather than aggregation over groups: the effects of both inflation and unemployment were cumulative over the duration of either, and cumulative for the individual as well as for the interest group that he belonged to. Aggregation over time was the first priority because the weakness of the government decision process led to shortness of horizon: the analysis should trace the effects of the various policy proposals over, say, ten years on each of the groups as well as types of invididuals within their lifetimes. Professor Koopmans asked Professor Leijonhufvud whether any such studies had been made. *Professor Leijonhufvud* replied that he had seen two such studies, but they suffered from not con-sidering the effects over time.

Professor Harcourt made three points:
(1) One of the consequences of inflation was that a state of unexpected inflation tended to institutionalise dishonesty. People learned at differential rates that it was a good thing to borrow and a bad thing to lend; as this became general, the interest rate effects seeped through the economy.
(2) In Australia indexation was a product of the Left.
(3) We must not forget that indexation by itself was certainly not a cure for inflation. It had to be part of a package deal intended to induce people to practise money wage restraint; sacrifices had also to be seen to be exacted from other sections of society.

Sir John Hicks believed that the subject was one of those matters which we could not get right if we looked at it abstractly and in an essentially time-less way. His own general picture of what had been happening was that we had started off with 'Keynesian' policies and a willingness to expand effective demand in order to create full employment. At the first round, the policies were very successful but they depended essentially upon 'money illusion', upon some class of the community believing that they could on the whole continue to work in terms of stable prices. As time went on that gradually broke down. In the British case, the expectation of some stability in prices disappeared first in relation to the Stock Exchange and purely financial trans-actions, and then gradually extended to trade union bargaining. Thus we arrived at a situation which was not so dissimilar to the expected inflation model and which, as Professor Streissler had observed, could under certain conditions be reasonably stable. But it was essential to recognise that it was basically an extremely unstable situation, because any major change in external or internal affairs could upset it. What seemed to have happened in face was that the rise in raw material prices in the early 1970s upset that equilibrium in many Western countries. When we had reached that point, it was difficult to know how to proceed; to return to even a stable 10 per cent rate of price rise seemed difficult. If governments stabbed at the problem, the result would be falls in productivity even if there was no increase in unemployment; on pessimistic assumptions inflation would in fact only come to an end when productivity had fallen so far that people found the fall quite intolerable.

On the costs of inflation *Professor Malinvaud* associated himself with what Professor Leijonhufvud had written in his paper. He thought that economists had in the past underestimated the costs of inflation, partly because we had not believed that inflation would become as rapid as it had in fact become. Among the costs of inflation, the difficulty of reducing inflation was one that should not be overlooked. When we took into account the costs of inflation we did not have to underrate the costs of unemployment One of the features of our capitalist economies was that we were faced with the costs of unemploy-ment and the costs of inflation and we had to cope with both of them. When he had looked at the French economy in the immediate postwar period, Professor Malinvaud had observed that the prices of basic commodities were revised in a disorderly manner; the increase in the erratic movements of relative prices should not be neglected when we were considering what inflation was doing to our economic system.

Professor Malinvaud did not believe that indexation was a way of stopping inflation; it might be something which had to be expected once one gave up the idea of fighting inflation or it might be something that would assist social acceptance of other measures to reduce inflation. In itself it made it more difficult to stop inflation, and that was why governments were resisting the pressure for the introduction of generalised indexation. In France wages were in fact indexed, even if not legally, by clauses in most wage contracts; what was under discussion was indexation for loans, which was being resisted because of the fear that this would make it more difficult to resist future inflation spurts.

Professor Parkin agreed with Professor Malinvaud that indexation on its own was not a way to stop inflation, but he disputed the claim that it made it more difficult to stop inflation, because if we were going to reduce inflation then we had to get prices actually rising at a slower rate than they had been expected to rise. On asset markets there was no way of reducing inflation without negative real rates of interest: the only way to produce high enough nominal rates of interest was to index mortgage loans, as had been done in Chile and Brazil. But perhaps indexation and democracy were not compatible.

10 Profits and Investment: A Kaleckian Approach*

A. Asimakopulos
M c G I L L   U N I V E R S I T Y

I INTRODUCTION

Kalecki's theories of effective demand and distribution are macroeconomic, but their development is very much affected by his views of the microeconomic arrangements in the economy. The economy to which these theories are applicable is a capitalist economy. A relatively small group of individuals (the 'capitalists') own the means of production, and they derive income from this ownership and from organising production. A much larger group of individuals (the 'workers') must sell their labour power to obtain an income. Kalecki's analysis of industrial production is based on the assumption that markets for manufactured goods are imperfectly competitive. In these markets changes in prices are characterised as being 'cost-determined', where 'cost' includes some provision for profits that depends on the degree of imperfection of competition or 'degree of monopoly'. Markets for manufactured goods are contrasted with those for primary products, which are generally competitive, and where changes in prices are 'demand determined'. This difference in microeconomic arrangements is an integral part of Kalecki's approach to the development of capitalist economies.

Labour markets in Kalecki's analysis are not perfectly competitive, individual firms may be rather large and they may be important employers in their localities with an influence on the wages paid. Workers may also be organised, with more or less effect, in trade unions. 'Equilibrium' is a term that is rarely, if ever, to be found in Kalecki's writings.[1] It is certainly not something that he uses to describe the position of workers with respect to employment. In his view 'The reserve of capital equipment and the reserve army of unemployed are typical features of a capitalist economy at least throughout a considerable part of the cycle (Kalecki, 1971, p. 137).[2] The

*I am grateful to J. B. Burbidge and J. C. Weldon for comments on an earlier draft of this paper. They are, of course, not responsible for any errors or for this treatment of the subject.
    [1] In his volume of *Selected Essays on the Dynamics of the Capitalist Economy* (1971) which 'includes what I consider my main contributions to the theory of dynamics of the capitalist economy...' (p. vii), the term 'equilibrium' does not appear in the Index.
    [2] All page references in this paper will be, unless otherwise noted, from Kalecki (1971) and only the page number will be given.

situations he analyses can, however, be identified with one type of equilibrium, with 'short-period equilibrium'. Keynes's short-term expectations are being fulfilled; firms in the short period produce the rates of output that they can sell at the prices they set; their investment in the period is equal to what they intended to invest; and saving is in the desired relation to income. The Kaleckian approach developed here will be restricted to situations of short-period equilibrium but it can be readily extended to other cases.

Kalecki's writings emphasised the double-sided relation between investment and profits. On the one hand there is 'the impact of the effective demand generated by investment upon profits and the national income and [on] the other . . . the determination of investment decisions by, broadly speaking, the level and the rate of change of economic activity' (p. 165). It is the second relation which, Kalecki wrote, 'to my mind, remains the central *pièce de résistance* of economics,' (p. 165) that has proved to be very elusive. Kalecki noted in the Introduction to his *Selected Essays on the Dynamics of the Capitalist Economy*, that 'there is a continuous search for new solutions in the theory of investment decisions, where even the last paper represents — for better or for worse — a novel approach' (p. viii). The examination of the relation between profits and investment decisions presented here draws on this work.[1]

The analysis is restricted to a capitalist economy that is closed and in which there are no government activities except in so far as monetary authorities affect the money supply and credit conditions generally. Kalecki distinguished between two types of capitalists: those who are engaged in the organisation of production ('entrepreneurs'); and those ('rentiers') who lend funds to the former. The entrepreneurs of a firm, those who manage it, would often be 'a controlling group of big shareholders' (p. 107) who make up the board of directors, and the senior management of the company or, in the case of very widely held companies, the board of directors and the senior management. Kalecki argued that 'the rest of the shareholders do not differ from holders of bonds with a flexible rate of interest' (p. 107). This distinction is important for Kalecki's analysis of the determination of investment. A firm's ability to invest is affected by the value (in wage units) of the capital it owns — 'The access of a firm to the capital market, or in other words the amount of rentier capital it may hope to obtain, is determined to a large extent by the amount of its entrepreneurial capital' (p. 105). A firm's expansion is thus, *inter alia*, circumscribed by the amount of capital it can accumulate out of its profits.

Kalecki's approach to the theory of economic growth and the determination of investment is not 'mechanistic', 'the rate of growth at a given time is a phenomenon rooted in past economic, social and technological developments rather than determined fully by the coefficients of our equations. . . .' (p. 183).

---

[1] The writings of Joan Robinson have also influenced this paper, both for her own contributions to this topic and for her interpretations of Kalecki's work.

There is no artificial distinction between 'short-run' and 'long-run' theories.[1]
'. . . the long-run trend is but a slowly changing component of a chain of short-period situations: it has no independent entity. . . .' (p. 165). The basic time period for Kalecki's analysis is thus a short period. Productive capacity is taken as given in this period, the investment activity in that period resulting in only negligible changes in its magnitude during the period. This short period is a segment of real, calendar, time. It will be identified here as a quarter of a year. Investment in plant and equipment (the only type of investment considered here: this analysis abstracts from inventories) in a particular short period is predetermined. It is limited by the productive capacity in the investment sector and/or labour available, but up to the lowest of these limits investment is determined by investment decisions made in earlier periods. This time lag between investment decisions and actual investment has a prominent role in all of Kalecki's discussions of investment. The time lag may be quite long, and in most cases is much longer than a quarter.[2] There is one other decision taken in previous periods that affects investment in the short period under consideration, and that is the decision to proceed with investment plans adopted earlier or to modify them.[3] The explanation of investment in a particular period therefore requires an 'investment decision function' which considers the factors determining investment decisions taken some periods earlier, as well as a 'realisation function' which considers the factors that might alter these investment plans just prior to the commencement of the period. Before discussing the effects of profits on investment through their influence on these functions, I shall sketch out some of the other important elements of a Kaleckian model, and briefly examine the effects of investment on profits.

II SHORT-PERIOD FRAMEWORK OF THE ANALYSIS

This analysis is restricted to industrial production. All plants are assumed to be fully integrated; they produce their own raw materials, and thus prime

[1] This contrasts with Kaldor (1955–56, p. 94) who made a distinction between 'short-run theory' and 'long-run theory' and wanted to use the Multiplier principle to explain variations in output and employment in the former, and to use it as a distribution theory in the latter.

[2] For example, the time-lag between the planning of big investment projects, such as private hydro-electric developments, new steel mills, etc., and the actual investment activity, may be a few years.

[3] As Kalecki noted '. . . investment decisions are not strictly irrevocable. A cancellation of investment orders, although involving considerable loss, can and does take place. This is a factor, therefore, which disturbs the relationship between investment decisions and investment. . . ' (p. 110 n.). A recent example of this type of change in investment plans concerns the building of oil tankers. With the fall in tanker rates and the laying up of ships 'Wherever possible, orders are being cancelled, . . . Norway's biggest shipbuilder . . . has been hit by cancellations for 10 tankers. . . . Foreign shipowners . . . had cancelled seven orders from Japanese shipyards since last December' (Report in *New York Times* 8 March 1975).

costs consist only of wage costs. Marginal costs in any plant are constant until normal productive capacity is reached, after which point they increase very sharply. There are also indirect, or overhead, labour costs which are part of variable costs. A core number of workers (included here are foremen, supervisors, quality-control personnel, etc.) are hired if the plant is operated in the short period, and this number is invariant to the degree of utilisation of plant as long as it is non-zero. Relative wage rates are used to reduce labour of different skills to comparable units. The assumption of a constant marginal product for direct labour plus the existence of indirect labour means that average labour productivity is an increasing function of direct labour employed until productive capacity is reached. Two sectors of production are distinguished: a consumption-goods sector and an investment-goods sector. The former produces a basket of goods whose composition is unchanged over time, while the latter produces plant and equipment, or 'machines', for itself and the consumption sector. Technical progress would affect the nature of the output produced by the investment sector.

Markets for the products of both industrial sectors are assumed to be oligopolistic. Prices are arrived at by marking-up unit prime costs. Among the factors entering into the determination of the size of the mark-ups in a particular industry are the degree of concentration in the industry and the barriers to entry. These features are summarised by the term 'degree of monopoly', and thus the mark-ups reflect, *inter alia*, the 'degree of monopoly'. The ratios of prices to unit prime costs are assumed to be relatively stable in the face of short-term variations in demand. Prices may be set by price leaders, with other firms following the leads given to them, or they may be arrived at by some other method that achieves the same results.[1] A price leader is visualised as determining the mark-up that is applied to unit prime costs to obtain price by having both a view as to an appropriate target rate of return on its investment, and a standard rate of utilisation of capacity — e.g., 80 per cent of capacity — that it uses to calculate unit overhead costs for pricing purposes. For a firm that is a price follower, the realised mark-up depends on its unit prime costs and the price set by the price leader. Given the price, the average mark-up for the industry is determined by the unit prime costs in the constituent plants and by the distribution of total output between these plants. The output shares of different plants are not explained here, they are assumed to be given for each short period and to be unchanged for any of the comparisons made within a short period. If the price leader's mark-up is unchanged then the average industry mark-up is also unchanged.

The changes in productive capacity during a short period, arising from investment activity in that period, can be neglected because they are very

---

[1] For example, if the firms in an industry use standard cost-accounting procedures, if they readily obtain information on changes in 'normal' costs in the industry, and if they have a common view of what constitutes a 'normal' rate of return, then concurrent pricing will produce the results attributed to price leadership above. See Asimakopulos (1975) for a critical examination of Kalecki's price equations.

small relative to the total capacity available. This model recognises that the time-lag between decisions to invest and the resulting investment activity is not shorter than a quarter of a year for most types of investment, and thus the investment in real terms (which is synonomous here with a measure of the value of investment in wage units)[1] in any period, is predetermined. Investment in the current period can be written as:

$$I/w = (1 + \mu_I)\, L_{II}; L_{II} \leqslant \bar{L}_{II} \tag{1}$$

where I is the money value of investment in the current period; w is the money-wage rate; μ_I is the average mark-up in the investment sector; L_{II} is total direct employment in the investment sector; and $\bar{L}_{II}$ is the maximum possible total direct employment in the investment sector given the available plants and the assumed distribution of output between them.

The value of total output in the consumption sector can be written as:

$$C = (1 + \mu_c)\, w L_{lc}; L_{lc} \leqslant \bar{L}_{lc} \tag{2}$$

where C is the money value of total output of consumption goods; μ_c is the average mark-up in the consumption sector; L_{lc} is total direct employment in the consumption sector; and $\bar{L}_{lc}$ is the maximum possible direct employment in that sector given available plant and the assumed distribution of total output between plants.

The price of the consumption good can be written as:

$$p = (1 + \mu_c)\, \frac{w}{b} \tag{3}$$

where p is the price; and b is average output per unit of direct labour in the consumption sector.[2]

Kalecki assumed no workers' saving in his models and this assumption is maintained here. It is not a critical feature of this analysis, what is crucial being the assumption that the propensity to save out of profits is greater than the propensity to save out of wages. Entrepreneurial saving is represented by retained earnings, only a portion of the gross profits remaining after interest payments is distributed. Rentiers are assumed to save a constant proportion, s_r, of their incomes. Their interest incomes, B, are assumed to be paid to them at the beginning of the current period, for they depend on the amount and terms of loans to firms outstanding as of the beginning of the previous period. Dividends in a particular period are some proportion, β, of gross profits in the

---

[1] In this analysis it is assumed that the average mark-up in the investment sector is constant.

[2] Average output per unit of direct labour is constant for the range of output considered, since output per unit of labour in individual plants is assumed to be constant, and the distribution of direct employment amongst plants is unchanged.

previous period less interest payments.[1] We have:

$$R = \beta(\pi_{-1} - B) + B = \beta\pi_{-1} + (1 - \beta) B \qquad (4)$$

where R is total rentiers income; π_{-1} represents gross profits in the preceding quarter. It is assumed here that rentiers' consumption is a function of their money incomes. This represents a departure from Kalecki's practice in most of his papers where he assumed capitalists' consumption to be given in real terms.[2] The present approach is adopted in recognition of the fact that many rentiers (in particular, pensioners) have relatively low incomes and these are often fixed, at least for substantial periods of time, in money terms. Rising wages and prices would thus result in a fall in rentiers' consumption. The value for consumption sector output is equal to total consumption demand because of the assumption that the firms' short-term expectations are correct, and thus:

$$C = W + (1 - s_r) [\beta\pi_{-1} + (1 - \beta) B] . \qquad (5)$$

Desired saving, S, can now be written as (since $S = Y - C$):

$$S = \pi - (1 - s_r) [\beta\pi_{-1} + (1 - \beta) B] ; \qquad (6)$$

where Y is the money value of total output, W is the total money-wage bill and π is the total money value of gross profits in the current period.

The necessary *ex post* equality between saving and investment, plus the assumptions that investment is predetermined and saving is in the desired relation to income provide us with a short-period equilibrium explanation for profits. They are determined by capitalists' expenditures.

$$\pi = I + (1 - s_r) [\beta\pi_{-1} + (1 - \beta) B] . \qquad (7)$$

This equation is the basis for one side of the double-sided relationship between profits and investment in a Kaleckian model. Gross profits can also be written in terms of the mark-ups, as

$$\pi = \mu_c w L_{Ic} + \mu_I w L_{II} - w(L_{oc} + L_{oI}) \qquad (8)$$

where L_{oc}, L_{oI}, represent the employment of indirect labour in the consumption and investment sector plants, respectively. From equations (1), (7) and (8) we obtain for the employment of direct labour in the consumption sector,

$$L_{Ic} = \frac{1}{\mu_c} \{L_o + L_{II} + (1 - s_r) [\beta\pi_{-1}/w + (1 - \beta) B/w] \} \qquad (9)$$

---

[1] The pay-out ratio of firms depends on the conventions used to calculate and provide for depreciation, the views of entrepreneurs about the firms' needs for retained earnings, and shareholders' and stock market constraints on their behaviour. (Cf. Robinson (1962), p. 38–9).

[2] For example, in his 1968 paper 'Trend and the Business Cycle' he assumed that capitalists' consumption in real terms is explained by an equation with a constant term plus a rather small fraction of profits in real terms (p. 167). Kalecki noted, however, in his 1943 paper on 'Political Aspects of Full Employment' that 'the price increase in the up-swing is to the disadvantage of small and big *rentiers* ...' (p. 144).

where L_O (= L_{oc} + L_{oI}) is total indirect employment. Employment in the consumption sector, and thus the rate of utilisation of plant in that sector, is directly related to employment in the investment sector and to rentiers' consumption in wage units, and inversely related to the average mark-up in the consumption sector.

The share of profits in this model, and not only the level of profits, is directly related to the level of capitalists' expenditures in wage units. This feature is due to the presence of indirect labour. Output per unit of direct labour is constant but output per unit of labour (direct *and* indirect) is positively correlated with the level of output. When there is a constant mark-up on unit direct labour costs, this means that the profit share is also positively correlated with the rate of output.[1]

III INVESTMENT DECISIONS AND INVESTMENT

A Kaleckian approach to the interrelations between profits and investment is based on the recognition of the firm (entrepreneur) as the key decision-making unit in the process, and the observance of a certain sequence of events. Preliminary plans for possible investment projects must be drawn up before any investment decisions that commit the firm to their implementation can be made. There is a further time lag between an investment decision, and the actual investment activity that it entails; and finally, there is another delay before the project is completed and productive capacity is changed. The time that elapses between these various stages of the investment process would differ for different projects, but this theory recognises some positive time lag, on the average, between each stage. In this context, the aggregate investment activity whose employment and distributional consequences were examined in the preceding section, would cover a series of separate activities. Some could be both initiating and completing a project in the current period; some could represent the initial stages of a project to be completed in later periods; some could be completing a project started in the past; or finally, some may be continuing a project that will be completed in the future. Whatever the

[1] Strictly speaking, this increase in profit share under these conditions must hold only for each sector separately. It is possible for the profit share in total output to be lower if the relative contribution of each sector to total output is changed.

Kalecki often abstracted from overhead labour, and assumed the ratio of profits to income to be constant over the cycle, (e.g., in 'Trend and the Business Cycle', p. 169), but this feature was noted in his path-breaking 1933 article 'Outline of a Theory of the Business Cycle'. He wrote '. . . aggregate production and profit per unit of output rise or fall together . . . . This results at least to some extent from the fact that a part of wages are overheads' (p. 11 n.). One of the contractual arrangements in this model relates to the overhead costs incurred by a firm as a result of its commitments with respect to the existence of its plant and equipment. Another relates to its commitments to indirect labour. The latter are entered into for the full short period if the plant is expected to be utilised at any positive rate. The commitments to direct labour are for shorter time-spans than the short period, they fall within the scope of Keynes's 'daily' reassessments of short-term expectations. (Keynes, 1936, p. 47.)

mix between these possible cases in any period, the requirements for short-period analysis are assumed to hold; investment activity in a particular short period has only a negligible effect on the productive capacity available to firms during that period. The shortest time interval over which changes in productive capacity are recognised by the model is a full short period.

The term 'investment decision' is used here to denote a commitment to purchase or build plant and equipment. This involves plans for all the physical aspects of the project, arrangements for financing it, plus a time schedule (which may allow for some flexibility) for carrying it out. The value of an investment decision may be estimated in terms of the expected money costs of its implementation or in terms of its cost in wage units. Before committing itself to a particular investment project a firm must be able to arrange for its financing. On this point Keynes has argued that

> The entrepreneur when he decides to invest has to be satisfied on two points: firstly, that he can obtain sufficient short-term finance during the period of producing the investment; and secondly, that he can eventually fund his short-term obligations by a long-term issue on satisfactory conditions [Keynes, 1973, p. 217].

The supply of short-term finance[1] is very much affected by conditions in money markets.

> ... the terms of supply of the finance required by *ex ante* investment [investment decisions] depend on the *existing* state of liquidity preferences ... in conjunction with the supply of money as governed by the policy of the banking system. Broadly speaking, therefore, the rate of interest relevant to *ex ante* investment is the rate of interest determined by the *current* stock of money and the *current* state of liquidity preferences at the date when the finance required by the investment decisions has to be arranged [Keynes, 1973, pp. 217–8].

The prospects for longer-term financing on satisfactory terms are affected by a firm's accumulation of reserves out of past profits, and its expected retained earnings (gross of depreciation) out of profits over the period of implementation of the investment project.

Firms make investment decisions because they expect the resulting investments to be profitable. In Kalecki's model current profits and the rate of utilisation of productive capacity, both of which are positively related to investment, as we saw in Section II, play an important role in the estimation of the likelihood of particular investment projects earning at least the standard rates of profits required to justify their implementation. Kalecki suggested (see particularly pp. 169–73) that the initial rates of return on recently completed plants are used by firms as indicators of the profitability

---

[1] In this connection Keynes used 'the term "finance" to mean the credit required in the interval between planning and execution' (Keynes, 1973, p. 216, n. 2).

of new investment. These rates of return depend both on total gross profits,[1] and on the extent to which embodied technical progress ensures a more than proportionate share of total profits for the newer plants.

The possibility for innovations and the example of successful recent innovations provides an additional stimulus to investment in Kalecki's model: 'In the year considered new inventions come within the compass of the entrepreneurs. Thus they expect to do better out of their investment than those whose investment materialised in the year considered' (p. 173). This stimulus[2] is seen as being conditioned by 'past economic, social and techno-logical developments. This semi-autonomous variable may be considered . . . a slowly changing function of time . . . ' (pp. 173–4).

IV   THE DOUBLE-SIDED RELATION BETWEEN PROFITS AND INVESTMENT[3]

These various strands of the Kaleckian approach to profits and investment will now be brought together. It is assumed that entrepreneurs know, when they make investment decisions in one period, their gross profits and the rate of utilisation of their productive capacity in that period (the introduction of a time lag here would not affect the essentials of the analysis in any way). Investment decisions are concerned with the acquisition and construction of various items of capital equipment and thus it is the command of profits over these items that would be relevant for these decisions. With the mark-up in the investment sector unchanged, this command could be represented by profits expressed in wage units. From equation (7) we can derive

$$\pi/w = I/w + (1 - s_r) \ [\beta \pi_{-1}/w + (1 - \beta) \ B/w] \tag{7a}$$

[1] Kalecki argued that this return 'may be assumed to be proportionate to the increment in "real" profits from the beginning to the end of the year considered . . . . Since ample unused productive capacities are postulated to be in existence . . . ' (p. 170). It is made proportionate to total profits here, rather than to the increment in profits, since new plants capture a share of the total market and thus a share of total gross profits, even when older plants are not fully utilised.

[2] An interesting sidelight on Kalecki's approach is cast by Joan Robinson's comment on her discussions with him on this point:

> He maintained that inventions (technical progress) raise the prospects of profit for capitalist firms and so encourage investment. . . . I pointed out that technical progress *permits* accumulation to go on faster than the labour force is growing but it cannot *cause* high profits, for if accumulation is actually going on steadily, Kalecki's own theory shows that the rate of profit on capital will be constant . . . he compromised with me, pointing out that at any particular moment some go-ahead firms are installing equipment embodying the latest inventions in the hope of gaining a higher rate of profit than the average at the expense of their rivals. Thus it can both be true that inventions may stimulate investment and that the overall rate of profits may be constant over the long run [Joan Robinson (1973, p. 90), emphases in the original].

[3] An earlier attempt to develop this relation along these lines is to be found in Asimakopulos (1971).

Gross profits in wage units are linearly related to investment in wage units, if rentiers' consumption in these terms is constant. There is no equation explaining money-wage rates in this model, but their rate of change is assumed to be positively related, to the demand for labour, to gross profits, to the rate of change of prices of consumption goods in the recent past, and inversely related to the rate of unemployment. The strength of these relations would not necessarily be invariant to the passage of time and to changes in attitudes, and labour market institutions. If the consumption of at least some of the rentiers in the current short period is determined by their (fixed) money incomes for that period, then the relation between gross profits in wage units and investment in wage units can be represented by a curve which, at least in its upper reaches, is concave from below. The concavity is due to the effects of the higher money wages that accompany the higher investment. A curve of this type is drawn in Figure 10:1.

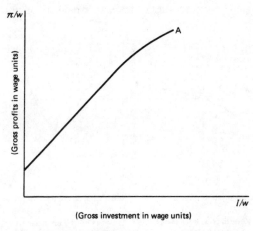

Fig. 10:1

For the purpose of illustrating the determination of investment decisions, the relation drawn in Figure 10:1 must be transformed into one showing the expected rate of return on investment. Such a transformation is not a mechanical matter. Profits, and the rates of return on new plants, in the current period are not the only elements affecting entrepreneurs' views of the future. The current period's experience may bulk large in the firm's balance sheets but the profits in the last few periods (which depend on capitalists' expenditures in those periods) as well as any more or less definite reasons for expecting changes, are also important, and enter into the firms' estimates of the expected rates of return on investment. A curve relating the expected rate of return on investment to current investment is shown in Figure 10:2. The height of the curve depends on the firms' experiences with the profitability of investments over the past several periods. Their current experience, if profits are higher than normal, may lead to more optimistic forecasts, while current profits lower than those expected would lead to less optimistic forecasts. This relation between current profits (investment) and the expectations of future profitability is reflected in the upward slope of the E-curve in Figure 10:2.[1] Increasing hesitation to project into the future profits much higher than those previously experienced, is reflected in the concavity of the E-curve. Given this curve, the expected rate of return on investment which is relevant to investment decisions made in the current period can be obtained from the current rate of investment in wage units. If the assumed rate of investment activity is $(I/w)_0$, as in Figure 10:2, then the corresponding expected rate of return on investment is r_0.

An upper limit to the value of investment decisions firms can make in a particular period is set by the plans that have been previously prepared. Given this limit, what they proceed with depends on the expected rates of return on the various projects, on the abilities of firms to arrange financing and on their

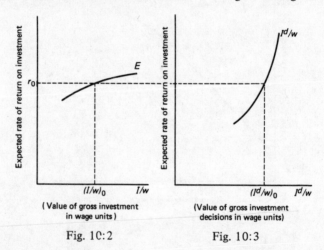

Fig. 10:2   Fig. 10:3

prospects for recruiting the necessary staff. The higher is the expected rate of return on investment in general, the greater are the number of projects that are expected to earn the minimum rate of return required to justify their implementation. Thus the investment decisions curve in Figure 10:3 is positively sloped. Our earlier discussion made clear that both short-term financing and the expectation of being able to eventually fund short-term

---

[1] Keynes's view of the importance of current events in forming expectations would bear out the upward slope of the E-curve: 'It would be foolish, in forming our expectations, to attach great weight to matters which are very uncertain. . . . For this reason the facts of the existing situation enter, in a sense disproportionately, into the formation of our long-term expectations; . . . ' (Keynes, 1936, p. 148).

obligations on satisfactory terms, are involved in the making of investment decisions. The position of the I^d/w-curve in Figure 10:3 is thus affected by both monetary conditions and the profits expectations of firms, as well as the number and types of projects that are available for consideration. Another factor influencing the position of this curve is the prevailing rate of technical progress, the higher this rate is the further to the right is the position of the curve.

The sequence in which the double-sided relation between profits and investment, depicted in Figures 10:2 and 10:3, is to be read as follows. Investment in the current period, $(I/w)_0$, is predetermined by decisions made in the past, and through its effects on sales and profits it helps determine the expected rate of return on investment, r_0. This rate then influences, along with current retained earnings, credit conditions, and technological developments, the investment decisions made in this period for implementation in future time periods. The time lag between most investment decisions and the resulting investment activity is substantially longer than the duration of our short period, and thus decisions to increase investment will have very little effect on total activity in the next period. There is more scope, however, for unfavourable conditions in the current period to have some negative effect. Firms might modify investment schedules that had called for investment next period, even though such actions involve losses on contracts, if to proceed with original plans now appears more costly. An investment realisation function must thus be added to this model and it is illustrated by the I_R-curve in Figure 10:4. The height of this curve indicates the value for investment in wage units scheduled for the next period.[1] Some scaling down of this planned investment is shown as occurring if the rate of utilisation of capacity

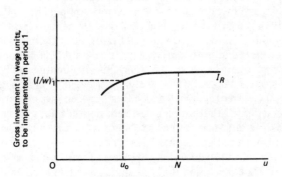

Rate of utilisation of productive capacity in the current period (o)

Fig. 10:4

[1] The I_R-curve also includes the value, probably very small because of the time lags between investment decisions and investment, of investment to be carried out next period that is the result of current decisions.

falls considerably below what is considered to be the 'normal' rate of utilisation (this rate is indicated by the point N in Figure 10:4).

We have now gone full circle in tracing the relations between profits and investment. Our analysis of a particular short period, as in Section II above, begins with investment in real terms predetermined by decisions taken in earlier periods. This investment plus capitalists' consumption in wage units determine the level of profits, and, given the average mark-up in the consumption sector, they also determine total employment and the rate of utilisation of plant. The current level of profits is an important influence on the expectations of the rate of return on investment and thus on investment decisions made in the present for future implementation. Investment in the succeeding period depends largely on investment decisions made in the past, but current conditions may lead to some modifications of plans. This combination of plans plus current conditions provides the investment which is to be carried out next period. This brings us back, one period later, to the situation described by the second sentence in this paragraph.

V   CHANGES OVER TIME

In a Kaleckian model the investment decisions of firms have a key role in determining the level of economic activity and the development of the economy, but they are not unaffected by current conditions. There is a feedback from current investment, through its effects on profits and utilisation of plant, to investment decisions. It is this feedback, and the inevitable time lags involving both the delay between investment decisions and investment activity, and this activity and the change in productive capacity, that are emphasised in the relations between profits and investment presented here. The relations between profits and investment have some stable components — they reflect the past economic, social and technological developments — but they may also be affected by changes in current conditions. For example, the relation between investment and profits in wage units would reflect not only the make-up of the rentier class, the mix of big and small rentiers and their propensities to consume, but it would also be affected by changing money wage rates in the current period. The relation between investment decisions and the expected rate of return on investment depends not only on the enterprise of firms and their readiness to innovate, it depends as well on their abilities to obtain financing for their plans and it could be affected by changes in current conditions brought on, say, by fears of inflation. This model does not give rise to the expectation that economic growth in a capitalist economy will follow a smooth path — a change in direction tends to be cumulative, at least for some time. A trend may be discernible through the business cycles but growth is unlikely to be uninterrupted by cyclical movements.

An expansion can be started by a burst of investment due, say, to particularly inviting opportunities for technical progress. Increased investment leads to rising profits and an increasing share of profits in total income as the more intensive utilisation of productive capacity results in higher output per man. This rising profit share does not require real-wage rates to fall; they may even be increasing if technical progress is increasing output per unit of direct labour. This upswing tends to feed on itself, but it may be slowed down by a variety of factors or combination of factors.

The rising employment accompanying the increased tempo of investment will improve the bargaining position of trade unions. Increases in money-wage rates are likely to be considerably higher than increases in labour producticity, as the firms' willingness to withstand strikes is weaker when markets are strong and individual firms expect to be able to pass on higher costs in higher prices. Rentiers' consumption, especially for those such as pensioners whose incomes are relatively small and largely fixed in money terms, will be squeezed by the rising prices that accompany the increasing money wage rates. This fall in rentiers' consumption in terms of wage units will tend to counteract the favourable effects of increasing investment on profits. Kalecki argued, in his posthumously published paper on 'Class Struggle and Distribution of National Income', that in these circumstances the substantially higher wages obtained by strong trade unions may lead to some erosion of mark-ups, since bargaining proceeds industry by industry and inter-industry competition acts as some restraint on price increases. Mark-ups may also be eroded in a period of rising wages and prices if firms calculate profits and the appropriate mark-ups to achieve target rates of return on the basis of historical costs.[1] All these factors may result in a falling share of profits, and possibly even in a fall in profits in terms of wage units, in the later stages of the boom, even though investment is increasing. These developments tend to have a dampening effect on investment decisions by lowering the E-curve in Figure 10:2. A further check to investment decisions may be caused by restrictions on credit imposed to counteract inflation which shift the I^d curve to the left.

The variety of time lags involved in investment makes it very difficult for monetary policy to stabilise activity. The restraints on investment required now to decrease pressures in the labour market will tend to discourage investment in later periods. Projects already planned may be modified and delayed, as illustrated by the realisation function drawn in Figure 10:4, as the rate of utilisation of capacity falls, and the volume of new investment decisions will be adversely affected. It would take some time before any subsequent easing in credit conditions is reflected in increased investment.

This analysis has abstracted from primary production. Primary production, as well as international trade and a government, must of course be introduced into the model before it can be used to explain actual economic developments. The presence of primary production in the model would strengthen the conclusion that capitalist development is unlikely to be smooth. The primary sector would be a source of 'exogenous' changes for the industrial sector and

[1] Nordhaus (1974) has argued that 'most businessmen . . . base their actual calculations of price, sales, and profits on historical cost. . . ' (p. 187). Such a policy would lead to an erosion of the mark-ups contained in our equations when wages and prices are rising.

it could also magnify the effects of changes emanating from the industrial sector.

Kalecki argued that

> Generally speaking . . . changes in the prices of raw materials inclusive of primary foodstuffs are 'demand determined'. . . . With supply inelastic in short periods, an increase in demand causes a diminution of stocks and a consequent increase in price. This initial price movement may be enhanced by the addition of a speculative element [p. 43].

Rising prices for primary products, brought on by increasing demand due to rapid expansion of the industrial sector, not only increase inflationary pressures in the industrial sectors by their effects on prices and wage demands, but also lead to a transfer of income from the industrial to the primary sector. Both profits in terms of wage units and real wage rates may be lower. Conversely, a slowdown of activity in the industrial sector would result in a transfer of incomes in favour of the industrial sector. The investigation of the interrelationships between these sectors is important, and it can begin with Kalecki's characterisation of the pricing process in each — it forms part of the microeconomic foundations of his macroeconomics.

REFERENCES

A. Asimakopulos, 'The Determination of Investment in Keynes's Model', *Canadian Journal of Economics*, Vol. 4, No 3 (August 1971) pp. 382–8.
A. Asimakopulos, 'A Kaleckian Theory of Income Distribution', *Canadian Journal of Economics*, Vol. 8, No 3 (August 1975) pp. 313–33.
N. Kaldor, 'Alternative Theories of Distribution', *Review of Economic Studies*, Vol. 23 (1), No 60 (1955–6) pp. 83–100.
Michal Kalecki, *Selected Essays on the Dynamics of the Capitalist Economy* (Cambridge University Press, 1971).
J. M. Keynes, *The General Theory of Employment, Interest and Money* (London: Macmillan, 1936).
J. M. Keynes, *The Collected Writings of John Maynard Keynes*, Vol. XIV (London: Macmillan, 1973).
William D. Nordhaus, 'The Falling Share of Profits', *Brookings Papers on Economic Activity*, No 1 (1974) pp. 169–208.
Joan Robinson, *Essays in the Theory of Economic Growth* (London: Macmillan, 1962).
Joan Robinson, *Collected Economic Papers*, Vol. IV (Blackwell: Oxford, 1973).

Discussion of Professor Asimakopulos's Paper

Dr Nuti felt he was not the most suitable commentator for Professor Asimakopulos's paper as he shared his sympathy and admiration for Kalecki's economics. He had been fortunate enough to be taught by Kalecki in Warsaw more than ten years earlier, and subsequently at Cambridge he had been persuaded by Joan Robinson that Kalecki was the man who had discovered Keynes's *General Theory* before Keynes. Dr Nuti also appeared to have unwittingly exercised undue influence on Professor Asimakopulos's paper. Although he believed Professor Asimakopulos was right in arguing that the notion of 'equilibrium' was not very important in Kalecki's writings, he would not rely too much on the evidence that the term 'equilibrium' does not appear in the Index to Kalecki's *Selected Essays on the Dynamics of the Capitalist Economy*: he had been responsible for that Index, and the absence of the term might be a reflection of his own way of thinking rather than Kalecki's. Nevertheless, Dr Nuti saw his role as that of devil's advocate, and in spite of his partiality he would go out of his way to discuss critically Professor Asimakopulos's paper in which he had brought together the main features of the Kaleckian approach with some modifications, and, although ending where Dr Nuti would have liked him to start, had come up with a number of conclusions that were highly relevant to the theme of our conference.

The framework was a capitalist economy, with classes of workers, managers and rentiers, permanently exhibiting unemployment of labour. Enterprises produced manufactured goods under constant variable costs up to capacity; they were price-fixers on a mark-up basis and total output depended on effective demand, determined by the multiplier and autonomous expenditure for consumption and investment (there was no foreign trade in the model).

Professor Asimakopulos considered what he called 'short-period equilibrium', where

> Keynes's short term expectations are being fulfilled; firms in the short period produce the rates of output that they can sell at the prices they set; their investment in the period is equal to what they intended to invest and saving is in the desired relation to income [p. 329].

This needed some qualification: in the model, firms produced the rates of output that they could sell at the prices they set, but their rate of capacity utilisation might very well disappoint them. Their investment in the period was determined by past decisions with a lag and *in that sense* was equal to what they intended to invest, but firms might regret past decisions committing them to a given level of current investment expenditure. If they found that level too high or too low this would be reflected in their current decisions committing them to investment expenditure in the next period, say six or twelve months later. The long period was simply a sequence of such short-run situations.

Investment decisions were taken in real terms and consisted of fairly irreversible commitments to expenditure on capital installation in the next period or periods. Someone in a hairsplitting mood could argue that investment was not properly accounted for, in that such an irreversible commitment to future expenditure should count as 'investment' even if it did not result in an actual current outlay. But then this kind of commitment to future expenditure did not have to be financed out of current savings, so that the Kaleckian use of current investment outlays was more appropriate than a rigorous notion of intertemporal transfers.

Unlike Kalecki, Professor Asimakopulos measured real investment in wage units. It was not clear why decisions should be taken in those terms in a Kaleckian context, though Professor Asimakopulos might have a simple answer for that. Nor was it simply a problem of normalisation.

In a closed economy, investment was financed out of profits. Workers consumed their entire earnings. In addition, rentiers consumed a constant proportion of their incomes (i.e., of interest on bonds and dividends on shares); Kalecki usually assumed that rentiers' consumption was decided in real terms, but this difference did not seem to be very important.

Kalecki had usually worked with an aggregate model, but then examined carefully trends in the relative weight of wages and of materials in prime costs. Professor Asimakopulos assumed that plants were vertically integrated and produced materials (though not machines) and that there were two sectors, consumption and investment goods. He therefore lost the potential impact of materials' prices on relative shares, which had undoubtedly been an important aspect of actual developments in the last three years in the industrialised world. He did not, however, always follow up the structural implications of having two sectors, and tended to neglect the problems raised by their aggregation.

Professor Asimakopulos's approach to the determination of profits was uncompromisingly Kaleckian. Kalecki himself had once summed it up by saying that 'workers spend what they get, capitalists get what they spend'. There was a reason for interpreting the *ex-post* equality between capitalists' expenditures and their receipts (in a closed economy without workers' savings) as a one-way causal relationship. Firms decide not how much profit they are going to make but how much plant they want to install. In the same way, capitalists as rentiers decide how much they want to consume (whether in absolute real terms as in Kalecki, or as a share as in Asimakopulos). *Therefore* (and Dr Nuti stressed this causal link because it might become the main target in the discussion), it was plausible to look at capitalists' current expenditure, and primarily investment, as *determining* the level of current profits.

There was a difference between this Kaleckian approach to income distribution, and the Kaldorian or neo-Keynesian approach: in Kalecki there was no mention of saving propensities, nor was any relationship established between distribution and the economy's growth rate. But the Kaleckian and Kaldorian approach had two things in common:

(1) the macroeconomic approach to profits and distribution;
(2) the notion of investment as *the* principal determinant of distribution.

It made no difference that Kalecki and Kaldor got there via different intellectual routes, Kalecki from Marx's reproduction schemes of Vol. II of *Capital* (Chs. 22–23) and Rosa Luxemburg's *Accumulation of Capital*, Kaldor from Keynes.

In view of the importance of investment, it was perhaps surprising that Professor Asimakopulos did not specify an investment function. His equations were accounting identities and their manipulations, embodying the statement that price-fixing followed a constant mark-up, wage-earners consumed all their income, rentiers a constant share of their income. Equation (1) was an identity saying that gross profits made in the investment goods sector were equal by definition to total investment times the mark-up in investment goods pricing. Equation (2) was an identity saying that gross profits made in the consumer goods sector were equal by definition to total consumption times the mark-up in consumption goods pricing. Equation (3) was obtained from (2) by dividing it by the quantity of consumer goods output, and was redundant; it was never used again in the paper. Equation (4) was an identity saying that rentiers' incomes were equal by definition to interest income (taken as given) plus their share of profits net of interest; such a share was taken as independent of the level of investment, though we had no reason to believe that it was not a *dependent* variable. Equation (5) stated the behavioural hypothesis that the value of consumption was equal to wages plus rentiers' consumption; together with equation (2) it determined the level of consumption output. Equation (6) used equation (5) to express savings as a function of profits. Equation (7) simply said that capitalists' expenditure depended on previous profits; this, in turn, must be equal to current gross receipts of capitalists, as in equation (8). Equation (9) was obtained by re-writing equations (1), (7) and (8).

The pay-off of this exercise consisted of three propositions. First, the employment and utilisation rate in the consumption sector were directly related to employment in the investment sector as well as to rentiers' consumption, and inversely related to the average mark-up in the consumption sector (p. 333). Second, the *share* as well as the level of profits was directly related to the level of capitalists' expenditures (pp. 333–4). Third, the profit share was also positively correlated with the rate of output (p. 334).

The trouble was that the prime mover, *investment*, in Professor Asimakopulos's paper was taken as given. It was a bit like a bullfight without *el toro*, to adapt a familiar expression to local conditions. It meant that we could not analyse the comparative statics, let alone the dynamics, of the system. Kalecki always had a specific form of the investment function in his models, and he experimented with several alternative types throughout his life: with and without inventories, with and without government expenditure and foreign trade, with and without lags and distributed lags, with and without the influence of short- and long-term interest, and so on. He stressed that there are many things that capitalists do as a class, but investing is the one thing they do not do as a class; he was interested in precisely how the dynamics of the capitalist economy are affected by alternative hypotheses about investment behaviour. Thus, for instance, in one of his latest essays, on 'Trend and the Business Cycle' (*Economic Journal*, 1968) Kalecki produced a model of capitalist dynamics yielding two solutions. One was a stable solution with fluctuations around a low growth rate, due to government intervention; one was highly unstable; the end of the capitalist system therefore appeared as a possibility, not a necessity. Kalecki was a Marxist but not a dogmatist.

By omitting an investment function, Professor Asimakopulos's paper lost a certain amount of Kaleckian flavour. What he had done was to emphasise the causal links in the system, and formulate a graphical presentation of some of these links.

The causal links were clear. Past investment decisions determined current investment expenditure, unless the rate of utilisation of productive capacity fell below a critical level (see Figure 10:4, p. 339). Current investment expenditure determined current profits (Figure 10:1) and current profitability (regardless of how this was measured by firms, whether as a rate of return or a pay-off period or a ratio between current profits and any arbitrary measure of capital invested) as *experienced* by firms (Figure 10:2). Dr Nuti suggested that we interpret Figure 10:2 as indicating 'experienced' rather than 'expected' profitability as Professor Asimakopulos seemed to imply, with the additional proviso that expected profitability was equal to profitability actually experienced. This was probably not what Professor Asimakopulos had in mind, but this way of interpreting his Figure 10:2 brought out an important feature of the Kaleckian model: namely, the dependence of microeconomic experience on macroeconomic behaviour, and the dependence of expectations on experience. If we contrasted Figure 10:2 with the familiar Keynesian diagram relating the marginal efficiency of investment to its total level, we were in a position to understand the opposition between the sum of micro-economic expectations (Keynes's marginal efficiency of investment falling with the level of investment) and the actual macroeconomic picture of Figure 10:2 according to Dr Nuti's interpretation (experienced profitability actually rising with the investment level).

In Figure 10:3, finally, expected profitability being equal to experienced profitability, the level of current investment decisions in real terms was an increasing function of expected profitability. If we could assume, in addition to Professor Asimakopulos's own assumptions, that the relationships depicted in Figures 10:2 and 10:3 remained constant over time, we could boldly combine them as in Figure 10:5 below, and illustrate various possibilities. In Case I the two curves do not intersect; the profitability required by firms to undertake any level of investment is higher than that afforded by the same level; whatever the starting position gross investment immediately falls to its lowest possible level, i.e. zero. In Case II the curves intersect once, and their intersection defines a stable equilibrium at which the profitability required by firms to undertake that level of investment corresponds to the profitability generated by that investment; whatever the starting position, the economy we are considering will get as close to that equilibrium as we wish given the necessary time. In Case III the curves intersect twice, defining one stable and one unstable equilibrium, a situation reminiscent of the Kaleckian 1968 model. This way of looking at Professor Asimakopulos's diagrams might violate their spirit, but at least it traced a time path of development, which we would not otherwise obtain from this model. There were clear reasons why the curves illustrated in the diagram should not remain unchanged over time: both the rentiers' share and the level of investment would be affected by the interest rate, which would vary during the cycle; expected profitability was not necessarily equal to experienced profitability, but rather to some weighted average of past rates and so on. Also, in a two-sector model of the kind tackled by Professor Asimakopulos, the very *structure* of investment affected the relative profitability of consumption and investment goods production. Here Professor Asimakopulos failed to follow through his division of the economy into two sectors.

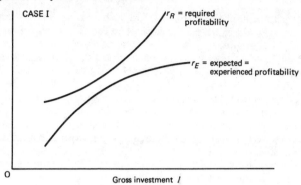

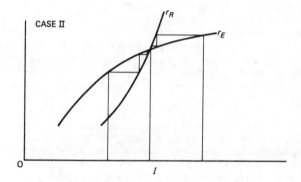

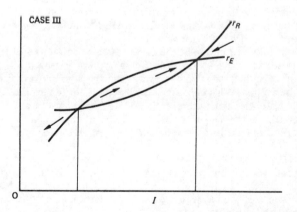

Fig. 10:5

Kalecki's pricing hypothesis, sketched in Section II (p. 331), required a fuller discussion. If the mark-up was defined in terms of a degree of monopoly, its microeconomic foundations were the demand elasticities for manufactured goods; Kaldor rightly classed this approach within the neoclassical tradition and accused it of tautology ('Alternative Theories of Distribution', *Review of Economic Studies*, 1956–6). If, following Section 5 of Kalecki's *Selected Essay on the Dynamics of the Capitalist Economy* (p. 44), we defined the firm's pricing behaviour in terms of its average prime costs and the prices of firms producing similar products, we had a non-tautological and statistically testable proposition. But although the mark-up hypothesis had the support of reasonably good statistical evidence (e.g., W. A. H. Godley and W. D. Nordhau 'Pricing in the Trade Cycle', *Economic Journal*, 1972), it raised more problems than it solved. For the mark-up theory to be a satisfactory price theory, we had to have an answer to at least three major questions:

(1) Whose costs were relevant for the pricing behaviour of an industry (i.e., we needed a theory of price leadership)?

(2) What level of capacity utilisation was relevant for the purpose of adding a mark-up to the price-leader's costs?

(3) What determined the leader's mark-up over and above its prime costs at the desired level of capital utilisation (here theories akin to the macroeconomic relationships between profit and growth were not acceptable because of inter-firm and intersectoral flows of investment funds)?

These were the microeconomic problems to which we should address ourselves within the context of the Kaleckian price model.

Finally, there was one aspect of Kalecki's analysis that deserved our attention, namely his awareness of the political economy of capitalism. His *Selected Essays* include, for instance, papers on the political aspects of full employment, and on class struggle and the distribution of income. Professor Shubik argued that we needed a mathematical-institutional economics; Dr Nuti took this to mean the recognition that there are classes, class-minded governments and class conflicts in a capitalist system. Kalecki was definitely in this tradition, and Professor Asimakopulos's paper was a step in that direction. Dr Nuti wished to contrast this approach with the current fashion, followed in one of the papers at this conference, of treating unemployment of labour as a form of self-employment in search activities for a better job, or even 'investment'; at a time when the unemployed were counted by the million, this approach was objectionable and even offensive. Following the Kaleckian path was more difficult than mainstream economics, but it was better to make a small step in the right direction than to rocket away at the speed of light into the emptiness of cosmic intellectual explorations.

Professor Harcourt reported that he and a colleague, Peter Kenyon, were investigating the relationship between the mark-up and investment, using a simple vintage model. they had first assumed that there was a price leader in the Kaldorian sense of the term, that firms had a certain amount of discretion in price setting, and that they had in mind normal sales rather than short-run profit maximisation and a fairly long time horizon. They had further assumed that the price set, and hence the mark-up, was determined by the investment which firms planned to do. Professor Harcourt wanted to know what others at the conference, particularly those from France, had found empirically about price-setting behaviour.

Professor Nell raised a problem about macroeconomic equilibrium conditions. In the Kaleckian framework fixed capital existed in each of the sectors. Suppose that the expected rate of return rose and that there was an increase in the demand for investment goods. Suppose also that the capacity of the investment goods sector was limited and the pressure of aggregate demand for investment raised the price of investment goods once full capacity was reached. Under those circumstances, since the capitalists' propensity to save was greater than that of the workers, the increase in profits would eventually provide the savings in value terms required for the investment. Since fixed capital was fixed, however, the macroeconomic equilibrium conditions would be satisfied only in value terms and not in real terms.

On the question of mark-up pricing, *Professor Streissler* said that he had often argued that there was a close relationship between investment decisions and the mark-up. The difficulty with Kalecki's model was that there appeared to be too little competition in it. One could, however, save the model if one assumed, for instance, that products had life cycles. After a new product was introduced the mark-up would decline over the life cycle of the product, because of competition from the products of rival firms entering the industry. Thus one might have a constant mark-up in spite of the fact that mark-ups were constantly whittled away by competition. If, however, the number of new products introduced increased over time, then the average mark-up would depend not only upon the initial mark-up, but also positively upon the growth rate and negatively upon the rate of decline of the mark-up over the life of the product.

Professor Henin made three points:
(1) There could be a middle way between the assumption of different market structures for raw materials and goods and the use of a vertically integrated model which assumed the same mark-up for raw materials and goods.
(2) Professor Asimakopulos and Dr Nuti had not mentioned Kalecki's principle of increasing risk. This had led Kalecki to derive not only an increasing supply curve of output but also a quantitative credit rationing constraint, which could perhaps help to explain the relation between expected investment and required profits.
(3) Although the degree of monopoly power could explain some dispersion of mark-up rates between sectors, it could not be used to explain the average mark-up in the economy, particularly in the long run; it would also be paradoxical for an economist in the Marxian tradition to explain income distribution by market forces. The difficulties of providing the Kaleckian mark-up pricing process with a satisfactory interpretation illustrated the ambiguities in transposing such pricing processes to the macroeconomic level. If no theoretical scheme of integration and aggregation was provided the resulting macroeconomic relation would be founded on mere analogy and would be *ad hoc*.

Professor Stiglitz discussed the two behavioural hypotheses in Professor Asimakopulos's model. He first raised the problem of the meaning of the mark-up hypothesis. At any point of time there was for any firm a price and a marginal cost and a ratio between these two variables. To turn that into an interesting hypothesis one had to add assumptions as to the constancy of the ratio and/or its independence of the level of unemployment and the level of aggregate demand. Further, the tests of this hypothesis were not encouraging; except for a few oligopolistic industries the hypothesis did not perform well. Although there were statistical problems, the tests suggested that the mark-up hypothesis did not characterise the behaviour of American manufacturing industry. The investment function was also unsatisfactory in several respects. There was the problem of trying to relate it to microeconomic behaviour: if there was excess capacity, why were firms investing? There was also the problem that it was conceivable that if the current rate of return on invest-ment rose the *expected* rate of return would fall, because if a high rate of profit corresponded to a high current rate of investment, then a high current return would mean a low future rate of return.

Professor Negishi intervened to point out that the asymmetric effect in Figure 10:4 of Professor Asimakopulos's paper assumed that it was no longer possible to increase investment even though there was negative excess capacity; this implied that there was already investment in progress. If the level of investment were reduced, then there remained some unfinished or semi-finished investments; would such unfinished investment have an effect on the current level of investment activity?

In response to Professor Nell's question, *Dr Sweeney* pointed out that in, for instance, a four-good model there were four equilibrium conditions: namely, excess demand for investment goods = excess demand for consump-tion goods = excess demand for money = excess demand for bonds = 0, of which only three were independent. When the excess demands for both money and bonds equal zero, then the sum of the values of the excess demand for investment goods and the excess demand for consumption goods equalled zero, savings would be equal to investment, but there was not necessarily equilibrium in *each* of the two goods markets.

Professor Koopmans asked whether Professor Asimakopulos's model was intended or suited for empirical testing. If it was, had any empirical tests been carried out? If so, what were the results?

Professor Marty, to the amusement of the other participants, adopted a 'Robinsonian' line. He pointed out that in Professor Asimakopulos's Figure 10:2, α and β did not refer to comparison between economies: one wanted to look at how the economy moved from position α to position β. In that case, there was a value of gross investment in wage units, but if labour markets were tight the wage unit might rise. Then the entire schedule would shift down-wards. Similarly, in Figure 10:3, the schedule would shift under the impact of technical progress. The question then arose: How could one know that these were stable functions, sufficiently stable to be verified by empirical work?

Dr Goodhart doubted whether the analysis of Professor Asimakopulos's paper was in fact particularly applicable to a capitalist economy. The main behavioural element in the Kalecki model was the savings function, which assumed that the propensity to save out of profits was greater than the propensity to save out of wages. In a capitalist economy this was debatable, given the life-cycle savings hypothesis; in a socialist economy it was more likely to be true. The other behavioural elements of the model were rather hazy, and the remainder of the model consisted of accounting identities.

Reacting to Professor Harcourt's question, *Professor Malinvaud* pointed out that there was a French macroeconomic model that had been built in the spirit of the Cambridge and Kalecki school. It was a short-term annual model which had been fitted on the data for the postwar French economy. Since Professor Malinvaud believed that in macroeconomics we should try to avoid being dogmatic, he was himself quite sympathetic to the model. When fitted on the data the model had turned out to be as good as but no better than any other short-term model, such as Klein-Goldberger. There was in it an equation relating the share of profits to a few variables, including the rate of increase of capital per unit of labour during the current and the two preceding years; in other words, there was a relation similar to the hypothesis that the share of profits was positively correlated with investment. This relation turned out to be statistically significant, but the interpretation was not clear; the definite six-year cycle in postwar France permitted alternative explanations. There was a basic difficulty in testing the hypothesis that the mark-up depended upon firms' investment: profitability was both an explanation of the importance of a mark-up and an explanation of the importance of investment.

Professor Parkin addressed himself to the question that had been raised by Professor Koopmans about empirical work. He had not been aware of the French empirical work but the work in Britain and North America had not favoured the mark-up hypothesis. The evidence there suggested that factors such as demand pressure systematically entered into the determination of the mark-up. The study by Godley and Nordhaus purported to show that the mark-up hypothesis was true; Godley and Nordhaus had computed the variable called normal cost by decycling the components of unit cost and then attempted to correlate price changes with the normal unit cost; in their regression equation they had found a positive intercept and a slope coefficient that was significantly below unity. But whereas they concluded that this constituted evidence for a constant mark-up, Professor Parkin concluded that some systematic factor had been omitted from the equation. With respect to the savings and consumption functions, matters were more nearly settled. The best empirical work was by Modigliani, who had compared the explanatory power of the life-cycle hypothesis and of the alternatives and shown that the life-cycle hypothesis won on several counts. That did not, of course, settle the matter, but it did mean that the hypothesis could explain many observed facts.

Professor Shubik intervened to report that in General Electric he had observed that for large-scale producer goods approximately 50 per cent to 70 per cent of the costs were lumped in overhead costs before the introduction of the large-scale computer; after the big computer was introduced only 35 per cent of costs were called overheads. What would be the basis of the mark-up in this case?

Professor Nell claimed that this had nothing to do with the issue; Kalecki's hypothesis was that mark-ups in different firms would be proportional to the different capital-output ratios in different sectors.

Replying to the discussants, *Professor Asimakopulos* first discussed the differences of interpretation between Dr Nuti and himself:

(1) The satisfaction of Keynesian short-term expectations was not *necessary* for the operation of his model, but it did remove the problems of unexpected undesired savings and inventories. It meant that firms' rates of sales were equal to their rates of output; it did not mean that their long-term expectations about, say, their rates of capacity utilisation, were satisfied. The condition of satisfaction of short-term expectations was necessary for the derivation of equation (5), where the rate of output of consumption goods was assumed to be equal to the rate of demand for them.

(2) Dr Nuti had pointed out that Kalecki did not use wage units. Professor Asimakopulos had used wage units to measure investment in real terms because capital goods were heterogeneous and changed over time.

(3) Professor Asimakopulos's paper represented only an initial step in a full Kaleckian approach. Hence he had at this stage left out the primary sector by means of the device of vertical integration.

(4) There were two basic differences between the Kaldor and Kalecki theories of distribution: first, Kalecki did not assume full employment; and second, Kalecki was much more careful in his treatment of historical time. In both theories investment was predetermined in the short period and the propensity to save out of profits was greater than that out of wages. Professor Asimakopulos had for simplicity assumed that the latter propensity was zero.

(5) In Professor Asimakopulos's model the timing of events was particularly important. In the short period with given productive capacity the investment decision in real terms was given. One could then, given the accounting and behavioural relations, work out the implications of this investment for the level of activity and the distribution of income. That was the point of the diagrams. Figure 10:1 showed the relation between investment in wage units and profits in wage units: the profit earnings of firms were positively related to investment in real terms. The expected rate of return on new investment was related to the rate of return on recently completed plants, as shown by the E curve. Figure 10:3 represented the dependence of investment decisions on the expected rate of return on investment. These investment decisions would be implemented in the future at a time to be determined by the nature of the investment. The curves in Figures 10:2 and 10:3 were not put together because they were based upon past history. It was not possible to use one set of curves to analyse the movement of investment over time, since these curves changed with changing historical experiences.

Professor Asimakopulos then turned to the other comments. With respect to Professor Negishi's remarks he pointed out that the undertaking of investment involved a lag between the decision and the implementation. In his model the short period was a quarter of a year; in this period it might be possible to reverse some investment decisions before they were implemented; by, for instance, the cancellation of orders for capital goods. On the mark-up hypothesis, he pointed out that in Kalecki's model the mark-up was not determined by investment decisions but by the degree of monopoly. The target rate of return was determined by both the normal rate of profits in the economy (determined in its turn by capitalists' expenditure) and, in some industries, barriers to entry. With respect to Professor Henin's second point, Professor Asimakopulos agreed that the principle of increasing risk was very important in understanding the growth of firms and their need to retain earnings.

In reply to Professor Koopmans, Professor Asimakopulos said that the model was conceived for empirical verification and the mark-up hypothesis was an empirical statement to be tested. The outcome of the tests that had been carried out were, however, difficult to interpret. He did not think that the evidence mentioned by Professor Stiglitz was necessarily unfavourable to the hypothesis. As for the life-cycle hypothesis of savings behaviour, he said that he believed that an advantage of the Kaleckian approach was its emphasis on the importance of firms' investment decisions in determining the distribution of income rather than on the savings decisions of individuals.

Professor Asimakopulos thought that Professor Marty's comment was based on a misunderstanding of the working of the Kaleckian model. The only comparisons that could be made in a short period were of the 'comparative statics' type. It was *not* possible to take two points α and β on the curve in Figure 10:2, and to speak in terms of going from α to β. The investment in this period, determined by decisions taken in the past, would place the economy at some point on the E curve, say α or β. We could compare the effects on the economy of a rate of investment that placed it on point α, as contrasted with one that placed it on point β, but these were alternative positions. In reply to Dr Goodhart, Professor Asimakopulos emphasised that the analysis applied only to a capitalist economy: the social relations were those of a capitalist system, the income categories reflected these social relations, and the key decision-makers for investment were individual firms and not a central authority.

11   An Aspect of the Economic Role of Unemployment

R. E. Hall

MASSACHUSETTS INSTITUTE OF TECHNOLOGY

INTRODUCTION

Economic thought on the role of unemployment has evolved in the past
decade from the view that unemployment is a simple waste of resources to
the view that at least some unemployment is privately and socially beneficial
because it yields a better match between jobs and workers. The papers by
Phelps, Holt, and Mortensen in the famous volume, *Microeconomic Foundations of Employment and Inflation Theory* (1970) have been especially
influential in bringing about this change in thinking. The literature on the
microeconomics of unemployment has not settled the issue of the
optimality of the equilibrium level of unemployment present in an unfettered
competitive economy. The extreme view that the private and social costs and
benefits are precisely equal is not widely held. In his thoughtful review of the
subject (Tobin, 1972), James Tobin has observed that the process of job
search involves externalities associated with congestion and queuing, but is
uncertain 'whether the market is biased toward excessive or inadequate
search' (p. 8). My purpose in this paper is to study one specific externality in
considerable microeconomic detail. The externality arises from the effect of
unemployment in the market on the hiring and firing policies of employers.
Earlier empirical work of mine has suggested the following hypothesis, which
Arthur Okun has picturesquely called the 'spare tyre theory': firms in
chronically tight labour markets try to minimise turnover by holding overhead
labour during temporary reductions in demands for their products. The costs
of recruiting in tight markets motivates this policy. In chronically slack
markets, on the other hand, firms treat the unemployed as a readily available
buffer stock from which they can draw whenever labour is needed. They do
not hold overhead labour because recruiting labour when it is needed is
inexpensive. Within the United States, there is a certain amount of evidence
in favour of the hypothesis. There are dramatic chronic differences in
unemployment rates among cities. Those with low unemployment rates have
strikingly low lay-off rates — the weekly probability of losing a job in Chicago,
a city with a tight market, is less than one quarter of the probability in San

Francisco, where the labour market is chronically slack.[1] International comparisons are even more striking — lay-off rates are virtually zero in countries with low unemployment rates.

This paper studies a microeconomic model with a structure that has been simplified in order to examine the particular issue of the external effect of unemployment. The model has no claim whatever to generality or realism. Rather, it serves as an extended example of the externality. In the model, a pathological equilibrium is possible, where output is far below its feasible level because an excessively tight labour market induces firms to hold overhead labour. The model also has an efficient equilibrium in which reserve labour is held only in the market where all firms have access to it. The wage is sufficiently high and recruiting sufficiently cheap that overhead labour within the firm does not pay for itself.

The structure and properties of the model of this paper cut very much against the grain of most recent thinking about unemployment and the function of labour markets. In the model, turnover is beneficial to both workers and employers, whereas most recent thought emphasises the costs of turnover owing to the dissipation of specific human capital and portrays employers as trying to minimise turnover (see Stiglitz, 1974, for example). Here, unemployment has no private benefits associated with the accumulation of topical knowledge of the labour market. It is not a search theory in the spirit of Mortensen (1970) and others. The contrast with other work is clearest in its conclusions about subsidies for the unemployed. Many economists favour unemployment compensation on grounds of equity while conceding the inefficiency it brings about by making the private return to unemployment exceed the social return. Martin Feldstein (1973), for example, has cited the generosity of unemployment compensation as an important obstacle to low unemployment rates in the United States. He favours tight labour markets achieved by making individuals bear more of the cost of unemployment. In the model of this paper, just the opposite is optimal· slack labour markets supported by full unemployment compensation. Driving unemployment out of the labour market only makes it reappear less efficiently in the form of overhead labour within the firm.

I THE MODEL

I will consider the problem of allocating a fixed labour force of size L to a fixed number of firms, N. Each firm produces one unit of output with one worker; however, there is only a probability of one half that it can produce at all. Agricultural firms dependent on stochastic rainfall are an example of the technology the model embodies. I assume that there is a sufficiently large

[1] There is weaker evidence that wages are correspondingly higher in cities with slack markets. This is necessary to attract labour to high-unemployment cities, and is possible because labour is more fully employed within the firm, and hence more productive, in those cities. See Hall (1972) for an extended discussion.

number of firms that the fraction of them who are able to produce is deterministic and equal to one half. It is possible for firms to put labour to work *after* they have determined whether they can produce. In the absence of any constraints on the allocation process, it is clear that all firms should wait until it is known which of them can produce and then to hire the $N/2$ workers they will need. With this scheme, if the labour force is exactly the right size $(L = N/2)$, every worker will produce one unit of output and every firm will produce as much as possible. Assigning a worker to a firm before it was known whether or not he could be used would make his expected productivity only half as high. Unconditional assignment would be efficient only if labour was sufficiently redundant to assign a worker to every firm $(L = N)$. For the rest of the paper I will assume for simplicity that $L = N/2$, so labour is not redundant.

Both a rational planner and a competitive market would arrive at the same conditional process of allocation if workers could be shifted costlessly among firms. The problem becomes interesting only when a more realistic view of the labour market is adopted. In practice, each firm has access to only a small fraction of the labour force, typically just those who enquire about work around the time when it is available. The danger of the conditional hiring policy to the firm is that there is a probability, v, that no workers will be available when needed. If v is high enough, it may be more profitable to hold workers permanently rather than to hire them only when work is available. A reasonable, general characterisation of the probability of failing to find a worker is that it depends on the total number of workers available in the market, say S (which may be less than $N/2$), and the total number of firms actually hiring, say D (which may also be less than $N/2$):

$$v = \phi(S, D) \tag{1}$$

I will make use of a particularly simple version of this general model. Suppose that each of the S workers visits one employer chosen at random and takes a job if it is available; if more than one worker appears, one is chosen at random for employment. The probability that a given worker will visit a particular employer is $1/D$. The probability that an employer will not be visited by *any* worker is

$$\phi(S, D) = \left(1 - \frac{1}{D}\right)^S$$

$$= \left[\left(1 - \frac{1}{D}\right)^{-D}\right]^{-S/D}$$

$$\doteq e^{-S/D} \tag{2}$$

Since I take D to be large it is reasonable to take $\phi(S, D)$ to be exactly $e^{-S/D}$. When supply and demand are equal, the unemployment rate is $e^{-1} = 0.37$. Later in the paper I will discuss more effective matching processes that achieve much lower unemployment rates when supply and demand are equal.

The probability v can be viewed as the vacancy rate.[1] It is linked to the unemployment rate, u, by the identity that the number of filled jobs is equal to the number of employed workers:

$$(1 - v)D = (1 - u)S \tag{3}$$

Firms may adopt a conditional employment strategy, hiring only if they are able to produce, or an unconditional strategy. Suppose that a fraction x of them operate conditionally and the remaining $1 - x$ operate unconditionally. Employment in unconditional firms will be $(1 - x)N$ and output will be $(1 - x)N/2$. Labour supply in the conditional market will be $S = N/2 - (1 - x)N = (x - \frac{1}{2})N$ and demand will be $D = xN/2$. The vacancy rate will be

$$v = \phi((x - \tfrac{1}{2})N, xN/2)$$
$$= e^{-(2x-1)/x} \tag{4}$$

Total output will be the output of unconditional firms who are able to produce plus the output of conditional firms who are able to produce *and* who are successful in hiring labour:

$$Q(x) = ((1 - v)x + 1 - x)N/2$$
$$= (1 - vx)N/2 \tag{5}$$

If the vacancy rate did not depend on x, Q would be a decreasing function of x, and the optimum would occur at $x = 1/2$, where all labour is employed unconditionally. Under the assumption that labour is not superfluous, however, the vacancy rate is low for x close to one and rises rapidly as x declines. Every firm switching from conditional to unconditional hiring reduces the supply of labour by one but reduces the demand for labour by only a half. The lower is x, the tighter is the labour market and the lower is the productivity of the conditional firms. The derivative of output with respect to x is

$$Q'(x) = - \left(v + x \frac{dv}{dx} \right) N/2$$
$$= (1 - x) \frac{v}{2x} N \tag{6}$$

Output *increases* with x over the whole range of x, so the optimum occurs at $x = 1$, where all firms hire conditionally. It is inefficient to hold any labour in reserve within any firm; even though the method of placing workers in jobs is severely limited, it is less costly than placing workers in firms with only a 50 per cent probability of being productive.

---

[1] This vacancy rate is the number of firms idled by lack of labour. It should be distinguished from the vacancy rate for jobs as collected by the government. Firms with vacant jobs may still operate at capacity if the firms are looking for workers in anticipation of future needs.

Next I will investigate market equilibrium in this model. I define equilibrium as the absence of opportunity for any individual economic agent to improve his situation. (Supply and demand for labour need not be equal in the model, so the usual definition of competitive equilibrium does not apply.) Two conditions are required for equilibrium defined in this way. First, if both employment strategies co-exist in the market, they must be equally profitable — were one strategy more profitable than another, the second would not be used. Second, employment must be equally attractive in the two kinds of firms. I will assume the absence of risk aversion among workers and employers. The only unattractive feature of the open labour to workers is the reduction in expected income associated with unemployment, not the uncertainty it causes. Then if the wage for stable employment among unconditional firms is w, the suitably higher wage in the open labour market with unemployment rate u is $\dfrac{w}{1-u}$. With these wage levels, the equal-profit condition for firms can be derived as follows: the expected profit for unconditional operation is $1/2 - w$ — a product selling at price one can be produced with probability $1/2$ but a wage w must be paid with certainty. The expected profit for conditional operation is $\frac{1}{2}(1-v)\left(1-\dfrac{w}{1-u}\right)$ — with probability $1/2$, neither production nor attempted hiring takes place, otherwise the firm has probability $1-v$ of hiring a worker at wage $\dfrac{w}{1-u}$ and selling the product at price 1. The equilibrium condition for co-existence (i.e., $x < 1$) is

$$1/2 - w = \tfrac{1}{2}(1-v)\left(1-\frac{w}{1-u}\right) \tag{7}$$

Given v and u, the only wage consistent with equilibrium is

$$w = \frac{v}{2 - \dfrac{1-v}{1-u}} \tag{8}$$

In terms of the relation between x and u and v hypothesised in equations 2 and 3, the equilibrium condition is

$$w = xv \tag{9}$$

At the minimum value of x, $1/2$, the vacancy rate is 1 and the wage is $1/2$, while at the maximum value, $x = 1$, the vacancy rate is $e^{-1} = 0.37$ and the wage is 0.37 as well. The equilibrium wage declines as x increases because the labour market is slackening and conditional hiring is becoming more attractive. With values of x close to one, only a low wage can make unconditional hiring as profitable as conditional hiring. At the point where there are literally no unconditional firms ($x = 1$), equal profitability no longer applies and the wage is free to take on a range of values, bounded below by the point where unconditional operation would be more profitable ($w = e^{-1}$) and above by the point where the profit of conditional operation is zero ($w = 1 - e^{-1} = 0.63$).

The equilibrium possibilities thus consist of mixed conditional and unconditional hiring in a tight labour market with the low wage prescribed by equation (9) together with totally conditional hiring in a slack labour market with a range of higher wages. I have already argued that the high-wage, slack market allocation is the only efficient one for this model. Although the efficient allocation is an equilibrium in the model, it is not the only equilibrium, but the others are inefficient. Under the constraints imposed on the labour market by the model, competitive pressures do not necessarily bring the economy to an optimal allocation of labour. In the inefficient, tight-market equilibrium, there is a genuine externality associated with unemployment. The movement of one worker from the unconditional to the conditional sector would raise output even though it would raise unemployment as well, yet wages are effectively equal in the two sectors and workers face no incentive to move.

II FURTHER STUDY OF THE TIGHT-MARKET, LOW-WAGE EQUILIBRIUM

The inefficient equilibrium of the previous section depends fundamentally on the hypothesis that firms can locate workers only in the way assumed. Many kinds of arbitrage within the market are ruled out by assumption. For example, a group of firms could raise their joint profit by forming a private labour pool. Even two firms can benefit by forming a pool containing a single worker. They could offer sure employment to the worker and thus pay the wage for unconditional employment, w. Their joint expected revenue would be the probability of producing, which is 3/4, less the wage bill, w. The expected profit per firm would be half this, or $3/8 - w/2$. By contrast, the expected profit of an independent firm, either conditional or unconditional, is $1/2 - w$, which is smaller than $3/8 - w/2$ for any w permitted by the model. In the model, firms are assumed not to have access to the workers of other firms in the way illustrated by this example. Firms either pay the cost of holding overhead labour or expose themselves to the chance of a vacancy together with the added cost of compensating workers hired conditionally for their exposure to the risk of unemployment.

The larger the scope of pooling workers among firms, the closer is the equilibrium to the unconstrained competitive equilibrium where all firms have free access to all workers, vacancy and unemployment rates are zero, and expected profits are $1/2 - w/2$. Belief in a labour market with unused resources attributable to stochastic matching of jobs and workers requires a belief that opportunities for arbitrage through pooling are limited. The model of this paper is a first attempt to characterise this limitation.

A second fundamental implicit assumption of the model is that firms are price-takers in the labour market. They make decisions on the assumption that they must offer the prevailing wage to get a worker at all, but that they have no higher probability of getting one by offering a wage above the prevailing level. The second part of the assumption is defensible within the model of job search, where workers get at best a single job offer and have no alternative to accepting it apart from unemployment. The first part has no satisfactory rationale. Under the assumptions of the model, the maximising firm should offer a wage only infinitesimally greater than zero when it actually comes to recruit, thereby taking full advantage of its power as a monopsonist. With this behaviour, no equilibrium is possible, because conditional employers as a group would have to offer a wage suitably higher than the unconditional wage to induce workers to enter the open labour market at all, yet each firm would have a large incentive to offer a much smaller wage if a worker actually appeared. This contradiction only demonstrates the inadmissability of the assumption that employers take the vacancy rate as given. The model counter-balances this unrealistic assumption with the equally unrealistic one that firms are also wage-takers. The result is a simple, workable model.

The next full step in this research is the creation of a model where firms take full advantage of their monopsony power but the power is limited because each worker visits more than one employer. A model extended in this direction is complex. Recent work of Gerald Butters (1975) and Daniel McFadden on a related problem in product markets suggests that under certain assumptions the only equilibrium will involve a distribution of wages, not a single prevailing wage. If all other employers offered the same wage, one employer could achieve a substantial increase in the probability of locating a worker by offering a wage only infinitesimally higher than the prevailing level. I will not pursue the development of a fully specified model with monopsony power here. Rather, I will assume that monopsony can be characterised in a certain way and then show that the pathological equilibrium with tight labour markets can arise even when firms recognise monopsony power and take advantage of it. The example I will give requires a slightly different specification of the matching process in the labour market slightly different from the earlier example. In the new example each worker meets with more than a single employer, so it is plausible that firms have a degree of monopsony power, but not the infinite power they had in the earlier example.

The new matching process assumes that the labour market has a second round where unsatisfied employers meet again with workers who did not find jobs in the first round. If S workers and D employers participate in the first round, $u_1 S$ workers and $v_1 D$ employers will remain to participate in the second. The first-round unemployment and vacancy rates u_1 and v_1 are determined as discussed earlier:

$$v_1 = e^{-S/D} \tag{10}$$

$$u_1 = 1 - (1 - e^{-S/D})D/S \tag{11}$$

The same process occurs in the second round, so the vacancy rate among participants in the second round is

$$v_2 = e^{-u_1 S/v_1 D} \tag{12}$$

The total vacancy rate is the probability of not finding a worker in either round and is the product of the two vacancy rates:

$$v = v_1 v_2 = e^{-(1 + u_1/v_1)S/D} \tag{13}$$

As before the unemployment rate is

$$u = 1 - (1 - v)D/S \tag{14}$$

It is apparent from these formulae that both the vacancy and unemployment rates are lower when there is a second round in the labour market. In the model of the previous section where firms are wage- and vacancy-takers, the character of the possible equilibria remains the same with the new specification of $\phi(S, D)$. At the efficient, slack-market equilibrium, $S = D$ and $u = v = e^{-2} = 0.14$. Since a larger fraction of the conditional labour force is employed, but the productivity of unconditional firms remains the same, the social cost of a tight-market equilibrium is higher. Further, the tight-market equilibrium occurs at lower wages – equation (9), $w = xv$, still holds, but v is lower for a given x.

Now suppose that workers choose among alternative employers in a way that makes the supply of labour to an individual firm upward-sloping in the following way:

Probability of locating a worker $= 1 - \tilde{v}$

$$= \min\left(\left(\frac{\tilde{w}}{w}\right)^{\frac{1}{2}}(1-v), 1\right) \tag{15}$$

Here $\dfrac{\tilde{w}}{1-u}$ is the firm's wage, $\dfrac{w}{1-u}$ is the prevailing wage offered by other firms and v is the vacancy rate for firms paying the prevailing wage. The expected profit for conditional hiring is then

$$\tfrac{1}{2}(1 - \tilde{v}) \quad 1 - \frac{\tilde{w}}{1-u} \tag{16}$$

Profit is maximised when

$$w = (1 - u)/3 \tag{17}$$

Since this calculation is performed by all firms, the prevailing wage, w, will in fact be $(1 - u)/3$. The possible equilibria in an economy with this process of wage-setting and the two-round matching scheme are shown in Figure 11:1.

The solid line in the Figure is the locus of equal profitability of conditional and unconditional hiring, $w = vx$; the broken line is the profit-maximising wage $(1-u)/3$. The new model has two distinct equilibria, an inefficient one with tight labour market and an efficient one with a slack market. Relaxation of the unrealistic assumption that firms are wage- and vacancy-takers does not change the fundamental conclusion of the paper that

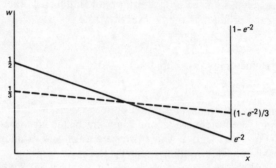

Fig. 11:1

an economy can achieve a pathological equilibrium where labour-hoarding is induced by excessively tight labour markets and where everyone could be made better off by moving some workers from employment in the unconditional sector to unemployment in the conditional sector.

III EFFICIENT SUBSIDY POLICIES

Within the simple model of the first part of this paper, many alternative policies could achieve efficiency. Most directly, the government could simply prohibit the hoarding of labour and require employers to make use of the open labour market. A sufficiently high tax on hoarded labour would have the same effect. However, existing policies rely largely upon subsidising unemployment, so it is of greatest interest to examine the role that such a subsidy could play in achieving efficiency.[1] Suppose that the government compensates unemployed workers at a fraction s_u of the wage they would have received in the open market had they found jobs. Then the gap between the wage for conditional employment and the wage for unconditional employment falls as s_u rises, and the two wages are equal if s_u is one. The conditional wage is $w/(1-(1-s_u)u)$, where, as before, w is the wage for unconditional employment. The condition of equal profit for the two methods of operation becomes

$$1/2 - w = 1/2(1-v)\left(1 - \frac{w}{1-(1-s_u)u}\right) \tag{18}$$

[1] The United States government has no important policies that encourage stable employment by taxing or controlling lay-offs. However, I believe that many other countries do have this kind of policy. Within the model of this paper, anti-lay-off policies are perverse.

Equality remains feasible even if s_u is one and unemployment is fully subsidised. High wages for conditional employment constitute only one of the two forces that make unconditional operation economically attractive, so elimination of the wage gap through an unemployment subsidy does not rule out the possibility of an inefficient equilibrium in which some firms operate unconditionally. The other force is the danger of vacancies in conditional operation. Suppose that the government compensates employers for a fraction s_v of the profit they forgo in case of a vacancy. Then the condition of equal profit is

$$\tfrac{1}{2} - w = \tfrac{1}{2}(1 - (1 - s_v)v) \left(1 - \frac{w}{1 - (1 - s_u)u}\right) \tag{19}$$

With high rates of subsidy, equality becomes possible only at very low wages but, in principle, an inefficient, tight-market equilibrium remains possible. When both unemployment and vacancies are fully subsidised ($s_u = s_v = 1$), the condition has the simple form

$$1/2 - w = 1/2(1 - w) \tag{20}$$

Equality cannot hold for any positive wage rate, so the only possible equilibrium has all firms operating conditionally and is therefore efficient.

IV CONCLUDING REMARKS

In a very simple model, unemployment has an important externality, in the sense that there is an equilibrium where total output could be increased by reallocating labour in a way that increased the unemployment rate. No claim can be made at this stage that a similar externality exists in a more realistic model where jobs and workers are heterogeneous and unemployment has a private benefit. The optimal unemployment and vacancy subsidies in a more realistic model would clearly be lower, since these subsidies distort private decisions along margins that are not considered in the simple model. The model does support the view, however, that unemployment cannot be conceived of simply as another use of individuals' time for which individual decisions can be relied upon to produce an efficient equilibrium. The presence of unemployed resources, whether labour or other factors, requires a thorough reconstruction of competitive economic theory.

REFERENCES

G. Butters, 'Equilibrium Distributions of Prices and Advertising', manuscript (1975).
M. S. Feldstein, *Lowering the Permanent Rate of Unemployment*, Joint Economic Committee, U.S. Congress (1973).
R. E. Hall, 'Turnover in the Labor Force' *Brookings Papers on Economic Activity*, No 3 (1972) pp. 709–56.
D. T. Mortensen, 'A Theory of Wage and Employment Dynamics', in E. S. Phelps, *et. al.*,

Microeconomic Foundations of Employment and Inflation Theory (New York: Norton, 1970).

E. S. Phelps *et al.*, *Microeconomic Foundations of Employment and Inflation Theory* (New York: Norton, 1970).

J. E. Stiglitz, 'Alternative Theories of Wage Determination and Unemployment in LDCs: The Labor Turnover Model', *Quarterly Journal of Economics*, Vol. 88, No 2 (May 1974) pp. 194–227.

J. Tobin, 'Inflation and Unemployment' *American Economic Review*, Vol. 62, No 1 (March 1972) pp. 1–18.

Discussion of the Paper by Professor Hall

Professor Stiglitz pointed out that Professor Hall had addressed himself to an important issue: What determined the equilibrium level of unemployment and was the market level too high or too low? He had focused on a particular aspect of frictional unemployment, the so-called 'spare tyre' theory of unemployment. One could call the spare tyre of an automobile 'unemployed', but this would clearly be misleading, for economic efficiency required keeping the spare tyre. In the labour market, it was argued, randomly an individual would have a low marginal productivity in a particular job. If there were no costs of reallocating labour, then in each period we should allocate labour to those uses where it had the highest marginal productivity. But if there were costs of reallocating labour, then we had to ask whether it was in fact better to leave labour in its lower productivity occupation.

Professor Hall had formulated a neat little model in which the only cost of reallocating labour was the associated unemployment. In this model each firm hired at most one worker, and half the time each firm was productive. Thus, if the output of a productive firm was 1, and if workers were not relocated, output per man was $\frac{1}{2}$. On the other hand, if there were S job seekers and D firms, and if individuals randomly sampled firms, $De^{-S/D}$ of the firms would not obtain any workers. Then, if a fraction $1 - x$ of the firms hired unconditionally, the demand for labour from the remaining firms was $xN/2$, while the supply of labour was $N/2 - (1 - x)N$. Hence the rate of unemployment in the conditional sector was $e^{-(2x-1)/x}$ and aggregate output $Q = [(1 - x) + x(1 - e^{-(2x - 1)/x})] \cdot N/2$. Then

$$\frac{Q'}{N} = -\frac{1}{2} + \frac{1}{2}\left[(1 - e^{-(2x - 1)/x}) + \frac{e^{-(2x - 1)/x}}{x}\right] \gtreqqless 0,$$

with inequality implying $x = 1$, while competitive equilibrium required, if both types of firm produced, equal expected wages, i.e.:

$$\frac{w_{uc}}{1 - u} = w_c,$$

and equal profits, i.e.:

$$\frac{1}{2} - w_{uc} = \frac{1}{2}(1 - w_c)(1 - v) \text{ where } (1 - v)D = (1 - u)S.$$

Together these equations yielded the basic equilibrium condition

$$w_u = \frac{v}{2 - \dfrac{1 - v}{1 - u}} = \frac{v}{2 - \dfrac{2x - 1}{x}} = vx = xe^{-(2x - 1)/x}$$

There was no theory of wage determination; hence it was argued that there might be too little (or too much) unemployment. The interesting policy implication of the model was that the only way to eliminate the possibility of an inefficient unconditional equilibrium was a 100 per cent unemployment and vacancy subsidy.

Professor Stiglitz thought that Professor Hall had provided a fine piece of modelling for an aspect of unemployment which had so far received inadequate attention; there were three questions about it that one could raise:

(1) How important were these derivations in practice?

(2) How robust were the results, within the 'spare tyre' theory of unemployment?

(3) Were there elements of the determination of the level of unemployment which were important and which biased the result in other direction?

Professor Stiglitz proposed to show that the model was in fact not very robust. There were five assumptions which played a crucial role in the analysis:

(1) firms hired only one worker;

(2) individuals could search only once;

(3) individuals searched randomly only among firms which were job seekers;

(4) each firm had a probability of $\frac{1}{2}$ of being productive;

(5) the number of firms was fixed.

In addition there was the further — and perhaps most fundamental — problem of how to close the system, i.e. the development of a theory of wage determination. Although Professor Hall had admitted that such a satisfactory theory was absent from his model, it was hard to see in the absence of such a theory how he could propose analysing the welfare properties or the market equilibrium.

Professor Stiglitz considered the case where there was a cost of establishing a firm, c. Output maximisation required

$$\max Q = \frac{x_1}{2} + \frac{x_2}{2} (1 - e^{-2(1-x_1)/x_2}) - cx_1 - cx_2$$

where x_1 was the number of firms hiring unconditionally and x_2 was the number of firms hiring conditionally. Then optimality required:

$$\frac{1}{2} - e^{-2(1-x_1)/x_2} \underset{>}{\overset{<}{=}} c,$$

with inequality implying $x_1 = 0$ or $x_1 = 1$, and

$$\frac{1}{2} - \left[\frac{1}{2} + \frac{1-x_1}{x_2} \right] e^{-2(1-x_1)/x_2} \leqq c,$$

with inequality implying $x_2 = 0$.

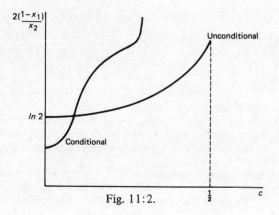

Fig. 11:2.

It followed that optimality entailed $x_2 = 0$: there should only be unconditional hiring. Hence any 'spare tyre' employment was excessive.

Professor Stiglitz considered another variation on the model, the polar case where individuals searched until they found a job. Since everyone obtained a job, net national output

$$Q = L \left[\begin{matrix} min \\ (-x, \hat{x}) \end{matrix} + \frac{1-x}{2} - c[2\hat{x} + (1-x) - xz] \right] (Lx, \hat{x}L)$$

where $2\hat{x}$ was the number of conditional firms and z was search costs. In general, z was a function of the number of firms and job seekers. Optimality entailed:

$$\hat{x} > x, \qquad -xLz_{\hat{x}} = 2c,$$

and if $\hat{x} > x$

$$\tfrac{1}{2} + c - (z + xz_x L) \geqslant 0 \text{ with inequality implying } x = 1.$$

Combining, we obtained

$$\tfrac{1}{2} = z + xL(z_x + z_{\hat{x}}).$$

Competitive equilibrium entailed, for an interior solution,

$$1 - 2 = 1 - w - z,$$

i.e., $w = z$.

In other words, only if wages were equal to search costs would there be an interior solution. Otherwise, competitive equilibrium entailed $x = 1$, and $\hat{x} > x$ if $\tfrac{1}{2}(1 - w_c) > c$. It was conceivable that, at $x = 1$, $\tfrac{1}{2} + c < x + xz_x L$ even though $z < w < \tfrac{1}{2} + c$. Thus again there was too much labour turnover.

Other modifications gave a qualitatively different picture. If one assumed, for instance, that only 5 per cent of the machines broke down in any period and let $N = 1 \cdot 08L$, then output *per capita* with complete unconditional employment was 0.95, while with complete conditional hiring it was $e^{-0.95} x \cdot 4$. In that case one could show that optimality entailed all unconditional employment.

Professor Stiglitz then turned to the broader issues raised by the paper. Was the equilibrium level of frictional unemployment too high or too low? One could list a number of factors that affected labour turnover and the associated unemployment. Professor Hall had stressed the spare tyre theory, and that might lead to too little unemployment; but on the other hand there appeared to be too much search unemployment, and the presence of unemployment insurance undoubtedly provided a subsidy for employment with some associated side-effects. Whether the latter were important enough to warrant a search for less disturbing forms of social insurance remained a moot question.

Professor Jané-Solá prefaced his remarks on Professor Hall's paper by saying that for decades unemployment had been one of the main points of interest in both theoretical and applied economics, because it was one of the principal problems which free societies had more or less been permanently

unable to resolve. The explanation of the unemployment problem and the
need to find ways to cope with it were the very roots of macroeconomics.
But as was well known, employment depended on the demand for labour as
well as the supply and also on many other variables because labour was not
just the nth commodity. Within the labour market four forces were found,
economic, social, power and organisational factors, which were of equal
importance. The non-economic forces might perhaps be of more importance
in wage and employment determination than economic forces in less
developed economies. There the workers' power might be negligible in terms
of the capacity for industrial conflict — strikes might be legally prohibited —
but it was often taken into account by politicians, and at the same time the
government played a very important role in fixing labour and wage conditions.
Nevertheless the unemployment problem had generally been analysed with
microeconomic or macoreconomic models. Professor Jané-Solá thought that
the different types of unemployment could be understood via microeconomics,
as in Professor Hall's paper.

Professor Hall had studied the specific externality which arose from the
effect of unemployment in the market on employers' hiring and firing policies.
Although Professor Hall did not claim generality or realism for his model,
Professor Jané-Solá thought that the model was applicable to at least one
real world case, Spain, where employers' hiring and firing policies were
absolutely controlled by institutional factors and governmental rules. The
Spanish labour market was not in fact a tight one because there were plenty
of people searching for jobs and still more people not drawn towards joining
the labour force — the participation rate was one of the lowest among
industrialised countries — but it worked as though it were a tight one. The
official unemployment rate was still very low and the lay-off rate was
virtually zero. When labour legislation was very restrictive with respect to
dismissing employees, as it was in Spain, firms were obliged to maintain
overhead labour during periods of low economic activity, just as in Professor
Hall's 'chronically tight labour markets'. On the other hand, one of the main
characteristics of the Spanish labour market was its lack of information,
which tended to keep workers in their jobs and to cause them to ignore better
offers even when work was reduced. Instead of hiring more labour in periods
of high economic activity Spanish employers offered well-paid overtime, which
was eliminated when economic activity was low. Consequently when work
was reduced the real wage was reduced but employment was not.

Professor Jané-Solá claimed that Spanish empirical data supported the
conclusion of Professor Hall's model, according to which 'unemployment has
an important externality, in the sense that there is an equilibrium where *total
output could be increased by reallocating labour in a way that increased the
unemployment rate*', at least in the short run. In the long run a new equilibrium could be reached at a lower unemployment rate, although this would
require measures to reduce structural and hidden unemployment and changing
the legislation which affected institutional, political and social factors.
Empirical studies of the Spanish case also corroborated Professor Hall's remark
that 'driving unemployment out of the labour market only makes it reappear
less efficiently in the form of overhead labour within the firm'. Since in Spain
the objective of maintaining a low unemployment rate was politically

important, important microeconomic objectives such as firms' efficiency were forgotten or put aside, even at the cost of misallocation of resources, a higher rate of inflation and a lower rate of economic growth. Professor Jané-Solá thought that Professor Hall's model was correct in indicating that 'competitive pressures do not necessarily bring the economy to an optimal allocation of labour'. Spain was not at all an efficient and equilibrated economy, as its economic performance in the last decade demonstrated. Therefore it was clear to Professor Jané-Solá that Professor Hall's model was not so unrealistic as he had claimed.

Professor Spaventa feared that there was not much to say about Professor Hall's model after Professor Stiglitz's presentation of it. What struck him was that Professor Hall was trying to provide an optimising model but had not taken into account workers' preference functions. Were workers indifferent as to whether they worked or stayed at home on the dole? If one was going to use an optimising model one should apply it to everybody. Since there was a lack of empirical evidence on workers' preferences Professor Spaventa drew attention to the different behaviour of firms in different countries at the present time. In Germany Volkswagen were dismissing 25,000 workers, while in Italy firms were hoarding labour. This was due to institutional constraints: in Germany the firms could sack migrant labour rather than German nationals; in other countries trade unions objected. Why did unions object? Firms would surely like to follow Professor Hall's 'advice', since a dismissed worker at home was not likely to be a militant worker and could often also be used as a blackleg worker.

With respect to Professor Jané-Solá's comments, Professor Spaventa wondered if it was true that in Spain some people were not interested in joining the labour force. Extensive empirical research had shown that this was not true in the Italian case, where the decline in the labour force could be explained by a number of institutional and economic factors.

Dr Sweeney said that Professor Hall's paper had prompted him to use the ingredients of the model to get a somewhat different set of results.

First, suppose that there were very few workers relative to firms, and that initially all firms hired 'conditionally': that is, only if they were allowed to produce in the given period. Virtually every worker would be employed because there were so many firms relative to job seekers. The real *demand price* for labour of each hiring firm was then 1, since there were no other factors in the model, and each employed worker produced one unit of output. No firm could afford to stockpile, for it could offer a wage of only $\frac{1}{2}$ (since it produces only half the time on average) and workers could do better by searching. Second, suppose the labour supply increases. At various times we might now find two workers applying to the same firm, and the firm might try to take advantage of this to lower its wage. This would, however, be stymied as workers learned to avoid that firm — there were costs to acting as a discriminator. The wage should remain equal to 1.

As the labour supply grew, unemployment would also rise due to the fixity of demand. When unemployment reached 50 per cent, it would become profitable for some workers to accept unconditional employment at a wage equal to $\frac{1}{2}$, since with conditional employment they would get a wage of 1 but have a 50 per cent chance of being unemployed and thus an expected wage of

$\frac{1}{2}$. If the labour supply grew further, unemployment among conditional workers would be held at 50 per cent by more and more firms hiring unconditionally; that is, removing workers from the pool of potential conditional employees. This would keep conditional and unconditional employers making the same level of profits (zero) and keep the expected wage the same for all workers. If the labour force grew so large that all firms hired unconditionally at a wage equal to $\frac{1}{2}$, further increases in the labour force would serve only to drive down the wage rate below $\frac{1}{2}$. In Professor Hall's example of a perfectly inelastic total unconditional demand and a perfectly inelastic aggregate industry labour supply curve, the wage was indeterminate. In his own version of it, the wage depended on demand and supply, and labour supply that was less than perfectly inelastic rendered the wage rate determinate. Output under all labour supply conditions was as high as the fundamental structure allowed. *Optimality* ruled in all cases.

Professor Frey wanted, like Professor Spaventa, to stress the unduly limited optimality concept in Professor Hall's paper. He made two points to show this. First, there was a trade-off between efficiency in terms of output and job security, as Professor Spaventa had pointed out. In Japan and most European countries workers had a strong preference for staying in the same firm, often for life. Dismissals not only affected the employees actually fired but also all the other employees of the same firm because they took it as an indication of an increased probability of being themselves dismissed. Second, if lay-offs were impossible as in most European countries, firms had an incentive to look for new markets and new products. This incentive was not a 'neoclassical' incentive, and it might well be that making lay-offs impossible *increased* dynamic efficiency of the 'Hirschman type'.

Professor Izzo raised the question that if the movement of one worker from unconditional to conditional employment would raise output and employment, provided that the subsidy was just a fraction of the wage, to whom would firms sell the increased output?

Professor Streissler had a question for Professor Stiglitz: Would he call Professor Hall's model a neoclassical model? *Professor Stiglitz* replied that he did not use such words because they gave rise to confusion. *Professor Streissler* said that he was concerned as to how neoclassical economists could present the pricing model given in Professor Hall's paper (p. 358); non-neoclassical economists could not believe in such a model because prices did not in fact change with changes in output.

Dr Goodhart said that he had noticed that lay-offs in the economics profession were not usually welcomed because they increased efficiency. The general feeling was that in such circumstances it was a personal tragedy with very little benefit for the profession or for the universities. He did not see why this should not also be true for other kinds of workers.

Professor Malinvaud said that he had been interested in what Professor Jané-Solá had told us in relation to Professor Hall's model, because when we had to understand what such a model meant we had to go into details on the institutional situation of the country or period of time that we were considering. Very often the models were very special. What inference should we draw from that? Some people might conclude that since these models were so special we should not try to develop them, given that they will always miss important facets of the phenomenon. If we did not take that point of view, then we had to recognise, as Professor Hicks had said the day before, that we were facing a very complex phenomenon and it was perhaps our duty to look at it in its complexity; i.e. to develop a number of different models and discuss them.

It was not a very pleasant job and one that was often put on the shoulders of mathematical economists. Generalists should be glad that they did not have to do it themselves; they should be kind to those poor fellows who were working hard on formalisations in order to help us understand the many facets of the unemployment problem.

Professor Stiglitz answered some of the specific questions. Several questions had related to workers' preferences; Professor Hall had explicitly taken that into account and made assumptions about the wage that would have to be paid to a worker to compensate him for being unemployed. On the question of institutional constraints, although one could not disagree that these were involved in the hiring of workers, Professor Stiglitz was not sure that they were the most important constraints; there were more real economic factors, like specific training costs. He had appreciated the attempt by Dr Sweeney to try to formulate a theory of wage determination for the model but did not think Dr Sweeney had succeeded: more work had still to be done. In answer to Professor Izzo, he pointed out that Professor Hall's model was one in which the people who were hired bought the goods that they produced. There was no problem of lack of effective demand; unemployment was purely frictional unemployment associated with a search disequilibrium. Finally, he agreed with Professor Malinvaud that one way these issues ought to be approached was by formulating a series of several models looking at the different aspects. His own criticism of Professor Hall's model was that he was not convinced he had provided a robust model even within that context; Professor Hall had none the less provided a framework in which we could discuss and evaluate the issues. For a final judgement about the costs of unemployment we needed more information about the magnitudes of the various kinds of unemployment.

Professor Jané-Solá answered Professor Spaventa's question. Professor Spaventa was in fact correct; it was not that some Spaniards were not interested in joining the labour force, but that though willing they could not. For example, the participation rate for women between twenty and sixty-five years of age was only about 25 per cent partly because of the lack of children's nurseries.

ADDENDUM

Professor Hall, who was unable to attend the conference, subsequently replied to the discussion of his paper:

Let me emphasise again that, in logical structure, the paper provides a counter-example to the proposition that the market equilibrium involves an efficient level of unemployment. Professor Stiglitz is quite correct in saying that the model is not robust with respect to this inefficiency − it can easily be modified to eliminate the inefficiency. I do not believe the lack of robustness diminishes its value as a counter-example.

At this stage I am unable to appraise the quantitative importance of the considerations addressed in the paper. Certainly, as Professor Stiglitz points out, other factors in the labour market bias it towards excessive unemployment. Still, I am unconvinced by the assumption, implicit in many recent discussions, that every subsidy to the unemployed is inefficient. Professor Jané-Solá's supporting remarks about the Spanish economy suggest that the perverse effects of excessively tight labour markets deserve further theoretical and empirical investigation.

Professor Spaventa raises the question of the motivation of workers within the model. Implicitly, I assume that workers have no alternative uses of their time. In the labour market, they are indifferent among alternative activities that yield the same income. I believe that these assumptions are compatible with the empirical evidence in the United States, which suggests a very low wage elasticity of labour supply. In any case, the model could easily be modified to make labour supply wage-elastic without affecting its major conclusions.

Dr Sweeney's remarks are based on assumptions rather different from mine. He assumes that firms make no profit and that labour appropriates the entire product. This assumption makes sense only if free entry of producers can take place. Then, as Professor Stiglitz demonstrated, inefficient unemployment cannot occur. However, my model assumes that the need to use capital or some other input imposes a fixed cost on firms. As the paper shows, limited entry makes inefficiency possible. Dr Sweeney's conclusion that 'optimality ruled in all cases' rests on his assumption of free entry and the absence of production costs other than wages.

12   Final Discussion

Professor Sir John Hicks introduced the discussion by explaining that we were holding this final meeting because our discussions had so far not done what we thought we were setting out to do. We had met to discuss a rather central issue in economics; but it had been shown that economists were not in a good state to discuss central issues. Economics was an expanding universe: we were each shooting off on our own paths, and we were lucky if we could keep in sight even of our closest neighbours; central issues, therefore, were almost lost from sight. We had been supposed to be discussing the microeconomic foundations of macroeconomics, but we had come to realise that there were several kinds of macroeconomics, each probably requiring its own foundations, and though they overlapped they were not wholly the same. One had to distinguish at the least between macroeconometrics and 'macro-political-economy'. The microeconomic foundations of macroeconometrics was a rather technical issue, which had not been our main concern; we had been much more concerned with macro-political-economy.

There was a close relation between macro-political-economy and social accounting, so he thought it might be useful to arrange our problems in relation to the social accounting framework in order to see how they fitted together. He took first the income-expenditure account of the household sector. This was in principle derived from the corresponding accounts of individual households, but Sir John believed that the aggregation raised no difficult problem: our theory of individual household behaviour made the passage from the individual to the collectivity smooth and easy. There were exceptions, arising in the collective but not in the individual case, from changes in distribution, but the theory enabled the exceptions to be identified. When we passed to the income-expenditure accounts of firms we came to much more awkward territory. Here we could not avoid such issues as the measurement of profits and issues relating to oligopoly. But the real core of the problem, which we had not sufficiently discussed, concerned the capital or saving-investment account. Sir John wished to pose some of the questions here rather sharply.

Keynes had said that saving and investment were always equal. We had learned to interpret that principle as an 'accounting identity' or an equality *ex post*, but we could not really make sense of Keynes's theory unless we admitted that there was another sense in which the equation was not an identity but was a condition for 'equilibrium'. These statements, which had got into nearly all the books, were both quite fishy. Aggregate saving was the algebraic sum of individual (positive or negative) savings. Individual saving was the difference between the value of the individual's capital at the beginning and at the end of the period; aggregate investment was the difference between the value of the capital of the collectivity at the beginning and at the end of the period. They ought to add up, but since the valuations often related to assets not marketed during the period and were made by different people, there was no economic reason for them to do so. They appeared in our social accounts to add up because of accounting conventions. Since most of the physical things which presented a difficulty of valuation appeared in saving and in investment, we could strike them out, constructing a form of the saving-investment equation ($S - I = 0$) in which every item would represent a market transaction, so that values would be unambiguously equal *ex post*; but this, which would look like an old-fashioned loanable funds equation, would be difficult to bring into relation with other macroeconomic variables.

The 'equilibrium' interpretation, while we were accustomed to it, did not fit comfortably into Keynes's theory. Sir John considered the simplest of all Keynesian models, that in which 'income' was determined by the confrontation of an upward-sloping 'consumption function' with an exogenously given level of investment. The meaning of the actual 'equilibrium' was clear; but what was the meaning of the other points on the consumption function schedule? They did not appear to be anything other than hypothetical positions. They showed that if I were different, Y would shift as shown. But they did not show that if Y were above its equilibrium level, savings would exceed investment; that was a pure geometrical construction, without economic meaning. There was no machinery shown whereby there could be a *tendency to equilibrium*. If that was to be achieved, S and I had to be re-interpreted. One way which was often suggested was to take them *ex ante*, but if this were done, even the items which were left in our *'reduced' ex post* $S - I = 0$ were no longer market items: they were just 'expectations' in the heads of the agents. There was no necessity for them to be consistent with one another or to be single-valued. They could have variances as well as means, and the variances could well be important. What then was meant by the statement that $S - I = 0$ (*ex ante*) in equilibrium?

A better way, he thought, was to take the consumption function and the investment function as expressing 'normal' relations. But it was only in quite simple (but useful) models that this made sense. There was a Keynes-type model, which he had himself set out formally in Chapter X of *Capital and Growth* (1965), where fixed capital investment was taken to be given exogenously, while investment in working capital was determined by a capital stock adjustment principle and consumption was similarly geared to normal income. Such a system could be said to be in 'equilibrium' when actual income and working capital were normal. This model was useful for the study of inventory fluctuations, but could not get us much further. Harrod had made fixed capital investment endogenous, using a capital stock adjustment principle. The resulting 'equilibrium' was, however, inherently unstable and was clearly not the equilibrium that Keynes had been talking about. In order to descend from this stratosphere one had to introduce frictions, lags or other 'coolants'. This again might be useful, but again not much was left of the concept of equilibrium in Keynes's sense.

Sir John emphasised that these were just models, within which one could define one's terms as one liked. But if one took these liberties with the terms, they could easily get far away from the conventional accounting concepts that we were bound to use in applied economics. What he had said about these models was probably most intelligible in relation to a 'fixprice' interpretation of Keynes, but many of the participants in this meeting disliked such an interpretation, being more at home with a 'flexprice' model. Sir John's own version of the flexprice system was still more or less the one he had given in *Value and Capital* (1939), but he did not now attach as much importance to it as he had done then. He would still be prepared to use it for some purposes, but for others he would want to use a fixprice model, and for others again some combination of the two.

However, since in *Value and Capital* there was no distinction between fixed and working capital, the *Value and Capital* model corresponded not to the inventory cycle model on the other approach, but to the Harrod model. It also had its 'knife-edge', when the elasticity of expectations was equal to unity. What he wished to emphasise was that he had been making no more than a first raid into what was then unexplored territory. There was, for instance, as much reason to introduce variances of price expectations here as there was to introduce variances of quantity expectations in a fixprice model. There were the same problems of varying expectations among individuals and of the formation of expectations from information about the past and the present. All this had been expressed, albeit inadequately, in the 'elasticity of expectations' formula.

In the *Value and Capital* model there was temporary equilibrium every day (or week) all the time, but there was no clear notion of any more comprehensive equilibrium. There was said to be an equilibrium when actual prices coincided with past expectations, but once one admitted variances of expectations this made no sense. No one to his knowledge had made much progress on this line, except in the direction of optimising models such as the one which Professor Koopmans had described. But these were not macro-political-economy.

Sir John concluded with an appeal to the members of the conference to stop searching the scriptures and to turn to the big task which remained to be done in the making of better theories.

Professor Henin wanted to explain why he was not in full agreement with the relative importance given to the different problems and approaches relating to the microeconomic foundations of macroeconomics. He thought that the participants had overemphasised markets and underemphasised financial problems.

Microeconomic foundations were concerned in the first place with the regulation of the macroeconomic system through the co-ordination of individuals' actions. The over-emphasis on markets arose from assuming that this co-ordination worked through markets. Professor Henin had thought that the core of the Cambridge School's message had been to combat the neo-classical assimilation of the economy to markets, but he feared he had been wrong when he heard that Marshall was still ruling the thought of many participants. In fact markets were only one way of co-ordinating individual behaviour, and prices were only one kind of relevant signal. There was some prior co-ordination of individual behaviour which simplified the work to be done by markets, namely the co-ordination by cultural patterns, by a common experience of life and common images of the world shared by groups of economic agents. These were sources of consistency and co-ordination, which might explain why real world economies were in general more stable than our models led us to expect. Herbert Simon's book, which was subtitled *Models of Man, Social and Rational*, would be a good programme for the development of microeconomic foundations.

The microeconomic foundations of macroeconomics should also include foundations for the integration of money. Here the conference had not achieved as much as Professor Henin had hoped. Putting money into a production function or a utility function was a typical *ad hoc* macroeconomic assumption, whereas in fact money mattered on three grounds: the technology of exchange, the production process, and short-run adjustments. The last two aspects had been neglected at the conference. With respect to the second aspect, the microeconomic foundation of money and finance derived in a simple and straightforward way from the fact that the production process was at the same time a process of combining inputs to get outputs and a circulation process involving money and the availability of financial resources. On this Professor Henin referred to O. Lange, 'Marxian Economics and Modern Economic Theory', *Review of Economic Studies*, 1935. The importance of the third aspect could be seen by considering the question: In short-term disequilibrium, with price rigidities and quantity constraints on the set of feasible transactions, which variable was the most likely to adjust? The answer was credit, since bankruptcy was no longer — at least in Europe — a normal way of performing the necessary adjustments and reallocations. The joint adjustment processes of inputs, financial assets and debt, and possibly prices, had more to tell us about the present inflation than a tale of M_{10} raining from a helicopter early one morning.

Professor Frey said that the microeconomic foundations of modern economics still assumed a purely individualistic and rational decision-maker. Economists should be aware that this '*homo oeconomicus*' was unacceptable to the other social sciences, especially sociology and psychology. On the individual level economists should be open to models different from the traditional decision-maker; the one different conception known to theoretical economists, namely Herbert Simon's 'satisficing behaviour', was now quite old, and one should ask what had happened since? Was satisficing an acceptable model on psychological and sociological grounds? Could it really make a difference to economic theory? There was also an *intermediate* level between microeconomics and macroeconomics which was of large and growing importance in modern societies. More and more reactions to changes in relative prices and constraints were on a collective basis. When, for example, a particular price rose, the groups of persons affected often managed to obtain compensation from the public purse, such as subsidisation of the particular product. There was then an endogenous economic process which made quantity reactions difficult or even impossible, and at the same time there was a growing gap between utility received and payments. Since there were many units operating which combined individual interests and which had also a specific and identifiable behaviour of their own, a general equilibrium theory which wanted to be relevant to modern society would have to take into account these collective modes of behaviour, and include interest groups, government and bureaucracy. There had been some theoretical moves in this direction, especially in the framework of the economic theory of politics or public choice. Olson's theory, for example, was intended to show which interests were able to organise themselves collectively and which were stable; Olson was able to derive reasons why consumers and taxpayers were difficult to organise compared to workers and producers. This intermediate level should not be forgotten when going from microeconomics to macroeconomics, and it might even be useful for some purposes to build general equilibrium models based on group rather than individual behaviour.

Professor Segura discussed (1) the use of empirical evidence and (2) the theory of the firm. In regard to empirical evidence he said he was surprised that whenever a participant mentioned the mark-up others asked about the kind of economy to which the theory was applicable, and that those asking for more empirical evidence seemed to feel comfortable talking about a long-run level of voluntary unemployment. He believed that we had been mixing up two different levels of empirical work, that designed to interpret the real world and that designed for forecasting. 'Black boxes' were useful as fore-casting devices but they did not explain any causal relationships. The complex actual world would never display the formal elegance of models designed to provide a general theory of resource allocation.

With respect to the theory of the firm, Professor Segura thought that a single target would not be able to explain the actual behaviour of firms. In a dynamic world with changes in technology and preferences, which were both difficult to forecast and interrelated, we needed a microeconomic theory which admitted different behaviour by different firms without making *ad hoc* assumptions. A theory of the behaviour of firms and prices in a dynamic world would probably have to take into account a variety of targets and constraints which reflected both the partially contradictory aims pursued by different members of a firm and the different environments in which firms operated. Alternative and even contradictory targets could also be considered as actual constraints on microeconomic behaviour; consideration of con-straints might change our views of such behaviour since the concept of competence included competence among groups and social and institutional frameworks, and not only among single firms. The analysis of industrial structure was therefore relevant to microeconomic theory.

Mr Younès pointed out that while until recently economists had on the one hand a microeconomic theory of general equilibrium in which only prices entered as variables explaining the behaviour of economic agents, and on the other hand macroeconomic theory where quantities explained economic agents' behaviour, it was now possible to provide a microeconomic basis for macroeconomic theory in the form of general equilibrium models where quantities explained economic units' behaviour. This was evident in many fields of economics, including planning theory. This theory was relevant to the subject of the conference because here on the basis of a microeconomic model we had to take account of the consequences of macroeconomic planning decisions. In such theory the relationships between the plan and the market were usually, and misleadingly, viewed through the mirror of classical general equilibrium theory in which there was implicitly an auctioneer who determined the equilibrium price level. Thus in 'market socialism' the central planning board would play the role of the auctioneer, and firms and households would maximise their objective functions given the price vector. If general equilibrium was instead framed in terms of contracts and contract proposals between economic agents, in the absence of an auctioneer, we could see that the market had to be defined in terms of relationships between agents. Thus 'market socialism' as classically defined was actually a case of centralised planning because the prices were fixed by the central planning board; the problems of contracts, and the terms of contracts, between economic units such as firms and households were not taken into account.

Roughly speaking, we could say that there was some market element in a planned economy if the terms of contracts made by an economic unit – that is, the precise definition and quality of the good or goods involved, the price of the good or goods involved, the quantity of the good or goods involved, the other contracting party or parties – were not completely and totally defined by the upper economic levels of the hierarchy. But, surely, this was a question of degree.

Similarly, indicative planning, or '*planification à la Française*', was usually analysed as an '*étude du marché généralisé*', but this did not show why the central planning board did not determine only indicative equilibrium prices as a guide to firms, in order to replace markets which either did not exist or were badly organised. In actual fact, the Commissariat Général du Plan established *quantity* signals. This could be taken into account in the new general equilibrium theory. However, this did not mean that macroeconomic theory had always to be founded on a microeconomic basis. Since economic science was a social science and we had to understand the social world, we had to accept the existence of social groups, social classes, the State and class struggles; in all problems in which these aspects of reality were important, we could construct a logical self-contained macroeconomic theory, which did not need a microeconomic foundation.

Professor Koopmans said that his comments had to be seen against the background of a somewhat restless personal history. From the mid-1930s through to the late 1940s he had had the good fortune to sit in on, and to some extent take part in, a good many discussions on the problems of macroeconomics — in the Netherlands, in Geneva, in visits to England, and later in Princeton, Washington and Chicago. After that he had wandered off into more tool-oriented fields, economic methods, the process model of production, and the theory of 'optimal' economic growth. The conference was thus for him like a return visit to the past. It provided the pleasures of recollection and recognition; it also provided a vista of the changing pre-occupations of macroeconomists, and of the growing awareness of the need for a basis in microeconomic analysis, both empirical and theoretical. At the same time, it gave the impression that, while the problems had evolved and changed, the style of discourse had shown remarkable continuity through time.

One aspect of the discussions that had puzzled Professor Koopmans was their history-of-doctrine flavour. It appeared at times that a hypothesis or a model obtained added credibility if it could be traced to the writings of one or more of the great names, whether Hayek, Kaldor, Kalecki, Keynes, Mrs Robinson, or any other, and that this rendered unnecessary a specification of the time period, the country, the institutions or the state of development of the economy to which the ideas or model referred.

Another impression of our discussions was that the tools of analysis used in research in macroeconomics had not changed or evolved much in the last forty years. In this connection Professor Koopmans pointed out that we now had the ideologically neutral tool of the computer. This could be used both for extending the reach of theoretical reasoning, and for empirical testing of some sub-set of its premises and conclusions; indeed, both aspects were intertwined in a computer simulation. Use of a computer to draw inferences from a complicated set of assumptions was more worthwhile if the numbers were not taken out of a hat, but chosen for their resemblance to specific economies. The computer also made it possible to build bridges between microeconomics and macroeconomics, by studying models of intermediate complexity; the field of 'development programming' contained several examples of this type of work. The computer might also help us to get around the compulsion of many aggregate concepts that created difficulties in defining the statistical categories relevant for measurement purposes. An example was the question of which assets were money: one could introduce several distinct money or near-money variables in an aggregate, weighted either by empirical estimation, or by some *a priori* weights which were not limited to the values 0 and 1. This activity shaded over into econometric model-building in which the element of empirical testing was more pronounced, although *a priori* or hypothetical inputs were by no means absent. As an example of its use half-way between microeconomics and macroeconomics, Professor Koopmans mentioned the work by Jorgenson and others for the Energy Policy Project in Washington: this had a small number of energy sectors embedded in a nine-sector model of the entire United States economy. Professor Koopmans believed that the conference would have gained if some econometric work of a type bridging macroeconomic and microeconomic analysis, or a survey of that work, had been included.

To *Professor Negishi* the microeconomic foundation of macroeconomics meant a bridge or at least some stepping stones over the water between the temporary equilibrium analysis of general equilibrium theory and the short-run Keynesian theory of involuntary unemployment. From the micro-economic side one starting point might be the generalisation of the Walrasian tâtonnement; analysis of the so-called non-tâtonnement processes had already suggested the need for the introduction of money. This also meant the possibility of involuntary unemployment. The principle of effective demand, or the dual decision hypothesis, had not, however, been properly introduced into non-tâtonnement processes. If demand constraints were properly intro-duced, the relation between price change and excess demand would be very different from the original Walrasian one. This could help us to explain (1) the existence of Keynesian unemployment equilibrium without assuming money wage rigidity, (2) unintended inventories, (3) the shapes of Phillips curves, and (4) the coexistence of unemployment and inflation, etc. Professor Negishi personally preferred to try to do this with other Walrasian simplifications being kept unchanged as much as possible, at least as a first step. As a second step, however, we had to leave the world of atomistic competition and take imperfect information, transactions costs, monopolies, labour unions, banks, government, minimum wage laws, unemployment compensation, etc., into consideration.

Professor Asimakopulos thought that it was important to ensure that the microeconomic foundations of our macroeconomics did not prevent us from understanding real economies. These foundations should include a characterisa-tion of the structure of markets and industries, since price and output behaviour was affected by structure: in competitive markets prices were very sensitive to short-period fluctuations in demand, while in oligopolistic markets they were not. This type of characterisation was found in Kalecki, and it also underlay Sir John Hicks's distinction between 'flexprice' and 'fixprice'. The foundations should also include a statement of the social relations of production: Who were the 'players'? What were the 'rules of the game'? Was the economy being analysed a capitalist economy, an artisan economy, or a socialist economy? Professor Asimakopulos regretted that these necessary elements were missing in some of the conference papers.

The microeconomic underpinnings of macroeconomic models that dealt with historical or calendar time, rather than logical time, had also to observe the necessary rules; namely, that the future was unknown, and the past could not be undone or 'recontracted', and set the stage for present actions. The notion of equilibrium had been used in economics in at least two senses: (1) as a chosen position – the best given the values of the parameters; and (2) as a position of rest – one in which, given the values of the parameters, there was no net tendency for the value of the variable being studied to change. Keynes had used the term in the second sense when discussing equilibrium involuntary unemployment, but there had since been unnecessary confusion because the two definitions were not distinguished.

Professor Asimakopulos also believed that there should be no artificial distinction between 'short-run' and 'long-run' theories. The long run was only a succession of short runs; if a particular result could not be seen to hold after the passage of a series of short periods, then it should not be said to hold 'in the long run'. He shared Kalecki's view that we should not have separate theories for growth and fluctuations, although the basic common model might sometimes be used to study growth possibilities by making special assumptions that the parameters changed in some steady manner, and at other times be used to study cyclical fluctuations.

Professor Garegnani thought that two rather negative impressions stood out from the last two days of the conference. The first was that the micro-economic foundations of macroeconomics were so thin that our macro-economic theories seemed to be somehow suspended in the air; the second was the indefiniteness of the results of those microeconomic theories which we could use. He believed that as far as microeconomics was concerned we were faced with an unhappy choice. On the one hand there was the theory of general intertemporal equilibrium, which, with its assumption of complete futures markets, not only lacked a sufficient basis in reality, but also, having failed to prove that its equilibria were generally stable, had failed to provide itself with a satisfactory logical basis. On the other hand, there were theories which were not sufficiently definite. An example of the latter might be the difficulty that Sir John Hicks had mentioned of speaking about a theory of the firm independently of the problem at hand: Professor Garegnani did not think that a physicist would feel happy about being told of the difficulty of speaking of a general theory of the fall of weighty objects independently of the problem in hand. A second example might be Professor Segura's dis-satisfaction with expectations. Professor Garegnani shared that dissatisfaction and referred to Sir John Hicks's comments about the 'method of expectations' in his 1936 review of *The General Theory*; namely, 'the more we go into the future the greater this source of error [the effects on expectations of changes in actual production] becomes, so that there is the danger . . . of the whole method [of expectations] petering out'.

Professor Garegnani believed that at the roots of the indefiniteness of results lay the obfuscation in recent theory of the notion that economic variables tended to gravitate towards central levels which could be explained by means of a limited number of persistent forces. This notion had been present in the writings of the English Classical economists who, seeing the real wage as determined by independent social and economic circumstances, obtained the rate of profits (and prices) from the ratio of surplus product to capital; the notion remained central to later theories which explained the division of the product by means of the supply and demand for labour and capital. It was only from the late 1930s that the notion began to be obscured in connection with a progressive shift of the basis of the theory of value from the traditional long-period general equilibrium — the 'full equilibrium' of Sir John Hicks's *The Theory of Wages* with its uniform rate of profits — to a 'short-period general equilibrium', where profits appeared in the shape of rentals of specified capital goods. This shift implied a parallel weakening of the notion of equilibrium as a centre of gravitation. The status of short-period general equilibrium as a centre of gravitation would in fact be doubtful even when it could be formally shown to be stable, since the forces determining it would not be permanent enough to be distinguished from those 'accidental forces' which might at any given moment of time keep the economy out of equilibrium.

These modern theoretical developments could be traced to difficulties which the dominant demand-and-supply explanation of the long-period centres of gravitation had met on two *connected* fronts. On the one hand, the concept of a long-period equilibrium of demand and supply for the economic system relied on the notion of a factor of production — capital — which must change in 'form' without changing in quantity, a notion which was beset with the difficulties of reswitching, etc. On the other hand, Keynes showed the difficulties that the gravitation towards long-period equilibrium could raise on the side of the savings and investment process. Thus the theory of value in attempting to preserve its basic demand-and-supply approach, had found a refuge in a 'short-period equilibrium' where the problem of capital did not arise. But this equilibrium could not be treated as self-contained in time and left us the sterile choice between the hypothesis of complete futures markets, and the introduction of price expectations with their attendant indefinite results. At the same time there were attempts to deal with the substantial problems raised by Keynes, by means of macro-economic theories, whose basis with regard to the behaviour of firms, prices, and distribution was far from clear.

Professor Garegnani thought that perhaps some of the energy which was being devoted to developing these two creatures born with such congenital defects could be more usefully devoted to going back to the roots of the trouble; i.e. to the attempt made in the second half of the nineteenth century to develop a comprehensive theory of value and output based on the idea of substitutability between factors of production, and to see whether our forerunners were wise in abandoning the different approach to value and distribution which had been dominant from Adam Smith to Malthus and Ricardo.

Professor Leijonhufvud said that he had always found the 'cognitive dissonance' between microeconomics and macroeconomics *intolerable*. He regarded short-run macroeconomics as the branch of economics where we studied the co-ordination of economic activities in large systems. Ultimately, the motivation for the quest lay in the social consequences of co-ordination failures — unemployment, serious inflations. Standard microeconomics and standard macroeconomics, seen from this vantage point, presented inconsistent images of the real world: the general equilibrium models portrayed worlds that always achieved 'full' co-ordination and could absorb virtually any shock without lasting trouble; the standard Keynesian model was one of a system lacking the minimal self-regulating properties to achieve co-ordination except by chance. In his view, there was *one* major problem and the various tasks for theorists that he wished to see done were parts of the larger problem: namely, to construct a class of models that would be representative of the temporal movement of a large, complex system that possessed certain *limited* self-regulating and self-organising capabilities. The system should be, on the one hand, less 'perfectly' equilibrating than the general equilibrium models and, on the other hand, less helpless than the Keynesian one.

In his article on 'Effective Demand Failures' (*Swedish Journal of Economics*, 1973), Professor Leijonhufvud had suggested a system which within certain bounds tended to restore itself 'automatically' to the near neighbourhood of an equilibrium time-path in much the same way that neoclassical models would suggest, but which, when exposed to severe shocks that displaced it beyond those bounds, showed co-ordination failures of a basically Keynesian nature. Even though the reasons he could adduce for trying to model this particular suggestion might be less than compelling, he believed that models fitting the same broad description would be worthwhile, because what we would have to learn in order to construct such models would be useful for further work on a more adequate theory.

On the question of the factors which were important in setting limits on the system's ability to absorb shocks and restore the co-ordination of activities, there had been several suggestions. The idea that had been most prominent in the Keynesian literature was that of institutional rigidities that caused wages or interest rates to 'stick'; another idea was to look for 'slippages' in the machinery: i.e. for ineffective price-incentives. A third would stress technological rigidities: i.e. that the capital stock inherited from the past was much less than perfectly malleable. His own hobby-horse was the 'fixity' of the knowledge that transactors possessed. In Marshallian terms, agents had the experience to enable them to cope with 'normal' situations, 'normal' variations in demand, etc., by following learned routines of behaviour, such as holding physical and financial buffer-stocks, etc. But when the system was shocked so severely that the new notional equilibrium lay outside the range of 'normal' experience, agents were not able to learn fast enough what the new world was like, and when buffer-stocks ran out or piled up, interaction in markets tended to teach agents some things that were 'wrong' in the sense of inducing them to undertake system-dysfunctional adjustments.

At one time Professor Leijonhufvud's attitude had been to drop the equilibrium conditions from neoclassical models and try to keep the rest of the

pieces, especially the individual behaviour experiments and the law of excess
demands (or 'Say's Principle') that guaranteed the coherence and consistency
of the system; but this raised difficulties at several levels. With respect to
individual conceptual experiments, equilibrium microeconomics was riddled
with assumptions that transactors acted 'as if' they had knowledge of diverse
and sundry things. For equilibrium states these could be seen to be workable
assumptions; that they were reasonable in that setting was part of the reason
why they were hard to ferret out. We had not unearthed them all yet; at any
rate we had not learned how to do without them in 'disequilibrium', where we
could see that they were purely *ad hoc*. With respect to market conceptual
experiments, we needed to work out the process-analysis of how interactions
worked out in various *types* of markets. One particular problem was the
pricing and production decisions of producers with increasing returns to scale.
Another was the formulation of the law of excess demands when we had a
mix of different types of markets; for if we developed theories of the consumption function, the investment function, and so on, separately and
independently we could not know whether putting them into the same model
would give us a consistent system. There was also, of course, the question of
money and financial constraints.

Finally, Professor Leijonhufvud believed that our theoretical modelling
should (for the time being at least) be limited in its forecasting ambitions. The
system should be modelled as open with regard to a number of variables whose
future values we — and the inhabitants of our models — could not hope to
divine. In terms of Wicksell's rocking-horse metaphor, we could hope to arrive
at reasonably well-validated statements about the curvature of its runners and
the distribution of its weight or mass, but we should refrain from trying to
turn those blows of a capricious Fate that knocked the horse about into law-
abiding endogenous variables of our theoretical systems!

Professor Spaventa had four contentions to offer:

(1) If we had been looking for new microeconomic foundations, we had
not found any. This was not surprising in view of the present state of
confusion about so-called general theory. In consequence, macroeconomic theories had not been questioned, contrary to what one
might have expected. Such theories seemed to possess the virtue of
leading an independent and unmicrofounded life.

(2) The issue of a more general *versus* a more partial approach was a barren
issue. The 'generalists' were right in maintaining that to account fully
for interdependence was better than to neglect it; the success of any
more general approach should not, however, be measured, as it often
was, by refinements brought to old and already known results and by
proofs that the same results obtained by simpler methods could also
be arrived at by more complex methods, but by *new* results which
were both macroeconomically relevant and could not otherwise be
attained. There was a danger of an increasing cleavage between
'relevance' and 'introspection', with 'introspection' becoming more

and more the pursuit of *l'art pour l'art*.

(3) The lack of uniquely determined results and of immutable laws was less worrying than the huge gap developing between the refinements of the analysis and the roughness of the tools used for policy problems by the most sophisticated analysts. The strictures increasingly passed on the profession by laymen and practitioners were not unjustified: better analysis should produce better tools, not for rationalising, but for explaining what happened around us and for solving the problems besetting us. The dispute on the causes and remedies of inflation, the unsatisfactory state of the explanations of business investment, the lack of a satisfactory theory of distribution, were all examples of the inability of current analysis to provide satisfactory answers to relevant questions. They were also examples of questions where a microeconomic theory would be essential for macroeconomic explanations.

(4) The one lead which the conference had given us was in the discussion of money, its definition, its functions, its influence on behaviour and its externalities, where one could see promising interactions between microeconomic and macroeconomic theories and problems. Only too often, however, money was introduced merely as an ornament, with all the problems to which financial assets gave rise assumed away. Further, the neglect of international monetary problems had deprived us of relevant insights not only into policy problems but also into some fundamental issues of monetary theory. This was perhaps another symptom of an increasing reluctance of the profession to concern itself with large issues.

Dr Sweeney believed that microeconomic phenomena were of macroeconomic concern in two related ways. First, individual firms reacted to demand conditions (which were dependent on the state of aggregate demand and perhaps on rivals' pricing policies) and to cost conditions (which were dependent on capital costs — the real rate of interest and the price of capital goods — and on rivals' wage offers and the state of the labour market). Second, households demanded goods and supplied labour on the basis of their beliefs about future consumption opportunities at expected prices, future wage and financial income, and future employment prospects at expected wages. Firms and households met in auctioneer-less markets that did not necessarily clear. All these phenomena had to be taken into account when discussing monetary and fiscal policy; most had to be considered in designing such microeconomic policies as social welfare insurance.

Within these overall requirements, however, each sector and problem should be handled as simply as possible. For example, Professor Hall's paper had come as close to certainty as possible in a stochastic framework, while also paring assumptions in a ruthless way; his model could provide plausible though intuitive bases for more general macroeconomic theoretical and empirical work. Complex formulations of problems often required powerful mathematical techniques, which in turn required stringent assumptions regarding economic phenomena to yield definite results. Since ambiguity could always be achieved, we should not be afraid of simplified models which often required less restrictive assumptions for definite results or yielded a limited number of results which could then be sorted out empirically. Dr Sweeney also believed that within the genre of perfect certainty, the consequences of uncertainty could often be handled by imposing *a priori* constraints on the problem or by *ex post* modification of the results. Since many of even the simplest uncertainty formulations could have clear solutions destroyed by seemingly minor changes in assumptions, the former strategy was not unreasonable.

Dr Sweeney favoured Professor Negishi's suggestion that aggregate demand impinged directly on the demand curves facing firms that had market power and yet were 'neoclassical' in, for example, the way monopolistically competitive firms were conceived to react to demand. It would also be useful to conceive of firms having some individual power in the labour market which varied with the state of macroeconomic variables. The key micro-macro interaction of firms and households turned on the concept of involuntary unemployment. Dr Goodhart's point that very few people chose to quit to search for a better job was well taken. Industrial employers often set a wage and hired up to the desired limit; when the hiring plans underestimated supply, qualified and willing workers were turned away. The theoretical nature and empirical extent of this phenomenon deserved thorough investigation. Dr Sweeney also agreed with the participants who wanted us to take models that applied to a general market economy and to give them content by imposing the institutional features of a specific economy.

Dr Nuti said that he had rather taken for granted, judging from the selection of participants, the title and the content of the papers, that the frame of reference of our conference was the capitalist economy; i.e. an economy with private ownership, monetary exchange, free enterprise and wage labour. Of course, we could, provisionally, abstract from some of these features; but then we presumably did this in the hope of understanding, eventually, the capitalist system; and, as long as we abstracted from the basic features of a system, we should refrain from making policy recommendations. However, it had become clear to Dr Nuti from the discussion that there was also a fairly widespread view that, somehow, economic theory was universal, applying to all economic systems; or, at any rate, that we could discuss the topic of our conference with reference to all *decentralised* economic systems.

In our subject it was most important to model not just institutions such as fiat money or insurance contracts, but the fundamental distinctive features of economic systems; in particular at least two features: the scope of ownership and the scope of exchange. The scope of ownership included what can be and is owned (means of production, consumption goods, slaves, etc.) and who can and does own (the State, groups of individuals, single individuals, etc.). The scope of exchange included the extent and mode of division of labour, in the broad sense of the relative scope of markets and plans, the levels of plan-making, the degree of centralisation.

To accept the importance of economic systems one did not have to be a Marxist. One did not have to believe in, say, a law of necessary correspondence between the level of development of productive forces and the productive relations prevailing in a system, or in the law of the necessary correspondence between the economic base of a system and its superstructure, with all the implications of dialectical materialism in the study of society (which was not to say that this approach did not have an important contribution to make to the study of society). Nor did one have to bring in at all the question of the relative desirability of one system or another. There were at least three reasons why a systemic approach was necessary to the study of the micro-economic foundations of macroeconomics.

First, economic systems determined whether decision-makers would be maximisers or satisficers, and what it was that they wanted to maximise or satisfy, and under what constraints. For instance, mainstream literature using standard general equilibrium analysis had investigated the properties of a labour-managed market economy, where there was no wage labour, and where co-operative firms maximised earnings per member (Ward, Vanek, Domar, Meade and others). It had been established that under simple conditions co-operative firms would react to an increase in their product price by reducing employment of labour and cutting their output. The macro-economic implications were important; it appeared that in that economic system Keynesian policies raised unemployment of both labour and capacity and raised the rate of inflation, though the economy was not easily displaced from full employment once it was reached.

Second, the informational flows generated by different economic systems differed, so that even if individual decision-makers used the same decision criteria, their information about the alternatives open to them and the repercussions of their choice differ; hence they would make different decisions. An instance was Professor Koopmans's notion of 'secondary uncertainty', like an investor's uncertainty about decisions made by other investors in competing and complementary fields. If investment was planned centrally this kind of uncertainty would not arise. This was not to say that central planning of investment was necessarily always superior; but it certainly was significantly different. (This incidentally answered a question raised by Dr Goodhart on the applicability of the Kalecki model of capitalism to the socialist economy.)

Finally, in so far as there was a conflict, or at least a difference, between microeconomic perception of economic phenomena and the collective macro-economic results of a number of microeconomic decisions, as Professor Streissler has reminded us, the nature of the difference and the resolution of the conflict would vary in different systems. Dr Nuti wanted therefore to stress the necessity of a systemic approach to the topic of our conference.

Professor Malinvaud explained the problems confronting us in terms of the three main areas of current research on the microeconomic foundations of macroeconomics, which were:

(1) clarification of the reasons explaining what were the prevailing economic institutions;

(2) foundations of the building blocks of macroeconomic analysis; and

(3) microeconomic formalisation of our macroeconomic models of the economy.

Under the first heading came such questions as: Why did we have money? Why were some prices sticky? Why was the use of forward contracts rather limited? Research on such questions certainly improved our understanding of economic phenomena, but Professor Malinvaud, being somewhat pragmatic, was not himself attracted by such questions; moreover, he did not think that this was the area in which we faced our most urgent problems.

The building blocks of macroeconomic analysis required extensive research. With respect to the behavioural equations, Professor Malinvaud agreed with Sir John Hicks that those concerning firms were the most difficult to clarify, given the great variety of industrial structures and of economic environment and the multiplicity of decisions simultaneously taken by a single firm. We were making progress in understanding the short-term variations of firms' decisions but we knew much less about their strategic decisions on long-term development. Other topics requiring and receiving attention included the formation of expectations. Some building blocks had a complex nature, notably the production function and the Phillips curve. The former had now been well clarified, and his own feeling was that we needed to leave the issue on one side for a while so as to let our ideas mature. He did not think that any economist would seriously eliminate the concept of capital from economic science or object to the notion that capital was productive; his own guess was that we would continue to use production functions in the same way that we used G.N.P. or the cost-of-living index: i.e. being aware of the fact that these tools had not the hard justifications that we would wish but were none the less very useful for many problems.

Under the third heading we should welcome the renewed interest in the concept of 'temporary equilibrium' introduced long ago by Sir John Hicks. This was fundamental for the macroeconomic analysis of short-run and long-run phenomena, since it provided a way of building a positive macroeconomic dynamics in which, starting from any given initial conditions, a process explaining the evolution of the economy was sequentially found. Professor Malinvaud thought that we had spent too little time discussing the recent temporary equilibrium models. Our research would also probably benefit from new purely static formalisations of the interdependence between economic agents and its consequences, as he and Mr Younès had tried to suggest at the first session of the conference. Finally, he pointed out that our macroeconomics was not always oriented only toward understanding the phenomena from the outside; we also needed planning models. In this respect all the microeconomic theory of efficiency in the face of time and uncertainty had a large role to play, a role that we had not discussed.

Professor Izzo wished to call attention to some aspects of the micro-economic foundations of macroeconomics that he considered important. First, with respect to the work that had recently been done to lay foundations of monetary theory – i.e., the theory of an economy in which money was essential – this work had not led us to modify significantly our view concerning the explanatory variables of the demand for money function and the characteristics of the transmission mechanism of monetary policy. The general equilibrium models of a monetary economy had so far confirmed that a time dimension, uncertainty and transactions costs were necessary and sufficient conditions for the use of money. Furthermore, Professor Izzo thought that Stanley Fischer was quite right in pointing out that, in order to understand the monetary mechanism and the working of monetary policy, the fact that money was the medium of exchange was less significant than the fact that the demand for money was a demand for real balances.

Second, dissatisfaction with the macroeconomic models usually used to explain what Keynes meant, had prompted a re-examination of one of the main contributions of macroeconomics, the possibility of an equilibrium with involuntary unemployment. Here again the tools of general equilibrium analysis were being applied. It was obvious that unemployment which was simply due to price rigidities was not the involuntary unemployment that Keynes had been considering. However, in some of the recent general equilibrium papers unemployment was simply due to the assumption of price rigidities. Furthermore, in these models there was no explicit role for the principle of effective demand, and movements in the autonomous components of demand did not influence output directly. As Professor Tobin had pointed out in his paper 'Keynesian Models of Recession and Depression', 'the proposition that Keynes was questioning' was the notion that 'the private market economy can and will, without aid from government policy, steer itself to full employment equilibrium'.

Professor Cochrane noted that the title of the conference had turned out to be quite an umbrella, which had sheltered a great range of territory. It seemed to him that nonetheless a major lesson to be drawn from the papers and the discussions was fairly straightforward; namely, in order to find ways to improve the thin foundations of aggregate economics, we had to learn much more about economic behaviour within financial institutions, within industrial enterprises, within government agencies, within trade unions, within households, and within all other phases of society related to material well-being, and to do this we would need to pay more attention to demographers, sociologists, political scientists, lawyers and engineers, as well as those working in the areas of operations research, accounting, information theory and finance. For example, the linkages between a firm's cost mark-up, pricing schemes and the environments within which it operated (including its sensitivity to the national political system) could not continue to be neglected. He thought that we should follow Professor Shubik's suggestion and move

toward a mathematical institutionalism. But methodological tolerance would
be required because there would continue to be, as Sir John Hicks had
suggested earlier, theories of macroeconomics, alternative 'visions' of how
economies work, grounded on alternative sets of microeconomic facts.

Professor Parkin said that he had been asking himself all week, 'What are
the questions?' His answer was: 'To explain unemployment and inflation
(and perhaps some other aggregate variables such as the rate of growth of
aggregate real income and the share of wages in national income).' Whilst
these questions were clear and straightforward at a loose, generalistic level,
they were not sufficiently well-defined to enable us to proceed with a
scientific investigation of them. When we got down to questions which were
sufficiently well-defined, we found ourselves using concepts such as voluntary
and involuntary unemployment and anticipated and unanticipated inflation.
This had led us to a class of models which explained purely voluntary unemployment; it had also led to a class of models in what might be called the
neo-general equilibrium approach which explained the possibility of persistent
involuntary unemployment. The former class also told a microeconomic story
about price change, which the latter so far did not. Thus we had 'search'
models which explained voluntary unemployment and inflation, and general
equilibrium models which explained involuntary unemployment but not
inflation; where was this present state of knowledge and activity leading?
Professor Parkin found himself increasingly wondering whether the answer
was nowhere.

Professor Leijonhufvud regarded macroeconomics as the study of decentralised systems which sometimes failed to co-ordinate; the systemic failure
that currently bothered Professor Parkin was that within the economics
profession. Too many theorists seemed to go about their theorising without
consulting the facts sufficiently carefully or sufficiently often. Yet in a world
where we could build an almost infinite number of models, how else were we
to discriminate between models? Matters were, of course, not entirely straightforward even here: macroeconomic models based on microeconomic theories
could fit the macroeconomic facts even though the microeconomic theories
were wrong, which meant that we could have a series of alternative microeconomic foundations which led to macroeconomic predictions all of which
were consistent with the facts at the macroeconomic level. The key to the
solution of this problem was often to attempt to discriminate between
hypotheses which had macroeconomic implications by using microeconomic
data. Unfortunately microeconomic data were very scarce. In addition, what
we wanted if we were to test our current theories was microeconomic data
which distinguished between voluntary and involuntary unemployment and
between anticipated and unanticipated inflation, and also, if we were to take
seriously the suggestions of Professor Marty and Sir John Hicks, information
about variances or other aspects of the dispersion of inflation expectations.
There was a crying need to generate more data in order to take matters
further. The present somewhat negative attitude toward data and testing of

many economists was perhaps one of the contributory factors to the scarcity
of such data.

The present state of our theories on the central problems of macroeconomics were not entirely in good shape. At the same time the real world
was generating high two-digit inflation and might very well be about to
generate a two-digit unemployment rate. What could we do about this?
Professor Parkin believed that we should adopt Professor Malinvaud's pragmatic approach in attempting to deal with the problems of the world in the
absence of solid microeconomic foundations. In particular, we should make
a great deal of effort to identify the 'hand on the rocking-horse'; much of the
discussion, and in particular that on Dr Goodhart's paper, had raised the
danger of losing sight of the main hand on the rocking-horse, namely central
bank and central government monetary and fiscal policy. There was a great
deal of careful empirical work supporting the view that the major variations
in aggregate economic activity had come from variations in aggregate demand
management and monetary policy. In an open economy operating with a
fixed exchange rate and full currency convertibility, expansive monetary
policy in a single country would, as David Hume had pointed out over 200
years ago, lead not to that country having an increased inflation rate, but to
the deterioration of that country's balance of payments and to an increase in
that country's and the rest of the world's inflation rate in proportion to the
effect of that country's monetary expansion on the world money supply. This
suggested that at least for an analysis of inflation in the fixed exchange rate
1960s we should focus on the world macroeconomy and on world monetary
institutions rather than on national considerations. In contrast to the massive
amount of careful empirical work pointing to monetary and fiscal policy as
the major sources of shock to the system there was a good deal of folklore
and conjecture about the role of real shocks; it was important to establish
whether or not this folklore added up to anything more than myth. We all
knew of individual shocks, e.g. the oil crisis, which had been sizable, but these
seemed to be small in number and well spaced in time. Indeed, only when we
had some harder facts about the major sources of the shocks to the aggregate
economy as well as better data on involuntary and voluntary unemployment,
on inflation and inflation anticipations, would we be able to get some
direction into the microeconomic modelling of macroeconomic problems and
thereby raise the marginal productivity of the scarce intellectual resources
being used in this activity.

Professor Davidson asked why did we want microeconomic foundations for
macroeconomics? As Sir John Hicks had pointed out, the choice of models
depended on the problems at hand. In mathematics, for example, we had
Euclidean geometry and non-Euclidean geometry; for some problems the
Euclidean model was appropriate, while for others its use would be disastrous.
In physics, there was a model of the electron as a particle and a model of the
electron as a wave. By using a classification method to decide when to use one
model or the other, other sciences had made progress; economics should not

be ashamed to follow this path. Professor Davidson believed that there were two basic types of models in economics, a timeless general equilibrium model and a historical (calendar time) humanistic model. An equilibrium model builder proceeded by specifying a sufficient number of equations to determine all the unknowns in the system and then concentrated on finding the existence, uniqueness and stability of the equilibrium where all plans were reconciled by market prices. An equilibrium model was, said Professor Davidson, bound to be a timeless system where all decisions were made and all contracts were signed without any false trades, so that all plans were *pre*-reconciled; once the future history had thus been determined, the economic actors merely read their pre-agreed lines. For certain questions the equilibrium model could be the most efficient model to provide an answer, but those who were interested in the macro-political-economics of the real world found such questions uninteresting. Moreover, the general equilibrium model was not designed to, and could not, answer the interesting macroeconomic questions of money, inflation, and unemployment.

The historical model, on the other hand, emphasised the one-way nature of time, the fact that economic activities involved the passage of calendar time, and the fact that the future was not merely a reflection of the past. Future history was created by current economic activity and was not merely discovered, while current economic activity depended upon expectations about a future which had not been created at the time expectations were formed. According to Professor Davidson, Keynes had developed a consistent historical method microeconomic theory to underly his macroeconomics. This recognised the simultaneous existence of spot and forward production markets, of stocks and flows over calendar time, of liquidity and the institution of catenated forward contracting over time. Professor Davidson said that he emphasised what Keynes wrote because his whole micro-macro historical model had never been spelled out. Once we got the model out on the table, we could analyse its many errors, but if we insisted on balancing Keynes's macroeconomic analysis on an incompatible general equilibrium base we would not make any progress in macroeconomics; we would also regress to the disastrous pre-Keynesian solutions to the macro-political-economic problems.

Professor Davidson concluded by listing the problems which he believed the micro-macro historical model could resolve (e.g., unemployment, inflation, and liquidity problems) and those in which timeless general equilibrium models had a comparative advantage (e.g., optimality and simultaneous pre-reconciliation of choices).

Professor Nell also thought that we might profitably have considered whether macroeconomics *needed* microeconomic foundations. The terms in which the title of the conference had been posed had in some sense begged the question: macroeconomics was aggregate economics, and aggregates were always aggregates of some smaller things. But economics had not always posed its problems, or constructed its methods, in such terms. Neither the classical economists nor Marx could be said to have developed their theories of the long-run development of society as a construction out of theories of individual behaviour; indeed, the distinction between macroeconomics and micro-economics would not have made much sense to them. The individual's behaviour took its meaning and motivation from its social context, the development of which the theory explained; the theory of the whole was therefore prior to the theory of the individual. For example, an individual's spending would be conditioned by his social class, which in turn was defined by the relationships in production, while the long-run development of the economy explained the changing relative prosperity of the social classes. One could try to derive different types of spending behaviour from individual preferences, but this was certainly not the approach of either the classics or Marx. It was unlikely that they would have thought that preferences could be taken as given independently of the economic changes they were investigating. On the contrary, it would be more consistent with their approach to suggest that economic pressures shaped individual preferences and defined the social positions in which individuals made their choices.

Professor Nell then suggested that the pure theory of exchange could not provide the basis for a theory of the whole economy, since the latter had to be concerned with the way goods and services provided the material support for society, and the requirements of such support, in turn, dictated a great part of the total pattern of exchange quite independently of individual preferences. The 'economy' was not separate from the society; it was simply an aspect of it, and the growth or development of the economy was necessarily also the growth or development of the society. Exchange alone could not provide the basis for understanding the activities of men in the ordinary business of life, because to use things was sooner or later to use them up; if the pattern of social activity was to be sustained and repeated, it had to be supported by the production of replacements for the goods and services used up. This was part of the traditional problem of 'maintaining capital intact', which Professor Nell believed should be moved to the centre of the stage. Then it would become clear that a careful examination of production, conceived as the material foundation of actual social practice, would yield a picture very different from that of neoclassical theory: in particular, production took place with specific, fixed and rigid equipment which could not easily be moved or adapted to other uses. These rigidities were important in understanding individual behaviour, for they provided economic agents with both information and opportunities. They were also essential to understanding both the level of employment and output and the long-run expansion of the system; assumptions of malleability and widespread substitutability suggested adjustment possibilities that were simply not there.

To model production accurately and realistically was, however, only a beginning; the next step was a correct model of who got the product and why. This required first a careful specification of institutions — in particular of property rights — and second a close examination of how these institutions worked as the values of economic variables changed over time. In this approach there was no room for a distinction between macroeconomics and microeconomics. The traditional descriptive economic problems of value and distribution were encompassed in the approach, and when financial institutions and the implications of social class for spending propensities were added, the problems of the level of output and employment would also fall into place.

Professor Nell also suggested that we had for a long time been victims of a certain methodological and terminological confusion. There was an important and crucial role for the optimising approach, but it was not in the realm of descriptive economics. We would not reject activity analysis because a business firm chose the wrong product mix. Moreover, if we determined that a certain product mix should increase profits, and it did not, we did not then reject the theorems of linear programming; instead we rejected the data that the firm supplied us. The theory of optimising behaviour was not a construction which we tested against the world; it was rather the standard by which we judged the world. The way the world worked was a matter of fact; the way it could be made to work better was a matter of optimising theory, provided such theory was firmly grounded in carefully specified institutional detail. Professor Nell therefore suggested that macroeconomics, conceived as the theory of the actual working of the economy as a whole, both with a given level of capacity and as it developed in the long run, needed no 'micro-economic foundations' in the theoretical sense, but could rest empirically on detailed institutional studies. What had traditionally been called micro-economic theory — the marginalist theory of the market, partial or general — made little or no contribution to descriptive economics, but when converted to operations research provided the basis for the economists' recommendations for improving the state of the world.

To illustrate his view that the conference discussions displayed many mutual understandings, *Professor Streissler* addressed himself to a particular problem. It had been suggested that we had not sufficiently discussed the microeconomic problems of macroeconometric models and the foundations of macroeconomic investment functions. His example in this area was intended to show that communication problems between microeconomics and macroeconomics were often due to a lack of patience of the two sides of the profession with each other; that the differences were frequently not as large as they appeared from a hasty assessment; and that concepts changed meaning and name in the rough-and-ready world of empirical application.

A production-theoretical derivation of an investment function, such as Jorgenson's, implied that the investment of a firm should depend on an accelerator, on the relative prices of the investment goods and the goods produced, and on the rate of interest. In applying such a concept to the econometric estimation of the amount of investment in industry as a whole (apart from building) the econometrician had first to ask himself if all individual plans in his period of study had been fulfilled. In an Austrian study that Professor Streissler wished to report this assumption had been thought reasonable and hence the microeconomic theory of investment applicable. In the results only the accelerator variable had turned out to be significant; what had happened to the other variables? As happened frequently, there were no data on relative prices and prices had been eliminated on practical grounds. The estimation was still very good, but this did not mean that a variable important to microeconomists proved unimportant. Since in microeconomic equilibrium theory everything depended on everything else and since that for an econometrician meant multicollinearity, the effect of relative prices could have been picked up not by the directly relevant variable, but by a dummy variable.

Interest rates had entered the estimated investment function more or less insignificantly; but in the period investigated political constraints had allowed very little variation in interest rates; what did not vary could not be seen to have much influence, even though it *might* have been decisive. The microeconomist assessing a macroeconometric piece of work might miss this point. As was usual in investment functions both past and present profits had entered significantly. The reason for present profits entering was institutional, the Austrian government's allowing depreciation in the first year nearly up to the value of the investment, which amounts to a loan at a zero per cent interest rate; profits therefore entered via their effect on interest rates. Past profits also entered because for tax purposes an invoice could be supplied in one year while the machine was supplied in the next. Thus, looked at from the right angle, an apparently completely different macroeconomic empirical function need not be inconsistent with traditional microeconomic theory, or for that matter, with satisficing behaviour or other models of decision-taking. Professor Streissler drew two conclusions:

(1) There was no one-to-one relationship between theory and empirical evidence; this was one of the reasons why there was so little agreement between economic theoreticians.

(2) As Professor Malinvaud had pointed out, the practical economist must be eclectic. He had to master the art of knowing what types of models were most useful for answering a well-defined question within a certain institutional set-up and then of adopting these to a second-best type of model within the straitjacket of data.

Lady Hicks pointed out that although the conference had been both enjoyable and successful, one could ask in what sense had it been successful? By and large little progress had been made towards the objective of identifying the general relations between microeconomics and macroeconomics. The mathematical papers were naturally bound by the limited range of assumptions necessary for their models; the writers of the non-mathematical papers had kept their eyes more strictly on the ball and provided useful (though not very incisive) contributions on general problems posed by constraints, preferences and other aggregation difficulties, but this was not enough to restore the balance. Moreover, there was a discernible lack of precision in the definition and use of a number of concepts such as equilibrium.

It seemed to Lady Hicks that we had reached general agreement on three propositions related to the general objective:

(1) while it was not too difficult to make considerable progress in relating microeconomics to macroeconomics in particular fields, to aggregate these into general propositions was extremely difficult;

(2) starting from the macroeconomic end a certain amount of disaggregation was essential in order to deal adequately with non-homogeneity in particular fields such as unemployment;

(3) analysis needed at all times to be tied definitely to particular countries and circumstances.

It was perhaps inevitable that a great deal of time and attention should be devoted to inflation and unemployment, the two major pre-occupations of the present. Some very useful work was presented in analysing the evils of inflation, but this again needed to be more closely geared to particular social and racial circumstances. Neither unemployment nor inflation was necessarily very relevant to what should have been the main theme.

Lady Hicks was somewhat disturbed by the time and attention devoted to the precise sayings of Marshall and Keynes, seeing that circumstances had greatly changed since they wrote. Keynes had drastically simplified his argument in relation to the circumstances of his time, but these were not the simplifications relevant to the modern world. Although there was much of permanent value in Marshall, it needed to be adapted to the problems of the 1970s. Indeed, we had devoted too much time to the economics of the 1930s and 1940s and too little to that of the 1970s. There had been a discernible tendency to attack micro-macro relations in terms of a single country reminiscent of the Keynes closed economy.

The big lacuna of the conference had been the lack of analysis of the working of money and credit in the present international world with its growth of central banks and other financial institutions. Again, scarcely anything had been said of the position of modern public sectors in macroeconomics; namely, the control by governments not only of income distribution, but also of large sectors of industry and its financing, through fiscal and especially public expenditure policies, as well as the predominant influence of governments on central bank policy. Surely it was along these lines that the setting for modern micro-macro economics was to be found and we could not afford to neglect them.

Index

Entries in **bold** type under the names of participants in the conference indicate their papers or discussions of their papers. Entries in *italic* indicate contributions by participants in the discussions.